Troublemaker

ALSO BY CARLA KAPLAN

Miss Anne in Harlem: The White Women of the Black Renaissance
Zora Neale Hurston: A Life in Letters
The Erotics of Talk: Women's Writing and Feminist Paradigms
Nella Larsen's Quicksand: A Norton Critical Edition (editor)
Nella Larsen's Passing: A Norton Critical Edition (editor)
*Every Tongue Got to Confess: Negro Folk-Tales from the Gulf States
by Zora Neale Hurston* (editor)
Dark Symphony and Other Works by Elizabeth Laura Adams (editor)

Carla Kaplan

Troublemaker

The Fierce, Unruly

Life of Jessica Mitford

HURST & COMPANY LONDON

First published in the United Kingdom in 2025 by
C. Hurst & Co. (Publishers) Ltd.,
New Wing, Somerset House, Strand, London, WC2R 1LA
© Carla Kaplan, 2025
All rights reserved.

The right of Carla Kaplan to be identified as the author of this
publication is asserted by her in accordance with the Copyright,
Designs and Patents Act, 1988.

Published by arrangement with *Harper*, an imprint of
HarperCollins Publishers, New York, New York U.S.A.
All rights reserved.

First edition designed by Michele Cameron.

Printed in the United Kingdom by Bell & Bain Ltd, Glasgow

A Cataloguing-in-Publication data record for this book
is available from the British Library.

ISBN: 9781805265375

EU GPSR Authorised Representative
Easy Access System Europe Oü, 16879218
Address: Mustamäe tee 50, 10621, Tallinn, Estonia
Contact Details: gpsr.requests@easproject.com, +358 40 500 3575

www.hurstpublishers.com

for Steve, and all the other troublemakers

CONTENTS

CONTENTS

Troublemaker

A NOTE TO THE READER

I t is a standard convention to refer to writers by their last names: Hemingway, Faulkner, or Fitzgerald, for example. This convention is especially important with biographies of women writers who are much more likely to be referred to by their first names than are their male counterparts. Jessica Mitford, however, was so unfailingly "Decca," even to funeral directors and other targets of her muckraking, that I have found it impossible to refer to her otherwise. She was, in fact, almost as famous for just being "Decca"—irreverent, passionate, obstinate, iconoclastic, and hilarious—as she was for exceptional investigative journalism. In those rare instances when I am referring only to her authorial self, and where confusion with other family is unlikely, I will sometimes call her Mitford. Jessica Mitford was an impossible person to diminish, and I hope that calling her Decca, her nickname from childhood onward, will bring her a little closer to readers, especially those who are meeting her here, for the first time. (Other family members, especially Decca's daughter Constancia, were also consistently known by nicknames which will be used when the narrative perspective is Decca's.) Names in letter citations are generally as addressed or approximations thereof.

Decca lived for letters at a time when letters were the principal means of communicating and staying in touch with others, and she continued to write letters even when phones and faxes became available. She left an unrivaled collection of correspondence, totaling well over twelve thousand letters.[1] This biography quotes liberally from those letters, in an effort to help readers hear Decca's voice and see how she thought, especially when she was out of the public eye.

INTRODUCTION

"God Careth for Us"

It never occurred to me to be happy with my lot.[1]
—JESSICA MITFORD

W hen *Time* magazine named her America's "Queen of the Muckrakers" in 1970, Jessica Mitford was delighted.[2] To this British aristocrat who became an American Communist, the mainstream recognition was a boost, especially since Mitford had only become a writer relatively late in life and was as surprised as anyone by her spectacular success. Most amusing, given her choice to discard wealth and throw over the rank of nobility, was being called a "queen." She'd known Queen Elizabeth as Princess Lilibet and never been much impressed with the royals. "When the princesses were little, I tried to spread a rumor in London that they'd been born with webbed feet which was why nobody had ever seen them with their shoes off," she once told her close friend,

Maya Angelou.[3] Queenliness combined with muck was a delicious contrast for someone who had a particular affinity for whatever was quirky, unconventional, contradictory, or odd. She also appreciated getting credit for reviving muckraking, a literary form that was nearly moribund when her blockbuster exposé of the funeral business, *The American Way of Death*, appeared in 1963; it was especially gratifying for someone completely self-taught to be so heralded as an expert.

As a muckraker with what she admitted was a particularly strong "appetite for tracking and destroying the enemy," Mitford excelled.[4] She was relentless in pursuit of anyone who preyed on the poor. An indefatigable researcher who couldn't help seeing the funny side of everything, she attacked by deftly combining facts and wit. Her disarming ways and upper-crust accent charmed targets into revealing more than they meant to, and she never hesitated to let them hoist themselves by their own petards. She skewered frauds and cheaters. Her readers adored her.

But Jessica Mitford, always known as Decca, was not raised to muckrake.

Decca was born on September 11, 1917, into one of the oddest families in England, as famous for its eccentricities as for its insularity. Even as a curly-haired, blue-eyed child, bubbling with energy and enthusiasm, Decca's look was quizzical, with raised eyebrows pointing distinctly downwards at the bridge of her small, pert nose. Her father, David Freeman-Mitford, also known as Baron Redesdale, was a right-wing British peer who had more land than cash, wanted women out of Parliament for fear they'd use the bathrooms, believed that schooling would thicken his daughters' ankles and make them unmarriageable, and kept a pet mongoose. He forced almost everyone out of his house and physically showed the "damn sewers" (as he called his daughters' young male acquaintances) the door. Decca's mother, Sydney Bowles Mitford, Baroness Redesdale, loathed doctors, eschewed modern medicine ("The Good Body" would right it-self, she was certain), distrusted refrigeration, pinched pennies, and refused to let her six daughters go to school because "the company of other children [was] unnecessary and overstimulating."[5] Both parents called everything outside of their home "Elsewhere" and pronounced themselves against it.

In St. Mary's Church, in the Cotswolds' Swinbrook Village, the Mitfords sat in the back two pews. They owned the small church, as well as the little village. They chose their seats so that they could watch the congregation unobserved. Behind them, on the dark oak wall, the family crest and motto were carved in a heavy scroll. "God Careth for Us" the wooden banner read. Some pronunciations might stress the second word: "Careth." But a proper Mitford family pronunciation stresses the last word: "Us": "God Careth for *US*." The family owned the "living" of the church and hired, and fired, the vicar at will. It was *their* music, *their* seating, *their* service. They let their six daugh-ters tow their pets along to services, where goat, dogs, lambs, and sometimes a pony were tied to the iron fence enclosing the adjacent graveyard. From inside the gray stone church, the animals could be heard bleating and barking as the girls giggled and pinched their way through the service. Outside St. Mary's, the tumult of World War I, the Russian Revolution, the global flu epidemic, unemployment and hunger marches, women's suffrage, anti-colonialism, and the birth of modern mass-media went unremarked by parents focused on what a very frustrated Decca called a "milk-bland life" of local concerns.[6]

Only Decca would describe her family as "bland." Behind their backs, they were called the "Mad Mitfords."

Decca was the second youngest of six exceptionally headstrong sisters. The "Mitford Girls," as they were known, were brilliant, am-bitious Beauties: slender, aqua-eyed, and graceful. Denied any of the outlets for their talents that were readily available to their one brother, Tom, and thrown back almost exclusively on one another's company, they constructed a private world of elaborate games and secret languages. From the nursery, tucked into the top of the house, they encouraged one another's rebellions and wild schemes. They hid themselves in linen closets and invented extravagant tales. They indulged in endless pranks. They teased one another mercilessly. Their nannies fled the house in tears. They could be a "savage little tribe," a family friend noted.[7] The Mitford Girls benefited from their parents' distraction. Decca's pet sheep, Miranda, was allowed to accompany her anywhere and sleep in her bed. Unity was permitted to shoulder her pet white rat, Ratular, or her snake, Enid, to debutante balls, which had the desired effect of discouraging "chinless wonders" and village squires.[8]

Animal indulgences notwithstanding, the Mitford Girls were cosseted in the extreme. They grew up thwarted and restless. Each pulled an imaginary future down from the air. Each had the grit to make that future happen. Not all their choices were worthy of their willfulness.

Nancy, the eldest, longed to be a famous novelist. Her early novels, *The Pursuit of Love* and *Love in a Cold Climate* were wildly popular, helping create the Mitford family mythology and cementing what Decca later called "the Mitford Industry." Second sister, Pamela, spent her life in the country, devoted to her horses and avoiding publicity. Diana left a wealthy husband, Bryan Guinness, to devote her life to Oswald Mosley, founder of the British Union of Fascists. Unity, Decca's favorite sister, declared early on that she would be a Nazi. As soon as she was old enough, she decamped to Germany and became Hitler's intimate. Youngest daughter, Deborah, was desperate to be a duchess. After marrying into one of England's grandest dukedoms, she restored Chatsworth House (the 126-primary-room ancestral home of the Cavendish family and the

Dukes of Devonshire) and lived out her dream as the Duchess of Devonshire.[9] Decca did not want to fulfill her designated mission to marry well and support Britain's class structure. She wanted to rebel. At eleven years old she opened a "running-away account" at Drummonds Bank, which she used to escape with her second cousin when she was nineteen.

The Mitford Industry has churned out seemingly endless books and movies documenting the sisters' gorgeous lives.[10] Before *Downton Abbey* and its many imitators, the Mitford Girls were emblems of a distant world—glamorous, naughty representatives of a vanishing way of life that they lived as if it could last forever.

No aristocracy maintains power through empathy. Aristocracies have always, as historian David Cannadine notes, "accepted, implicitly and absolutely, an unequal and hierarchical society, in which their place was undisputedly at the top. The members of the titled and genteel classes were not merely the lords of the earth, they were also the stars of the firmament." Normalizing inherited privilege, Cannadine adds, requires generations of aristocrats impervious to how others see them, as well as "to reason, to common sense, and to the historical evidence."[11] Aristocracy, in other words, requires insularity. The Mitfords personified that protocol. As Nancy Mitford once acknowledged, in the face of a rapidly changing world, they all continued to "drink and drive about in large Daimlers. Mitfords are like that."[12]

Decca was not "like that." Even as a child, she felt like an outsider. The village poverty that her family took for granted:

> *worried me and filled me with uneasiness. They [the villagers]*
> *lived in ancient, tiny cottages, pathetically decorated with*
> *pictures of the Royal Family and little china ornaments. The*
> *smell of centuries of overcooked cabbage and strong tea lurked*

in the very walls. The women were old, and usually tooth-less, at thirty. Many had goiters, wens [cysts], crooked backs and other deformities associated with generations of poverty. Could these poor creatures be people, like us? What did they think about, what sort of jokes did they think funny, what did they talk about at meals? How did they fill their days? Why were they so poor?[13]

Decca once confronted her mother: "'I say, wouldn't it be a good idea if all the money in England could be divided up equally among everybody? Then there wouldn't be any really poor people,'" Decca said. Her mother replied: "'Well, that's what the Socialists want to do . . . It wouldn't be fair, darling. You wouldn't like it if you saved up all your pocket money and Debo [sister Deborah] spent hers and I made you give up half your savings to Debo, would you?'"[14] Decca set herself "in headlong opposition" to her family's unshakable view that "upper class, middle class, and working class were destined to travel forever harmoniously down the ages on parallel tracks which could never meet or cross."[15] Being against "everything the family stood for" was a "lonely opposition" at first.[16]

Decca wasn't lonely for long. Her inability to suppress her humor—her sisters always turned everything into a joke as well—annoyed a few comrades but appealed to many more. She had a predilection for silliness and a gift for making politics fun. And she kept faith, even as a Communist, with some unusual aristocratic tics and games. That fidelity to her past—what we might now call being true to herself—made her an exotic and unlikely combination to Americans. She was not just an ex-aristocrat. She was an aristocrat-activist, imbuing her later life as a Communist "foot soldier" in Oakland civil rights work with the hijinks of her childhood. Playfulness, joking, wit, clever phrasing, and huge confidence—all the hallmarks of a privileged upbringing—were key aspects of her success. She knew that others saw her as remarkable. She deployed her singularity brilliantly.

Most activists who eschew personal privilege move as far from their breeding and background as possible. Many devote their lives to doggedly imitating those for whom they would advocate, giving us the politician who tries to talk like a factory worker, the white activist desperate to dress "street," the environmentalist attempting a pure, plastic-free life. Decca did none of that. She showed that we need not *be* like others to care about their struggles.

We are currently living through a crisis of caring so profound that some social commentators contend that we have lost "the critical core skills of not only empathy but connection," and that our brains need rewiring for sociality.[17] Decca's life proves that such rewiring is possible. She demonstrates the difficult process through which true empathy can be learned and practiced.

Decca lived a wildly productive and sometimes painfully tragic life. Yet, her road map is as much to pleasure as it is to effective political agency. Many writers, including some of muckraking's best practitioners, have wondered if "shouting at society" really accomplishes very much.[18] Decca was sure that shouting matters.

She transformed herself from isolated aristocrat into engaged, effective ally without the benefit of social media, affinity groups, or retreats, before widely circulated essays such as Peggy McIntosh's "White Privilege: Unpacking the Invisible Knapsack" or books such as Ibram X. Kendi's *How to Be an Antiracist*. She sought out others who had reshaped their lives through personal sacrifice. She read. She listened. She learned from Black activists in Oakland, California, who taught her how to partner with others, although they were justifiably wary of training white women, let alone British Honorables.

Those who seek to become good allies can learn a great deal from Decca's ways of change. So can anyone who would like to start a life over, anyone who would seek a do-over that goes in unanticipated, improbable directions.

Decca's unlikely choices made her the most complex and interesting Mitford Girl of all. Yet, to date, she has received far less attention than her wealthy, beautiful sisters.[19] Alone among her sisters, Decca became a fierce advocate and ally for others, finding a lifetime of fulfillment in fighting for social justice. By putting the spotlight on Decca's unlikely choices, in their larger context, this biography demonstrates not only what Decca's remarkable self-transformation cost her—all that she gave up to join the social struggle—but equally important, what that transformation from aristocrat to activist brought her in return, and why she always felt the exchange worked so strongly in her favor.

"The Gooey Parts"

The kind of thing that I enjoy is any confrontation.[1]
—JESSICA MITFORD

I n the early spring of 1962, Jessica Mitford faced a crisis. Her publisher demanded that she cut her favorite part of her forthcoming book: a detailed description of embalming a dead body. Using a fictional corpse named Mr. Jones, Decca had lingered over how a trocar device, "jabbed into the abdomen," extracted cavity fluids, how the blood was drained, how "three to six gallons of a dyed and perfumed solution of formaldehyde, glycerin, borax, phenol alcohol, and water" is pumped into the body, how the mouth is sewn shut "with a needle directed upward between the upper lip and gum and brought out through the left nostril," and how products such as Suntone, Lyf-Lyk Tint, and Flextone were used to "soften tissue, shrink or distend it as needed" until the corpse—"sprayed, sliced, pierced, trussed, trimmed, creamed, waxed, painted, rouged, and neatly dressed"—was transformed for viewing into a "Beautiful Memory Picture."[2] Take the offensive chapter out, Houghton Mifflin warned, or they'd pull the book.

Decca was approaching fifty. She'd been imagining success as a writer for thirty years. Her publisher had accepted her first book, a memoir called *Hons and Rebels*, after a dozen publishers had turned it down, and they'd promoted it vigorously. For this, her second book, they'd given her a hefty advance, which Decca had already spent and might now have to repay. The embalming chapter must go, they repeated.

Most early career authors would cave. But Decca was committed to describing her grisly details. She had tested the chapter on friends (her Writing Committee, she called them) and on the few family members with whom she was still "on speakers." "Hen I bet you don't even know what is the best time to start embalming," she wrote her sister Deborah, the Duchess of Devonshire, "so I'll tell you: Before life is" over.[3] To stir up empathy for the poor people funeral directors fleeced, Decca believed, meant exposing the gruesome practices undertakers engaged in, revealing the many unnecessary steps for which they charged grieving clients.[4] She refused to back down. "To leave the gruesome parts out would, I think be wrong," she maintained.[5] If necessary, she decided, she and her husband, Bob, would mimeograph the book on their dining table and distribute it themselves.

All her life Mitford faced difficult, high-risk, potentially disastrous choices. She received lots of advice, almost all of which she ignored. Being a radical, for her, meant always questioning authority. It meant doing things differently. And then accepting the consequences. Decca's instincts were generally sound. When she made bad decisions—and a few of them were doozies—she did not whine. Combining her aristocratic training with her refusal to leave out the gooey parts— whatever was difficult, unpleasant, or wrong in the world—allowed Decca to create a life that was entirely her own. She hated being a role model—"ghastly thought, misleading Louts & their ilk about the pursuit of happiness . . . an absurd idea."[6] But she became one in almost every way, largely because of her bravery. She left lessons not only in writing and advocating for social change, but also in creating a life that was remarkable, and remarkably joyful, for its stubborn embrace of difficulty, contradictions, and mess.

Decca didn't listen to the seemingly good advice she received because she intuited something about herself that most others did not. Her infectious, enviable joyfulness was not tied to winning. She didn't *mind* winning, of course. But what she really loved was the fight itself. She thrived on struggle because she genuinely enjoyed the mucky work of trying to fix things: identifying problems, researching solutions, collaborating with others. Decca often seemed unreasonable. She broke rules, raised hackles, caused offense, and took huge chances. Her way was not for everyone. But her constant troublemaking liberated her from the constraints of her background, allowed her to retain what she valued from her upbringing, and offered freedoms that for most people were unimaginable, at least until Jessica Mitford made them seem more normal.

If she caved now, Decca believed, and took out the parts of her book that she valued, she'd be trading her self-respect for safety. At the same time, Bob had taken a year off work to write the book with her and if she pulled it now, to print it on the dining table, their debts would be immense—far more money than she could reasonably make up as a writer, especially one who would be known henceforth as a difficult woman and unmanageable professional. Bob said it was up to her. Decca was frozen but she had to act fast. She was like a spring thaw rushing under ice, waking at night to scribble calculations on the backs of envelopes, making dawn phone calls to trusted friends, pressing angry doodles into her notepad. She and Bob talked it over again and again. Then Decca decided.

1

"The Feudal Remnant and the Fem"

Edwardian by chronology but Victorian in ideology.[1]
—JESSICA MITFORD ON HER PARENTS

Nancy's novels and Decca's memoirs turned their parents, David and Sydney, into popular caricatures of eccentric British aristocracy, immortalized in what Decca called "the Mitford Industry" for their quirks, prejudices, refusals to modernize, and the beliefs to which they clung.[2] Known to the world through their daughters' writing as General Murgatroyd or Uncle Matthew for David and Aunt Sadie for Sydney, the fictionalized Mitfords let readers peek around the baize door shielding the aristocracy and offered gentle mockery of those to whom so much had been given.[3] Decca professed puzzlement over the allure of "Mitfordiana"—why did anyone care about the Mitfords, she'd ask—but she and Nancy both mastered the push-pull of fascination and derision, ensuring that David and Sydney would be forever synonymous with their fictional counterparts. Following Nancy's 1945 novel about the world in which she was brought up, *The Pursuit of Love* (so successful that two hundred thousand copies were sold in the first year alone), the first thing that visitors to Swinbrook, their large brick home in the Cotswolds, wanted to see was David's "entrenching tool . . . still covered with blood and hairs," with which he'd "whacked to death eight Germans." Nancy had hung it in the entry hall on page 1 of her novel, but it did not exist.

David had the starring role in Nancy's novels, as an eccentric bellower stomping about in corduroy jacket, canvas gaiters, and a moleskin waistcoat, terrorizing all about him with his dislikes, yet beloved by his daughters, who teased him mercilessly about his habits and rules. Fictional David "roared," detested books and would not read them, "loathed clever females," had "medieval . . . standards of chaperonage—the principle was that one never saw any young man alone, under any circumstances until one was engaged to him"—and sat in scowling silence in Parliament, unless the plumbing issues with which he was obsessed were under discussion (in real life, David was indeed chairman of the House of Lords Drains Committee). Nancy captured David cracking his whip on the lawn and raging that "abroad is unutterably bloody and foreigners are fiends." She made a family game of hide-and-seek with their hounds so famous as a "child hunt" that locals felt they had to investigate whether Lord Redesdale was, in fact, hunting his offspring.[4]

Nancy's genius was for caricature, for distilling people to their one dominant trait. Linda teases. Fanny observes. Uncle Matthew roars. Jassy (Jessica) runs away. Aunt Sadie (Sydney) drifts, lost "into a cloud of boredom," distracted, distant, and vague. "My mother," Nancy wrote in a later letter, was "abysmally detached."[5]

Decca's portraits of her parents, written fifteen years after Nancy's, struck similar notes, cementing "Muv" and "Farve" (short for "Muvver" and "Farvver") as isolated eccentrics.[6] "According to my father," she wrote, "outsiders included not only Huns, Frogs, Americans, blacks and all other foreigners . . . in fact, the whole teeming population of the earth's surface." She said he spent so much of his time shut up in his study that everyone, servants included, called it the "Closing Room," because "inevitably, his old eyes would close there, never to open again." Like Nancy, she pictured him as a "man of violent temper, terror of housemaids and gamekeepers, who spent most of his time inveighing against the Hons and growling . . . 'Stinks to merry hell!'"

Decca devoted more attention to Sydney in her nonfiction memoir than Nancy did in her satiric fiction. Decca's version of her mother was a combination of the parental vagueness Nancy noted and something more serious. Her mother's neglect was such, Decca wrote, that when Decca broke her arm twice before turning ten, Muv merely sighed, "Poor Little D., she doesn't seem to have bounce." Her "complete distrust of doctors" was so extreme that she poured all medicines down the sink—"Horrid stuff! The Good Body will throw off the illness if left to itself"—and "in defiance of the law, she refused to allow any of us to be vaccinated ('pumping disgusting dead germs into the Good Body!')." When Decca had a frighteningly sharp stomach pain, her mother went off to attend her chickens, leaving the barely adolescent Decca to telephone the doctor in neighboring Burford and ask if he'd "mind coming over to take out my appendix?"[7] But as abstracted as she was with her children, in Decca's view, Sydney was also an efficient economic manager, unencumbered by sentiment. She practiced:

> *various rather oddly chosen economies. She worked out the*
> *cost of washing and ironing an average of nine napkins,*

17

three meals a day, 365 days a year, found it staggering, and
eliminated napkins from the dining table forever. Paper ones
would, of course, have been unthinkable, and individual
napkin rings too disgusting for words. To her annoyance, the
Daily Express *ran the story of our napkinless meals under the*
headline "Penny Pinching Peeress." Muv made sporadic efforts
to interest us in the subject of household economy, and once
offered a prize of half a crown to the child who could produce
the best budget for a young couple living on £500 a year; but
Nancy ruined the contest by starting her list of expenditures
with "Flowers . . . £490."[8]

She was not as outsider-hating as Farve, Decca remembered. "My
mother rather enjoyed having visitors."[9]

However eccentric Decca's fictionalized parents were, the real
lives of David and Sydney were, if anything, even more unusual.
Understanding how Decca came to throw off everything in her
background, and then devise ways to make use of so much of what
she'd tossed away, requires starting with her parents, the world they
inherited and perpetuated, their peculiarities and their strengths,
and, especially, the models they offered of parenting, marriage, and
gender roles.

IN THE WINTER OF 1894–95, Sydney Bowles was an unusually
mature and self-possessed fourteen-year-old. She had already traveled the world and managed a large London household.[10] So she was
particularly put out about having to wear a child's blue sailor suit—
traditional daywear for Victorian children—when she accompanied
her widowed father to visit his friend and fellow Conservative member of Parliament, Algernon Bertram Mitford. Known as Tap, Thomas
Gibson Bowles was the founding editor of the magazines *Vanity Fair*

and *The Lady*.[11] The train trip from London to Gloucestershire could take more than six hours, but Bowles owed Mitford a favor, so when Mitford asked that he come, Bowles agreed. Bowles and Mitford stood politically to the right of their fellow Conservatives in Parliament, and Mitford sought Bowles's political support. Sydney, her older brothers, George and Geoffrey, and her much younger sister, Dorothy, set out from London's exclusive Belgravia neighborhood and traveled along the Great Western Railway to Mitford's Batsford estate in Gloucestershire, at the edge of the Cotswolds. Fathers did not then typically tow children along on business. But Bowles was both a widower and an eccentric. Mitford had more than enough staff to look after a few stray children, so he indulged Tap's unusual request to bring his children.

The Bowles family arrived at the station at night. A formal coachman and uniformed footmen met them at the small Moreton-on-Marsh train station with a large horse-drawn wagon. Sydney, who was not easily impressed, felt awed. She was also cold. Their drive was long and dark, passing through the black woods where Cotswold falconers gathered to challenge their birds. But the Great Hall of Batsford, nicknamed "Mastodon" for its enormous size—a one-hundred-room, neo-Tudor, sprawling mansion with five different staircases—was warm.[12]

In spite of her youth, Sydney had a keen eye for domestic spaces. Passing through the Great Hall she experienced "the most delicious and special odour. It seemed compounded of wood-fire, beeswax-polish, and . . . rare spices," as she later wrote in her diary. Sydney and her family were led into Batsford's library, which held one of the best book collections then in private hands, thanks to Mitford's wide-ranging literary interests.[13] Mitford, known as Bertie, was both an avid reader and a popular writer, especially about Japan, where he had been an ambassador, following diplomatic service in France,

St. Petersburg, Moscow, and Peking. Like many British Victorians, Mitford was entranced with the Far East; Japan, he felt, was unique in keeping venerable medieval traditions alive.

In the library, a large fire blazed. Sydney took in Bertie Mitford's "glittering" blue eyes (the Mitfords all had startlingly blue eyes) and his wife Clementine's "fine presence."[14] A slender girl, who would stay thin all her life and whose daughters would be famous for their excellent figures, Sydney also noted that Clementine "like all middle-aged women then . . . [was] too fat." For Sydney, as for many women of the upper class, fat was a moral failing, signaling inept handling of the social, economic, agricultural, and culinary excess that the aristocracy enjoyed. Nancy Mitford, in her wildly popular book on England's class consciousness, would later note that the English aristocrat "seldom overdoes anything. It is his enormous strength."[15] Bowles especially abhorred overeating. He observed a lifelong practice of eating only a light breakfast and dinner: no lunch, no snacks. At least Bertie and Clementine's daughters, Frances and Iris, were not overweight, Sydney noted, approving the lithe, well-mannered girls and envying them their dresses.[16] But most of her attention was fixed on David Mitford, the lanky young man who ten years later would become her husband: "With his back to the fire, standing half on the fender, and wearing an old velveteen coat such as keepers wore in those days, stood the wonderful figure of a young man. It was David, aged 17. So, when I was 14 and he was 17, I fell in love with him."

Sydney's crush on David was the way Victorian aristocrats fell in love. Young people of their social class were almost never alone. They spent little time with one another. They did not search for soulmates.[17] The goal was to marry a familiar stranger.[18]

David and Sydney were ideal familiar strangers. Both were tall and handsome. With long faces, slender noses, and bright blue (almost aqua) eyes, they looked, in fact, like brother and sister. David's resting expression was annoyed. Sydney's mouth had a naturally and sharply downward cast; it gave her a permanently pouty and disapproving look, as if she'd been sucking something sour. Both loved to ice-skate, and both wanted children. More importantly, both had experienced profound life changes early in life: Sydney lost her mother, and David's father suddenly and unexpectedly inherited a large fortune, including the Batsford estate, from a cousin.

But in spite of her longing to make a good impression, the Batsford visit did not go well for Sydney. Her outfit compared poorly to the elegant clothes of Frances and Iris. Tap Bowles was a professional contrarian, and on this occasion, behaved badly by insisting that Sydney be seated with him at supper, although it was evident that Clementine Mitford wanted the children served upstairs. "Dinner was always a grand affair" in English country estates, and Sydney, Bowles, and the other guests were served soup, fish, an entrée, meat, fowl, and a dessert. The practice was to "take very little of a course or refuse it entirely."[19] When Tap Bowles spied an elderly guest across the table taking more than he perhaps should, he did not hold back. "My dear Sir, the part of your dinner that does you the most good is the part that you *don't* eat," Bowles bellowed across the room.

That outburst—and the hateful sailor suit—were bad enough for Sydney. But then a fishbone stuck sideways in her throat.[20] She showed her mettle, going back to her room alone and getting the fishbone out by herself with a buttonhook.[21] Sydney was lavishly praised for her cleverness—and for not causing further drama. David, never considered excessively clever or handy, took note. Sydney made a better first impression that night than she knew.

While this was David and Sydney's first meeting, their connection went back further. Sydney had been born on Bertie Mitford's estate.

Sydney's mother, Jessica Evans-Gordon Bowles (for whom her

21

daughter Jessica was later named), had suffered miscarriages and difficult childbirths with Sydney's siblings George in 1877 and Geoffrey in 1879. When she found herself pregnant again in 1879, for the fifth time in five years, she wanted to be near the recently completed Royal Victoria Hospital. Wealthy women had begun relying on male physicians, rather than female midwives, to assist them in childbirth, a choice that did not always serve them well.[22] The Royal Victoria Hospital boasted every modern medical advance. Bertie Mitford's estate was thirty miles from the hospital. Bowles appealed to Bertie for help relocating Jessica nearby. The estate included a separate, ten-bedroom house, named Inchmerry, sited above a private beach. Bertie let that to Tap for a year. For some reason, in spite of the hospital's proximity, Jessica and Tap Bowles's daughter, Sydney, was born at home, at Inchmerry, on May 10, 1880.[23] If David and Sydney met in 1880, as toddler and infant, neither remembered it. Their fathers would not have arranged playdates for their children.

Mitford and Bowles were classic Victorian adventurer/entrepreneurs—though Bowles excelled at making money and Mitford at spending it. Both were eccentrics who thrived in Parliament, wrote, and studied languages and linguistics. They shared a passion for yachting and foreign travel. They were curious, energetic, lively, and highly social. They were colonial enthusiasts, heavily involved in Britain's imperial economy—Bowles through sugar in Trinidad and Mitford through tea in Ceylon.[24] They took both social inequality and British rule for granted, as they took for granted that men of their milieu would marry much younger women and leave them behind when they traveled. Both men were obsessed with cleanliness, had bright blue eyes, and spoke French.

Bertie Mitford was educated at Eton and proud of his family connections. There were family seats at Airlie and Cortachy castles on one side, and the vastly wealthy Stanley family of Alderley on the other. He was fascinated by other cultures but believed them inferior to Britain. His "snobbery grew as he got older."[25] When he inherited his wealth unexpectedly in 1886, he spent it with abandon, creating showy gardens in the long-standing British tradition of lavish spending on houses and grounds, something that David would later do as well. As a traditionalist, Mitford wanted his own sons, Clement and David, to understand both "the right of Europeans" to govern others and the importance of "good breeding." His own mother, Lady Georgina Ashburnham, had left when Bertie was three, divorcing his father and marrying her lover: highly scandalous behavior that gave Nancy the idea, decades later, for a character she called "the Bolter."

This bent branch in Bertie's family tree may have made Bertie sympathetic to Tap Bowles, whose parentage and upbringing were far more difficult. Tap was illegitimate, "the most common of family secrets" in the British aristocracy.[26] He was the son of Susan Bowles, a servant who lived in "grinding poverty" before working for Thomas Milner Gibson and having his children. When Gibson's wife, Susannah, agreed to accept young Tap into the household and to raise him as her own, Susan had little choice but to give up her son to her employers.[27] While the Gibsons accepted Tap, the rules of their class did not. He was denied admission to the best schools and sent away to France. Yet even more than Mitford, Bowles promoted the system that excluded him. He viewed the lower classes (from which he sprang) as naturally inferior and considered women "uneducated nuisances . . . incapable of ethics or high principles," and fundamentally ineducable.[28]

Both men were fiercely anti-Semitic, even more so than was then typical of their class, sharing what Decca later called "a sort of innate antisemitism, an innate anti-foreignerism, jingoism if you like, you know, directed against everybody except their own class and their own country," just the attitude Mitford's son David would later

23

embody.[29] For modern readers, the nonchalant brutality of these men's hatred may be shocking. Bertie Mitford wrote an introduction to notorious anti-Semite Houston Stewart Chamberlain's "rambling, ranting meditation [on] . . . the innate superiority of the Teutonic people."[30] Tap Bowles was even more hateful, excoriating Jews in the most dehumanizing terms of his time. "I don't see what the Jews have to whine about," Bowles declared: "There is absolutely nothing . . . to excite any sympathy for the Jew. On the contrary, all that one sees of him produces loathing and contempt. His filth, his effeminacy, his degradation . . . the ungenerous cunning that gleams in his eye. There is, I suppose, no human animal more utterly devoid of all dignity and nobility . . . [they are] a race that has been oppressed for centuries, and that has so deserved oppression as to make it hard not to oppress it."[31] Decades later, Diana would also blame Jews for their own oppression, but with some care not to repeat the most offensive strains of this language.

While raising his children to despise Jews (Sydney would later be stubbornly loyal to Hitler, whom she found charming), Bowles was also convinced that Jews were immune to cancer and that their diet should be imitated. He forbade white flour, white sugar, most medicines, and all vaccinations: "Trust the Good Body," he intoned.[32] He prescribed fresh air, clean bath rinses, whole grains, and fresh, unprocessed foods.[33] Sydney adhered strictly to his ideas of "the Good Body."

Bowles often roared. "Don't . . . talk . . . such . . . RUBBISH," he bellowed at anyone who disagreed with him.[34] He dismissed most others as "brutal . . . insipid . . . lunatic . . . or niggling."

Sydney said that she was "always miserable as a child."[35] Her mother died, from yet another difficult pregnancy, when Sydney was eight years old. The usual thing would have been for Bowles to hire extra nannies, nurses, and governesses to care for Dorothy, three,

Sydney, eight, Geoffrey, nine, and George, eleven, at home, ideally in a wing of their own. Instead, he scooped up his children and took them out to sea for almost a year, on his yacht, the *Nereid*.[36]

Life on the *Nereid* was difficult. It had only four cabins, no engine, and was entirely dependent on wind and tide. Packed on board, in addition to the four children, were Tap, two crewmen, a cook, a nurse, and a governess. In all likelihood the crew slung hammocks after dark and slept on deck, exposed to the elements. Unlike the sturdy children, the governess and nurse were ill most of the time.[37] When there was strong wind, they were all locked into their tiny cabins, with their skylights blocked with boards to protect the glass. Breathing stale air, with a single, swinging oil lamp casting ghostly shadows, they all felt pummeled as choppy waves slammed the boat up and down. Lack of wind was worse than gales, because in still weather the *Nereid* baked in the heat. The children had brought their beloved terrier, Smiler, along on ship. For safety, Smiler was tethered to the deck. One day he jumped overboard in excitement and was hung to death by his leash. Another day the ship was visited by dolphins "playing and tumbling round the ship," considered a great omen in becalmed seas, and a thrill for the children. A crew member speared one of the dolphins and butchered it on deck; he nailed the tail to the bowsprit.[38] Their father insisted that Sydney and Dorothy visit a Turkish bath in Alexandria; they caught lice there. Since their cook frequently had to contend with unfamiliar ingredients, their food was often inedible. During one cyclone their ship was nearly smashed to bits off the coast of Africa. In a hurricane off Syria, their mast snapped, and they were nearly driven onto the rocks. Years later, Sydney wrote Decca that "a week at sea in rough weather is no joke."[39]

Bowles loved it all. For him, being on the sea was "a consolation and a refuge from the trivialities, the meanness, and the confusions of land life."[40] The sea's great lesson, he would say, is "that we are all of us utterly unimportant; its dangers made him feel like a "real man."[41] His young children did not want to learn about their irrelevance. They wanted to matter.

At some point during the *Nereid*'s voyage, Bowles seduced the children's governess, Tello. She shared a cabin with Sydney, and her ensuing pregnancy became obvious.[42] Bowles maintained that it was all fine for his children and insisted that they were "neither sick nor sorry" to live with him on ship.[43]

Bertie Mitford was considered an ideal British "type," even a "sort of Prince Charming."[44] Japan had captured his imagination. But he was also captivated by the Mormons and their magic, secret-scripture-revealing glasses and fascinated with America's "true pioneer spirit" toward the "howling wilderness."[45] With the supreme self-confidence of his class, he moved easily between worlds, and gracefully in and out of wealth.

It was challenging for David to be his son. Much of what came easily to his father was difficult for David: scholarship, languages, and social acceptance, especially. David could be funny and creative. But he lacked his father's poise.

Sydney and David did not marry for ten years after their introduction in 1894. When Sydney first met David, Britain was two years into an economic depression, but little of it had touched either of their lives. David had just finished boarding school at Radley and was en route to Ceylon, for the beginning of what would be an education in maintaining the British empire in the colonies, specifically as a tea planter, an economy that was heavily dependent on enslavement. His father and older brother Clement, set to inherit the family fortune, had both attended Eton, considered distinctly superior to Radley. He was "very much a second son" and he had all the grumbling resentments common to that set.[46] David was unpopular at Radley: bad at team sports, a poor student, and difficult to get along with.

Ceylon (Sri Lanka) was one of the colonies where British second sons were sent to make their fortunes. David spent four years there, learning the "colonial ruler kind of thing" in a world "modeled on the slave plantations of the Caribbean."[47] His time in Ceylon coincided with Ceylon's agricultural transition from coffee to tea planting, and with various attempts to break the "semi-slave" state of indentured workers on plantations. David was faced with labor challenges, diminished profits, and illness—cholera and smallpox were especially rampant.[48] In later life, he hardly spoke of his time there.

From Ceylon, David joined the military, the "profession I always wanted," he said, convinced that "being a soldier and a gentleman . . . [was] the most you could say for any man." He fought in the Second Boer War, receiving two leg wounds.[49] The British fought the Boer War over gold and diamond rights, to keep open routes to India, and to repress Dutch competition and secure territorial expansion in Africa. The war was especially bloody, expensive, and drawn out. Illness ravaged British troops. Great Britain utilized concentration camps and a scorched-earth policy that was heavily criticized, even within the country. While learning to oppress others there, David had his first experiences of being without his accustomed privileges. His leg wounds healed. But he lost a lung. Surrounded by dying soldiers in the hospital, he wrote Sydney a love letter, for her to read after his death. He was invalided home in 1902 and survived, proud of his service and survival. Nothing he saw in the war induced him to critique the British Empire.

Sydney also received an imperial education. She came out into society with a string of potential suitors, including a Swedish ice-skating teacher she allowed to kiss her, a young soldier, and a young man who broke her heart, she said. Sydney found the romantic agonies of other young women self-indulgent. She was set on making a sensible match to "a man of my own station" and promised not to be a "sentimental vain foolish little ass" and marry for love alone.[50]

By the time they married, on February 6, 1904, at St. Margaret's Church in Westminster, Britain was on the cusp of enormous social changes that would include a recession, the establishment of Britain's National Insurance, challenges to hereditary privilege in governance, widespread labor and general strikes (as many as one thousand strikes a year between 1911–1914), pressure for universal education and women's suffrage, and, in the distance, the war that would sweep up almost half of all British men of military age.[51] What social historians call the "niceties of rank and etiquette" were vanishing.[52] But David and Sydney set forth as if nothing in their world was changing or would ever change.

They honeymooned on Bowles's second yacht, *The Hoyden* (perhaps an odd choice for Sydney, given her earlier shipboard experiences) and visited Paris. They secured a house near Bowles, off Sloane Square in London, and employed five female servants to run it.[53] Later they moved to a larger home off Kensington High Street. They lived mostly in London, and David worked for Sydney's father, taking the unlikely position of office manager of *The Lady* magazine, a job for which he was eminently unsuited, but at which he plugged away for a decade. They had his income of roughly 600 pounds a year, and Sydney had an allowance from her father of 400 pounds a year (a combined amount equal to roughly £110,000 today), as well as Old Mill Cottage in High Wycombe, which gave them a country retreat and allowed them to rent out their London home, when needed, for extra cash. They spent considerable time at Tap's home in Lowndes Square. Sometimes they stayed with Tap at his home near the Isle of Wight.

At this point, Bertie Mitford's vast inherited fortune was largely depleted, and after taxes and bequests came to under £20,000 (£2.2 million today), not including the value of lands and property. He had spent lavishly and beyond his means on Batsford, razing a perfectly good Georgian home to replace it with his large neo-Tudor manor and an expensive Asian garden, complete with different species of exotic bamboo. In this, Mitford kept alive a long British tradition of conspicuous consumption of a very particular sort. "Only the wealthy could afford expanses of scythe-mown lawns," and until the invention of the modern lawn mower the lawn symbolized not only enough wealth to devote valuable land to useless visual ornamentation—meant to showcase the large house it surrounded—but enough wealth, as well, to commend workers to the backbreaking task of hand mowing.[54]

David did not keep journals or write memoirs as his father did. Records of his feelings about Ceylon, the Boer War, fighting in France in World War I, or his father's squandered fortune are scant. He was more effusive, however, about his first years with Sydney. "I am afraid that in my happiness I forget others who have not been so happy although they deserve it far more," he wrote his mother, Clementine. "I *am* grateful."[55]

David tempered his boredom at *The Lady* by chain-smoking, playing the banjo, and hunting rats. He had brought a mongoose home with him from Ceylon, and upon discovering that the cellars of the magazine office were rat infested, he turned his mongoose loose. Sometimes, he was taken with get-rich-quick schemes, such as papier-mâché radio cases. He decided to take up gold mining, inspired perhaps by newspapers accounts of huge successes in the Klondike, and he staked a claim in the small Canadian town of Swastika, Ontario, taking Sydney with him. There, Unity was born, and they lived in a small wooden shack where Sydney did all the housekeeping herself, including pumping water from a well. A neighbor struck a massive vein of gold, but David and Sydney found nothing.[56] Deborah later described her father's financial management—which should have been in Sydney's able hands—as a series of "unlucky financial decisions."[57]

David leaned far to the right of his right-wing father in all matters. While he could be appealing, he always had to be appeased. And he insisted on being in charge. Sydney indulged him and took his rages in stride.

Where Bertie and Tap had thrived on travel, the upper-class tradition of long visits was anathema to David, as was dining at anyone else's home. "Farve seldom stayed in other people's houses. . . . My parents seldom had friends to stay," Deborah observed.[58] He was a homebody who no one wanted to be home with. As a consequence, the Mitfords were socially landlocked. As Deborah put it: "My father did not wish for a social life. Muv would have enjoyed one but seldom suggested anything he would not want—she was aware of the hazards."[59]

Nancy described their father as "one of nature's fascists." He despised all things non-English—"Never shake hands with . . . Catholics or Germans"—and he could not bear the slightest inclination to modernism spied in his offspring.[60] Sydney gave him the traditional home he craved, complete with seven children. She erred only in that six of them were girls. Nancy was born on November 28, 1904, roughly nine months from Sydney and David's wedding day. She was followed by Pam in 1907, Tom (the only boy and everyone's darling) in 1909, Diana in 1910, Unity in August 1914, Decca in 1917, and Deborah in 1920.

After war was declared in 1914, David rejoined his former regiment from the Boer War, serving as a Transport Officer in Belgium. Sydney moved the children out from London to Bertie's Batsford estate, just as Jessica and Tap Bowles had done many years ago. In

May 1915, David's brother Clement was killed in battle.

Clement's death put David next in line to inherit the family estate, after his father's death (provided that Clement's widow, Helen, who was pregnant when Clement died, did not give birth to a son). Bertie Mitford died suddenly in August 1916. Helen gave birth to a girl, Clementine. David, who'd spent a lifetime as the second son, now inherited the estate with virtually no time to learn what would be expected of him.

Yet, after the war, Sydney and David moved surprisingly easily into what Decca later called their "narrow . . . conservative" roles as Lord and Lady Redesdale, the inherited title they acquired in addition to their family name of Mitford.[61] Batsford was much different than it had been when Sydney met David there in 1894. Most of the rooms were now closed off or covered. But it was still an enormous and grand estate, and it included homes and lands in Northumberland that totaled almost twenty thousand acres and the ruins of a twelfth-century castle. There were also large estates in Gloucestershire and Oxfordshire.[62] Clement's widow and children were moved elsewhere, and David's grieving mother, Clementine, was exiled to Redesdale Cottage in Northumberland, where one day David would also retreat to grumble and expire.

Between David's tempers and Sydney's detachment, most people found Decca's parents intimidating. From the proprietor of the inn whose livelihood depended on their approval, to the tradesmen who served their needs, to the self-trained engineer who devised river-driven electricity for their manor house, Lord and Lady Redesdale inspired equal measures of fear and respect. But as she grew up, Decca liked to tease them. She especially liked to poke fun at their traditionalism. Her favorite nicknames for them were the Feudal Remnant and the Fem.

2

"That Dread Place"

One had to get away from that dread place at all costs.[1]
—JESSICA MITFORD

A "Feudal Remnant" needs a "feudal stronghold," Decca said. Over the course of her childhood, her parents provided five of them, each house profoundly affecting the shape of family life. A favorite tease of Decca's was naming the houses in descending order of grandeur—"Batsford Mansion to Asthall Manor to Swinbrook House to Old Mill Cottage"—to mark the family's fading fortunes (a very grand London house that didn't quite fit the joke went unmentioned).[2] Like many men of his class, David Mitford, Lord Redesdale, paid more attention to his houses than his daughters, and he was more enthusiastic than wise with his property. He scrimped when he should have spent and spent when he should have saved. He sold property at the worst possible times and bought properties he could not afford when they were selling at peak prices. He sank far too much money into his purchases, then tried to make up for that with doomed schemes to make a sudden mint.[3] Sydney could not, or would not, contain him.

Decca was two years old when her father sold Batsford, with its hundred rooms and ten thousand acres of land, unable to afford the massive upkeep his father's home required. He moved the family to Swinbrook village, where he'd inherited over two thousand acres of land and an estate that included three dozen village houses, stables, an inn, a mill, a post office, a blacksmith's shop, a public house, a village school, an estate-keeper's lodge called Furzyleaze, a cricket field, remnants of an old Roman road, and a church, but no family house he considered suitable for the estate owner. There, David made the one truly good purchase of his life: Asthall Manor, the only home that everyone in the family adored.[4]

Asthall was easy to love. A Jacobean two-story sixteen-room home, originally built in the early 1600s, its honey-colored limestone and many mullioned windows were beautifully sited on a tree-lined lane and surrounded by a walled garden. While Asthall was so large that it was used as a convalescent home during World War I, the family called it a cottage and felt that, unlike Batsford, it was a true family home. As such, however, Asthall had a few peculiarities, including looking straight onto an adjacent graveyard.

The home needed extensive renovations when David purchased it. He had an engineer build turbines for a system of water-generated electricity, allowing the house to be wired for electric lights and heating—unheard of conveniences in the Cotswolds of 1919. He put in a phone (which only he was allowed to touch), a light board to ring for the servants, indoor plumbing and bathrooms, and modernized the kitchen. For the family, he created a swimming pond from a river bend, with a dock, benches, and a Victorian-styled thatched summer changing house which looked like something out of a fairy tale. Between house and pond, he installed a terraced rose garden and a willow walk. In place of a loving father, the Mitford children had a lovely, embracing home.

Asthall required a staff of between eight and eleven people working as maids, cooks, butlers, or nannies, and another half dozen outside working on the water turbines (housed in a large, oily room behind the house), or as engineers, gardeners, gamekeepers, and grooms for the family stables. In the large, bright kitchen, on an uneven plaster wall beneath a low ceiling, servants' bells sat in their dark oak box. At any time, dining room, hall, morning room, study, drawing room, west bedrooms, east bedrooms, staircase to the bedrooms, large spare room, small spare room, blue room, bathrooms, guest bathrooms, nursery, school room, governess's room, or front door might light up.

David's most important renovation, and the one that mattered most to Decca and her sisters, was connecting a barn to the main house with a covered stone walkway that the family called "the Cloisters." More than sixty feet long and over twenty feet wide, this annex had a coved ceiling, carved curved beams, massive chandeliers, a bay with oversize casement windows and built-in window seats, teak floors, electric light, four upstairs bedrooms (which the older Mitford children were allowed to claim), a bathroom with running water, sofas, richly colored Persian rugs, and a grand piano. The walls of what now became The Library, as David always called it, were lined with built-in teak bookcases and filled end-to-end with Bertie Mitford's extensive Batsford book collection. The Mitford children were free to peruse The Library at will, provided they returned each book to its exact spot. They spent almost all their time in the library, reading, inventing games, playing piano. Sydney and David spent almost no time there, so the children had a world apart, and they took every advantage of that freedom from the grown-ups to invent their own society of rules, rank, games, languages, pranks, cruelties, and occasional kindnesses. The Mitford Girls were preternaturally lively. Natural competitiveness drove them to greater and greater heights of cleverness in order to best one another in reading, storytelling, conversation, and creative games. Teasing was their pilot light. Prodded by one another, itching for more activity that their social script allowed, straining at the dual bits of gender and class, each of the Mitford Girls lit up every room they entered, setting everything about them either aglow or ablaze. "It was paradise and I knew it," Deborah later said.[5]

David wanted a modern home, not one as quirky as the family inhabiting it, and he always intended Asthall to be temporary. He started building a new house even before the war, and in 1926, when Decca was nine, he sold Asthall and moved the family a few miles away to Swinbrook, which Decca and her sisters hated and secretly called Swinebrook.

Swinbrook sat on a barren rise: a blocky three-story brick square with a dozen bedrooms, a nursery and schoolroom, garages, greenhouses, tennis courts, and stables. Swinbrook required an inside staff of nine or more. They wore "Redesdale Blue" uniforms, David's favorite color. Swinbrook, Decca said, had "the utilitarian look of . . . a small barracks, a girls' boarding school, a private lunatic asylum . . . [it] had many aspects of a fortress or citadel of medieval times."[6]

The home was a family failure from the first, with plaster walls which had not cured properly and remained damp to the touch and elm doors, made to David's specifications, which had dried incorrectly and were consequently so warped that the children complained they had no privacy in the bathrooms. David had taken great care to install modern conveniences. But despite its many fireplaces, eight chimneys, and central heating, the house was always drafty and cold. Its biggest failing was its utter lack of charm. Unlike Asthall, which was full of surprises, Swinbrook had no nooks or crannies, sudden twists, unexpected stairwells, or tiny doors. It had no library, no special place for a children's world. All the books from Asthall were installed in the freshly-built bookcases of David's new bespoke study, into which only he was allowed.

The warmest place in Swinbrook was a large linen closet through which the house's hot water pipes ran. The girls ventured there, at first, to get warm. They found that the linen closet, now immortalized by Nancy's novels as the "Hons' Cupboard," was an ideal place to tell stories and speak in secret languages. "Here we would sit, huddled up on the slatted shelves, and talk for hours about life and death," Nancy later wrote.[7] Hon was not a shortened form of "honorable," a title any of the girls could have claimed (and which they all, to their credit, refused). "Hon" was derived, Decca explained, "from the Hens which played so large a part in our lives. . . . We kept dozens of them."[8] The "Hons' Society" met in the "Hons' Cupboard" to speak "Honnish" and "Boudledidge," an invented language so complete that Decca and Unity found they could tell dirty jokes in front of the grown-ups without being detected. Nicknames "Hen" and "Henderson" were also nods to the chickens. In addition to Honnish and Boudledidge, the sisters developed a distinctive idiolect, a "curiously cadenced sing-song" that one young friend remembered as quite annoying—a language partly modeled on the speech of the "Bright Young Things" of Nancy's generation, the disaffected artists and aesthetes for whom everything, mockingly, was either "divine" or "dread," and in which people were always "longing."[9]

Nicknames were a Mitford staple. The sisters had many of them over the years and held on to them all their lives. Decca was Hen, Henderson, Squalor, Steake to Pam, and Susan to Nancy. Nancy was Naunce, later French Lady and Lady, but usually Susan to Decca (since they both called one another Susan, their letters could cause confusion). Diana was Cord, Honks, Nard, or Nardy. Unity was Boud, Birdie, or Bobo. Deborah was Nine to Nancy (Debo's mental age, Nancy said), but Hen or Henderson to Decca; she was Debo to everyone else. Pam was Woman or Woo. Tom was Tuddemy or Tud. David and Sydney were Muv and Farve to everyone, even the neighbors. They were sometimes the Revereds to Decca or the Poor Old Male (TPOM) and the Poor Old Female (TPOF). Decca also called her father the Old Subhuman.

Muv and Farve were even more absent than was typical for their class. Muv's "detachment" was flawless, Decca said.[10] Decca used to bet that she could go twenty-four hours without seeing her mother, a wager she usually won. Once, Unity ran into the drawing room where Sydney was seated at her writing table. "Muv, Muv, Decca is standing on the roof—she says she's going to commit suicide!" Unity announced. "'Oh, poor duck . . . I hope she won't do anything so terrible,' Sydney said, and then went on writing."[11]

In their parents' absence, the sisters became an intense and feral tribe. All the sisters knew exactly which buttons to push, and they kept one another in stitches or in tears: "shrieks and floods," Decca called it. They patented what Decca called "an unrelenting form of ridicule," known as "the Mitford tease." The Mitford tease could be painful to the point of torture but was also irresistibly funny. Nancy and Unity were especially good at it. Debo was not.[12] An interviewer once asked Decca to confirm that sisters stood between her and life's cruel circumstances. "Sisters *were* life's cruel circumstances," Decca replied.[13] She was also an excellent tease. Braver than her sisters, Decca even teased her father, sometimes poking fun at his financial woes. "It is fun to tweak up your gorse dear," she said.[14] Unity was "the one I really adored," Decca said, because she was funniest and most stubborn, and because her "dissatisfaction with life mirrored my own." Unity had a "huge, glittering personality . . . [a] rare brand of eccentricity . . . a kind of loyalty" that she preserved even when the two sisters grew apart.[15]

As Unity became increasingly drawn to fascism, Decca was seized by socialism, becoming as passionate about ameliorating social inequality as Unity was about maintaining it. Their differences were childish declarations at first—"'I'm going to Germany to meet Hitler,' Boud announced. 'I'm going to run away and be a Communist,' I countered." When they took a diamond ring and carved competing swastikas and hammer and sickles into the glass window of their nursery, both were still young.[16] But the divide proved serious. Decca "had a sad and uneasy feeling that we were somehow being swept apart by a huge tidal wave of which we had no control; that from the distance a freezing shadow was approaching which would one day engulf us."[17]

She remembered a "bewildering succession" of haphazardly trained governesses whom the sisters tormented, shocked, and sent packing. One taught the children to play cards. She was followed by one "whose main contribution to our education was to teach a little mild shoplifting. 'Like to try a little jiggery-pokery, children?'" she would ask on the way into town.[18] Decca desperately wanted to study science. But "a cold No was the only answer, no reason given."[19] Her mother insisted that any education her girls received could be provided at home. "Interwar Britain was still a very undereducated society," social historian Martin Pugh explains; this was as true—if not more so—across social ranks as within them.[20] Using the PNEU system, (Parents' National Education Union), designed for homeschooling, Sydney read aloud, then asked the girls what they remembered. She taught them geography from maps—there was Britain in the map's center and the rest of the world on its edges—and encouraged reading. Indifference to seriously educating girls was common in the Mitfords' milieu. "The thing that *absolutely burned into my soul*," Decca said, "was the business of not being allowed to go to school. So much so that . . . [decades later when] the subject came up . . . I found myself literally fighting back tears of rage."[21]

Decca's parents opposed education because their daughters were raised for marriage. To support that future, they took a large London house to use for each girl's coming out, during the time of her presentation at court, and for chaperoned London courting. The house, 26 Rutland Gate, in London's fashionable Kensington neighborhood, was a six-story cream-colored building, trimmed in black iron, with a ballroom, an elevator, and a rudimentary intercom system that David installed as soon as he acquired the property.

Placing six daughters in British society was costly. The London house was expensive to buy and to run, requiring at least nine staff people. Often, it was more than David and Sydney could afford. Sometimes they had to let out the London house and squeeze into their mews cottage (an apartment over the house's garage). Occasionally, they had to rent out both Rutland Gate and Swinbrook and retreat to Sydney's Mill Cottage in High Wycombe.

One after another, Decca's sisters made their choices. Nancy was supposed to marry first, but she spent years pining after Hamish Erskine, a homosexual friend. After Erskine ended the nominal engagement to marry a wealthier woman at the end of 1933 (when Decca was fifteen), Nancy married Peter Rodd, a young man of bad habits and constant infidelities (they separated shortly after marrying and divorced after the war). Diana had a grand society wedding in 1929, when Decca was twelve, to the beer dynasty heir, Bryan Guinness. She soon divorced him to embark on an affair with Oswald Mosley, head of the British Union of Fascists, who was married at the time and having an affair with his wife's sister. After Mosley's wife died suddenly, Mosley and Diana married in Germany, at the home of Joseph Goebbels. Hitler was a wedding guest. In 1936, Pamela married wealthy scientist Derek Jackson, a bisexual, notorious womanizer, and thoroughly undomesticated. Unity had an unsuccessful debutante season in London, traveled to Germany, attended the Nuremberg Nazi rallies of 1933, and became obsessed with Hitler, stalking him relentlessly at his favorite lunch restaurant until he finally invited her to his table. Thereafter, Unity spent every moment she could with Hitler. She never married.

In 1928, when Decca was eleven, Nancy (then in her early twenties and still unmarried) prevailed upon her parents—after "titanic rows"—to let her attend art school in London.[22] Decca could not contain her jealousy. She imagined Nancy in "a world of London bed-sitters, art students, writers . . . a world of new and different ideas . . . a world from which Swinbrook would seem as antiquated as a feudal stronghold."[23] After one month at the Slade School, however, Nancy quit and came home. "How could you!" Decca wailed. "If I ever got away to a bed-sitter I'd never come back." Nancy had found herself "knee-deep in underclothes . . . I literally had to wade through them. No one to put them away," she explained.[24] "You are very weak-minded," Decca replied. "You wouldn't catch me knuckling under because of a little thing like underclothes."[25] Not surprisingly, Decca "did not particularly relish the idea of following in the footsteps" of the women in her family.[26] Their pathways looked as empty to Decca as flat roadways with nothing on either side.

Shortly after Nancy's disappointing knuckling, Decca decided to run away from home: "[I] had saved enough money to support myself for a while. I wrote immediately to Drummonds Bank; in a couple of days I had their answer. 'Dear Madam, We respectfully beg leave to acknowledge receipt of ten shillings as initial deposit in your Running Away Account. Passbook Number 437561 enclosed. We remain, dear Madam, your obedient servants . . .' I triumphantly flashed the letter around the family. Look! And fancy Drummonds being my obedient servants! What bliss!"[27]

At a certain point, Decca later wrote, "you discover suffering." When she was twelve, she began to experience "vivid glimpses of the real meaning of poverty, hunger, cold, cruelty." She said that she "fretted and fumed at my inability to discover a solution."[28] She began to understand that "class was everything" and the key to the suffering to which she was, increasingly, attuned. In her home "class was a delicate matter, a subject for intuition rather than conversation . . . deeply felt but never discussed."[29] Refusing to acknowledge class differences was common in Decca's milieu. But her parents were excessive in those denials, Decca felt. They were both, she wrote, "extremely narrow, narrow and conservative. . . . My father was . . . an extreme conservative."[30] As labor unions, death taxes, inflation, and agricultural collapse threatened the largest estates, other British aristocrats began to worry that they might be what Andrew Cavendish, 11th Duke of Devonshire (and Decca's eventual brother-in-law) called "a spent force."[31] But not David and Sydney. They behaved as if their way of life was the globe's fixed axis. It was inevitable that Decca, anti-authoritarian to her core, would go in the opposite direction.

As a child, she experimented with "new and more revolutionary notions of how to solve the world's ills." Her experiments were typically terrible failures, and she never forgot them. When she was thirteen, she joined a British organization called the Sunbeams, designed to pair rich and poor children as pen pals and to facilitate the rich children's donations of used clothing and toys to the poor ones. Decca's Sunbeam was named Rose Dickson, and Decca "spent hours packing up old jerseys and skirts into exciting-looking parcels . . . I imagined that my letters, which consisted of a highly romanticized account of life at Swinbrook, must bring great rays of joy into her otherwise drab existence." Decca found Rose's life "fascinating," especially the "miserable over-crowded conditions in which they all lived—all six of them in two beds in one tiny room." She became "obsessed" with rescuing Rose and begged her mother to invite Rose to visit Swinbrook. Instead, Lady Redesdale hired Rose, fourteen years of age, as a "Between Maid" or "Tweeny," at Swinbrook. Rose cried herself to sleep every night. "I didn't see her much," Decca remembered. After a few wretched days, Rose went home.[32]

These were the kinds of experiences that, combined with the total isolation of her life—"It was neither necessary, nor generally possible, to leave the premises for any of the normal human pursuits . . . all were provided, either in the house itself or within easy walking distance."—made Decca want to flee.[33] Not being able to talk about her feelings of guilt and rage with either her parents or her sisters only made them worse. She felt like a kettle, left boiling far too long on the burner.

A segment of the Mitford Industry has nevertheless argued that Decca was a malcontent whose childhood was ideal and her bitterness about it was "inexplicable." According to Diana's daughter-in-law, Jessica lacked her sister Debo's "well-adjusted disposition," which another family biographer laments as "inimical to Jessica."[34] On this theory, questioning one's privileges is either misguided, ill-mannered, or dishonest. But Decca was both grateful and miserable. She enjoyed all there was to enjoy about her sisters and their special, funny world, and appreciated having time to read, horses to ride, family forests to walk in. She also resented being uneducated as well as the social cost of the comforts she enjoyed. The "haze of contentment" that enveloped the rest of her family was not available to her.[35]

Decca was just thirteen in 1930 when the Cotswolds became an especially choice tourist spot, a coveted place to visit on "the weekend" (itself a new idea then), imbued with nostalgia for an imaginary form of British country life. The picturesque Cotswolds villages had always had a dark side, however. They had given up disproportionately large numbers of young men to war. The region, moreover, rested on an economic model requiring confining labor and social inequity. Its textile industries polluted the air with sulfur and poured poisons into the rivers.[36] "One wasn't really aware of the undercurrents that were going on most of the time," Deborah claimed.[37] But Decca *was* aware. She made a point of looking past the charm of that "exceptionally beautiful part of England," as Deborah put it, to see the foundation it rested on.[38]

According to Diana Spencer's brother, Charles, a certain absence of social curiosity lies at the heart of the British aristocracy. Successful aristocrats, he maintains, were those who had "read the code, accepted its terms, and fused it into their DNA."[39] They did not question or scrutinize the system that made them the winners and so many others the losers. "I always believed that everything that happened to us was the unvarying norm," Decca's sister Diana said.[40] Dismissing Decca's awareness of those undercurrents as "teenage angst" avoids having to confront what Decca saw.[41] Reducing her commitments, as many of her relatives have done, to merely a "lasting sense of grievance" from childhood is convenient, but it is inaccurate.

Decca did not accept "the terms," as Spencer puts it, of her family's class. Yet she deeply loved her difficult, charming, incomparable right-wing siblings and quirky, distant, and unloving parents. She was, however, incapable of seeing as normal the inequalities they all accepted. But she was equally incapable of excising all the Mitford in her. Diana dismissed Decca as "unforgivably callous & hard."[42] Nothing could have been further from the truth. The greatest challenge in Decca's evolving social critique would never be that she didn't care about her family. It would always be that she cared about them too much. Decca's search for viable alternatives to the class system was especially compelling because her longing for social justice was fueled not only by anger, but at least as much by her enormous and enduring family affection.

3

"It Will All Be Terrific Fun"

More than just a wild exciting adventure[1]
—JESSICA MITFORD

Decca didn't know any successful runaways. She "endlessly mulled over possible running away plans." Nothing would be worse than being "ignominiously discovered and hauled back home."[2]

She did have a second cousin who was famous for running away. If only she could contrive to meet him. Esmond Romilly, one year younger than Decca, had been enrolled in a military boarding school. There, in early 1934, he'd started an underground magazine to "champion the forces of progress against the forces of reaction" and to "oppose military training." The first issue of *Out of Bounds: Public Schools' Journal Against Fascism, Militarism and Reaction* asked its young readers to criticize "the men [including themselves] who shall rule our empire" and to "question their unique privileges and powers."

Shortly after starting *Out of Bounds*, Esmond ran away from Wellington, his boarding school. Because he was Winston Churchill's nephew, and Churchill was such a powerful, prominent voice in Parliament, the British press followed him with attention-getters such as BOYS' MAGAZINE MENACE, RED MENACE IN PUBLIC SCHOOLS, WINSTON'S RED NEPHEW . . . UNDER INFLUENCE OF LONDON COMMUNISTS, and SECRET DASH OUT OF COLLEGE. He was often a subject of conversation at the Mitford dinner table. Decca consumed the news reports about him. "My admiration for Esmond was unbounded," she said.[3]

After he published four issues of *Out of Bounds*, Esmond wrote a book with his older brother Giles, which was published when Esmond was fifteen. It argued for an end to corporal punishment, greater intellectual freedom, and distrust of authority. From his book, Decca said, "I almost felt as though I knew Esmond . . . He emerged as a person of unlimited resourcefulness, with that extra degree of good humor which comes from absolute self-confidence." She felt enraptured that Esmond's life "revealed so many exact parallels with my own" and wondered "if I could somehow arrange to meet him, but his whereabouts were apparently unknown even to his parents."[4]

Unbeknownst to almost everyone, Esmond—living in London—sometimes slept on the floor of a Bloomsbury bookshop and sometimes on the streets. He didn't much care. "Esmond was born indignant," his biographer writes.[5] His "violent antipathy to Conservatism," as Esmond described it, made anything preferable to the stockbroker's life his parents imagined for him.[6] From a difficult, hyperactive child, he'd grown into a "ruthless" young man: easily bored, unable to tolerate authority, quick to anger, but also enormously charming when he wanted to be. He was strong, handsome, and highly intelligent. He had the gift of making whoever received his attention feel special.

It was inevitable that Esmond would get into trouble soon after running away. Along with his good friend Philip Toynbee, Esmond was arrested for drunkenness and sent to a remand home for young delinquents. Mixing the mentally ill with those arrested for everything from housebreaking to fighting, the Ponton Road Remand Home offered no treatment, training, or activities beyond cleaning and marching up and down. Beatings were frequent. Meals were bread and gravy.

Esmond's time in remand was brief but hugely influential. He'd been spoiled as a young man trained to believe that boys like him did not ever suffer. Remand showed him how many kinds of people there were in the world. He also learned that he could survive not because he was privileged, but because he was tough. Esmond always liked to imagine that he was of the "race of outcasts, tramps, and bohemians" and could "hold his own" with anyone. Esmond, Toynbee concurred, "was at his ease with anyone and with every social class."[7] He came out of remand more determined than ever to challenge the status quo. After remand, Toynbee said, Esmond's fearlessness had a quality of "self-sufficiency."[8] "People from universities and public schools are not content to deplore the misery and waste that they see," Esmond wrote:

> There is something inherently wrong with the system under which we live; that the world is divided into a large class of exploited and a small clique of exploiters, that capitalism can offer them nothing—not even a job.

> The youth has [sic] a clear choice, there can be no half-way house. Either they must side with the parasites and exploiters to "make the world safe for plutocracy," or with the working class to smash the capitalist system and lay the foundations of a classless society.[9]

While living out of the Bloomsbury bookshop, Esmond experienced fighting for the first time, battling Oswald Mosley's Blackshirt fascists, the most violent wing of a fascist party that had then grown to fifty thousand followers and always embraced political violence, appealing to a particularly brutal and hostile constituency. Esmond was injured on June 7, 1934, in a demonstration at the Olympic Coliseum, and again, later, in the infamous Battle of Cable Street. The threat that Mosley posed was reinforced by both the Blackshirts' violence and by widespread aristocratic support for fascism. That Britain might fall to fascism, through an aristocrat like Mosley, seemed plausible to many ordinary Londoners, "well within the realms of possibility."[10] During the Cable Street demonstrations of October 4, 1936, when the Blackshirts attempted to march in London's Jewish East End, citizens stopped them with the Spanish chant "No Pasarán" (They shall not pass).

The Blackshirts were so notorious for brutality that Nancy Mitford made their crude responses a refrain of her 1935 satiric novel *Wigs on the Green*. Her primary character, Eugenia, a fascist sympathizer modeled on both Unity and Diana, responds to every problem by saying, "Push their faces in the mud."[11]

In the fall of 1936, Esmond became one of the first Englishmen to join the volunteer brigades fighting fascists in Spain, brigades that would eventually swell to tens of thousands from dozens of countries. He was not alone in believing that "volunteering to fight in Spain was a natural extension of the struggle against Mosley."[12] Other British volunteers were also veterans of the Cable Street fight. "As a result of what happened at Cable Street, [we] felt that we had to do something to defeat fascism," one volunteer wrote.[13]

Spain was blockaded and difficult to reach. Esmond took a boat across the English Channel to Dieppe, then cycled ten days through France to Marseilles (more than six hundred miles, mostly over mountains). He lost his wallet, money, passport, and letters of introduction along the way, and spent five days subsisting on charity before finding boat transport to Valencia. "My main memory of the journey is of the excessive cold of cycling at night," Esmond said.[14]

He was penniless when he finally arrived in Spain, without a proper change of clothes, and he could speak little Spanish. At the time, there was not yet a British-based International Brigade. He linked up with a few other British, Italian, and German volunteers who'd formed the Thaelmann Batallion, joining other fighters in a violent battle to defend Madrid. Based for weeks at the University City of Madrid, Esmond's unit engaged in such heavy battles with the fascist forces seeking to take over Spain that the university buildings were dotted with bullet holes, some of which survive to this day.[15] "We were bombed, shelled, machine-gunned from the air, practically frozen . . . instructed in the use of trench mortars . . . one hardly ever got more than an hour's consecutive sleep."[16] From there, Esmond's unit went to Boadilla del Monte, where the fighting was even more intense—battles Romilly later described in great detail in his second book, *Boadilla*. Esmond was one of only two survivors of his battalion. Suffering from life-threatening dysentery, he was invalided back to England in early January 1937, a story carried by all the London newspapers. Esmond was determined to return to Spain as soon as he recovered, but first he was assigned to travel across Britain and tell the families of fallen volunteers how their loved ones had died.

That same month, in a "mood of unrelieved gloom, hating myself and everyone else, cross and bitter to sisters and parents alike," Decca was invited to spend the weekend at the home of a distant cousin, Dorothy Allhusen. Decca had just completed her London debut. "It became cruelly evident," she said, "that it had been a complete waste of time. I had made no real friends, had learned nothing, was no further advanced in planning my life. I cursed myself for not having the brains or ability to find my own way out." Allhusen had been acting as Esmond's guardian—his parents gave up on him after he ran away from Wellington—and Decca had the "thrilling" idea that perhaps she'd meet Esmond at her cousin's.[17]

She took a Friday afternoon train to Marlborough, south of Oxford. On arriving at Allhusen's country home, she was informed that other weekend guests would include "your cousin, Esmond Romilly. He's just back from Spain, I expect you saw it in the papers." Decca "had been in love with Esmond for years," of course, "ever since I first heard of him," she later wrote. Before going down to dinner, she took a very long pause in her room, dressing her hair, worrying that her dress smelled of storage, imagining that all the other women Esmond knew were thinner, braver, more accomplished, and more beautiful.

At dinner, seated next to Esmond, she was surprised to find him shorter and slighter than she'd expected. But she thought him handsome, heroic, and charming. At the first opportunity she asked him, "Are you planning to go back to Spain? . . . I was wondering if you could possibly take me with you?" He agreed immediately.

They hatched a quick plan for Decca to accompany Esmond to Spain as his secretary—Esmond now planned to return as a journalist. They figured on his salary and her Running Away money. Decca would have to devise a way to deceive her parents, however, or they'd certainly stop her from going.

She had two friends, Mamaine and Celia Paget, known as the Paget twins, who were then traveling in Austria. Her parents did not know them well, and they would not reappear in England for months. On February 3, Decca presented her mother with a letter purportedly from the Pagets, inviting her to visit them in Dieppe:

Darling Decca,

Twin and I are so anxious to see you. . . . Now I have a suggestion to make—sorry it's such short notice, but do try and fall in. We have *taken a house in Dieppe—that is, Auntie has taken it! We mean to make it the centre of a sort of motor tour to all the amusing places around. We are going there from Austria on Wednesday, and we should so <u>love</u> you to join us . . .* [18]

The letter was a fake, written by Decca and Esmond to buy some time. "Muv was completely taken in," Deborah later wrote.[19] Decca purchased a brown corduroy jumpsuit for fighting in Spain, tucking it into her luggage next to an expensive camera she'd charged to her father's account. Decca and Esmond left London from Victoria Station on February 8, 1937, sitting in separate cars of the same train. Decca's family saw her off at the station and gave her spending money to use with the Pagets, cash that she immediately added to her Running Away funds.[20]

On February 9 Decca wrote another fake letter, postmarked from Dieppe, telling her mother she'd arrived safely, that the weather was not good, and that "the Pagets send their love." A few days later she wrote again, closer to Spain, to say that she was having a wonderful trip and would be "staying a bit longer." "All the cherry trees are in flower already. . . . The Twins send their love."[21]

By late February her parents had contacted the Pagets' mother and realized that Decca was not with the them. The Redesdales were frantic. Fearing that Decca might be dead, David contacted Scotland Yard. "Rutland Gate was like a morgue," Deborah said. When the twins' aunt, known as Ging-Ging, visited to offer condolences, she found a "gloomy" scene, everyone "distraught" and consumed by "heartbreak."[22]

Later that February, Esmond's friend Peter Nevile brought the miserable Mitfords another letter. "I'm afraid this will come as rather a shock. . . . By the time you get this we shall be married. . . . I am longing for you all to see Esmond. . . . You will honestly <u>adore</u> Esmond when you know him."[23] Her father's response was: "Worse than I thought, married to Esmond Romilly."[24]

Esmond once joked that "'the only thing to do with the English upper class is to marry into it.'"[25] He and Decca, in fact, were remarkably well suited, both very much members of the class both wanted to escape. "We . . . egged each other on to ever greater baiting and acts of outrage against the class we had left."[26] Like Decca, Esmond was clever, stubborn, and charming, with a gift for pranks and practical jokes. Like her, he was domestically inept, without, Decca said, "the slightest sense of dealing with the physical world around him. One had the feeling that he had never really learned to tie his shoes. The simplest act of opening or closing a perfectly ordinary suitcase was a mystery to him."[27] In all that, he was completely of his class, as was she. Both also abhorred looking inward. Toynbee described his friend Esmond as "the least introspective person I have known," and felt that Decca, "pretty, incautious and enthusiastic" was "probably the only member of her class who was suited to be [Esmond's] wife."[28] He was certainly the only man she'd met of her class who was suited to be her husband.

Yet Decca and Esmond were also quite different. Esmond had firm political views.

> *Esmond's encounter with fascism in Spain, and above all the horror of his final action in the battle of Boadilla, had done much to solidify the direction his life had taken since the age of fifteen. He was no longer a dilettante, playing around the edges of the struggle of his generation, nor a mere enfant* terrible, *baiter of the traditions of the rich and powerful. He had become a committed partisan of the fight against fascism.*[29]

Decca, by her own description, "was still only on the threshold." And her personality was also still taking shape. Unlike Esmond, she had feet in both worlds. "I was secretly shocked and disturbed," she said, "at Esmond's assumption that I should never again see my family. Life at home, with all our silly jokes and private languages, huge Christmas gatherings, Nancy's bright clownishness and Boud's immense, strong personality, still meant something to me." But Esmond "regarded my family as the enemy and discouraged all discussion of them. . . . My quality of what he called upperclassishness irritated him."[30]

From Dieppe, they traveled to Bordeaux, hoping for a cargo boat to Bilbao, or farther into Spain. In Bordeaux, they had their first fight. A Basque man came into their café with a muzzled dog, which he began to beat. As the dog yelped in pain, Decca begged Esmond: "Tell him to stop." "Esmond became furious"—not at the man but at Decca, lashing into her "upperclassishness." "I can tell you," he harangued her, that

> *when we get to Spain you'll see plenty of horrible sights, bombed children dying in the streets. French people and Spaniards don't give a damn about animals, and why should they? They happen to think people are more important. If you're going to make such an unholy fuss about dogs you should have stayed in England, where they feed the dogs steak and let people in the slums die of starvation.*[31]

Decca knew that "running away meant more than just a wild, exciting adventure."[32] But she did expect to enjoy herself. She'd written her mother to say not to worry, asserting, "It will all be terrific fun."[33] She'd not thought much beyond that.

The day after their fight, February 13, 1937, they received word that passage to Spain had finally been secured. Hurrying from their hotel to the docks, they found a cargo boat with decrepit decks called the *Urbi* (or "Princess"). Across the gray, uneven planks, sick chickens were scrabbling dejectedly; bad luck for a "Hen," thought Decca.[34]

The crew of the *Urbi* did its best to make the young travelers comfortable. After a midnight feast of soup, fish, beef, chicken, dessert, fruit, and way too much wine and brandy, Decca felt certain she'd "enjoy the voyage immensely." While the mates pleated themselves into hammocks swung from beams and masts, the captain ushered Decca and Esmond into the ship's only cabin (his own). "Furnished in the style of a cheap hotel," she noted, the cabin's heavy furniture groaned with every "sputter of engines." Under an alarming "creaking of timber," as the *Urbi* steamed toward sea, Decca and Esmond crawled into their narrow berth and attempted sleep.

"Grinding sounds and loud thuds . . . [and] banging of furniture" woke them in the small hours of the night. The movement of the ship became so violent," Decca later wrote, "that Esmond and I had to take it in turns to hold each other in the bunk." One of Franco's submarines came in range, and they were confined to their clanging quarters as the crew prepared to fight. A battle was averted, but Decca became acutely seasick, too weak for the next three days even "to make the effort to reach the basin." Esmond, who detested illness, nevertheless "worried about me and brought drinks of water," Decca wrote, revealing "glimmerings of kindness [in him] . . . not often seen in those days."[35] Her stoicism seemed to reassure him.

Days later, when the *Urbi* landed, Decca staggered onto Spanish soil dizzy, shaking, with stringy hair, stained clothing, and a sour smell. She was "filthy and crumpled." Her best suit skirt had "large gashes."

Although she was proud to have catapulted herself, in the space of a few weeks, from one world to another, Decca would have much preferred to slip into Spain unnoticed. But, as defectors from their class, she and Esmond were instant celebrities. The foreign minister of the Basque Republic came to greet them personally as they disembarked. He took them, via limousine, directly to a four-hour exhibition boxing match as the Republic's guests of honor. Decca endured the match in a silent agony of waiting for "a nice hot bath and clean bed."[36]

Room and board were provided to Decca and Esmond at the Hotel Torrontegui, a large Art Deco building and Bilbao's grandest hotel, occupying one of the city's busiest intersections.[37] Even as guests of the Republic, conditions were spare. "There was hot water only twice a week . . . food was scarce . . . Meat, milk, eggs, [and] butter were completely unobtainable," Decca noted. They ate mostly garbanzo beans and coarse "grayish bread. . . . Breakfast, lunch and dinner were indistinguishable."[38] Decca found the "grey seaport town . . . grim." She saw children begging by the side of the road. "Garbage was piled up in the nearly deserted streets."[39] Bilbao's residents were cut off from the rest of Spain, surrounded on three sides by the fascists, and facing the Bay of Biscay on their fourth side. They lived in "anxious anticipation" of invasion. "Life in Bilbao," Decca said, "had for me far more the quality of a dream than of a dream come true."[40] She'd written her mother that Esmond would get "a very good job as a journalist" and they'd "have a mass of dough."[41] Now she was not so sure.

Most international volunteers arrived in Spain poorly prepared. Few, however, were as ill-prepared as Decca. She spoke no Spanish. She'd been dressed, fed, and amused all her life. She had no skills. She'd traveled rarely and mostly to visit family. She and Esmond, moreover, were nearly strangers. "I often reflected," Decca wrote, "on the strange beginnings of our life together. Most honeymoons, after all, are preceded by at least some period of acquaintance, family introductions, or engagement. Here we were, strangers only a few weeks ago, now suddenly alone together against the world—or at least against our families! It was a little like being castaways meeting for the first time on a desert island, or explorers coming face to face in a lonely jungle." Most honeymoons were, in fact, preceded by a marriage, which had not yet taken place. For Decca, "reality still seemed to be centered at home, with the family . . . [she] was consumed with curiosity and anxiety about what must by now be happening at home."

Esmond had insisted that she cut all ties with her family. But she wrote them on the sly, begging for news of "the Season," other debutantes, family news. Sydney sent care packages, including, at Decca's request, up-to-date copies of *Vogue*. Decca worried that her best dress, a purple satin gown, would be "out of fashion" before she ever wore it. "Sell it for me and send me the money," she wrote Debo.[42] Decca asked what people were saying about her sudden departure. "It's so fascinating to think of my old Hen in love that I must hear everything," Debo asked.[43] "He has got blue eyes & beige hair about the colour of mine and he talks rather like Michael Farrer only with a slight cockney pronunciation—for instance he says riowd instead of rood for rude. Also, he can do awfully good imitations of people like Winston Churchill & he talks French so well you'd take him for a Frenchman. . . . He is frightfully good at languages," Decca replied.[44] "Hot it up," Debo responded. Unity sent Decca silk stockings. "I was in Munich when I heard," Unity wrote, "oh I *was* sad, it seemed like my old Boud had died or something. Of course I came scramming back at once, but thank goodness I saw my friend [Hitler] before I left & he . . . comforted me like anything . . . Oh Boud do come back & see us all, even if it's only for a bit. . . . Poor little Debo has had a dreadful time & misses you dreadfully. . . . I'm dying to see Esmond, & hear all about him."[45] Nancy also tried to convince Decca to return. "I saw the family yesterday & they are miserable. Susan it isn't very respectable what you are doing & I see their point of view I must say. . . . after all one has to live in this world as it is & society (I don't mean duchesses) can make things pretty beastly to those who disobey its rules. Susan do come back."[46] Decca may have felt too shy to ask her sisters about birth control, information that might have been useful to her.

Decca had no intention of coming back. Her parents had no intention of letting her stay. They attempted to have Decca declared a ward of Great Britain so that Esmond could be charged with her capture.

Esmond also had no intention of backing down. He was a year

behind Decca in age, but many years ahead in experience. He'd had to duck under a "hurricane of lead" in the trenches, seen friends killed on either side of him, been part of frantic attacks and equally frantic retreats, been lost, been so sick to his stomach that he wished he was dead. His time in Spain had left a "mark" that, Esmond said, "does not diminish but grows with time."[47] He was at least as fierce as any Mitford. A few of his friends found him "unscrupulous."[48] But with those he loved, his "natural desire to give pleasure" came to the fore, others said.[49]

Esmond was naturally inclined to dictate. Nineteen years old and in love for the first time in her life, Decca was happy to fall in line. Decca was rebelling from her class, but not yet from the gender script she'd been born to. Toynbee felt that their relationship was "in many ways an old-fashioned [one] . . . in which both partners clearly recognized their well-defined functions. It was for Esmond to establish their views and decide on their actions—for Decca to cheer him on and to look after the house."[50] All the sisters were capable of a certain "Honnish adoration," as Peter Sussman puts it, of men who satisfied their "Byronesque" ideals.[51] Handsome, clever, and daring, Esmond was certainly cut in the Byronic mode. Decca's first weeks with him were filled with what she could only call "strange emotions": "Of course I would never confide these feelings to Esmond. He was very unsympathetic in those days, and was not about to take any nonsense from anyone, me included. He could be delightful company, though, and he had me doubled up with laughter for much of the time. . . . I never had any real misgivings about having run away with him. Really, if it hadn't been for Esmond where would I be? In a loony-bin, I guess."[52]

As one historian of this period notes, it is "difficult to exaggerate the significance of the civil war" in Spain to young radicals at this time. Many saw Spain as "the centre of the world, the place where the great issues of the time were being decided."[53] For them, the Spanish Civil War was "the defining moment" in global politics, a people's war.[54] To an unprecedented degree, it was fought by citizens and against citizens, "over social identities and values." The fundamentalists who sought to overturn Spain's democratically elected government "targeted the socially, culturally and sexually different," historian Helen Graham writes.[55] All "those who symbolized cultural change and thus posed a threat to old ways of being and thinking"—progressive teachers, educated workers, and New Women, especially—were vulnerable. No wonder that young people around the world saw the fight for Spain's democracy as "the pivotal battle for modernity in the 1930s."[56]

Many British aristocrats had fascist sympathies. In a general sense, Graham explains, "Britain's elites knew the Francoists [and other fascists] socially."[57] This was especially true of the Mitfords. Diana said Hitler was "kind and sweet . . . the kindest man in the world."[58] Hitler had now become Unity's special "friend" and "perfect angel," and for a brief period the international press reported that Unity and Hitler looked likely to marry.[59] Decca's mother was also devoted to Hitler. "Nazism is from every point of view preferable to Communism," she declared.[60]

The Spanish Nationalists were violently opposed to freedoms for women. New Women were a particular target, and the Right "used rape as a weapon of war . . . [and to express its] loathing of emancipated women."[61] Women who failed to conform to Nationalist conservative ideas were publicly humiliated, assaulted, and tortured, sometimes forced to march naked in public, under the influence of drugs that made them soil themselves in the streets.[62] For Decca, as for so many international women, "the Spanish Civil War was genuinely emancipatory" in its resistance to gender norms and in opening "new roles" for women.[63] The first British volunteer to die in Spain was a woman, Felicia Browne, a sculptor and painter, killed on August 25, 1936, in a mission to "blow up a munitions train near Tardienta in Aragon."[64]

Most remarkable about the Spanish Civil War, as historians such as Sarah Watling emphasize, "is how much it mattered to people who had nothing to do with Spain." For the sixty thousand volunteers who supported the Republicans in Spain, the war was a profound experience of solidarity with others. "Solidarity," Watling writes, "meant identifying the ways in which a phenomenon like fascism was not confined by national boundaries; it meant finding common cause with people not like you—and that sometimes meant bringing your own experiences and causes to the table."[65]

Although "there was very little going on in Bilbao at the time," as Decca later put it, their days "began to assume a routine." They would check at the Press Bureau for news, then conduct interviews if they could find any officials to talk to them. In the afternoon they'd type up what they had for the British *News Chronicle*.[66] Decca, who very much wished she could practice journalism also, had little to do but follow along in Esmond's "wake:" "briskly trudging to government offices, press headquarters, information centers, lining up arrangements for interviews and news stories," as she put it. After waiting days, they were taken to the front "in an Army car over miles and miles of rough mountain roads" by the Republican Press Bureau. At that time "the front was still quiet." They were driven to a ravine where, from a distance, they could see enemy soldiers and cannons. Decca was allowed to fire at the enemy. She hit a tree. The enemy fired back "in much the same desultory fashion."[67] And that was that for Decca's experience of combat, the only time that her "special suit . . . to fight in"—her brown, corduroy ski suit bought with her father's charge account at the "Army and Navy" store—ever saw action.[68]

After their arrival, Decca and Esmond found themselves marooned in Bilbao, with little to do of value to the cause. At the same time, the remnants of Esmond's Thaelmann Battalion were fighting a grisly battle in Jarama, one of the worst of the war. Historians call it a "slaughter."[69] Esmond was consumed with news of the front, thoughts of his comrades still in the brigades, and his brother, Giles, whom he could not locate. Decca sensed how much he "minded being separated from the struggle in Spain. . . . It was plain from his occasional deep moodiness that the decision had been a hard one to make."[70] He probably did not notice the degree to which, for Decca, the biggest war—"total war" she called it— was still with her family.[71] In his new position as a reporter, Esmond was painfully aware of the "large groups of British soldiers [who] were taken prisoner" and the horrific prison conditions they faced: no toilets, no running water, no bathing, starvation rations of thin soup and small chunks of bread, fleas, lice, typhus, dysentery, scurvy, and malaria; no medication or medics, and hospitals, should they be lucky enough to get transferred, that simply let people "die off."[72]

Unfortunately for Decca and Esmond, they were even more in the news than those British prisoners or the suffering Spaniards. The *Daily Express* reported PEER'S DAUGHTER ELOPES TO SPAIN. Almost every detail of the story was wrong. (The paper reported that Debo had eloped with Esmond, and she was able to later sue for a considerable sum.) On March 3 the *Daily Mirror* wrote that the couple were trapped in a "hut." Another story blared JESSICA MITFORD FEARED LOST IN PYRENNES! MR. ROMILLY AND DECCA BELIEVED IN BARCELONA. *The Daily Telegraph* wrote that they were in Spain, and possibly still unmarried (which was, in fact, true, and considered quite scandalous at the time). ANOTHER MITFORD ANCARCHIST; CONSUL CHASES PEER'S DAUGHTER; MIXED UP MITFORD GIRLS STILL CONFUSING EUROPE, other British papers headlined.[73]

Following all the news stories about them, Decca and Esmond were visited by Ralph Stevenson, a representative to the British consul. He had a coded telegram from Anthony Eden, Britain's foreign secretary (and later, prime minister): "Find Jessica Mitford and persuade her to return." Decca and Esmond wrote the consul's response for him: "Have found Jessica Mitford. Impossible to persuade her to return."

A few days later, Stevenson, undeterred, demanded that they meet with him. Decca must return immediately to England, he insisted. They declined. The next day, Stevenson appeared at their hotel. He informed them that Nancy and her husband, Peter Rodd, were steaming toward them on a British destroyer, HMS *Echo* (a massive ship over 320 feet long, mounted with machine guns, depth charges, and torpedoes), with messages from Decca's parents. Stevenson expected Decca and Esmond to be humbled at being fetched, by their government, via destroyer. When they refused to be cowed, Stevenson got angry. They must travel thirty miles and meet the destroyer in Bermeo, Stevenson demanded. Everyone needed to see that Decca was fine. "I was actually very excited at the thought of seeing Nancy," Decca remembered, "and extremely anxious to hear news from home."[74]

Decca went. Esmond did not. In Bermeo, Stevenson tried to tempt Decca onto the destroyer with "roast chicken, bread sauce, peas, mashed potatoes, chocolate cake." Suspecting his offer was a trick (it was), a hungry Decca sat in the rain, for hours, on a hard wooden bench, waiting for Nancy and Peter to come out to her. They didn't. When she returned damply to Bilbao, a bit like a wet puppy who'd been hoping for treats, Esmond told her how proud he was that she'd seen through Stevenson's ploy. While she was in Bermeo, eating nothing and getting drenched, he'd received news that the Mitfords had involved Scotland Yard. There was a chance he'd be jailed.

Stevenson upped the stakes and engaged in what Decca called a "fantastic piece of bargaining." Britain was scheduled to evacuate hundreds of Spanish refugees. Unless Decca and Esmond "agreed voluntarily to leave the Basque territory," he'd leave the refugees stranded. He would also, Stevenson warned, have their press status—and therefore their lodging—revoked. Finding themselves at the center of international policy and responsible for hundreds of lives, Decca and Esmond had no choice. They left Spain aboard another destroyer, now filled, thanks to them, with refugees from Spain.

Decca later said they'd "capitulated" to British pressure. This was largely true. But they had their own reasons for giving in. "We felt,"

Decca wrote, "that all the recent publicity about us had already harmed the cause of the Spanish Republic. The endless stories about our adventures had driven the war news off the front pages, as well as making a farce of our own convictions."[75] Getting refugees out of Spain was a way to use that notoriety and help expose the British policy of nonintervention (the "charade of nonintervention," many called it).[76] Stevenson believed they'd be on the destroyer all the way to England. The moment it reached French soil, however, in Saint-Jean-de-Luz, a Basque fishing village in France, they jumped ship.[77] From Saint-Jean-de-Luz, they made their way to Bayonne, a slightly larger French town.

They had "exactly nine shillings between us" and "very bleak" prospects in Bayonne. Decca was "miserably wretched" at this "dead end."[78] They took a room at the Hôtel des Basques, a small, seedy establishment on Rue des Lisses, in a working-class neighborhood of dark narrow streets known as "Little Bayonne." Esmond quickly secured a job, of sorts, with Reuters. He was to report news from the front, which was largely impossible to get, so he made up most of his dispatches. The job paid for their tiny hotel room. Esmond began writing *Boadilla*, an account of the war, for which he received a windfall advance of fifty pounds.

A photograph of Decca and Esmond survives from this time. It was taken in April 1937, in the Hotel des Basques. It shows a simple room, so small that Decca had to sit on the bed for the photo. Esmond sits in what appears to be the only chair, pulled up to a dainty round table, with his manual typewriter and stack of manuscript pages. He is dressed in a suit and tie, looking down at a book he holds in his lap. Decca sits demurely, with one knee crossed over the other, and her hands on her thigh. She is either gazing down at Esmond or has her eyes closed—because of overexposure, it is impossible to tell. The metal frame of their double bed dominates the center of the photo, and next to it their clothes are hung, one on top of another on the room's few pegs. Decca looks like a perfect lady, idle and devoted. Ironically, the photo presents the very passivity she left England to escape, the unhappiness of "many girls" like her, with "nothing to do."[79]

Alone in their tiny room, Decca read *Vogue* and wrote her sisters. Esmond wrote about mortar explosions "like someone slamming a book just in front of one's nose . . . crouching in the valley . . . the dull thudding sound of artillery fire . . . being under fire . . . a crash . . . a continuous racket . . . the flashing of rifle fire."[80] Decca's closest correspondent in April 1937 was Unity, in Munich, with her "dear friend" Hitler, and the Goebbelses. On April 11, Unity wrote Decca about Esmond's "feeling for fascists." While admitting that she wouldn't "hesitate to shoot him if necessary for my cause" and also acknowledging that "I hate the communists just as much as he hated Nazis," Unity averred that this was no reason why she and Esmond "shouldn't personally be quite good friends, though politically enemies . . . family ties ought to make a difference." As for her "turning against my Boud," Unity wrote, it was simply out of the question, and she would always be on Decca's side, ready for a "good chat" and "longing" for her letters.[81] Decca never showed such letters to Esmond.

After much back-and-forth about where to register and who might attend, Esmond and Decca were finally married in Bayonne on May 19, 1937. Both mothers managed to be present. Esmond wore a brown suit. Decca wore a simple summer dress which her mother had purchased for her. It hid her stomach, since Decca was pregnant by this time. "It was really great fun," Decca wrote Debo. "We nearly giggled from nerves during the ceremony. . . . Being a married Hen is not at all unlike being an unmarried Hen," she added, "except it seems rather extraorder to have a wedding ring & a mother in law & everything."[82] Unity lamented missing the wedding: "I suppose I should skeke [hardly] be very welcome among the comrades at Bayonne," she teased.[83] Even more "extraorder" no doubt, than having a wedding ring and a mother-in-law, was the irony of Esmond Romilly and Oswald Mosley now being brothers-in-law. Decca and Esmond did the traditional thing—they went to Paris for a honeymoon and "jollied ourselves up in nightclubs," which was also "fun but rather tiring," Decca wrote. Her sisters sent impractical wedding presents such as jewelry so expensive it could not clear customs and a gramophone, which Decca said was "heavenly." "I do adore it," she affirmed.[84] Other gifts included a brush set from her mother, with her new initials, JLR, a ruby-and-diamond ring, a handbag, and money.[85] Unity wrote often. "I have seen the Führer a lot lately which has been heaven," she confided happily.[86] Deborah wrote about a crush on a Hungarian orchestra leader, about debutante dances (the young men were all CHs, or "chinless horrors," she said), and her dogs. She also wrote Decca about her "nice" tea with Hitler and Unity—"I think Hitler must be very fond of her," she reported. "He never took his eyes off of her."[87]

During the summer, Decca worried that as her pregnancy developed, she'd suffer "agonies." She did have a difficult first trimester, but kept the usual Mitford stiff upper lip, writing playfully that she wouldn't "call it Nancy . . . as I have a feeling it's going to be a boy & being called Nancy might prove a handicap . . . I do hope it will be sweet & pretty."[88]

Esmond had to return to England to work with his publishers on *Boadilla*. Decca went to Dieppe to wait for him. While there, she had a tooth out, a process she described in detail:

I went to the dentist here day before yesterday & he pulled out a <u>huge</u> back double tooth without any anaesthetic. . . . I felt <u>everything</u>. Susan I never have in all my life of broken arms, appendicitis, typhoid etc. known such agony. I nearly fainted & couldn't stop trembling for about 2 hours. The dent said the reason it hurt so was because it was seriée between 2 other teeth, but I said that was a stupid excuse because all teeth are serieés between two others unless one is a toothless deformity. Altogether I teased him quite a lot & was glad to see I made his hand bleed by digging in my flags while he was pulling. I expect he will get blood poisoning now because they are engrained with dirt.[89]

"I do hope it wasnt too frightful darling," Esmond wrote from London, pleased with her bravery.[90]

By early September, with Decca due in a few months, both she and Esmond returned to England, wanting to be there when Esmond's book was published and also be near English-speaking doctors. Decca, though she dared not say so, also wanted her family close by when her baby was born.

From a good friend named Roger Roughton, they rented one floor of an odd, industrial-style house in a working-class London neighborhood, with a good view of the commercial ships going in and out of London, a "wonderful place . . . right on the river so that you look onto the barges going down all the time."[91] It was not, Toynbee recalled, "a house like anybody else's; it was a thin little slice of a building, sandwiched between the warehouses which line the south bank of the river at Rotherhithe."[92] More or less a commune already, Decca and Esmond helped to fill the house with even more friends. They opened a gambling parlor, complete with a bar and admission. They were having great fun, and the world seemed to open itself to their wishes.

Esmond took one job as a door-to-door salesman, then another in advertising. Decca found work as a marketer. *Boadilla* came out in the fall to good reviews, making Esmond an accomplished two-book author before he turned twenty. Decca saw her family on the sly. Toynbee deeply admired what he saw as their "loving and lawless life."[93]

On December 20, 1937, their daughter Julia was born. With Julia's birth, it began to seem to Decca that one could have it all, could be a rebel, mother, wife, daughter, and sister. It seemed plausible to reject family values but still have family. It seemed that one could leave one's class yet stay in one's country. One could even be married to a revolutionary, who went off to work each day in advertising.

Decca was a devoted, proud mother. "You can't *imagine* how sweet it is," she wrote to Debo. "I long for you to come & see it. She hasn't got any of the disadvantages of so many babies such as excessive redness & baldness & smelling of sick."[94]

Measles was rampant in Rotherhithe just then and no vaccine was widely in use, but breastfeeding infants, like Julia, were thought to have immunities from their mothers, who were presumed to have been exposed to measles at some point in their own childhoods.[95] Decca refused to allow her family to hire her a private nurse. Her public health nurse, assuming Decca had been exposed to measles as a child, advised her not to be concerned. Infection rates were down, and girls usually fared much better than boys, the nurse said.[96] Working-class children who played together in dense quarters were, in fact, usually exposed to measles. Aristocratic children like the Mitfords, however, often had very little contact with others and, hence, very little immunity.[97] "Perhaps," Decca later wrote, "they [public health nurses] did not know that immunization can only be conferred by a mother who had had the disease; or perhaps in that teeming part of London, it never occurred to them that a person might reach maturity without having had all the usual childhood illnesses at some time or other."[98]

At four months old, Julia contracted a bad case of measles. Decca caught it too. Both were deathly ill. Decca recovered. Julia did not.

Julia died on May 28, 1938, leaving Decca feeling like someone "battered into semi-consciousness in a vicious street fight."[99] Julia's death, Toynbee recalled, "was received almost with satisfaction at the dinner-parties of Kensington and Mayfair," as if it were Decca's comeuppance for flouting social rules, for being "triumphantly indestructible."[100] No one appreciated the price Decca had paid to change who she'd been.

Decca and Esmond attended carefully to household details, even remembering to leave specific notes for the next tenant.[101] Esmond, Decca wrote, "took charge of all our plans, drew out our savings, made the necessary travel arrangements, and the day after the baby was buried, we left for Corsica. There we lived for three months in the welcome unreality of a foreign town, shielded by distance from the sympathy of friends, returning only when the nightmare had begun to fade."[102]

Decca never spoke of Julia's death. Her grave may have been unmarked; it has not been located.[103] In later life, even close friends were unaware that Decca once had a young daughter who'd died. This reticence to revelation was part of a lifelong pattern for Decca. It baffled friends and associates, who sometimes misinterpreted it as absence of feeling. The opposite was true. The deeper the hurt, the less Decca would speak of it. Esmond looked for a way to leave England again. Decca withdrew from her family.

Esmond had gone to Spain a committed activist and become a hero. Marrying Decca made him a husband and father who cared as much about individuals as about the Cause. Decca had gone to Spain a very young woman, with little experience of suffering—her own or that of others. In Spain, she had met people who sacrificed their own lives for strangers. And just as she was coming to see the world in larger patterns and to think in terms of social forces, she suffered her first personal tragedy, one that marked her for life.

In Nancy Mitford's *Wigs on the Green*, a character named Poppy worries that "people can't be divorced from their status in life."[104] That was just what Decca had most feared—that she'd be stuck in the class she detested all her life. Her upbringing had made her feel as if "people outside the immediate family were two-dimensional, half-men and -women, part of the scenery."[105] But Spain and Rotherhithe made life very real.

After losing a baby daughter, some people might retreat back to safety. Decca was not one to go backward. Having set out to change her status, she now kept moving forward, taking huge risks and accepting the consequences.

4

"Let's Go to America"[1]

I would support anything he wanted to do.[2]
—JESSICA MITFORD

As soon as Decca and Esmond returned to Rotherhithe, they hatched a plan to leave. With a 100-pound windfall Decca had received for her twenty-first birthday, September 11, 1938, Esmond planned a group lecture tour of American women's clubs. "They have them all over," he said.

Esmond had heard that Americans wanted lectures about Britain. So he approached nearly four dozen U.S. lecture agencies offering such topics as "Sex Life at Oxford University," "How to Meet the King," and "The Truth About Winston Churchill." "This'll be just the sort of thing they love," Esmond said. There would be five lecturers—Esmond, Decca, Philip Toynbee, and their friends Sheila Legge and

Tony Hyndman. Esmond and Decca were to lecture on such topics as "The Inner Life of an English Debutante" and "I Ran Away from an English Public School."

Esmond was "congenitally incapable of dwelling on the pitfalls and difficulties in a situation," Decca said.[3] First, Legge and Hyndman fell away. Esmond plowed ahead with only Toynbee in tow. Esmond had "hallucinatory powers over me," Toynbee said, and he described being swept up by Esmond's wild enthusiasms. But finally, even Toynbee could not "envisage a long adventure in the company" of the Romillys." "My personality," he said, "would have been obliterated in their tremendous company . . . their undeliberate but crushing domination."[4]

Decca said that Esmond "never doubted that in the long run I would support anything he wanted to do."[5] She held fast to his scheme. Rather than focus on her grief over Julia's death, she concentrated all her concerns on getting her husband out of England. She had "never seen Esmond so depressed and restless."

Decca believed that Esmond was "above all a person of political action" and that sitting on his hands now might do him in.[6] He had expected to return to Spain and to fighting. He had expected a happy fatherhood. And he'd expected a vigorous global defense of Spain. Chamberlain signed a September agreement reinforcing their fears that Britain would purchase peace at any price. "There was a real possibility that the Chamberlain government might go full circle," Esmond cautioned, "that England and Germany might team up against Russia" and the British might accept "a kind of half-life" under Hitler's thumb.[7] Upper-class British lack of "sympathy for democracy" just when "a vigorous support of democracy was essential"[8] made England "one of the saddest places in the world," they felt. [9] Decca worried that England's "drab limbo" was overtaking Esmond.[10]

While she worried more about Esmond than herself, the global turn toward fascism was personal, cutting her off from her family. "I hardly ever saw any of them," she said.[11] Unity and Diana were now Hitler confidantes. Decca's parents had also warmed to Hitler. Sydney fiercely defended Hitler's "very good manners" and sociability.[12] "Dear Prime Minister," she wrote Chamberlain, "Hitler is a person of heart."[13] Bring Hitler over for a "friendly visit" on English soil, she urged. Unity wrote her cousin Winston Churchill, passionately defending her "dear" new friend Hitler.[14] Unable to discuss her predicament with Esmond, Decca wrestled with her disgust over her family's politics and her affection for them, which persisted. Being, as she later put it, on "opposite sides in the central conflict of our day" produced daily miseries for Decca.[15]

In the end, debt, not politics, determined Decca and Esmond's departure from England. At Rotherhithe, they'd tried living ordinary lives: without servants, paying rent, working, using the public health system. *Boadilla* did not sell well. Esmond, a lifelong gambler, thought he could make money with boule—in which players bet on which of seven spots a rolled ball will stop at. He set up a weekend boule gaming table on the first floor of their Rotherhithe home. One friend who lost to Esmond remembered his "cherubic grin, his hands gently clapping" as he scooped up his friends' coins.[16]

Unfortunately, Decca and Esmond had seen little of how ordinary people actually managed day-to-day. "No one had ever explained to me," Decca observed, "that you had to pay for electricity; and lights, electric heaters, stoves." Faced with an enormous electric bill, the stunned couple slunk off to hide in a furnished room near Marble Arch, seven miles away. The electric company dispatched a process server—"a pale, sad-looking youth"—who they tried to dodge with fake mustaches, fancy hats, dark glasses, and days spent under the covers, because they'd heard that process servers were prohibited from disturbing debtors in their beds.[17] As much as Esmond and Decca relished the game, they couldn't evade bill collectors forever. More sad-looking servers were on the way, they knew. "We'd go and live in America until the war began," they decided.[18]

Going to America was a huge gamble. But Esmond was a gambler. Whenever he could see success in his mind's eye, he was incapable of countenancing defeat, driven by faith in what Toynbee called his "tremendous simplicities." Decca went along with them all.

In late January 1939, they gathered birth certificates, marriage license, passports, character references, and permission to travel from Esmond's mother (Esmond was legally a minor at twenty). Medical examinations were required by the American consulate. Esmond nearly failed his. The examiner asked Esmond if he had varicose veins. Esmond had no idea what they were, but he was anxious to please. "Yes, I do," he replied. Esmond's examiner explained varicose veins and invited Esmond to retract, which he promptly did. "No, I don't," he answered gamely. When asked about their finances, Decca and Esmond said they had bundles of money (although they had only Decca's birthday cash), and they just squeaked through.[19]

They emerged from hiding on February 17, having paid none of their outstanding bills, and threw themselves a grand farewell party, to which they invited all their friends, as well as "tough journalists and advertising agents, Communist Party bosses, Bohemian pub-crawlers and a sprinkling of half-liberated girls who had once been debutantes."[20] Halfway through the party, tired, a little bored, and very ready to get on with their American adventure, they left their guests and went up to bed.[21]

Prior to departing, friends Peter Nevile and Roger Roughton helped Decca and Esmond assemble more than two dozen letters of introduction to famous Americans.[22] "All our hopes for making a real break in America were based on a large bulky brown envelope marked Letters of Introduction."[23] "Magic things" Esmond called them.[24] Their letter writers represented a dizzying array of ideological perspectives, from racist and fascist sympathizers to radicals and fellow travelers. Decca and Esmond had absorbed their class's credo that everything depended on whom you knew, a notion reinforced by Decca's mother—*Debrett's Peerage*, the *Who's Who* of aristocracy, was far more important than the Bible to Sydney.

With their letters firmly in hand, Decca and Esmond took a train from London to the Southampton docks. There, they were seen off by Philip, Decca's nanny, and her brother, Tom.[25] From Southampton, they boarded a Cunard-built Canadian passenger ship, the SS *Aurania*, which had five hundred first- and second-class cabins and fifteen hundred third-class (steerage) cabins. For the considerable sum of £34 (roughly £2,200 in today's currency and a third of their money), they secured third-class passage, joining refugees from Nazism and fascism.[26] By February 18, 1939, when they sailed, third-class cross-Atlantic passage had improved slightly.[27] On the *Aurania*, steerage included bed-size berths, some with a tiny sink, but most without fresh air. Their section of the ship lacked the upstairs opulence of parlors, lounges, chandeliered dining rooms, game rooms, and elegant smoking rooms, but it provided spartan spaces for smoking and dining, and a small, shared deck space: cramped, dirty, and loud. Amidst the many immigrants seeking to escape the war, anxious about their futures, Decca saw tense faces and heard stories of lives upended by forced departures, stolen monies, and death. She knew that, by comparison, she and Esmond had it easy.

On ship, Esmond amused himself by "outsnobbing the snobs," Decca later said, taking up for the Poles, to whom the Canadians were nasty, and making a great show of escorting a group of Polish travelers about the decks and into the bar.[28] In spite of some similarly amusing moments, the passage was "rough, long and uncomfortable."[29] (Later that year, Pan Am would launch the first transatlantic flight, destined to replace long ocean crossings with air travel.)

The *Aurania* landed in New York on a wet Sunday, February 26, 1939, the day that Hitler ordered the forced evacuation of one hundred Jews a day from Berlin and the same day that Jewish shipboard emigrés were turned back from ports in Uruguay and British Guiana, just as German Jews were also being turned away from Hungary and Yugoslavia.[30] Decca, always mindful of her parents' and sisters' politics, said it was an "enormous relief to put three thousand miles between the family and myself."[31]

Nevertheless, the Mitfords' influence remained strong. Based on family recommendations, Decca and Esmond went straight from the docks to the Shelton Hotel at Lexington and Forty-Ninth Street, one of New York's premier hotels. Celebrity tenants such as Alfred Stieglitz and Georgia O'Keeffe had helped make the Shelton an icon of modern New York.[32] Decca adored the Shelton's "mass-produced luxury . . . magnificent lobby and bellboys, the immense size of the place, the thickly carpeted corridors had nothing in common with any English hotel. . . . We seemed to have stepped on to another planet." She was especially taken with the private bath and shower, a great relief from common bathrooms on the *Aurania*.[33] After ten days of sightseeing, room service, and shopping—a suit for Esmond, a pleated black silk dress and matching hat for Decca—half of her windfall was gone.[34]

In Greenwich Village, they found a short-term furnished sublet at 16 Christopher Street, for forty-five dollars a month. It was cheap by New York standards, but even that much they could not afford for long. In the main room was an orange plaid trundle bed with a thin mattress doubling as a couch and a curtained kitchenette—emphasis on "ette," Esmond said. The only other room was a tiny bathroom. Decca had always longed for a bedsitter. Now that she had one, she was surprised to find it so small and dirty. Esmond and Decca's friends described them as "impervious": to danger, the possibility of failure, physical surroundings, and sometimes to others' feelings as well. Decca was so indifferent to domestic comforts that Debo nicknamed her "Squalor." The Greenwich Village apartment must have been seedy indeed.

Nevertheless, Decca was very taken with the Village. It's "lovely," she wrote her mother, even prettier than parts of Paris.[35] Both she and Esmond took stabs at domesticity. Decca sewed curtains. Esmond brought home a cat. When he was out, she wrote letters to her family. New York was quickly eating into her birthday money. But both found exploring the city wonderful.

Every day, they were reminded of their comparative good luck. Hitler's march into Prague in March and Mussolini's invasion of Albania in April, "a dangerous game" of incremental fascist expansion, the newspapers said, filled them with rage.[36] Esmond expected that eventually he'd have to fight again. Until then, he wanted to have fun. The "form" as they both put it, was best-foot-forwardism. While they would not trade on Esmond's experiences in Spain (one of the only things both regarded as sacred), they considered anything else that might help them get ahead in America to be fair game.

"The people here are far nicer than I expected & of course very hospitable and kind," Decca told her mother. Rich Americans, she reported, "have fine wirenetting round their windows to keep out moths & slow flies."[37] Central heating and American bathrooms both captivated her, as did American generosity and open curiosity. Americans were so *interested*, she marveled, so unrestrained in their enthusiasms. Whenever she could, Decca detailed her new American purchases to her mother, drawing pictures of the black short-sleeved silk dress she'd purchased at Klein's, so that her mother could see how cleverly it was cut.[38] Distance had restored some of Decca's warmth toward her family, and she was writing her mother much as she used to. "America is such heaven," she reported.[39]

Their letters of introduction did yield a varied crop of invitations to tony dinners and cocktails, as well as weekends in Long Island,

Connecticut, and Cape Cod. They typed up a contact list, made careful notes about each person and what help they might provide, but they promptly lost the list, leaving them, Decca lamented, "like hunters not knowing if they're stalking a deer or a rabbit."[40] Decca and Esmond might receive a delightful message, such as, "Call us at Plaza 5-8324 anytime, and come along one evening," but have no idea who'd made the invitation.[41] From then on, and for the rest of her life, Decca maintained meticulous contact lists, often in triplicate, updated as she was traveling and heavily annotated.

Each weekend Decca and Esmond visited a different contact. Familiar with British upper-class country-house traditions and trained to be good guests, Esmond especially was a sparkling conversationalist full of flattery for their hosts. Decca's guesting had been more limited, since Farve so detested "Elsewhere," so Decca took guesting instruction from Esmond. Esmond had a seemingly endless repertory of funny stories (in which he generally figured as the foil), and Decca played his straight man, saying little. Their weekend visits were lucrative. At each visit, and at Esmond's prodding, Decca filled a large black British leather handbag with whatever toiletries and household staples she could grab. If their hosts noticed the pilfering, Decca or Esmond made a joke of it, usually without returning what they'd pocketed. Americans were then new to the practice of maintaining second homes, and many sought to emulate the centuries-old British country-house traditions, even building America's beach houses to look like English cottages.[42] Two young, aristocratic Brits added a sought-after authentic ambience to a weekend's atmosphere. Esmond was quick to take advantage of this cultural capital. "It's a distinct advantage to be English here," he noted. "That is if you continue repeating what a wonderful country America is."[43]

On their country weekends, Decca's job was to sit next to Esmond and look lovely, which her eager, large aqua eyes, dark wavy hair, model-thin figure, and great sense of style made an easy task. When prompted, she was sharp and witty, with a British accent even more rarified than Esmond's: the characteristic headlong Mitford pitch, heavy on adjectives and nouns as verbs, an Asthall dialect that persisted over the years and deepened whenever Decca particularly wanted something from others. Esmond's boyish good looks and humor, combined with his shabby style and irreverence, made others eager to win his approval.[44] He understood that Americans were both afraid of being drawn into European conflict and also anxious not to be judged for doing too little. A visible friendship with a British radical could be invaluable to an ambivalent American's self-esteem.

After Hitler's annexation of Czechoslovakia on March 15, it was becoming clear that Britain would either be drawn into war or fall to fascism. Esmond and Decca were isolated, unable to get the reliable news they longed for and mostly feeling useless. They welcomed distractions. Peter Nevile had hoped to marry a young American woman named Elizabeth. They had quarreled, and she'd returned to America. Nevile did not know how to reach her. "Please find her for me," Nevile pleaded. "Tell her I did not mean all that I said and that I must marry her before I join up."[45] Esmond was a "master planner" with an instinct for complex logistics, and he and Decca threw themselves into the search. They found Elizabeth. But Peter failed to secure permission to come to the United States and Elizabeth's parents wouldn't allow her to travel to England. She became another new friend for Decca and Esmond instead.

Peter's failed engagement reinforced Decca and Esmond's sense that they were more determined and capable than their friends were, a conviction that solidified their operation as "a self-sufficient unit, a conspiracy of two against the world," as Decca later put it. "Even our best friends," she admitted, "the ones we loved fondly and looked on as our nearest and dearest . . . had for us an almost two-dimensional quality, for more and more we only really minded about each other."[46]

Decca and Esmond were deeply interested in others, but sometimes not very sympathetic to them. Just as they resolutely minimized their own pain—keeping a stiff upper lip—they also tended to minimize the pain of their friends. Esmond, Philip Toynbee said, "made me feel without expressing it . . . that unhappiness is a dirty disease which must never be encouraged, or even tolerated."[47] Shortly after Esmond and Decca arrived in America, Toynbee wrote that his brother, also a friend of theirs, had killed himself, in despair over a bad romantic breakup. "Remembering how much you dislike gloomy people," Toynbee wrote that he'd say no more about it.[48] Esmond wrote back, mostly with a lengthy, highly comic, description of his various attempts to find work.

Esmond wanted advertising work and better pay than he'd earned in England. Unaware that Americans then considered the British inept at modern marketing, he was characteristically confident. Decca got a job first, at Jane Engel's Dress Shop, a high-end, Upper East Side establishment, for twenty-five dollars a week. The process presented one of Decca's first experiences with American racism. For weeks, she'd been filling out job applications by writing in "light brown" as her answer to the always requested question of "color." She received no job offers. Finally, someone at Engel's explained that when an American application requested "color," they wanted skin, not hair.[49]

The American press was fascinated with Decca and Esmond, always framing them as Unity's sister and Churchill's nephew.[50] "Getting one's name in the paper in England is tantamount to a death in the family," Esmond once acknowledged. In aristocratic circles, "friends send flowers."[51] He and Decca now welcomed reporters and courted press attention as something they could turn to advantage. In April, *The Boston Globe* reported breathlessly on their "American adventure," comparing Decca's radicalism to her sisters' fascism. Accompanying the story, the *Globe* photograph captured a very poised Decca—in her new black dress—smiling directly into the camera. A wildly gesturing

Esmond is caught in mid-expostulation.[52] With singular insight, the *Globe* reporter noted that "pretty and blue-eyed" Jessica . . . was "silent most of the time—Esmond talks so much." Anticipating the modern obsession with branding by more than fifty years, Decca and Esmond realized they could trade on their sobriquets, such as "Rebel" and "Mad Mitford" to promote themselves as wacky aristocratic American-loving foreigners, a story that sold smartly to American audiences. They were "Blue Blood Adventurers" having "madcap adventures," *The Washington Post* reported.[53] They were "gay and exciting . . . young lovers . . . making their dreams come true in America . . . top-drawer immigrants" for whom "slammed doors and empty pockets have only been fun."[54]

As he continued waiting for a job, Esmond focused on writing, impelled by his ideas of what the writer's life could look like in America and inspired by the story he and Decca had begun concocting about themselves. He hired a secretary to come daily, an extravagance they could ill afford, but which Esmond was sure would prove a wise investment. He began churning out essays and opinion pieces. But Esmond's perspective—he wrote that war was inevitable, democracies were being crushed, and most British politicians were fascists—lacked commercial appeal. In May, after months of trying, he sold an essay called "Escape from England" to *The Commentator*, for a respectable ninety dollars. In the process, he met Selden Rodman, editor of *Common Sense*, who quickly became a good friend. Like many progressive Americans, Rodman opposed U.S. military intervention in any coming European conflict. He was also anti-communist and a critic of the New Deal. But Rodman and the Romillys agreed on many things, especially the danger of the Red Scare that Martin Dies's House Committee on Un-American Activities had been fomenting since 1938.[55] To Decca, the Rodmans and their artistic-political circle felt familiar, like "American Rotherhithe Streeters."[56]

Decca's family always claimed that she and Esmond were doctrinaire and unyielding. The opposite was true. Their social circle was broadly drawn, embracing a wide range of views. "The essence of enjoyable living," for Esmond, Decca noted, was "contrastiness."[57] More than anything else, they sought out people who were active and engaged, who were making things happen and who could converse and debate.

This ideological flexibility led, in July 1939, to another of their great early friendships. Through Peter Nevile's letters of introduction they were invited to spend the Fourth of July weekend with Nevile's friend, John Cook, at the summer home of Cook's uncle, Eugene Meyer: investment banker, former head of the War Finance Corporation, the Federal Reserve Board, and later president of the World Bank, and owner of *The Washington Post*. Meyer was a capitalist, a Republican, Jewish, a "big shot," and much older than Decca and Esmond. But he was also strongly anti-fascist and the most potentially useful "contact" they'd yet met. Most importantly, he liked Decca and Esmond. "We immediately assigned him to the top of the list of Possible Job Getters." Eugene and Agnes Meyer were kind, well-informed, generous, and had strong senses of humor—a prerequisite for friendship with Decca and Esmond. In short order the Meyers were elevated, in Esmond and Decca's categorical scheme, to "Fairy Godparents." They called the Meyers "Genoowinely Innaresting People." There was nothing fake or faux about the Meyers. Their home, Decca said, was "the most luxurious place I had ever seen . . . like an English country house in size and surroundings, only twice as comfortable. There were none of those unexpected inconveniences—cold bath water, electric lights that don't work, inedible food—so often suffered in similar settings in England."[58]

Meyer was almost as interested in using Decca and Esmond as they were keen to take advantage of him. He immediately sensed how well Decca and Esmond's story would sell and signed them up for a nine-installment series about coming to America. This *Washington Post* series was designed to be in both voices, carrying each of their names as separate bylines, with competing versions of their American adventures laid out in facing columns. Capitalizing on an image of harmless haplessness, they were to share anecdotes about their own naivete in job getting, job doing, and job losing. Esmond's many setbacks would star: how he was outsmarted by American con artists, his inability to adapt to American efficiencies, and so on.

It was Decca's first shot at journalism and her first experience with how effective her humor could be in winning over readers. It was Meyer's idea to have the columns face off, and as he may have surmised, that energized Decca's competitive instincts. In print, she did not demur to Esmond. The first double column they wrote, "Two Young Adventurers Explore New York," featured Esmond on the left, describing the lobby of the Shelton Hotel and the money they were spending. "I started looking for a job as soon as we arrived," Decca's right-side column began. Their second double column, "English Adventurers Stalk Job in Wilds of New York," featured a cartoon of Decca going off to work in a suit and tie, while Esmond lounged in bed in striped pajamas, dreaming of success. Esmond's column described being fired from an advertising job. Decca's was about being hired for a new one, at the World's Fair. His column ended, "My job did turn out to be a sort of joke." Hers ended: "Now it was time to leave and get a job somewhere else." By their third column, Meyer had reversed the placement. "By Jessica" was to appear first, on the left-hand side. Their fourth double column would be a single, carrying only her piece on working at the World's Fair. Her distinctive voice was already evident in the drafts she prepared for Meyer: "I picked my way through the drooping ranks of wet-collared college boys with their empty chairs to the entrance of the Eighth Avenue subway . . . I had visions of soon becoming an assistant buyer or division superintendent, bossing all the other girls around . . . public relations director or head buyer . . . after three weeks in junk jewelry, I ended my department store career."[59] Meyer gave them feedback on their columns and stockpiled them as they turned them in. But with extraordinary prescience, he held off publication until he had the full series in his hands.

Esmond continued to search for work. After weeks of looking for advertising work, he was suddenly offered a job paying a hundred dollars a week (just under £1,500 today), four times what he'd been earning in London. The advertising firm was called Topping and Lloyd, and the job, as he excitedly wrote to both Peter Nevile and Philip Toynbee, asked virtually nothing of him. Unbeknownst to Esmond, Topping and Lloyd was a tax scheme designed to lose money. But Esmond thought his workday reflected the American way of business:

10.10 a.m.	Arrive. Seat myself in huge office towering over Madison Avenue, which I share with Vice-President.
10.15 a.m.	Open and begin study of *New York Times*.
11.10 a.m.	Cheerfully greet Vice-President. Put *New York Times* in waste-paper basket.
11.10–12.00	Do a bit of work
12.00	Wash, pack up shirt, shorts, etc., and depart to play tennis with somebody at Tudor City.
12:20–1:25	Play tennis
1.20–2.20	Changing, lunching, drinking, relaxing.
2.40	Arrive back at office
2.40–3.00	Read *New York Post*
3–4	Work.

4–5	Chat with someone.
5–5.30	More general chatting.
5.30	Depart[60]

Had Esmond understood that he was only hired as window dressing, it wouldn't have mattered. The easy money mesmerized him. "We're rich," he boasted to his friends.[61]

While Esmond loafed at Topping and Lloyd, Decca worked at the 1939 New York World's Fair selling tweeds in Ye Merrie England Village for twenty dollars a week. The fairgrounds were over three miles long. Merrie England Village was tucked away in the vast amusement zone, which also contained Old New York, a replica of Victoria Falls, Sun Valley, a parachute jump, a beer hall, and an Artist's Village. The fair's theme, "Building the World of Tomorrow," was celebrated in booths ranging from General Motors' wildly popular "Futurama" of cars to Kodak cameras and Bissell carpet sweepers.[62] "Our shop," Mitford wrote, "was decorated as an old Scotch cottage with a spinning wheel and handloom. It has a weaver, imported direct from Scotland, who was the barker, shouting over and over again: 'Only 10 cents to come in! See the old Scotch cottage.'" Merrie England was designed as a safe antidote to the Russian, Romanian, and African pavilions, a familiar alternative to Jungleland or Cuban Village. In Merrie England Village were also a castle, Shakespeare Craft Shop, two English-style inns offering dinner, a miniature Globe Theater, and a Highland Home. Decca's job was to persuade wealthy customers that the tweeds were "made in little Scottish homes."[63] As the weather warmed, however, the tweed market shrank. By summer, Decca spent most of her time dodging drunks. King George VI and Queen Elizabeth came from Britain to the fair and Decca met them. Her sister Pamela also made an unexpected visit, accompanying her husband, Derek, on business. "I was amazed at Woman suddenly turning up here," Decca wrote her mother. "I had no idea she was coming & in fact the night before she rang up I dreamt that she & Nancy had died of old age. They came out to see me at the fair & last night we all had a wonderful dinner together at their hotel."[64] Pamela's visit was Decca's first contact with family since Nancy's ill-conceived destroyer caper, but the "wonderful" feelings did not last.

After Topping and Lloyd lost a sufficient sum, Esmond was fired. Decca's wages were reduced at the fair. It was late summer. Their apartment was stifling. Decca had managed to save nearly five hundred dollars (about £6,500 in today's currency). They decided it was time to take a Grand "Tor."

Assembling a second batch of letters of introduction, "this time to people in all parts of the States," they bought an old Ford and studied maps. Esmond took a one-week crash course in bartending while Decca sorted their clothing. Their Grand Tor covered two thousand zigzagged miles of New England—"much more like English people they talk the same way & one sees village idiots in the country just like England"—stopping every ten to twenty miles to add water to the Ford's leaky radiator.[65] The highlight of their drive was to be a long visit to the Woods Hole estate of plumbing heiress Mrs. Murray Crane, whom they had met once in New York and whose casual invitation they had reserved ever since. "We had been told that [she] . . . had quite a penchant for young authors, artists, and poets, and that she had even been known to pay a fee on occasion to foreign visitors in these fields of endeavor for an evening lecture to her guests."[66] Woods Hole was a bust, however. It was dull. There were few other visitors. There was nothing good to filch. So, they made their way to Martha's Vineyard, to visit Selden and Hilda Rodman, who were renting a cottage on the island.

By the time they arrived at the Vineyard's Menemsha Inn in late

August, they'd received news of the German-Soviet nonaggression pact. True to form, Decca's family made light of it. "Stalin how could you let him," Nancy teased.[67] Both Decca and Esmond were on edge, Esmond especially, struggling to gin up the charm that guesting required. The Rodmans were renters, not owners, and had no room for company. Esmond was agitated and easily goaded, feeling betrayed on all sides. His defense of the Soviet Union, however, was relentless and "took on all comers."[68] "Arguments raged," Decca wrote, and "political arguments raged louder than ever."[69] They had neither money nor anywhere else to go, so they resorted to squatting: sleeping every night in a different unoccupied cabin. Each morning, they packed up their suitcases, stashed them, and posed as day visitors. They usually enjoyed that sort of cat and mouse. But now, with war so clearly on the horizon, the game wore thin. Esmond was "wound up like a spring watch . . . as exasperating as a buzz saw," Rodman said. He noted that Decca's patience had frayed and that she and Esmond were getting on one another's nerves. When they became "querulous . . . the tension was terrific," Rodman said.[70] "I began to lose my temper," Rodman remembered. "We speculated whether Esmond was mad or childish, brilliant or foolish, funny or disagreeable."[71] Decca struggled to charm the Rodmans on her own.

On September 1, news reached the Vineyard that Germany had invaded Poland. Sitting with the Rodmans, Decca and Esmond waited for Chamberlain to declare war. Esmond predicted that his Uncle Winston would now become prime minister. Intrigued, Rodman commissioned Esmond's analysis for *Common Sense*. Esmond's article offered Churchill as a thoroughly consistent conservative and a "staunch British Imperialist" who could, unlike Chamberlain, be counted on to fight Hitler. Churchill would fight, Esmond surmised, not because of anti-fascist sentiment or in defense of democracy. He would fight to defend the British Empire, and it would be "on his terms and his alone."[72]

Since setting foot in America, Decca and Esmond had anticipated war. They were still shocked when it came. "I can't believe it has actually happened," Decca wrote her mother.[73] She reproached her family, but she also sympathized with them and longed for news of them. Decca imagined Debo, back in England, and felt badly for her. "Poor Henderson, I suppose she is dancing alone in the deserted ballrooms now," she wrote.[74] Unity was in Germany and news of her was hard to come by. In spite of the fact that Roosevelt continued to insist that "we are not going in," Decca remained positive about America.[75] Their English friends advised them to stay put. "Much as I would like to see you," Peter Nevile wrote from England, "I sincerely hope you are not considering coming back here."[76] It seemed best to go to Washington, find work, and fulfill their remaining obligations to *The Washington Post* from there, since they'd so far written few of their promised installments.

In the installments they had completed, Esmond and Decca had promoted an image of carefree, youthful hijinks. They were self-consciously selling optimism, enthusiasm, and love of America to an American audience hungry for that affirmation. They were supposed to be having "terrific fun," as Decca had put it to her mother. But the events of September 1939 tested that story. Hitler's "unspeakable evil" changed everything.[77] Shut off from home and comrades, they watched the speed of Hitler's move across Europe, horrified that no one had the strength—or will—to stop him. The British and French were ineffectual in demanding Hitler's withdrawal from Poland. The Soviet nonaggression pact took Russia out of the equation. The Spanish Republicans were no match for the Fascists. Defeat in Spain seemed inevitable, and Esmond's brother, Giles, still fighting in Spain, was in the thick of it. Roosevelt had begged for an end to the "bombardment from the air of civilian populations" in Spain, but he nevertheless reiterated his resolve that America would "remain a neutral nation."[78] To Decca and Esmond, it now seemed that the American government was prepared to sit on its hands while Europe's fate hung in the balance.[79]

For two days after Hitler invaded Poland, Chamberlain hedged. Finally, on September 3, he reluctantly declared war, demonstrating profound sadness rather than the resolve that Esmond and Decca hoped for. By September 3, 1939, between the declaration of war, "Decca's increasingly querulous voice," and "Esmond's wearing bumptiousness," Rodman's nerves were shot. "We still laughed, but almost hysterically now and at almost nothing," Rodman said. It was registering with them all, as he put it, that the "world will never be the same." Tennis and drinking, gossip and swimming suddenly seemed unimportant.[80] Rodman's other friends—tennis player Babe Alexander, journalist Max Eastman, and a "pale youth" whose name no one seemed to know—all were anxious to depart.

Roosevelt officially recognized the war on September 5. His action triggered the total arms embargo mandated by the Neutrality Act, deepening the desperation of anti-Nazi Europeans. Britain and France were now cut off from all possible U.S. assistance, which was just what isolationists like "America First" Charles Lindbergh had asked for.[81]

It was time to pack up and leave the island.

The earliest morning ferry left at 6:30 a.m. and everyone but the Romillys and the Rodmans were aboard. Decca and Esmond had overslept. When they stumbled out of bed late, they asked Rodman to make another trip to the Vineyard Haven Ferry terminal, just for them. In a rage, Rodman dropped them off, then beat the Romillys back to New York in his private plane. As far as he was concerned, they could now be someone else's problem.

5

"America Is Such Heaven"

History was the shocker.[1]
—VIRGINIA DURR

Two against the world.
—JESSICA MITFORD

Decca celebrated her twenty-second birthday, September 11, 1941, by visiting with Rodman, who had forgiven her and Esmond for causing such trouble on Martha's Vineyard. Sydney sent a beautiful new green suit and Pam gifted a singing telegram, just the sort of uniquely American thing Decca loved. Decca wanted news of Unity, still in Germany.[2] "Do let me know about her as soon as possible," she pleaded.[3] But Sydney had little news to share. She wrote vague reassurances.

Decca threw herself into the driving tour. Esmond laid out the route: "Washington D.C., get jobs in the New Deal. New Orleans or Miami, something in the restaurant business. Texas: Cowhands. Hollywood: Be movie stars, or at least extras. San Francisco: Longshoremen. Chicago: Underworld."[4] His notions of America were shopworn stereotypes, yet to Esmond, they seemed reasonable. A Hollywood producer did, in fact, find Decca photogenic and offered a screen test. But he had nothing for Esmond. So Esmond and Decca turned him down. The president of an Arizona cattle company offered them jobs punching cows. Esmond thought they could find something both more thrilling and also more lucrative. He turned the cattle offer down as well.

Their first Southern stop was Washington, D.C. Esmond found it dull. Selden Rodman sent them to his friend Michael Straight, who seemed to know everyone in Washington's liberal Democratic circles. Before they knew it, they found themselves "in the centre of everything," as Esmond glowingly reported back to Rodman.[5]

Decca desperately needed a role model and friend. Straight provided one for Esmond. Like Decca and Esmond, Straight was a rebel with a pedigree. He was the son of Willard Straight, an investment banker who had died in 1918, and heiress Dorothy Payne Whitney Straight. His mother, remarried in 1925, founded *The New Republic* and the New School for Social Research with her second husband. She supported unions, the Junior League, and service. Michael Straight was one year older than Decca, shared her and Esmond's playful streak, and like them, carried the confidence born of wealth. He had the enthusiasm Decca associated with Americans. In spite of his youth, he had already worked as a speechwriter for Roosevelt and as an economist for the State Department. Decca thought him "extraordinarily handsome" and accomplished.[6] She did not know (none of Straight's associates did) that Straight was a spy. He had been recruited by Anthony Blunt in 1937, while still an undergraduate at Cambridge University.[7] Unlike Rodman, whose patience they'd exhausted, Straight was charmed by Decca and Esmond. They stayed on in Washington a few extra weeks, meeting Straight's many friends.

Straight believed that the New Deal was "more dynamic than Fascism and more revolutionary than Communism." His friends were also passionate New Dealers, keeping alive a passion for government programs that had waned somewhat nationally by 1939.[8] They saw New Deal social welfare reforms in wages, working conditions, housing, labor relations, relief, banking, and social security as "equal opportunity in a classless society." And they believed the New Deal had alleviated the cruelest effects of the Depression, saving it from its own worst tendencies, as Doris Kearns Goodwin puts it.[9] Many of these young New Dealers were born to wealth and social standing, people whose worldview had been shaken, like Decca's, by poverty and war, and by the Spanish Civil War especially. Like Decca and Esmond, they'd had to come to terms with assumptions that wars took place elsewhere and that indolence, rather than injustice, caused hunger and homelessness. They'd pulled their heads out of the sand and were still clearing grains from their eyes. Historian David Kennedy explains that the New Deal created a "momentous shift in perception" through the precept that "the well-being of ordinary" people was a shared obligation.[10] This paradigm shift in understanding social fairness and taking responsibility for human misery resonated with Decca. The "cutting edge of New Deal politics," Southern social activist (and, later, close friend of Decca's) Virginia Durr said, was "part of a broader personal transformation," grounded in an awareness of "how class distinctions shaped people."[11]

Esmond and Decca were not theorists. It was the pragmatic spirit of the New Dealers that really hit home with them. "I'd no idea," Esmond wrote Rodman, "how terrifically keen and enthusiastic the spirit would be among the New Deal people."[12] "Far from being the dreamy-eyed, muddleheaded idealists portrayed by almost all the press," the New Dealers were canny and hard-working strategists, Decca said, "doers of deeds, planners of projects, and above all translators of their country's principles and ideals into real life."[13] Decca felt that "much of what was best in America was . . . represented by this bright, sincere group of liberals."[14] She and Esmond visited New Deal offices of youth programs, agriculture, and the arts. Could they get New Deal jobs, they asked. Could one of the bright, busy offices be theirs? Straight introduced them to many influential people, but he could not conjure up government jobs for two young Brits without experience or advanced education.

Esmond was deeply interested in educational systems. Dartington Hall, the free school founded by Straight's mother and stepfather, was precisely what he and his brother, Giles, had argued for in *Out of Bounds*: permissiveness, no corporal punishment, no uniforms, no Greek or Latin instruction, no celebrations of empire, and no compulsory religious services or competititve games.[15] At Dartington, even classes were voluntary.

Like Esmond and Decca, Straight had married young. At twenty-three, when they met him, he had just married Belinda ("Binny") Compton, eighteen years old and so sheltered that her nanny went on her honeymoon.[16] "We often had dinner with the three of them," Decca remembered.[17] Binny was striving to be a traditional Washington wife.[18] She gave cocktail parties, organized social fundraisers for liberal institutions such as the Highlander School and Bethune-Cookman College, and sponsored teas for Chinese orphans. As a member of the Junior League, she ushered at events where her husband gave speeches.[19]

Straight thought Esmond "brilliant, colorful, often hilariously funny" and considered his incorrigible petty thievery hilarious, at first. He initially admired the way Esmond and Decca "captured Washington by defying all of its conventions."[20] He was less amused, however, when

Esmond pilfered Straight's own clothing, including his socks and his neckties. Straight was troubled by Esmond's "contrastiness."[21] While he could be exceedingly mature—ready to lay down his life for his principles—Esmond was also childish: always up for a game, a prank, a dodge, or a gamble. Stealing his host's toothpaste could engage his attention as fully as dodging bullets. He immersed himself in the present, while hatching wild schemes for the future. Decca accepted, even loved, his variability. But Straight became annoyed, then alarmed, by Esmond's relentless opportunism.[22] "He showed no restraint," Straight said, "no discipline. He was an adventurist. Where the action was he was there. He seemed incapable of settling down."[23] He could never fully "come to terms with Esmond," as he put it.[24]

Sometimes, Esmond's contrastiness also confounded Decca. He'd finally found a temporary job, selling stockings door to door. How could he be so "disturbingly successful" at sales, she wondered?[25] Usually such a nonconformist, Esmond never questioned the Silkform script: "a deft combination of mental torture and physical manipulation designed to reduce the subject to a state of helpless passivity, bereft of independent will, and ready to sign anything as a condition of freedom from torment," Decca said.[26]

Decca's ability to embrace undersides, messiness, paradoxes, and oddness would eventually translate into a keen ability as an investigative journalist to ferret out hidden information and dive beneath the surface. At twenty-two years old, in 1939 it largely took the form of open-mindedness about her mercurial husband. No stranger to contrastiness in those she loved, including her sisters who were personally kind but fascist, and who were fiercely independent but always subordinate to their men, Esmond's juvenile side may have even been a relief to Decca, making him that much more familiar as she struggled to please him. All the people she had grown up caring about were contradictory and complex; even her parents had their tender, sentimental side.

Perhaps because he'd noticed Decca's "fine satirical mind" or possibly because he wanted to unload Esmond and Decca onto someone else, Straight brought Decca to the perfect person for her—Southern activist Virginia Durr. In Durr, Decca found her first truly feminist role model, one of three strong feminists who would influence her, and a lifelong friend she felt she could trust completely. Durr was very nearly a sister.

The parallels between Decca and Durr—fourteen years Decca's senior—were striking. Born in 1903, Durr was raised an "almost completely apolitical" Southern belle in Birmingham, Alabama.[27] She had the full-fledged coming-out that Decca had mostly ducked. Her Southern ancestors were wealthy slaveholders, many in the Ku Klux Klan, and Durr was raised in a socially stratified world. Black domestics might be beloved, but "I was taught that they were not like us."[28] Class lines were similarly sharp. "We were brought up . . . to believe that the distribution of wealth was ordained by God. It was 'in the blood.' You were born to be either wealthy and wise and rich and powerful and beautiful and healthy, or you were born to be poor and downtrodden and sick and miserable and drunken and immoral. . . . It was a very comforting thought."[29] Rail-thin and self-assured, Durr was talkative, unflappable, and energetic. She had also married young, choosing fellow Alabaman Clifford Durr, a lawyer, in 1926, shortly after completing her education at Wellesley, a path, then, to marriage as career. As a young wife, Durr had tried to follow the rules. She had children, joined the Junior League, sewing circles, and bridge groups, and she entertained her husband's associates. The Depression's effect on Southern steel mill workers radicalized her. The shock of meeting starving children never left her. "It was absolutely terrible. . . . I had been a conformist, a Southern snob. I actually thought the only people who amounted to anything were the very small group I belonged to. . . . What I learned during the depression changed all of that."[30] "More accumulated misery than you can imagine," she said.[31] Being a good wife and mother was no longer enough.

In 1933, Clifford Durr was called to Washington to work in the Reconstruction Finance Corporation by then senator and later, Supreme Court Justice Hugo Black, who was married to Virginia's sister. Leaving the South, as Decca escaped England, gave Durr the chance to reinvent herself. "I was brought up to be utterly useless with only one aim in life, which was to get a husband," Durr explained. All her aunts "ever did was sit on the front porch and rock."[32] In D.C., Durr looked for other women who used their connections to build power and influence change. She attached herself to Eleanor Roosevelt, following the First Lady into social justice initiatives. She emulated the First Lady's steel. She did not emulate how Eleanor deferred to Franklin in order to get her way. Durr decided she'd operate in front of the scenes, in her own name, on her own terms, and without deference to her husband. She respected and adored Cliff, but she would be treated as an equal by him.[33] Yet Durr made canny use of her former debutante's toolbox: batting her blue eyes, flirting, and playing on her delicate, white femininity when it suited her objectives.

At the same time, she had a knack for not taking herself too seriously, and she mocked her own privilege and pretensions. She put social problems above her own feelings. Decca thought her principles were sound. "I do think 'feeling personally let down' is a sin," she once wrote Durr. "What it boils down to is putting one's feeling on a special plane, as if one's personal feelings were more important than those of others."[34]

Durr launched a campaign against the poll tax, which had been designed to keep Blacks, poor whites, and women from voting and to consolidate social and political power in the hands of the South's traditional white segregationists. She had grown up with those men, seen what their power could do, and was determined to break their grip. By

1939, she had organized the South's most important conference on labor and economic conditions: the Southern Conference for Human Welfare, which both Eleanor Roosevelt and Mary McLeod Bethune attended. Durr was also beginning to confront the racism of her up-bringing, preparing for a leading role in Birmingham's emerging civil rights movement. She was like a political endurance athlete, able to put in exceptionally long hours and never asking others to perform tasks she was unwilling to do herself. Durr, like Decca, had been raised to be popular. In Virginia's world, as in Decca's, social acceptance and stand-ing had been highly prized. But she'd grown willing to be disliked. If she ruffled feathers, then so be it. Decca still very much wanted to be liked. Durr's willingness to burn bridges to get her way made her, like Esmond, "one of nature's rebels."[35]

At first, Durr struck Decca as too aggressive. "Her approach to conversation was that of the frontal attack . . . she fired question after question. . . . I was a little ruffled by the insistent barrage. . . . Mrs. Durr made me feel outnumbered, as though I were being cor-nered by a roomful of reporters."[36] Durr, however, barely remembered meeting Decca because Esmond so thoroughly bowled her over. To her, he was "the world's most marvelous young man. . . . so incredibly brilliant . . . charming . . . extremely funny. He was absolutely dedi-cated to a better world . . . I was . . . bedazzled." What Durr noticed about Decca was that she was "exquisitely beautiful . . . beautiful in a really classic sense," and that "Decca never said anything." Esmond "completely dominated every situation he was in . . . [he was] center of the stage. . . . She [Decca] seemed to be just an echo of Esmond in a way." Durr said, "I've never seen any two people so completely in love."[37] The Romillys were "as one . . . [but] Esmond was the one."[38]

In early October, Decca and Esmond headed South again, aiming for New Orleans and from there to San Francisco. Michael Straight helped them assemble another set of letters of introduction. Their rattletrap Ford needed its radiator filled every twenty miles. Pulling over, turning off the engine, getting out the water jug, and waiting for the engine to cool made for slow going. While they were traveling, there was a sudden burst of American newspaper articles about Unity. She was ill. She had committed suicide. She and Hitler had a violent quarrel. She had overdosed on sleeping pills. She had sunstroke from waiting outside for Hitler. She had been poisoned. She was having a serious operation. She was pregnant with Hitler's child. She had shot herself.[39] The London papers reported that she'd died. Hitler had imposed a strict news blackout, so no news of her came directly out of Germany. Transatlantic mail service was long delayed, at best. "One just doesn't know what to believe," Decca wrote her mother.[40] "No one knew . . . what had become of her," she later added.[41] Decca was largely on her own with her anxieties. "The only area of my life which I could not share," she reflected, "was my attachment to Boud. Perversely, and although I hated everything she stood for, she was easily my favorite sister. . . . I had tried, most of the time unsuccessfully, to banish her from my mind after the war broke out. . . . I mourned my Boud of Boudledidge days, my huge, bright adversary. . . . I knew I couldn't expect Esmond, who had never met her, to feel anything but disgust for her, so by tacit understanding we avoided discussing her."[42]

Unity had declared that if war broke out between Britain and Germany, she would "commidit." That meant kill herself, in Mitford-speak. Unity had always taken every dare further than anyone else. Decca had loved that boldness. If Unity's influence over Hitler proved to be largely in Unity's head, there was no telling what she might do.[43]

On September 3, when Britain declared war, Unity wrote a farewell letter to her parents. My "best love to you all and particularly to my Boud [Decca]," she said.[44] "See the Führer often when it is over," she requested. She dispensed with her most precious property—a signed photograph of Hitler and her Nazi Party badge. And she left a sealed letter for Hitler: a second suicide note saying that she could not stand the idea of war between the two countries. Then she left behind all her cash and apartment keys, and drove to Munich's English Garden, a large park on the Isar River. There, in the warm autumn sun, Unity sat down on a park bench, took out her pistol, placed it on her temple, and pulled the trigger. Visitors strolling in the park heard the shot and saw her slump. They called the police. Before they could arrive, a Luftwaffe car pulled up and spirited Unity away to a Swiss hospital in Berne.

Unity survived. The bullet she had pressed into her head lodged at the back of her skull, pressed between brain and bone. Inoperable, the Swiss surgeons said. Unity spent a week in a coma. Hitler sent roses, paid her hospital bill, and visited, although Unity—a still body in a stark white room—did not know he was there. When she finally regained consciousness, she tried again to kill herself, swallowing a jagged Nazi brooch. The large pin was surgically removed and, again, Unity survived. She phoned Hitler and said she'd like to return to England. Please arrange that, she asked him. She was now partly paralyzed, and her face was badly swollen. Very few people could make out her words.

Told only that Unity was ill in Switzerland, the Mitfords were frantic. International travel papers were almost impossible to obtain, but David used all his connections as a member of the House of Lords to obtain special permission, from both warring countries, so that he could access Switzerland via Germany and bring Unity home.[45] Moving a patient with a bullet in her head was a nearly insurmountable logistical problem, made much worse by Unity's notoriety and by press fascination with her story.

Decca and Esmond missed New Orleans (neither was good with a map) and landed in Miami, Florida, instead. Miami, Decca said, was a "horrible, tinselly town with its maddening eternal sunshine pouring incessantly down on white stucco [and] . . . sham-looking poinsettias." Its people, she said, were a "humorless, suspicious, narrow-minded lot . . . [who] matched their surroundings. . . . Many of those with whom we came into contact exhibited a sort of smarmy bonhomie reminiscent of sugary German *gemütlichkeit*, a front behind which lurked the foulest racism." She found the whole place saturated with "a crawling, mean sordidness."[46] Decca considered the South revolting, and she described it in language that harkened back to her first revelatory upsets over village poverty in Britain. "Some of the shacks where the poor farmers live are simply incredible," she wrote her mother, "they are wooden & look like old, broken-down chicken houses." She didn't think much more of the people. "I don't really like Southerners much, they are absolutely different from Northerners (as they never stop pointing out) and are mostly rather snobbish."[47]

In Miami, they rented a small, furnished apartment that was filthy, even by their unexacting standards. Decca heard insects rustling inside the cane chairs. The floor was so grimy that their shoes stuck to it. Their solution was to take their shoes on and off from the bed and never go barefoot.[48] She described it all to Debo, living up to her nickname, "Squalor."

Never one to voluntarily admit defeat, Decca told her family that Miami was "a heavenly place . . . boiling hot and with people bathing all through the winter."[49] She wrote Unity that "Miami's rather like the South of France or Venice, all the people here have got something extraorder about them."[50] She did not feel quite as positive as she claimed. Nevertheless, she and Esmond filed an intent to naturalize as American citizens.

Unity lay stiffly in a metal hospital bed in Berne, still barely conscious. David, Sydney, and Debo reached Switzerland in early January 1940. In an antiseptic, unadorned room, they found Unity guarded, glassy-eyed, bewildered, and unwashed, but conscious. "She could not walk," Debo wrote Decca, "talked with difficulty and was a changed personality, like one who had had a stroke. Not only was her appearance shocking, she was a stranger, someone we did not know. We brought her back to England in an ambulance coach attached to a train [personally arranged by Hitler]. Every jolt was agony to her."[51] When their special ambulance train arrived in Calais, they put up in a hotel close to the ferry terminal, with Unity's fourteen pieces of luggage and a phalanx of reporters setting off flashbulbs as fast as machine-gun fire. Unity stared at the reporters, completely bewildered. She did not seem to know what they were. Some of them offered as much as £20,000 (£370,000 in today's currency) for a statement, which David refused.[52] But he asserted: "I am not ashamed of anything my daughter has done in Germany."[53]

A large ship was cleared of all other people so the family could travel in privacy from France to Folkestone, south of Dover. "Soldiers with fixed bayonets . . . military policemen, railway policemen, local constables and special officers" escorted Unity off the ship and into a waiting private ambulance for the hundred-mile trip to the Cotswolds.[54] Crowds gathered to glimpse "HITLER'S ENGLISH GIRLFRIEND," the "PEER'S DAUGHTER," "HITLER'S ADMIRER," and "HITLER'S FRIEND." "Are you all mad?" David fumed at the assembled onlookers.[55] Again, "the photographers raced ahead" to snap pictures, *The New York Times* reported.[56] The family's home was placed under armed guard to protect Unity from protesters who wanted to know why "the Mitford Girl who has openly been consorting with the King's enemies," was allowed to go "scot-free?"[57] A hastily produced newsreel stirred further resentment by revealing that Unity's private train cars and ambulances had cost the government an amount of money equivalent to the annual combined wages of more than half a dozen average laborers.[58]

In Miami, Decca scratched for any news she could get. "It is of course absolutely impossible to get anything reliable from the newspaper reports," she complained. She read that Unity had declared herself a "Jew Hater" in Julius Streicher's *Der Stürmer*, that Unity said that Jews should be put on an island to die, and that she visited four different Munich apartments offered her by Hitler, touring and inspecting them at her leisure, while the Jewish owners to be dispossessed of their homes watched in despair.[59] She begged her mother for updates: "Do write & tell everything because I have no other way of knowing & I can't think of anything else, it is all so frightful."[60] Decca found it nearly impossible to accept that the sister she once knew as kind and funny was the subject of these stories.[61] The Unity she knew had never been a political person. The Unity she knew liked to talk about dogs, walks, lunch, what people said, and what they were wearing. Could that really be the same lovelorn Nazi maniac the newspapers described? "Why had she," Decca asked, "to those of us who knew her the most human of people, turned her back on humanity and allied herself with those grinning beasts? . . . How could Boud, a person of enormous natural taste . . . have embraced their cruel philistinism? . . . She had always been a terrific hater—so were all of us, except possibly Tom—but I had always thought she hated intelligently."[62] Afraid she would end up completely "off speakers" with her family again, Decca avoided politics in her letters home.[63] "Darling Boud," Decca wrote Unity, "your Boud is so sorry you are ill. . . . I've been so longing for news of you."[64] With assistance, as she recovered, Unity replied: "Darling Boud, When I got your letter I nearly went off my head! You SEE I had ached for you because I do love you so much."[65] Neither mentioned events in the world.

Decca took the first job she could find: selling junk jewelry in a large Miami drugstore. "Once more . . . the family breadwinner," she joked.[66] She worked almost fifty hours a week, for fourteen dollars (about £250 today). Esmond finally found work waiting tables at the Roma, a local Italian restaurant. His first day was a "nightmare," which was hardly surprising, given that, as Decca noted, he was "known for his inability

to carry a teaspoon from one room to the next without dropping it."
Esmond had lied about having experience when he applied, imagining from what he remembered about *being* served, that serving must
be easy work. After crashing into another waiter and drenching him
in chicken cacciatore, Esmond was fired. He then talked the owners
into keeping him on as a handyman. "An unhandier man I can scarcely
imagine," Decca said. Failing miserably as handyman, Esmond next
convinced the owners to try him as a bartender. For that, at least, he'd
had a week's training. Almost immediately he procured a $1,000 loan
from Eugene Meyer and became not only bartender, but business partner as well. Decca quit her drugstore job and became the "buyer of supplies, bookkeeper, and bouncer." Looking back later, she reflected that
"Esmond threw himself into the project "as though he was deliberately
trying to shut out, for the time being, the realities of life and politics."[67]

Decca said that Esmond "developed all sorts of wild plans for the
future of the bar . . . the center of a whirlpool of activity of his own
making," while she awaited news from home and while they both followed news of the war.[68] The war was called "phoney" because there
were no battles on British soil, but already more than one million British troops had been mobilized, gas was rationed, and children were
being evacuated to the countryside. To Decca, it seemed real indeed.

Unity remained on the front pages. Just after New Year's, 1940,[69]
her story even "drove Mr. Roosevelt off the [British] front pages."[70] As
The New York Times's reporter put it, "a beautiful woman with a bullet
in her head is news in any language."[71] Reports repeated the rumor
that Unity had shot herself "for love of Adolf Hitler."[72] "Do you know
if it is true," Decca asked her mother, "that she had a terrible quarrel
with Hitler as the papers say?"[73]

On January 7 there were three articles on Unity's return in the
Times.[74] That same day, the *Chicago Tribune* ran a photo of Decca and
"Edward" at the Roma bar, under the headline UNITY'S SISTER A MIAMI

WAITRESS. It described Decca as the "Sister of Hitler's English Friend."[75] *The Washington Post* published a piece that day saying that "while Unity Freeman-Mitford, daughter of an English peer, was living a court life as Hitler's 'Perfect Nordic Beauty,'" her sister, Jessica Freeman-Mitford Romilly, was taking orders in a Miami restaurant bar.[76] Decca was now an American celebrity as Hitler's girlfriend's sister. "The telephone rang continually with reporters from newspapers all over the country demanding to know the 'inside story'" of Unity.[77]

Decca and Esmond were dodging international reporters while still owing Meyer stories for *The Washington Post*. Their series had finally been advertised and was scheduled to run, no doubt based on assurances they'd given Meyer. But, as yet, many of the installments remained unwritten. They'd stopped working on it once they'd gone on the road. They needed to hunker down now.

On January 28, the announcement of their series appeared on page 1, under a banner reading BLUEBLOOD ADVENTURERS DISCOVER AMERICA, complete with cartoon images and photographs. The paper promised "a gay and exciting salute to reality by two front-page young lovers who bought the world for a song and are making their dreams come true." As the female half of these "two top-drawer immigrants," Decca's role was depicted as pouring tea and imagining the fortune that Esmond would earn. Their first essay, "How to Spend Newly Acquired Fortune of £200," was credited solely to Esmond. Decca was described as having a "song in her heart" and an enviable new lifestyle, but she did not speak for herself. Pictures of her appeared alongside Esmond's voice and articles asking, "Should Married Women Work?" as well as yet more news of Unity. On page 11, the *Post* confirmed that Unity had brain damage. There was also speculation over how many gunshot wounds Unity had suffered, and questions about why a British woman so loved Adolf Hitler.[78] International fascination with the Mad Mitfords had not abated. If anything, the public was more fascinated than ever with a family whose lives touched so many aspects of contemporary history and yet seemed to lodge themselves so firmly in the past. As one historian put it, they were "such a perfect reflection of the times that it was often difficult to believe that the Mitford family had not been invented."[79]

Both Decca and Esmond projected a lightheartedness they could not now feel. In April, Hitler attacked Denmark, Norway, the Netherlands, and Belgium. Esmond received word that Giles had been captured in Norway, in the chaos that ensued as Narvik fell to the Nazis. When the Germans learned that they'd nabbed Churchill's nephew, they locked Giles in their notorious Colditz prison, where they kept most of those they intended to use as hostages. For a long time, the Romillys didn't know if he was living or dead. As all their attempts "to get some news of Giles" failed, Esmond and Decca felt increasingly isolated.[80] In May, they learned that Esmond's father had died of cancer, some of the only family news to reach them for weeks.

They were thrown back exclusively on one another, at a very difficult time for each of them. "We had more reason than most to feel bound to one another in a way that excluded people around us," Decca later wrote. "Estrangement from our families, the circumstances of our marriage, our constant wanderings about, the death of the baby [Julia], all had conspired to weld us into a self-sufficient unit, a conspiracy of two against the world."[81]

Tourists kept popping in to see "Unity's sister." "Well, she's not here just now," Decca always said.[82] And running a business was more demanding and less profitable than they had expected. So in the late spring of 1940, they gave up on the Roma bar. They piled back into their car and headed north, from Florida to New Orleans, through Alabama and Georgia up to Washington, sightseeing all the way. While they were traveling, Oswald Mosley and Diana were arrested and imprisoned under the Defence Regulation 18B, as enemies of Great

Britain who posed a public danger to the nation. Originally held in separate cells, they were soon allowed to share a cottage on London's Holloway Prison grounds.[83] Decca read all about it on the road, grabbing every newspaper she could find on their travels.

Back in Washington once again and staying with the Straights, Esmond was determined to volunteer for military service. He thought that Virginia Durr's "large, disorganized, and animated" farmhouse on Seminary Hill, where both toddlers and prominent New Dealers wandered in and out at will—was the perfect place to deposit Decca once he went back to war.[84] In July, he asked Durr if Decca could stay with them "over the weekend" while he registered with the Royal Canadian Air Force.[85] Durr later recalled exactly how Esmond approached her. "He came into the kitchen while I was fixing dinner," she remembered. "'Don't you think you could keep dear Decca while I'm gone? . . . I am sure that she will be so lonely. If you will just keep her for the weekend, I can't tell you how I would appreciate it.'" No, Durr said, explaining that she was just then en route to the Democratic Convention. "Wonderful," Esmond replied. "Take Decca with you." Esmond "persuaded me to take her," Durr conceded.[86] Esmond left for training with the RCAF, nominally autonomous but a training ground for British pilots. He told Decca, "I'll probably find myself being commanded by one of your beastly relatives.'"[87]

After enlisting, in mid-July 1940, Esmond wrote to Decca, he'd traveled north to Canada via the Rodmans (where he went to a "dull" baseball game, played some poker, and overslept his alarm clock). He signed up successfully in Ottawa ("the dullest place on earth"), barely made it through a four-hour medical examination, and spent days in a filthy rented room while he waited for his paperwork to clear.[88] "There's no sign of a war on," he wrote.[89] Esmond had bicycled into Spain and signed up by showing up. But in Ottawa he'd discovered that the Royal

Canadian Air Force required paperwork—a school certificate from Wellington (which he'd dropped out of and publicly mocked), as well as character references. Get those from Meyer, he urged Decca, but ask him not to "draw attention" to the fact that they never wrote the last article they'd contracted for their series.[90]

Esmond had also neglected to mention to Durr that Decca was pregnant and experiencing violent morning sickness. As Durr and Decca started the seven-hundred-mile trip from Washington to Chicago, a long hot drive in pre-interstate July 1940, Decca needed to stop "every fifteen minutes" to be sick.[91] Durr was attending the 1940 convention as a guest of her friends from Texas, Lyndon Baines Johnson and Lady Bird. On arriving, her party was given large hats and lariats as convention souvenirs along with their credentials, and were seated, with the Texas delegation, at the far end of the immense hall. "I've got a young English girl with me who throws up all the time. What in the name of god are we going to do?" Durr asked her Texas friends. One Texan offered Decca his ten-gallon hat, which she kept on her lap, just in case. They joked that the baby was kicking up its heels like a small Democratic donkey, a dinky donk, which is how Constancia Romilly acquired the nickname "Dinky" even before she was born.[92] Decca thought the convention was remarkably undemocratic and hierarchical, but she was thrilled with the Chicago stockyards, the site of the Memorial Day Massacre of striking steel workers in 1937, and other local spots she toured.

It was a dramatic convention. There were conflicts over isolation and intervention. There was tension over whether Roosevelt would run. He had declined to attend (unthinkable for a candidate today). Infighting threatened to shut down the process. He was nominated at last, on a third balloting, but chose the controversial Henry Wallace as his running mate. Another standstill loomed. Roosevelt sent in Eleanor. Decca was able to witness one of Eleanor's most famous speeches, on July 18, reminding the assembled that "this is no ordinary time." Eleanor took the podium in a large, flowered hat, with more large flowers pinned to her bosom. She carried only one page of quickly jotted notes. Calmly and easily calling for party unity and principles, Eleanor carried the day and saved the convention from collapse. It was an enormous victory.[93] Aside from the Queen, Decca had never seen a woman address such a crowd. She never forgot that speech.

After the convention, the Durrs invited Decca to stay on. Decca seemed fragile, Durr had a big heart, and in spite of herself, she soon felt "devoted" to Decca.[94]

Ultimately, Decca stayed almost three years, under constant surveillance—"watched all the time," Durr said, because her family were fascists and her husband was purported to be a Communist. Her own politics were, in fact, still unformed. To Durr's dismay, Decca swung between the New Deal politics of the Durrs and the "virulent anti–New Deal talk" of her friends the Meyers. Decca thought it fine to have a "wonderful time" both "Durring & Meyering."[95] Her morning sickness improved. But "she thought it was ridiculous to make a bed every day when you got right back into it at night . . . [and] she absolutely had never done one single domestic task. She either had not done them or had servants to do them," Durr realized.[96]

Decca and Esmond were especially susceptible to feeling bored, one of the prerogatives of privilege. The Durr household offered Decca a "kaleidoscopic mix" of Americans and "an unforgettable education." There was Justice Hugo Black, Lyndon Johnson, Lady Bird Johnson, John Kenneth Galbraith, Supreme Court Justice William O. Douglas, Congressman Tom Eliot, journalist Eric Sevareid, "New Deal functionaries, earnest young radicals."[97] But Decca worried terribly that the Canadian Air Force was not amusing Esmond. "I'm terribly sorry things are getting so boring. . . . Please try not to have a boring time," she wrote him. "It's so awful to think of an old boot be-ing bored all by its self in Canada."[98] "Please have a nice time because that's the one thing I think about,"[99] she wrote.

Nevertheless, Decca was maturing. Even as she tittered about bore-dom, she read her way through all five volumes of Roosevelt's speeches, a feat that even Durr had yet to master. Anxious to contribute money to the Durr household, Decca got a job at Weinberger's department store, for thirty dollars a week (equivalent to over £370 a week in to-day's currency), modeling dresses, to give "the place tone."[100] It was good money for something that wasn't "at all hard work," and it would enable her to become a "P.G." (paying guest) at the Durrs, as she told Esmond.[101] To enhance her sales, she socialized with "better, smarter & richer circles" of people—"International Smart Setters" ideally—who might come in and buy her dresses (even if politically they really were "a filthy mire"). Decca was "keeping my mouth shut" at work and also persuading friends like Virginia to come in and buy dresses they could not afford.[102] She was also corseting her pregnant stomach (a practice common to the Victorians but now unheard-of outside the aristocracy because it posed such risks of miscarriage and prolapse) so she would not show while modeling. Immediately after work she would slip into Clifford Durr's office to wriggle out of her corset. If his office was unavailable, she wriggled out of her corset in the crowded car where they all pooled rides home, sometimes wriggling out of a corset as she perched on someone's lap in the overcrowded car.

Durr was amused by the wriggling but horrified at the corseting. She made Decca "go to a well-known, very expensive Washington gynecologist for checkups." It is not clear what the doctor did about the girdling, but he did provide Decca with an excellent first muckraking experience. Decca discovered that he was charging menopausal women, including Josephine Durr Black, Virginia's sister, ten dollars a shot for injections of pregnant women's urine, then considered a treatment for hot flashes. Decca was being charged five dollars a visit for checkups and testing, which included urine samples. Realizing that the doctor was profiting from her pee, she stopped producing and promptly accused him of fraud.

Decca missed Esmond terribly. But she was working hard on becoming independent and that was keeping her busy and absorbed. And she now had a public image which she had helped to craft. She had an exterior to focus on, which helped her bracket her feelings.

The *Washington Post* series painted Decca and Esmond as "madcap" in 1940, lost in a "giddy whirl of social activities."[103] That image was published just as Esmond was training in the military and as Decca was pregnant, working, and studying politics. As their image as a funny couple went public, both were struggling with separation. "I have missed you enormously the last few days—it has been similar to a prolonged dull kind of stomach ache," Esmond wrote Decca from Buffalo, en route to Canada. He added that "The car, driving around, having meals, club banquets, arriving in new place etc. have all point removed when done sans squirrel . . . Be sure to write me exactly what you are doing, & be sure to have . . . a exciting time & enjoy yourself in true man like fashion. I shall be doing the same."[104] They were not "madcap." And the great adventure was over.

Nevertheless, they were living, still, as characters in a narrative. From the moment they'd whispered together at Dorothy Allhusen's dining table, in fact, they'd begun inventing themselves as characters in a wild story written, first, for one another's pleasure, and then for the public's. Even if they'd wanted to, they could not now avoid seeing themselves as protagonists of their own wild tales. They would never fully excise from their personalities the imaginary characters they'd fashioned that year.

6

"A Prolonged Dull . . . Ache"

The unutterable blankness . . .[1]
—JESSICA MITFORD

On July 27, 1940, *The Washington Post* featured a large photo of a beautiful young woman in a dark, lace-collared dress, with a wide-brimmed hat and a big, cheerful smile. The picture was part of the *Post*'s coverage of how the war abroad was affecting Americans at home. The smiling lady representing American service and sacrifice was not an American, however, but Decca, twenty-two years old and at the height of her beauty. "Husband fights for Britain" and "War means separation," the captions read. Invisible in the photo were Decca's recent pregnancy or her anxiety for Esmond's welfare, especially reasonable as death and casualty rates continued rising for

Allied troops, and of particular concern regarding Esmond, well known for his clumsiness and inability to follow orders.[2]

Decca and Esmond embraced American slang with abandon. "Punch-packing"—willful refusal of all obstacles—was one of their favorite phrases, constantly dropping into their conversation and correspondence, peppering their letters back to England. The *Post*'s puff piece was classic "punch-packing," performed with the brio they both embodied, as if they could make the world conform to the story they wanted to tell about themselves. As if saying something would make it so.

Decca had never spent more than a night or two by herself. Although the Durrs' household was overstuffed with family and friends and offered her "warmth and affection—qualities that seemed very important just then"—the truth was that Decca was on her own now.[3] Her world had shrunk to a guest room, letters, and putting on a brave face for the many people coming in and out of Seminary Hill.

There had never been any question of whether Esmond would fight. After Kristallnacht in 1938, France's fall to Germany on June 22, 1940, and with news of Nazi persecutions and exterminations, Esmond could never have gone "dilly dallying along in the same slow way," as Decca put it.[4] Throughout the hot summer of 1940, Decca alternated between being captivated by Americans and confounded by them. Spain had taught her that there was no neutrality. Most Americans, it seemed to her, were determined not to grasp the lessons of Spain or the hope, in fighting fascism, that "in the course of the war the 'spirit of Madrid' would once more emerge."[5] The vast majority of Americans (94 percent) expressed opposition to Germany, but still opposed allowing more Jews into the country, even when First Lady Eleanor Roosevelt pushed hard for immigration expansion.[6] Americans said that they supported Britain, but they resisted offering any meaningful military help. In the fall of 1939, almost 50 percent of Americans said that the U.S. should not get involved in the war, a percentage that swelled to almost 80 percent by summer 1941.[7] American interventionists, like the Durrs, faced deep resistance. "No matter what, no matter how awful Hitler was or how many children died in the gas chambers," Virginia noted, most Americans believed "we should not go to war. . . . There was still a terrific fight going on between the isolationists and the interventionists."[8]

Esmond had signed up to fight without consulting Decca, but she never complained about it. She understood that "Esmond was of the opinion that the only thing which really mattered in life now was the defeat of the Axis powers. The horrors they were visiting on Europe made it unthinkable to stand aside from the war."[9] This war, Esmond felt, represented exactly what he had fought for in Spain, "only on a much larger scale, for now the survival of the whole of Europe was in the balance." But Decca knew that this war would "be no replica of Spain, no thrilling adventure of self-propelled action directed against the oppressors."[10] It would be an interminable slog, and Esmond's uncanny luck might not hold.

Unable to handle their anxieties about Esmond's well-being or express them—lest they deepen each other's fears—Decca and Esmond leaned into the privileged affectation that nothing was worse than being "dogged by boredom," nothing more terrible than not being amused.[11] "I so hate to think of how dull & lonely it must be for you," Decca wrote her soldier husband.[12]

If they could not share their fears, they did share how deeply they hated being apart.

"I will never be able to explain how tremendously I miss you," Esmond wrote after enlisting.[13] Being without Decca was like a sudden physical illness, he added, telling her he felt constantly sick and in pain. Decca felt similarly. "The unutterable blankness of such a separation" in wartime disoriented her.[14] Everything that she'd done to date had been as one half of a team, a partnership others noted as unusually close. With only letters to work with, Decca now devoted herself to keeping that team—parted by war and by miles—together.

Some people found both Decca and Esmond difficult to understand. Decca's teasing about money, American neutrality, and American Anglophilia—she was always finding herself referred to snobbily as "Winston's Churchill's nephew's wife," usually by self-described anti-aristocrats—could strike the wrong note.[15] Too often she felt that she could only "make a very good impression . . . by dint of keeping my mouth shut."[16] Esmond could be very charming, but he rarely inspired trust.

They believed in one another, however, and Decca, at least, understood her spouse very well, with a keen grasp of Esmond's "complicated and many-sided" character, as she put it.[17] Where Esmond's friends saw a ruthless quality in his nature, she saw his rock-solid sense of fairness and his resolute insistence on putting his life on the line for his principles. She knew that Esmond was at his best when the challenges were great and the gamble was large. A razor-thin edge was his finest perch. She saw him as he wanted to see himself, invisibly performing the time-honored emotional, gendered work of supportive wives shoring up male self-confidence.

With only occasional phone calls and telegrams and very rare visits, their daily correspondence had to hold them together. Decca intuited perfectly what could—and could not—go into her letters to Esmond. She described the enthusiasm with which she was planning trips and also looking for work, and all the energy with which she was volunteering for interventionist groups such as Fight for Freedom, staying busy and moving forward: "completely punch-packing," she said.[18] She wrote little about her pregnancy, which she managed on her own, an effort that Esmond approved: "I do admire you for your wonderful attitude on everything," Esmond told her, adding in another letter that he was "so glad the man [another of their inexplicable nicknames] is . . . generally punch packing."[19]

A "proper" letter between them was at least two pages long, filled with news, highly detailed, and vividly giving a sense of things, requiring considerable writing skill—the "form," they called it. "I so adore learning all the form about the characters & can completely visualize them . . . your letters are simply wonderful," Decca wrote. Decca and Esmond treated themselves as characters, using the third person, as if they were still writing for *The Washington Post*.[20] Such self-imagining was not artifice, although it was artful. It was a chance for each of them to become, and to practice being, the people they now felt their circumstances demanded (brave in Decca's case; organized and detail oriented in Esmond's). Their correspondence put them into a story that they needed, about a pragmatic, patient wife and her valiant, enduring husband.

Neither gushed. Neither moaned. Their nicknames were all inside jokes—"Old boot" and "Thinger." "Writer's boot," "the Man" or "slipper," "slip," and sometimes "squirrel" for Decca—never the syrupy and common language of "darling," "sweetheart," or "dearest." They rarely wrote about politics, although politics consumed their lives. They almost never complained. When they did grouse, it was largely about either boredom or other people complaining.

Esmond wanted Decca to see the "form" of the Canadian "military mind" and how different it was from Spain.[21] RCAF stations were well built, well equipped, and provided easy access to local towns as well as goods and services: "eggs, bacon, milk, terrific medical attention, tennis courts, YMCA, canteens, movies almost every night," Esmond reported happily on July 29.[22] But military life in the RCAF was filled with arbitrary rules of exactly the sort Esmond had never managed to master (and that had not been enforced in Spain). His challenges were serious and frustrating. But his descriptions were tongue in cheek:

*The place of the maid answering a bell is taken (and very ade-
quately) by a singularly strident bugle note. . . . At this point I can
already claim my day is better than yours, for I have a 3½ hour
start and waste none of the precious hours of these long summer
days—i.e. Reveille goes at 6 o'clock. . . . Social life at this moment
projects itself into the scene in the form of the two dangling feet of
the man in the bunk above. After an ample breakfast of cereal and
milk, I decide that the day is too good to be wasted indoors. So I put
in an appearance at the physical training squad, at which roll call
is taken to find out whether everybody else took a similar decision.
After a lot of creaking and groaning of joints to get my right hand
to touch my left foot and generally pivot and wheel and bend on
various hips, balls (of feet) etc., we go indoors. Drill ends at half-
past eleven, starts again at one and at 4:15 . . . the day is officially
over.*[23]

Decca saw that successful military service would require Esmond
"to overcome the habits of a lifetime."[24] She hoped he'd have an easier
time of it than she was having. She still could not wash "stockings or
underwear," Virginia groaned. She "never had to, either didn't do it
or had servants."[25] But Decca was eager to master working. In a ten-
page letter to Esmond—her "Bumper Sundayer," she called it—she
gave Esmond the "form" of succeeding at dress-selling and modeling
while disdaining the customers and hiding her pregnancy. "Complete
bulletins from the Slipper front for the entire week:"

*As a first move I thought I'd better try & get into better,
smarter& richer circles . . . I do think this is the best way I can
make a success at Weinbergers. . . . [Thursday] I made my first
really big sale—$140 worth of clothes to one customer, a v.
drear girl wearing a Woolworth fishnet hat, & Miss Wain kept*

*whispering to me not to waste time on her, then it turned out
she was buying her trousseau & she bought her wedding dress
& a suit! Clever Man. Miss Weinberger was very pleased &
was all congratulaty. . . . Virginia came into the shop yesterday
& caused a great furore by complaining loudly how expensive everything was. . . . However I sold her a dress, with great
difficulty & by pretending it was brown instead of purple (she'll
be furious when she sees it in the daylight) . . . Only bad mark of
the week: a new dress came in & Miss Weinb. asked me to put it
on & model it for a while, saying 'it will be too large on you, it's a
size 16.' When I got it on it was too large, but fitted PERFECTLY
round the waistline and Miss Weinb. said 'you've got rather a
thick waistline, Mrs. Romilly!' So you see my chief hope lies in
making myself indispensable before they note the facts.*[26]

Decca's letter was written on September 8, one day after the start of
the Blitz. On September 7, 1940, more than six hundred bombs were
dropped on London, killing over four hundred people. Decca and Esmond's beloved Rotherhithe neighborhood had been one of the first
targets. Aiming for Rotherhithe's industrial docks, German bombers
ignited the worst fires in British history, burning more than a million
tons of wood and turning the night sky, as one Rotherhithe resident
put it, as "bright as day." The river that Decca had watched from her
windows was now "like a lake in Hell" with "burning barges drifting
everywhere."[27] *The Washington Post* described the "fiery glow . . . [of
the] fantastic dreamworld" London had become, the "bedraggled men
who looked as if they had not slept in weeks" amidst the total destruction of East London's warehouses and docks, where people wandered
"staggering under loads of clothing, mattresses, household goods . . .
their faces haggard in the fitful glare."[28] Any "detailed disclosure of
what actually was hit" was strictly off-limits, and Decca and Esmond

had no way of knowing how their friends had fared or if they were alive.[29]

Feeling "terribly cut off," they said little to one another about the Blitz.[30] On September 15, the day the Germans launched their largest single attack on London, with fifteen hundred planes battling in the skies, Esmond wrote only: "I suppose the main thing now in Washington is the news from England." A week later he added: "It seems as though what everyone expected in the first weeks of the war is happening now, and London will soon be in ruins."[31] They focused on the realities closest to them. Esmond described the "endless succession of polishing, sweeping up, parading, waiting around, falling in on marches, right dressing, carrying kit somewhere else, answering roll calls, being assembled in alphabetical groups, waiting to see what's next, being formed in new groups, drilling in the sun, preparing barracks for inspection, and folding sheets and blankets 'Camp Borden style,' as opposed to the 'Manning Depot' style."[32] Decca wrote about her plans to crack the "rich ladees" who might be induced to shop at Weinberger's, following her theme of "The Man Crashing the Smart Set."[33] Her twenty-third birthday was September 11. The Durrs had a party for her. She described the food for Esmond: "fresh curried shrimp & rice, succotash & garden green lettuce salad & hot rolls, followed by the Grand Entrance of a cake." He sent a funny birthday telegram that made her "roar."

In late October, in spite of Decca's extremely cheerful letters to him, Esmond worried that she "seemed a little fed up with things" and especially exasperated with boring people. He thought that "the Straights would be quite a haven of civilization in these critical days."[34] In November, Decca worried when Esmond was disqualified from pilot duty because of an ear problem/hearing problem with his mastoid, which had been operated on when he was five.[35] He had little experience with failure, and even less patience for it. Fortunately, the doctors certified

that his health and hearing were perfect, but military regulations prohibited anyone with mastoid problems from flying, and Esmond found,
to his shock, that he could neither bend the rules nor get around them.
He told Decca that "this last week was just about the most hellish thing
I've known in my life . . . the most awful disappointment I think I've
ever had."[36] He took a room in town, showed up only for roll call, and
was hoping to be discharged (a condition of his enlistment entitled him
to a discharge if his medicals failed). He planned to go to England and
join the RAF. He was even prepared to appeal to his Uncle Winston.[37]
Discharged on November 22, he was almost immediately reinstated
as an Observer (later termed a Navigator), allowing him to participate
in piloting again. "The only snag is, of course," he wrote Decca, "that I
don't think observation has so far been my main quality—in fact even
recently I've lost my way on a number of occasions" inside the buildings
on the base. "Anyway, I shall have to work very hard indeed to overcome one or two little practical obstacles."[38]

Observation (or navigation) was very precise work. And Esmond
could hardly have been more ill-suited for it. His inattention to detail
was legendary. Observers were trained to fix targets with logs, com-
passes, aeronautical charts, ground training, and air practice. It was,
as he wrote to Decca, "the most responsible, most difficult, and most
highly paid" of the jobs available in the RCAF.[39] As Decca aptly put it,
"Fancy the old Boot at the controls of an aeroplane. I just can't imagine
it."[40] That very month he'd lost their car on the streets of Montreal.
He'd parked it, forgotten where, and the car was towed away. Esmond
made light of his "struggle to avoid committing some ghastly blun-
der such as losing my protractor under the seat, plugging my oxygen
tube into the aircraft radio circuit, breaking the points of all twelve
of the pencils I shall persuade myself it's necessary to take, taking an
astro sight on an enemy searchlight, releasing a few thousand pounds
of high explosive bombs accidentally on the ground while checking the

bombsight before take-off, using the nautical mile scale instead of stat-ute miles, mistaking the Atlantic for the North Sea, and other farcical items of this nature."[41] All these mistakes would, of course, have proved fatal, not farcical.

By December 1940, Decca was too pregnant to continue mod-eling dresses for sale at Weinberger's. Esmond wrangled a leave and came back for the holidays. "He'd never had a Christmas tree which he considered fully decorated," Durr recalled, "so we had a tree which was the most gorgeous thing you've ever seen in your life. And he made stockings for everybody, and when we woke up they were pinned to the bed full of gimmicks and things . . . Everything he did was an event."[42] He was only able to visit for a few days, and they packed them as full as they could.

As the end of Decca's ninth month neared, Agnes Meyer wanted to get her a private room, but Decca, determined to do her wartime part as a regular American, refused. In early February, she entered the public maternity ward at Columbia hospital, where she took one quarter of a four-bed room, hoping to keep the charges down to fifty dollars for a ten-day stay (then the typical length of a maternity stay), including the anesthetic and induced labor. She'd been reassured by her doctor, she told Esmond, that if there were complications, he'd move her out of the public ward into someplace more private.[43] She gave birth on February 9, 1941, the same day that Churchill, in his first speech in months, again pleaded to the U.S. to "give us the tools" to fight the war.

Decca was the only patient in the public ward to receive photog-raphers from the national press. Great boxes of food arrived from the Meyers and Kay Graham. Huge bouquets of flowers came in baskets and vases: roses, daffodils, irises, and exotics from Miami. Esmond wanted to visit Decca and "the Piker," as they were calling the baby, but another leave proved impossible to obtain so soon after Christmas, and

Decca feared it would be way too expensive. The baby couldn't be called "the Piker" indefinitely. Decca wondered about naming it Esme, after Esmond. She also suggested Carmen. Esmond countered with Carol. "You do agree, I hope, that Constancia must be out," he wrote—a letter that arrived too late.[44] The baby, always known as Dinky, was officially named Constancia after Constancia de la Mora, whose book about turning her back on the aristocracy to fight for Spain had been so influential for Decca.

Decca stood out from the other women in the ward and also organized them, naturally assuming a position of leadership. "When the nurses weren't responsive enough with bedpans" for one of her roommates, Decca, in what she called her "'first successful effort at organizing for mass action'—staged a communal 'pee-in.'" She made light of her success, but it was an important moment for her, reinforcing both her skills as an organizer and the advantages of humor in organizing work. There was silliness in the "pee-in." But it was instantly effective. The medical team did not dare ignore its public patients again after that. According to Virginia Durr, when they brought her home, "the nurses were very glad indeed to get her out of the hospital."[45]

Esmond was also trying to minimize distinctions of rank, and, like Decca, he had some success. When he discovered that he had received a commission but his friends had not, he wrote Decca about his feelings of seeing "officers segregated in a separate barracks and separate mess, exultant ordering of officers' uniforms and other fancy adornments in the Halifax stores, groups of disappointed sergeants sitting together bleakly in cafes in the evenings . . . the logical sublime climax of the competitive promotion seeking, mark-grabbing, on-with-your-career ideology which has been nurtured by the powers that be."[46] He had hoped for some of the same democratizing experience he'd had in Spain, part of the "spirit of Spain" that he and Decca both still looked for. "The main thing," he proudly confided to Decca, was "that things have so worked out that I have definitely not lost any of my friends who are still sergeants—as a result of getting a commission."[47]

Decca had very much wanted a baby. She had little idea of how to care for one, however. The first February night she brought the baby back to the Durrs, it screamed all night long and would not be comforted. Decca wrote Esmond that she felt defeated by motherhood and wondered if it was always so difficult. She pondered whether she had made good choices and worried that the lax Durr housekeeping (to which she contributed) would pose hygienic risks for the baby. So she hired a nurse to take over and fight "the general Durr sloppiness" and assume some of the baby's dispiriting care.[48]

Decca wanted to visit Esmond right away, but her doctor advised against it, making her feel that even considering such a trip was as unmannered as "eating asparagus with a fork."[49] In the spring, ignoring her doctor's advice and believing the baby and she would manage just fine, she took a monthlong rental at the Mayfair Mansions in Toronto, an Art Deco set of apartments built in 1937. At Mayfair Mansions she had a phone installed, set up housekeeping, and tried to hire a maid and nurse to help her with little Constancia, settling for the help of a fourteen-year-old girl who washed the baby's diapers and clothes. While she never saw as much of Esmond as she'd hoped, being nearby was a great relief. Even more wonderful was watching Esmond get to know his baby daughter.

After her Toronto trip, and back at the Durrs with Dinky, Decca socialized with "f. traveler types & a rather dull girl called Ladybird Johnson" and considered her options.[50] One possibility was to go back to Canada, but Esmond was likely to be shipped out at any moment. She could look for work, or train for future work. Journalism appealed. A seven-week program of study at Columbia University and a rooming house in New York would be particularly "punch packing," she told

Esmond hopefully.[51] Meanwhile, she was writing long letters to him, sending out care packages, and trying to learn to cook.

Toward the end of June 1941, Esmond received another short leave. Decca arranged to meet him at the Rodmans on Martha's Vineyard, leaving Dinky with the Durrs in D.C. Esmond and Selden were able to play tennis and poker. There was lots of drinking. And the swimming was good.

Then the war intensified. Together, on June 22, they all listened to Churchill address the world on the German invasion of Russia, just as in 1939 they had listened together to announcements of the German-Soviet nonaggression pact. Now, the Russians would be forced into the fight. "I do think the war has become much more exciting if not to say worthwhile," Decca wrote shortly thereafter, reflecting the faith she and Esmond shared that the tide of the war would now turn.[52] Rodman noted that Esmond had never lost all his faith in Communism. "He thinks that now the communists will fight hardest to win the war and win it for socialism," Rodman said.[53] Nor had Esmond lost any of his upbeat faith in himself. "I have no doubt at all that I will survive this war whether shot down or not," Esmond told Rodman, shortly before they all left the Vineyard.[54] From the Vineyard he was called back to Halifax, to ship out to England. Their few good days were over.

"It was frightful when you left," Decca wrote him. "I was so miserable," she wrote in late June. After that visit, Decca felt unsettled and anxious. Biding her time became more difficult. She was uncharacteristically finding fault everywhere she looked. The Americans, she complained, weren't nearly excited enough about the new role that Russia was playing in the war. Liberals like their friend Michael Straight were much too critical of Communists. She grumbled that the Durrs were intolerant of the heat just as they were of the cold in the winter.[55] Selden Rodman was unsanitary and ought to take more baths, she declared. She groused that Esmond was not writing enough. "I keep trying to imagine where you are & what you are up to, but of course it's impossible," she wrote in July.[56]

By early August 1941, Esmond was in England, at Operational Training Unit Abingdon in Oxfordshire and more comfortable than he'd been in months. No one around him seemed worried, and he began to feel that perhaps he shouldn't be either. He wrote Decca that "the totally amazing thing about England is that there is nothing amazing going on at all . . . really, everything's just the same, you wouldn't think there was a war on at all." He felt disappointed that the "spirit of Madrid"—the great democratizing force of the Spanish struggle—was nowhere in evidence. "Tho' individuals' lives were broken up & habits of a work & pleasure radically changed, yet the economic structure— the class divisions, the central organization of society as a whole has not changed," he wrote.[57] He was able to see a few old friends, including Philip Toynbee, who found him mellower and more "emotionally forthright," especially about his "dismay at human unhappiness" than he'd ever been before.[58]

In August, Decca learned that she was pregnant again and that the new baby would be born in March 1942.[59] She told no one. The Durrs were, she thought, terrible gossips, and if word got out she feared it would ruin her chances of going to England if she should try to go. Decca didn't yet show, wasn't sick, and the Durrs had already agreed to look after Dinky. So Decca decided to continue on with plans for a trip south, with their friends, John and Janet Manwaring, to visit the Tennessee Valley Authority, the Highlander School (famous later as the training center for nonviolent civil rights resistance), and Birmingham, where the Durrs had friends and connections. But Decca came down with the flu. The Manwarings gamely offered to wait until she recovered before they all headed out. Decca knew she should feel grateful to the generous Manwarings, but she found them dull. A few days into the trip she felt ill again, this time with sharp abdominal pains. Locking herself into a roadside gas station bathroom, Decca miscarried, alone. Demonstrating the same stoicism that enabled Sydney to take a buttonhook to her own throat, Decca kept her roadside miscarriage a secret, sharing it only with Esmond and only in a highly edited version, in line with the upbeat tenor she'd chosen. She tucked a brief mention of her miscarriage (omitting all details) into funny stories about the trip. "Now it has actually happened," she wrote "the only thing to do is just forget it was ever up & pack one's punch accordingly." She added that she was "not all shaken up as I was yesterday."[60]

Even when she did not hear from Esmond for an entire month, Decca tried to stay light and cheerful. She did not want to seem "worried or whiney" to him, which may be why she also never mentioned to Esmond that she was being spied on by both the FBI and the British Embassy, still being "watched all the time" as Durr had put it earlier, now because of Esmond's partisanship in Spain on the one hand, and Unity and Diana's fascism on the other.[61] She was "watched both for left and right tendencies," Durr later recalled. "It got so that the FBI would come so often that the children [Virginia's] would just call upstairs, 'Mother, the milkman's here,' 'Mother, the grocery man's here.' 'Mother, the FBI's here.'"[62]

Decca had increasingly come to think she should join Esmond in England and wanted him to like the idea. "I do think the war has become much more exciting," she wrote in early August, "so therefore to come to England would be quite as punch-packing as any other scheme or more so."[63] She wouldn't need any luxuries, she was quick to reassure him, and Dinky could stay behind. "I know you think of the man as one who relies on good food & lighting up but do admit that is not really its form. However the whole decision is yours & whatever happens don't worry about it, but just say what you really think because I will be terrifically all right & happy whatever we decide."[64]

Esmond didn't realize how much Decca wanted to come to him.

Perhaps he saw it as too dangerous. Perhaps he was distracted by the realities of military service. He told Decca a series of stories meant to be funny, but that fed all her worries. In September, he told her about falling off his bicycle and ruining a new pair of pants. Then he told her about falling into a four-foot-deep hole, followed shortly thereafter by a story about getting his gas-mask straps caught in his bicycle hub and completely ruining the bike, and then another story about using a flashlight to try to read bomb markings but realizing afterward he'd turned the light against himself, as a fellow pilot pointed out to him "rather crisply."[65] He did not encourage a family visit.

Esmond flew a few missions, his first on October 16, 1941, followed by three more that month. He was not especially successful. He struggled with his equipment, could not decode messages that were given him to decode, had a terrible time understanding what was said to him over the intercom, lost all his notes and instruments off the tables for failing to secure them in flight, bumped his head, and generally fumbled about. In his letters he bracketed the actual work of bombing, and told Decca, instead, about "cold and worry and hard work and complicated problems of navigation."[66] He cast all his problems as solvable, merely requiring that he exercise more discipline or control.

Waiting around was hardest for him. He said the fall of 1941 was "really agonizing—just like the way it used to be from Spain." Waiting to see which way things would go, he wrote, had "the same dull torturingness that the news about the war in Spain used to have."[67] For some of their friends, the torturingness was too much. That fall, they learned that Roger Roughton, their Rotherhithe friend and landlord, had committed suicide in April 1941. The long delay in getting the news spoke both to how out of touch they were with most of their English friends and also to the unreliability of wartime correspondence.[68]

Thanks to Esmond's military pay, Decca went to secretarial school and was learning to type. So she left Dinky with a succession of babysitters and Durr's housekeeper Mrs. Daniels watched her in the afternoon. She wrote Esmond about a "sample man's day:"

7 a.m. angry sounds are heard from the other bed; the Donk is changed & given her rattle, which she waves violently thus giving a pleasant waking up period. Sometimes if I'm not very sleepy she is taken out & played with. 8 am breakfast now fixed by VA & quite good—8:30 a mad rush for the car by Ann, Cliff, Viola (Daniels' little girl) & me; nearly always a different car as Bill is away & VA is usually to be heard hopefully phoning all round the neighborhood so she wont have to take us in. 9 am the man arrives all efficient & secretarial with case of books & settles to its typewriter . . . The typing instructress is rather like a horse trainer; she steps around the room saying 'SNATCH the keys! ONE two! ONE two!' We type to the tunes of marches which is rather fun.

Dinky was now nine months old, "all crawly & half chatty," and Decca wondered if Esmond received any of the photographs she sent over of her, since he never seemed to comment on them.[69] All fall she pressed, delicately, for more of a response. "The Donk [for Dinky Donk] is so terrifically nice, she has absolutely made the whole difference to things—when she roars the old Boot sarcastic expression comes into her face in fact she is exactly like you altogether & rather a scene I should say."[70]

Decca also began pressing harder to come to England. She wrote out a long argument, describing herself in the third person, asking Esmond to admit that they'd agreed she'd come, that coming was "actually part of the punch in a roundabout way," and that it was not good for "Slipper morale" for things to be so undecided and suspended for months at a time. "Bird darling," she wrote, "I so tremendously want to be with you." Then she quickly reassured him that she'd be fine either way: "you do know that if it doesn't seem possible yet all will be ok. completely so."[71] Whenever she pressed to come, she was also quick to reassure him that not coming was also fine. Her language—through third person references to herself and calling herself "it"—downplayed the difficulties of her situation and let Esmond off the hook if he didn't see things her way. "The man is now completely punch-packing for whatever is decided—for instance, it's not all downed & pregnant—& miscarriage-y as it was a few months ago; & it specially doesn't want to be a constant worry to you, I mean so you'll feel you have to tell me to come over even tho it was not really the best thing."[72]

With so much uncertainty about the outcome of the war—in October he asked Decca if Russian resistance would generate "more enthusiasm now among the New Dealers and one time fellow travelers" for getting into the fight—Esmond remained cool to the idea of Decca coming to England.[73] On November 11, four of his closest friends from the base were shot down over the North Sea: two Canadians and two Brits. "They were the people I used to discuss things with all the time, they . . . had more or less the same views on most things as me, and so we formed quite a circle. . . . there is no sort of attitude or line you can take to a thing like that happening, the truth is one is very untough, and this sort of thing makes you cower down for a second like a cruel blow from something against which it is utterly impossible to strike back, it is so huge and powerful and at the same time so vague and shadowy there is no place on which you can grip at it." Esmond had spent much of his free time with the four, "discussing books and politics and life in general and the changes that we hoped would be made after the war."[74] Suddenly, he very much wanted Decca to come. "[I] want to be with you again more than anything else in the world" he wrote on November 23.[75] "I know that when you come here you will terrifically want to be taking part in the war and the general life of everybody and all the changes, etc. . . . If one is in it, there is the barrackdom and grumbling and the overwork and exhaustion and meeting new types of people and general fascinatingness, but if one is out of it, then the whole thing is utterly bleak and pointless."[76] His longing to share his story with Decca now felt urgent.

It was difficult to secure passage, but Decca was determined. She went to the British Embassy, which told her that regulations were much the same as before the war, and that so were the accommodations, but that there were fewer spots available. The cost would be, she told Esmond, about $125 (just under £1,500 today), and she put in her application on November 9, expecting a wait of weeks or months. One week later, in mid-November, she wired Esmond that she thought she'd done it. "GOOD POSSIBILITY SHIP TRANSPORT HAVE MADE ROUTINE APPLICATION BUT WILL ONLY COME IF YOU ARE 100% PRO."[77] She had decided to bring Dinky and was worried he'd object. On November 13 she telegrammed, "PLEASE DON'T VETO BEFORE GETTING MY LETTER ALL LOVE."[78] Decca secured passage and cabled him on December 1 to tell him. She wrote: "LEAVING FRIDAY SO TERRIFICALLY EXITED DARLING STOP DECIDED TO BRING DONK DO WIRE THAT YOU AGREE HOW SHALL I CONTACT YOU JOURNEY WILL BE VER COMFORTABLE GREATEST LOVE—ROMILLY."[79] She spent the first day of December at the Durrs, packing and repacking to leave the next day.

On December 2, she received the following cable:

REGRET TO INFORM YOU THAT ADVICE RECEIVED FROM ROYAL CANADIAN AIR FORCE CASUALTIES OFFICER OVERSEAS YOUR HUSBAND PILOT OFFICER ESMOND MARK DAVID ROMILLY CAN J FIVE SIX SEVEN SEVEN MISSING ON ACTIVE SERVICE NOVEMBER THIRTIETH STOP LETTER FOLLOWS.

Esmond had set out on a raid on Hamburg on Sunday, November 30. The aircraft signaled low oil pressure in an engine and then sent out an SOS at 8:42 p.m. There was heavy fog. The search the next day, December 1—the day that Decca cabled—showed no sign of the aircraft. A few hours after taking off, they regretted to inform her, Esmond's plane had radioed three times. First there was a distress signal about mechanical problems with oil pressure. Then there was a request for bearings and coordinates. Finally, an SOS followed, sent from somewhere far out over the North Sea.[80] Then there was silence. Three rescue boats from the British Air Sea Rescue searched for five hours. They found only a large patch of oil on the ocean's choppy surface. Stormy weather forced them back to shore. After the fog lifted, the search resumed. They found no wreckage, no dinghy, and no sign of survivors.

For weeks, even months, Decca held out hope that Esmond had survived, as he had always insisted he would do if shot down. According to Virginia Durr, the only person who saw Decca cry, Decca masked and tamped down her agony with constant occupation. Every day she awaited news that he'd been taken prisoner and plucked from the water. "It was very hard for her to accept the fact of his death," Durr wrote. "She kept believing that he wasn't dead and that maybe by some miracle he had escaped. . . . In the night I would hear her saying, 'Oh the water was so cold, the water was so cold.'"[81]

Esmond's death is a footnote in Decca's memoir *Hons and Rebels*. Having referred to Esmond's "short life," the note reads, "He was killed in action in November 1941, at the age of 23."[82]

7

"A Concrete Upper Lip"

I remained in America and carried out our resolve.[1]
—JESSICA MITFORD

There was no funeral or memorial service for Esmond.[2] Officially, he was missing.

"The circumstances all point to disaster," his mother was informed.[3] Esmond's supervising officer, Commander Clark, asserted that since Esmond's plane had vanished in the dark, far from shore, and in icy water, "there is little or no chance of . . . survival." Royal Canadian Air Force officers, chaplains, lawyers, and numerous Red Cross officials all wrote Decca with similar details.[4] The British Air Sea Rescue eventually became legendary for the motto "The Sea Shall Not Have Them." In 1941, when Esmond's plane vanished, however, only about 20 percent of aircraft downed in the North Sea were located.[5] Rescue ships searched for two days in high winds and low visibility, then pronounced future efforts futile. The sea was too cold for survival, they said.

Decca was having none of it.

Esmond had posted her one last letter, just before his plane disappeared. It updated his instructions about what she was to do if he ever went missing. Do not presume me dead, he'd admonished. "When people are missing," in war, he wrote:

It is of course a very long time before any definite news can be reached of them, i.e. as to whether they have landed anywhere and been captured. In a very large number of cases this turns out to be the case . . . one always imagines the worst somehow, which is so utterly irrational.

Incidentally, if, which I certainly think is an inconceivable improbability, I should ever find myself in this sort of situation, I have absolutely determined to escape in some way or another, and I'm sure that if you are sufficiently determined of anything you can achieve it. However I'm equally sure the need will never arise, so please don't attach any sort of significance to the above, or imagine it indicates a resigned or nervous frame of mind.[6]

It was the last word she'd received from Esmond, and Decca would not disregard it. She was also not the only one Esmond had thus reassured. Just before leaving for England, he'd told Selden Rodman that he would "survive this war whether shot down or not."[7] On December 7, Rodman wrote Decca: "it would be easier if I didn't feel so inwardly sure that he is all right, and that we will hear of him (or from him) soon. . . . It is, of course, the feeling that anyone who knew Esmond would inevitably have about him—that he is indestructible."[8] Other close friends saw things similarly. Peter Nevile telegrammed: "AM HOPEFUL

ESMOND IS PRISONER MAY TAKE THREE MONTHS TO FIND OUT BE CHEERFUL."[9] No one who knew Esmond well could accept his death. "Decca kept thinking that somebody might have rescued him or a submarine had come along . . . [she] wouldn't believe that Esmond was dead," Durr observed.[10] Not until mid-January did Decca manage even a cursory telegram to her mother. On January 17, 1942, she cabled: "WELL HAVE NO PLANS YET WAITING FOR BETTER NEWS."[11]

She was not merely in denial.[12] Esmond had always had remarkable luck. Even in the especially brutal battles of Spain, under heavy fire, surrounded by dismemberment and death, Esmond had felt optimistic. And true to his word then, he'd walked out alive. His positivity was why, in a Spanish trench, with gunfire overhead, amid a "racket of rifle and machine-gun fire," he was capable of sitting down and reading a "book about snobbery in the United States of America."[13] He simply did not accept his own finitude. He "wore his ability to survive," Philip Toynbee recalled, "like a halo."[14] His risk-taking and boyish hopefulness sprang partly from his class and gender, of course, part of what Toynbee described as a "brusque hostility to anything at all 'deep,' at all contrived, at all emotional."[15] But Esmond's faith in good things was also a signature aspect of his individuality, his idealistic view that things could always get better. Failure and death were not in his vocabulary. When Giles was found alive in the fall of 1940, living as a prisoner of war,[16] Decca, poring over the military's "Memorandum of the Steps Taken to Trace Missing Personnel," took it as a sure sign of Romilly indestructability.[17]

Durr was so worried about what seemed to her Decca's inability to face facts that she wrote secret letters to Decca's mother, Sydney. She knew how Decca would object to that. To risk what Durr called Decca's "porcupine quills"—Decca never held back when angry—Durr must have been deeply concerned over how this young mother, only twenty-three years old, thousands of miles from home and family, in the midst of world war, could make it on her own in America. Decca is "so worn with anxiety and crushed with alternate hope and despair," Durr wrote, "that she cannot look ahead."[18] Can't you bring her home and look after her, she pleaded, adding that she believed Decca still felt "an intense family feeling."[19] "I am afraid," Sydney responded, "that dreadful word missing is by far the worst to bear."[20] She wrote Decca letters filled with family news, saved her condolences for the end of her long, chatty letters, and always kept them simple. "We think all the time of you darling," she wrote, "it is such a terribly bad time for you."[21] Esmond's mother, Nellie, wrote Sydney also. Nellie was willing to provide a home for Decca and Dinky, she stated, and would be happy to take over both Decca's finances and Decca's plans for the future.

Nellie Romilly was the last person whose advice Decca would have sought. But money was, in fact, a pressing problem. She had a small widow's pension from the RCAF, but that would expire in six months, and Decca wasn't convinced, yet, that she *was* a war widow. She wasn't sure she should take it. Esmond, to whom death had been unimaginable, had left no will, no estate. Wartime regulations made sending money from Great Britain to America almost impossible, although Sydney tried.[22] She was able to send very small checks, which Decca left uncashed, unwilling to take money from the "filthy fascist family" she blamed for Esmond's death. She promised to visit, someday, and resolved to raise Constancia in America.

A few newspapers published stories about Esmond's presumed death.[23] Friends and family published memorial poems. Nellie's contributions were saturated with the maudlin emotional excess that Esmond had always detested and mocked, and that Decca also could not bear:[24] "Did nobody see my Esmond? . . . Flying through the night . . . St. Michael and his angels / Could you not ground his flight?"[25] Giles wrote a poem from his prison cell in Colditz about Esmond's "justice-loving urgency" and his "powerful instinct for justice."[26] Nellie published it in the *Evening Standard*, with a photo of Esmond.

Decca did not memorialize Esmond in public. Her way was to honor him by carrying out his plans. Her way was also to channel him, to resemble him, to keep him alive by adopting as much as she could the qualities of his she'd always loved most. With her large widely set blue eyes, slim figure, upper-crust manners and accent, and with her much-lamented lack of education, she still seemed vulnerable and fragile. But Esmond's death steeled rather than shattered her. Almost overnight, the young forward-looking, frivolous optimist became a bold, driven pragmatist. The young woman who'd spent her whole life following others became fiercely self-directed. Confidence replaced caution. Courage replaced uncertainty. Her personal grammar dropped question marks and now everything Decca did or said ended with a period. Durr was astounded. She declared that Decca was the bravest person she'd ever known. She didn't have a *stiff* upper lip, Durr said, but a concrete one.[27]

On Sunday, December 7, just days after Esmond's plane vanished, the Japanese attacked Pearl Harbor, killing sixty-eight civilians, wounding over one thousand, and killing more than two thousand American military, including more than a thousand men on the USS *Arizona* alone.[28] Americans were glued to their radios, nowhere more than in D.C. The next day, December 8, the United States declared war on Japan, amid widespread and nearly universal calls for vengeance. The House and Senate voted overwhelmingly to extend the draft, requiring registration of every American man up to the age of sixty-five.[29] "Overnight," the nation had become, Walter Lippmann wrote, "an awakened people—wide awake to the stark truth that the very existence of the nation, the lives, the liberties, and the fortunes of all of us are in the balance."[30] The Durrs were one of the most political couples in the country, and that put Decca in the midst of the nation's response. Pearl Harbor, Durr remembered, was the shock that created common purpose. "People really backed the war . . . there was very little dissent." For many, she added, "it was also a terrific relief to be finally fighting the horrors of Nazism and fascism."[31] Decca took hope from seeing citizens accepting rationing, massive labor changes, and sending their own sons into war. "It seemed inconceivable," she thought, "that the war against Fascism would not eventually turn into a world revolution against all forms of repression, sweeping capitalism into the dustbin of history, as Lenin would say. Having but one life to live, what could be better than to devote it to this noble cause?"[32]

The collapse of American isolationism closed the gap between Britain and the United States and helped Decca feel less alone as she was coming to realize that Esmond's death was looking incontestable. "We are all in the same boat now," Roosevelt told Churchill over the phone on the day of the attack." "England would live; Britain would live," Churchill concluded, accepting Roosevelt's swift invitation to come at once to Washington.[33] By December 11, provoked by Hitler as well as the widespread Japanese attacks on the Philippines, Malaysia, Guam, and Hong Kong, Congress also declared war on Germany and Italy. Decca's private grief was part of the international story.

As Virginia noted, Decca faced that grief by both remaking herself anew and by also falling back on what was familiar to her. She was "essentially English, and so bound to England by her affection that she could never be anything else."[34] Her aristocratic heritage of understatement, of not "drawing attention to oneself" or "getting all earnest and emotional," as one historian puts it, suited Decca best when she was wrenched by feeling most deeply.[35] "Heroic self-control," a kind of class pride taught to Decca from infancy, reasserted itself as a reasonable, even honorable, norm, making Decca even more of a Mitford, just as she was pushing all Mitfords away.[36] Debo wrote in December to express her condolences. She could hardly get the words out:

Dearest Hen

I am so appalled by the news I heard from Muv that I simply don't know what to say or even how to begin . . .

This is a hopeless letter but I can't make it any better because of being so hopeless at explaining what I mean.

Much love, Hen[37]

Embodying now the "stoical pride in 'getting on with it'" so funda-mental to "the mythical forging [ahead] of the English," Decca waited for more news.[38] "Something that gets one out of the house, with a certain amount of routine to it is a very good thing," she said. That was the way to handle grief.[39] Like some British tanks, which lacked reverse gears, Decca kept plowing forward, initially at a crawl.

Her family continued providing outlets for her rage. On December 12, Winston Churchill, Esmond's uncle and Decca's cousin, departed En-gland on HMS *Duke of York* for Washington, D.C.[40] On a mild, windy December 22, 1941, President Roosevelt met Churchill to escort him back to the White House personally. Churchill was welcomed by Eleanor and shown to the Rose Suite, which had been specially prepared. At din-ner that night they all toasted the "common cause."[41] The Monroe Room was made over as a war room, and Roosevelt and Churchill pored over maps, drinking and smoking cigars into the small hours of the morning, as they shared strategies for beating back Germany and Japan.

On Christmas morning Churchill awoke to an overflowing schedule packed with map-reading, war councils, and planning and strategy ses-sions with Roosevelt. He was drafting what he considered one of the most important speeches of his career, to be delivered the next day to a joint session of Congress, and he needed more time. Yet Churchill summoned

Decca to the White House that same day to discuss Esmond's death. Two Secret Service agents were dispatched to fetch Decca from the Durrs and bring her to meet Churchill and Roosevelt at church. It would "take more than two men to get Decca into church," Durr noted wryly.[42] Decca was with the Straights, and Durr phoned Michael and Binny, telling them to get Decca to the White House immediately.

Michael and Binny drove Decca to D.C. in their rattletrap car. By the time their old Ford completed the drive, "rumbled up the elegant driveway" of the White House, and came to a stop under its white columns, Churchill had started his afternoon nap and left orders that he was not to be disturbed. Eleanor waited on the portico in the unusually warm weather to greet them, and Michael, Binny, Decca, and Dinky all piled into the White House for tea and a lively debate, between Eleanor and Michael, about the Reconstruction Finance Corporation and the Federal Loan Administration.[43]

As soon as Churchill woke up, he sent immediately for Decca, who arrived at the Rose Room with Dinky in tow. Dinky was dressed in her Christmas best, a white wool dress so fetching that Churchill remembered, and later described it to Clementine, his wife. In the "loose dressing gown" in which he'd napped in the huge four-poster that had once been Andrew Jackson's, Churchill leaned toward Decca and told her that the private investigation he'd ordered had yielded no new information. He was "quite sure that Esmond had drowned."[44] Decca later told Straight that Churchill "strode around the room, rolling off sonorous phrases about the enemy striking with brutal fiendishness at the British home and hearth."[45] For years, there had been rumors that Esmond might be Churchill's son. Churchill did not behave like someone who believed those stories.[46] He spoke of Esmond with real affection, however, and described him as a hero. He advised Decca to remain in the United States and offered his assistance if she preferred to return to England. In a blundering moment, he began talking about Diana's imprisonment, aiming to reassure Decca that he would intercede personally for Diana and that he would personally see to her comfort in Holloway Prison. He apologized for jailing Mosley, but said it had been the "best way to protect him." He also proudly relayed his ingenuity in having arranged that other prisoners would clean and housekeep for the Mosleys.[47]

Decca erupted. The last thing she wanted, she let Churchill know, was to see Mosley comfortable. Both Diana and Oswald deserved to die, she said. She blamed them—and all their fascist associates—for Esmond's death, she declared. Moreover, she was not convinced, she went on, that everything had been done that could have been done to track Esmond's plane. Being so certain of Esmond's death seemed to her an "utterly stupid point of view since there must be many German submarines and other boats all over the North Sea which could pick him up." She suggested that Churchill do a better job of tracking Esmond's last radio contact in case he'd been picked up by a boat. On her way out of the Rose Room Churchill directed his secretary to give Decca an envelope. It contained five hundred U.S. dollars (the equivalent of £7,500 today). Decca donated Churchill's "blood money," as she called it, to Virginia Durr's anti-poll tax campaign.[48] She refused to touch it for herself.

Decca's Christmas day meeting with Churchill at the White House is rarely mentioned by historians. It may help explain why, as some have noted with consternation, the prime minister was particularly "out of sorts on Christmas Day. . . . He retreated into silence at the formal dinner" at the White House that night, excusing himself early to work on his speech.[49]

Durr thought that Decca believed Churchill. "Finally, Decca accepted the fact that he was dead," Durr believed. "She used to wake up at night and I would hear her weeping.[50] But Durr was mistaken. Decca continued to wait for good news. "I'm absolutely <u>certain</u> that Esmond is all right," she wrote her mother in February 1942, "although the officials (C.O. etc) take a very unhopeful view; so many different things could have happened, & he might even be in Norway or somewhere. Sometimes it takes as long as 6 months to hear about prisoners . . . at first I kept expecting every day to hear from him but now I realise it may be a very long time perhaps till the end of the war."[51] As late as 1943, Decca still held on to some hope. "About what I think of the chances of Esmond coming back," she wrote Rodman, more than a year after Esmond had vanished, "I literally don't know anymore exactly what I believe . . . although I am still just as sure as ever that he will come back, I can't see it in such concrete terms."[52]

Gaps were narrowing between the United States and Britain, but they were widening between Decca and her family. Too many Mitfords, she felt, were able to remain untouched by the war. True, Tom had joined the military and was getting ready to be sent overseas (he left to fight in January 1942). Sydney was helping with school lunches. Diana, of course, remained in Holloway Prison. But the others, Decca felt, went on altogether too much in the same old way. David moved between London, the country, and the Scottish island of Inch Kenneth, always with a small staff in tow. Pam was raising Diana and Oswald Mosley's two sons in luxury while the Mosleys remained in prison. Unity regained the capacity to drive in 1941 and motored about the countryside, visiting various friends. Debo, whom Decca compared to Scarlett O'Hara because she seemed *so* removed from the war, recovered from her son's stillbirth in November only to return, in Decca's view, to a narrow round of shallow interests. Nancy, while doing some volunteering, had an affair and continued writing.

In the Durr household, on the other hand, politics dominated. Durr remained laser-focused on her poll tax campaign. War reports and international news were closely followed on Seminary Hill. The Durrs distrusted mainstream sources and dug deep for facts. They understood that the worst horrors of the Nazi regime, often discussed in their house, were not yet widely known in the United States. "The horrors were real. They were actually true," Durr said.[53] The "Final Solution to the Jewish Problem," Hitler's genocide, was effected only weeks after Esmond's plane went down. It did not become common knowledge in the United States until the fall of 1942, and even then many did not believe it. By the time of Pearl Harbor, and Esmond's death, Decca and the Durrs hoped the news would kindle the feeling that Decca and Esmond had about Spain—that this was the fight of their lives and almost any sacrifice was worthwhile. Most of the front-page news in U.S. papers, in fact, was war news, almost exclusively so in the case of *The New York Times* and about 50 percent in the case of *The Washington Post*. Kristallnacht had been widely covered by the American press in November 1938, even if the depths of anti-Semitism it revealed were not fully understood. The plight of the Jewish refugees on the ship the *St. Louis*, turned away from the United States with over nine hundred Jews on board, was also well covered in the U.S. press (although it would be years before most Americans learned how many of those passengers were sent back to Europe and died in the Holocaust). While both the United States and Great Britain continued to limit immigration, news of the Kinder Transport of unaccompanied children from Germany drew widespread attention, both as news and as so-called "human interest."

In the winter, the Durrs took in a Japanese family in need of safe haven. This added three more people—Hitomi and Saiko Yamasaki and their baby Hiroshi—to a household that already included nine people (the Durrs, their children, Decca and Dinky, Mrs. Daniels, the Durrs' maid, and Mrs. Daniels's daughter). The addition of Japanese houseguests drew more FBI agents to Seminary Hill: "two big old dumb goofs who wanted to look around and see if there were any aerials and if we were transmitting messages to the Japanese," Durr said.[54] Housing a Japanese family was a bold move after Pearl Harbor, with anti-Japanese hysteria rampant.[55] Calls for putting Japanese citizens in concentration camps came even from the U.S. Congress, leading to frenzied retaliations and to Executive Order 9066, signed by Roosevelt in March 1942, creating internment camps for Japanese Americans.[56] Taking in the Yamasaki family was representative of the Durrs' view that social justice had to be both personal and inconvenient, that activists had to take risks. The Durrs still had Black domestic help; they seemed not to find that odd. But they housed a Japanese family and a notorious British war widow, and saw both activities as part of doing their share.

Decca wanted to do her share as well. In hopes of landing an important job as a secretary to a Party leader or important political person, she enrolled at Strayer Business School in Washington, taking stenography, typing, and shorthand. It was a time of such shortages in clerical workers, Decca said, "that the applicant for a government job was taken into a room with a typewriter and a washing machine; if she could identify the typewriter, she was hired."[57] Decca graduated Strayer in March 1942 and landed a secretarial job almost immediately. She was hired by the Royal Air Force Delegation (RAF) at about £26 a month as a part-time typist, working out of the British Embassy.[58]

Decca imagined that business training would loft her out of "the dead-end world of market research, retail selling and the like" and propel her "into realms of ideas and action."[59] Her actual work at the RAF proved disappointingly dull. But she quickly became known as a hard worker and earned the respect of her colleagues. In spite of working out of the British Embassy, she managed to keep her family a secret.

Most of the Seminary Hill women stayed home. They created a lively social round of lunches, dinners, teas, parties, dances, and fundraisers. After Pearl Harbor, they organized neighborhood light wardens, cooperated on making blackout shades, shared rationed goods, and traded childcare. For the most part, Durr remembered, it was the wives who ensured that everyone could "live together and disagree and yet keep a personal relationship," precisely the kind of emotional management that women in the 1940s were presumed to exercise effortlessly (and that

Decca had watched her mother, Sydney, work so hard to accomplish).[60] Decca discovered that Saiko Yamasaki was an exceptionally competent nanny and hired her to look after Dinky while she worked. Riding with Hugo Black, Justice William O. Douglas, Congressman Tom Eliot, journalists Leonard Niall and Eric Sevareid, economist John Kenneth Galbraith, and others, on the seven-mile route from Virginia to the capital, she picked "furious fights about capitalism and socialism," asked policy questions, and gathered legal background. For the most part, the New Deal men of Seminary Hill accepted Decca's code-switch. In a matter of months, she went from being an "exquisitely beautiful" woman who "never said anything"[61] to being highly political—"quite a storm center,"[62] Durr said. Rage and grief gave Decca voice. Widowhood and cultural difference allowed her to exercise it.

In the early summer of 1942, when the Straights bought a farm in Virginia, Decca took over their Washington, D.C., apartment, determined to live independently. It was a good-size apartment, with two bedrooms, and it was near her job, enabling her to walk home at lunch. At sixty dollars a month, the apartment's rent came to half of Decca's monthly salary. She hired a nurse for Dinky and found a roommate for the second bedroom, taking in "a terrifically nice girl called Anne Hopkins."[63] In the fall, when Anne went back to Chicago, Decca promptly took in two boarders: "one sleeping in the drawing-room and the other in Anne's bedroom. Everyone in Washington has arrangements like that now."[64]

Taking in boarders had been routine for the working class and now became more widespread, promoted as a patriotic and civic duty. No less an authority on social rules than Emily Post provided guidance to the public on the proper way to take in boarders in wartime. Newspapers featured stories about how to handle boarder conflicts.[65] Decca got a great kick out of her boarders. "The 2 boarders are extraorder," she wrote her mother, "I call us the three Boards: one is a bawd, and other just an ordinary board, and I am the bored (by them). Actually, they only sleep here and don't have meals with me, thank goodness." She was, in fact, so pleased with how her boarders had turned out, and with her ability to contribute to the war effort, as Durr had done with her and the Yamasakis, that she planned to take in more: a refugee Italian mother and her two children. They could "sleep in the bathroom or somewhere," she figured.[66] The boarders linked Decca to her family, and to her mother especially, who had often rented out the family homes when money ran low and who now, like many Londoners, had strangers living in Rutland Gate.

Housing, in fact, was a prime Mitford complaint during the war, as family members shuffled about among their various homes. They were unusually lucky during the Blitz, suffering only minimal damage to Rutland Gate and no damage at all to their mews house behind it. Their country homes and Inch Kenneth remained largely untouched by bombs for most of the war. British Defense Regulations requisitioned mostly large country houses, but not the Mitfords' home. When city homes were seized, they were generally used for civil servants, the military, or as hospitals.[67] But in September 1940, during the Blitz, a Jewish family was placed at the Mitfords' London home, occupied at the time by Nancy and her father, David. Nancy loved having the family there. She spoke of them almost as her pets. "As for my sweet refugees no kind of person could possibly in any way be nicer—I shall always love Jews for their sake," she wrote family friend Violet Hammersley. David was less enamored: "roaring like a bull because everything is not just as he always has it," Nancy said.[68] Shortly thereafter, the rest of the house was requisitioned for Jewish families, bringing fifty Jews into Rutland Gate. Sydney, who came to London weekly to visit Diana in prison, was "beastly," according to Nancy. She "says if she had all the money in the world she would not ever live in the house again after Jews have had it."[69]

Sydney remained a faithful correspondent, and Decca warmed to her mother in the wake of Esmond's death, although she still blamed her family for his loss. She largely exempted Unity, Nancy, and Sydney from her vitriol, which she reserved for Diana. Perhaps Decca now needed her mother too much to blame her. Perhaps she never realized—and Sydney certainly did not tell Decca—just how deep her mother's fascist and Nazi sympathies now ran. Decca may not have known that Sydney's stubborn support of Hitler was the wedge that was just then driving her parents apart. For all his conservatism, David was a loyal British subject. Like other British aristocrats at the time, national loyalty made him turn away from fascism once actual war was declared. He and Sydney now lived separately. Decca's letters to her mother never referenced Esmond directly, never mentioned being lonely, and never relayed how difficult it was to raise Constancia on her own.

Brutal heat had been hovering over Washington for weeks. In September, it finally broke. Decca got a new job, at the slightly higher pay of $1,440 a year (about £15,500 in today's currency), as a typist in the "sub-eligible" category in the recently created office of the newly independent Office of Price Administration (OPA).

"The OPA seemed as close to the front line of the war against Fascism as anything in Washington," Decca believed. It was an antidote to the "boring and oppressive American preoccupation with material comforts . . . the unseemly scramble for affluence."[70] Being an OPA investigator gave her an official perch from which to scrutinize her new country, a reason to stay in America. "Reality was back in England, where the Nazi invasion seemed imminent, where people were stoically preparing for the onslaught. Yet after Esmond's death it seemed pointless for me to return—I had nobody to return to, and encumbered by the infant Dinkydonk I should not be in a position to be of much help in the war effort," she said.[71] Ever since her childhood days of waging "Honnish" war against the "dreaded Counter-Hons," Decca had loved doing battle. The OPA provided a way to do that. "My new-found colleagues—lawyers, investigators, economists, rationing experts—were for the most part young, dedicated, immensely energetic, and hard-working anti-Fascists. It was our job to hold the line against war profiteers, price gougers, greedy landlords, violators of rationing regulations."[72]

Unfortunately, even the "sub-eligible" category into which she'd been hired could not disguise Decca's clerical incompetence, which Strayer Business School had done little to mitigate. As she later told Betty Friedan, who became an editor and sometime friend, she was "only able to hang on to my job by a series of subterfuges (such as taking my copy to a typing pool in some other agency and pretending to be a boss: 'I want twelve copies of this by noon, please,' and then lurking in the ladies room until noon."[73] Her subterfuges caught the attention of her new boss, Bob Treuhaft, an enforcement attorney at OPA. As he recollected it years later:

> *In the OPA I met a fantastically beautiful woman who attracted me not only by her charm and wit but by her frugality. I watched with fascination as she moved down the line of the block-long counter of the cafeteria in the huge OPA temporary building. As she passed the beverage section, she would pick up a glass of tomato juice, down it, and set the empty glass down on a handy little shelf below the counter. Next she would scoop up a salad and dispose of the plate in the same way. Then a sandwich. When she reached the cashier, she had nothing on her tray but a cup of coffee—cost of lunch, five cents. This, I decided, was the girl for me.[74]*

Decca's lunchline stratagem was the kind of antic she'd learned from Esmond. Her boss, who had "slanting, twinkling black eyes," a joy in exposing corruption, and deep veins of kindness and intelligence, found it delightful, rather than disapproving of it. This endeared him to her no end.

For his part, Bob was instantly smitten, "tremendously enamored of her right away," he said.[75] "She shines with a kind of fierce honesty and

courage," Bob told his mother, Aranka, admitting to a "wild, uncontrollable and completely futile infatuation for the most terrific female the
world has ever seen." Bob escorted her to dances, and even a fancy ball or
two. Bob made Decca laugh, something she'd hardly done for months.

Decca received a promotion at the OPA, to the rank of Investigator
I. It carried a nice raise, of four hundred dollars a year. More importantly, it introduced Decca to the joys of investigating. She could now
take down powerful people who abused their power. While many of
her assignments took her into completely unfamiliar territories, such as
machining and its pricing, Decca discovered that she had a real knack
for rigorous undercover research. "It is so extraorder," she wrote her
friend Kay Graham (soon publisher of *The Washington Post*).[76] "One
gets sent out all over Virginia and Maryland on 'field trips.' . . . Right
now one of the landlords I have been investigating, who masquerades
under the pretext of being a sweet old lady of 85, is about to get sent
to jail. . . . Next week I have to go and be a witness in court, so you can
see what a fascinating job it is."[77] Assigned to work with Bob, Decca
started with an investigation into pleasure-driving, a serious violation
of wartime gasoline rationing. At night, Decca and Bob staked out
popular New York nightclubs. One night, they apprehended the Norwegian ambassador. Other joint investigations followed. During their
long stakeouts, plastered to the bench seat of Bob's car, they shared
stories. Decca reexperienced some of the joy she'd felt with Esmond of
pulling schemes and undermining the authorities. Bob told Decca that
she was a great investigator and had much to contribute. He was not
"snobbish" and did not assume, Decca noticed, that she was "incapable of understanding or contributing to policy."[78] He treated her as an
equal. They had dinner almost nightly, sometimes alone and sometimes
with friends. Decca had never known an American Jew, and certainly
not a Jew from the Bronx. She found him fascinating, and different.
Believing that Decca was entirely out of his league and never expecting

her to return his affection, Bob made light of his feelings. Decca could not tell if he was really interested.

While Bob treated Decca as *his* equal, he was not confident that he was hers. Decca was a "stunning," stylish, dark-haired, blue-eyed, vibrant beauty with a steely gaze and a dazzling smile. She was brave and accomplished. He only became serious about politics after graduating college, largely because of the impact the Spanish Civil War had on him, as it did on so many American progressives. Decca, by contrast, had *participated* in the Spanish Civil War, even picking up arms to fight.[79] She was smart and self-educated. By his own admission, Bob had gotten into Harvard by what he called "a freakish kind of chance." Once there, he glided through—"I was just interested in having a good time and enjoying it . . . I had a rather easy time going through college."[80] His greatest challenge had been epilepsy, which first appeared in college and proved difficult to medicate. "I'd have grand mal seizures, and they were pretty horrible and frightening."[81] By the time he met Decca, he rarely suffered seizures, but Decca's robust health made him self-conscious. She mocked her mother's medical views of "the Good Body" but did come out of the Cotswolds with a vigorous country constitution.[82]

Bob had dated often, and even been engaged in a desultory fashion, but he'd never been in love before. Decca had not only been married, but she was now the war widow of an International Brigade hero and bomber Navigator. Where Bob was an American Jew of barely middle-class Hungarian extraction, Decca was a British aristocrat, related to royals and prime ministers.

Bob was too gobsmacked to see the many ways in which he and Decca were well suited at just this moment in Decca's life. He had enormous energy and a wonderful work ethic. He was adept at the minutiae of American politics and skilled in navigating bureaucracies. He had a terrific sense of play and a great sense of humor. He was witty, could turn a good phrase, played a mean game of Scrabble, and could quote—and parody—most of the literary classics.[83] His particular mix of qualities—generous, quick-witted, playful, hardworking, funny, mischievous, warm, stubborn, and loyal—matched Decca well. He shared her irreverence (when others found it annoying). He loved teasing, pranks, and word games as much as she did. He did not demand the kind of introspection Decca abhorred. He understood perfectly well that Decca was extraordinary. Bob did not need to be the smartest person in the room. He did not have to grab the microphone. He was happy for Decca to shine.

In D.C., with three of his housemates, Bob had cooked up a group of silly songs that he produced as a record on a do-it-yourself phonograph machine. As a spoof, he mailed copies to various girlfriends and ex-girlfriends, proposing marriage to them all:

Dear Joyce, please come to Washington—
[Bob] . . . wants to marry you;
Dear Joyce, please come to Washington—
No government girl will do.
I think of you night and day;
I think I'm with the REA, the FSA, the CAA,
When I'm really going dopey in the OPA . . .
Think of rations, rent, and price;
No need to hoard that wedding rice . . .
Don't think twice, be nice—
Come to Washington!

Unfortunately, some of the women receiving the phonograph record *didn't* think twice. They came to Washington, believing they were engaged. Decca thought Bob might marry one of them. She decided that Bob was "faithless" and put in for a transfer to the West Coast.[84] She had accepted being the single mother of a toddler, finally accepted being a widow, embraced having her own independent, autonomous career. She did not have time for emotional ambivalence, romantic games, or uncertainty. In or out.

Many years later, Decca told Maya Angelou that she "tended to flee the scene if things had gone too wrong" or gotten too intense. Now she fled. The OPA badly needed investigators on the West Coast. Decca requested a new post in San Francisco, where she and Esmond had often planned to go. Her transfer was granted immediately. San Francisco was far from Washington, where all her American friends were. It was almost impossibly far—especially during the war—from her family and England. Decca didn't know a soul there.

> *Was I running away, not only from Bob, but from the fresh and bitter memory of Esmond's death, blindly putting distance between me and all those past connections? Separated by six thousand miles from family in England and by three thousand from my nearest American acquaintances, I could be virtually reborn as an anonymous bit of human flotsam in this remote outpost. I was both excited and a bit desolate at the prospect.*[85]

Decca arrived at Washington's Union Station on a cold February day in 1943, juggling thirteen pieces of luggage (most of them shopping bags), a twenty-month-old toddler, and a tricycle. Bob showed up at the station, staying on board for three stops until the conductors tossed him off, and then Decca and Constancia were on their way to San Francisco alone.

Between channeling what she most admired about Esmond and absorbing her experience at the OPA, almost everything that Decca would later be and do—fighting for justice, exposing corruption, trusting in facts, forging ahead, withstanding both tragedy and tedium, managing expectations, learning to be useful—traces back to this watershed year after Esmond's death.

8

The "New Life"

I really suffered from loneliness.[1]
—JESSICA MITFORD

Looking backward is not much in my nature.[2]
—JESSICA MITFORD

Decca always viewed her first months in San Francisco, in the spring of 1943, as the worst time of her life. She told herself that happiness was not a matter of "outward circumstances" but rather of having the right attitude and making "practical decisions about life,"[3] so she secured housing and work. But she remained miserable. "I really suffered from loneliness for the first time in my life . . . for about 3 months I really went through tortures," she said.[4] Being alone, only twenty-five, with Constancia, in San Francisco, from

March to June of 1943, was even harder for her, in some ways, than coping with Esmond's death. As she later reflected about this period in her life, "I longed to be a person considered on her own merits."[5] But someone had to do that considering, had to see her new autonomy. Having narrowed her world down to work—at which she only sometimes excelled—and motherhood—at which she felt she rarely did—Decca was trying to make the largest decisions of her life with uncharacteristically little input from others. As a "not specially introspective type," as she admitted about herself, her difficulties were not eased by her own disinclination to ruminate.[6]

After more than a year of forced optimism, the certainty of Esmond's death had now sunk in. Decca had no idea what to do with that. The pain was like a crater she had, somehow, to edge her way around. Even as a child, she could not abide dwelling on difficult feelings. She and her sisters "roared" at the notion of processing feelings or sitting with sadness. How unnecessary, they would have said. How self-indulgent.

She'd chosen San Francisco impulsively because she and Esmond had dreamed of seeing it. Being there shortly after Pearl Harbor, halfway around the world from England, with only work associates and almost no money, was not, however, the madcap fun that Esmond would have made it. She was a widow, a single mother who'd already lost one child, and "horribly, chronically lonely, as though shrouded in a fog of unhappiness through which I could descry but dimly the cast of characters at home and at work. I even developed an illness [persistent fever and sore throat] which I thought might be psychosomatic, attributable to this state of mind."[7]

On her first night in San Francisco, Decca checked herself, Dinky, Dinky's tricycle, and their thirteen shopping bags, into a hotel. Then she promptly left Dinky in the care of a surprised hotel maid and went out. It was a cold, wet, dark March night. Decca slipped into the first bar she found—a dingy neighborhood hangout—and ordered a drink.

148

"I can't serve you," the bartender said. "Wartime restrictions prohibit unaccompanied women from drinking in bars." Decca argued that war industries depended on women working as mechanics, crane operators, factory workers, ship and airplane builders, truck drivers, lumberjacks, and federal workers, like herself.[8] She got her drink.

Decca didn't believe in making too much fuss over children. But she knew that hotel rooms weren't right for them either. The next day she rented a "Dickensian" room in an unsanitary boardinghouse that had advertised in the newspaper.[9] It was located at 1350 Haight Street, on a relatively flat stretch of the street, in a crowded neighborhood, mostly comprised of two- and three-story Victorians, many with storefronts, turrets and gables above.[10] Famous as a hippie enclave in the 1960s, the Haight in 1943 was a small hilly section of mostly working-class houses, small shops, and streetcars. Side streets had brick cobbles. Everything a person might need—from chop suey to hardware—was easily accessible. Most shop windows were filled with patriotic displays. A few doors down from Decca's boardinghouse, the Cherry Blossom Bakery at 1573 Haight Street sponsored an "AmeriCake" donation drive and raffle that filled two large plate-glass windows: "Hi Neighbor. Do Your Bit to Fill a Kit." The neighborhood was one of many areas where once-affluent homes had been subdivided in the boom that followed the 1906 earthquake. Rents had been inflating ever since.[11] California experienced more wartime population growth than any other area of the nation, and even the shabbiest rentals were scarce and at a premium now.[12] The war industry suspended all housing construction and "you were lucky if you got a room," as one worker put it.[13] Some new arrivals slept in tents, basements, refrigerator lockers, and cars. Those with children found the housing search especially hard.[14] Decca expected a salary of $1,800 a year at the OPA,[15] which made her twenty-five-dollar monthly rent for room and board a bargain. Her standards were not high.

In the rundown boardinghouse were two other boarders, who kept her up to date on the war. She craved conversation and had constant questions for her housemates. The landlady, Mrs. Betts, had two young boys, and Dinky took to both immediately.[16] Millions of women had entered the wartime labor force. Yet day care hardly existed.[17] Decca persuaded Mrs. Betts to babysit Dinky while she worked and to charge her less than half the going rate.[18] Being able to "solve at one blow the problems of housing and Donk care, both of which loomed large because of drastic wartime shortages of apartments and domestic help," boosted Decca's confidence.[19] She focused on the fact of having found work and a place to live, not on the quality of her housing or her lack of a social life.

Between 1940 and 1945, more than a fifth of the nation's population moved in search of new jobs in the war industry. Millions went West, increasing the population of the Bay Area by almost 40 percent and drawing large numbers of Black workers. San Francisco was a hub for Pacific military transport and for shipbuilding, processing, distribution, and defense industries, as well as all the social services that went along with that population explosion. "Each day, weekends especially, the roads and highways into San Francisco were lined with young men in uniform hitchhiking into the city on pass," California historian Kevin Starr notes.[20] Many of the new arrivals were workers seeking professional opportunities previously foreclosed to them. San Francisco drew more than its share of the over six million women who entered the labor force during the war to fill jobs in the new defense and war-related industries.[21] Some were war widows, like Decca, or separated from husbands by the war.[22] Some were divorced.[23] All needed safe housing and a range of social services. Factory workers like Rosie the Riveter did exist, and they changed expectations for women's labor, but so did the many middle-class and nonindustrial women workers, like Decca, in suit, pumps, hat, pearls, and handbag, carrying briefcases with their gloves.[24] The steady influx of new workers upended the Bay Area's social and political fabric. A formerly conservative region became progressive almost overnight.[25]

Among all these other recent arrivals, Decca might have alleviated her agonizing loneliness and experienced the sense of community and belonging she longed for. But she kept to herself, "preserving my anonymity," she said, concentrating on taking care of Dinky and becoming good—very good—at her job.

Decca's boardinghouse was less than a block from Buena Vista Park and only two blocks from the Panhandle and the entrance to Golden Gate Park. But she and Dinky had arrived during one of San Francisco's extended periods of cold, drenching rain. Decca's coworkers caught the flu and had high fevers. Decca didn't have rain gear. She could not afford to be sick. For most of that long soggy month she traveled only when necessary and only from home to work and back again, seeing only a narrow band of the city between her boardinghouse and office, visible from the trolley windows or on a rushed walk.

The OPA offices were on Market Street between Ninth and Tenth streets, in a massive Art Deco building that had been built as a Furniture Mart and that now exclusively housed war-related offices.[26] It occupied a full, square city block and was nine floors high, accessed through a glorious lobby with expensive marble and massive dangling lights. It was just down the block from the enormous new center for servicemen, part of the city's increasingly important war role. Decca went from shop fronts encouraging civic volunteerism to a downtown city block that was 100 percent dedicated to the war effort.

Decca, who loved chatting more than anything, had almost no one to talk to now. Looking back, she reflected that Dinky was her "constant friend and companion."[27] "In hopes that she [Dinky] would soon learn to talk," Decca admitted, "I treated her more or less as a grownup."[28] When she could afford it, she called Bob in D.C.

Counting mostly on correspondence to ease her isolation, Decca exchanged frequent letters with Bob and also revived a lively correspondence with her mother, who kept Decca up to date on the family. When

Decca's landlady told her a peculiar story about the "odd sex habits" of her ex-husband, a dentist—"'He ruined my bladder,' she confided mysteriously"—Decca wrote Bob about it straightaway, and he turned it into a funny song: "In a fit of depravity, he filled the wrong cavity / What's the madder, you ruined my bladder, you took advantage of me." It was just "the sort of letter that made my day," Decca told Bob.[29]

Somehow, Decca intuited that her mother would rise to the challenge of not realienating her daughter. Sydney played a nonjudgmental, sympathetic, interested, and open-minded role with extraordinary finesse. There were no "I told you so's," no demands, no recriminations, no plays for pity in Sydney's letters to her daughter. She trod her thin line gracefully. And she mailed clippings and magazines, the same sort of popular magazines—filled with fashion and gossip—that she had sent her daughter in Spain. For Decca, the massive distance between them was convenient. Her mother was in no position to challenge the upbeat story that Decca now crafted about her "glamorous" life in San Francisco.[30] Decca's loneliness affected her perception of how much her mother could understand. And perhaps, in referencing so many things outside of Sydney's sphere, Decca was also showing off, demonstrating her distance from all things Mitford. "My job is heaven," she wrote her mother, "tho unfortunately the reactionaries here are trying to prevent a lot of the things we want to do, & it may even result in us all losing our jobs. If so I know I can get another job very easily; but I do love the O.P.A. The FBI (like Scotland Yard) are investigating a lot of people in our division at the moment, including me. This is part of a general Red-baiting program. The Durrs were investigated too."[31] Sydney was thoroughly befuddled.

Unbeknownst to Decca, the FBI had begun assembling a file on her San Francisco life at this time. Since she did little besides go to work and, later, to her union offices, and care for Dinky, the file was dull. But her FBI investigator commented on what an adept enforcer Decca was becoming: "capable, reliable, a good worker, efficient, intelligent." "An interesting personality," he added. Her file also noted, quite correctly, how much Decca was then keeping to herself. "According to _____ Mrs. Romilly never discussed her personal affairs with any of the office force," one comment in her FBI file stated.[32]

Almost everything shaping wartime San Francisco, and therefore Decca's new life, was absent from her letters to Sydney. She did not mention Executive Order 9066, evacuating Japanese and Japanese Americans to detention centers and concentration camps in the California desert, although it touched her deeply, especially after living with a Japanese family at the Durrs. Even many liberal Americans harbored racist feelings about the Japanese in 1943.[33] Not Decca. The last few hundred Japanese and Japanese American residents were taken from San Francisco in May 1942 by six Greyhound buses. Fear of attack from the Japanese was so persistent that in January 1943, the Air Force dropped torpedoes and a bomb on what turned out to be a whale, spotted on radar as a "large object" in the North Pacific. In August 1943, War Gas Self-Aid Stations were established in the belief that the area might come under Japanese gas attack. Decca said nothing to her mother about the tense atmosphere in California. Nor did she mention the race riots of summer 1943 that broke out in Detroit and Harlem—crowding out the national news for days and profoundly affecting Decca's thoughts about America and race.

Decca celebrated the enormous social and cultural changes wrought by thousands of Black workers who were rushed into the void left by the relocated Japanese. Years later, long after they'd become close friends, Maya Angelou described the civic turbulence that Decca experienced in San Francisco in 1943. "As the Japanese disappeared," Angelou wrote, "soundlessly and without protest, the Negroes entered with their loud jukeboxes, the just-released animosities and the relief of escape from Southern bonds. The Japanese area became San Francisco's Harlem in a matter of months."[34] Or, as one Black woman worker, newly arrived in

San Francisco from the South, put it more pithily: "Hitler . . . got us out of the White folks' kitchen."[35]

Decca had chosen the Bay Area without much consideration. But it turned out to be more than an escape for her, providing opportunities for remaking an independent life, as a woman, that the Durrs' house in Seminary Hill could never have afforded. In myriad ways the war economy encouraged female independence, even if some constraining gender messages persisted. For example, since metal was needed for the war effort and consumer goods such as vacuum cleaners were not manufactured during the war, women were encouraged to maintain and repair their own vacuum cleaners, sewing machines, irons, radios, toasters, and other devices.[36] These small changes had massive impacts both during and after the war. Decca had no interest in becoming another Rosie the Riveter. Like Durr, she intended to break gender barriers while also adhering to gender norms. But she was paying close attention to all the available models for female activism and ambition. She absorbed the message that women could be not only domestic engineers—fixing appliances and managing budgets—but elbow out some space for themselves in public as well.

Decca was responsible for enforcing the OPA's mandate—to keep businesses from taking advantage of consumers by profiting unduly from the war—by investigating individual business owners to ensure their compliance with unpopular wartime regulations and by defending an agency that was in the "doghouse of public condemnation," as *The New York Times* put it.[37] The ban on all pleasure-driving, which Decca and Bob had drafted, was especially unpopular.[38] One *Washington Post* reporter spoke for many citizens, arguing that while individual sacrifice in times of war was a sound principle for the Republic, "OPA regulations ought to conform to American folkways."[39] *The New York Times* questioned the OPA leadership and its fairness.[40] Few critics went as far as the right-wing *Chicago Daily Tribune*, which called the OPA "the most ugly and brutal tyrant the New Deal has raised," but many called the OPA the "Office for Persecuting Americans."[41] Decca's job required her to assert authority over male-dominated industries and worksites. She discovered that she did best when she felt most besieged. She was happy to defend the beleaguered agency. She found that she enjoyed challenging men. She loved it when they underestimated her.

Decca also relished playing a role in forcing Americans to sacrifice; they'd gotten away with doing far too little for much too long, she thought.[42] Individual Americans were great. But Decca deeply resented how the nation had held back, letting Britain and other allies pay the cost of America's wavering indecision. For most Americans, the war had only recently become real. For Decca it had been an intimate reality for years, claiming her husband and her sister, shattering her ties to her country and her family, imprisoning Giles, and turning Diana—the sister Decca had most admired—into a monster. It was time for the Americans to pony up some pain of their own, she felt. The OPA gave Decca a panoply of small, manageable, targets. She was relentless. So much so that her boss, who praised what he drily called her "commendable zeal for enforcement," cautioned her to be *less* enthusiastic.[43]

Across the spring and summer of 1943, the fractured marriage of Decca's parents finally gave way entirely. David could not bear Sydney's continuing support for Hitler. Sydney would not back down. David moved out, going first to Inch Kenneth in the Hebrides; then he decamped to Redesdale Cottage, in far Northumberland, with Margaret Wright, the under-parlourmaid. Sydney tried to carry on as if nothing had changed, but she soon moved permanently to Inch Kenneth with Unity, isolating herself almost completely.

The OPA's mandate was sweeping. As *The Washington Post* put it, "The functions of OPA cover practically the whole field of producing and distributing commodities of every kind."[44] The OPA exposed seams of hypocrisy, and Decca tore into those. Americans might say they supported the war effort 100 percent. But in practice they wanted cars, gasoline, silk stockings, vacuum cleaners, and waffle irons. When coffee consumption was restricted to one cup a day per person, so that coffee-carrying cargo ships could be used for weapons and troops, even Eleanor Roosevelt's personal appeal to the nation could not stem the loud affronted outcry.[45] Many consumers, small businesses, and landlords opposed the OPA.[46] Decca was all in.

The OPA and the War Labor Board were cobbled together quickly and rarely managed efficiently. They were large agencies—the OPA alone employed over three thousand investigators and nearly a quarter of a million volunteers—beset by bureaucratic tangles, sometimes conflicting goals, and criticized from all sides.[47] Conservatives in government saw the OPA as a liberal extension of New Deal overreach. Trade unionists opposed OPA-enforced price ceilings that made it hard to organize workers and no-strike deals, which deflated collective bargaining. Progressives inside the OPA felt the administration was too soft on enforcement and pushed for more restrictions, rationing, ceilings, and inspections. Decca found like-minded thinkers in the United Federal Workers Association (UFWA or FWA), which supported wage ceilings and a no-strike pledge. She began spending more and more time at the offices of the FWA and even less time with her daughter Dinky. In April 1943, Roosevelt imposed a "hold-the-line" order on wage and price controls, designed to reinforce the regulators.[48] The move drew new critics, who saw it as an ill-timed departure from the milder redistributions of the New Deal.[49] It made Decca a fervent FDR supporter, in spite of his support for Japanese internment, recasting him in her eyes as a social radical, cracking down on the weak and wishy-washy.

In her first assignment for the San Francisco OPA, Decca was sent to enforce secondhand-machine-tool pricing, a task that depended on familiarity with each piece of equipment's condition, age, and make. She knew absolutely nothing about machine tools. Her solution was to go undercover and pretend to be a customer with a lot of questions. She started in the waterfront industrial district, walked up to the counter of a secondhand-machine-tool shop, and asked to see a lathe. "Looks very nice, lovely. What year is it, actually?" she asked, batting her eyes.

> *I was scribbling down in a notebook the names, descriptions, and prices of these objects as given by the dealer, who squinted suspiciously and answered in monosyllables. He did not seem at all keen about making a sale; perhaps he was a front for a vast secondhand-machine-tool black market ring? If so, here was a marvelous opportunity to work up a major criminal case against this unprepossessing man and his evil confederates. . . . I returned to the shop, waited in a nearby telephone booth until I saw the owner go out for lunch, then went in to speak to his secretary. "Will you please fetch out all your sales records for the past month? I'm here on OPA business, and we need them to determine if you're complying with the regulation."[50]*

When the secretary handed over the records, Decca scooped them into her briefcase, ran out the door, and spirited them back to the office, to try to understand them at her leisure. Her boss, John McTernan, asked that she not steal documents in the future.[51] Decca could not resist anything that was the least cloak-and-dagger, however. Her OPA methods were eclectic, strategic, and not always ethical. But they were effective.

From her OPA work, Decca was, without knowing it, training herself to do investigative journalism. She was learning to get the information she needed by any means necessary—the talent upon which much of her later success as a writer would ultimately rest. Almost every quality that would later make Decca's writing so successful, in fact—urgency, passion, in-depth research, joy in exposing corruption, delight in involving collaborators—can be traced to her early experiences as an unusually zealous OPA enforcer. She also had an extraordinary capacity for work, and remarkable focus.

What Decca lacked was a capacity to simply plod along without some sense of fun or adventure. And while her coworkers were "exceptionally promising"—"a good cut above the average run of war-agency personnel," she thought—and the union brought her like-minded people doing interesting and important work, loneliness ate away at her accomplishments. "Try as I might, I could not recapture the spirit in which I had departed from Washington; the 'new life' would not take shape."[52] She wasn't sure she would stay. "If I don't like it in San F. after a few months," she wrote her mother, "I may skeke off to Mexico."[53] She wrote upbeat letters, to Bob especially, trying to recapture the spirit that now eluded her. Bob wrote back, full of good humor and jokes about the boardinghouse and also tales of government bureaucracy, which he excelled at deciphering. He started letting Decca know how he felt. "It's no good, Dec, having all those miles of Field between us," he wrote. His letters were also filled with the kind of chatty details she craved—"crammed with amusing Washington gossip." Decca said that "more and more I found my only source of real pleasure and sustenance was Bob's letters."[54]

Decca took courage from the Warsaw Ghetto uprising in April, following the end of the Battle of Stalingrad in February. Both seemed to augur well for an eventual end to war. Churchill's May 19 speech to the U.S. Congress, heard by more than fourteen million Americans and printed in its entirety in the next day's *New York Times*, expressed optimism and reasserted the strength of the British-American bond. It reassured many Americans—but by no means all—that Great Britain would not leave America to fight Japan alone. "We will wage that war side by side with you," Churchill pledged, "while there is breath in our bodies and while blood flows in our veins."[55]

The rains and cold weather finally let up and Decca found San Francisco a different city. "We love San Francisco," she decided in April.

"The Donk is getting much healthier out here, which is partly why I came, Washington has a horrible climate. The people here are terrifically nice. . . . We are definitely going to stay."[56]

Decca worked long hours at the OPA. She added to those by taking on more work for her union, becoming an officer of the United Federal Workers Association, which Bob had helped to found in Washington.[57] "I threw myself into the work of the union," she later recalled.[58] According to Decca's FBI file, the "Federal Workers of America in the OPA offices had gone beyond the purposes of an ordinary union and was endeavoring to promote communism."[59] The FBI was wrong about most of the union members, but Decca was recruited into the union by her OPA coworker Al Bernstein, who was also involved in Communist Party politics.[60] At the Union, she'd warmed to UFWA President Doris (Dobby) Walker, in spite of their marked personality differences. Dobby "ran the union as a *very* tight ship"[61] and brooked no nonsense, and Decca desperately needed nonsense. Nevertheless, the two drew close, eventually becoming lifelong friends.[62] Dobby was Decca's first San Francisco friend and the first woman she became friends with all on her own. With her support, Decca was elected to an important union position: Membership director of the War Agencies local, which was also an enforcement position—responsible for making sure the locals all carried out official policy. Decca was getting noticed. Dinky spent even more time with Mrs. Betts.

In May, Decca persuaded Mrs. Betts to let her fix up a damp, shabby basement apartment for herself. It was an awkward space, long vacant, and accessible only by traversing a dark, outside alley and then climbing a fire escape: a "very rum dwelling" consisting of two rooms and a kitchen behind a boarded-up storefront. It was essentially unlivable and certainly illegal. It could not have been more inconvenient. Mrs. Betts could not imagine why Decca wanted it, but Decca persisted, and Mrs. Betts gave in.

Yet, even as she seemed to be settling down, Decca also traveled to

Seattle for work and considered another move. In Seattle she was training other investigators to enforce prices in the lumber industry, a notoriously sexist field with a long history of excluding women. She was so successful in teaching other women to stand up to sexism that the OPA asked her to relocate and concentrate on lumber investigations. They offered a huge raise. "I suppose I shall leave here soon," she told her mother resignedly. "I'm sorry as this is a really fascinating town & I like all the people in the office so much. . . . It is rather a nuisance about the Seattle job, as I just got moved into my new flat and bought all the furniture."[63] Decca ultimately turned the Seattle offer down, but no one seemed to know why.

Decca was alternately scattered and offhand. She dropped something about wanting a vacation in mid-June to spend time with a "friend." The apartment seemed secretly connected somehow. She let slip that she'd developed an idea involving her "friend" Bob Treuhaft, but didn't know how viable it was and wouldn't say what her idea was. Bob was also dropping "tantalizing" hints in flirtatious letters and calls. But he had not declared himself. Until he did, Decca could not admit to anyone what she had not yet admitted to herself—that she was ready to marry again and build a new family.

Bob had not revealed the depth of his feelings because he assumed they were futile. He could not have devised a more successful strategy for winning Decca than letting her chase him. In holding back, Bob created the only conditions that could have succeeded with Decca at this time, offering just the combination of devotion and irreverence she required. He did not put her on a pedestal. He teased her. He helped her not take herself, or others, too seriously. Yet he seemed to also get Decca, and to understand her needs. Now that Decca was alone in San Francisco, he looked more and more like the bright light at the end of a very dark tunnel. She confided her thinking to no one but began quietly putting a plan into motion which would solve her intractable problems and banish the loneliness still plaguing her.

Just then, in the early summer of 1943, Decca received the startling news that Virginia Durr "had a sort of nervous breakdown . . . brought on by the defeat of the anti-poll tax bill in the Senate last year and by the fact that Cliff is in the middle of constant fights in his agency & is on all the Dies lists." Decca did her best to explain. "Dies," she wrote her mother, "is one of the congressmen over here who is constantly attacking government workers, suspected of left-wing tendencies." He is "one of the chief Red-baiters," she wrote.[64] Decca had taken Durr as a model, and to Decca she had seemed indomitable. The news was both shocking and deeply unsettling.

Durr was "one of the most effective organizers of the anti-poll tax movement," able to prevail against restraints placed on women.[65] "There was no women's movement at that time," Durr later told interviewers, and no clear way to protest her exclusion from the important political work, mostly on the Southern Policy Committee, taking place in her own living room. "I wasn't allowed to take part," Durr recounted. "No women were allowed. I just had to feed them."[66] But Durr had jostled her way into power, "becoming something of a feminist," she said, and mentoring others, like Decca, to challenge their backgrounds, fight constraints, and unlearn prejudices and racism.[67] Durr had told Decca that breaking free of her heritage was "like having escaped from a prison."[68] When Clifford Durr found himself in the crosshairs of Martin Dies, Virginia felt undone. "Both our families," Durr said, "had come over here in the early 1700s and had fought in the Revolutionary War. We had a sense . . . that we owned the country, . . . I felt absolutely safe. I was an American. It was my country. . . . The wife of the president was my friend. I went to the White House for receptions. My husband was in the government. My brother-in-law was on the Supreme Court of the United States. I felt perfectly safe."[69]

If the Durrs, with their high-level social and political connections, could be not only imperiled but also scared stiff, Decca realized that no one was safe. She had moved to San Francisco determined to *be* alone, to avoid entangling herself with another man so soon after Esmond's death. The plan had been to forge ahead independently, just as she'd seen Durr do. Durr's breakdown cast all that thinking into doubt. Forging ahead alone was not only harder than she'd thought. It was also more frightening. Once again, she felt "horribly . . . lonely."[70]

Bob arrived, as planned, in June. They went to Izzy Gomez's, a famous leftist bar. At a table across the room from renowned labor leader Harry Bridges, they got down to business. "I asked Bob what his plans were for the future. 'To marry you, and move out here to live' was the inspiring answer."[71] Done and decided before they'd ordered second drinks. They married the next day, June 21, 1943, in the small Russian River town of Guerneville and honeymooned nearby, making an impromptu arrangement for Dinky on the way out of town. Sussman writes that "they took a bus to the quiet river town north of San Francisco, passing Constancia and her suitcase out the window to a family to whom they'd been given a letter of introduction—friends of Katharine Graham—who had agreed to babysit during their absence."[72] As Bob told it, "I came out here knowing that Decca loved me, but with little hope of persuading her to marry me. The second day here I asked the question and she said yes before I had a chance to finish—because she had been thinking about this for months, and had already made her decision. When Decca makes up her mind, she <u>never</u> changes it." Bob had spoken to his mother, Aranka, over the phone, but could not say much about the marriage. "The wonder and the beauty of it all just left me speechless," he admitted. He had not expected to win Decca. And he was still catching up to his own happiness. "She is the only person that I've ever known that I <u>know</u> I can be completely happy with, whatever may happen," he wrote.[73]

"You will be v. surprised to hear I am married to Bob Treuhaft," Decca wrote her mother. "I know I haven't told you about him before, so will do so now: I have known him since last December (he works for OPA too & is an attorney in the Enforcement Division). . . . I am tremendously happy & all the bitter, horrible past months seem to have vanished . . . I do hope you will realise how wonderful everything is." She claimed that she was entirely surprised to find herself married again. "I hadn't even thought of such a thing till Bob came out here on his hol," she wrote, burying the truth of her planning.[74] She and her sister Deborah had a warm exchange about being wives and teaching their husbands how to be affectionate.

Decca's marriage was a surprise to everyone but Decca. No one was more stunned than Bob. He'd spent five days crossing the country, rehearsing a proposal he never expected to deliver. He did not ask Decca, then or apparently ever, what had made her decide so firmly, and so suddenly, in his favor. Perhaps he was afraid to jinx his good fortune.

Bob's fake marriage proposal record caper should have given him pause about practical jokes. Decca had also told him that one of her worst fears was press exposure as Unity's sister or a "Peer's Daughter." She was now devoted to preserving her anonymity and being "merely an English war widow who happened to fetch up in San Francisco." She "longed to be a person considered on her own merits," no longer dogged by identification as an aristocrat. She was sure that her OPA and union colleagues would not understand her "family notoriety." On their return from Guerneville, Bob went shopping for a celebration dinner. Decca had done her best with Mrs. Betts's basement apartment—painting, buying used furniture, even making curtains. She still could not sweep stairs (from the bottom up? she asked) or make a bed (wasn't one just getting back in at night?). She was indifferent to ironing and cooking. From the day they returned to San Francisco on June 22, 1943, and continuing thereafter for more than fifty years, Bob assumed the lion's share of shopping, cooking, and running their small, disorganized household.[75] Now, failing to take Decca's "terror of discovery" seriously, or to understand the labor that had gone into

163

distancing herself from her family, he bounced back in, brandishing a tabloid with enormous headlines that read: OPA SNOOPSTRESS WEDS SLIDE-RULE BOY: STUNS S.F.[76] When Decca nearly passed out, Bob had to admit that he ordered the fake newspaper from a nearby joke shop specializing in such pranks. His apologies were "profuse."[77]

He made up for it by quickly getting an offer from the San Francisco office of the National War Labor Board.[78] He went back to D.C. to wrap up his work and to pack. But wrapping things up proved much more daunting than expected, with a new delay every week. In the end, it took months for him to finally relocate. Some of Decca's old friends were baffled by her choice. Bob seemed so different from Esmond, whose charm was effervescent and whose courage was legendary. Durr was especially shocked. She liked Bob and "thought he was very attractive" (though Bob was adorable where Esmond had been handsome), but she found it almost impossible "to accept Bob as her [Decca's] husband, when I thought of Esmond as her husband."[79] In spite of his flaws, however—such as occasional lapses in judgment and not always paying attention to what Decca said—and sometimes because of them, Bob proved an inspired choice for Decca's mate.

Decca was less impatient for Bob's return than might have been expected. The fact that she was no longer on her own seemed to have mattered more than actually *being* with Bob, who was still on the other side of the country. Decca's second memoir, *A Fine Old Conflict*, describes this period of waiting for Bob to return from Washington to San Francisco in telling detail. Even recounting events that occurred when Decca was still alone, and Bob was on the other coast, the narrative slips from "I" to "we:" "we thrilled to the sights and sounds of the convention;" "we exclaimed;" "we learned;" "we joined," and so on.[80] Decca's pronominal slips tell a larger truth. The moment she married Bob, she quickly put behind her, once and for all, the only time in her life when she would ever be alone.

9

"A Serious Person"

[Among] "Real Communists" you had to be a
serious person of single-aim sincerity.[1]
—JESSICA MITFORD

One is . . . quite incapable of taking everything as seriously as one should.[2]
—JESSICA MITFORD

Decca returned from Guerneville as relieved as she was happy. "All the bitter, horrible past months seem to have vanished," she said.[3] Bob had to return quickly to Washington. But that hardly mattered. Being half of a couple freed Decca to be on her own. She felt such a rush of energy and focus that it was like bursting up through the water to breathe. Housing, work, and family uncertainties seemed resolved, but a social life and, more important, a political life, both remained to be secured. She had always said she wanted to be a Communist. "Finding the Communist Party" now became her main objective.[4]

She did not have to look far. San Francisco was a union town and a progressive stronghold, especially after the General Strike of 1934, led by the Longshoremen's Union. Its Communist Party was unusually large, innovative, and successful, and its offices were just downhill from Decca's apartment.[5] Centrally located on Turk Street, a couple of blocks from the city's town hall, was the Party-affiliated California Labor School, which had just expanded in 1942, and which combined a vibrant community center, concert and theater venue, bookstore and print shop, art studio, lecture hall, meeting area and library open to the community, with classes that ranged from Marxist and labor theory to music and fine arts. The school had been through various incarnations of community service, from seminary, to cultural center, to YMCA, to Hebrew Association, before becoming a workers' school, founded by famous muckraking writer Lincoln Steffens and others. Designed as a program "for the strengthening of democracy and the deepening of knowledge which will implement the democratic desire for a better world," under the patriotic motto of "Education for Victory," the California Labor School had massive wartime appeal.[6] It "became enormous almost overnight," historians note.[7] Early Black Studies and Women's Studies classes were pioneered at the school.[8] Underwritten and supported by every union local in San Francisco, as well as by national organizations such as the NAACP, it attracted top-notch faculty from Stanford and state universities, as well as visiting lecturers from across the country.[9] Tuition was only six dollars a semester, and free to anyone in active military service. Special students were offered scholarships and encouragement. (As a teenager, Maya Angelou received a California Labor School scholarship to study drama and dance.) On request, classes were brought into union halls and community centers.

The school printed posters, leaflets, pamphlets, and flyers, ran a Christmas market, had a well-regarded chorus (Decca loved to sing), and sponsored nightly public programs in addition to its rich array of evening courses.[10] Its many parties were in what art teacher and political cartoonist Pele de Lappe called "the old art school tradition:" lots of drinking, dancing, music, and bohemian dress.[11] Decca had always wanted to go to school. The Labor School was ideal for her.

In 1943, the Communist Party resonated with many young people, as it did with Decca, providing a powerful sense of optimism and hope. One of the leaders of the California Communist Party said that "we had a feeling that history was on our side and that we were making history every day."[12] In the words of Marge Frantz (daughter of Durr's friend Joe Gelders and later one of Decca's closest friends), "you felt that you were really going to make a difference in the world."[13]

The Communist Party had suffered a steep drop in membership after the Nazi-Soviet Pact of 1939.[14] By 1943, however, what Popular Front historian Michael Denning calls a strong "anti-fascist common sense in American culture," combined with the growth of labor unions, made Communism an appealing political choice for left-leaning Americans, especially in California.[15] With the Soviets now as critical allies, Americans became more accepting of both the Party and the Soviet Union. In 1942, according to Denning, 25 percent of Americans favored some form of socialism, while 35 percent—more than a third of the nation—described themselves as open-minded.[16] For Decca, these shifts meant that becoming an American and becoming a Communist need not be in conflict. For the first time since leaving England, it seemed possible to have everything she wanted. Decca, in her mid-twenties, had been dragging herself from home to work. San Francisco's steep, picturesque hills now felt like flatlands to her, and she felt young again.

Before moving to San Francisco, she had worried that becoming a

Communist might require qualities she lacked. Esmond had met many "Real Communists" in Spain, and he'd told Decca it required "a serious person, a rigid disciplinarian . . . lacking in any such selfish motive as fear or reckless courage." He did not believe he had the "single aim sincerity" that Party membership demanded.[17] He insinuated that Decca was even less qualified for membership. Like him, she could not tolerate authority, always had multiple aims, loved to tease, and could work phenomenally hard, but only if she could have fun doing it.

Luckily for her, San Francisco politics were stamped with the city's unique character as a place open to new ideas and new people, as if its constantly surprising geography had seeped into the soul of its citizenry. The Labor School's day care, dinner parties, and experimental forms of collective living arrangements were all unconventional, run by activists awash in drive, refusing to let their wild enthusiasms be dampened.[18]

On every visit back to San Francisco, Bob found Decca "in the swing already in local politics, clubs and unions."[19] She was "busy, busy, busy," he said.[20] While Decca began studying at the California Labor School and continued her OPA work, Bob was in D.C. One of the first things he did there was visit Virginia Durr so that he could report to Decca that she was improving.

Decca shared an OPA desk with Al Bernstein. He was a Communist and a character. Although he was a skilled and admired organizer, Bernstein could be so absent-minded that socks turned up in his desk drawers. He was always disheveled, with mismatched, wrinkled clothing and a shirtfront dusted with cigar ashes. A Columbia University Law School graduate who ran a laundromat for extra money, Bernstein had an irrepressible sense of humor. Union President Dobby Walker once told Bernstein's son Carl (later famous for exposing the Watergate scandal) that Al's humor was what made him politically effective. "You knew you were going to have a good time around your dad and it was going to be interesting."[21] His colleagues loved him. So did Decca. His esteem proved to her that the Party made room for individuality, even eccentricity.

To Decca, Dobby Walker was clearly one of Esmond's "few Real Communists." Walker suspected that Decca was superficial. Their initial meeting did not go well. "I guess," Decca told Dobby, "you are a bit rigid and sectarian, and you think I'm a bit sloppy and opportunistic."[22]

Her first words to me were, "Which committee would you like to work on?" I responded, "Where do you need the most people?" Dobby sternly said that was not the point of the union, which was engaged in serious struggle on behalf of the working class against the forces of reaction. After a few more mystifying exchanges, it developed that she thought I had said, "Where do you meet most people?" While this might not have been an unreasonable question from an unattached newcomer to the area, to Dobby, "a serious person of single-aim sincerity," it must have smacked of irresponsible frivolity.[23]

Two years younger than Decca, Dobby had joined the Communist Party when she was seventeen and an English major at UCLA.[24] She graduated from UC Berkeley's Law School at twenty-four, the only woman in her law school class. Slight, with a high forehead, prominently ridged nose, and fierce stare, Dobby was a no-nonsense Jewish Texan. She was also an ardent hiker and a nature lover. Decca was a distinctly indoor person; "nature, nature, how I hatecher," she liked to quip. Yet Dobby, like Decca, had often felt like an outsider. She grew up Jewish in racist and segregated Dallas. She was an early feminist when few—either in law school or in the Party—prioritized the "woman question," as it was then called.[25] Dobby was conscientious and an especially exhaustive researcher, which interested Decca even then.[26] Decca came to adore her.[27] And she absorbed myriad feminist lessons from Dobby, even if she resisted claiming them.

By this time, Decca and Bob were both battling with the OPA, which was not as liberal as they had thought. The Washington office delayed Bob's transfer to San Francisco and demanded thousands of dollars—money Bob did not have—as reimbursement for having written off his trips to San Francisco as business expenses. "It really is a nightmare," Decca said.[28] Bob rounded up supporters, filed mounds of paperwork, and refused to pay.[29]

Decca had recently been reassigned to the rent-control division, with a new boss she liked. He was fired by conservatives in what Decca said was "just another dirty manoeuvre" almost as soon as Decca got there.[30]

In August, the San Francisco OPA office, exasperated by Decca's "increasingly obnoxious presence as a union trouble-maker," exploited a regulation that prohibited government employment of aliens, and they fired her. Dobby Walker and Al Bernstein rallied the Federal Workers Union to Decca's defense and helped her quickly apply for U.S. citizenship. She was swiftly reinstated. "Soon all the government offices in San Francisco were blanketed with leaflets announcing: UNION SCORES DOUBLE VICTORY! . . . OPA KEEPS TRAINED INVESTIGATOR! Decca later wrote: "in my enthusiasm, I mailed a copy of the victory leaflet to my mother. She replied, 'I wish I knew what the "union" is, to me it means the union of South African Republics.'"[31]

Decca had embarked on a long campaign to win over her mother-in-law, Aranka. Aranka, as Bob put it, "was rather put out when I married Decca without consulting her."[32] Aranka did not think "a *Shiksha* of radical persuasion with a two-year-old child" was right for her son, and she did not hesitate to make that known.[33] She was a first-generation Hungarian Jew who had clawed her way up from routine millinery work (one of the few occupations open to female Jewish immigrants) to proprietor of a fashionable Park Avenue hat shop. She was a shapely, round-faced woman with a very sharp verbal edge and deep ambitions for her Bobby, as she persistently referred to Bob.[34] She acknowledged that Decca was very beautiful: she could see in the photos Bob showed her that Decca was slender and poised, with arresting eyes, a strong chin, wavy hair, and a warm smile. But Decca, Aranka feared, failed to understand the importance of social codes and would hold her Bobby back.

Decca said that Aranka was "vile" to her in the early days of her marriage.[35] Yet in her letters to Aranka, Decca was warm, chatty, light, and amusing. She flattered Aranka, mocked herself, and focused on things she knew Aranka would like, such as what a star Bob was at work. "Everybody in the office here is so much looking forward to Bob getting out [here], as I've told them what a wonderful source of ideas etc. he will be.[36] Nevertheless, "it took some time for her to accept the idea," Bob admitted, of Decca as a daughter-in-law.[37]

In September 1943, though she had just learned she was pregnant and was finding all travel exhausting, Decca took Dinky on a twenty-hour flight from San Francisco to New York (Bob was still in D.C.) to meet Aranka and Bob's sister, Edith.[38] In her Upper East Side apartment on Sixty-Eighth Street, Aranka showered Constancia with toys. She lavished Decca—even more beautiful than Aranka expected—with all the things Aranka wanted Bob to strive for: linens, good clothes, and fine bone china.[39] Aranka gifted what she would have liked for herself, Decca learned.

Decca's desires were not for things. Later that month, "in a dark corner," Dobby finally popped the question. "Would you two be interested in joining the Communist Party?" Decca and Bob, both elected along with Dobby as delegates to the National Congress of Industrial Unions (CIO) convention in Fresno, said an enthusiastic "yes" and had a "thrilling" time, joining thousands who sang "Solidarity Forever" and meeting some of their heroes, a few still carrying the "scars of picket line battles, impressive arrest records, service in the Abraham Lincoln

Brigade."[40] We "wondered when" you were going to ask us, they both teased Dobby, beaming over their invitations.[41]

Waiting to be invited might seem odd today. As Bob later explained: "They [members of the Party] would exercise great care. They had to know you for some long period of time. . . . You had to wait until you were asked."[42] Rose Podmaka, a former steel mill worker and Communist, remembered: "They weren't having mass recruiting; you had to prove that you were a worthy individual that they could trust."[43]

Invitations were formal. Initiations were not. Those who joined the Party, like Decca and Bob, received a membership card in a fake name and began attending fundraisers, meetings, and Educationals (what we would now call study groups). Bob kept his membership card all his life. It was made out in the name of Rufus Timebolt (R.T.) and listed membership rates on the back for the upcoming period of July 1–December 31, 1944: "$1.00/month for those earning over $30/week; .50/month for those earning $20–30/week; $.25/month for those earning less than $20/week."[44] Each member joined a unit—or club, sometimes called a local after the unions—closest to their home, and each club was run democratically, with rotating leadership among all members. Clubs were social. "You had a kind of a whole total world that was very rich in many ways," one member from the time remarked. "Shared passions for social transformation" created "social bonds" that members did not experience elsewhere. This was especially true for women, as feminist historians explain.[45] "Our lives had purpose," one California Communist remembered. "We made lasting friends . . . and we had fun."[46] A California Party leader put it this way: "We had a counterculture from the thirties and forties that I would suggest was far more all-powerful, all-inclusive than anything that the generation of the sixties had created."[47] Decca worked best when she worked closely with others. The club culture was perfect for her.

No other political organization addressed the range of issues Decca and Bob cared about. As he later put it:

It was the only place where Blacks, called Negroes in those days, were respected; the only place where women's rights were being talked about; and if you had a liberal point of view, the Communist party was the liberal party. . . . And we knew the people that we were associating with were joining, not out of any interest in advancing themselves, but they were doing it in recognition of the fact that they were exposing themselves to loss of jobs and to loss of advancement in the government and that part of society. So we didn't ever feel that we were sacrificing anything at all. We were in there, not purely from the point of view of doing good, but because we enjoyed doing things with the people that we liked, and we also enjoyed the kind of struggle that we were engaged in.[48]

Decca was "enchanted by the flesh-and-blood Communists" she met. Party membership, she discovered, required intense study and self-education, in history and economics especially. It was just what she craved. It countered, Decca said, "the scorn in which intellectuals were held by my parents." She and Bob read *Capital* to each other in bed. Their local San Francisco Communist group, the Southside Club, "held meetings that lasted far into the night to study and dissect draft resolutions from the national office, to scrutinize papers submitted by club members. . . . It is hard to convey," Decca wrote, "the sort of alchemy at work in those discussions." She was proud not only to be a "carrier of the torch against Fascism," but also proud to be a student, at last.[49]

Decca joined the Communist Party at what she later called "a curious moment in its history: the Browder Period."[50] Unlike his predecessor in 1942, William Z. Foster, Communist Party General Secretary Earl

Browder felt that the Party should be a form of "20th Century Americanism," a viable ally of capitalism and government. In May 1944, in a highly controversial move, he effectively dissolved the Party to replace it with a political association called "the Communist Political Organization." National membership in the CPUSA had suffered from the non-aggression pact the Soviet Union had secretly signed with Hitler, and also as a consequence of the 1940 Smith Act, which made advocating or encouraging the overthrow of the U.S. government a crime. Browder thought he could increase membership and build alliances.[51]

In Decca's view, he was setting aside "the goal of socialism for the foreseeable future." She agreed that defeating fascism and supporting the war effort had to remain the Party's most important goal, but she was "secretly disappointed that its revolutionary goals seemed to have faded away." She was not alone. "Many comrades," Decca wrote, "had deep reservations about the Browder policies."[52] The California Communist Party had more than six thousand members.[53] It prided itself on concentrating during this period on issues that other progressive groups were weak on, especially civil rights and racial justice. The women members of the Southside Club were almost all feminists. The club's priorities, however, were not.

The Southside Club spent long hours discussing and debating Browder's policies. They believed in the practice of democratic centralism, where everyone voted, and every vote was binding. Decca bent rules at work but played by the rules the Party laid down. Loyalty was one of her core values. The Browder period allowed her to demonstrate her political loyalty. She showed herself "more than willing to accept the leadership of those far more experienced than I," even when that meant having little influence on agendas and priorities.[54]

Decca's club recognized her talents almost immediately. She was quickly drawn into organizing, invited to lead discussions at the one-hour weekly Educationals, and proved herself to have a particular genius for fundraising, much of which was designed to support the San Francisco Party's daily newspaper, *The People's World.*[55] After years of wanting to study journalism, Decca's fundraising—part of her uncanny and lifelong ability to get others to do her bidding—finally brought her closer to another goal. For the rest of her life, persuasion and reporting would remain strongly linked.

The People's World, founded in 1938, was ambitious and original. It bowed to neither Communist nor journalistic conventions. According to its first editor, Al Richmond, "in the California Party there was an openness that may not have existed elsewhere" and that allowed the paper a "spontaneity and improvisation" that gave it a "distinct flavor."[56] Richmond, barely older than Decca, was willing to try things that a more established Communist paper, like *The Daily Worker*, was not. He gave a young Woody Guthrie a column, and he gave journalists such as writer, editor, and illustrator Pele de Lappe an unusually free hand. The paper operated with essentially no budget, a daily crisis, and a great deal of frenzied activity.[57]

Decca was allowed to go at fundraising in her own way. Where most people dreaded asking for money, Decca rather enjoyed it. *A Fine Old Conflict* devotes a chapter to her fundraising antics:

> *I gave a PW [People's World] fund-raising party in our flat at Mrs. Tibbs's [Mrs. Betts], at which we charged fifty cents admission and fifty cents per drink, phenomenally steep prices for those days. Since the attendance was small, and I feared we should fail to raise the sum we had had hoped for, I started improvising more rules: fifty cents a drink, but twenty-five cents to* refuse *a drink; ten cents for use of the lavatory, five cents extra for toilet paper; a seventy-five-cent exit fee for those leaving before 1 a.m. This terrible party became the talk of the town, and word of it soon reached the county leadership. Shortly thereafter, I was called by Oleta [Yates], who*

informed me that I had been nominated for the full-time job of county financial director.[58]

According to one attendee, Decca followed the notorious party with an even more notorious apology. She sent letters to everyone who'd attended, apologizing if they were offended. Then she promised not to hold another such party *if* they'd immediately remit the amount that such a second party would cost them.[59] Finding the fun in situations that seemed odious to others would later become a signature of her writing and the core of how she lived her life.

Decca's CP fundraising also drew her attention to what she would later dub the American way of death. CP members were urged to donate blood to raise funds and support the war effort. Decca did so as soon as she was asked. In the process, she made the discovery that when people died away from home, funeral directors paid escorts to bring their bodies back. Party members, she immediately proposed, should put themselves forward as escorts for the dead. They could not only raise money and meet new people, but with a little careful planning, pay their way to conventions and meetings located where the bodies were, she explained. She also proposed that Party members register to donate their bodies to science and give their seventy-five-dollar payment back to the Party. "Motions Defeated," Decca noted sadly.

"Motions Defeated" aside, the fall of 1943 was a peaceful season for Decca. San Francisco's autumn was spectacular that year, with lots of dry weather and wonderful, golden light. Bob finally returned to San Francisco full time and began working for the War Labor Board, which shared office space in the Furniture Mart with the OPA. Focused on arbitrating grievances to forestall wartime strikes, the War Labor Board exercised broad authority over American labor relations. It pushed for changes that Bob and Decca cared deeply about, such as equal pay for equal work for women and restrictions on racial discrimination.[60] Once again, Decca and Bob could eat lunch together every day, trading strategies and gossip. Decca told Bob that she still wanted to become a journalist. She thought she might leave the OPA.

Through *The People's World*, Decca became especially close to Pele de Lappe. Pele was just a few months older than Decca, but she'd been an activist and a feminist for years. Her Party bona fides were unimpeachable. Where Dobby Walker was admirable, but often severe, Pele had a silly side. She offered a more relaxed model of activism, which Decca found appealing. At *The People's World*, Pele had created an illustrated column offering a Communist pin-up girl to dispense advice on organizing and Marxist theory, while dangling a mule and smiling seductively.[61] The "Vicky Says" column was controversial. It was both feminist—a bombshell as Marxist dialectician—and irreverent toward both feminist and Marxist axioms. Decca loved it.

As an artist, Pele worked in the spirit and style of Thomas Hart Benton, Reginald Marsh, and other social realists, the sort of representational work Decca understood and liked. She was a young mother and, like Decca, the wife of a left-wing Jewish lawyer, Bertram Edises (whom she married in 1935 and whose law firm Bob later joined). A stylish, attractive woman, with dark hair, wide-set eyes, a thin face, and a very full mouth, Pele did what she wanted to do, secure in both her talent and her left-wing credentials. She wore makeup and loved to dress in costumes, the bolder her clothing, the better. As the daughter of bohemians, Pele had an upbringing that Decca envied. She had studied at the Art Students League in New York; been a habitué of black Harlem in the 1930s; had a large jazz collection; knew the great Mexican artists Siqueiros, Kahlo, and Rivera; modeled for Rivera and Kahlo; traveled in Europe and Polynesia; and been arrested twice before she was eighteen. Her drawings of strikers, workers, and demonstrators appeared on political posters and book covers throughout the Bay Area.[62] Pele and Decca were in the same Communist local.[63] Decca struck Pele as "very jolly and . . . friendly and . . . amusing right off the bat . . . terribly brave . . . and deliciously funny, with a great sense of humor that a lot of other people just don't have."[64] She encouraged Decca's playfulness.

The gender politics of the Party in the early 1940s were deeply contradictory. War industries brought women into factories. Vast new federal agencies, such as the OPA, also opened up new jobs for women, many of whom were newly college educated but having to fight to be heard and taken seriously. But women were told to hand those jobs back to men, at the drop of a hat, when men returned from battle. The Communist Party drew attention to what it called "the woman question" throughout the war. Yet, it both "idealized women's roles," as one historian notes, and "pushed them [women] to transcend those roles and to work alongside men in political organizing."[65] Dobby largely ignored sexism, outperforming all the men around her. Pele mocked sexism with powerful sex appeal. Both strategies had a big impact on Decca.

California Communists had unusually strong female political leadership, including Dorothy Healey, head of the Southern California Party; Oleta Yates, chair of the Northern California Communist Party; Celeste Strack, State Communist Party education director; and Louise Todd, State Party secretary. David Jenkins, director of the California Labor School, remarked that "the Party leadership itself was dominated by women, at least in the San Francisco area."[66] Women were also prominent in the California Labor School and *The People's World*, which serialized Mary Inman's hard-hitting "In Woman's Defense," contending that women were subjugated as a group. "In Woman's Defense" attacked sexism in child-rearing and mass culture, argued against the denigration of housework, and deflated the sexual double standard.

Decca's sensational fundraising for *The People's World* fueled her promotion to local financial director for the Party. In her new position, she shared an office with Clarence Rossman, another of her "first Real Communists." Decca admired his "single-minded devotion" and called him "my mentor." Like Al Bernstein, Rossman had retained the "unwavering optimism of childhood." While female role models like Dobby and Pele encouraged Decca to forge a significant role in the Party, male role models like Bernstein and Rossman strengthened her resolve to do so without becoming grim or joyless. In the fall of 1943, Decca truthfully could say that "our lives as Communists were informed by a supremely optimistic view of the human potential."[67]

Her optimism was both generative and hard won. While both she and Bob were safe and comfortable, the war remained brutal and unpredictable. From fuel shortages to fierce fighting in faraway places like the Solomon Islands, to increasing awareness of Nazi genocide and fascist repression, each day was a steady drip of bad news. Both Decca and Bob felt deeply for those who were suffering in ways that they were not. They wanted to avoid guilt and take responsible action. Decca particularly wanted to compensate for her family's complicity with fascism and Nazism, their refusal to see their many privileges as she saw them—as unearned and unfair.

On November 3, 1943, the war took an especially dark turn, with the largest single-day Nazi massacre of Jews.[68] Intense fighting continued in the Pacific and the Atlantic, between American and German submarines and between Japanese and American forces on the ground. There were bombings in Greece and Austria. The Germans expanded their extermination plans, rounding up those they called Gypsies and sending them to concentration camps.

Decca was not spared reminders of her family connections to the horrors. Mitford hell broke loose on November 18, 1943. Oswald Mosley had become seriously ill with phlebitis, a potentially life-threatening vein inflammation for which little treatment then existed.[69] As a result, after almost four years in jail, he and Diana were suddenly released from Holloway Prison. A "storm of protest" erupted in Britain and in America. Releasing Diana and Mosley was a "gross betrayal" and a "stab in the back to the British people," protesters said. Tens of thousands of demonstrators immediately took to the streets to protest the release. Resolutions were passed demanding reinternment. *The Daily Worker* mockingly asked, "How much phlebitis is Rudolf Hess going to have soon?"[70] The Communist Party circulated petitions demanding that they return to prison immediately. Protests in Trafalgar Square became a "tidal wave" of rage, with demonstrators also swarming the London Underground stations.[71] Decca's sister Nancy wrote Diana that protests were so universal that to get onto the tube one had "to join a queue & shout in unison 'Put Him Back.' If you didn't shout you were flung out of the queue & no chance of getting to the Underground!"[72] Stickers reading "Put Mosley back in GAOL!" were pasted onto British mail.[73]

Decca was "furious . . . to hear that the Mosleys have been released. . . . I think it is a real act of treachery against everybody who is fighting in this war," she wrote her mother.[74] "I do hope they are not staying with you because if they are I feel I shall have to stop writing to anyone in the same house with them."[75] Diana and Mosley had been granted special privileges inside Holloway Prison, including their own apartment and inmate servants. Spirited out of a side door at Holloway, they'd been whisked away by police to a "wonderful welcome" from Decca's sister Pam and her husband, Derek, who showered them with "delicious food, beautiful wine," "soft, fine linen," and "soft warm beds."[76] Now they were granted additional special privileges upon release. Not allowed to live in London or to own a car, they were nevertheless free to establish a luxurious residence in the English countryside. A British police officer was detailed to guard them.[77] Decca did not know that Sydney had interceded on their behalf. At Diana's request, Sydney had gone to see her cousin Clementine Churchill, Winston's wife, with the hope that Clementine would put in a good word to Churchill. As Esmond's aunt, Clementine might well have felt some of the same rage that Decca felt toward the Mosleys. "It was a difficult interview," writes one biographer of the family, with Clementine suggesting that "the Mosleys were better off in prison as they would probably be lynched if released."[78]

Decca learned little of this from her mother's letters. Those remained cheerful and filled with news such as Debo being pregnant again, the challenges of hiring good help, and "ordinary housework" being really "so easy" that she could manage just fine without extensive staff.[79] Decca knew there had to be more. She again stopped communicating with her mother.

Reporters dogged her relentlessly. They could not get past Mrs. Betts, but they showed up at the OPA, pleading for a comment on the Mosley release. Finally, she broke her "cherished anonymity" to denounce the release.[80] First, she wrote a public letter to Winston Churchill, then published a version of it in the *San Francisco Chronicle*:

Dear Cousin Winston:

I am writing to you to add my protest to the thousands which I imagine you are receiving against the release of the Mosleys.

Their release is being interpreted in this country, even by the reactionary press, as an indication that there is a real cleavage between the will of the people and the actions of the ruling class in England, and that the Government is not truly dedicated to the cause of exterminating fascism in whatever place and in whatever form it rears its head. Unless the Mosleys are immediately put back in jail where they belong great harm will be done to the cause of friendship between Britain and America.

My personal feeling is that the release of the Mosleys is a slap in the face to antifascists in every country, and that it is a direct betrayal of those who have died for the cause of anti-fascism.

The fact that Diana is my sister doesn't alter my opinion on this subject.[81]

Decca acknowledged that she might be seen as unsisterly. If there had been "an element of hostility or prejudice" toward Decca in the Party, given "her background . . . you know the whole Lady Redesdale Syndrome," Decca's statements that "family ties should [not] be allowed to influence a person's convictions" did much to lay those to rest.[82]

Decca was now thoroughly disenchanted with the OPA. On December 15, more than four months pregnant (but telling only Bob), she quit. With Bob's salary coming in, she felt free to devote her working hours—sometimes as many as sixty hours a week or more—to the Federal Workers Union, the Party, and the Joint Anti-Fascist Refugee Committee (JAFRC), which she'd recently joined and where she'd been promoted to San Francisco director, her second promotion to a directorial position in only a few months. Dedicated to providing aid to refugees of the Spanish Civil War, especially in France, the JAFRC was largely comprised of veterans of the Spanish Civil War. It was supported nationally by many famous progressives, including Leonard Bernstein, Albert Einstein, Lillian Hellman, Langston Hughes, Paul Robeson, and Orson Welles.[83] Decca was not only a skilled fundraiser; she was also excellent with celebrities: unfazed, direct, and unselfconscious, regardless of anyone else's renown.

After Christmas, Decca and Bob were both laid low with flu. While they were still sick in bed, in early January, Aranka decided to visit. It was not a good time. Yet since Decca was still off speakers with Muv, who had not answered the question of whether or not she was seeing Diana, she did not want to turn away what little family she had.[84] The visit, she later wrote, was "a total disaster":

Aranka arrived via the Tibbs boardinghouse, descended the wooden fire escape [the only way to access their apartment without going

*through Mrs. Betts's home] burdened with furs, hatboxes, luggage,
and a little yapping black dog on a lead, took one look at us, and
burst into tears . . . After this inauspicious beginning things did
not improve. I tried to be a good daughter-in-law, to fall in with
Aranka's ideas about the proper care and treatment of Bob, yet I
seldom succeeded in pleasing. She confided that Bob, like his father,
was not sufficiently motivated to rise in the world, to get ahead,
to earn more money. My role as a wife should be to instill these
aspirations by being more demanding. I should insist on having a
fur coat, a better car, costly objects that would compel him to set his
monetary goals ever higher. . . . The next morning as Bob . . . set off
to catch the Haight Street trolley, I leaned out the window and . . .
bellowed, "Get to work, you lazy good-for-nothing bum! . . . I want
a new coat! . . . I want a car!" . . . But my performance did not find
favor with Aranka.*[85]

Decca had the gift of complete indifference to domestic chaos.
Her fierce concentration allowed her to work anywhere. If the clut-
ter of Communist daily life—leaflets, books, diapers, clippings, white
papers, bills, posters, and groceries—covered every surface, Decca swept
the mess sideways and got down to work. All her life she worked in
pass-throughs and public spaces, hallways and foyers, never seeking
a walled-off study, even when there was space and money enough to
afford one. She was undisturbed by people nearby when she worked.
Aranka was horrified.

After the holidays, Constancia started school. Decca's U.S. citizenship was finalized, and she was naturalized on January 3, 1944. By
March, she was missing communication with her mother. She decided
to write, thank Sydney for her homemade Christmas gifts (so much
better than Aranka's store-bought ones), and explain her long silence.
"I see in the papers that they [the Mosleys] are living in Shipton [about

183

four miles from Swinbrook], so I suppose you do see them—I was so disgusted when they were released, & so much in sympathy with the demonstrators against their release that it actually makes me feel like a traitor to write to anyone who has anything to do with them," she wrote. Decca was now twenty-six. Her next lines would probably not have been possible a few years earlier. "I see," she added, "that it is difficult for you & not your fault!" This was an olive branch letter. Constancia was then in the habit of packing her little suitcase whenever she was angry. "We think she has running away blood in her," Decca joked to her mother.[86]

Nancy reached out that same March. "I do long for news of you," she wrote Decca warmly.[87] Decca replied. She sent pictures of Dinky. She invited Nancy to visit after the war, reprising a bit of their old teasing rapport. If you don't visit, Decca wrote, "I shall probably never see you. Do come Susan I long to see you not getting on with Americans."[88] Visiting America was the last thing on Nancy's mind. The previous year, 1943, she had fallen hopelessly in love with Gaston Palewski, a charming, but irrepressibly womanizing commander in the Free French forces and Charles de Gaulle's cabinet director. In March 1944, she was focused on finding a way to move from England to Paris, in wartime, to be nearer to him. Her affair with him would dominate the rest of her life. Palewski enjoyed Nancy's company, but not to the exclusion of other women.

On May 16, 1944, at Stanford University Hospital in San Francisco's posh Pacific Heights neighborhood, Decca gave birth to Nicholas Tito Treuhaft. She had her first experience with caudal anesthetic (also known as an epidural) and loved it, not in the least interested in so-called natural childbirth and thrilled that she and Bob were able to return to a bedside cribbage game only hours after the birth. (Much later, in *The American Way of Birth*, she came to question the highly medicalized, physician-attended, hospital birth—still a relatively new phenomenon nationally—that she enjoyed at Stanford Hospital.) She "felt really swell" up to, during, and after Nicholas's birth, she told Aranka, still working to improve their relationship.[89] Decca said that the baby was "named after Lenin & Marshal Tito to annoy the P's [parents]," but they called him "Mong"—"because of his Mongolian eyes . . . Bob is partly Mongolian," she said, though he was, in fact, Hungarian."[90]

Nicholas's birth, to Decca's surprise, brought a letter from her father, the only direct word she'd had from him since eloping (and the last time she would ever hear from him). Stirred, perhaps, by a traditionalist's gratification at the birth of a son (he did not reach out after Julia's birth, nor after Constancia's), David wrote "just to send you my love and every good wish for him and his future. Some day, when things are in a more settled state, I greatly hope to see you all, and judging from all news and the look of things it seems to me there is some prospect that I may last that long—I should much like to."[91]

In June, Decca received yet another promotion, this time to financial director of the California Labor School. She went back to work shortly after D-Day, leaving Nicholas and Constancia both in the care of Mrs. Betts. By 1944, the California Labor School had taught more than six thousand people. With that number now doubling yearly, it had outgrown its suite of rooms on Turk Street, above a car dealership and showroom. The school purchased a five-story building on Market Street, which allowed for considerable expansion of facilities and curriculum. It also opened a school in Oakland. Decca was hired to direct the Oakland branch by David Jenkins, an old friend of Bob's. Jenkins had only an eighth-grade formal education and was only three years Decca's senior.[92] He had high regard for her self-education, intelligence, and work ethic. In her new position, Decca would be responsible for everything from budgeting to curriculum and hiring faculty.

Oakland's branch of the Labor School had an almost exclusively male board of directors, but Decca joined many women who taught there and worked on the staff. (The financial director of the San Francisco

School in 1944 was also a woman, Lucille Austin.) There were fewer classes than in San Francisco, but the branch had its own library and scholarships.[93] In its first semester, in fall 1944, classes varied from Postwar Reconstruction to Science for the Future (everything from hormones to insecticides, taught by representatives of Shell Oil and the California Spray Chemical Co., among others) to Photography and Childrearing and Development (taught by professors of Psychology, Home Economics, the superintendent of Berkeley Public Schools, and the day care director of the local Council of Churches). As with the San Francisco campus, the Oakland branch was funded by nearly one hundred unions and designed, as its catalogue declared, "to forge a progressive anti-fascist program. . . . representative of the great majority of the common people."[94] There were also lectures that were offered free. Director Dave Jenkins said it was "the most popular lecture series in the city.[95] "My job is to raise funds to keep the school going, write publicity, etc. I think it will be very interesting," Decca wrote her mother.[96]

Decca's memoirs say little about directing the California Labor School. But it was a remarkable job for a woman who had always felt diminished by her lack of education. Along with the Party's readings and Educationals, the School also gave her a crucial opportunity to engage in the kind of in-depth, intense study she craved. *The People's World* provided Decca with journalistic experience. The California Labor School offered many journalism classes and extensive training in a range of skills useful to journalists. Not surprisingly, especially for a school run by Communists and originally founded by Lincoln Steffens, the California Labor School especially prized exposés and investigative reporting.

Decca was loving her new life, although it did have its challenges. She had a long daily commute from San Francisco to Oakland. After traveling back home, getting inside was always daunting. She either had to climb back down the fire escape or traipse through Mrs. Betts's living room. "When we get home at night," she wrote Aranka, "it is like moving an army with all its equipment; Bob carries Nicholas in his cradle, I carry Donk & her clothes for the morning, then we have to get his bottles & her dolls."[97] She and Bob looked for a better apartment without luck. "No landlords will rent to those with children (I mean in San Francisco, which is fearfully overcrowded)."[98] Bob joined the radical labor law firm Gladstein, Grossman, Sawyer & Edises (Decca called it "Gallstones, Gruesome, Sewer & Odious") founded by Pele's husband, Bertram Edises, which had its offices in the East Bay, not far from Decca's new office.[99] "It is exactly the job he has been wanting, so we are awfully pleased," Decca wrote her mother.[100]

A brilliant lawyer, Jewish and Marxist, like Bob, Bert Edises was "attractive, with beautiful brown eyes and a thoughtful manner," wrote Pele. Like Bob, he was "a fiendish prankster." But Bob was even keeled, while Bert suffered from undiagnosed mental health problems, producing extreme mood swings and occasional collapses that rendered him unable to work, or get out of bed, for days at a time.[101] Both Bob and Decca were fond of him, as they were of Pele, and Bob willingly took up the slack when necessary.[102] Decca believed she'd had little prior exposure to mental health issues—to her, Esmond's volatility and Unity's obsessiveness were just personality quirks—and she found herself very interested in Bert's struggles.

In the late summer of 1944, still unable to find a suitable rental, Decca and Bob bought their first home, at 956 Clayton Street, about half a mile uphill from their boardinghouse, in an area of mostly two-family homes, in the heart of Haight-Asbury, on a street lined with large southern magnolias. Their neighbors were mostly salespeople and stenographers, cab drivers and librarians, warehouse workers and machine operators. There were few doctors or lawyers, but an optometrist practiced around the corner.[103] The house they bought—heavily remodeled and gentrified now, but still standing—was substantial.[104] It had a small yard, bay windows overlooking the street, a large fireplace, a formal dining room, and three bedrooms, which Decca quickly filled with a nurse and the nurse's large family. "They are all going to live with us," Decca wrote her mother. "So you can see the bedrooms are going to be fairly packed."[105] Compared to Asthall, Swinbrook, or even the Durrs' home on Seminary Hill, the Clayton Street house was modest. But compared to anything Decca had lived in since leaving her family, it offered what felt like palatial excess.

Decca expected recognition in the Party for eschewing the comforts of the class she'd been born to. At the same time, however, and in a manner that sometimes confounded her closest associates, she clung to certain vestiges of her background. She used Mitford as a surname often, even when she also used Treuhaft. She never shed her distinctly aristocratic accent and lilt; some friends felt she *used* it, noting that it seemed to get more pronounced whenever she was arguing with recalcitrant Americans.[106] She also clung to domestic ineptitude. "Bob never ceased to marvel," she wrote, that she had so little grasp of "the rudiments of cooking . . . some minimal understanding of the properties and uses of various cleaning materials . . . but in my culturally disadvantaged childhood (I kept explaining) one did not actually see the housework done, as it would have all been finished early, before we came down in the morning."[107] Over the kitchen sink, she hung quotes from Lenin on the "unproductive . . . barbarous . . . arduous . . . petty" labor performed by women in the home.[108] She might not have called these critiques of domestic labor feminist—to her they were straightline Marxism—but she never organized her households on traditionally gendered lines. At twenty-seven, owning her first home, what she liked were labor-saving appliances. She even invented "an automatic bed maker & an automatic machine for picking up soiled diapers," fanciful machines that she sketched out in detail and that, of course, were never made. "I don't want a Bendix any more since seeing an ad for a Thor combined washing machine & dishwasher," she wrote Aranka. "I spent yesterday hunting for one & enquiring for additional fixtures which will put the children to bed. No luck so far."[109]

Through the fall and winter, Paris was liberated and Roosevelt was re-elected (Decca spent months campaigning for him and often took both children leafleting door to door). As the Red Army moved into Auschwitz and Birkenau, Decca continued trying to "do all in my power to overcome the handicaps of birth and upbringing."[110] Occasionally she tried to disguise her background altogether, making up professions for her ancestors.

On March 24, 1945, her brother, Tom, was hit in the neck and chest by Japanese sniper machine-gun fire in Burma, where he was leading Indian troops. His infantry regiment, the First Devonshire, had been in Burma for almost two years, following the Japanese capture of Rangoon, Burma's capital, in an attempt to hold one of Britain's valuable colonies. Tom was in Burma as a representative of the Empire. He had never told the family about the difficult and disease-ridden conditions he suffered there. They heard about it after his death, adding to the "ghastly blow," as Pamela put it.[111] Decca had loved Tom dearly and in spite of years with little communication, his death devastated her. She wrote to her mother:

My Darling Muv,

I have tried to write several times since getting the terrible news about Tudemy [the family's nickname for Tom]. I felt so awful about it & couldn't think of anything comforting to say, because to me it seems that anyone who was killed in this war has died for the most magnificent cause in history—but I don't know if you would agree . . . I think that at last you do agree, and that you see that it would be better for us all to be wiped out than to live in the same world with the Nazis. Esmond used to say that long ago, in the days of the Spanish war.[112]

Sydney said little in reply, leaving Decca to wonder "whether developments in the last ten years have yet proved to you what a criminal thing it was to have supported Hitler."[113]

By what she called a "fluke" of Scottish inheritance law after Tom's death, Decca came into one-sixth ownership, along with all her sisters, of Inch Kenneth, the small Scottish island in the Inner Hebrides which David and Sydney had purchased in 1938. They'd bought the island after Decca and Esmond left England, so Decca had never seen it. Inch Kenneth is one the smallest of three hundred or so islands in the Hebrides, about a mile long and half a mile wide. When David and Sydney purchased it from Sir Harold Boulton, the hilly island contained sheep, outbuildings, a generator, and a white stucco fifteen-room manor house, tucked between hills across a channel from the tiny hamlet of Gribun, on the Isle of Mull.

Sydney hated the "absolutely hideous" house, she said initially, but she adored the island.[114] She furnished the house with books, a piano, French furniture, an enormous dining table, Harold Acton's sketches of her daughters, and paintings. She gardened. She had groceries delivered from London and sent her laundry back to London to be cleaned at Harrod's. She hired help. On warm days she took a frigid dip off the small beach below the house.[115] Every window offered views of dark blue water framed by gray-green cliffs that seemed to float on the surface rather than rise from the sea. The nights were a rich dark black, thick with stars. A profusion of hardy wildflowers grew out of Inch Kenneth's mossy granite rocks. As soon as she could get clearance to take Unity out of England, Sydney had taken her there, away from the flashbulbs of the press.

After Tom's death, Debo, Diana, Nancy, and Pamela promised their mother a life tenancy on Inch Kenneth. They neglected to consult Decca. Her sixth, she decided, would go to the British Communist Party. "Since a share of the island has come my way, I am determined that it shall be put to a good use," she wrote her mother. "My share will go to undo some of the harm that our family has done," she added.[116] Inch Kenneth was expensive to maintain. It was extremely difficult to access, requiring an overnight train from London to Oban, a ferry crossing to Mull, a long one-track drive across Mull to Gribun, and a rowboat to the island. The roof leaked. The kitchen was, unaccountably, built below grade. In any rainstorm, the navy-blue kitchen floor filled with one to two inches of water. This was not the sort of donation the Party was accustomed to receiving. In the end, unable to give the island away, Decca agreed to Sydney's life tenancy and provided for it herself, buying out her sisters' shares and becoming sole owner of the island.

For years, Decca had been looking into whether any funds were due to her, as Esmond's widow. The process so severely strained her relationship with Esmond's mother, Nellie Romilly, that Nellie did not inform Decca when Esmond's brother, Giles, was finally rescued from Colditz in May. Aranka, of all people, was the one to give Decca the startling news that Esmond's brother, Giles Romilly, imprisoned by the Germans since 1940, had been rescued. "Aranka read it in a New York paper," Decca wrote her mother.[117]

Decca's feelings about her family were intense, conflicted, and troubling. In spite of how profoundly her family feelings determined her choices, Decca was, and would remain, as disconnected from the Mitfords as she could manage. Yet her feelings for them threaded through all aspects of her life.

By September 1945, at war's end and at twenty-eight years of age, Decca had found her own political footing and was a woman others looked to for political leadership, information, and strategies. Yet even the end of the war, on September 2, prompted no political commentary in her personal letters home to her family.

10

"A Terrific Hater"

Venom against the enemies of humanity.[1]
—JESSICA MITFORD

itfords were stubborn. Decca's first memoir, *Hons and Rebels*, ends with her fond remembrances of "terrific haters": those who did not prevaricate or knuckle under. Even when they were misguided, she wrote, her family demonstrated a consistency of purpose and belief that she admired. It was one of the things she loved most about Unity. Unity, she said, "was always a terrific hater." The trick, Decca explained, was remaining steadfast to the right causes, and that is what Unity, Diana, and Sydney all got wrong. Unity, Decca proudly recalled, could reduce others to near panic with "one of her smoldering looks of loathing." But she smoldered indiscriminately. Esmond had also smoldered. He was an especially "gifted hater." And he remained discriminate. Esmond's "venom against the enemies of humanity, peace and freedom" was fueled by a "strong and perfectly genuine love for his fellow man."[2]

Decca admired fierceness. But unlike both Esmond and Unity, who stomped through the world largely oblivious to how others saw them, Decca cared deeply about how she was perceived. Praise and recognition meant the world to her. She worried that she was too apt to anticipate others' concerns (perhaps a writer's greatest gift). Was it a weakness, she wondered, like her constant need for dialogue? What did it mean to be so critical of society and yet also so profoundly, almost desperately social? "Empaths" are highly attuned to others' emotions, aware of how others think. Must an empath approve of what they discern? Could one be an angry empath? Decca was. She couldn't understand why others saw her as "terribly brave," as Pele put it, "totally gutsy," in Marge Frantz's words, the bravest woman Bob had ever met, he often said. She didn't see herself that way. In fact, she wished that her convictions were firmer.

The second half of the 1940s seemed designed to test Decca's fortitude. Becoming the activist she envisaged meant questioning every norm and convention of an increasingly conformist postwar world. It meant being skeptical of all calls to national loyalty, doggedly resisting mainstream thinking, and always standing up to the hysterical anti-communist Red Scare by fighting loyalty oaths, the Smith Act, the McCarran Act, and the many state and national Un-American Activities Committees that coalesced by the end of the decade into McCarthyism. Meeting her own political aspirations meant not only refusing to name names—that went without saying—but also ruthless rejection of those who caved to such pressure and those, like her English family, who aided and abetted the enemy.

The postwar period challenged all progressives to make hard choices about their alliances. The emergent Civil Rights Movement and a nascent feminism also challenged radicals, like Decca, who had already pledged allegiance and energy to workers and labor. Throughout the Left, struggles over alignment led to factionalism and infighting.

Decca scrutinized her own choices carefully. For her, the personal and the political would always be intricately knotted. When she persisted, across the decade, with efforts to give Inch Kenneth to the Party, comrades such as Claude Cockburn detected a telltale "light in her eye . . . she had in mind something a little more spicy than just the welfare of ozone-starved Communists."[3] Postwar consumption promoted goods as compensation for the sacrifices of war. As Decca and Bob settled into their new marriage, and Bob eventually began to earn money as a lawyer, they could afford a few indulgences: a house, appliances, a new car, desert vacations, fresh paint. Decca liked nice things. She just wanted them equally distributed so that everyone could enjoy them. Would letting herself have the things she craved make her less sensitive to what others lacked? Could she avoid becoming a sellout, she wondered?

Hard work kept Decca humble. In the early winter of 1946, she accepted Communist Party assignments hand over fist. She served on the board of directors of the Oakland Branch of the California Labor School. She became financial director for the San Francisco Communist Party. She represented her local CP branch—the Twin Peaks Club—at conferences and meetings, as an usher, and as a member of the Arrangements and the Credentials committees. She was an official representative to the Lenin Memorial meeting, the Northern California Conference on Industry, and the 1946 Party Leadership Institute, where she presented a paper on "Why and How to Achieve the Maximum Financial Contribution to the Party." She raced from event to event, as speaker, coordinator, organizer, or moderator. Bob was working. They had a new housekeeper. Dinky seemed fine. Decca rarely said no.

Decca's pace was frenetic, reflecting her growing sense of being under siege. A series of legislative moves laid the groundwork for what Decca called "a grotesque period in American history," creating "the soil for the noxious growth of McCarthyism."[4] On February 15, 1946, twenty-two Communists were indicted in Canada and charged with being Soviet spies. Labor strikes turned bloody. Decca and Bob were under such relentless government surveillance that even their most minor meetings were clocked and noted. The scrutiny seemed absurd, but added to their sense that even little actions might have big consequences. To Decca, that meant they could not afford any slips.

"The CP was a great believer in forms and charts," Decca complained.[5] Her Party responsibilities came with lots of the paperwork she loathed—the thankless jobs that went into being what Decca called a dedicated "foot soldier" in the Party. Sometimes she deliberately dropped the ball on record-keeping. At one point in 1946, she was charged with failing to account properly for campaign funds and asked to resign. She dug in her heels and was reinstated. At another point that year she barely survived "a big blowup" involving new paperwork designed to prove that Party leaders came from the working class. Decca, as a leader, was prepared to adapt her own biography by putting down "miner" for her father's occupation (his gold mine in Swastika), "gardener" for her grandfather Bertie (his extensive Batsford grounds and garden), and "domestic" for her mother (her bread-baking, home-schooling, and refusal of doctors). She was spared the subterfuge. Local friends pushed her appointment through without the new forms.

Sometimes Decca still denied her background completely. Sometimes she freely acknowledged that her background had shaped her. She'd become a rebel, she occasionally admitted, as an extension of the "strong streak of delinquency" she and Esmond had shared. Their "carefree intransigence . . . supreme self-confidence—a feeling of being able to walk unscathed through any flame" was "not hard to trace to an English upper-class ancestry and upbringing," she acknowledged.

As she became more radical, her attacks against the upper class and its interests remained linked to her past, with "a number of old scores to settle along the way."[6]

Now, as a committed member of the Communist Party, Decca tasked herself with dropping all privilege. It was a tall order. She decided to model what she saw as the dignified behavior of workers, Blacks, and Jews. She wrote: "The qualities of patience, modesty, forbearance and natural self-discipline that the worker brings to his struggle for a better life, the instinctive respect for the fundamental dignity of every other human being—even his enemy—so often displayed by the Negro or the Jew in his own fight for equality, were on the whole conspicuously lacking in us, or only present in the most undeveloped form."[7] This was an idealized, even a romanticized, vision. But it exerted a powerful pressure on Decca, who, at twenty-eight was young enough to believe in self-improvement and old enough to lay out an ambitious agenda for her own transformation.

She could never escape being reminded, however, that she was a Mitford. Across the winter of 1945–46, her sister Nancy's novel *The Pursuit of Love*, published in December 1945, kept a spotlight on the family. Extensive U.S. press attention—three reviews in *The New York Times* alone—meant that comparisons between herself and Nancy and reminders of her childhood, since "it's about us when we were little," Nancy said, were unavoidable.[8] *The Pursuit of Love* sold over two hundred thousand copies in its first months, earned Nancy more than £1.1 million in today's currency, was widely translated, well reviewed, and its film rights sold immediately. The Royal Family even chose the novel for its yearly Christmas gift book. Its immense popularity was largely due to its descriptions of naughty aristocratic adolescents (hunting, riding, playing pranks, and telling stories). It was "an exact portrait of my family," Nancy claimed, and its tone was much in the style of Decca and Esmond's prewar series for *The*

The Pursuit of Love's second half was a peculiarly anti-feminist tale of the love affair of Linda, a stand-in for Nancy, and her beguiling older French lover, based on Colonel Gaston Palewski. In overblown tributes to the wonders of Fabrice, Nancy (still married to Peter Rodd at the time) created a portrait of herself as a willingly subjugated and submissive lover, perversely undercutting her professional success just as her career was really taking off.[10] Nancy's novel dripped with her lifelong refusal to take anything seriously, demonstrate effort, or display honest emotion; the Mitford Tease was on every page. Decca, working so hard to be taken seriously at just this time, left little evidence about her reaction to the book.

Photographs from 1946 vividly display how different the two sisters now were. Nancy was so slender that she seemed artificially elongated, like a fashion designer's sketch: dark-eyed, dark-haired, sharp-chinned, and elegant.[11] Sitting lightly in her Paris apartment, or posed in front of her writing desk, she embodied rarified detachment with just the faintest hint of a wicked sparkle in her seductive, sidelong glance. Photographs of Decca in 1946, on the other hand, depict her looking so directly into the camera that she seems startled. She leans in. Her face is round and open. She smiles guilelessly. Nancy styled herself, and her novel, in accordance with the cardinal principle that life was a great joke and that one was never, ever, to make a fuss. Decca was in training, quite literally, to make the biggest fuss possible.[12] With war-crime tribunals, labor struggles, lynchings, famine in the Soviet Union, growing anti-communism, and at the end of the year, the start of yet another war, in Indochina, she believed that people of good conscience should never treat injustice as a joke.

The world Nancy depicted was, as one reviewer noted, "a way of life" that was already "obsolete" before the war and "now extinct."[13] All Decca's sisters, with their country homes, traditional marriages, and burnished aristocratic aesthetic, were clinging to that vanishing life. Deborah trounced them all when she attained Chatsworth, one of the largest estates in England, with hundreds of rooms, thousands of priceless artifacts, and miles of gardens and grounds. Decca and Bob lived in a modest, overcrowded house on Clayton Street in San Francisco, which they shared with housekeepers, comrades needing a place to stay, and for some months with a Japanese family needing postwar housing. Yet, even as Decca and her sisters moved farther apart, she still expressed her longing to visit and reconnect to her roots.[14]

Decca read the newspaper cover to cover first thing every morning. She read about the worst winter that Britain had seen in decades, with snow falling for fifty-five days straight. She read about food, coal, and energy shortages. She read that Unity had recovered slightly but still remained childlike, mercurial, and prone to unpredictable tempers. She read about Truman's Cold War and his many measures to deepen anti-communist sentiment: from new laws barring Communists from teaching, to investigations into Communists in Hollywood, to increased government surveillance.

In March 1947, Truman issued an executive order requiring all federal employees to sign loyalty oaths. Soon local boards were working with the FBI and the attorney general to dig into the beliefs of millions of federal employees, including all of Decca and Bob's OPA and Washington friends, the beginning of a long effort to list and register all American Communists. Decca increased her already exhausting organizing, attending conferences up and down the state of California, including the Party's Press Conference in April, its Press and Building Conference in June, and its William Z. Foster Conference in the fall.

In the summer, Decca and Bob purchased a house in Oakland and moved to the East Bay, where Bob was working.[15] Their house at 675 Jean Street was an adobe Craftsman bungalow at the bottom of a steep street across from a municipal rose garden. It had four bedrooms, a

Sydney Bowles Mitford ("Muv"),
Jessica Mitford's mother, as an
adolescent in her sailor suit, 1895.
*Unknown photographer, photo courtesy of
Constancia Romilly, Benjamin Treuhaft,
and Ben Weber.*

Sydney Bowles Mitford in 1916, painted by
Philip Alexius de László.
Photo courtesy of Mitford family.

David Freeman Mitford
("Farve"), Jessica Mitford's father,
as a young man, 1896.
*Unknown photographer, photo courtesy of
Constancia Romilly, Benjamin Treuhaft,
and Ben Weber.*

David Freeman Mitford in 1910.
*Unknown photographer, photo courtesy of Constancia Romilly,
Benjamin Treufhaft, and Ben Weber.*

David Freeman Mitford, Sydney Bowles Mitford,
and Nancy Mitford, 1906 or 1907.
*Unknown photographer, photo courtesy of Constancia Romilly,
Benjamin Treuhaft, and Ben Weber.*

Sydney Bowles Mitford in 1897
(age seventeen).
*Unknown photographer, photo courtesy of Constancia
Romilly, Benjamin Treuhaft, and Ben Weber.*

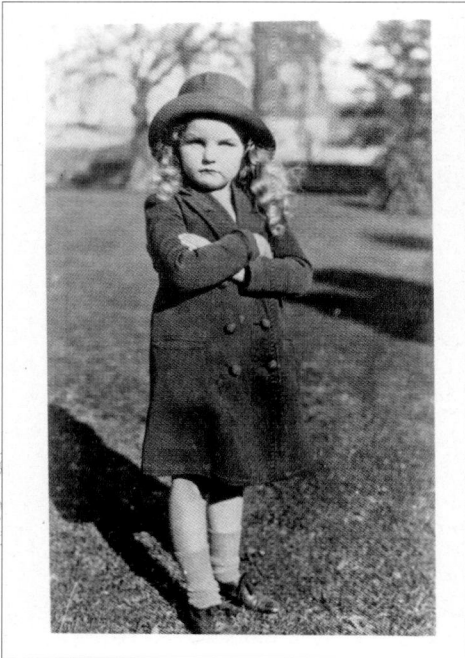

Jessica Mitford, five years old.
*Unknown photographer, photo courtesy of Constancia Romilly,
Benjamin Treuhaft, and Ben Weber.*

The Mitford family in 1925 or 1926—Unity, Jessica (holding cat), and Deborah
in front row; Diana and Pamela in second row; Nancy and Tom in third row;
Sydney and David on sides.
*Unknown photographer, photo courtesy of Constancia Romilly,
Benjamin Treuhaft, and Ben Weber.*

Asthall, currently a private home and sculpture garden.
Photo courtesy of the author.

Jessica (seated) and Unity Mitford at Asthall, 1922.
*Unknown photographer, photo courtesy of Constancia Romilly,
Benjamin Treuhaft, and Ben Weber.*

The Mitford family in 1934 at Swinbrook; Jessica (age sixteen or seventeen) is in the middle front, wearing a black coat, seated between Unity (holding her pet white rat) and Deborah; Nancy, Diana, Tom, and Pamela are in the back.

*Unknown photographer, photo courtesy of Constancia Romilly,
Benjamin Treuhaft, and Ben Weber.*

Jessica with her spaniel, Tray, when
she was fourteen years old, in 1931.
*Norman Taylor photographer, photo courtesy of
Constancia Romilly, Benjamin Treuhaft,
and Ben Weber.*

Jessica in 1935 (seventeen years old),
about a year before eloping
with Esmond Romilly.
*Unknown photographer, photo courtesy
of Constancia Romilly, Benjamin Treuhaft,
and Ben Weber.*

Detail of Jessica Mitford, from
Acton sketch of Mitford sisters.
Courtesy of the Mitford family.

Swinbrook.
Photo courtesy of the author.

William Acton sketch of
all six sisters: Jessica is in
the middle bottom row,
between Unity (left) and
Deborah (right), and in the
top row, left to right, are
Nancy, Pamela, and Diana.
Courtesy of the Mitford family.

Jessica Mitford in the family church
pew at St. Mary's, Swinbrook.
*Unknown photographer, photo courtesy of Ohio
State University and Mitford family.*

Detail of the Mitford family
crest, St. Mary's church.
Photo courtesy of the author.

Jessica Mitford as a debutante,
ready to be
presented to the queen.
*Photograph by Yevonde Portrait Studio,
courtesy of Mary Evans Picture Library.*

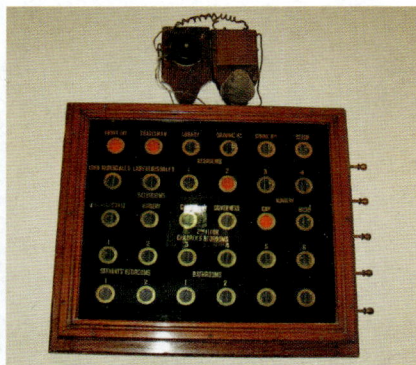

Servants' bells from Asthall
and Swinbrook.
Photo courtesy of the author.

Five Mitford sisters: Jessica, Nancy, Diana, Unity, and Pamela.
Unknown photographer, photo courtesy of Pictorial Press Ltd / Alamy Stock Photo.

Rutland Gate, the Mitford family
home in London.
Photo courtesy of the author.

Esmond (left) and Giles Romilly,
1935.
*Photograph by Howard Coster, photo courtesy of
Constancia Romilly.*

Jessica Mitford and Esmond Romilly
in Greenwich Village, 1939.
*Photograph by David E. Scherman
(later a good friend of Jessica's) for* Life.

Jessica and Esmond on
the French coast, near
St. Jean de Luz, 1937.
*Unknown photographer,
photo courtesy of Mitford
family.*

Jessica and Esmond on the beach
in Corsica, 1938.
*Unknown photographer,
photo courtesy of Mitford family.*

Jessica and Esmond in the Hôtel des Basques, Bayonne, France.
Unknown photographer, photo courtesy of Mitford family.

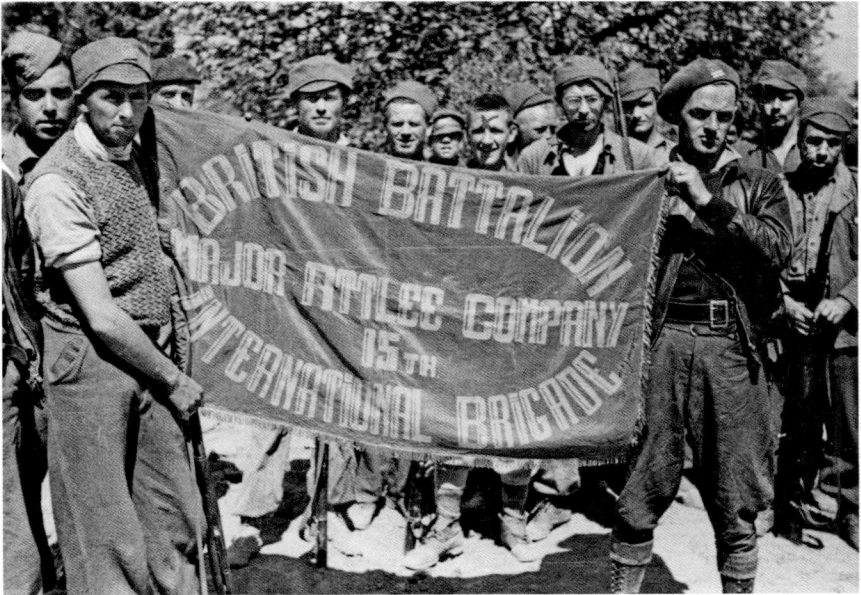

British Battalion, Spanish Civil War.
Unknown photographer, photo courtesy of Constancia Romilly, Benjamin Treuhaft, and Ben Weber.

Jessica and Esmond in the Roma bar,
in Miami.
*Unknown photographer, photo courtesy of Constancia
Romilly, Benjamin Treuhaft, and Ben Weber.*

Jessica and Esmond, late 1939 or early 1940.
*Unknown photographer, photo published in
The Washington Post to accompany their series.*

Esmond and Jessica in Greenwich Village.
Life *magazine photograph by David E. Scherman.*

Esmond at Martha's Vineyard, 1940.
Unknown photographer, photo courtesy of Constancia Romilly, Benjamin Treuhaft, and Ben Weber.

Esmond as an RCAF Observer/Navigator.
Unknown photographer, photo courtesy of Constancia Romilly, Benjamin Treuhaft, and Ben Weber.

Esmond in the Royal Canadian Air Force (RCAF).
Unknown photographer, photo courtesy of Constancia Romilly, Benjamin Treuhaft, and Ben Weber.

Jessica with Constancia, 1941.
Unknown photographer, photo courtesy of Constancia Romilly, Benjamin Treuhaft, and Ben Weber.

Jessica with Constancia, 1942.
Unknown photographer, photo courtesy of Constancia Romilly, Benjamin Treuhaft, and Ben Weber.

Jessica with Constancia, October 1941.
Unknown photographer, photo courtesy of Constancia Romilly, Benjamin Treuhaft, and Ben Weber.

Durr family—front row, Tilla and Lucy;
back row, Virginia, Clifford, and Ann.
*Photo courtesy of the Alabama
Department of Archives and History.*

Virginia Durr and Rosa Parks.
Unknown photographer.

"Blueblood Adventurers Discover America," *The Washington Post.*
Courtesy PARS International Corp.

Jessica selling dresses, probably 1940.
*Unknown photographer, photo courtesy of Constancia Romilly,
Benjamin Treuhaft, and Ben Weber.*

big flat backyard, sweeping views of the hills from the front, and—important for Decca who was a lifelong self-described "pack rat"—many built-in cabinets and lots of closet space. It was designed for family life, with a fireplace in the living room, a large dining room, and a big eat-in kitchen with a separate pantry. "Our house here is much nicer than in San Francisco," Decca told her mother; "it's right near a beautiful park."[16] Decca related that Nicholas suffered from food allergies and eczema, recovering from both just in time to develop asthma, and that Dinky was improving her reading and writing. She did not tell her mother that they'd moved partly because she was pregnant again. Moving in, Decca had one of her last bursts of domesticity. She spent quite a bit of money getting the Jean Street house painted. One room was white and chartreuse with scarlet and white curtains. The dining room was gray and chartreuse, the living room was gray and yellow, while the fireplace wall was plum-colored. She even had stationery printed to match. "Mrs. Robert E. Treuhaft," the stationery announced. Her nesting enthusiasms proved short-lived.

Oakland was much more a labor town than San Francisco. During the war, workers had poured into Oakland war industries such as shipbuilding. In 1947, their unions remained energized by Oakland's General Strike of 1946, the largest one in U.S. history, which had been ignited, in part, when police shepherded strikebreakers through picket lines. Over one hundred and fifty unions and one hundred thousand workers supported the strikers.[17] In 1947, when Decca and Bob bought their house, the aftershocks of that strike were still reverberating. Solidarity swept Oakland. "At the time it looked like the dawning of a new era," Decca wrote, "the beginning of a worker-led rebellion against the established order that might spread through California and ultimately throughout the nation." Bob's partners were the most radical lawyers in the region, and in the thick of it. Richard Gladstein and Aubrey Grossman had successfully defended Harry Bridges, president of the

Longshoremen's Union. His cases were, to date, the most important in thwarting attempts to use the 1940 Smith Act (which prohibited advocating overthrowing the government) to curtail free speech and oust Communist organizing from worksites.

Bob's firm was also involved in civil rights cases. "My partners and I considered ourselves civil rights lawyers from the beginning," Bob said.[18] In addition to police brutality cases, the firm's lawyers were heavily engaged in the work of the national Civil Rights Congress (or CRC). Founded in Detroit in 1946 and labeled, by HUAC, a "subversive Communist Front" in 1947, the CRC logged case after case of Oakland police beating civilians.[19] They investigated incidents, took affidavits, and gave victims a voice.[20] "We were the only ones in town— and I mean the only ones, who ever sued the police for damages for these beatings," Bob said. The firm managed to get the state's Committee on Crime and Correction to investigate police brutality in Oakland: "the first time in the history of the nation," Decca wrote proudly, "that a specific probe has been conducted into the over-all practices of a major police department toward minority groups." Decca told Aranka that "Bob is becoming famous throughout Oakland, the Bay Area, California, & probably the U.S. for winning impossible cases."[21] Of course, that was not quite the success Aranka had hoped for.

The CRC was formed from a merger of the International Labor Defense, or ILD (famous for defending the Scottsboro defendants, who had been falsely accused of raping two white women), and the National Negro Congress. Combining international attention to groundbreaking legal cases with militant street actions and protests, the CRC had a dual focus from its inception: defending Communists from loyalty oaths, the Smith Act (and later the McCarran Act) and other measures designed to contain and control so-called subversives; and taking the most difficult civil rights cases, specializing in those left behind by the slow, careful politics of the NAACP. Black Communists such as lawyer William L. Patterson, who, as the executive secretary of the ILD, had defended Sacco and Vanzetti and also the Scottsboro Nine, were prominent in the leadership of the CRC. Bob and Decca had joined the San Francisco chapter of the CRC, one of the organization's strongest chapters, as soon as it was founded in 1946. The CRC was organized, Bob said, "to have a broader, and more active, activist approach to fight for civil rights—not only in court but in the streets—to picket, to do things that were considered beneath the dignity of an organization like the NAACP."[22] Bob and Bert Edises served as primary counsel for the Bay Area CRC as it took on more and more difficult cases. The firm's lawyers were all developing notorious reputations for taking "unpopular positions," as Governor Edmund "Pat" Brown later put it, and for never wavering from their principles.[23]

Beginning in 1947, the CRC became increasingly involved in what began as a local case, in Laurel, Mississippi, when Willie McGee, a Black man, was accused of raping a white woman, and found guilty by all-white juries who deliberated for mere minutes. Cases like this were replicated in courtrooms across the American South, but McGee's drew national attention, partly because Laurent Frantz, Decca's and Durr's old friend from Alabama, had gone to Mississippi to look into it.

Oakland was not fashionable. It was heavily industrial: a transcontinental railroad terminus, major port, and a manufacturing center for ships and chemicals, as well as a canning and food-processing center. Oakland's Black population was the largest in the area, largely because of Black wartime workers, some of whom came straight from Southern agricultural work as sharecroppers, and many of whom now discovered that Oakland's wartime industries were often not able to easily convert to postwar production.[24] This led to layoffs, unemployment, and unrest. Decca's Washington friends saw Oakland as a "wasteland" renowned for "its cultural barrenness." But for Decca, Oakland was the political frontier. "There was nothing abstract about the class struggle in Oakland," Decca said.[25] "Oakland, we decided, was the place for us."[26] The East Bay Communist Party, which Decca had now joined, was led by a veteran of the Spanish Civil War. Oakland, perhaps unaccountably to anyone but Decca, felt like home to her. A never-published essay of Mitford's, "Why I Live Where I Live," explained her love for Oakland:

> Oakland provided scope for my subversive nature in a way that glamorous places like San Francisco, Manhatten [sic]—let alone Sag Harbor and Honolulu—never could. [In Oakland I] enjoyed a sense of hand-to-hand combat with our neighbors, the city's administration, its police department, its District Attorney, its monopoly, all-powerful newspaper the Oakland Tribune, that would only be possible in a city that is essentially a small town grown big, where Vendetta can flourish and become all-absorbing.[27]

Decca said that the city was too raw for subterfuge: "parts of Oakland seemed a microcosm of some Alabaman or Louisianan town, replete with white prejudice in its most savage form." Oakland's workers and Black residents had given their all in the war effort. They now organized a broad-based coalition demanding just the kinds of changes Decca and Bob had been fighting for: publicly owned mass transit, public housing, better funding for public education, more social programs. For anyone like Decca, whose political education had begun with New Deal politics, these were familiar fights. Oakland's political machine, dominated by Oakland Tribune owner and power broker Joseph R. Knowland, provided a political focal point for Bob and Decca. Decca was always at her best when she faced a powerful adversary. Knowland's "stranglehold" on her new town was a spur that worked well for her.[28]

She was seven and a half months pregnant when they moved into the Jean Street house. "For a few depressing months I stayed at home trying to cope with the tidal wave of washing and cleaning that daily threatened to engulf us."[29] As a junior associate, Bob earned a very modest salary (Decca later claimed it came to less than £26,000 a year in today's currency). Aranka supplemented that with frequent checks for fifty or one hundred dollars. The baby was almost three weeks late by the time he was finally born on October 17.[30] It was a very difficult birth, and Decca did not receive the anesthetic she'd requested, an experience she never forgot.[31] "I've been in the hospital one week today," she wrote Aranka on October 21, "most of the time being what they call 'induced,' consisting of a total of 5 big doses of castor oil, 5 Triple-H enemas (so called by the nurses—it stands for High, Hot & a Hell of a lot) and 45 shots of something or other. Also innumerable pills." The doctor, she added resentfully, "says it was a very easy birth—which it probably was for him." To her mother she wrote that "you would be horrified at the things they do to the Good Body." The baby, later named Benjamin (for Benjamin Davis) and always known as Benjy, "is wonderful," Decca was quick to assure Aranka. "Very large & a terrifically strong sucker . . . extremely handsome, in his own way, has big eyes."[32] Benjy's birth was followed by a painful breast abscess, which sent Decca back to the hospital for nearly a week in November and required both surgery and intense drugs. "I have heard Bob erroneously refer to this as a 'slight infection,'" Decca wrote to Aranka.

Decca left Benjy's care largely to Dinky, who taught him his first words: "Dinky's always right, Benjy's always wrong."[33] His health was not good. In the new year he suffered a frightening bout of pneumonia. Of Decca's four children, only Dinky, it seemed, had robust health. Decca never talked of Julia's death. But losing such a young baby, when she was still a very young mother, must have made her anxious about her children's health. She was proud that her children were socially conscious, and she took them leafleting as soon as they could walk. She insisted that Benjy was talking at only four months of age, which was not very likely.[34]

Juggling family and politics was a constant in Decca's life. Never a helicopter parent—in fact, the opposite—she both worried about her children and figured that they could mostly look after themselves. As her activism increased, her ambivalence about her old family remained. She felt suspended. On the one hand, she wanted to put Mitfords behind her. But she also needed them to see her do it.

Her mother continued writing with news of the weather, the births, marriages, and deaths of cousins, family friends, cows, and horses."[35] Decca responded with letters about what mattered to her, heedless of what her mother hoped to hear about. "P.S. A shocking new case of police brutality came to us this week. A Negro, arrested for being drunk, had both jaws & two ribs broken by the Oakland police. This gives you some idea of the reign of terror here."[36] Even when her letters were passive-aggressive jabs, however, they were also engaging, conversational, close to spoken speech; Sydney could almost hear her daughter talking. Decca was perfecting a style, crucial to her later writing, that credited her reader with both comprehension and agreement, a prolepsis that proved a winning strategy for her. She still longed for her family's understanding. Since that understanding seemed unlikely, she behaved as if she had it. She attempted to reestablish ties with her sister Nancy. Mosley had renewed his political movement, holding meetings of his new fascist Union Movement in London's East End, near where Decca and Esmond had lived. "Don't be weak-minded about Diana," Decca wrote Nancy, "or I shall have to be off writers again for several years."[37] Nancy was, in fact, seeing Diana quite often.

In the winter of 1948, Constancia, then eight, sent her English grandmother a thank-you note for a Christmas sweater. "Granny Muv," she wrote, "would you come over here some day? We live in Oakland—675 Jean Street is our address. I go to school."[38] Accepting the invitation by return telegram, Sydney sent an itinerary for a flight she'd already booked. Decca went straight to Party leadership. Did rules against consorting with "enemies of the working class" include mothers, she asked, half hoping for a "yes." "No," she was told, "the restriction didn't apply to visiting mothers."[39] Decca was moved, but also very anxious, that her mother so wanted to come. She was not at all sure what she wanted her mother to see. "In the nine years since I had seen Muv, she had receded further and further into the background of my life and thoughts, out of sight and almost out of mind; it would be like seeing a phantom suddenly materialized out of the dim past. I was at once immensely excited at the thought, pleased and touched that she would make the long, expensive journey, and deeply apprehensive that the visit would be a disastrous failure."[40]

Sydney flew over in April 1948, a trip that at that time entailed more than thirty hours of flying.[41] She arrived at dawn, tired, disoriented, and glad to see that Decca still seemed her funny, enthusiastic self. On the way home from the airport, in the car, Dinky asked, "Granny Muv, when are you going to scold Decca for running away?"[42] That broke the ice. To Decca's enormous relief, her mother proved to be a great sport: wonderful with the children, and an easy houseguest with few demands. She slept in the children's playroom. The visit, Decca told Aranka, was "a great success."[43] Asked about what she wanted to see in America, Sydney had replied: a supermarket, a women's club, and a funeral parlor. Sydney was fascinated by the funeral parlor, helping Decca to see it from the outside, which would prove important later. "Never once did she cast aspersions on our political views or on the company we kept," Decca said.[44]

Decca was now working three Party jobs: executive secretary for the Alameda branch of the Party, financial director and principal fundraiser for the Bay Area Communist Party, and as of February 1948, press director for the Party in the Bay Area. She and Bob were both heavily involved in the Willie McGee case, which took a great deal of time. She reduced her activities as much as she could during her mother's visit, but she did not suspend them. Sydney, who had raised her daughters to put family before everything else, was sometimes left to her own devices while Decca worked.

Her mother's visit softened Decca's family feelings, but she was not privy to the nasty barbs her sisters were trading about her, based on Sydney's reports. Diana and Nancy took swipes at her marriage, at Bob, and at Decca's housekeeping: "Such a slattern . . . so dirty," Nancy wrote to Diana.[45] "We screamed with laughter about the Treuhafts," Diana wrote Nancy; "after all the talk & trouble only ONE Mitford has ever done any harm to a Jud–Decca."[46]

Shortly after her mother's return to England, on May 28, Unity died of pneumococcal meningitis, in a small hospital in Oban. She was buried in June, at Swinbrook, with all the sisters, excepting Decca, in attendance. Decca wrote her mother that she'd already mourned her sister long ago. "I so hope you won't be terribly lonely," Decca added, asking if Sydney shouldn't consider moving to London.[47] Deborah's sister-in-law Kathleen "Kick" Kennedy was killed in a plane crash over France, also in May. When her body was brought back to England to be buried at Chatsworth, Decca was very sympathetic, without an unkind word to say.

Decca and Bob now feared they might be imprisoned. On July 12, Party leaders were arrested and charged with violating the Smith Act. J. Edgar Hoover tried to make a case that Party philosophy amounted to advocacy of violence. Hoover even had some of his undercover informants reveal their identities by testifying in the trials. He wanted them to perform close readings of Marxist writings to prove that they advocated violence. On the stand, these informants "dissected the works of Stalin, Lenin, and Marx," historian Beverly Gage writes, as if they were giving classes in dialectics.[48] Few officials opposed the arrests, since public opinion was overwhelmingly anti-communist and many people accepted Hoover's premise that beliefs could be crimes.[49] Defending the Party members indicted was enormously expensive—their bail alone came to over £2.2 million in today's currency—and the CRC was responsible for all the fundraising for their case. Bob's law partner Richard Gladstein was one of the chief trial lawyers, which meant that he might well be indicted as well. "Anti-communist hysteria" threatened to disable the Party, which was trying to hold its sixty thousand members.[50] It was an all-hands-on-deck moment for American Communists and everyone in Decca's circle was swept up in it.

Decca and Bob tried to keep a normal family life going at home. In August 1948 their two older children went to camp, Benjy went to Bob's sister, Edith's, and Decca and Bob took a camping trip to Big Sur. After stealing a mattress from a nearby cabin, Decca said they were "very comfortable" in their tent.[51]

Decca accepted yet another new position as assistant to the director of the East Bay Civil Rights Congress, in September 1949. This position moved her from fundraiser to organizer, drew on a wider array of skills, including her talent for investigation, and proved to be an excellent match. The position was designated as part time but demanded all her time and energy. The CRC, still responsible for raising money for the twelve Party leaders indicted in 1948, had also embarked on a groundbreaking document called *We Charge Genocide*, developed from the United Nations 1948 Universal Declaration of Human Rights. *We Charge Genocide* detailed cases of racial violence and lynching and laid out a powerful, comprehensive case for systemic and institutional racism, an argument that would set the agenda for all the CRC's work. Racism is "everywhere in American life," it argued, "the result of the consistent, conscious, unified policies of every branch of government," creating "psychological terror and mass intimidation."[52] It linked America's "institutional oppression" to both incarceration and fascism.[53]

We Charge Genocide also focused on the taboo against discussing interracial sex: analyzing how the myth of Black rape maintained white supremacy by criminalizing Black masculinity. Well before modern historians unpacked the ways that Jim Crow and "white fright" were built "on the foundation of anti-miscegenation laws," *We Charge Genocide* argued that rape had become "a weapon of terror and death . . . a capital weapon of white supremacy."[54]

The CRC also argued that the criminal justice system was genocidal. "State prisons in the South were really reservations," Black CRC leader William Patterson wrote, "concentration camps for Black political prisoners. Millions of Black Americans are aware that when they leave home in the morning they may not return at night if by chance their general demeanor or manner of response to a question rubbed a white person the wrong way."[55] Laying the groundwork for prison abolition, the CRC argued for abolishing the death penalty because of racial disparities in the justice system and its application.[56] The CRC went into prisons and jails and it helped organize the incarcerated. "Work with prisoners was a solemn obligation for the CRC," as historian Gerald Horne noted.[57]

The Willie McGee case had now become a central focus of CRC work and a particularly important case for Decca and Bob. In February, Willie McGee's third trial had begun, this time with the support of the Civil Rights Congress, the Communist Party, Aubrey Grossman of Bob's old law firm, and New York lawyer and future Congresswoman Bella Abzug, along with local lawyers from Mississippi. McGee had become an international cause célèbre, attracting the support of Albert Einstein, Josephine Baker, Richard Wright, Norman Mailer, Frida Kahlo, Paul Robeson, William Patterson, Ethel and Julius Rosenberg, and others. As Horne put it, in the most comprehensive history of the CRC to date, "the case was a microcosm, a cross section, a sliver of Americana."[58]

McGee's local defense team refused to state that relations between McGee and the woman who accused him, Willette Hawkins, were consensual. Too controversial for a Southern courtroom, the lawyers claimed. Instead, they leaned on the absence of Black jurors and the fact that the death penalty for rape was only used against Black defendants, never against white ones.[59] Abzug, who came on as chief outside counsel for McGee before she turned thirty, felt strongly that consent should be used.[60]

In August 1949 a Paul Robeson benefit concert in Peekskill, New York, to raise funds for McGee and the Smith defendants was attacked by a white mob wielding baseball bats. The injured that day included Bella Abzug and many of Decca and Bob's friends and associates.[61] Their friends were also well represented among those who showed up at Peekskill, a few days later, to form a human chain around the second concert attempt, keeping the white mob out. Any Communist who didn't develop a siege mentality during this time, as they saw it, when even the NAACP and ACLU were moving toward anti-communist resolutions, simply wasn't paying attention.[62]

Decca's CRC boss was Hursel Alexander, a charismatic Black Irish leader. According to Harry Haywood, he was "one of the party's finest orators."[63] Alexander was notorious for overworking associates with what Decca called a "mesmeric ability to wring the last ounce of effort from those within his orbit." She thought him a "terrific charmer" and appreciated his "restless *joie de vivre*." Their local Party chapter was particularly successful, with more than five hundred active members and its own radio show.[64] Decca credited Alexander with the CRC's success during a period of national decline in the Party. Some felt Decca deserved the credit for that.[65]

The CRC shared office space with the Independent Progressive Party (IPP), which was still active after Henry Wallace's loss in the presidential race of 1948. The local IPP office was directed by Decca's friend and Bob's associate Dobby Walker, a position then taken over by Marge Frantz, daughter of Joe Gelders.[66] Marge's husband, Laurent Frantz, had served as an investigator on McGee's case and been badly beaten because of it. Marge was, like Decca, a brilliant organizer, a young mother, and a progressive lawyer's wife. Decca was immediately drawn to Marge, five years her junior, with her Birmingham roots, her activist pedigree (she had joined the Young Communist League when she was only thirteen years old), and her "laser-beam mind."[67] Sharing office space allowed for constant consultations and quite a bit fun. Like Decca, Marge loved to sing, and they serenaded one another while they worked. Marge had boundless energy and little respect for conventions. Decca, Marge said, "was a total, total delight to work with. She was nothing but fun and the most incredible sense of humor . . . we hit it off immediately and became bosom friends until she died."[68]

Virginia Durr, Decca's first female friend in the States, was fiery but also conventional, willing to be Mrs. Clifford Durr in spite of her critical civil rights work. Decca's new circle of friends—Dobby, Pele, and Marge—were unconventional, strong feminists. Around this time, Decca stopped being Mrs. Bob Treuhaft, becoming Decca Mitford again from then on, in all but the rarest of circumstances. Decca's estrangement from her sisters had not diminished her longing for them; her new feminist comrades became sisters who helped fill that gap.

Decca was motivated in her CRC work both by outrage over racial injustice and by a powerful longing "to be accepted into black homes, black churches." Her main CRC job was to investigate police brutality complaints lodged by Black residents. An interviewer once asked Bob, "How effective was Decca, as a white English aristocrat" in a mostly Black organization? He replied that she was "extremely effective," and that her accent might have proved an advantage, distinguishing her from run-of-the-mill white women.[69] Decca's very authentic curiosity, her deep interest in others' lives, often won over those she worked with. She was on fire about injustice and people she worked with appreciated her outsider's outrage and her dedication.

Decca was now learning how to make her Mitfordness an asset. Coiffed and well dressed in suit, pumps, and pearls, she presented as a mid-century British housewife. Her warm, eager manner, coupled with her upper-class accent and considerable charm, could be disarming. Her contagious enthusiasm and sense of humor—she was always ready to laugh—made her seem harmless, when she was anything but. Decca scrunched up her eyes, smiled widely, looked deeply at others. She seemed guileless. But she was very judgmental, and astute in her judgments. She made others feel that they'd *earned* her approval. Those she approved felt special. Faced with an opponent, her sparkling eyes went from turquoise to an intense steely blue in a fraction of a second. Adversaries underestimated her at their peril.

Anticipating by decades current discussion about allyship and racism, the CRC was devoted to a large-scale educational anti-racist mission.[70] It rigorously disciplined whites who denied their racism or took refuge in having good intentions. Decca understood that someone raised as she had been had a lot to unlearn, and she willingly subjected herself to reeducation. She signed the CRC's pledge stating: "As a white American . . . I pledge eternal hostility against discrimination, segregation and prejudice. . . . I pledge no peace with those who support these alien and abhorrent evils."[71] Decca credited William Patterson with teaching her to listen to those most affected (something that made her a good investigator and, in Marge Frantz's view, a "phenomenal organizer").[72] "It would be an act of white chauvinism for me," Decca said, "a white person, to try to dominate or manipulate our predominantly black membership, to deflect their attention from the very issues that had led them to join the organization."[73] In the main, CRC's strength came from workers, church

211

people, and community members. "We strove to make the CRC a living example of racial integration and equality," Decca said.[74]

Most national branches of the CRC balanced what Horne calls "Red cases with Black cases," or defense of Communists and African American civil rights.[75] Decca's branch, responsive to local concerns, was largely involved with civil rights cases. One month after she assumed her directorship, a local case intensified that focus. Soon it drew national and international attention.

On October 22, 1949, white pharmacist Robert Savage and his light-skinned Black assistant Marjorie Wilson were found in the back of the Rose-Waterman drugstore in Oakland. They had been assassinated execution style, shot while kneeling with their fingers over their eyes. Jerry Newson, an eighteen-year-old shoeshine operator with a stand near the drugstore, had just been indicted for robbing the administrative offices of the housing project where he lived, a clumsy break-in to which he admitted. Newson was now charged with both murders as well as the robbery. Decca read the story of Newson's "confession" in the *Oakland Tribune* and was immediately suspicious. "I have been convinced since the beginning that it's a frame-up," she wrote her mother.[76]

Bob became Newson's defense counsel. Decca was chief investigator on the case, and it was her job to speak to people from every place Newson had frequented.[77] "Day after day, with little hope of success, I trudged through the pool halls and bars of West Oakland," she later wrote.[78] The investigations were exhausting, but also life-changing. Ever since peeking inside a poor villager's cottage, Decca had wanted to truly understand how the "other half" lived. Now that was her job. At the OPA, she had honed important investigative skills. Now she could apply them to something that really mattered. She shone. She helped turn the Newson case into a study in "a transparent pattern of official conspiracy. . . . The pall of police oppression fell from the outset of the trial over a daily packed courtroom."[79] Thanks in no small measure to

Decca's work, Newson's case, like McGee's, was able to teach hundreds of activists about systemic racism and racial injustice. "It was the big case of the decade," Bob said.[80]

Bob challenged the all-white juries used in Newson's case, and his coerced confession, as well as shaky evidence, especially ballistics. "Bob is now a local hero for his work in the case," Decca wrote her mother.[81] Nevertheless, Newson's first trial on murder charges ended with a conviction. He was sent to San Quentin and put on death row. Blacks in Oakland overwhelmingly believed he'd been framed.[82]

When Hursel Alexander left the CRC in the spring of 1950, Decca became executive director (or secretary), yet another promotion. "My day to day work in Oakland as executive secretary of the CRC consisted in carrying out the directives of the largely black board of directors: local cases, police brutality directed against blacks, police frame-ups of blacks in criminal cases, the physical defense of black homes against threatening white mobs."[83] She was joined by Black Party member and journalist Buddy Green, who, like Decca, was an autodidact. Green had dropped out of school in the sixth grade, ran an Oakland café, and was politicized there by his patrons. He'd worked as a farmhand, dishwasher, longshoreman, truck driver, and in the sawmills. He'd driven trucks, served in the military in World War II, and now, still in his twenties, was rapidly rising in Communist Party leadership when he joined Decca at the CRC. Decca greatly admired him and his "meteoric" rise. She was especially impressed by how quickly he'd become "one of the best reporters on [*The People's World*], his vivid, idiosyncratic style in refreshing contrast to that of some of his stuffier and more verbose colleagues."[84]

Decca had never lost the interest in journalism she'd developed after watching Esmond in Spain and working on the "madcap" *Washington Post* series. She was mostly writing fact sheets, press releases, and chronologies on both the Newson and McGee cases. But she took heart from Green's example. Working on legal cases, Decca discovered that she had a knack for synthesizing research and for making confusing details clear. She had a gift for streamlining and sharpening confusing timelines. It was excellent training. While she never took credit for it, she also helped Buddy Green and Steve Murdock (Pele's husband) write a short book about the Jerry Newson case.[85] Going door to door throughout Oakland in the fall and winter, Decca helped sell a remarkable ten thousand copies. Esmond's door-to-door Silkform successes had not been lost on her.

As Decca and Bob's political work intensified, their social circle narrowed. They drew back from much socializing with anyone but other Communists, largely because Communists were so under attack. "We tended to drop our friends and associates from pre-Party days because we now had so little in common with them," Decca said.[86]

She admitted to her mother that her letters were often about jails and prisons. "Sorry, but that is where most of our friends are," she added.[87] She was visiting Newson (and also other prisoners) as often as she could, sometimes accompanying Bob and sometimes going to the prison alone.

Her mother's visit had reignited Decca's desire to see England. She wanted her new family to see where she was from. And she had not given up the idea, however unlikely, that her old family might appreciate the life she'd now made. Simultaneously with "working literally day & night on the [Newson] murder case," Decca was trying to figure out how she and Bob could possibly afford such a trip. Maybe, she said, Nancy could "buy my horrid old furniture which she is using" or perhaps "Debo could be induced to fork over a decent rake-off of the £1000 she got for libel" when the British press misreported that she had eloped with Esmond.[88] "We should like to see Farve," she told her mother, "on condition he doesn't insult Bob or Dinky." She continued her habit of writing as if she and her mother lived in the same world: "Could you possibly ring up the *Daily Worker* next time you're in London," she asked Sydney, "& ask them whether they know of any interesting mass meetings or demonstrations" that she and Bob might attend while visiting?[89]

Decca and Bob didn't manage to get to England that summer. But in the fall they spent two blissful weeks at the San Cristobal Valley Ranch in New Mexico, the start of many family trips to left-wing, interracial resorts where the children could be in "natcher" while Decca stayed inside for cocktails and conversation.[90] From the ranch, Decca and Bob traveled to Denver to see the Durrs for the first time in seven years. While Decca got to show off her new family to Virginia and Clifford, she also needed a backup plan if she and Bob were imprisoned. Would the Durrs take in her children, Decca asked, if the need arose? "Virginia says she will take the Children," Decca told her mother, "if anything should happen to us, the only problem is that it will probably happen to her, too"—not, perhaps, the most reassuring aside.[91]

Decca's concerns were well founded. Alger Hiss had been convicted in January. McCarthy made his most inflammatory speech—alleging Communists had overrun the State Department—in February. Eugene Dennis, the general secretary of the Party, began a jail sentence in May. By late August 1950, both Ethel and Julius Rosenberg had been arrested. Aubrey Grossman was badly beaten in Mississippi in August, when he went South to aid in the defense of Willie McGee. The Korean War—"Complete madness," Decca called it—ended the decade of peace Decca had known, providing cover and justification for a growing wave of additional anti-communist measures.[92]

All summer, Decca worked on planning a trip to England, in addition to all her political organizing. With enormous demonstrations happening nationally in support of McGee—more than a thousand demonstrators in Times Square in July—it seemed to Decca and Bob that they could not help but prevail. By late August, Decca was forced to the "dreadfully sad decision" that they could not take time off from the case. "You have no idea how horribly disappointed we all were," she wrote her mother. In addition to their political commitments, she and Bob had not yet received the passports they'd requested. Going abroad seemed neither possible nor fair. "There is now a very immediate danger of people being rounded up & jailed here," she wrote, "and of course we wouldn't want to be away if that should happen."[93]

The McCarran Act, also known as the Internal Security Act, and the Subversive Activities Control Act, was passed in September 1950. It required that all Communists register with the attorney general and submit their membership and financial records (books Decca had been keeping for the Party as organizational secretary and financial director, and also in her various roles at the CRC). It limited citizenship and travel, subjected all Communists to possible arrest based on Party membership alone, and provided for the indefinite detention of Communists in concentration camps. One section of the Act, particularly relevant to Decca and Bob, prevented Communists, including American citizens, from obtaining or using passports.

The contrast between Decca and her family of origin had never been sharper. While she was working day and night to stay out of jail, save the lives of imprisoned Black men, and expose white complicity in systemic racism and injustice, her sisters were rebuilding prewar lives along completely traditional class trajectories. "Politics, do I loathe them!" Nancy wrote Diana.[94] Decca tried to make light of the differences. "Nancy is dressed by Dior," she joked. "I'm dressed by J. C. Penney."[95] Having her own American family helped her perspective. Her life was richer and fuller, she could say to herself. "Family life and political life merged into one. Dinky and Benjy, loyal supporters of the cause, accompanied us on many a demonstration. Their weekend treats would consist of picketing the Oakland police department of a Saturday morning, turning out on

Sunday with CRC contingents for leaflet distributions to church-goers in West Oakland, canvassing in the neighborhoods during election campaigns—diversions highlighted by an occasional PW picnic, a CRC evening songfest, a Paul Robeson concert."[96]

In January 1951, Decca and Bob moved from Jean Street to 730 Fifty-Ninth Street, closer to central Oakland in a more diverse neighborhood. Decca said that the move "to North Oakland, on the fringes of the black ghetto," was so that "the children could go to a mixed school and have black playmates."[97] On the day of the move, Nicholas had a fever of 104, and Decca, who hated illness almost as much as her mother did, was too busy to care for him. She took him to the hospital and "just made them keep him there all day. The hospital people were furious but there was nothing they could do as I just left."[98] Their new house was larger, with a separate apartment for governesses. The family got their first TV.

The Rosenbergs were convicted in February. The Martinsville Seven was another important case for the CRC, with many parallels to McGee's. They were executed. Newson's appeals were still moving through the courts. Willie McGee had been convicted in a third trial and, once again, sentenced to death. Bella Abzug traveled to Jackson, Mississippi, in early March to intercede for McGee. Forewarned of her coming, all of Jackson's hotels refused her a room. Local papers urged violence. Abzug spent the night terrified, sitting on a toilet in a stall of the Greyhound Station bathroom. In the morning, she fixed her hair and renewed her efforts in court. Abzug, who was seven to eight months pregnant at the time, miscarried soon after.

Decca headed to Jackson one week later as part of a White Women's Delegation to support McGee and to show local residents that white women could refuse complicity with racism. She went door to door in Jackson's white neighborhoods. Believing she'd be part of "scores or hundreds" of delegates, Decca found herself one of only four white women, dressed to the nines in "hats, stockings, and white gloves at all times," randomly stopping at homes. Again, local newspapers "threatened violence and encouraged it," but Decca's delegation, which grew to twelve women over her eleven days in Jackson, met with no violence. As Horne puts it, the delegation "laid the foundation for the 'Freedom Riders' of the 1960s" and also "prepared the ground for Montgomery" and the bus boycotts.[99] "I went to Mississippi with a delegation of white women from all over the country to intercede for a Negro, Willie McGee, who was charged with rape & sentenced to die," Decca wrote her mother.

> The charge is a frame-up, that is, he is not guilty but they are determined to kill him.... When we arrived, the newspapers ran stories every day trying to incite the people against us. The mayor called a special meeting about us & urged people to call the police if they saw us coming.... We drove a total of 7700 miles, in my new car. It was the most thrilling experience I ever had. Finally there was a stay of execution, so we did some good.... The Negro people here & throughout the country are tremendously enthusiastic over our going.[100]

The delegation's goal was to challenge the "rape myth" and "arouse the conscience of the white community."[101] "We are very proud of you," Buddy Green wrote Decca. "You guys have accomplished far more there than I ever dreamed possible."[102] From Mississippi, Decca also wrote a series of articles for *The People's World*, on McGee's case and the delegation's work. Not yet displaying the distinctive conversational voice of her letters, Mitford's pieces were nevertheless clear, strong, and dramatic. Unlike in her *Washington Post* stories, she did not make herself a character.

After a few days in Jackson, Decca and her delegation drove to

Oxford, Mississippi. Unannounced and uninvited, the four women marched up a long walkway, stood under the Spanish moss–draped pillars of a wide front porch, and rang William Faulkner's doorbell. To their surprise, Faulkner spent two hours charming the women and agreeing with them on all counts. As soon as she got back to Jackson, Decca wrote up a quick press release, then returned to Oxford and asked Faulkner to initial it. Faulkner backtracked quickly. On March 27, the Memphis *Commercial Appeal* published his statement that he believed the women were being manipulated by the Communist Party. "I did tell them," Faulkner was quoted as declaring, "if they wanted to save Willie they should talk to the women in the kitchen and make their arguments there rather than to the men and the politicians."[103]

On March 23, McGee's defense team succeeded in securing an execution stay from Supreme Court Justice Hugo Black, Virginia Durr's brother-in-law. Black's stay was an example of the authority that powerful networks could wield. But it was not supported by the other justices and the stay did not hold.

The California Supreme Court, however, reversed Jerry Newson's murder conviction on April 27, 1951. District Attorney J. Frank Coakley enforced an unusually draconian fifteen-year sentence on Newson for the housing project robbery, assuring that Newson would not see daylight until his mid-thirties. And Newson was charged, again, with the drugstore murder, for which a new trial was ordered.

Both cases showed Decca what extraordinary resources it took to free one Black man. Before Newson's murder conviction was finally dismissed definitively in the summer of 1952, there would be thousands of demonstrators, multiple lawyers working full time for years without charge, dozens of expert witnesses researched and located, investigations, hundreds of interviews, three trials, a book, and radio shows. As *We Charge Genocide* demonstrated, cases such as Newson's filled courtrooms and jails, most without the attention Decca had made sure Newson would receive. When *We Charge Genocide* was finally presented to the United Nations by William Patterson, Jerry Newson was one of its signatories, along with Paul Robeson, Mary Church Terrell, Ben Davis, Howard Fast, W. E. B. Du Bois, Bob and Decca Treuhaft, and Rosalee McGee, Willie's wife.[104]

By the time Newson's conviction was initially overturned in April 1951 (a process that would subsequently drag on for more than another year and two trials), Willie McGee had already endured six years of trials and appeals, three convictions, two lynching attempts, six execution dates, and just as many stays. *Life* magazine featured McGee.[105] Hundreds of "Save Willie McGee" protests across the globe had demanded justice as the most "well-known case" in CRC history "lanced the ugly sore of U.S. racism."[106] On Sunday, May 6, demonstrators in "Free Willie McGee" T-shirts chained themselves to the Lincoln Memorial. On Monday, May 7, Willie McGee reiterated what he'd claimed all along—that he and Willette Hawkins had a consensual relationship of many years, and that Willette had always threatened to cry rape if Willie broke up with her. "Taking my life doesn't end such things," he said.[107]

McGee was transported from the Hinds County jail back to Laurel, Mississippi, and taken to the top floor waiting cell of the courthouse, where a traveling electric chair was installed. On May 8, hundreds of white Laurel residents gathered on the courthouse lawn. They watched as a portable generator was set up from a truck, with enormous electric cables strung along the sides of the courthouse up to the top floor windows. By evening, more than five hundred people had gathered across the lawn—men and women, children, and the elderly. Some brought chairs. Many ate and drank.[108]

McGee was executed just after midnight on May 8, 1951. The execution was broadcast live on two local radio stations, WAMC and WFOR. Over their radio, Americans could plainly hear the "mass

surge" of the portable generator as it pushed power up the black cables and then, more loudly, the "blood-curdling cries" of the hundreds
of white Laurel spectators, giving "the rebel yell of victory" as Willie
McGee died.[109]

Decca turned thirty-four on September 11, 1951. She spent her
birthday on the witness stand in court, answering a subpoena from the
state's Fact-Finding Committee on Un-American Activities. The subpoena had demanded all of Decca's CRC membership and financial
records, its meeting agendas and strategy notes. Decca appeared at San
Francisco's ornate City Hall, walking up into the Rotunda on an unusually warm and windy day, carrying only her handbag. She had a new,
shorter haircut. Bangs made her seem even younger than she was, as did
her unusual thinness. She'd recently lost quite a bit of weight (Nancy
would have been so pleased), probably from the anxiety of the Newson
and McGee trials. In a pastel-colored suit with a rounded, feminine
collar and a dark silk blouse, Decca looked proper and ladylike as she
took her seat in the Beaux Arts hearing room and adjusted her cat-eye
glasses.[110] From then on, she refused to answer questions. At one point,
enraged by her polite refusals, the committee sarcastically inquired if
she'd confirm whether or not she was a member of the Berkeley Tennis
Club, a notoriously conservative outfit. Decca heard "Berkeley Tenants
Club," which sounded radical to her, so she declined to answer that one
as well. The gallery audience broke into such explosive laughter over
Decca's refusal of the Tennis Club query that her case was dismissed.
The committee was so flustered they forgot to ask Decca to produce
the papers that she'd declined to bring with her. Had she been asked for
them and refused, as she planned, a jail sentence of up to twenty-five
years might have been imposed. "A stretch in prison . . . [had] loomed
as a very real possibility." Decca went straight from the hearing into
hiding until the committee's work wrapped up.[111] "One became adept
at subpoena-ducking in those days," she said.[112]

11

"A Most Un-Duchessy Life"

I see . . . [that my writing] is full of references to jails,
sorry, but that is where most of our friends are.[1]
—JESSICA MITFORD TO HER MOTHER, SEPTEMBER 23, 1951

From the outside, Decca's new life as she reached her mid-thirties looked easier than it was. She made it look easy, with her incorrigible humor and unselfconscious smile, with an open, heart-shaped face invariably turned outward. She broadcast pleasure. It was true that after losing the love of her life and her first family as well, she had secured a second, also adoring, husband, created a new family, found meaning and work, and centered herself in a close-knit community of friends and comrades. But nothing had, in fact, come easily for her; she won her happiness through dogged determination and paid for it with grit. She was forward focused as a matter of principle.

The 1950s were an unsettling time for progressives. The anti-communist drumbeat and arrests made life for American Communists especially precarious; the simplest acts of leaving for work, registering children for school, or scheduling a medical procedure were fraught with uncertainty of never knowing when one might be snatched and imprisoned. Whenever Party members gathered, their conversation inevitably turned toward evictions, surveillance, lost jobs, children punched on playgrounds, snubs from neighbors, slashed car tires, and worse. When Decca wrote her mother that she was always referencing jail because prison was where most of her friends were (or were headed), she was not exaggerating. Popular culture has memorialized the white American 1950s, as journalist David Halberstam noted, as "an orderly era," characterized by "personal freedom" to consume goods, a decade of "material well-being," "security," and "expanding affluence." In the 1950s, "few Americans doubted the essential goodness of their society," Halberstam asserted.[2] That was not the world that Decca and her comrades inhabited. For them, the 1950s were chaotic, anxious, constricted, and paranoid. Unlike most postwar Americans, they lived with what Decca's friend Al Richmond called "the sense of being in a war of attrition with the overwhelming odds against you."[3]

Much has been written about the oppressiveness of the McCarthy period, the lives that were ruined and the talent that was wasted when people went into exile and were pushed out of their careers. That was the point. David Caute, an historian whom Decca admired, explains that the House Un-American Activities Committee, or HUAC, was *designed* to be an "agency of misery." Its "ultimate mission and highest delight was to hound radicals."[4] Communists were denied the right to assembly, speech, housing, safety, and economic security, the right of association, the right to counsel (simply defending Communists was such a risk that often they could not find lawyers), the right to travel (seizing of passports and denials of visas), the right to citizenship (denaturalizations and deportations), the right to organize labor (breakup of unions), nonprofit status, and more. According to some estimates, well over fourteen thousand federal employees were forced out of their jobs during the Red Scare, hundreds of people were deported, and thousands of teachers were fired for "subversion."[5] As one "unrepentant leftist" puts it, "There was no aspect of . . . life unaffected by the political repression of those days."[6] Howard Fast, jailed as a Communist, wrote that the "fear and suspicion" of those times operated like a "rasp" that filed down people's lives. It was, he said, a "living hell" for progressives.[7] The toll was immense. Marriages broke up, physical and mental health suffered, families were separated, children were traumatized, people suffered insomnia and depression. Suicide rates spiked. Decca's training in not giving way to her feelings was, in this instance, an asset. She was immensely brave by nature. She was unflappable by conditioning and background.

The early years of the 1950s were so uncertain for progressives that some, like Durr, developed a "fortress mentality."[8] "I have learned that to survive I can't look ahead all the time," Durr said.[9] Public opinion polls conducted in 1954 reveal that 80 percent of all Americans wanted Communists stripped of their citizenship, 52 percent were in favor of imprisoning all Communists, and 42 percent wanted to deny the press the right to criticize the U.S. government. "Hundreds of local papers across the nation were committed to this furore, clutching at circulation by feeding their dazed readers ever stronger doses of panic and hatred," David Caute wrote.[10]

Fearing mainstream sentiment, people Decca knew shrank back from ordinary social discourse with neighbors, store clerks, mechanics, and postal carriers. Decca had already largely given up her family of origin. She wasn't about to give up the ordinary Americans of Oakland. Where some activists pulled inward in response to the Red Scare, Decca did the opposite. In the fall of 1951, she was active in so many different campaigns that she attended a different meeting each night. Bob felt that arrest was imminent, for one of them at least. Nevertheless, neither altered their course, and Decca, in fact, increasingly involved the children in leafleting, ticket sales, and other activities. At one point, her son Nicholas, age eight, was arrested for selling Jerry Newson Defense benefit tickets door to door. "I took all 3 children down to the Chief of Police to protest Nicholas' arrest. The only trouble was Benjamin kept having to go to the loo which rather ruined the delegation."[11] Decca encouraged her children to laugh at the enemy.

The psychological damage of constant surveillance is incalculable. Many women in the Party, consumed with anxiety for their children, felt the pressure keenly. California Communist Party leader Dorothy Healey wrote: "The FBI was following my every move. There was always three carloads of FBI men sitting in front of my house. . . . I'd go shopping at a market nearby and the agents would come into the market with me while I did my shopping."[12]

Some bold activists pulled off an occasional tease. Party member Alexander Trachtenberg, for example, would sit through the same dull Soviet film three times in a row so that the FBI agent tailing him would have to do likewise.[13]

Decca had grown up with servants and staff always present, and she did not place the premium on her personal privacy that most Americans did. But she was nevertheless worn down by being watched. The government's demand that members turn against friends and associates by naming names of other Communists was designed to erode one's sense of self and undermine any feeling of belonging. As Victor Navasky put it, "The naming of names had shifted from a means to an end." HUAC aimed to "poison social life in general, to destroy the very possibility of a community."[14]

Loyalty was a Mitford family value that Decca held dear. She remained convinced that Spain fell largely because of Western disloyalty.

HUAC's tactics devastated her. Every day brought another heartbreak. As she struggled to stabilize herself and her family, and looked to what resources, material and psychological, she could rely on, she took sustenance from the lessons of her childhood, especially the robust tribal ethos of the Mitfords.

The American Communist Party encouraged its leaders to go underground. In June 1951, it issued what it called a "five minutes to midnight" prediction that American fascism, comparable to Germany, Spain, or Italy, was poised for victory. Some Party members saw this as precisely the reason to remain in the open and appeal to the widest number of people possible. The success of organizations like the Civil Rights Congress (CRC), which brought many nonmembers into the fight, was offered by such thinkers as a model. Those, like Decca, who retained some faith in the fundamental fair-mindedness of everyday people soon found themselves pitted against friends and comrades who believed that the new culture of surveillance made trusting anyone outside known circles just too risky to hazard.

Roughly two thousand Party members went underground at this time. One of them was Adam Lapin, a good friend of Decca and Bob's. Eva Lapin, his wife, noted that "for Adam, it was a lonely time, and for the children, a time of fear and worry. For me, a painful time of fear, anxiety, responsibility and gnawing anger."[15] Writer Kim Chernin, whose mother, Rose, was arrested on July 26, 1951, vividly recalled what it was like to be a young child at the time. "I went into the closet," she remembers. "I climbed upon the shelf . . . there were extra blankets, for the winter. I tried hiding myself under them, piling them on top of me."[16] When members of the Party were arrested, some were not given the opportunity to make arrangements for their children. Toddlers were left standing in empty kitchens and living rooms, as their parents, pressed into police cars, begged indifferent neighbors to please look after them. Decca had heard such stories for years.

Party trials often dragged on interminably. Since the Smith Act "allowed perfectly legal acts to be criminalized," as Dorothy Healey put it, no one was safe.[17] Defendants did not need to be accused of violent acts. Conspiring to perform violent acts wasn't even necessary. "Conspiring to teach and advocate" that violent acts might be necessary was a charge vague enough to be used on anyone.[18] As Decca's friend and self-exiled Communist Cedric Belfrage put it, "the [Smith] Act's patent unconstitutionality multiplied the agony of the victims, plunging them into a murk of unreality and spinning out their ordeal into ever costlier months and years."[19]

The political threat, grave as it was, was not the only source of insecurity for progressive parents at this time. The 1950s were also the most difficult years of the polio epidemic. For Decca, who had lost her infant daughter, Julia, to measles because of misassumptions about immunity and vaccination, and who now had three young children, the anxious wait for a polio vaccine throughout the "plague year" of 1952, as it came to be known, coupled with the anxieties of the Red Scare, was excruciating.[20] With no known cause (at the time) and no reliable treatment, "polio did not behave like other diseases," as a young friend of Decca's who contracted the disease later recalled.[21] The daily newspaper printed box scores of polio cases on page 1, near articles about the national rout of Communists.[22]

Concerned as she was not to end up in jail, Decca forged ahead with her many prison visits. She insisted on getting inside as an advocate, witness, and investigator. She visited the Oakland jail—a grim, gray box in the heart of downtown—so often that she became well known there. When entertainer-turned-activist Josephine Baker expressed interest in learning more about the cases the CRC was pressing, Decca escorted her to San Quentin. Traveling north from San Francisco to visit Jerry Newson in prison, Baker and Decca passed through some of the most beautiful and privileged communities in the world. In San Quentin's immense visiting room, they sat on benches on either side of a wooden partition as high as their chins, while guards watched Baker listen intently to Newson's story. Baker was convinced of his innocence. She told Decca that she was going to pay one of her own attorneys in Chicago to assist with Newson's case.[23] Bob was working pro bono on Newson's case and swamped with complex preparations. Help from people like Baker was invaluable.

Decca's hands were full with meetings, prison visits, death row and rape cases, civil rights battles, police brutality investigations, fundraising, and a range of home and childcare responsibilities. Deborah reached out in the fall of 1951 to see if she might come visit. How would Decca make time for her? Would Debo be as open-minded as Muv had been? How could they possibly bridge their now vast differences: Debo renovating one of the largest ancestral estates in England and preserving its precious antiquities and Decca visiting jails? What on earth would they talk about?

In November 1950, Deborah's father-in-law, Edward Cavendish, the 10th Duke of Devonshire had died suddenly, making Andrew, Deborah's husband, the 11th Duke of Devonshire.[24] Edward's oldest son, Billy Hartington, married to Kick Kennedy, had died in the war.[25] Deborah, who had always said she'd be a duchess someday, became one at thirty. She and Andrew inherited one of the wealthiest estates in Great Britain, although Edward Cavendish's untimely death meant that the estate was entailed with high taxes, a truly "monstrous debt," Deborah said.[26] Chatsworth House was one of the grandest and most beautiful homes in Europe, perched atop twelve thousand Peak District acres of gently rolling parkland, bordered by a river.[27] Its lavish grounds were designed in the 1700s by renowned landscape architect Capability Brown, its gardens were laid out by Joseph Paxton in the 1800s, and family portraits were painted by Lucian Freud in the 1900s.

At over 1,704,233 square feet, Chatsworth's nearly three hundred total rooms dwarfed most other British estates.[28]

During the war, Chatsworth House had served as a girls' boarding school, housing three hundred students and staff, "like a barracks," Deborah complained.[29] In 1951, when she proposed visiting Decca's seven-room Oakland home, Deborah had just begun supervising the remodeling, rewiring, refurbishing, and restoring of all its rooms and outbuildings, and adding 17 new bathrooms to the building's 32 kitchens, 17 staircases, and 112 fireplaces.

Deborah and Decca's other sisters had inspired most of Decca's passions and cast the mold of her pleasures. The separate world they created, drawn from the Library and Hons' Cupboard, had been a self-sufficient universe, rich with its own language, rituals, rules, games, and social hierarchies, a mirror of the larger world, perhaps, yet a world that was under their control. Deborah had played a crucial role as the youngest, whose willingness to take direction from Decca was part of what Decca remembered fondly.

Decca kept alive her fondness for the "Hons' Cupboard, our secret meeting place at Swinbrook, [and for] talking our secret language." Clearly, an aspect of her joy in what Communist leader Dorothy Healey called the "kind of a whole total world" of the Party was rooted in that past. Although she took almost nothing to Spain, she carried photos of her childhood homes. She kept those close by until her death. Her childhood as a "Hon" was embedded in her adult character, part of her profound sense of loyalty and her need for group activity.

She wrote back to Debo quickly, on October 19, 1951, to express her enthusiasm for the proposed visit and to lay out some ground rules:

I think it's a wonderful idea about you coming out here, I long to show you the children, I'm sure they are quite unlike yours. However, before you take the plunge, I must warn you of a few things—

*1. We lead an <u>extremely</u> un-Duchessy life here. For instance, if
you stay with us you would have to sleep on a couch in the dining
room, we don't have a spare room here. Of course you could stay
in a hotel, only how to pay for it? Which leads me to 2:*

*2. You can't bring more than $25 out of the country, so you would
be completely at our mercy once here—we'd <u>love</u> to have you, but
wouldn't be able to afford to pay for a hotel. However people often
do come to stay on one's couch, so maybe you would do that. . . . A
lot of our friends have been thrown in prison & one never knows
who's next (Not that we expect to be, at least not before February,
but I'm just warning you) . . .*

*There is one more thing: I work quite hard, in fact night & day—if
you come I would plan to take off for a week or two, but then
if some emergency should arise I might have to scram back to
work.*[30]

Decca was informed that far from disapproving such a visit, "the
comrades craved to meet Debo" as well, news that she promptly shared
with Deborah.[31] "Now that you've heard the worst, I DO hope you'll still
come," she urged.

Decca had never abandoned the idea, even if she would not admit
it to herself, that her two lives might somehow merge. Her vision of the
duchess bedding down on her lumpy old couch was half Mitford Tease,
but also half hope that her current life could seem normal to Debo. It
did not seem outlandish for Decca to imagine that she and Debo, now
thirty-four and thirty-one, might make a space for one another in both
their new lives.

Deborah arrived in February of the following year, 1952.[32] Decca
was intensely busy, serving on numerous executive boards, more than

full time at the CRC, organizing many conferences, and increasingly in demand as a speaker—a big, always funny, always authoritative voice, tinged with a slight British accent, booming out from a highly animated small body she deployed with the grand gestures of a slapstick comic. Audiences loved her. Local events included protests of racist films and plays, protecting Black homeowners, picketing residents who wore Confederate gear, and exposing officials. She and Bob had also begun hosting frequent parties. Crowded and lively, filled with cheap liquor and too many guests, their gatherings sometimes continued into the early morning hours. They hosted welcome-back parties for jailed Communists, fundraising events, folk song parties, readings, and parties for any of their comrades celebrating birthdays or anniversaries. The night before a big party they stayed up late, writing funny songs and poems, which were often distributed as song sheets. Their parties were oases of exuberance in a sea of grim anxiety, and Northern California's Left community was mad about them. Decca took these parties very seriously, typing up detailed guest lists, checking them carefully, and keeping them in her files, along with carbons of party songs, poems, and programs. Bob's caseload had continued growing. Their house overflowed with papers, posters, pamphlets, guest lists, shopping lists, calendars, legal briefs, and files. Twelve-year-old Constancia looked around and quietly arranged for Debo to stay at the Hotel Claremont in Berkeley, one of the most elegant hotels in the greater Bay Area. Decca scrambled to clear as much time for Debo as she could.

Decca picked Debo up from the airport, helped her settle into her large room at the Claremont, and left her to rest. Almost as soon as Decca closed the door and stepped into the hotel hallway, Debo began a long letter to Diana, detailing all her first impressions of Decca's new life. The impressions were not kind. There was no one, moreover, Decca wanted to know less about her life than Diana. But Debo was hot to share.

I got off the areroplane after all night and was walking to where you go out and a figure appeared who somehow was Decca and yet completely different. Oh dear it was frightening and in a way so terribly sad, I couldn't believe that this complete American could ever have been her . . . Oh Honks. Decca has lost all colour even her eyes look different but I suppose people do change between twenty & thirty-four, and also this dreadful airless climate must be bad for people. The accent is what struck me most, I still can't believe it, she not only does the accent but says completely American sentences like when I asked her how old Bob was she said 'Pushing forty.' The house is a little suburban house, they seem very pleased with it. It is a sort of box painted like a child would, red doors in one room, blue in another. It had a very peculiar smell and they said they had a negro family in the basement so of course that was it. . . . as for Dinky she is heaven. She has got a beautiful face and fat body but she really is sweet . . . somehow it is awfully frightening seeing someone like that after so long, and I feel that her blasted causes has become so much part of her that she can never forget it for a minute. . . . But it's the voice that I can't get over. . . . I am so thankful to be in this luxurious hotel.[33]

Photos of Decca at this time show her trim, lively, and very energetic, with a lovely round face full of color, glittering blue eyes, and prominent cheekbones. In spite of often working herself to the point of exhaustion, she had a beautiful complexion. It is almost as if Deborah were seeing a different woman altogether.

Deborah, late in her life, still remembered her dinners with Communists, Decca's friends, whom she did not like. "The sarcasm that spewed from Decca's dinner guests," Deborah recollected, "was relentless and difficult to bear; none of them had ever been to England yet they launched into bitter criticism of everything I knew. Whatever I tried to say in defence of the King and our way of life was laughed out of court or greeted with a 'You would say that, wouldn't you' sort of look. One evening, the conversation turned to how to do away with the royal family. Manners were not their priority."[34] According to Marge Frantz, Decca was always very careful about who she introduced to Deborah, choosing her most established and well-dressed acquaintances over close friends like Frantz, who looked exactly like the feminist-activist she was. Frantz resented being sidelined, she confessed, but she also felt that Decca's relation with Deborah was difficult for Decca and not something she wanted to make any harder.[35]

In a memoir published fifty years after this visit, and after Decca's death, Deborah expressed her frustrations with the visit. While expressing appreciation for the effort Decca and Bob made—taking her to Carmel and "introducing me to her friends and political colleagues"—she wrote that her sister's life choices made no sense to her. Decca was "a new person, trousered American in appearance and accent—someone I did not recognize. It was the oddest sensation and filled me with a feeling of intense loneliness. What was I doing, thousands of miles from home, meeting a stranger who had once meant more to me than anyone in the world?"[36] Decca's assessment of the gulf between them was similar. But she did not blame her sister for her own disappointments. "We loved having Henderson here," she wrote her mother soon after the visit. "She met quite a few of our friends but they couldn't quite make each other out. Tell her I'm sorry not to have written much since she left."[37] Deborah wrote an amusing letter after getting back to England, one that masked her real feelings about the gulf between her and Decca.

In typical Mitford fashion, both tried to joke away their discomforts about the visit. Referring back to a large dinner Decca had thrown for her, Deborah teased about the way the comrades introduced themselves—"CP fashion, in which one indicates the area of a person's political work. 'This is Andy Johnson, he's active in the Youth Movement.'" At Christmas, she sent a card showing herself and Andrew in full royal regalia, dressed in their "ducal robes." She captioned the photo "Andrew & Me Being Active."[38]

On an early March morning in 1952, a few days after Deborah's departure, Decca read in the *San Francisco Chronicle* that a Black family had moved into an all-white California neighborhood north of Oakland and been attacked. She phoned her CRC coworker, Buddy Green. In Decca's car, they sped to the house, "where a huge crowd of white men and teen-agers was gathered." As many as four hundred angry whites had surrounded the small Richmond house, while the family cowered inside. "It was the first time I had witnessed the horrifying sight and sound of a mob in action," Decca said. She knew that as a white woman trying to thread her way through that mob with a Black male coworker she was risking her life and Buddy Green's as well. Assailed by curses and shouts, they moved gingerly toward the house. Small clutches of policemen and deputies looked on, just "standing by, watching bigots hurl rocks at the Garys' home and not making an arrest or even asking them to stop,"[39] Decca said. They reached the front door and slipped inside as the mob advanced up the lawn, howling and brandishing weapons. Someone burned a cross. Someone threw bricks. Some yelled that they'd burn down the house.

Huddled around a small kitchen table, Decca learned about the Gary family, Wilbur, Borece, and their seven children—the war workers' housing they'd been stuck in, how most of Oakland's strong unions excluded Black workers, how the city of Oakland was pushing out Black residents. Black workers who had fought the war, built its ships, and maintained its planes were now denied opportunity.[40] Wilbur Gary was a Navy veteran. He thought he could change things. The small white house they purchased on 2821 Brook Way was in the Rollingwood neighborhood of Richmond, an area that still enforced racial covenants outlawing Black residents, although such restrictions had been ruled illegal.

Decca and Buddy began making phone calls from the Garys' kitchen. Within hours, over a hundred white and Black supporters—Communists and unions folks, church people and teachers, even local businesspeople—encircled the house in a human chain, facing the screaming mob as Robeson's supporters had done at Peekskill. Over the next days, whenever one person needed a break, someone else replaced them. The human circle held fast. The Rollingwood Neighborhood Association tried to buy the Garys out. In downtown Richmond, Black realtor Neitha Williams, who had sold the Garys their home, found her plate-glass store window shattered by a brick.

Decca "hardly slept" for days. Even when she was miles from the Gary house, she thought she could hear the mob pushing forward, thought she could feel the floor shake as they advanced. But she was determined not only to defend the Garys, but also to model an interracial, cross-class, cross-gender coalition, what Martin Luther King, Jr., had called a "Beloved Community" and what Marxists imagined as a revolutionary, classless society.[41] "Defenders had to be organized into round-the-clock shifts, in itself a formidable job . . . we strove for a careful balance of blacks and whites, of men and women. . . . Simultaneously we had a dozen other activities going on in an effort to mobilize support for the Garys throughout Northern California . . . our primary goal . . . [was to] seek out whites in Rollingwood who would come forward to condemn the mob violence and would themselves undertake defense of the Gary home."[42]

For two weeks, the white mob in front of the Garys' home ebbed and flowed. But nearly two dozen members of the Rollingwood Neighborhood Association broke ranks to write a letter welcoming the Garys to Richmond. Decca printed twenty thousand copies of the letter and distributed them throughout Richmond (with a population of roughly one hundred thousand people, she provided at least one leaflet for every five households). She mailed an additional two thousand leaflets to news outlets and civic organizations. On March 18 she led a large delegation to the County Board of Supervisors, demanding investigations, protection, and arrests. She organized eight hundred volunteers—"only a fraction . . . were CP members."[43] Nor were the Gary family Communists. The CRC's greatest success was the breadth of its reach. But the NAACP issued its own leaflets, warning local residents not to "get sucked in" by "subversive and un-American movements" like the Communist Party and the CRC.[44] As Robert Self puts it in his history of Oakland, "The NAACP's bowing to anticommunism in Oakland, as nationwide, further crippled the possibility of a true interracial progressive politics."[45]

The Gary case was not Decca's only cause. In late May 1952, she went south to Los Angeles to attend the Smith Act trials of Dorothy Healey, Rose Chernin, Bernadette Doyle, and others, including her friend Al Richmond. Most of the plaintiffs held Party positions like Decca's, as secretaries and chairs of state or local Party committees. The prosecution was attempting to prove that membership in the Party constituted a crime. The rationale, once again, was that violent revolution was inherent to all Marxist-Leninist thought. If true, any advocacy of the ideology in any form was potentially criminal. To make their case, the prosecution often went toe-to-toe on Marxist theory with the nation's best Marxist theorists, giving courtrooms the occasional, and highly ironic, appearance of Party study groups and Educationals. The whole thing was, in Richmond's words, a "theater of the absurd." "You can't think of how horrifying it was," Decca wrote. "Of the 15 on trial about 7 are friends of ours, they face 5 years in jail if convicted."[46]

Bail had been set so high that most of the plaintiffs had spent all their pretrial months in jail. By February, they were drained of energy and resources. Nevertheless, the California Emergency Defense Committee, which worked closely with the CRC, mobilized significant support, using the trial as a chance to educate the public about the dangers of antidemocratic hysteria. Defendant Dorothy Healey wrote that "every day there were lines of people waiting outside for the start of the trial, to come in and observe. The Defense Committee spoke of the observers as a 'people's jury' and encouraged representatives . . . to report back what they had seen. We couldn't sway the jury or the court's decision in the case, but at least we could see to it that in areas of public opinion important to us the government's case would be understood for the frame-up it was."[47] Al Richmond wrote that "the government sought a political and psychological atmosphere in which . . . putting and keeping Communists in jail was to be made routine."[48] The trial observers were there to display outrage at government attempts to criminalize speech and thought. "Comradeship, devotion, generosity, affection . . . [that were] the human element of the Communist movement at its finest," as Richmond put it. Consequently, the trial sometimes took on a "circus-like" atmosphere, forecasting the political theater of conspiracy trials in the 1960s, as the defendants strove to antagonize, challenge, and expose the prosecution.[49]

The trial cemented Decca's profound distrust of authority. It reinforced her view that American justice was capricious at best. The trial also reinforced the importance of solidarity and the value of putting herself on the line. Both the New York and California trials ended in convictions, as Decca had suspected they would.

Exhausted by his legal work, Bob came down with pneumonia and was hospitalized early in 1953, very frightening at a time when antibiotics were not so widespread. Stalin's stroke and death the next month, March 1953, raised questions about the future of the Communist Party. In April, Deborah's infant daughter, Mary, died. Decca and Bob were beginning to feel that bad news was their only certainty. In June, the Rosenbergs were executed. Their killing hit the whole family especially hard. Even teenage Constancia had become involved. Earlier that year, she'd reached out to Churchill, begging him to intercede, but he did not respond.[50] The Korean War, opposed by American Communists as interventionist support for a right-wing tyrant, seemed to be winding down at last, but another war was already looming on the horizon.[51]

Decca still wanted to see her English family. She and Bob kept applying for passports and not getting them. Bob dropped Decca's connections to Churchill at the passport office, to no effect. So Decca wrote to her mother, suggesting that her mother "ring up Cousin Winston & tell him we just want to come for a visit, no politics, and see if he can't arrange it?"[52] Sydney wrote back: "I'm afraid there's nothing doing as regards asking favours, it would not be possible for me anyhow & surely not for you either, as you are heart & soul against him. As for Nelly, she thinks you cordially dislike her, & I think she is right, unless you have changed."[53] Decca had not spoken to Churchill since storming out of their White House meeting in December 1941. Her willingness to appeal to him now reflected her longing for her family and for England and her belief that there was a way to get what she wanted, rather than a softening toward her cousin.

That year, she'd become heavily involved in the case of Wesley Robert Wells, a Black prisoner on San Quentin's death row, who'd been originally imprisoned for a petty crime, then sentenced to death under an obscure statute for hitting a prison guard with a spittoon. The guard was not seriously injured, but Wells was scheduled for execution on April 9, 1954. He was seen as a problem inmate, and the system was determined to make an example of him.[54]

Taking on the Wells case, Decca added many more hours to an already intense workload, developing one of the earliest critiques of the "prison Jim Crow" system and helping to lay the groundwork for what has now become the prison abolition movement.[55] Wells was represented by Charles Garry, a partner in a firm that included John McTernan, Decca's old boss at the Office of Price Administration.

Garry was largely self-taught, like Decca. She admired how he used "the courtroom as a platform from which to attack the status quo."[56] He was never "boring." He enjoyed a good fight. He also never let other white folks off the hook. William Kunstler remarked that Garry had "the best set of questions" to deal with white jurors; if one claimed not to be racist, Garry knew that person was a liar.[57] Garry saw every trial as an opportunity for "educating the jury" about American racism. Garry and Decca were cut from the same cloth and were happy to learn from one another.

Through her work on the criminal cases of Black defendants, Decca was developing the habits of persuasion she would rely on for the rest of her life. Stories were her main strategy. She wanted to get Wells's story out to the public. At her urging, the CRC put out a fact sheet in the form of a letter from Wells to the reader: "The purpose of this letter is to give you the facts on one of the most amazing stories in the history of California's prison system," it read.[58] This gesture—*I am talking to you; don't look away*—was already a signature of Decca's new style. It appeared in both her political and personal writing as a kind of bossiness born of urgency—a shared resolve that made Decca and her reader, when the strategy worked, into one community of concern. "I'm sending you some pamphlets about cases we are working on," Decca wrote her mother. "Do read them. Also, do write Gov. Earl Warren, State Building, Sacramento, Calif, and ask him to free Wesley Robert Wells. Send me a copy of the letter."[59]

The CRC published a small booklet, which it sold for fifteen cents a copy, called *My Name Is Wesley Robert Wells*. The cover showed Wells before incarceration and after. "On these dramatic pages," read the foreword written by Buddy Green, "you will find the story of what it is like to be a negro in the prison system of the supposedly enlightened state of California." In what purported to be in his own words, Wells argued that he had become violent in prison as a direct result of the racism he encountered there. Prison racism and prison Jim Crow, he maintained, created the very problem that prisons purportedly existed to solve. "I am the result of what inhuman, brutal and ignorant treatment can do and cause," Wells wrote.[60] This argument later became one of the central tenets of prison abolition advocacy.

Thanks in part to Decca's organizing, the Wells case generated a remarkably diverse coalition that included church groups, the Black press, a large group of doctors—three hundred of whom signed a letter urging Wells's release—and eventually the white, mainstream press, including the *San Francisco Chronicle*: "the broadest civil rights movement in our history," Dorothy Healey claimed.[61] The Wells coalition was a large-scale version of the human chain that had formed around Paul Robeson and the Gary family home in Richmond. For Decca, it reanimated the hope she'd drawn from the Women's Delegation that went to Jackson for Willie McGee, showing that change was possible, and that white people could make a difference, even under conditions of brutal racism and bitter constraint.

Inspired by that diverse coalition, Decca shifted tactics. Increasingly, she focused on bringing in supporters who could not be dismissed as Communists. She wanted to demonstrate that people could understand and support struggles that may not have been their own. Looking back on the Wells case more than ten years later, Decca said that breadth was key to saving Wells; the "CRC, with the best intentions, simply couldn't do it alone," she wrote.[62] All spring of 1953, Decca continued working the case, building diverse constituencies and developing a new sense of what it meant to be accountable to other individuals within the machinery of oppression.

Late that spring, she and Bob moved yet again. "Did I tell you we moved again? Our new house is <u>much</u> nicer, also it has a beautiful garden," she wrote her mother.[63] Their new house, at 574 Sixty-First Street, was less than half a mile from Jean Street, but in an area of somewhat bigger houses on nicer lots. Their new eight-room, four-bedroom, Craftsman-style house, built in 1912, included an attic dormer and a garage.

Decca was now doing critical research for many of Bob's legal cases. She was an excellent investigator, fearless and thorough. She was especially brilliant about discerning which tactic would work best on a given individual: flattery, threats, cajoling, wheedling, or aristocratic imperiousness. She carried herself with such confidence that most people found it impossible to say no to her. Those who did, Decca could charm. She was a gifted listener: locking in to her interlocutor, her face would light up at the least inflection from others. When she disapproved, her eyes fixed like lasers. When something struck her as funny or absurd—and inevitably something always struck Decca as funny or absurd—her whole face would scrunch up, her eyes would roll up, and her laughter was unchecked and abandoned. She was deeply appealing, and most people found it impossible to refuse to answer her questions.

Both Decca and Bob were subpoenaed by HUAC at the end of 1953. They'd expected it for some time but still felt shocked and scared when it happened. Left to mostly fend for themselves, their children took over the house—Benjy gorged on mustard and jam sandwiches—while Decca and Bob spent the week in court. Every day, Decca appeared in the defendants' box dressed to the nines. She inveigled Aranka to send what Decca called her special HUAC-hearing hat: an expensive and fashionable item from Aranka's Upper East Side shop. Republican women who came to jeer the defendants mistook her for one of their own. "I'm sure it was the hat you gave me that did it," Decca wrote Aranka.[64] "Old Bob" was a great hero, Decca added, telling her mother-in-law how he managed to read a four-page statement that "ripped into the committee" and was greeted with "terrific cheering & applause" from the many supporters in attendance. After a long and anxious week, Decca and Bob both walked away. No conviction. They felt more guilt than relief. Decca thought it was evidence that she and Bob had too much privilege.

While Decca and Bob emerged from their HUAC hearings relatively unscathed, most of their friends did not. "The witch-hunt," as Decca put it, wreaked "havoc" for most of the people they knew.[65] By the spring of 1954, the Durrs were again in the crosshairs. In March, Virginia was subpoenaed, along with Myles Horton of the Highlander School. Outraged at being called up before someone (Jim Eastman) she considered "just as common as pig tracks," she phoned her friend Lyndon Johnson, waking him to complain. Even Johnson, then majority leader in the Senate, could not stop Eastland.[66] Virginia and Cliff Durr were forced to appear at hearings in New Orleans that Virginia said were "insanity." "It is hard to describe the horror of it," she said, a "surreal quality of craziness."[67]

Clifford Durr had been suffering from mild angina for the previous two years. At one point, he became so enraged that he rushed at the prosecutor and then blacked out.[68] He spent the next two months in different hospitals, trying to recover. "We were sort of shellshocked after it was all over," Virginia Durr wrote to Decca. "The horror of the sort of thing we went through is that it is done under Government auspices, and the use of perjured testimony is deliberate, and the complete lack of any fairness or due process—and the deliberate intention of trying to lynch you publicly, but you know all about it." Clifford Durr returned to his law practice, but many of his clients "began to slide away."[69] "You can't imagine how revolting they [the hearings] are," Durr said. "Many have lost their jobs as a result, including teachers, university professors, waitresses, electricians, carpenters, just about every kind of person you can imagine."[70] In the summer of 1954, the government began exploring ways to denaturalize and deport Decca, as it had done with other foreign-born Communists. Decca and Bob were able to thwart those efforts, but they did not feel secure, and Decca was still not able to travel freely. That same summer, William Patterson was given a six-month jail sentence for refusing to hand over membership lists of CRC fundraisers to HUAC. Cedric Belfrage later said it was a death knell for the struggling CRC.[71] About this time, some of her friends began to notice that Decca was drinking excessively.

That year, as part of a monthlong investigation, Decca took a train trip to Salt Lake City and then St. Louis, where she also attended a national CRC conference. On board the Southern Pacific Line, she picked up a magazine lying on a nearby seat. Its bright pink cover featured a large photograph of Nancy (complete with pearls), next to a large portrait of Madame Pompadour, the subject of Nancy's latest book, steeped in anti-feminist sentiment and nostalgia for the lost glories of aristocratic life.[72] Responding to the stark contrast between her life and her sisters' lives, Decca said they all lived in "Cloud Cuckoo Land."[73]

Decca did not live on a cloud. On an early summer evening, walking to a CRC meeting after dark, thinking about the meeting's agenda, Decca crossed a desolate corner of Berkeley, bordered by hills, and was suddenly grabbed from behind by a Black man in his twenties. He dragged her downhill into a ravine. He was dirty, disheveled, and clearly desperate, maybe mentally ill. In a frenzy, he pawed at her clothing, tried to rip it off, grabbed Decca's breasts and her genitals, kept one hand across her mouth and threatened to kill her if she screamed.

Decca later told many different versions of this attack. In all but one of them she was nearly raped by the attacker, but Bob arrived in the nick of time, also on his way to the same CRC meeting. In these versions, Bob heard the scuffling and was able to chase Decca's attacker off. It is likely, however, that no such rescue occurred. Years later, Decca told one friend that she'd been raped by the man, and that she told him to "get it over with" as quickly as possible.[74] In what she told that friend—and the doctor from whom she sought treatment immediately after the attack—no one came to her aid or assistance. In every version Decca told, she related how she tried to make her attacker see her, how she told him about her anti-racist work in the Willie McGee case, how she invited him to come to a CRC meeting and talked to him nonstop throughout the assault.

She refused to call the police. She would not file a report. She downplayed the attack. She was not going to be another Willette Hawkins, the white woman who accused Willie McGee of rape. She would not endanger a Black man's life. She joked about rape. She claimed that the problem with American feminists is that they made altogether too much fuss about sex. She distanced herself from American feminists who were concerned about pornography, sexual violence, or women's objectification, and ultimately from feminism itself.

Decca rarely took time off. In August 1954, while trying to quit smoking and visiting Aranka in New York with her young son Nicholas, she let herself be persuaded to go on a hiking trip with Dobby Walker. She was probably still recovering from the attack, although she was not discussing it. Dobby took Decca on a two-week camping trip in the Sierras. The trip reinforced Decca's dislike of camping and hiking. She'd bought two mismatched hiking boots from different used bins at the Army Navy store and spent her time alternately cursing Dobby and nursing blisters. Her milieu was indoors, wherever people gathered to talk, drink, and debate. Throughout 1954 she continued to attend meetings on an almost daily basis—board meetings, executive committee meetings, fundraising meetings, special event meetings, Educationals, organizational meetings, and editorial meetings. She was also heavily involved in the midterm elections of fall 1954. She wrote her mother: "We are all awaiting the elections with tremendous interest, on their outcome may depend the application of the Anti-Communist legislation. The whole family is campaigning, even Benj."[75]

Off speakers completely now with both her father and Diana, Decca nonetheless kept apprised of their difficulties. She knew that her father suffered increasingly ill health and that he felt ashamed of being ill. And when Diana's family home, Clonfert Palace in Ireland, burned to the ground, Decca followed the reports and thought often, and with deep sympathy, about how awful it would be to lose almost all their books, papers, and letters.[76] Esmond's mother, Nellie Romilly, from whom Decca had long been estranged, had been ill since October with cancer. On the first day of February 1955, Nellie died, cutting one of Decca's last ties to Esmond's family.

Decca had little time to think about Nellie's death. On February 15, 1955, a sunny morning, Decca's son Nicholas, an effervescent and easygoing child, hopped on his bicycle, as he'd been doing every day for weeks, since getting a newspaper route for the *Oakland Tribune*. Two blocks from home, he was struck by a bus, which threw him off his bicycle and into the curb. Constancia somehow heard the commotion from blocks away and ran to the corner. She found her young brother, surrounded by neighbors. The fourteen-year-old girl crouched in the gutter, lifted him into her arms, and cradled her brother as he died. By the time Decca and Bob could be located, the ambulance had come and gone. Friends surrounded Decca and Bob through the day's inquiries and arrangements. At night, they retreated to separate rooms to pace and grieve. Decca telegrammed her mother the next day:

DARLING MOTHER NICHOLAS WAS KILLED YESTERDAY
BY A BUS WHILE RIDING HIS BICYCLE FUNERAL IS FRIDAY
AFTERNOON DINKY AND BENJAMIN TAKING IT WONDER-
FULLY WILL WRITE SOON GOING TO COUNTRY FOR A FEW
DAYS BOB MOTHER COMING PLEASE DON'T WORRY WE ARE
ALRIGHT OUR FRIENDS ARE WITH US BEST LOVE DECCA.[77]

Decca was, of course, not all right. She and Bob were both in a heavy fog of grief, keeping to themselves, unable to comfort each other. The funeral director took advantage of them. He talked them into an elaborate, conventional funeral with a white coffin and wreaths of white flowers—the "whole gloomy horror," as friend Pele put it—attended by two hundred people.[78] Dobby, one of the many friends who attended the funeral, said: "My feeling [is that] she was so traumatized by Nick's funeral. Big white coffin wreathes with flowers [—] so depersonalized." After the funeral they took Nicholas's body up to Guerneville and buried him in Redwood Memorial Gardens, near where they'd been married.[79] "Afterwards we went to a home of a friend who lived above the Russian River and had a memorial feast" outside, to remember their "unusually bright sweet, happy boy."[80] Decca and Bob stayed away from Oakland as long as they could. They avoided anyone who might try to sympathize or offer condolences. Constancia developed an ulcer in the weeks immediately following her brother's death, highly unusual in someone so young. Decca could not bear to grieve openly. She took down all photos of Nicky. She did not speak of him. She went to bed with a bad case of flu. He is not mentioned in her memoir. As Dobby put it: "She (concealed) it . . . repressed it—She toughed it out—you wouldn't have known anything had happened if you didn't know her very well. [She was] not one to go around mourning."[31]

Three weeks after Nicholas's death, at the end of her flu, Decca wrote to Aranka. The only way to repay the kindness, she added, was by "living a normal life which includes laughter and happiness—(Anyhow, one can't live any other way—for long)."[82] This was the formula Decca had used with Julia's death, and then with Esmond's. It was the formula she and Esmond dubbed "forging ahead." It was the only way Decca knew to live. This "form," as she and Esmond would have called it, was entirely future focused. Its success depended on building, creating, and imagining futures, a perspective that comes easiest with youth and stability. Decca now had neither.

Fortunately, a remarkable opportunity for distraction presented itself, unexpectedly, in July of that year. It was an opportunity Decca had longed for but given up all hope of expecting. She was going back to England.

12

"Going Home Again"[1]

You have no idea how difficult it is to write to all of you as you don't know any of the people here.[2]

—JESSICA MITFORD TO HER MOTHER

O
n a temperate, dry Tuesday, July 19, 1955, Decca's mailman came up the steps and dropped "one of those cheap beige envelopes inscribed 'On Official Government Business'" through the mail slot. Fearing a subpoena, she held it out from her body, cautiously tearing off the edge. Two passports slid out. "Terrific news," Decca wrote her mother, "we got our passport <u>at</u> <u>last</u>! It just came today." Decca and Bob had been traipsing downtown for weeks, going through the "irksome ritual" of having their photographs taken, standing in line, and filling out passport application forms, mostly to help out radical lawyers Leonard Boudin and Victor Rabinowitz, who

were assembling data for a Supreme Court challenge to the travel restrictions imposed on American Communists. "It was as unbelievable and stunning as winning the Irish sweepstakes," Decca said about actually receiving a passport. She immediately began planning a trip to England.[3]

Decca hated packing. She could never decide what to bring, always gathered far too much and could not fit it into her luggage. What she liked, on the other hand, was making complex travel arrangements, plotting out the logistics of getting from place to place, typing up itineraries, navigating how she'd get her family entourage from place to place, and where they'd stay once in England. "I had a dream," she told her mother, "that I was showing Bob & Dink round Swinbrook & Asthall."[4]

Decca had no intention of wasting this opportunity on personal pleasures alone. With most American Communists unable to leave the country, she and Bob had the chance to be emissaries and ambassadors, reporters and investigators, travelers with a mission rather than mere tourists: representing their Party and also bringing important information back home. Both Decca and Bob loved public speaking, Decca especially. When they came home, they could look forward to sponsored talks about what they'd seen. Decca began arranging her post-trip lectures before she even booked her passage.

A trip to England in 1955 for a family of four was an expensive proposition. Decca and Bob were good economizers, and they worked out ways to save money, including having Decca, who hated to fly, take Benjamin to New York by train, sitting upright in coach for five days straight. Bob and Dinky would fly and meet them in New York, and from there they'd all travel on to England. With food, airfare, boat travel, train travel, and incidentals, Decca calculated they'd need about $2,000 a month (almost £19,000 today), a fortune for her and Bob. Do "I have any money there still, if so, how much," Decca asked her mother. She again raised the possibility of selling her share of Inch Kenneth to fund her family's trip.[5] For almost twenty years, Decca refused financial help from her mother. Now she eagerly agreed to her mother's offer to underwrite most of the visit. "It really is wonderful of you to be paying," Decca wrote her.[6]

Dinky and Benjy had both been ill off and on since the death of their brother five months earlier. In addition to ulcers, Dinky had developed a persistent sore throat. Benjy had such a high fever in the days after Nicky's death that their family friend and physician Ephraim Kahn made daily house calls. Benjy got over his fever within days, but even months later, he still seemed delicate. "We feel that his long illness was partly due to unexpressed unhappiness," Decca admitted to Aranka in an unusually reflective moment.[7] They decided it would be best to leave him with Aranka. At eight years old, he was too young to fully appreciate the trip, they reasoned.[8] Decca borrowed three good dresses from friends and began thinking of how to amuse Dinky, on such a long trip in another country. They planned to tour various Communist Party sites in Europe, and Decca did not want Dinky to be bored. She invited Dinky's friend Louise (Nebby Lou) Crawford, a young African American girl and the daughter of good friends and associates, to come along with them as Dinky's companion, provided that the Crawfords covered Nebby Lou's expenses. This meant last-minute fundraisers for Nebby Lou, and Decca helped with those as well.

At the last moment, the trip was almost canceled. When Decca's train pulled into the New York station, she was greeted by a breathless Constancia, running full tilt down the platform and shouting: "the police are after you and Bob." The phone had been ringing day and night in Oakland for days. State Department telegrams came to the house. The passports had been issued by mistake and the State Department says that they must not be used, Dinky said.

Decca went into high gear. With the same brio with which she'd eluded British bill collectors decades earlier, she hid the family at Bob's sister, Edith's, apartment in Queens. The ship they had ticketed was not scheduled to leave for a few days. Decca secured last-minute cabin-class tickets for the four of them on a ship leaving in four hours. This meant dashing back to Manhattan from Queens and forfeiting the cost of their original tickets as well as paying for the new ones. Aranka found all the frenzied scheming annoying, especially when it turned out that Dinky's luggage had been forgotten in Queens, with all her new clothes bought for the trip, which Aranka would now have to have shipped to England. But she paid the new fares and saw them all off from the docks. Safely on board the SS *Liberté*, Decca, Bob, Dinky, and Nebby Lou Crawford stayed on deck until the tugboats left the ocean liner and they were well into international waters. Then they went down the narrow flights of metal stairs to find their assigned cabin.

Decca and Dinky were both prone to seasickness. They expected the worst. The seas were smooth, however, and their crossing was easy. Decca, in fact, found their five-day passage a pleasure. "Words cant describe the utter blissfulness of the ship, the food & life generally on board," she wrote friends in Oakland. In addition to unlimited food and wine, there was even free French brandy. "The girls" had found their way out of cabin class and snuck into First; they were "in heaven—there's swimming, dancing, movies, all one could desire—we'll bring back some menus for you to drool over."[9]

Decca, Bob, and their friends often poked fun at such decidedly bourgeoise comforts. They did not do so then, however. After Nicholas's death, her children's illnesses, and their frenzied departure, Decca welcomed every indulgence. Her enthusiasm for sumptuousness now was undiminished by her earlier decision to relinquish it.

Decca had never stopped missing her sisters and had never—excepting Diana—relinquished *them*. The prospect of introducing them to her new family, and being able to show off Bob and Dinky, made her giddy.

On ship, Bob was reading *Lifemanship*, Stephen Potter's wildly successful 1950 booklet: a send-up of upper-class stratagems for making others ill at ease. Potter's very funny little book focused on modes of speech designed to make people feel inferior: "the slight put-off, the well-timed provocation, which will get the other fellow down."[10] Don't try "beating the English at their own game," Decca warned Bob. With "ten centuries of practice" under their belts, he could not hope to compete.[11] Bob was not deterred.

Five days later, when they docked, Debo met them. Decca wanted time alone with her, to adjust. Straight from the terminal, however, Debo "rushed us off to lunch in a very fancy French restaurant where we were joined by a rather ghastly friend of hers." He "had obviously been invited to view the outlandish American relatives," Decca believed.[12] It was not an auspicious beginning.

After lunch, Debo carted the family directly to Inch Kenneth, where Sydney awaited them. Getting to the island was a chore, especially after a long transatlantic voyage. First, they took an overnight train to Oban, sitting up all night. From Oban, they took a ferry across the North Atlantic to the island of Mull, spending hours on hard wooden benches in an icy spray. Sydney met them all at the small, windswept terminal in Craignure, where she shoehorned them into the twenty-five-year-old car she kept in a shed on Mull, strapping their luggage around the tiny Morris until it resembled a small, prehistoric tank. Sydney was not a good driver—"The drive was a bit terrifying, we went with my mother in her 1930 Morris, she has quite bad palsy but drives like a New York cabdriver, honking like mad at anything and everything in sight." Tooting and swerving, Sydney propelled the overloaded Morris across Mull's single-track dirt road, up and down hills, to the tiny hamlet of Gribun, where the Inch Kenneth caretakers maintained a home and boat.[13] From Gribun, leaving the Morris behind, it was a short open boat ride across the channel to the family's large white haystack-shaped house. For the next nine days, however, Decca could rest. There were no meetings, no telephone, no agendas, nothing but walks, talks, food, reading around in the house's substantial collection of warped and mildewed novels, listening to the crackling radio and looking through her mother's enormous black scrapbooks. Decca slowed down for the first time in years. Sydney's scrapbooks told the whole family's history in clippings and photographs. They took Decca back to a period before her own losses, between wars, away from jails and printing offices, demonstrations and meetings.

Decca was generous and expansive, eager to get along with everyone (except Diana). She would even reconcile with her father, she said, if he'd agree not to "roar."[14] She did not know that behind her back her sisters were exchanging small-minded, mean-spirited, anti-Semitic letters about her, letters that gave no quarter for the recent tragic loss of her son. As soon as Debo arrived at Inch Kenneth, she wrote Nancy a "full report" on "these Americans" while her impressions were still fresh. She found Bob "pretty odd" and called him "an Old Yellow Peril."[15] She liked Dinky's looks, but not her views of aristocracy. "Dinky thinks Andrew gets money from selling slaves, I do wish I could buy some, I wouldn't dream of selling." Debo continued:

> Oh the SAGA of it all here, it's a great strain . . . to write any of it let alone all. I do wish you were here to study it. . . . Oh dear, Decca's appearance, she has got an Eton crop & specs and wears men's trousers and smokes without stopping, it really is too sad. She doesn't seem to care in the least. . . . Decca is being terribly nice & much less violent as far as one can make out without actually getting involved on some subject which means

arguing which I can't do. . . . Progressive is a terrific word with
them, it always makes me scream. Oh dear it does all seem so
sad in a way but they seem happy with each other I must say.[16]

The woman Debo saw as sad appears, in photos from this trip,
to be glowing. "I can't tell you how much we are loving this trip," she
wrote Aranka.[17] Nancy was absorbed with an article about to appear
in *Encounter* magazine, but she found time to reply that Debo's "letter has filled me with gloom & apprehension. TROUSERS!"[18] A few
days later, Nancy reiterated her apprehension to Diana. "Oh dear how
I dread their arrival—& I have to keep hypocritically writing to say I
die for them," Nancy wrote.[19]

The article preoccupying Nancy was "The English Aristocracy,"
a tease about upper-class mannerisms that built on the Stephen
Potter book Bob had been reading on board ship. Potter's tease targeted upper-class pretensions. Nancy's tease, on the other hand, was
aimed at those who pretended to upper-class manners that were not
their own. In spite of deriding commoners, Nancy's article proved
immensely popular. She lengthened it into an edited book, *Noblesse
Oblige: Sophisticated Fun About the Speech and Manners of the English
Upper Class,* which became a bestseller.[20] Nancy liked to pose as a critic
of the aristocracy, but no one more fully embodied its disdain for excess enthusiasm. "Zeal," she wrote coolly, "has always been frowned
on." Zeal was Decca's way.

Decca and Bob found the island's "haunting beauty" entrancing.[21]
Decca wrote back to Dobby, it is "quite beautiful" and "the house is
much bigger than I thought . . . life on the island is not <u>exactly</u> rough-
ing it by our standards. . . . This thing about my mother living alone
has also been somewhat exaggerated since she has six employees living in nearby cottages."[22] With fresh produce, eggs, and mutton all
produced on the island, Sydney's staff made wholesome and delicious

meals. Bob told Aranka: "we're having a blissful, restful time," adding that "Dec and Muv are having a fine old sentimental reunion."[23]

Not until leaving Inch Kenneth and arriving in London a few days shy of her September 11 birthday—her thirty-eighth—could Decca catch up on the news. Almost two weeks after its occurrence she learned of the murder of fourteen-year-old Emmett Till on August 28, killed by white men for allegedly flirting with a white woman. From London, as best she could, she followed the groundswell of rage over Till's murder, the national outrage that the CRC had tried, not always successfully, to ignite.

Decca would not have been able to take a break from the CRC earlier. But the Red Scare and attrition in the Party had decimated and weakened the organization. The rise of autonomous and organic civil rights organizations that would soon coalesce into Martin Luther King, Jr.'s, Southern Christian Leadership Council (SCLC) and the powerful student group Student Nonviolent Coordinating Committee (SNCC) would render organizations like the CRC redundant and superfluous. Already, the energies the CRC had been able to mobilize were beginning to go elsewhere.

Indeed, Virginia Durr was now closer to the real action in national civil rights struggles than Decca was. On March 2, a few months before Decca left for England, Claudette Colvin, a fifteen-year-old African American, had had enough. Influenced by stories of Sojourner Truth and Harriet Tubman, Colvin refused to give up her bus seat to a white woman in Montgomery, Alabama. Colvin's arrest was swift. Local Montgomery activists such as E. D. Nixon and Rosa Parks, a good friend of the Durrs, worked with Clifford Durr to spearhead Colvin's defense. It paved the way for similar actions later, including the better-known arrest of Rosa Parks, which sparked the bus boycotts that ignited the Civil Rights and, later, Black Power movements.[24]

Decca spent her birthday in London, staying in her family's small mews apartment behind Rutland Gate and writing long letters to her American friends. In London, Constancia and Nebby Lou went sightseeing, while Decca and Bob acted as Party ambassadors (Bob lamented that he couldn't go sightseeing too). They met with Party leaders, giving reports and sharing strategies and forecasts. They toured the offices of *The Daily Worker*. Paul Robeson had been one of many Americans denied a passport. Decca started a London campaign for the return of his passport. Her remaining time she divided between showing her family old haunts, attending demonstrations, touring Party facilities, observing the British court system (of particular interest to Bob), and meeting Party members. She also met with some old friends, including Philip Toynbee, and had a very unsatisfying meeting with Giles Romilly, who seemed strange and stilted to her. And then the group drove to Chatsworth, on the eastern edge of what is now the Peak District's national park. Approaching Chatsworth, small in the distance, then grander and grander, Decca waited to see what Bob thought, bracketing her own first impressions, perhaps because they were too difficult to process.

In the long letters Decca wrote home, she acknowledged that she was more comfortable with Bob's reflections than her own. She felt "inhibited" about sharing her reactions, she said. The "Bob's-Eye View" of her family was funnier and less ambivalent. She quoted Bob's thoughts on her family instead of her own:

We made our tour of the dukeries. Our first stop was with Debo at her little hideaway in Derbyshire, where we spent three ducal days. The main establishment, "Chatsworth," is only slightly larger and grander than Versailles, 178 rooms and no baths. . . . Because of the monstrous death duties the poor dears can no longer afford to live in Chatsworth, so they live in the "lodge"

*(which they own) in the village (which they own), and they
make do by opening Chatsworth to holiday trippers 6 months
of the year. This year they led the league with 250,000 trippers
[at] 2 ½ shillings a head.*[25]

They all were, Dinky said, "fish out of water" in that "bizarre" and "intimidating" estate.[26] Bob had it easy, Decca felt. "For him, my family was a hilarious spectator sport; he was by turn amused and bemused by them, whereas I was in a constant state of ambivalence. . . . I had longed to see them, yet felt myself constrained in their company."[27] Decca's constraint was more well founded than she could possibly have known, given what her sisters were saying behind her back. "I don't know what it is about them," Debo wrote to Nancy, just before their arrival at Chatsworth, "perhaps the *voices*, the screaming American sounds made by the children, or the fact that one feels the other two are waiting to attack one on a million things. I really don't know what it is, perhaps it is just that there isn't one single point of contact with any of them. They come here tonight, . . . Oh dear me how difficult it all is . . . I'll write again after this VISIT, oh dear."[28] To her friend Raymond Mortimer, Nancy admitted that "I don't die for her as much as I pretend to when I write."[29]

Unaware of her sisters' letters, Decca blamed herself for the awkwardness she felt. "They were wonderful hosts and I was not a good guest," she thought. Sometimes the entire trip home felt like a mistake. "You <u>can</u> go home again, I reflected, but only at some risk. I sometimes wondered why I had left the satisfying world I had carved out for myself in Oakland to revive often oddly painful memories and relationships from the vanished past."[30]

From Chatsworth, in an old Austin borrowed from Deborah, Decca gave her family the long-awaited grand tour of Swinbrook and Asthall, showing off the picturesque Cotswolds villages with their narrow rolling streets and honey-colored stone buildings. The new owners of Swinbrook let them come inside to see the Hons' Cupboard—the linen closets where Decca and her sisters had spent their time as children telling stories, teasing, and creating their own language. "The Tour of Childhood Places was a great success," Decca informed her mother. "Bob discovered swastikas and hammer-and-sickle cut in the . . . windows in diamonds by Bobo [Unity] and me when we used to live there, he did roar."[31] Away from Debo, Decca could still tell the funny old familiar stories.

She took the family to meet cousins. She was nervous and guarded. "You were very thorny, darling, when you first came back," her favorite cousin reported. "Prickly is the word, none of us felt we could get near you."[32] She stopped at all the Cotswolds places she had loved as a young woman. She put the family up at an inn in Burford, the nearest market town to Asthall and Swinbrook and a village famous for its winding roads and low, green hills along the Windrush River. Bob made a good impression, as did Constancia. "Needless to say," Decca wrote Aranka, "all my family simply adore Bob, they keep taking me aside one by one to tell me so."[33]

Following a brief stop back in London, Decca and company traveled on to Communist Hungary, which they called "the continent" for their friends at home, in an attempt to foil their FBI trackers. The Hungarian People's Republic was idealized by many global Marxists as a model of republican rule, national self-determination, economic justice for peasants and laborers, and a mutually beneficial Soviet alliance. Getting to Hungary had been a major objective of their trip—as much longed for as family reunions, and perhaps more so. "We yearned to see for ourselves a country in which Communism had triumphed," Decca wrote.[34] Also, Bob's ancestry was Hungarian.

After seeing her family, traveling to Hungary was a welcome return to Decca's sense of herself and her values, a reminder of who she was and why her choices mattered: a reset. She could see a way of life for which she'd been advocating for years. She could support Bob's experience of reconnecting to his ancestry, rather than thinking about her own.

Neither Decca nor Bob had visas for Hungary. They stopped in Vienna to try to arrange travel papers. The Emmett Till case was front-page news there. "Friends here in Austria tell us the press coverage is unprecedented," she wrote, adding a bit wistfully, "I imagine there must be a tremendous amount of activity at home."[35] The Hungarian consulate in Vienna was exceedingly slow. On impulse, Bob told the officials that Nebby Lou was Paul Robeson's niece. (She wasn't.) The effect, Decca said, was "explosive." Travel permission to Hungary was granted immediately.[36]

In Hungary, she and Bob were honored guests. They visited schools, courtrooms, housing developments, farms, and factories. They were impressed with Hungary's development, and especially, its emphasis on culture for everyone, a kind of universal access to education that seemed like a national version of the California Labor School. In Hungary, it appeared, anyone could study photography, sculpture, Marxist theory, astronomy, or poetry. Everything seemed a "triumphant" improvement over the Hungary Bob remembered visiting as a child. Decca said that seeing Hungary was truly "ex-hilarating."[37] Based on the limited information they received about Hungary—soon to explode in anti-totalitarian protests that their handlers carefully kept out of their sight—both received a rosy picture. Needing an antidote to her family visit, Decca may have been especially inclined to see any socialist country in purely positive terms. Hungarian officials worked overtime to show them the best of socialism, and Decca and Bob were only too happy to accept "the authorized view," which screened out growing Hungarian discontent and dissent.[38]

Decca wrote glowingly about their visit for *The People's World* in an upbeat piece of reportage called "We Saw Socialism." In spite of years of writing for the CRC and various causes, no publication in roughly fifteen years—nothing since the series for *The Washington Post*—had carried her name. This article was bylined, "Decca Treuhaft."[39]

Unfortunately, her article was almost wholly inaccurate. While the Hungarian uprising against Stalinist policies would not become a forceful movement for another year, in 1955 there were indications of the revolution to come throughout Hungarian society and especially from workers. She and Bob had missed all the signs, although two workers did try to take them aside for private conversations, attempts that both she and Bob waived away. "Bob and I had entirely failed to perceive the widespread discontent that must have seethed below the surface," Decca later admitted.[40] Her published article was embarrassing.

From Hungary, Decca had scheduled a visit with Nancy in Paris. She hadn't seen Nancy since the failed attempt to lure her onto a British destroyer off the Basque coast in 1937 and felt equal measures of trepidation and excitement. Here, at least, was a family member with whom one could discuss ideas. "Of all the relations seen so far," Decca wrote friends in California, "at least Nancy reads, is still funny, & is not a fascist or an idiot."[41] Most important, for Decca, who was still processing her visits with the rest of the family, Nancy, at least, "had been ardent, even passionate, at the prospect" of their reunion.[42] "'Oh darling Susan it will be like a dream to see you again,'" Nancy had written.[43] Given Nancy's usual cool reserve, this unexpected warmth was especially welcome. Decca had no idea that Nancy was telling Deborah and Diana just how much she dreaded the visit. "Oi am in great & terrible despair," Nancy wailed about their impending arrival. "I can't bear it."[44] Nancy decided to go to Debo, in Chatsworth, to avoid them.

Entirely unaware, Decca made the complex two-day journey from

Hungary to Paris bursting with anticipation. They reached Nancy's Paris apartment on a cold, wet October 21, exhausted. Nancy's maid told them that Nancy had gone to Chatsworth because they'd failed to give Nancy definite arrival information (information Decca and her family had no way to transmit from Hungary). After hours of trying to navigate the French phone system, they finally reached Nancy at Chatsworth. Furious that they were running up her long-distance bill, Nancy hung up on them. She called back after a while. On Debo's dime, she was friendlier, but very concerned that they had been let into her apartment in her absence. She promised to return to Paris quickly if they'd wait for her. I have to "dislodge" them, she wrote Diana. She begged Diana to contact her maid and "tell her once they've gone they're not to be allowed into the flat again—she must shut up & pretend to be away."[45] Decca waited patiently for Nancy to return.

By the time that Nancy made her way back to Paris a few days later, Bob and Nebby Lou had already left to go home. The apartment was not trashed, as Nancy had so feared. In fact, "they behaved perfectly," Nancy confided by letter to Diana, blaming Debo for making her fear the worst. "Debo rather hotted me up," she wrote indignantly. "Oh the relief."[46] Nancy installed Decca and Dinky in the cheapest Paris hotel she could find: "just above the bug level."[47] To her surprise, they proved uncomplaining and flexible. Also, to her surprise, Decca seemed "unchanged—and so svelt."[48]

Nancy was "marvelously good company," Decca said. But she could not penetrate Nancy's well-constructed facade. "One could only guess," Decca lamented, "at any . . . aspect of her private life. She was "adept at erecting barriers."[49] Decca was, of course, similarly adept, "not at all inclined to impart confidences about the subjects nearest to my heart—Bob, the children, the CRC, and the Party," she admitted. The "conversational barrier with Nancy worked both ways."[50] Nevertheless, Decca said she was satisfied with her time in Paris, delighted to find so much of what she'd always loved about the city still intact after the war, and relieved to renew relations with her sister, whatever the limits.

Decca and Dinky returned to London from Paris and both went on diets. Before long, Decca proudly reported being back to her usual weight of 125–130. Much of her time in London was spent in the offices of new solicitors, attempting to settle Esmond's estate after his mother's death. They advised Decca to negotiate with the family and suggested that she ask for something between £1,000 and £5,000 (a sum roughly equivalent to between £20,000 and £100,000 today). Decca wanted to know what she could put into trust for Constancia.[51]

Toward the end of her time in London, Decca caught wind of a scheme that Sydney was hatching to arrange a "chance" encounter between her and Diana. Decca quickly put a stop to it. "I could not have borne to see Diana again . . . too much bitterness had set in."[52]

Before returning to Oakland, however, she was able to visit other family and friends, including her sister Pamela. Pamela seemed well, was quite wealthy, and had become a lesbian—"a you know what bian," as Decca put it in a letter home to Bob.[53] Decca and Pamela had never had the intense connection that Decca had with her other sisters, but it was gratifying to see her happy and making bold choices. Decca also had numerous visits with Giles. In her first meeting, she'd expected him to argue with her about Esmond's inheritance. But Giles never brought it up. They met for lunches, teas, and dinners without discussing either Decca's claims, or her British estate attorneys. Decca warmed to Giles and his family. She learned that he was living on next to nothing. She thought his wife was "quite nice." She found his young children charming and gave them gifts she'd purchased for Benjy.[54]

Giles came down to the docks to see Decca and Dinky off on November 24. They had a warm parting. The crossing home, on the other hand, was very difficult. "Oh the roughness, Decca moaned."[55] They followed it by three days straight spent sitting upright on a train. It was a huge relief, however, to come back to the circles in which Decca felt comfortable. She was greeted by many parties and gatherings celebrating her return. If she had expected England to feel like "going home," her return confirmed that Oakland was where she now belonged.

But she remained assiduous about maintaining contact, especially with her mother. She wrote Sydney letters from the ship, from Aranka's apartment in New York, and from the Santa Fe train back to California. Decca had never lost her British accent. She returned from this trip with a much stronger version of it, which she retained until her death. After her 1955 trip, Decca restored all the quirks of her original Mitford voice, as Dinky, and Decca's closest friends, all noticed.[56] As she had done when Esmond died and she embodied her favorite traits of his, Decca now took on the aspects of her past that she could use best, and that would best serve her purposes. It was a thoroughly singular combination of both self-protective and assertive gestures, the kind of paradoxical double, and nearly contradictory, trait that increasingly marked Decca's character.

Although she'd been gone only a few months, Decca found a changed landscape when she came back. Nicholas was gone. Aranka, who'd been widowed for years, had remarried a man named Al Kliot. Kliot quickly revealed himself to be a scoundrel who wanted to fleece Aranka. Aranka wanted to divorce him, and he was making her pay.[57] The CRC had been floundering when Decca left. Now it was "in shambles." The FBI was systematically invading the workplaces of members and former members. From the "privileged position as wife of a solvent self-employed lawyer," Decca had to witness friends, associates, and clients hounded out of jobs and houses, lose their livelihoods, lose their families, and sometimes lose their sanity and even their lives as a result. The Party, meanwhile, was struggling for both membership and relevance.[58] "I felt useless," she said.[59]

What Decca now saw as the truly interesting struggles were happening elsewhere, mostly in the South. The Southern bus boycotts first began in the late 1940s and became powerful, controversial, sometimes violent—and successful—while she was in England. The December 1955 bus boycott that ignited a mass movement put Virginia and Clifford Durr at the center of the most explosive events in the nation, turning the tables from North to South and shifting the center of gravity in civil rights organizing away from the Communist Party and toward more mainstream groups such as the NAACP.

Rosa Parks, who picked up the gauntlet Claudette Colvin laid down, was the Durrs' seamstress and friend. She was also a long-time NAACP activist. She'd been an investigator on the 1944 case of Recy Taylor, a Black woman raped by six white men, and when she refused to give up her seat to a white bus rider on December 1, 1955, Parks was secretary of the Montgomery chapter of the NAACP. Parks's action was the final straw in a rising national rage over discrimination. It brought together a series of efforts, including a landmark 1946 Supreme Court ruling on interstate transportation, the 1951 arrest of civil rights activist Lillie Mae Bradford, the 1953 Baton Rouge bus strike, and the March 1955 Colvin arrest.

When Parks was arrested, she immediately called the Durrs to the jail. Virginia was shocked by what she saw there, by the "terrible sight" of "this gentle, lovely sweet woman" behind bars. Virginia and Cliff, along with Black political leader E. D. Nixon, would make her arrest a high-level test case, they strategized, to be represented by young Black attorney Fred Gray and Clifford Durr. Parks was the right person, they all agreed, to ignite outrage over the indignities of Southern Jim Crow. Planning and fundraising for the case, organizing supporters and gauging opposition took over Virginia and Cliff's lives. Virginia wrote Decca that the new movement "has a quality of hope and joy about it that I wish I could give you . . . I feel like I am in touch with all the rising forces in the world and the end of fear and slavery is in sight."[60]

Decca wanted to help. "If you can raise any money to send to Mrs. Parks that is the thing to do," Durr replied.[61] Decca fundraised. The bus boycott required Black residents to walk many miles a day when they could not carpool with those who had cars. Decca organized shoe donations. "Theirs are wearing out from walking," she explained to Aranka.[62] In April she organized a speaking tour in Oakland for Rosa Parks. When a good friend of Decca's complained of intractable, debilitating headaches, Decca's response was: "Start collecting shoes."[63]

As busy as she was, Decca also began looking for paid work. She wanted an income, even if all she did with it was donate it away. In the spring she secured the only job she could find, a "rock bottom" position in Classified Advertising at the *San Francisco Chronicle*. "It's a very lowly kind of job," Decca confided to her mother, but "you can't think how I love going to work again after all this time."[64] Drawing on her early sales skills, her observations of Esmond from his silk-stocking days, and especially on her great success as a Party fundraiser, Decca quickly proved herself to be phenomenally proficient. She made a quick ascent through the ranks, received bonuses, and was in line for a promotion when suddenly she was fired. A coworker at the paper let the reason slip: The FBI had appeared at her workplace to warn her supervisor that she was a dangerous "subversive."

With no job, no prospect of work, the CRC officially now disbanded, and the Party hemorrhaging members, Decca found herself at loose ends. She described herself as having: "a) no marketable skills, b) no education, c) blacklisted for being a Subversive."[65] She turned her attention to writing, later joking that she was "more or less driven into the field of writing because of inability to get other work."[66]

Writing was her most realistic option, but it was hardly the accident she claimed. Pretending she was not really serious about writing was a convenient way to insulate herself against the possibility of failure and also to mask her rivalry with Nancy. Decca's first serious writing experiment in this period was very much in Nancy's mode. In fact, it was a direct takeoff of Nancy's article "The English Aristocracy" and her book *Noblesse Oblige*. Where Nancy poked fun at upper-class speech, Decca took aim at Party lingo, a target that her comrades, obsessed with precise vocabulary, made almost too easy. Playing with Stephen Potter's titles, Decca called her booklet *Lifeitselfmanship, Or How to Become a Precisely-Because Man: An Investigation Into Current L (or Left-Wing) Usage.* "If ever a book wrote itself . . . this one did," Decca later declared.[67]

In place of Nancy's U (upper class) and non-U language, *Lifeitselfmanship* offered L and non-L versions of statements. The non-L version was: "Time will tell whether that plan was OK." The L equivalent was: "The correctness of that policy will be tested in the crucible of struggle." There was a quiz on proper word use, with vocabulary words for different sectors of society. In the Needles Trades Section, Decca put: "Pinning (down responsibilities) . . . Hemming (the Labor Movement in with contradictions) . . . Cloaking (with demagogic phrases, or with left-sounding slogans . . . [and]Vested (interests)." She included poetic translations: "with a heart for any fate" became "to a realization of their historic task within the political climate." She concluded with what would later become her signature gesture as a writer—letting her adversary hoist himself by his own petard with a set of self-important, obfuscating quotes from *Political Affairs*, including: "at this juncture we should particularly stress the next immediate stage of progress . . . which is inseparably bound up with, and requires the crystallization of a broad . . ." At the very end, Decca offered a list of "appropriate criticisms" the reader could level at "The Author," making fun of the Party's "Crit, Self-Crit" sessions. The possible boxes to check included "Right-Opportunism," "Left-Sectarianism," "Rotten Liberalism" and "Fails to Chart a Perspective."

Lifeitselfmanship was a home production. Lavishly illustrated by Pele, it was printed on a mimeograph machine and stapled on the dining-room table. Decca printed a few hundred copies, which she and Pele thought would be more than enough. Once the booklet began "selling like mad" they had to keep reprinting.[68] Decca sold it for fifty cents a copy, raising the price to a dollar as demand increased. Any profits were designated for *The People's World.* This was an especially self-serious time for the American Left, and Decca expected to be excoriated, maybe even excommunicated, for making jokes when things were so dire. She couldn't resist turning her family's notorious "Mitford Tease" on her comrades, however, and skewering their pretensions. While Decca was "constitutionally incapable of subordinating her humor," as Peter Sussman aptly puts it, there was more to *Lifeitselfmanship* than that.[69] She was developing a style of argument that continued family traditions of using humor rather than direct confrontation. But she was doing this—entirely at odds with family tradition—in the name of larger social confrontation, agitation, and conflict. Mitford tics were increasingly becoming key to Decca's troublemaking.

Decca had abundant insight into readers' emotions. She intuited that no one would want to see themselves as the target of her tease. Her quiz cannily anticipated and dispensed with an outside reader's objections and criticisms, consolidating the position of those on the inside of the joke. She got away with her tease because everyone in the Party wanted to believe themselves capable of laughing at Party ostentatiousness and no one wanted to feel like the butt of her jokes. "The extraorder thing about 'Lifeitselfmanship,'" she wrote her mother, "is that the worst offenders love it best."[70]

Decca "basked in the sudden, unexpected fame" her pamphlet brought her. She "thrilled to the praise." As she would do for the rest of her life, she "conjured up" images of her readers "sitting around their dinner tables, actually reading something I had written. I do not know if other writers indulge in these fantasies about their readers; I do, and am kept afloat by them," she said.[71] She adored getting fan mail, something she always found especially gratifying as a writer who so wanted to reach her audience. "How I reveled in those fan letters!"[72]

On June 5, 1956, *The New York Times* published a version of Nikita Khrushchev's revelations about Stalinist brutality. The admissions shook the world and destroyed most of what was left of the American Communist Party. Known originally as the "Secret Speech," Khrushchev's information was revealed to Soviet leaders in a closed conference early in 1956. His report laid bare what Vivian Gornick later called "the incalculable horror of Stalin's rule."[73] In numbing detail, Americans learned of labor camps, property seizures, deliberate food shortages, torture and execution of dissidents, assassinations of supporters, and more. Worse, the so-called secret revelations were not really secret. As early as March, the atrocities had been made known to American Communist Party leadership, and their meaning was extensively discussed in national meetings of Party leaders in late April and early May. Inevitably, the word reached Party members. Indeed, the Party talked of little else that spring.

Diminished by the Red Scare, Smith Act trials, and its own ill-conceived strategy of encouraging leaders to go underground, "demoralization and confusions were already spreading" throughout all ranks of the Party, as one historian writes.[74] The immediate question was how to move forward. What responsibility did American Communists who'd been loyal to the Soviet Union bear for Stalin's crimes? Steve Nelson, Decca's friend, wrote that "the words of the speech were like bullets, and each found its place in the hearts of the veteran Communists. Tears streamed down the faces of men and women who had spent forty or more years, their whole adult lives, in the movement. . . . I thought, 'All the questions that were raised along the way now require new answers . . . we're on our own.'"[75] Shocked and betrayed, tens of thousands of Party members resigned in the weeks after the revelations. National Party membership, according to some estimates, fell to about ten thousand. Others put the figure even lower, at about five thousand.[76]

"I did not join this exodus," Decca said.[77] Neither did Bob. Looking backward, critics often ask why all American Communists didn't immediately do so. Some accuse those who did not resign instantly of being apologists for Stalin, or for Russian leadership.

Decca was a fiercely loyal person and felt a strong sense of responsibility to the Party and those who had supported its work. She felt especially responsible to those she'd recruited and did not want to abandon them. Her local clubs had always been focused on American concerns, especially after the Nazi-Soviet Pact, and it seemed to Decca and others that critical local work should continue, without any obedience to Stalin or Moscow. All her friends and associates were Communists or fellow travelers. Like her, all were trying to figure out the most just response. The values that had brought Decca to the Party had not changed. If anything, they were now more urgent. Decca needed to see if the American Communist Party could be fixed before she gave up on it.

For many, Decca and Bob included, the Communist Party was their entire life. Through shared meals, cooperative day care, close friends, resorts and camps owned by Party members, Party-sponsored education, campaigns, newspapers, parties, demonstrations, and fundraisers, the Party circumscribed their world. "One of the reasons I stayed in the Party long after others," Decca's good friend Pele told an interviewer, was "because it was my family."[78] Decca's recent trip "home" still served as a painful reminder that she could not go backward and had no refuge in England. She was strongly motivated to right what was wrong with the Party rather than to abandon it, if at all possible.

To Decca, moreover, while the revelations were indeed "grisly"—"ghastly disclosures of rigged trials and summary executions of revolutionary heroes"—the "very fact that Khrushchev had seen fit to lay them out for all the world to see" seemed proof that "untrammeled, critical reexamination" would usher in a new and more open and democratic spirit: "a new dawn for an indigenous, American-style revolutionary movement led by the Party."[79] Such optimism later seemed naïve, but Decca was not alone in this hope. Others, like Al Richmond, found the "titanic" reappraisals and discussions invigorating. The Party was now "shook" by "untrammeled debate" that many found healthy.[80]

In the fall of 1956, Decca was surprised to learn that her inheritance was, in fact, significant. Giles had not mentioned—"cool" of him, Decca thought—that she would be coming into a third of his and Esmond's father's estate, which included considerable real estate wealth in docks and rents. "I don't suppose I'll ever actually get it," Decca lamented, "rather difficult to get the docks out of England."[81] She didn't say much about the irony of being a committed Communist coming into a sizable inheritance. Before she'd seen a dime, however, she was already taking orders from her friends for the presents they'd like and beginning to give her new "Fortune" away. By December, she'd learned that she might be expecting even more. "If only I had my passport we'd all come back to England to spend it."[82]

The "Fortune" came to about 8,000 pounds (roughly £55,000 today). After gifts and clothes for friends and family (each of her female friends received an expensive new dress), she banked what remained for Constancia, just as she'd done with the small Canadian pension she'd received after Esmond's death.[83]

In October, Decca got away for a week by herself to Laguna Beach, enjoying gatherings in Los Angeles with Party friends and associates. Many were aflutter about Nancy's spectacular success. "Almost every issue" of *The New Yorker*, Decca observed to her mother, seemed to contain some mention of *Noblesse Oblige*.[84]

She wanted to talk to Bob and Dinky and Benjy about it all but didn't want to pay long-distance rates. She invented a ruse, adopted a decade later by dozens of American young people, for avoiding expensive charges. This trick was a word game, as well as a way to stick it to The Man, and Decca had always had a passion for both. The tactic depended on coming up with just the right name to send a clear message to someone without their having to accept the call. It made telephone operators into unwitting intermediaries. Wondering if Dinky would be joining her in Los Angeles, Decca put through a call for Mrs. S. Constancia Cumming (Is Constancia coming?). Other examples included "Mrs. Esther Annie Mehl" (Is there any mail?), "Mrs. Alice Okie" (All is OK), "Mr. Needham Ormony" (Need ham or money), "Mr. Juarez Cocoa" (Where is Cocoa the dog?), and "Lesbioff Tomex" (Let's be off to Mexico). Decca loved cheating major corporations out of their excess profits and never suffered a moment's compunction about doing so. She was immensely proud of her own ingenuity, and she and Bob competed for the most ingenious names to use. Some of her friends got in on the game as well.[85] It caught on nationally. Decca could never prove that she'd been the one to invent it.

Still hoping that the Party would prove itself capable of "fundamental change," Decca traveled to New York in February 1957 as a delegate to the Party's first major national conference since the Hungarian revolt and the Khrushchev revelations. Being elected as one of only four delegates from the San Francisco area was a "high honor," she said. She expected lively debate and a complete rethinking of Party strategy, goals, and priorities. She "welcomed the chance to participate" in that process of creating a "home-grown program for radical change."[86]

She arrived in New York wearing an old beaver fur, handed down from Deborah on Decca's departure from England and now so bedraggled and patchy that even *The People's World* rummage sale had refused it. Aranka was appalled. "You cannot go to the convention in that awful-looking thing," she declared, promptly lending Decca a good mink coat stored by one of her clients. Decca was preparing to turn forty, still very slim and attractive, and she worked hard on keeping her weight down, finding it necessary now to diet periodically. She didn't bow to pressures of conspicuous consumption, generally traveled second or third class, and she furnished her home with whatever was cheap and available. But she cared about her looks. And she took real delight in any luxuries she could afford. She'd accepted the loan of Aranka's fur coat without thinking much about it, glad to have something warm she could wear, and enjoying the fur's soft silky feel.

The next morning, she traveled to the convention hall on Houston Street through a biting snowstorm.[87] Belatedly, she realized how out of place she would be sashaying into the conference in an expensive mink coat and what kind of attention her coat was likely to draw. Not wanting to take the chance that some smart reporter might write up the "Mink-Coated Delegate" in the next day's newspaper, Decca paused out of the driving snow in the subway station, "wrapped the mink in the *Times* and dashed through the snowstorm (and past the photographers)" in a thin rayon dress and pumps, the balled-up mink coat tucked under her arm.[88]

Various reports survive of this convention. All paint it as sad. According to Dorothy Healey, "Three hundred delegates came from all over the country to meet on a snowy weekend in mid-February in a dismally cold hall with the misleading name of Chateau Gardens on the Lower East Side of New York."[89] To demonstrate a spirit of transparency, outside observers were invited to attend, although the press was closed out. One of the observers, Catholic activist Dorothy Day, published a lengthy account of the convention's controversies, "colored" by Khrushchev's speech. In spite of her opposition to Communism, Day could not help but be impressed by the commitment she witnessed, especially from those who'd been arrested on Smith Act charges. "All of these people are convicted," she wrote, "not for having done anything, but for having believed in something, and it is a strange and remarkable thing to see such numbers of people assembled in convention and having served or being willing to serve long terms in prison for their convictions." At the same time, Day could not help but be surprised at "the barrenness of the delegates' terminology" and by the way they "clung to their cliches."[90]

Decca did not disagree. The "sharp turn" she'd hoped for, away from the "hidebound, orthodox leadership of past decades," did not come. What pleasures were to be had from the convention, unfortunately, were not political but personal. Because of *Lifeitselfmanship*, Decca "found myself something of a minor celebrity, and thrilled to the praise of comrades from all over the country, my hitherto unknown readers."[91]

In spite of her disappointment, Decca persisted with the Party once she returned to California. She attended regional conventions, state conventions, and more national meetings. She took on numerous extra tasks for her local district and regional Party chapters, both at *The People's World* and for the East Bay sections of the Party, joining an ever-dwindling band of stalwarts trying to keep Party functions afloat. Decca was an exceptionally responsible Party member. Yet she welcomed opportunities to take a break from what was undeniably a sinking ship. She tried to plan another quick trip to England, which did not come off. Debo pretended enthusiasm but wrote that "I don't terribly want to see her" to Diana.[92] She was invited to the June wedding of Virginia Durr's daughter, Lucy, who was marrying historian Sheldon Hackney, and she was looking forward to seeing the Durrs.

Decca had no idea that she'd become a lightning rod for controversy within the Durr family. Virginia's sister Josephine, wife of Justice Hugo Black, objected to Decca's attendance, arguing that a known Communist at the wedding would endanger her husband's reputation. Virginia refused to withdraw Decca's invitation. "We have never felt that we could disassociate ourselves from old and loyal friends," she said. Virginia wrote Josephine and Hugo that it would be cruel to now ask Decca not to come "as she has lost her boy recently" and also "softened a lot and regards Cliff and me as her best friends." In that case, Hugo wrote back, his and Josephine's attendance "would be most unwise." They did not attend.[93] Unaware of most of this, Decca had a wonderful time at the wedding. She described its "innumerable lunches, evening parties with *Ladies Home Journal* type food (croquettes, creamed asparagus, ice cream in shape of bridal shoes, jellied salads, et. et." to friends back home.[94]

From Alabama, she and Bob stopped off in New York, visiting with good friends Abe and Judy Glasser and seeing Aranka. Aranka might be a pain in the ass half the time, but she was Decca's pain in the ass, and Decca made sure to pay a lot of attention to her.

Decca's English family was shrinking. Decca had never spoken to her father again after running away with Esmond. He died in Northumberland on March 17, 1958. His body was brought back to Swinbrook for burial at St. Mary's Church, where Unity was buried, and Tom was now memorialized. All of Decca's living sisters accompanied their mother to the funeral. Decca did not go.

Dinky planned to start college in the fall. Decca and Bob were working on her applications with her, especially puzzled about all the questions colleges asked about Dinky's parents and their educational backgrounds. "Since both Esmond's parents and mine were quite

273

uneducated and unemployed, that part of the form is full of dreary blanks," Decca moaned to Aranka.[95]

By April 1958 there was little left to hope for from the Party. The only real reason to stay was "inertia." Most of their friends had already resigned. Without fanfare, Bob and Decca did so as well.[96] They felt that they could now do better work outside the Party, where "movements for radical change" were building in Black communities and on college campuses. Informing local leadership of their decision, Decca later recollected, they faced "no recriminations, no bitterness—and certainly no regrets, on our part, that we had devoted all those years to the Party's cause."[97] Bob later recollected that he "never announced that I had left the party. I never avoided red-baiting by saying, 'Well, I'm not a Party member anymore.' As a matter of principle, I didn't think it was a thing that needed to be publicly discussed." He added that "we remained on friendly terms . . . with a lot of the Party people. In California, unlike the East especially . . . you could leave the Party and still remain on friendly terms."[98]

Neither Decca nor Bob said much about what this decision cost them. It would have been painful. Their friend Eva Lapin noted that "to leave the Communist Party was a momentous decision, not only a political one, but a deeply personal and emotional one. . . . Once you left the Party, you were free to move in any direction, but you had to look within yourself to find what that direction might be." Those who left continued to support one another. "The Ex-es, as we called ourselves, kept in close touch, networking," Lapin said, "about possibilities in the outside world."[99] An enormous hole opened up for Decca when she left the Party, a void made especially alarming with Dinky going off to college, Benjy old enough to look after himself, Bob busy at work, and Nicky gone. Something very large would have to now fill that space. It would need to replace both the structure the Party had given her life and, just as important, the identity it had afforded and secured.

13

"Action Man"

I don't like not doing anything.[1]

—JESSICA MITFORD TO HER DAUGHTER, CONSTANCIA

Decca called herself an "action man." The key to getting over grief and having a good life was to stay busy, she believed. "I've always found hard work the very best cure," she told Dinky.[2] "The best one can do," she felt, "is to make the best practical decisions about life that seem right, and hope for the best."[3] "One is only inwardly comfortable, so to speak, after one's life as assumed some sort of shape," she went on. "Not just a routine, like studying or a job or being a housewife, but something more complete than all of those, which would include goals set by oneself and a circle of life-time type friends."[4] The Communist Party had given Decca all that. Losing its scaffolding in 1958 had "knocked [her life] out of shape" and forced her "to start over again."[5] She planned to replace that foundation with writing.

Decca excelled at new beginnings. At forty-three, she'd started over more times than most people could conceive of: from British aristocrat to teenage runaway to refugee to young anti-fascist to American Communist to federal investigator to activist to widow to wife and mother. With neither education nor training she'd established her competence as a federal worker and also risen through Communist Party ranks as an adept organizer, speaker, writer, and fundraiser. Her social life was so full that her family rarely ate dinner at their own dining table alone. With her help, her husband had become a beloved people's lawyer. She behaved as if all these beginnings-again had been effortless, admitting only to loneliness in San Francisco and never to deep anxieties or emotional paralysis. Each new beginning had been as arduous as trying to crawl out of quicksand unaided.

Now, Decca took a steely look at things through the cat-eye glasses that were her only concession to fashion (she was indifferent to popular trends). *Lifeitselfmanship* had been a hoot. But it was clearly a one-off. So, now what?

Recently, she'd rediscovered her box of Esmond's wartime letters. Prompted by a fresh reading of them, she conceived a book about the Spanish Civil War and her first marriage. As she worked on "filling in some of that" background, the book's focus began to shift until it had metamorphosed entirely, becoming her story rather than Esmond's. She wrote in a kind of imaginary dialogue, almost as if she were writing letters, sharing daily drafts with a group of friends she called "the Book Committee." As the project grew into a full-blown memoir of her family—competing with Nancy's fictionalized versions—a central theme began to take shape. Her story was becoming about not fitting in, always feeling like an outsider, seeing things from a different, more critical, perspective. The problem was memoir itself, hardly an obvious genre for someone as forward focused as Decca. "I'm not a specially introspective type," she readily acknowledged. Looking backward is not much in my nature."[6] She'd shared her manuscript with a New York agent who was "tremendously encouraging," she reported to Dinky, and she took his enthusiasm to heart.[7] The writing offered an opportunity to put her own spin on her family history, something she especially needed after her complicated first trip home. Decca had not fared well in Nancy's versions of the family, dismissed as an angry runaway and a lightweight, yet also as grimly doctrinaire, unbending, and irresponsible. She saw no reason to cede Nancy full control of the family story. Enough Mitford mythology was present in Decca's *Washington Post* series for her to believe that she had first claim to Mitford family material as intellectual property.

The easiest part of writing a memoir turned out to be setting up a "very workmanlike" routine.[8] With Benjy in grammar school, Dinky in her final year of high school, and Bob at work, Decca had more time on her own than she'd ever had before. She got down to work as soon as the house was empty. Her goal was to write every morning, leaving her afternoons free for political work and socializing. "I think I've discovered the Secret of Eternal Youth," she said. "It is, keep on the move, and time seems to stand still."[9] She placed her typewriter on the dining table, as close to the center of household activity as she could get. Before doing any writing for the day, she answered correspondence and returned phone calls, surrounding herself with dialogue before she surrendered herself to solitude. As part of her new writing routine, she became more disciplined: got up earlier, lost weight (at forty-three, Decca was the slightest bit plump), tried not to procrastinate, kept up with errands. She joined an exercise class and attended a few times before dropping out. She attempted to corral eleven-year-old Benjy's incurable carelessness. "We are in the midst of a crash program to de-sloppy him," she wrote Aranka. "It consists of buckling the old thing down to his homework and practising [*sic*], making him straighten his room, not letting him eat with his fingers, etc."[10] Decca felt very organized and professional as she took a page from her stack of fresh paper every morning and rolled it into her typewriter.

Her greatest achievement in workmanlike routine was defeating writing's solitude. While she claimed to like "leading a quiet life," in fact, she could not stand it and always wrote with one eye open for any possible distraction or good excuse to stop.[11] At lunchtime, she'd call her friend Betty Bacon to get advice on what she'd written so far. Bacon, a librarian, was a "marvelous editor" who could root out structural flaws "like a truffle pig sniffing for its quarry." Decca would then share her draft with Pele—"infallible at spelling and grammar"—and make corrections. She would share it with Pele's husband, Steve, a little later—"he was much harder to please"—and make more edits. Then, later, she would try it out on Marge, her former serious-minded CRC office mate, hoping for success with Marge's "Roarometer" as Decca called Marge's rare but much sought after laughter. At different times in the day, she shared her drafts with Bob, sometimes calling him at work to read choice bits over the phone. "Writing is said to be a lonely task," Decca noted. "I did not find it so."[12] Every day she'd write as many pages as she could force out, the words often whistling onto the page in a headlong rush at her keyboard, always propelled by the happy anticipation of sharing her pages with others. By making her writing such a "thoroughly collective endeavor," as she proudly called it, she was not only keeping herself at it, but also constantly learning how her written voice sounded to others, how she could create a written voice that felt intimate, chatty, and as if she were speaking.[13] Decca loved it when the Writing Committee disagreed. She would open her bright blue eyes wide, squinch up her face, and "roar" over their opposing views. It was just like fighting over political strategy at the CRC, arguing about the best ways to achieve their shared aims. Decca was almost never defensive about negative feedback; she simply ignored advice she did not agree with. Being one of six sisters, part of a "tribe," as she called it, had deeply imprinted Decca's character.[14] As an adult she could only work effectively when she was collaborating with others, leading them, if possible. Then she shone. Her Writing Committee worked brilliantly.

Various readers urged her to be more forthcoming, but Decca could not be pushed into sharing much emotion. "What it boils down to," she wrote Virginia Durr, "is putting one's own feelings on a special plane; most unwise, if you come to think of it. Because the bitter but true fact is that the only person who cares about one's own feelings is ONE. Oneself. That's the trouble in this country, Americans are always going on about their mothers and fathers, their friends and siblings or whatever it's called, and the letting-down of them by one and all. I must say I never felt 'let down' by, for instance, anybody in my family; I expected nothing and got nothing."[15] A book about personal expectations and life's disappointments struck her as pointless. And it would have felt like a defeat. Instead, she triumphed at telling funny stories and showing, through her own story, how a life is both shaped by its world and a reflection of the world that shapes it. She focused on her own rebellion because it was what she knew best and because she believed it might encourage others to rebel. Otherwise, she believed, there was little value in focusing attention on herself.

At first, she could crank out ten or eleven pages a day. The writing came so easily that she thought the whole memoir would be a pleasure to write. Through Dobby, she'd acquired a well-known literary agent, Barthold Fles, a Dutch Jew who established a New York agency in 1933 and was known, in the fifties, for his work finding publishers for blacklisted writers. Fles was initially so encouraging, relaying early interest from Henry Simon at Simon & Schuster, that Decca believed a contract was forthcoming. "So relentlessly did I broadcast this exciting news to anybody who would listen that Marge Frantz threatened to have a button made . . . 'Yes, We Know Decca Has An Appointment With Henry Simon.'"[16]

As the writing slowed down and became more difficult, she worked on her memoir in fits and starts, taking on other projects as well that seemed more manageable to her.

The principal product of this period was an essay called "Trial by Headline" about a macabre murder case (the assailant bit his victims) that had dominated local newspapers for months. Focused on a "media frenzy" of false rape accusations, the essay was accepted by *The Nation* and carried the byline of Decca M. Treuhaft, followed by a descriptor reading "Decca Mitford Treuhaft, a San Francisco free-lance writer." It was published on October 26, 1957, and Decca was paid a seventy-five-dollar royalty (about £500 in today's currency). "Trial by Headline" was disjointed but heartfelt.

Being published in a prestigious, liberal/Left mainstream journal was a watershed. In spite of her *Washington Post* series, her extensive writings on the Willie McGee and Jerry Newson cases, her published essay on Hungary in *The People's World*, and her self-published send-up *Lifeitselfmanship*, she called "Trial by Headline" her "first" published piece. "The publication . . . was for me a turning point . . . it made me for the first time, begin to think of myself as a 'writer' . . . I adored seeing it in print," she said.[17] Although she considered "Trial by Headline" her first true publication, she already had a philosophy of investigative writing: "The main purpose of the exposé type of article is to generate corrective action," she said. Distrust of authority, combined with a high regard for facts, was the literary extension of Decca's anti-fascist politics. Decca's work was thoroughly researched. Never forgetting her lack of education, she always made sure to know more than her readers. At the same time, she took care never to make her readers feel inadequate. Decca could create a community of shared values through her writing by treating her readers with respect and her targets with ruthless mockery. Skills she had used to organize communities in Oakland she now transformed into strategies for building a readership that could be moved to outrage and action. She used case history to drive home larger points about the importance of accuracy and truth. *The Nation*, however, cut out her call-to-action conclusion. From that, she learned never to give editors a free hand.

Writing gave Decca an outlet for her strong, distinctive voice. It realized long-held ambitions. It gave her authority. Where other kinds of work, even for the Party, had required that she prove her abilities, sometimes in the face of skepticism from male bosses, sometimes in the face of skepticism from those who distrusted her British manners and aristocratic lilt, as a writer she could stand on her own, facing her reader, backed by her prodigious research and self-confidence. Writing was also flexible. She could write anywhere, answer to her own sense of what was needed, set her own schedule. Writing utilized her extraordinary investigative skills and her ability—as long as she remained curious—for boundless reading and research. Editors weren't exactly bosses. She kept them at a distance and used her no-nonsense English imperiousness to treat them more as her helpers than as constraints. In one sense, however, writing, so fraught with potential rejection, was a risky choice. Decca expected the swift success she usually achieved with whatever she undertook, and which so rarely attaches to writing's slow grind. She needed her writing to make important contributions to the causes she cared about. She wanted a large and ready audience. Her memoir was an activist's remembrances. It measured her personal growth in terms of her growing political understanding, not against individual self-awareness. As she composed it, she continued her political activism, but writing and activism were not yet fully joined for her.

In 1958, Decca's activism, loosed from both the CP and CRC,

was not notably different. She was fronting for Black acquaintances who wanted to buy houses in white and restricted areas (she especially enjoyed that as it involved subterfuge and the satisfaction of routing racists), trying to organize visits for Jerry Newson, who remained in prison on robbery charges, and supporting Ruby Bridges, a New Orleans six-year-old whose attempts to integrate an all-white school were met with jeers and violence. She was still raising money for Smith Act defendants. She was supporting the nascent student movement in Berkeley that sprouted in 1958 through an organization called SLATE, with Aversion to Conformity as its motto, and that was soon to ignite into the Free Speech Movement. SLATE was formed to support fair housing and to protest anti-communism, racism, and mandatory campus Reserve Officers' Training Corps.[18] Decca loved the young students' anti-authoritarian irreverence and their understanding that all social justice struggles were linked (though she often failed to follow their thinking on gender). Unlike many older Exes, she took the "Yut," as she fondly called them, seriously as a political force. This endeared her to them as well.

At this time, Decca was also working on a long-running whistle-blower case involving three journalists who had reported on U.S. use of biological warfare in Korea and been charged with sedition for their work. Whistle-blowers were Decca's people. She watched their case drag through the court system while the defendants remained behind bars, draining left-wing legal and financial resources.[19] Decca worked "like mad" on their defense committee in 1958.[20]

While Decca had not yet merged her activism and writing, she and Bob never partitioned their lives, always mixing the political and the personal. In June, when they celebrated their fifteenth wedding anniversary, they threw a large party that doubled as a *People's World* fundraiser. The morning after, before they had a chance to gather glasses and ashtrays, carry dishes into the kitchen, vacuum and throw out the trash, they learned that the leaders of the Hungarian Revolution had been executed. Decca felt sick over how she and Bob had misread the Hungarian situation on their trip. She had fallen into the trap of believing what she wanted to believe, not what the facts should have shown her. She did not want to make that mistake again.

Late in June, she headed off with Dinky, Benjy, and two of Dinky's young friends for a 1,650-mile car trip to Mexico, a trip for which passports were not then required. Dinky was planning to attend Sarah Lawrence College in New York in the fall. She had grown into a dependable, mature young woman, a little too serious, some people thought. Decca worried that she might be too introverted, perhaps even inclined to depression. Decca had no idea how best to counsel—or console—her daughter, and she hoped the Mexico trip would be a distraction to redirect Dinky's inward drift. Decca was a flexible and noncomplaining traveler. She loved luxury but was also unusually tolerant of spartan, even unsanitary, conditions. She was impervious to heat—the hotter the better—which her friends thought odd for someone from cold, wet England. They also thought her love of economizing, tracking every penny and always looking for a bargain, was a little odd for someone from her aristocratic background. Benjy was a joy, but also a handful. At eleven years old he had become hyper, curious, wildly energetic, smart beyond his years, athletic, and mischievous. He had a wicked wit (the Mitford Tease came naturally to him) and a grown-up's sense of irony. He was a quick study yet had a perplexingly short attention span. Nothing was safe with him: his lunch, his shoes, appointments, even his bike. He seemed to lose or forget everything. He also continued to suffer from a series of confounding health problems—everything from skin inflammations to bed-wetting.

Crammed into their old De Soto, with way too much luggage and four young people, driving through the ferocious desert heat, Decca was in her element, as happy as her mother in her rickety old Morris. The De Soto had no working starter, and its radiator was prone to overheating. Bob had tried tying a large water bottle to its side mirror so that they would not die of thirst in the desert and could fill the radiator; so now the De Soto lacked a side-view mirror as well. Dinky and her young friends learned to "goose" the old car along. They drove at night and spent the hot days in cheap air-conditioned motels with small concrete swimming pools. In each musty room, Decca pulled out her manuscript, tinkered with a few words, then packed it away again.

Once they reached Mazatlán, Decca wrote glowing letters. "Mazatlán—it is sheer bliss. This hotel ($5.44 a night for the 5 of us) is a huge, cool, breezy place, we have a large bedroom, a closet the size of a small room, a very comfortable sitting room, & on & on."[21] But one of Dinky's friends turned out to be a whiner—"because of the gnats & mosquitoes & general boilingness"—and Decca had no patience for complainers or bad travelers.[22]

Even in Mexico, Decca could not escape "Mad Mitford" stories. This time it was about her and her father's will, which had just been probated. *The Times* (London) wrote that the Mitfords were "a family which has never found it easy to stay out of the news, largely because fascination with them seemed never to fade."[23] Reporters were bowled over by the fact that none of David's estate, worth $361,000 (about £2.6 million today), went to Decca. The *Chicago Tribune* reported that LEFTIST DAUGHTER LEFT NOTHING BY HER FATHER, in a story that gave Decca seven sisters, instead of her actual five.[24] The Associated Press picked up the story and reported that "cut off without a cent was Jessica, who married a Left-Winger and named her child for Lenin."[25] The *San Francisco Chronicle* pictured a sad-looking Decca with the caption "I ran away to Spain." One of its reporters tracked Decca down to Mexico, hoping for a quote on her "split" with her father, who they misrepresented as "a friend of Hitler."[26] Back home in Oakland, Bob was bombarded with requests for quotes. *The Washington Post* also phoned Decca in Mexico, hoping for a quote from "Nobility's Out-cast."[27] Decca found all the interest in her "non-legacy" completely baf-fling. "Really," she wrote to friends, "you must say the papers are pretty odd in their concept of what constitutes news."[28]

One clear takeaway, for Decca, was that Mitford stories sold. So, she was surprised, on returning to Oakland, to learn that Fles, who'd been so warm about her memoir, could not sell it. Simon & Schuster, Dial Press, Morrow, Dodd, Mead, Atlantic Monthly Press, and Doubleday had all passed. "My early confidence seeped away," Decca said.[29] Unsure of whether the rejections reflected her skills as a writer or a lingering anti-communist sentiment, Decca determined that she'd keep working on the book and, if necessary, try it with British pub-lishers. If they rejected it as well, she'd give up her writing ambitions.

She was still trying short pieces when she could find a good subject. The consumer cooperative movement came to her attention through Bob. When they'd moved to Oakland in 1947, they'd joined the Berke-ley Food Coop. Everyone in their circles belonged. Bob did the family shopping and Decca paid little attention to the Coop, although the co-operative movement had a long history of fighting economic exploita-tion and criticizing corporate capitalism.[30] To her, it was crunchy-feely terrain of little interest. Bob, on the other hand, was totally taken with cooperatives. He threw himself into the Food Coop, serving on its board of directors. This, along with his work with labor unions, alerted him to the exploitive practices of commercial funerals. Funeral costs invari-ably claimed 100 percent of working people's death benefits and often a family's life savings as well. How, Bob wondered, did undertakers know exactly how much money survivors received in death benefits? How did they always contrive to siphon off every cent of it?

Bob helped organize the nation's second funeral cooperative, the

Bay Area Memorial Association. He served as president, did the association's legal work, and in Decca's view, became ridiculously obsessed with its problems. She waved away "Bob's funeral thing" as a dismal pursuit. Decca "showed no interest in it at all until I started bringing home some of the trade magazines," Bob explained.[31]

These magazines—*Mortuary Management, Casket & Sunnyside,* and *Concept: the Journal of Creative Ideas for Cemeteries*—spun a macabre, shadowy world of burial negligees, street wear, and brunch coats for the dead, devices such as "Natural Expression Formers" and expenses such as the "True Companion Crypt, where husband and wife may truly be together forever." They appealed to Decca's fascination with anything weird or secretive. Oblivious to what outsiders might make of their "apoplectic flights of rhetoric," the stories in these trade magazines handed Decca a wealth of self-damning material, proudly boasting of their strategies for shaming vulnerable customers into expensive purchases they could not afford.[32]

Bob suggested that Decca consider an article on the memorial societies. She opted for "horror stories about fleecings at the hands of unscrupulous undertakers."[33] She hoped the article would "provide me with some comic relief and a needed break" from her memoir and she dashed off an article called "St. Peter Don't You Call Me," detailing how Americans could not afford to die.[34] Her agent tried to sell "St. Peter" to all the mainstream periodicals. Every one of them rejected it as "too distasteful a subject." Finally, *Frontier,* a small regional magazine with a circulation of two to three thousand, bought the article, Decca's second mainstream sale, for forty dollars. "No great shakes," Decca wrote Aranka. "But I'm glad it will be printed somewhere."[35]

Her article proved to be far more successful than she could have imagined. It showcased her ability to handle serious, even "gruesome," topics in a breezy, inviting voice.[36] It revealed her uncanny knack for letting her subjects humiliate themselves. She used their own words against them, such as an undertaker's pronouncement that "in keeping with the high standard of living, there should be an equally high standard of dying," or a glossy offer from the National Casket Company to pay fellow funeral directors "$5 each" for examples of tactics used successfully to trick buyers into unnecessary but higher-priced goods. Funeral directors called her merciless. Readers loved her. Decca reveled. Funerals began to seem a "very lively subject" indeed.[37]

Thanks to a *Saturday Evening Post* feature that credited Decca with "leading the shock troops of the rebellion in one of the most bizarre battles in history—a struggle to undermine the funeral directors, or 'bier barons,' and topple the high cost of dying," her obscure exposé prompted what she called "a really astonishing response."[38] The *Saturday Evening Post* writer, Roul Tunley, called her "the sharpest thorn in the morticians' sides" and said that she had "iron nerve."[39] Decca was suddenly in demand as a speaker, especially on television and radio.

She had stumbled onto a subject whose time had come. People were hungry to avoid being taken advantage of by the "Dismal Traders," as Decca called undertakers. Her critique of "the American way of death" combined two cultural strains rarely found together: an anti-consumerist/anti-materialistic perspective and a less familiar aristocrat's disdain for American bourgeois taste—anything faux, new, or fake. Decca struck a chord.

At the same time, she was struggling with the memoir. "No more of this 8 to 10 pages a day, more like 0," she told Dinky. Sometimes she truly hated "the cold, hostile look of the typewriter when you are stuck. . . . Remind me not to start any more books once this one is out of the way," she pleaded.[40] Her work would go OK for days, then hit an unexpected logjam. "I'm always setting optimistic deadlines and not meeting them," she admitted.[41] Oddly, although Fles could not place her memoir and she could not bear to finish it, she embarked on a second memoir (which she would not publish for another twenty years).

She also looked for essay subjects, took on book reviews, and courted commissions. She declared herself self-employed on her joint taxes with Bob and deducted her writing expenses. She wanted to make good on that declaration and pushed Fles to try selling her memoir in England, where "Mitfordiana" meant ready-made audiences. At the very end of 1958, Decca and Bob unexpectedly received their revoked passports and were suddenly cleared for international travel. This made selling her memoir in England appear even more viable.[42]

Decca told her mother that she was glad to have the passport but had no immediate plans to return. By the spring, however, she had departed California for London, with Benjy. Bob was expected to find short-term renters for their Oakland home (their practice whenever they traveled) and to fly over later in the summer, so that they could travel together, in other parts of "Yurrup." Decca was especially excited to show Benjy England and introduce him to his British roots. Her biggest worry—drilled into Benjy as a grave matter about which he could not breathe a word—was keeping her memoir hidden from the family. She hoped to sell it before the family caught wind of it. She did not want them meddling with her version of their lives.

From their first day on ship, Benjy found his way to First Class, where he spent the day in the pool and made new friends. Decca found Benjy to be a delightful traveling companion. He was funny, helpful, and people universally found him to be charming and mature beyond his years, already imbued with the family's dry wit and quick bon mots.

Their cruise started out very smoothly. Decca was surprised at how well she handled it, not feeling seasick in the least. Halfway to England, however, a storm rolled in and the sea became rough. Decca rode out the violent turbulence with Benjy in the cruise ship's bar. "We sat out the storm making lists of which of our fellow passengers to save, which to let drown. I was glad to find we were in substantial agreement on both lists."[43]

In London, she experienced "none of the awkwardness and strain which rather dogged me on the last visit."[44] She lunched with Sydney at the Mews, visited with Nancy who came in from Paris, and with Pamela who came in from Ireland, met new friends, saw old friends, dodged reporters, saw a performance by Paul Robeson (who'd finally gotten his own passport back as well), and missed Bob. "Do remind me not to plan these long trips without you any more, as I miss you fearfully," she wrote him.[45] Giles dodged her initially, but Decca succeeded in seeing him: "He is just completely loony," she told Bob sadly.[46] Friends confirmed "the battiness of Giles," reporting that he went for his wife "with a knife a few times, also he left home one night without a word and didn't show up 6 weeks; he just went off to France by himself."[47]

Decca's "Red Letter Day" was April 26, 1959, when she received word that her new agent in the UK, James MacGibbon (a "heavenly" ex-Communist), had sold her memoir to Gollancz in Britain and Houghton Mifflin in the United States for the "huge advance" of $1,500 (about £10,000 today).[48] Decca telegrammed Bob "in a haze of unbelieving excitement." She was bursting, but she kept the news from her family.[49] She told her sisters only that she was working on a "sort of memoir of my life with Esmond."[50] With input from her Book Committee and help from MacGibbon, Decca fired Barthold Fles.

Decca's memoir of family life in "the Cotswold country, old and quaint," rehearsed many of the same anecdotes of eccentric behavior made famous by Nancy in *The Pursuit of Love*. Decca opened her book with a prologue previewing the Hons Cupboard, the hammer and sickle and swastika window carvings cut by her and Unity, her parents' peculiar dietary notions and their rigid rules about "Outside" and "Elsewhere." Then she went on to the infamous Mitford Tease, the sisters' play and private languages, their parade of bolting governesses, their mother's refusal of formal education—all the comic rituals of

Mitford family life, rich with "all our silly jokes and private languages, huge Christmas gatherings, Nancy's bright clownishness and Boud's [Unity's] immense, strong personality."[51] Decca brought her parents to life as formidable and peculiar, and also as much loved by their children, herself included. Often funnier than Nancy's novel, Decca's memoir also took the family and its milieu seriously enough to take it to task. She included long sections on marriage, dwelling on a young girl's desperation to avoid "normal virtues." She was careful to depict a young girl's growing awareness of class inequality, the pain of losing loved ones to fascism, and the everyday life of war. The memoir painted a very positive picture of idealism and rebellion. Seen through Decca's and Esmond's eyes, the world is troubled but worth fighting for. Sacrifice and struggle matter. Her memoir ends with Esmond still alive (his death appears in a footnote), driving "slowly off down the Durr's drive," and Decca watching him go, wondering what is ahead of her.[52]

Her publishers moved quickly. They wanted a better opening, a stronger ending, more about Unity, and a less "bald" (i.e., more self-revealing) narrative. They needed the edits right away, so Decca set up on Inch Kenneth, where she had no choice but to work right under her mother's nose. Decca fell under Inch Kenneth's spell, alternating work with long, slow walks and beautiful views, and spending time with her mother's enormous scrapbooks, "every clipping about any or all of us, gathered and pasted in huge bound tomes." Dismayed, Decca saw that her mother was nearly deaf, frail and weak, but tossing away her prescriptions, hearing aids, and canes and refusing to see her doctors. Decca let her mother read a little bit of the manuscript. Wisely, Sydney said little about it, though she hated the title so much that she wrote Decca's publishers, behind Decca's back, imploring them to change it. Victor Gollancz refused.

Decca now decided that she wanted to buy Inch Kenneth from her sisters and offer her mother a life tenancy there.[53] The sale of the sisters' island shares was completed in June, for about $12,000 (a little more than £70,000 today), largely with funds from the final settlement of Esmond's estate (Nancy generously offered her share for free, feeling that Decca had been ill-treated by David in his will). While the purchase might seem an odd choice—few places are farther from Oakland, California, than the Inner Hebrides of Scotland—Decca justified the purchase as a "good investment." The poetic justice of purchasing Inch Kenneth, through her husband's estate, when she held the family accountable for his death, was a factor. Owning Inch Kenneth was also a way—like reclaiming her British accent in 1955 or like writing her own family memoir—to keep her ties while besting some members of the family. Decca finished her memoir revisions in mid-July. "The pleasure of having it done is indescribable," she said.[54]

At the end of August 1959, Decca and Benjy returned to America on the *Liberté*. Decca never traveled light. She disembarked with sixteen pieces of luggage, all of which had to be located (she'd neglected to put her name on her boxes) and transferred first to Edith's, then to Aranka's, and finally to the train station in New York. Then the luggage was transferred again at the train station in Chicago, where Decca and Benjy boarded the City of San Francisco train for the final leg of their travels. Aristocrats who travel with that much baggage also travel with servants to wrangle it. Decca had kept the custom without the means to make it workable.

Hons and Rebels appeared first in the UK, at the end of March 1960. The cover, drawn by Pele, showed a young Jessica Mitford in a British skirt and flat shoes, trapped under a glass bell jar, desperate to join an exciting world of glamorous women, men of color, beatniks, and activists, all doing fascinating things, just outside the glass. It was the first major publication to carry her name as Jessica Mitford, undoubtedly to capitalize on the interest for all things Mitford in England. She went from identifying herself exclusively as "Jessica Treuhaft" in her first publications, to "Jessica M. Treuhaft" or "Jessica Mitford Treuhaft" in the late 1950s, then back to "Decca Treuhaft" in *Frontier* in 1958, then Jessica Mitford for her memoir. As Peter Sussman puts it, "Decca's search for her public identity as a writer was reflected in her changing byline."[55] She copyrighted the book under "Jessica Treuhaft." From the time *Hons and Rebels* appeared, however, she always used "Jessica Mitford" and never again reverted to her married name in bylines.

Decca was nervous about the reviews. She needn't have been. It received what she called "amazingly favorable" reviews.[56] The reviewer for the all-important *Times* (London), praised the book as "extremely funny" and got that the "binding theme of her book is an assessment of the things she was running away from." Decca had worried especially that she'd be seen as too critical of her upbringing, but that reviewer wrote that "she depicts a childhood of uproar, and contrives a damning and yet hilarious spectacle of home life without ever taking refuge in malice." Most gratifyingly, the reviewer added that the book displayed "not a trace of self-pity." As an almost instant British bestseller, *Hons and Rebels* appeared on lists alongside Joy Adamson's *Born Free* and Gavin Maxwell's *Ring of Bright Water*, tales of natural triumph of a very different sort but perhaps appealing to readers who wanted to immerse themselves in unfamiliar worlds.

A few months later, on June 6, 1960, *Hons and Rebels* appeared in the United States, to even more glowing reviews. Critics dubbed it "one of the funniest books of reminiscences anyone ever wrote." It received two reviews in *The New York Times*, and two in *The Boston Globe*. To Decca's relief, American reviewers did not dismiss the book as merely a funny romp that "catches the English nobility with their hair down." They noted that the book served important social and historical purposes—just what Decca had hoped for. The Mitford family, *The New York Times* reviewer wrote, especially seen through Decca's eyes, was "emblematic of the troubled, divided, dramatic times." Presciently, that reviewer also described Decca's escape from her family as a "ruthlessly patrician rebellion."[57] Decca was thrilled with the "instant respectability."[58]

Decca longed for Nancy's response but also feared it "more than anyone's even the reviewers."[59] She hoped that all her sisters would respond favorably. She should have known better. Diana, probably stung by the reviewer's description of Decca as "the most brilliant" of the sisters, responded to *The Times Literary Supplement*'s admiring review by countering that Decca's portrayal of the family was inaccurate and "grotesque."[60] Only Nancy wrote directly to Decca. She praised the book as "easy to read & very funny in parts." Then she slammed it as sending "a very cold wind to the heart." In her view, it didn't "seem very fond of anybody." She was dismissive of Esmond, who she'd never liked, as an original "Teddy Boy," or delinquent.[61] Aside from that letter, Decca encountered "total silence" from her other sisters, some refusing even to admit whether they'd read the book or not.[62]

Debo hated it. In some profound way, Debo lacked the social sense, the social consciousness, at the core of Decca's personality. She could not understand taking politics seriously. In spite of the very public responsibilities of being a duchess, Debo's world was insular and lived always on her terms. To Nancy, she wrote that Decca's memoir "becomes so dreadfully sad, the baby dying and Esmond too, oh she has had a tragic life. I would understand anything bitter now, but why then, before all the dreadery set in. I will never understand it."[63] That the "dreadery" of fascism could profoundly affect Decca's life, and that her family's complicity with Nazism and global suffering would, in turn, cause Decca to suffer also, never made any emotional sense to Debo. In her view, Decca's depiction of a life embedded in its times was just "dishonest . . . ninety per cent lies & rubbish."[64] Nancy reported some other sisterly "Reactions," all ones that Decca could have done without. She told Decca that Diana "was not pleased at being presented as a dumb society beauty & is really down on the book."[65] Privately, Nancy confided to Pamela that she considered Decca "beastly" and "insensitive."[66]

Decca was acutely sensitive, especially to social conditions. After the Khrushchev revelations and the collapse of the Party, many Exes, like Decca, were drawn to movements rooted in concepts of participatory democracy, in place of centralized, authoritarian organizations. In the spring of 1961, working on three journalistic assignments at once, she stumbled into what she'd been looking for.

She was commissioned to report on the growing student movement in Berkeley. She wrote an uncharacteristically dull article, "The Indignant Generation," an excerpted version of which was published in *The Nation* in May 1961. It differentiated the many varieties of student dissent and lauded the students for "being do-gooders in the . . . best sense of the word, raising the banner of humanity and freedom not for themselves but for their fellow-man in distress."[67] While the essay was not her best effort, the student movement grabbed her attention. Additional assignments helped focus her political energies. She was commissioned to write two more essays, one called "Proceed with Caution," about long car trips in the U.S. and the luxurious standards typical of American motels—part of the "American genius for comfort"—for *Life*; and another for *Esquire* on the American South.[68] For some time, she'd been contemplating a book project on the South, imagined as an outsider's perspective on intransigence. The *Esquire* commission enabled her to take a trip to the South that spring of 1961, allowing her to spend time in a number of Southern states, participating in anti-segregation demonstrations and "Testing Committees"—groups that went out into Southern communities to see if anti-segregation laws were being observed. In Kentucky, Decca visited with Carl and Anne Braden, renowned white civil rights activists. Anne Braden was a strong feminist, a proud "traitor" to her Southern white heritage, and an "Action Man" in her own right. Braden found a "place to live" in politics. She believed that being part of the political struggle "gives life a meaning."[69]

Decca was especially interested in how political women like Virginia Durr and Anne Braden found their voice.[70] She was also influenced by their aversion to celebrity leadership. Unusually open to the politics of the "Yut," Decca was particularly drawn to groups such as SNCC (the Student Non-violent Coordinating Committee), and the principles of Ella Baker, who maintained that political decisions had to be made by those who did the work and stood to be most affected.

Decca's Southern journalism was not particularly influential or successful, but her experiences in the South, and the activists she met there, gave her a feminist, anti-racist, and anti-authoritarian political model. Southern activists inspired Decca with an idealistic but fierce sense of social justice. Their ability to identify and empathize, across racial and national lines, was what she'd witnessed in both Spain and the CRC and had looked for ever since. The Southern activists she met all embodied the principle that "injustice anywhere is a threat to justice everywhere," which Martin Luther King, Jr., made the core of his influential organizing.

Decca happened to arrive in Montgomery, Alabama, to spend time with the Durrs in mid-May 1961. She was there just a few days after a group of Freedom Riders were nearly killed in Anniston and Birmingham, when their bus was set on fire by a white mob, which trapped them inside. When they finally did escape, they were badly beaten. The Freedom Rides were a watershed political moment, one that participants regarded as "our generation's Spanish Civil War."[71] Those who sacrificed their own safety for others' freedom were criticized as outside agitators, just as the supporters of the International Brigades, like Esmond, had been criticized decades ago. In the young people who "willingly put their bodies on the line for the cause of racial justice," as historian Raymond Arsenault puts it, Decca saw the activism she most admired.[72]

On May 20, a contingent of Freedom Riders from Birmingham filled out their wills and boarded a bus. The Alabama governor had promised Attorney General Robert Kennedy there would be police protection for the Freedom Riders. And from Birmingham, the bus had an initial escort of highway patrol, reporters, and a highway patrol airplane. At the Montgomery city lines, all that accompaniment disappeared. When it reached downtown Montgomery, the solitary bus pulled into a terminal with not a single policeman in sight. Instead, the double-decker Greyhound bus was met by a large, vicious white mob.

Clifford Durr's law office was adjacent to the bus station. Decca, there with Virginia, had a clear view through the plate-glass windows as the mob dragged John Lewis and the other Freedom Riders from the bus and beat them with bats and lead pipes.[73] "The only law enforcement presence," Taylor Branch writes, "was a stone-faced FBI agent," who simply took notes as a large wooden Coca-Cola crate was smashed over John Lewis's head, and a Black teenager was doused with kerosene and set afire. As the mob systematically knocked out the teeth of white Fisk University student Jim Zwerg, "a few adults on the perimeter put their children on their shoulders to view the carnage."[74]

Decca ran directly into the melee. "Decca's down in the mob," Virginia Durr yelled to Bob Zellner, a young friend of the Durrs who later went on to become famous as a white SNCC organizer, as the police arrived and began spraying tear gas through the crowd and arresting the Freedom Riders, not the white mob.[75] Zellner pulled Decca to safety. "These were the people I was living among," Durr wrote, "and they were really crazy. They were full of hatred and they were full of bigotry and meanness."[76] As Decca noted in her *Esquire* article, she had planned only on observing the South, but "violence followed me and unwittingly I found myself in the middle of it."[77]

A rally was scheduled for the next night, Sunday, May 21, with all the Freedom Riders, and special guest Martin Luther King, Jr. It was to take place at Reverend Ralph Abernathy's First Baptist Church in Montgomery, an imposing redbrick building three blocks uphill from downtown Montgomery. Decca borrowed the Durrs' car to drive to the church. She'd been instructed to park a few blocks away. But as she pulled near the church, she saw a white mob beginning to amass around the church. So she parked right in front and dashed inside, dressed in her best Southern outfit of green chiffon and pearls.

Inside the church were fifteen hundred mostly Black Montgomery residents, gathered to hear from King, Ralph Abernathy, Fred Shuttlesworth, Diane Nash, and the Freedom Riders. Everyone crowded onto wooden pews while a "howling mob" encircled the building. They were "a living mass of formless hate," one attendee remembered.[78] The white throng swelled to over three thousand people. It began hurling rocks and stink bombs, breaking random car windows, and trying to set fires, most of which sputtered out in the thick spring humidity. A few federal marshals with tear gas stood between the attendees inside and the crowd outside. That frustrated the white mob, and it grew more enraged. It overturned a green Buick and set it ablaze, cheering as the flames caught the gas tank and exploded. A few marshals were injured by flying debris from the burning sedan, and they left.

The church windows were shut to block rocks and stink bombs, but gases seeped in. Heat waves rose to the pressed-tin ceiling and settled back down over the crowd, smothering those in the upstairs pews of the high balcony in a solid blanket of nearly 38-degree thick air. "The ceaseless flutter of paper fans, bearing the imprint of a local funeral parlor, merely stirred the soupy air." From the pulpit, King urged calm. But almost everyone in the room knew someone who'd been lynched. Decca worried that if even one person panicked and began to run, there might be a stampede inside the church. All remained stoic.[79] Not one

297

person broke ranks. "Searching that sea of calm, determined faces, I felt as though I'd stumbled on the very source of strength," Decca said.[80] Every day, she realized, these people tamped down rage, found a way to carry on with their lives, and had the fortitude to feel joy.

Inside the church, the civil rights supporters sang, held hands, and prayed. In the basement, seated at a gray metal desk, with his shiny black shoes firmly planted on the brown linoleum floor, King held a heavy desk phone and tried to convince Attorney General Robert Kennedy to send troops. Members of SNCC gave short speeches. Ministers preached. Freedom Riders read poems. Children played in the hallways. Women made tea and coffee. At home, the Durrs sat up all night trained on the radio. Inside the church, the heat continued to rise.

Kennedy was distantly related to Decca through his deceased sister, Kathleen, known as Kick, who had married Andrew Cavendish's older brother, Billy. John F. Kennedy and Debo were close—perhaps a bit too close, a few friends cautiously hazarded. But Decca attempted no personal appeal. She kept her place on the pew, fanned herself, and waited. At 4:30 in the morning, the National Guard finally arrived, circled the building, and told the white crowd to disperse. As the sun rose, many of the fifteen hundred people assembled inside the church walked out, finding their own way home as best they could. Decca and a young college friend of the Durrs came squinting out a side door to discover that the burned car was the Durrs' Buick.

Writing about her ordeal, Decca tried to use a light touch, starting her essay with an aside about long meetings and attempting to mock the rioters for looking exactly like "mob scene extras" from Hollywood. The article was commissioned by *Life*, but never published, though *Life* paid a five-hundred-dollar kill fee for it. Decca incorporated one page from it into an essay about the South called "Whut They're Thanking," but somehow it didn't quite work there either.[81] None of her letters contain an account of that night. Characteristically, she said least about what mattered most. As with Esmond's death, the impact of that night cannot be sought directly in her writing but must be measured otherwise, in how it changed her life. When she wrote Bob the next day, Decca focused on the Buick. The Durrs had no insurance, and they'd need to buy them another car, she said.

Back in Oakland by late May, Decca regrouped. In the fall, she and Bob moved for the last time. They bought a larger house on the edge of Berkeley and Oakland between Telegraph and College avenues, slightly set back on a quiet residential street lined with large homes on good-size lots. The house was a wood-framed, 1910 Craftsman-style house with a wide front porch, a large living and dining room, a big kitchen, five bedrooms on the second floor, a fireplace, and a sunroom addition that looked out over the backyard. In between the dining room and the addition was a wide hallway with built-ins along one side. Decca put her desk and files on the other side and that passageway became her office, tucked away from the rest of the house but in sight of everything that was going on.[82] There was a small front yard, perfect for roses. "It's a lovely house, much nicer than any heretofore," Decca wrote Durr. "Special little room for my writing things, so they won't overflow the living room, and v. nice living room, dining room, kitchen etc. Also, masses of rooms, and a huge attic."[83] Every time Decca would finish a project, she would cart boxes of research material upstairs into the attic, where she never had to look at them again and did not have to spend time sorting.[84]

In her new study, staring at her garden and down the street from the growing university protests, Decca thought about what to work on next. She raised funds for a variety of Southern anti-racist causes. The South, she concluded, was a "mass of contradictions."[85] Believing that she lacked the background to sort them out, Decca abandoned the idea of a book on the South and decided she might be better suited to work on other things.

14

"The Making of a Muckraker"

I had a wild & woolly time. . . . Oh, absolute wildness.[1]
—JESSICA MITFORD

Decca was a superb planner, detail-oriented and disciplined. At forty-four, with her first published book under her belt and doing well, she wanted to move deliberatively to capitalize on that success. Appreciating the need to keep her name before the public, she was on the lookout for an excellent new topic while also accepting almost any writing assignment that would carry a byline. A few fluff pieces and book reviews, on the other hand, quickly found good homes.[2]

Planning was one of Decca's strengths, but pivots were her superpower. She tended to be most successful when seizing on opportunities that presented themselves, and her knack for making hay from the unexpected was uncanny.

Tunley's *Saturday Evening Post* essay, "Can You Afford to Die?" continued to generate an "absolutely astonishing" response. The Bay Area Memorial Society had to hire extra staff to respond to the thousands of new inquiries the article generated. Bob received a phone call from the United States Postal Service: "We have hundreds of letters here addressed simply Jessica Treuhaft, Oakland," the Oakland Postmaster groaned. Decca's favorite envelope was addressed to "Jessica Mitford, Cheap Funerals, Oakland."[3]

Clearly, there was a market for a book on the subject of funeral expenses. Decca offered Tunley all the research materials she'd assembled for "St. Peter Don't You Call Me" and volunteered to introduce Tunley to her contacts and also to Bob's Memorial Society associates if he'd take it on.

"Why don't *you* write it?" Tunley replied.[4]

On the face of it, a book about expensive funerals was a far cry from the social justice and civil rights topics Decca had been pondering. What could such a book contribute to racial justice, freedom of speech, fair housing or labor? How could overcharges for caskets compare to firebombed buses, battered protesters, besieged churches, murdered children, voter suppression, student radicalism, or an impending war?

Decca recognized, however, that larger issues were at stake in the fight for dignified dying. She saw political potential in any cause that could give voice to the voiceless. She perceived a broad constituency for the subject: everyone dies, after all. And she imagined a future in organizing consumers—"Trade-Unionism for Corpses" Evelyn Waugh called it—as yet unappreciated by most American radicals.[5] If consumers imagined themselves as agents of change, Decca felt, they might exert enormous power in a culture increasingly focused on commodities as compensation for everything that was wrong with modern American life. Tunley's article credited memorial societies such as Bob's with bringing collective bargaining to funerals, but the insight into consumer power was as much Decca's as anyone's.[6] She and Bob anticipated by four years the arguments Ralph Nader's *Unsafe At Any Speed* would make about car manufacturers' emphasis on profits over safety, the ensuing creation of the National Highway Traffic Safety Administration, enactment of seat belt laws, and the birth of a consumers' rights movement in 1965.[7]

While she never admitted as much, some of Decca's friends saw personal motivations at work. Friends Martin and Judy Bernal, young writers who were very close to Decca and Bob at this time, believed that "at some level . . . she was dealing with all the deaths she had had to face . . . Esmond . . . her brother Tom . . . two children, a baby . . . and Tito [Nicky], a son whom she adored."[8]

Tackling a book about funeral practices, however, would be nothing like writing her memoir. A book on the funeral industry would demand a great deal of historical, medical, civic, legal, scientific, and cultural research. Decca did not want to do it alone. "Bob and I discussed this possibility. I said I would consider it only if he would help, and work with me on it full time."[9]

Decca's new agent as of that year, Candida Donadio, thought a book on American funerals was just nutty enough to work. Donadio was game.

Bob took a year's leave of absence from his law firm, and they divided up the work. "The book was a completely joint effort . . . We each wrote about half," Decca said.[10] Bob took the legal, financial, and mortuary school research. Decca would do most of the interviews and go underground. As a "pre-need" funeral shopper, she'd infiltrate funeral homes and cemeteries. Bob "is the cemetery man around here. I am the funeral parlor man," Decca bragged to her mother-in-law, Aranka.[11] Both would work through the industry's trade publications and attend its professional conferences and conventions. They managed to get inside many funeral homes, often by pretending to be customers, so that they could see how the business was done and how merchandise was displayed. They even received permission for Decca to observe an embalming session. She didn't think she could bear it, so Bob went in her stead.

Soon, every surface of their home—Decca's desk, the dining table, the coffee table in front of their saggy velvet couch, sometimes the couch cushions themselves—supported stacks of *Casket & Sunnyside*, *Mortuary Management*, *Concept: The Journal of Creative Ideas for Cemeteries*, and other such publications. Some were high-production glossy affairs resembling *Time* or *Ladies' Home Journal*. Others were small-scale productions, mimeographed, stapled and clearly intended only for insiders' eyes.

Decca loved collaborating. Bob, like her, had a seemingly bottomless capacity for work. Decca cut out her favorite advertisements from the industry magazine—backless "fit-a-fut Oxford" cardboard shoes, for example—and taped them to the walls of their small downstairs bathroom to amuse their guests, eventually also taping them to her study walls, to the dining-room doors, and the kitchen refrigerator. When funeral directors noticed all the subscriptions going to a Treuhaft address in Oakland, cancellation notices arrived. Decca enlisted her neighbors and friends to resubscribe on her behalf. Soon, these trade publications—filled with tips on fleecing customers, highfalutin rhetoric about the sanctity of the business, and a dazzling array of expensive items for dressing up corpses—became Decca's special purview. She was at her happiest poring over them, marking ever more bizarre products and promotions to share with Bob and add to the book.[12] It was like the heady first days of *Lifeitselfmanship* all over again. "I am rather loving doing it," Decca confided to her mother. "It's sort of like having a job again."[13]

The undercover research, especially, was "rather bliss" for Decca.

She had a wonderful time in mortuary "slumber rooms," dressed up in her best pastel suit, pearls, pumps, and one of Aranka's good hats, deciding between expensive caskets for imaginary Loved Ones, and dabbing her eyes with a hanky. She was in her element on cemetery tours and in casket rooms: collecting samples, slipping ashtrays into her large black handbag, purchasing cemetery coloring books for children, and filching whatever other memorabilia she could palm.[14] She gloried in working the undertakers up for a "Big Sale" that would never materialize.[15]

Decca had envisioned a little project, intended for a small audience of like-minded anti-capitalists, Unitarians, and progressives—something like *Lifeitselfmanship*, but slicker. "The whole thing shouldn't take very long to write," she promised her agent.[16]

As soon as they began to work in earnest, however, the book's scope exploded. Decca and Bob wanted to cover every aspect of the funeral industry's corrupt and distasteful practices: markups, manipulation, self-aggrandizement, price fixing, advertising, lobbying, and lying. They were particularly astounded by the industry's bold claims for the necessity of embalming, an extraordinarily expensive and grisly practice with no demonstrated health benefits and no demonstrable purpose. They wanted to enrage their readers, so they focused on stories of poor people tricked out of their life savings and widows terrorized into buying expensive caskets with threats of shame and humiliation. One grieving widow was told that to fit her husband into the moderately priced coffin she'd chosen, the mortician would have to chop off his feet.

Decca and Bob wanted unassailable facts to shore up their commonsense values. So they uncovered every tasteless detail of the business from collusions between florists and undertakers to the self-inflated claim that undertakers were professional "grief therapists" for distraught mourners. They wanted to keep their readers' interest, so they made it as funny as they could, constantly deflating "funeralese" and exposing the industry's euphemisms for the sham operation they were. In the trade magazines they found instructionals for undertakers that fed their sense of the absurd and that they happily reprinted. One such instructional directed undertakers to say:

Casket Coach	*not*	Hearse
Display Area	*not*	Casket Room
Internment Space	*not*	Grave
Opening Interment Space	*not*	Digging Grave
Closing Interment Space	*not*	Filling Up Grave[17]

The funeral industry's "ornately shoddy" language made it almost too easy for Decca and Bob to poke fun at them. They had only to pull direct quotes and use them verbatim: "Futurama, the casket styled for the future." Or "funerals are becoming more and more a part of the American way of life," which they chose as the epigraph for their book. Self-seriousness was always the butt of Decca's best jokes. The stratagems the death dealers used to transform their "grubby" work into a so-called social service encouraged her to stop at nothing in parting the "formaldehyde curtain" to expose all the "gooey details" of a very distasteful business.

Decca was an autodidact. Her curiosity was unbounded by disciplinary norms. So she delved into hundreds of years of history on death and dying, comparing cultural rituals from across the globe, researched the world history of undertaking and all its American permutations, studied the clergy's role in death, and became expert in medical donation, cremation, embalming, and entombing. She mastered the history and economics of cemeteries. She went through each record in the extensive archives of the Bay Area Memorial Society. She also began collecting artifacts used in embalming, including a number of gleaming trocars (used to pull fluids from dead bodies). Inevitably, her research slowed her writing. Like most researchers, she vacillated between delight—"I soak up books and articles"—and despair—"the behindhand feeling" of not being far enough along.[18] To cheer herself onward, she peppered her letters with descriptions of favorite funeral home devices—"Bra-Form, Post Mortem Form Restoration" for making a corpse's breasts look perky. Sometimes she enclosed individual items, such as burial lingerie, or makeup samples in her letters to family and friends.

In addition to their detailed descriptions of embalming, Decca and Bob covered the effects of "so-called protective caskets" in graphic detail. The most expensive metal caskets, marketed as a means to preserve the body against decomposition and sealed "to prevent alien and foreign objects from reaching your loved one," accelerated decay, they explained. "Using an impermeable, inexpensive rubber gasket as a sealing device causes a buildup of methane gas, a byproduct of the metabolism of anaerobic bacteria, which, thriving in an airless environment, have a high old time with the contents of the sealed casket. Exploding-casket episodes" were one result. Quoting San Francisco's chief of pathology, they wrote that "an exhumed body is a repugnant, moldy, foul-looking object . . . the silk lining of the casket is all stained with body fluids, the wood is rotting, and the body is covered with mold."[19]

"Cut out the foolishness," her editor tersely demanded.[20] "I am not," Decca countered, "in favor, generally of writing horrors for the sake of horrors . . . this is something different.[21] The point was not to tarnish "the occasional miscreant" but rather to try to take down "the profiteering and monopolistic tendencies of the industry as a whole as exemplified by its most respectable and ethical practitioners." Bob agreed that they had to "go for the jugular."

It was a blow to contemplate losing their contract "after the months and months of work we've put in, and Bob leaving his practice to work on it,"[22] Decca said, but she dug in her heels. With Bob's support she "decided to go ahead, finish the book . . . and sell it ourselves."[23]

Houghton Mifflin canceled her contract.

Robert Gottlieb, Simon & Schuster's young wunderkind, had always wanted to publish an exposé of the funeral industry. He said it was his "one good idea" and had been terribly disappointed, a year earlier, to learn that Jessica Mitford was writing just such a book, but for Houghton Mifflin. "If the funeral book ever comes free," he told Candida Donadio, "let me know and I'll pay twice whatever they paid."

As Houghton Mifflin readied to kill the book contract, Donadio turned to Gottlieb, who happily slapped down the twofold payment he'd promised.[24] "I jumped," Gottlieb recalled of his chance to publish the book, gooey parts and all. Decca and Bob were happy to move over to Simon & Schuster, or Simon's Shoestore, as Decca always called it. Decca found Gottlieb, who would later become one of the most legendary editors in the history of American publishing, "an uncommonly good editor, at once perceptive, amused, tough, adept at ferreting out one's weak spots, yet sympathetic with one's difficulties."[25] Gottlieb said that "it was love at first sight . . . we saw everything the same way."[26]

Working with both Donadio and Gottlieb put Decca at what *Esquire* magazine dubbed the "red . . . hot center" of a new publishing world that understood and knew how to use marketing and public relations.[27] The shift from Houghton Mifflin to Simon & Schuster was the first indication that *The American Way of Death* might have an appeal larger than a few progressives, coop fanatics, and earnest clergy members.

While the book had developed over a year's work, its mission evolved beyond exposing an exploitive industry to a more general "protest not just against high costs, but against something more sinister: destruction of standards, tastes, etc."[28] Although her sisters derided Decca as a bourgeois frump without style, she was, in fact, ideally suited to illuminate the poor taste of America's culture of consumption. Her critique drew on her aristocratic background— its disdain for anything faux or new—and at the same time, on her left-wing scorn of capitalist display. Gottlieb felt that Decca's humor was the key to the success of *The American Way of Death*. "Death & dying were a dirty little secret . . . the fact that she could do it in so funny a way . . . really made it possible."[29] Decca's humor encouraged readers to pit themselves against pompous, predatory undertakers. Her peculiar blend of aristocratic snobbery and Communist values, however, was the engine that drove her humor. In this way, though the research was evenly shared, and Bob drafted nearly as much of the book as Decca did, *The American Way of Death* bore Decca's indelible stamp. In the end, it was her matchless view of the world that made the book such a hit.

Decca and Bob had always assumed that their coauthored book would carry both their names. Simon & Schuster pushed back, insisting that coauthored books never sold as well as single-authored ones. The publisher had begun expecting a wide audience, good reviews, and strong sales for the book. They were heavily invested. They wanted the Mitford name out front, infinitely more marketable than Treuhaft, they insisted. Bob never planned on writing a book and certainly did not plan on writing another. Decca had her doubts. But Bob quickly ceded the point.[30]

Both Bob and Decca were possessed of the ability to work anywhere, under any conditions, regardless of distractions. This allowed them to continue the travel they loved, even under strict deadline pressure for finishing the book. In June, Decca returned to England for her third visit and stayed for most of the summer. Bob accompanied her initially, then returned to California for work. At Chatsworth, Decca mingled with Debo's friends, who included well-known artists and scientists such as Duncan Grant, Cecil Beaton, and Julian Huxley, some of whom Decca dismissed as the kind of people who "sucker up to dukes."[31] In London she saw family and friends, but reported that Giles's marriage had collapsed and that Giles had "gone off his head" and kidnapped his two children, taking them to California.[32] She still found Inch Kenneth a "haven of peace" and reveled in its wild flowers and Muv's improvements, which included redecorating and adding a washing machine, but not a refrigerator because Muv "said it always seems to make the food so <u>cold</u>."[33] On the island, she tried to finish revisions of her book and also turned every page of "the most extraordinary haul of old letters"—all of those received after running away, a stash that had only just surfaced.[34] Sydney kept little alcohol on the island and Decca keenly felt the lack, she told Barb Kahn, of "a good stiff drink in the p.m."[35] Decca's later problems with alcohol were just beginning to show.

In Paris, she spent time with Nancy, with a group of Nancy's lesbian friends—who Decca thought affected and unlikable—and had a visit with Pam and her "German wife, a ghastly one called Jedita, to whom I cottoned not," Decca wrote to a friend.[36] There, she could drink as much as she liked. Nancy took her dress shopping and, as always, encouraged Decca to spend more than she should.

Back home in Oakland in the fall of 1962, Decca was also visited by Giles, who she confirmed had indeed gone "quite a bit mad." She found it "hard to make any sense of him, or his plans." Giles, she reported to their mutual friend Peter Nevile, was both avoiding her and yet sticking close by, somewhere in the San Francisco area.[37]

Bob had returned to his practice as soon as they'd finished a final draft of the manuscript. Throughout the spring of 1963, Decca struggled on her own to keep pace with the frenzy of copyediting, permissions, and indexing. In early May, overwhelmed with book pressures, Decca received word that her mother, then eighty-three years old, had suddenly become gravely ill. She considered trying to make the trip—a two-day journey at best—but her sisters dissuaded her. Muv, they said, was likely to slip away at any moment and then Decca would be stuck, they pointed out, somewhere en route, where they probably couldn't even reach her.[38] As it happened, Sydney held on for nearly two more weeks, slipping in and out of consciousness, attended by nurses and her other daughters. "Susan it's really awful," Nancy wrote to Decca, using their childhood nickname for one another. "So difficult to die," Deborah added sadly.[39]

Sydney died on May 25. Her body was ferried from Inch Kenneth to Mull, then driven to Swinbrook, where she was buried next to her estranged husband, David, on a bright, warm, green spring day. Decca, in Oakland, felt sad and alone. "I do wish in a way I had come," she wrote Debo.[40] In an unusually sympathetic moment—her insight triumphing over her customary cruelty—Nancy noted, "It's worse for you, seeing it from afar."[41] To a friend, Nancy added how sad it was for Decca to miss the funeral, all the "tears" and also the "shrieking with laughter."[42]

Decca was comforted to know that Muv had died naturally, and at home—without hospitalization, intensive care, useless intervention or extreme measures, all the modern medical advances Muv had always avoided. She had an old-English death and an old-English funeral.

Debo sent flowers to Muv's funeral in Decca's name, not realizing that Decca's forthcoming book had a section, under "Allied Industries," on how the florists colluded with the undertakers, and were often owned by them, to persuade the public to spend more on funerals than they could possibly afford, strong-arming newspapers not to print obituaries that omitted directions for sending memorial flowers.[43] Decca attempted to joke about it—"My new book is all about the ridiculous waste of money on funeral flowers."[44] But Nancy took umbrage. Decca had to write her, apologetically, that she "didn't mean to annoy about the flowers."[45]

Had Decca's sisters seen the cover for *The American Way of Death*, they might have understood. The book's design, "the best symbol for a book I've ever seen," Gottlieb declared, was an enormous pink and green funeral wreath, shaped into a dollar sign. It signaled Decca's intention to go after those who profited, handsomely in most cases, from the suffering of others.

Simon & Schuster organized an unprecedented publicity campaign for *The American Way of Death*. For the annual booksellers' convention in Washington, D.C., they planned a giant version of the wreath design, as well as a full-size casket. "We all knew that the book had enormous possibilities to be a bestseller and certainly to be a very controversial book," noted Dan Green, the young publicist assigned to promote the book.[46] Decca could hardly contain her excitement.

The publicity team at Simon & Schuster deliberately goaded the undertakers, hoping to incite controversy and publicity. Some came out with prepublication denunciations of the book, bemoaning it as unpatriotic and mean. "The more they protested," Gottlieb noted, "the more fun she [Decca] had."[47] And the more fun Decca was having with the press, the better the buzz was for her upcoming book.

Advance sales for the book quickly exhausted the seventy-five hundred-copy print run that had been planned. Simon & Schuster doubled the run to fifteen thousand, then raised that to twenty thousand, then raised their numbers again, only to find that the entire first print run sold out on the day the book appeared. They were "bombarded," they said, with booksellers "screaming for additional copies."[48]

Decca hired both British and American clipping services and also enlisted friends and relatives to send any reviews her way. She read them all, excerpted them in letters, and delighted in the extensive international praise for her book. Reviewers applauded its "good sense" and "clear-thinking" as well as its "strenuous research and uncounted hours" of interviews. Placing *The American Way of Death* "in the best tradition of muckraking," they commended its civic-minded mission. "This is not an objective inquiry," the *New York Times*'s reviewer observed. "Miss Mitford is outraged." Humor was widely extolled as the book's special "blessing" and the key to its success, especially whenever the authors "let the perpetrators of the outrage satirize themselves." While death "doesn't readily lend itself to laughs," *The Boston Globe* remarked, *The American Way of Death* was a "howler."[49] *Time* magazine dubbed Decca "Queen of the Muckrakers," a moniker that she loved. Decca was suddenly doyenne of the cultural dictate to question authority, the bedrock impulse of all good muckraking.

"The book leaped up the bestseller list to number one," Gottlieb boasted. Even more importantly, for Decca, "not only were the reviews almost universally dazzling, the subject became topic A in the media."[50] To Decca and Bob's delight, "one had but to tune in to any radio talk show," to hear the funeral industry denounced. Undertakers became the butt of cultural jokes in feature stories, television skits, radio programs, and political cartoons. CBS covered the book in a program that drew forty million viewers. "You're the author of the number-one best seller in the country. You're a major authority whose opinion is sought by legislators and public agencies," Dan Green informed Decca.[51]

Unlike most of the Mitfords, who excelled at emotional restraint, Decca was an unabashed enthusiast. Her openness to excitement and her capacity for hard work, in fact, were the two qualities her friends most often admired. With rave reviews, a bestselling book, national media attention, and sudden elevation to the position of cultural "authority," Decca had to work hard not to "become swell-headed over it all," she confided to Bob.[52]

By September, there was so much coverage of the book that Decca had to hire someone to help her "do a scrap book of them" of her own. Indeed, *The American Way of Death* was such a hit, Decca joked, that "Benj is angling for a $2 weekly increase in his allowance. . . . [and] I've already done a couple of daring things, such as to buy a salad bowl (to replace the beat-up old mixing bowl we've been using) at cost of $12, without consulting Bob. I shouldn't have; he doesn't like it, so am returning it tomorrow."[53]

Simon & Schuster hired a top Madison Avenue public relations firm, Addison, Goldstein and Walsh. Addison sent books not only to other writers and newspapers. They also sent advance copies to labor leaders, airline executives, Congress, the funeral trade journals, as well as florists, medical professionals, and others—anyone who might pay attention to the book, positive or negative. By early October, Decca could report to her sister Debo "they've now gone into a 5th printing, nearly 100,000 books printed."[54]

Almost overnight, Decca went from being a moderately successful writer and very successful local activist to being a nationally celebrated public figure and a wildly successful author. She had no time to keep up with her own fans, let alone attempt any activity that was not book related. She embraced the change, although it meant being sidelined from the center of the political activities that had defined her life. Like most other Americans, she now kept pace with news such as Medgar Evers's murder, Wallace barring the doors to Black students at the University of Alabama, and King's "I Have a Dream" speech from newspaper, radio, and television reports, rather than the first-hand accounts, strategy sessions, or frontline protests and demonstrations that would have formerly shaped her days. On September 17, two days after four Black girls were murdered by a bomb in the basement of Birmingham's 16th Street Baptist Church, Decca was not spearheading the response from California. Instead, she was finalizing the hiring of her friend Judy Bernal to collect and scrapbook her press clippings and reviews and to answer her letters.[55]

The American Way of Death generated so much attention that Simon & Schuster decided to pioneer ways to invest more resources in it. They now planned to send Decca out on the kind of extensive national book tour that was then quite rare, reserved only for authors with enormous reputations and followings. It was, Decca later reflected, "another example of the Shoe Store's innovative and go-ahead merchandising."[56] Accompanied by Dan Green, "a Love," Decca traveled from one end of the country to another.[57] She came alive on the stage, her engagement with her listeners so electric that strangers felt instantly that they'd known her all their lives. "Decca turned out to be a fabulous promoter," Gottlieb proudly noted.[58]

The book tour included radio and TV interviews as well as live appearances in over twenty cities, including New York, Boston, Detroit, Chicago, Cleveland, D.C., Houston, Dallas, Tulsa, Atlanta, and elsewhere. In New York, Simon & Schuster put her up in a suite at the Savoy Hotel, threw a book party for two hundred people, and pulled its editorial staff off other projects for two days to handwrite every invitation. Decca was booked on the *Today* and *Tonight* shows. Tony Richardson called and asked her to come to Hollywood in order to write the script for Evelyn Waugh's *The Loved One*, also about death and dying. In diners, trains, taxis, and lobbies, Decca was flabbergasted to find herself recognized by admirers. "I saw you on television last night, it was marvelous," someone remarked in the Ambassador Hotel.[59] "So now I'm a Public Speaker," she crowed to Bob.[60]

As much as Decca loved being admired, she thrived on being attacked. In fact, Decca had expected more of a fight. She'd expected to see her political history dredged up and used against her and the book. So far, only a few morticians' societies and one weekly newsletter called *The Tocsin* had tried to make anything of her past, claiming, without irony, that her goal was to "bury capitalist America's funeral customs."[61] No one paid any attention.

The book's gruesome parts on embalming remain the most re-printed passages of Mitford's most celebrated book, excerpted dozens of times to teach journalism students how to narrate chronologically and nonfiction writers how to use detail, and as a general example of excellent prose. "Is there a moral here?" Decca asked.[62] *The American Way of Death* became the biggest success of Mitford's life, "smashing an industry," changing federal laws, and helping to energize a growing movement of consumer rights.[63]

On a cool, dry Denver afternoon, October 17, 1963, Decca was in her room in the Brown Palace, Denver's finest hotel, hunched over her typewriter with a bottle of whiskey at her side. She'd already put in a long day of television interviews, lunched with an old friend, gone to meetings and newspaper interviews. She had set out her best French silk dress and was trying to finish her speech for the evening, where she'd be featured at the *Denver Post*'s authors' dinner in the hotel's enormous ballroom. The hotel was filling up with old friends who had traveled to see her, including the Durrs. Before turning back to her speech, she typed a letter to her friend Barbara Kahn, mock-ing the "filthy" food she'd been fed in the West—"Hamburgers and hotdogs"—and the "lad didah" university wives in "flavored hats" she'd been meeting along the way.[64] Letter-writing usually calmed Decca down. As she was typing, however, her phone began ringing off the hook and reporters banged on her hotel room door. News had just broken that a right-wing California congressman named James B. Utt had taken to the floor of the House to denounce Jessica Mitford as "Anti-American" and "Anti-Christ." Utt's lengthy speech identified Decca as the author "of a recent book entitled 'The American Way of Death'" and claimed that her "tirade against morticians is simply the vehicle to carry her anti-Christ attack." CBS, Allen Dulles, and Adlai

Stevenson, Utt said, were all suspect, in his view, for giving her book attention.[65]

Decca wanted to make her Denver address a counterattack on Utt, but was dissuaded by Dan Green, who was "distraught," Decca said, over the sudden negative attention. Their next tour stop was Boston, where a bomb threat met them after their arrival, adding to Green's fears. At the last minute, a scheduled excerpt in *Reader's Digest* was canceled.[66]

To Decca's surprise, and Green's relief, after the Boston bomb threat and *Reader's Digest* recoil, Utt's attack largely fizzled. *The New York Times* helped blunt the attack with a short editorial on Sunday, October 20, called "How Not to Read a Book," noting that Utt's "credentials" as a critic were "nil" and scoffing at his view that the United Nations was a "tool of Communism."[67] If anything, the brief dust-up was good publicity, and the attacks, as Green put it, mostly "backfired."[68] "The undertakers seemed to have misread the mood of the country," she noted. America was now "on the turn, stirring out of the deep spell cast over it by McCarthyism." Largely thanks to the student movement, Decca believed, Red-baiting "had lost much of its magic" to harm. She wove that sea change in attitudes into many of her remaining speeches.[69]

Decca had Bob Gottlieb's support. He was not especially rattled by Utt's ham-fisted attempts to sabotage her and accepted her refusal to become defensive in response. She would not denounce the Communist Party. If the question came up, her strategy would be to "make thousands of jokes in succession" and change the subject, she told Gottlieb.[70] It worked. As Peter Sussman noted, "Americans . . . shrugged off the Communist charges and innuendo, laughed along with Decca . . . and kept buying the book."[71] Decca continued to receive rave reviews, extensive media coverage, and stacks of fan mail in every delivery.[72] Privately, she had worried that the book's success might signal some kind of failure. Perhaps she and Bob had not been radical enough if they were now "reaching people by the millions."[73]

Decca was in Dallas on November 13, in Tulsa on the fifteenth. She'd been home for only a few days, joking that she'd "stayed one step ahead of the bombs," when she heard, on November 22nd, the "utter horror" of President John F. Kennedy's assassination.[74] Her thoughts went immediately to her sister, Debo. "Lots of love" and condolences, Decca wrote.[75] There were many intimate visits between Kennedy and Debo in 1961, 1962, and 1963, including one visit to Chatsworth a few months before his assassination, and a trip together to Palm Beach not long thereafter.[76] Kennedy had taken "an extraordinary amount of time" to dine with Debo in the midst of the Cuban missile crisis. Debo kept Kennedy's portrait in her personal drawing room. She traveled with him whenever possible and received calls from him at all hours. All the sisters, Decca included, believed that Debo and JFK were having an affair in the years immediately preceding his death. They all called him "the Loved One," a play on Waugh's title and a classic Mitford Tease. Kennedy's reputation—"doing for sex what Eisenhower did for golf," Nancy quipped—fueled their speculations. More importantly, Debo did nothing to dispel them. She came closest to confirming her sisters' suspicions when Kennedy announced an important, upcoming national address. The sisters believed he'd be announcing his "abdication" of the presidency to be with her. Instead, he spoke about the Cuban missile crisis. "It was a shame it wasn't what you thought," Debo then confided to Diana.[77]

Debo told Decca that Robert Kennedy was an admirer of *The American Way of Death*. Influenced by its arguments, he refused the expensive metal casket sent by the Dallas undertaker who handled the president's body. Instead, he chose a less expensive wooden one.[78] If Decca still had any question about the reach of her work, she could now, as she would have put it, lay such questions to rest.

15

"Do Something"

We have to do something . . . What to do?[1]
—JESSICA MITFORD

ecca's fans now pressed her with suggestions for further exposés in the mold of *The American Way of Death*, "hundreds
of letters suggesting other infamous rackets that should
be investigated and exposed." "Why don't you expose Bar Mitzvahs,
Why don't you write about the high cost of weddings, hearing aids,
Christmas—but 9 out of 10 say DOCTORS NEXT!"[2] She was happy
to accept spin-off and follow-up assignments related to death and dying
while she pondered what was next.[3] But she made a firm decision that
she'd not write another book about either American taste or consumer
capitalism. Her celebrity imposed a responsibility, she felt, to use her
new platform carefully. She wanted to capitalize on her unexpected

triumph with work that would advance civil rights, free speech, and social justice. Some of her fellow Exes were still floundering. Steve Nelson said that he did not know how to "rebuild my life with that central core missing." Yet, he said, "I couldn't just sit and do nothing."[4] Other Exes, such as Marge Frantz and Eva Maas, were swept up by feminism; for them, the women's movement replaced the "whirlwind of activities" Party life had provided.[5] Feminism did not resonate in the same way for Decca. White feminist politics at that time were often taken up with consciousness, what Adrienne Rich called a personal "awakening" to the political reality of seemingly private life—"seeing with fresh eyes" to "understand the assumptions in which we are drenched"—a way of digging into the personal, which would always be anathema to Decca.[6]

Writing offered a form of activism that could contribute to the causes Decca cared about and offer some of the energy of collective action she missed from CP and CRC work, if she could find the right subject and continue to work collaboratively. As excited as she was with her new success, however, she had reservations about her influence. *The American Way of Death* had been remarkably effective. In fact, *The Times* proclaimed that "Miss Mitford's impact on the transatlantic scene is only slightly less than the Beatles." This was a white, mainstream assessment, and Decca knew it. She saw a wide gap between consumers' rights advocacy, however powerful, and the fight for racial and economic justice. Compared to Medgar Evers's murder, the 16th Street Baptist Church bombing in Birmingham, or the murders and beatings of civil rights activists, all the "hoop-la" over her book sometimes seemed rather "silly" to Decca. She wanted to contribute fully to the most significant social struggle of her day, which she saw as systemic racism. "One really should be figuring out a way of doing something useful about it all," she wrote a friend. "But what, is the trouble."[7]

Decca had achieved a status she'd never dreamed of. She was the kind of literary celebrity who could make demands—a better room, a deeper bathtub, more expensive Scotch, a bigger byline, a car and driver. "I still have not recovered from the excitement of it all," she declared.[8] It was wondrous to be flooded with offers and invitations "on a peak of middle-age," Decca (then forty-six years old) wrote a close friend. Being a celebrated author was "terrific fun," she said, and she believed she deserved a bit of fun.[9] She was torn between wanting to enjoy all the perks of her hard-earned success and wanting to use it for deeper political work. For months she had turned down dinners, fundraisers, demonstrations, and exhibits to keep her nose to the grindstone and complete *The American Way of Death.* The year 1963 had been all frenzy. Maybe 1964 was her chance to bask. Decca, however, was not a good basker. Inactivity agitated her. Praise only made her hunger for more praise. To recover from the exhausting overwork of *The American Way of Death* she'd have to keep working, but perhaps at a less punishing pitch.

While she considered her next steps, Decca kept up her usual grueling pace, accepting every speaking invitation that came her way, whatever the venue. She addressed local book groups, coop board potlucks, high schools, colleges, professional organizations and societies, bookstores, church basements, anywhere she was asked. She marketed as if every single book sale mattered, in spite of the fact that her book was selling like hotcakes and had gone into its fifth printing before officially going on sale.

At this time, she also accepted most of the essay requests that came her way, either because they paid well, or because they were easy to do. She wrote fluff pieces on how she came to write her bestseller and how it felt to suddenly become rich and famous, as well as pieces on other death and dying writers, such as Evelyn Waugh.[10]

In 1963, Constancia had become heavily involved, as had dozens of other radical young anti-racist whites, with SNCC. Founded in 1960, SNCC brought together students across the South to fight racism with voter education drives, sit-ins, Freedom Rides, and other forms of direct action. What Spain had been for Decca's generation, the Southern civil rights struggle was for Constancia's cohort of young white radicals. Some Black SNCC activists worried about the dedication of the white volunteers, wondering if they would sap energy away from Black issues and if they truly understood—after the murders of Herbert Lee, Jimmy Travis, Medgar Evers, Louis Allen, and others—just how dangerous nonviolent resistance could be. White volunteers, they warned, would have to earn Black trust. As one Black senior SNCC staff member put it, "These white kids were unsteady vessels . . . [we] weren't at all sure that these were the allies . . . [we] wanted."[11]

Decca had spent years, in the CRC especially, proving that she was a good ally. Now Dinky followed her mother's model. After devoting all her time to organizing an intercollegiate conference on civil rights and turning her dorm room into a movement control center, Dinky dropped out of Sarah Lawrence. She followed SNCC's Chairman Charles McDew, a charismatic Black leader famous for being "unwilling to bend to Jim Crow" to New York City.[12] From there, she moved to SNCC's Atlanta office to work as a full-time organizer, fundraiser, and liaison to other white radical college students being recruited as Friends of SNCC.[13] In 1964, SNCC's logo was an image of black and white hands, clasped in friendship, superimposed on a global map. It was good marketing during a time when most Americans were averse to both integration and social activism. But the image belied SNCC's shift away from reliance on whites—including those Dinky was tasked with recruiting—in favor of local Black leadership. Dinky's Atlanta office was pushing a transition to Black-only staff just as Dinky moved there to raise support for Mississippi's Summer Project. Yet, Dinky played prominent roles in Atlanta's SNCC. She served on a finance committee that included Marion Barry, Ella Baker, John Lewis, and James Forman, on the voter registration committee, and as principal organizer of a high-profile national tour featuring Dick

Gregory and the Freedom Singers.[14] She was notably successful as a white ally when such success was especially difficult and contested. Decca and Bob told her they were proud.

Dinky thought her parents were "very happy" about her decision to work with SNCC rather than finish college.[15] Privately, Decca had steam coming out of her ears over Dinky squandering the education she'd always longed for. Decca knew that Dinky could be every bit as headstrong as her biological father, Esmond. What she lacked in Esmond's playfulness, Decca's warmth, or Bob's adaptability, Dinky made up for in a kind of intense competence; there seemed to be nothing she could not do well. Dinky's exceptional beauty—she strongly resembled her fascist Aunt Diana—and her sharp intelligence made her seem haughty to some. She did not suffer fools or brook much disagreement. Dinky did what she chose.

Bob enjoyed writing and researching *The American Way of Death*, especially exposing undertakers' secret practices. Taking a year off from his legal practice was challenging, however, and the moment they handed their final manuscript to Gottlieb, Bob had returned to his firm. Now, only a year later, he was well on his way to becoming one of the nation's well-known "movement lawyers," along with more recognized associates such as Victor Rabinowitz, Leonard Boudin, Charles Garry, and William Kunstler. Most of his cases concerned either police brutality or defense of student activists.[16] "For many, many years," he said proudly, he and his associates "were almost without exception the only lawyers to ever sue the police." Peter Sussman relates that "Decca was once told by Black Panther Party co-founder Huey Newton that when he was a young boy growing up in Oakland, Robert Treuhaft was a 'hero to all the kids' in his neighborhood because of Treuhaft's—and the CRC's— dogged defense of wrongfully accused murder suspect Jerry Newson."[17] Bob's status as "Public Enemy No. 1 with the Oakland Police Department" earned his clients' trust.

In 1964, Oakland and Berkeley were hotbeds of social justice protests. Oakland's industries had seen years of labor struggles. Its schools gave birth to the Free Speech and anti-war movements. Calls for Black Power and community control fueled protests over employment and economic segregation, housing restrictions, and police brutality and led to the rise of the Black Panthers and to demands for "Power to the People." Workers, students, and Black activists questioned authority, tested limits, challenged existing norms, and resisted traditions in powerful ways that were also reflected in the rise of Women's Liberation and gay rights movements and even in the calls for new lifestyles and sexual freedom identified with San Francisco's burgeoning hippie culture. Every social movement of significance used the language of revolution to indicate that incremental reforms would not do; the world would have to be remade from equality outward. "No more training for obedience," as one Berkeley student activist put it.[18]

Decca never had much use for lifestyle issues. Struggles for sexual freedom and the intimate politics of the Women's Liberation movement left her cold. But when "the civil rights movement came to the Bay Area with a bang in the fall of 1963," as Jo Freeman put it, she was profoundly stirred.[19] Disobedience was Decca's default.

In 1963, the *Oakland Tribune* was still running "Whites Only" real estate listings for Oakland properties, even as Oakland's Black population doubled from 1950 to 1960, then doubled again in the early 1960s. Redlining separated most of white and Black Oakland, with some streets, as Oakland historian Robert O. Self explains, such as Telegraph Avenue, operating as dividers. Decca and Bob lived in a mixed section of Oakland. They identified and agitated across divides, and they hoped to be a fulcrum aiding in the destruction of such social barriers.

Meeting the relentless demands of *The American Way of Death* had sidelined Decca's political work during a watershed period of the struggle for civil rights. She had missed the March on Washington, the demonstrations in Mississippi and Alabama, the chance to shout at white supremacist Sheriff Bull Connor in Birmingham or Alabama Governor George Wallace as he barred the doors against Black students. She wanted to make up for lost time. The threads of rebellion that made the Bay Area the nation's prototype for resistance to oppression all connected to Bob and Decca.[20] Led by seasoned civil rights workers, the Berkeley Free Speech Movement was fueled by young leaders who had gone to the South with SNCC, CORE, or the SCLC, and who could not conceive of defeat. They were also the same young people who had come to Decca's defense when she and others were arrested by the House Un-American Activities Committee (HUAC) and who'd been violently firehosed down the gray granite steps of City Hall for their efforts. They operated with contagious anti-authoritarianism. And they were brave. SNCC volunteers, like Free Speech leader Mario Savio, were training in Oxford, Ohio, when they learned that fellow civil rights workers James Chaney, Michael Schwerner, and Andrew Goodman had vanished after a June 21 trip to investigate a church bombing and that they were now targets as well.[21] "There is no guarantee that you will get out of this summer alive," Black SNCC leader Robert Moses told them. Almost all stayed.[22] In their "defiance of authority," Decca saw the young volunteers of the International Brigades.[23] These Northern activists, often called SNCC's "shock troops," had grown up privileged. Like Decca, they were not born allies, but rather self-taught ones. SNCC taught young white people to stop talking and listen to others.[24] In their stories about the lessons they learned on ramshackle porches and in unlit kitchens, Decca could hear echoes of the dank, unheated Cotswold cottages in the shadow of the Mitford mansions, where she'd first learned about social inequality.[25] The Oakland civil rights movement was also unlike any place else in the nation, powered by a militancy unique to the region. Many of the activists who would go on to create the Black Panther Party had parents whom Decca had worked with in the CRC or Bob had worked with on police brutality and housing discrimination cases. The Bay Area's Communist Party had always worked closely with area unions, dockworkers and industrial workers especially, and always collaborated in progressive labor fights.

Decca admired the young activists. "I think we should only applaud the efforts of the kids," she wrote Virginia Durr. "The one really new and hopeful thing about the youngest generation, as distinct from the 30-ish, is their refusal to listen to their elders and their insistence on discovering things and ideas for themselves. They really don't want to be told. In some ways this is tiresome of them, and also leads to silly mistakes they could avoid. I happen to think the disadvantages are outweighed by the advantages of them taking what amounts to real, total responsibility."[26]

On a cold December 2, 1964, thousands of such rebellious students gathered outside the University of California Berkeley's administration building, Sproul Hall, to defend student leaders who'd been singled out for reprisals. Mario Savio jumped on top of a car and called on his fellow students to throw their "bodies on the gears" of the machine. One thousand students then occupied the building, creating a highly organized sit-in, with different sections devoted to study halls, teach-ins, music (Joan Baez and others arrived to lead sing-outs), strategy rooms, a folk-dancing area in a linoleum hallway, and a makeshift kitchen.[27] As the night wore on and the administration's obstinacy hardened, Savio contacted a lawyer to mediate between the students and the university administration. He called Bob Treuhaft.

Bob arrived close to midnight. The police blocked him from meeting with the students. After a heated exchange, in which Bob insisted on seeing his clients—"my legal right," he recited—a clutch of heavily armed officers in full riot gear arrested him.[28] Bob's arrest was followed over the next few hours by 767 student arrests.[29] Bob was charged with trespassing and held in solitary confinement. His repeated requests to call his wife and let her know where he was were all denied. It was, he later said, "a sign of how far the police would go to repress those they consider part of the Left."[30] Decca spent the night on her lumpy living-room couch, willing the phone to ring. She finally heard from Bob, mid-morning on December 3, and catapulted Bob's legal associates, whom she'd called in the middle of the night when Bob did not come home, into action.[31] They were glad that Decca woke them. "From the perspective of lawyers with a social conscience the decade of the 1960s was a dream come true," one of Bob's junior partners said.[32]

Decca bragged about Bob's arrest to Aranka and Edith. "The whole free-speech fight has been simply thrilling," she wrote, the "dear boy rather thrives on this sort of thing." Decca thrived on it also. In a long-standing tease of writing to conservatives as if they were her comrades, she described Bob's arrest in glowing, unsparing detail to his mother:

He was booked in the basement of Sproul Hall (where they had set up a full-scale booking procedure, fingerprints, photos, the works) and eventually was taken to Santa Rita prison farm along with the other 860 arrested. There he was given a v. bad time, put in a solitary cell with stone floor and nowhere to sit so he stood for about 3 hours. Meanwhile I was going quietly bonkers as our British cousins say. I had been called at 4 a.m. to say he was arrested, but natch I thought he'd be out at once. He wasn't released till 11:30 Friday. He is livid, as you might think, planning massive false arrest suits against all concerned. . . . P.S. At one point the cops in Sproul Hall started locking up the johns, presumably to discourage students with weak blads. So some of the men students took the doors off the hinges, and they had what you might call a shit-in. Bob said he met Joan Baez in one of the johns! Also the other night Bob addressed the 860 defendants at a mass meeting, starting off

with 'Fellow Jailbirds.' He got a standing ovation. They simply
adore him.[33]

She had nothing nearly so interesting to report about herself, but it
was not in her nature to begrudge her loved ones their moment. As Bob
and Dinky plowed ahead in their new movement roles, she continued
her own quest for the next right thing.

That year, Betty Friedan was asked to follow the publication of *The
Feminine Mystique* by editing a special issue of *Ladies' Home Journal*, the
nation's most popular women's magazine. It would be called "The Fourth
Dimension." The remit was to showcase women who'd found fulfilling
work, giving the magazine's more than ten million readers a glimpse of
overcoming challenges to a meaningful life.[34] Friedan planned to put
feminism's best foot forward for a readership new to its ideas. Decca was
one of the first potential contributors Friedan approached.

Although Decca was not known as a feminist, Freidan saw her as
one and offered her the lead article. She wanted Decca to explain her
trajectory from aristocracy to authorship and make work outside the
home attractive to the magazine's middle-class, white readership. The
other contributors—all white and middle or upper class—included
well-known artists, playwrights, journalists, and a diplomat.[35]

Friedan's offer of star billing to Decca was gracious. It was probably also strategic. *The American Way of Death* was published at almost
the same time as both *Silent Spring* and *The Feminine Mystique*, and
while both would ultimately outsell Mitford, Decca's initial publicity
was much stronger than either.[36] Decca had also just shown Friedan
up in *The New York Times*. The *Times* had asked the year's most popular
writers to share their experiences. Friedan confessed to "torturous personal self-doubts" about challenging gender roles. Decca, on the other
hand, said that "ruffling feathers" was a thrill. "The praise and blame my
book has received afford almost equal satisfaction," she declared, making

Friedan's angst look foolish.[37] Friedan may have wanted to recruit Decca as a friend, rather than having her as competition. And no doubt she wanted to entice Decca into taking feminism more seriously.

Decca was relieved to have an assignment necessitating none of the painstaking research *The American Way of Death* required. She woke early every day, took her coffee—and a shot of vodka if she needed a boost—into her small, windowless study, sat down in a fuzzy robe at her huge green electric typewriter, and clacked contentedly away.[38] "Public Figuredom," she wrote, came as a particular surprise given "the paradoxes and surprise my life has afforded." Stressing her complete lack of formal education, Decca wrote about being raised to run "a well-staffed English household." She described running away to marry "a penniless fascinator," working odd jobs, being a terrible housekeeper, and other Mitford material she repurposed from her memoir.[39]

Her article, "The American Way of Success," was surrounded by American advertisements of just the type she lampooned—apricot-scented tissues, dubious slimming products, hair dyes, pastel-colored refrigerators, and Chef Boyardee spaghetti and meatballs in cans. Scare ads queried: "The Women Your Husband Works With . . . Are You as Interesting As They?" Cartoons mocked women. Famous men, such as writer Alvin Toffler, acknowledged a few "advantages" to feminism while worrying that it damaged male self-esteem. "The Fourth Dimension" trod very lightly on men's feelings, with most of the contributors expressing anxiety about wanting anything beyond domesticity. All but Decca tried to avoid insulting men.[40] She happily declared that she'd thrown over the "feminine mystique" as soon as she could. "My husband positively drove me from the nest, urging that the housework be put in more competent hands," she wrote. She blithely dismissed "tidal waves of cleaning and washing" as altogether too "depressing" for smart women to be bothered with.[41] Despite refusing to embrace the label, Decca's essay was far and away the most feminist one in the journal.

Its light tone was very much in the spirit of her early *Washington Post* stories, the comic mix of superiority and self-deprecation she excelled at, with no dreaded "grubbing about" into her inner psyche. Beneath all the lightness, her message to other women was sharp.

Had she "grubbed about," Decca would have had to admit that her recent triumphs had a downside. She had always disdained radicals who mellowed with age, calling them traitors, fools, or worse.[42] While holding herself up as a role model for other women, Decca was, in fact, uneasy. She was now in real danger of finding herself a middle-aged success. Bob was on his way to becoming a radical hero. So was her daughter. Decca went back to weighing her options.[43] Feminist work, she decided, wasn't one of them.

Instead, she signed a contract for a second memoir. Her heart wasn't in it. She took advantage of a long, sad summer stay—"the past encloses me here . . . I dread being alone"—in England, France, and Inch Kenneth in 1964 to finish an essay on the Hebrides for a travel magazine, masking her melancholy with sunny descriptions of the island as a "perfect haven of warmth and hospitality . . . one of the few truly isolated spots left in a crowded world."[44] She dashed off a gossipy piece for a Hollywood glossy. *Redbook* asked her to write a profile of Julie Andrews, but she found that she liked Andrews too much to write it. "I'm much better at what you might call combative writing—that is, sticking in the old knife," she admitted.[45] She also wrote a short piece criticizing the rise of talk shows, an essay that is prescient now but seemed inconsequential then.[46] She had "masses of things ¼ cooking," but little done that she liked.[47] Most of her time, oddly enough, went into a series of essays on women's weight, about which Decca cared not one whit.

Decca's descent into dieting began with an article on Elizabeth Arden's fat farm. A more unlikely journalist for such a piece is hard to imagine. At forty-eight, Decca was energetic, attractive, and trim. She was not skinny, like her sisters Diana and Nancy, who placed a moral premium on weight. She was medium height, and at just over 140 pounds, an average size for her age. She occasionally lamented a thickening middle and longed to wear old Scottish wool suits that no longer buttoned, but her dieting had always been desultory at best, abandoned at the first fundraiser. She never exercised. Nevertheless, in the 1960s Decca wrote nearly half a dozen articles on dieting—the most attention she paid any topic other than funerals and death. A "preposterous" distance from what she thought she'd write about, the dieting articles gave her ample space to tease. And they earned a steady income.[48]

The idea for the first one came from Vivian Cadden, Decca's editor at *McCall's*. Opened in Maine in 1934, with an Arizona branch called Arizona Maine Chance in 1946, Arden's weight-loss spa was the first in the country. Cadden thought there was a great story in such spas, if she could get a smart, funny writer to do it. Dangling the catnip of an all-expense-paid luxury trip combined with the desert heat Decca loved, as well as a chance to go undercover, Cadden told Decca that she could write about Arden's "lucrative avoirdupois" any way she liked.[49]

Dieting was nothing new in 1965, when Decca set out for Arizona. For decades, women had been urged to make themselves smaller. Some, like Fannie Hurst, became as famous for their dieting as for their accomplishments.[50] Arden's insight was in monetizing an already existing link between weight, class, and race by linking weight loss to expensive vacations. By 1964, her exclusive spas were a snobbish alternative to middle-class pursuits such as Weight Watchers (launched in 1963, the year of *The American Way of Death*). Catering to the same middle-class audience Arden eschewed, Friedan's "Fourth Dimension" issue of *Ladies' Home Journal* had also pushed weight loss through advertisements for slim-mints, low-calorie salad dressings, apple cider vinegar, bathroom scales, and impossibly slender long-legged models in low-backed black leotards. Arden's clientele, by contrast, would pay experts to solve their weight problems for them.

Decca was appalled by the spa and wrote Bob a daily letter in which she let loose about her very pink room, "like a fairly good motel room," but with pink curtains, white wall-to-wall carpet, pink roses, and a bathroom full of Elizabeth Arden beauty products. She was particularly scornful of the guests: wealthy, bored, Republican women who complained about their servants and were lost "in the utter concentration on themselves." These women amounted to "a ton of human flesh in various stages of disintegration," she told Bob.[51] Their bland "sort of chatter" about global events was especially repellant, Decca said, and she felt like a "fish out of water" in their company.[52] We all "get the newspaper with our breakfast trays. The headlines are full of bitter battles raging in Vietnam . . . [and] historic Supreme Court decisions over civil rights. But we, who are being fiddled while Rome burns, do not discuss such matters."[53] Using her letters to get her notes safely off-site, lest someone discover that she was not just another guest, Decca detailed the spa's exercise regime, massages, steam treatments and 900-calorie-a-day meals. She took especially careful notes on the ways that, not unlike a corpse in an embalming room, she was plucked, waxed, manicured, brushed, and arranged: "kneaded, stretched, massaged, manipulated, creamed, steamed, cooled."[54]

Many female journalists in 1965 would have taken Arden to task for how insulting her message was to women and how narrowly her regime viewed their bodies. Decca did make one historical connection, noting the spa's similarity to the notoriously misogynistic Victorian Rest Cure—"A big part of the therapy is a reversion to infantile ways," Decca wrote, "you do not have to make a single decision. You are lulled back into the life . . . of a good child."[55] But she did not defend women's bodies. In fact, she traded in age and gender stereotypes of her own for her humor. "The fact is," she wrote, "that middle-aged women in their natural state, sans girdle, bra, or make-up, do not present an attractive sight."[56] She took Arden to task only for ridiculous gadgets such as her "shakeaway" chairs for "juggling" off fat, for monetizing every single aspect of the spa experience (more or less as Decca had done at some of her most notorious fundraising parties), and for prohibiting alcohol on the spa premises, which proved especially challenging to Decca, who was now a heavy drinker.[57] In her published article, Decca faithfully reported her own loss of two inches from her waist, one half inch from her upper arms, and five pounds overall, wryly adding that it was probably all dehydration, because she looked just the same.[58]

What she called "odd pockets of American enterprise" followed "Maine Chance Diary." She wrote about Weight Watchers, taking special aim at gimmicky before-and-after pictures. She experimented with syndication, publishing different versions of the same pieces in multiple venues.[59] Her oscillation between feminist messages and snarky views of feminism continued. In an essay for *Vogue*, she skewered women who strove for domestic perfection—they iron their husband's underwear, she revealed! She also blamed Friedan's brand of feminism for helping to foment "an obsession with being Interesting, a new mass movement, a craze for Individuality."[60]

In December, Decca traveled to New York to spend time with Dinky and her new partner, SNCC leader James Forman. Dinky and Forman were launching a national fundraising campaign for SNCC and had moved from Atlanta to organize Northern white volunteers. They were living in a "miserable little apartment" on Tenth Street: a fifth-floor walk-up with one bedroom, a living room, a tiny, barely functional kitchen, and a bathroom. In their bedroom they'd built a loft bed with a desk and bookshelves underneath so that Forman, a big man, who was serving as executive secretary of SNCC (a position he held from 1961 to 1966) could crunch himself underneath to work. They offered Decca a cot in their narrow hallway. She stayed either with friends or Aranka instead, but came over every day, made lunch, and tried to help by tidying up. She was delighted with her "daughter's sloppy hospitality" and her choice of a partner, she reported in her letters.

Forman was midway between Decca's age and Dinky's, born in 1928. The son of a hardworking single mother, he'd joined the Air Force when every other door slammed shut. Constant experiences of racism, including a brutal beating, arrest, and very bad night in jail, forged the "philosophy and strategy of struggle" Forman brought to SNCC. He could be impatient. His distrust of white people ran deep. To "lay bare the injustices perpetrated upon black people . . . to expose the dirt of the United States," Forman felt, demanded discipline and constant effort.[61] Forman made sure that SNCC "had the best research arm of any civil rights organization before or since." Julian Bond called Forman a "master propagandist" and a brilliant leader.[62] Forman's work ethic was exemplary: he never asked anyone to take a task he did not also do.

Forman's and Decca's backgrounds were antipodal. Yet Decca warmed to him quickly and found herself complaining to Barbara Kahn that Forman was showing "no indication of intentions" of marrying Dinky.[63] Forman was a natural muckraker, phenomenally disciplined and diligent, and he fiercely loved those he loved, as did Decca. Beneath his formidable sternness, Decca—also intimidating—discerned an optimistic, even playful nature. "I'm getting to adore him," she wrote a friend. "He has a merry quality, and above all . . . he makes my daughter ha-ppee," she added. She called him her "commonlaw-soninlaw," read the manuscript of his memoir-in-progress, and bragged about him to her friends.[64]

While in New York, Decca met with her editor, Bob Gottlieb. Their "soul-searching session," she wrote a friend, resulted in a renewed commitment to meaningful work. "I've really and truly and definitely decided to cut out all the crappy articles."[65] Her agent,

Candida Donadio, said that based on the sales of *The American Way of Death*, she could secure an advance of $50,000 to $125,000 for the memoir book (between half a million to well over a million dollars today), on which Decca had made very little progress. "I warn you this book won't sell," she told her agent. "It will be a sympathetic account of life in the CP." You said the funeral book wouldn't sell either, Donadio reminded her. "And look what happened."[66]

No sooner had Decca signed the new contract for her second memoir than she found the perfect excuse to avoid it. Bob decided to run for district attorney against Frank Coakley, "America's #1 Prosecutor," in Coakley's self-description. Coakley had prosecuted the Jerry Newson case in 1954 and personally ordered Bob's arrest in Sproul Hall.[67] An "utter brute," Bob and Decca thought, Coakley's administration was "marked by the most vile sort of racial bigotry."[68] He was, Bob said, "an extremely right-wing district attorney . . . who had a lot of control over the police and police procedures and over the judges in the courts."[69] Decca turned their family home into Bob's campaign headquarters. She welcomed volunteers at all hours, covered the dining table with campaign materials, and turned the kitchen over to anyone willing to make coffee, sandwiches, or cocktails to get them through late-night strategy sessions and long days of canvassing.

Coakley's machine was too entrenched for Bob to have any "expectations of winning."[70] "I was running," he said, "because I thought somebody should get the word out about the anti-consumer, anti-people attitudes of the current incumbent." The campaign was part of a larger war against government corruption, and it included radical East Bay journalist, founding editor of the *Berkeley Barb*, and *Ramparts* editor Robert Scheer's bid for Congress. It was a heady time in Oakland, with the energies of student activists and Black radicals coalescing against Ronald Reagan's gubernatorial campaign. Jerry Rubin and Alice Waters managed Scheer's campaign, coordinating with Decca and

Bob's campaign office. The Scheer campaign focused on the growing war in Vietnam, mobilizing students, and the New Left. Bob drew on his base in Oakland's Black neighborhoods to emphasize civil rights and economic justice. Decca's wide networks, carefully maintained through her avid correspondence, brought in establishment Democrats and donors, such as publisher Katharine Graham.

Bob lost soundly to Coakley; but he won more than 80 percent of Oakland's Black vote, greatly expanding Black voter participation. "Every Black precinct, every precinct that had substantial Black votes, I carried," Bob said.[71] Scheer came close to winning, garnering almost 50 percent of the overall vote.[72] He felt that Decca deserved the credit for much of that success, both for running a "stupendous" campaign and also for building bridges between generations of activists under the slogan "Squares for Scheer," which cracked up everyone. "They came to us; they really came to us," Scheer said.[73] Decca told Leonard Boudin how proud she was of the "lovely stink" their campaign stirred up. She was exhausted, but she'd had "tremendous fun."[74]

After the fall 1966 election, Decca decided to spend four months in England, to try to get a good start on her memoir. "I've been having a perfectly beastly time not getting on with it," she admitted to her editor at the end of a year that she spent, in her own words, as "the prize goofer-off of all time."[75]

Dinky was expecting a baby. Decca was overjoyed.[76] She worried about Dinky and Forman being unwed and wished they would marry. Interracial marriage was then rare (under 1 percent of all American marriages) and frowned upon by most Americans.[77] The Supreme Court's ruling in *Loving v. Virginia* would not overturn prohibitions against interracial marriage for months to come. Her favorite joke was now to mimic an average American racist posing the standard racist question, "Would you want your daughter to marry a Negro?" To that, she would quickly answer "Rather," in her thickest British lilt.[78] Decca believed in marriage—hers had never held her back—and she wanted it understood that it was the non-marriage she disliked, not the fact that her grandchild's father would be Black. "Beige power is my slogan," she told everyone.[79] By June she was in New York for the birth, doing all that she could to help. "Oh dear I hope I last in this job," she joked to a friend.[80]

Behind her back, her sisters had a field day with the news of Decca's Black grandchild. "Well Lady, the inevitable has occurred," Deborah wrote to Nancy, "Dinky is going to have a baby by a black man." Such, she asserted, was "the outcome of a liberal upbringing." Decca must "MIND" very much, she wrote.[81] "Liberalism," Deborah added, "naturally results in coffee babies & no wedding."[82] Diana threw herself into the conversation, taking it for granted that others shared her unrepentant, racist views. "Do you think," Diana asked Deborah, "really & truly all those people [who claim not to 'MIND'] are just pretending most of the time & underneath the pretence are rather like ONE?"—which was to say that underneath, they were as appalled as she was. Diana's theory was that having found her happiness with a Jewish husband, Decca wanted her daughter to marry a Jew as well. But now, Diana wrote, she "will never find a kind intelligent Jew to marry her. . . . Thank goodness Lady Redesdale wots not of this."[83] Nancy shared some of her thoughts directly with Decca. She'd "think of Dinky, down on the plantation when the days' work is done, crooning," she wrote.[84] Nancy, so used to communicating with Diana, no doubt thought such racist humor was acceptable.

Around this time, for reasons she never made clear, Decca decided to sell Inch Kenneth, the island she had worked so hard to wrest from her sisters and that kept her tied to her family's history. As with everything closest to her heart, she turned a private and painful decision into a colossal, public joke. Using her connections to Robert Scheer and *Ramparts*, she took out a full-page *Ramparts* ad. It described a "fifteen room manor house . . . a staff cottage . . . two jetties with matching motor boats . . . a garage protecting a 1924 Morris . . . the ruins of a crusaders' chapel [and] a graveyard"—hardly what most *Ramparts* readers wanted. The advertisement ran for nearly half a year, producing no serious interest but generating a lot of attention. Decca took the joke further later in the year. She invented a fictional sister island for Inch Kenneth called Innersk, promising potential buyers of Inch Kenneth "fine, sober, industrious and quiet neighbors—Us."[85] While waiting for a real buyer (which took some time and came through a conventional realtor), Decca invited her sisters to come and take whatever keepsakes or furniture they might like. At enormous expense, she shipped family paintings back to her home on Regent Street and hung the dark, brooding portraits of her parents and other relatives on her bright Oakland walls.

A long history of discrimination was bringing Oakland to a political boil. Unemployment dominated Black communities torn apart for construction of the area's rapid transit system, communities already devastated by environmental damage from shuttered defense and shipbuilding plants, communities long enraged by police brutality and redlining. What area historians describe as a highly "contentious and variable political terrain" was marked by both extreme inequality and "a new politics of community empowerment."[86] Conditions were perfect for the rise of new resistance. Black activists called Oakland America's "urban plantation," linked its struggles to global anti-colonialism, and developed political statements about racism, capitalism, and class inequality that put Oakland at the center of the national stage when the national Black Panther Party was launched in Oakland in October 1966.[87]

Forman worked to broker partnerships between the Panthers and SNCC. He felt that "the creation of the [Black Panther] Party by Huey P. Newton and Bobby Seale was the extension of work that many of us in SNCC had been doing over the past seven years and a natural outgrowth of the intense struggle that had been waged since 1960."[88] Decca also saw the Panthers as continuing the work of SNCC and the Civil Rights Congress.

Decca was a Black Panther supporter from the day of their inception. The Panthers now joined the Free Speech rebels, anti-Vietnam protesters, labor and civil rights activists as political leaders for whom she hosted fundraisers, spoke at events, and with whom she marched.[89] Reagan had campaigned on a promise to "clean up the mess in Berkeley." For Decca and Bob, no place made more sense than Oakland and Berkeley.

By May 1967, Decca was in England again, when Nancy's novel *The Pursuit of Love*, opened as an elaborate musical at Bristol's Royal Theater, thrusting the family's eccentricities and privileges back into the British spotlight. Nancy had just moved from Paris to Versailles, finally accepting that her longtime love, Gaston Palewski, would never reciprocate her feelings.[90] Nancy, of course, was upbeat, claiming that she'd always preferred Versailles to Paris. But her sisters could easily see how lonely and unhappy she was. Decca went way out of her way to try to cheer her sister, organizing a large "Theatre Party" to travel from Debo's estate at Chatsworth to Bristol, with an overnight stay at a Bristol hotel. Written and produced by popular composer Julian Slade, *The Pursuit of Love* featured dialogue written by Nancy, catchy music, beautiful sets and costumes. Nevertheless, the play was a flop. Audiences tired of the two dozen similar songs and the three-hour performance. Critics said there was only one joke and that it went on far too long. The play offered the usual dazzling Mitford exterior but little interior. Fans came away with unanswered questions: Why did such rebel women never warm to feminism? Why were so many of them fascists? Were the Mitford Girls representative of their class or the last gasps of a dying life? Were they great successes or tragic failures? Nancy's cool play skittered across the surface of the Mitfords' well-rehearsed lives.[91] Decca was underwhelmed. But reluctant to hurt Nancy's feelings, she kept her opinions to herself.

Shortly after her return from England, Decca came home to one of the worst family crises she had faced. In early August 1967, Giles Romilly committed suicide in a shabby room of Oakland's Hotel California. It was a largely Black hotel, in a Black section of Oakland, where Giles knew no one. He and his recent bride, "a hopeless sort of girl" named Coral, much younger than Giles, had been living out of this room for weeks, and Decca "had no idea they were even there."[92] For years he had been "popping into our lives, then popping out again."[93] Giles had first appeared at Decca and Bob's home in 1962, having kidnapped his own children and acting "quite a bit mad."[94] He showed up again earlier in 1967, with his then fiancée, Coral, addicted to drugs, uncooperative, needy, and difficult. Decca felt sure that he'd returned to the area to be near her, perhaps to seek her help, and she couldn't fathom why he hadn't reached out.

Decca had always admired Giles—he'd been one of the first volunteers to go to Spain—and she'd long been convinced that his time in Colditz prison, combined with Esmond's death, had broken him. Over the years she'd tried to help him, especially with finding publishers for his writing. Now she tried to help Coral, who'd survived the suicide pact. "It made no sense at all," Decca said, unable to comprehend such giving up on life.[95] She and Bob took Coral home, cared for her, and made arrangements for Giles's cremation.

Giles's death unmoored Decca in ways she hardly knew how to talk about. She'd seen the ill effects of his drug use (his addiction began during his imprisonment), when he'd shown up at her house on previous visits: sometimes raving, sometimes intimate.[96] But "the horror, the squalor, the dreadfulness" of his suicide was so much worse than any outcome Decca, who always overcame her own adversities, imagined.

He was an important tie to her past, more important than she'd realized, and there was no one she felt she could turn to who shared her memories of Giles as she'd once known him: young, handsome, capable, and brave—the most daring of the two dazzling Romilly brothers. She leaned on Virginia Durr, who had so adored Esmond, the closest thing to a friend of Giles's she could find. When she wrote of Giles's death to others, including her sisters, she downplayed its effect, even making jokes about it all. Giles's son, Edmund, sixteen years old and away at boarding school when his father died, never felt that Decca and Bob had done enough. He blamed Decca for Giles's death, for the madness that soon engulfed Coral, for the cremation arrangements they made, for not consulting the family. They "wanted to brush the whole thing under the carpet," he said. "I didn't forgive her."[97]

Giles's death contributed to Decca's concerns about Benjy. He remained as engaging as ever—a true charmer and a very handsome young man—but his mood swings, carelessness, and chronic disorganization were beginning to look like something more serious than youthful overexuberance. Approaching twenty years old, he still seemed as unsettled as an adolescent: in and out of schools, in and out of jobs, suddenly leaving one place and just as suddenly appearing in another, erratic and unpredictable. At one point, at Inch Kenneth, Benjy suddenly decided he had to study in Paris. Having forgotten to pack, and running out of time, he threw his things into his oversize rainboots and ran with them down to the dock, just making the last boat of the day. Clearly something was not quite right. In September, just after Giles's death, Bob threw Decca an elaborate fiftieth birthday party on a boat, complete with a live band, roast pig, and Chinese dragon dancers. Decca loved the party, but she was not herself, shaken by the death of Giles and her anxiety about her son.[98]

Decca was then caught up, as was everyone she knew, in anti-war protests and discussions of Vietnam. Sometimes it seemed as if the entire Bay Area was one anti-war protest.[99] By 1967 there were ten thousand U.S. soldiers and many more Vietnamese citizens dead. War protests ramped up, culminating in Stop the Draft protests at the Oakland Inductions Center. At these demonstrations, protesters were brutally beaten by the Oakland police, yet the demonstrators returned day after day, facing mace, nightsticks, and arrest to draw attention to the war. Some of the demonstrators (known later as the Oakland Seven) were arrested; they turned to Bob for advice and counsel. Decca focused on how to "turn the tide" of public opinion and engender distrust in government authorities. In organizations such as the anti-war Jeannette Rankin Brigade, she fought for strategies that would appeal to "wider circles," clashing with other activists who distrusted the mainstream but urging tactical flexibility and remaining open to the possibility that supporters of the war could change their minds.[100]

Baby doctor Benjamin Spock was nationally beloved and a celebrated war veteran. His 1946 guide to raising infants was in almost every home in the country. It was a close second only to the Bible in sales. Spock had come out against the Vietnam War early on, largely on moral grounds. On January 5, 1968, this gentle, patrician, well-dressed, soft-spoken icon—America's family physician—was indicted by the U.S. government and charged with conspiracy. Specifically, he was charged with conspiring to counsel, aid, and abet draft evasion and with hindering the Selective Service Act. The indictment claimed that Spock had conspired along with Yale Chaplain William Sloan Coffin, think tank president Marcus Raskin (father of Jamie Raskin), novelist Mitchell Goodman, and Harvard graduate student Michael Ferber. Spock did not know most of the other men. These were extremely serious charges in 1968. The basis of the indictment relied on an obscure and little-used statute. It was brought by Attorney General Ramsey Clark in hopes of creating a show trial that would dissuade other high-level protests. The foundation of Clark's case were the demonstrations that the defendants had attended, and statements to which they'd added their names—an increasingly common show of support by successful American citizens. Clark gathered anti-war messages from across the movement, such as "this war violates international agreements," "the combat role of the United States troops in Vietnam violates the Geneva Accords of 1954," and "resistance against illegitimate authority is courageous and justified." Then he claimed that such statements were not free speech but rather unlawful interference in crucial government affairs.[101] The individuals he charged hence stood in for every single person who then opposed the war. The stakes of the case could not have been greater. The government construed legal protest as a criminal act. It claimed that merely sharing a view or thinking along the same lines as others, even thousands of others, could be defined as conspiring criminally. If the government won its case, Spock and others rejoined, free speech in America was dead.[102]

The indictments shocked America. Many saw the government's attempt to compel loyalty to an increasingly unpopular war as overreach. Clark would not back down, however. Leonard Boudin, a longtime friend of Bob and Decca's, was immediately pulled into the case, as were many other progressive attorneys. Since the Smith trials, Decca had focused on the government's "vindictive justice": ways that political resistance was suppressed through legal charges, fines, and sentences that were not otherwise administered.[103]

On March 16, 1968, Boudin asked Decca to write the definitive book on the Spock case. She and many others believed it would be the "political trial of the decade."[104] Gottlieb was to edit the book at Knopf, to which he'd recently moved. Certain that the book would be her most important yet and a chance to make a significant contribution to the movement, Decca immediately began to pack her bags. "It's the first truly exciting thing that's come my way for a long, long time—even beats undertakers for sheer thrill," Decca wrote to friends.[105]

16

"Do Admit"

The political trial of the decade . . .
—JESSICA MITFORD

Decca may not have been an obvious choice for the definitive account of this conspiracy trial, usually called the Spock
trial and sometimes called the Boston Five. She was not lo-
cal, a trial reporter, nor especially active in draft resistance circles. She
was glancingly familiar with the Quakers and Unitarians who proved
essential to draft resistance (they had been interested in her memorial
society work), but she was not part of those groups. In 1968, in fact,
Decca was more famous as a writer for her eccentric aristocratic background and her exposés of American excess—funerals and fat farms
particularly—than she was for the grim subtleties of American law.

Asking Decca to take on the project was a brilliant stroke on

Leonard Boudin's part, however. Decca was well known and admired in anti–Vietnam War work. With her two children grown and Bob in constant demand defending radicals, she had unhampered time to devote, and could drop everything, travel to Boston, and stay as long as she was needed. She was tough, and Boudin knew it. She was not only a dogged researcher, but also someone who could sit uncomplainingly all day long on the straight, high-backed wooden pews reserved for observers. Her energy was infectious; she infused whatever she was part of with *joie de vivre*. Her excellent publishing connections guaranteed visibility. Most importantly, she was deeply, innately, sympathetic to the anti-authoritarian strains of the war resistance movement, warmly supportive of their sometimes wild, dramatic antics. Courtroom #3 on the twelfth floor of Boston's Art Deco federal building was imposing. The high dark doors, massive leaded windows, and iron and glass pendant lights of the McCormack Court House were designed to make defendants feel small. The courtroom was unadorned, except for the wall behind the judge's bench. There, a large New Deal–style mural, framed in dark oak, depicted a map of the United States with a banner reading "Justice Is the Guarantee of Liberty."[1] Decca was unimpressed. Despite decades in a middle-class Oakland house, she could still turn on a dime and summon aristocratic disdain, her wry half smile suggesting that she'd seen things far grander than this. Boudin knew that Decca would not show deference to authority. And he probably discerned that his friend was not yet satisfied with her literary success, that she still wanted to prove herself to a more radical readership.

Decca had been scheduled to leave for Mexico to see the Belfrages and take a much-needed rest in the heat she craved. She canceled all travel unrelated to the Boston case. "This is the political trial of the decade," she told the Belfrages, explaining why she simply had to beg off her visit.[2]

She had done all that she could to avoid working on her second memoir (it would not be published until 1977). She did not waste a second now, however, researching the principals of the Boston Five conspiracy case and digging into all the background material she could find. She was at her desk off the dining room early every morning making lists and arrangements for Boston. Late into the night she was still there: poring over legal articles on the use of conspiracy charges, reading history, parsing anti-war statements, rereading the Geneva Convention, amassing newsletters and broadsides from religious associations supporting conscientious objectors, as well as veterans' groups and others advocating draft resistance. She filled spiral notebooks and typed up things to check and contacts to pursue. She made what Bob thought were endless phone calls. He derided cold calling, but she found it surprisingly successful. Few people refused her melodic English voice. Decca liked to refer to Bob as "the Old Trial Hand"; she pumped him for legal information constantly.

As soon as she could, Decca rushed to Boston, New York, New Haven, and Washington, D.C., for interviews. She was on a train into D.C. on April 4, when Martin Luther King, Jr., was assassinated in Memphis. Making her way up through the "dense smoke" that filtered down to the tracks, she threaded a path through National Guard troops, demonstrators, and rioters, finally reaching the home of friends. Did a book on the Boston Five still matter, Decca wondered? Didn't King's murder change everything? Her friends reassured Decca that a book on the Boston case, and the Vietnam War—a war that King had so recently and so powerfully opposed—was, indeed, still relevant. They all lived in what Coretta Scott King called a "sick society . . . infested with racism and violence."[3] That sickness *had* to be exposed, they said.

Decca was hardly alone in hoping that the conspiracy trial would have huge cultural impact. Since the government had targeted unusually high-profile people, like Spock, it seemed certain to be "a broad test of the legality of the Vietnam War," as *The New York Times* predicted.[4] Conservatives looked to the trial to curtail a growing culture of disrespect for established authority. Progressives like Decca believed that the trial, if it didn't help bring an end to the war, would strengthen the opposition. Dr. Spock was an establishment icon, as a gold-medal Olympian, Yale graduate, and elegant, trusted physician. Putting him on trial, along with a respected Yale chaplain who had served as a CIA officer, seemed likely to underscore dissent's morality.

The Spock trial, as the press always called it, was not the government's first attempt to squelch dissent with conspiracy fears. "Originally adopted as a weapon of organized crime," conspiracy laws were "regularly used in times of stress against political offenders, from trade union organizers to communists," as Elinor Langer explained in *The Atlantic*.[5] "The public," Boudin later commented, "has always been more frightened by the word 'conspiracy' than by any other . . . word in the criminal . . . lexicon."[6] Decca was more familiar with this history than most people. She had lived through the government's use of such charges in the Smith Act trials against leaders of the Communist Party in the late 1940s and 1950s. She was angry, but unsurprised, to see such charges now used "to intimidate opponents of the Vietnam war."[7]

Conspiracy had also been used in Oakland, in January 1968, against the seven young men, known as the Oakland Seven, indicted by Decca and Bob's arch antagonist Frank Coakley, charged with felony conspiracy charges for misdemeanor offenses of trespassing and resisting arrest during the October 1967 "Stop the Draft Week." Coakley acknowledged that "the indictment procedure in such instances is a new one." It should, he insisted, "serve as a warning." Many of the Oakland Seven defendants were veterans of SNCC and the Berkeley Free Speech Movement. Their lead attorney was Decca's old friend, Black Panther lawyer Charles Garry.[8] As Langer put it, "the Spock defendants were the respectables, the Oakland Seven were the *enragés*."[9] Decca and Bob were now involved with both, one on each coast.

With decreasing popular support for the war, the government's case against the Boston Five for aiding, abetting, and counseling draft resistance was a gamble.[10] Because most of the defendants did not know one another, had acted only openly and in public, had understood everything they'd done to be in accordance with their free speech rights as citizens, it was a tough case to prosecute. Boudin felt that it boiled down to a "personal prosecution" ordered by a frustrated president who took defiance badly. Spock "had gotten under Johnson's skin," Boudin believed.[11] Defendant Michael Ferber, a graduate student at the time of the trial, also believed that "Johnson must have ordered it."[12] The government's ability to prosecute the case depended on the judge conducting it within the narrowest possible channel, without discussion of the war or First Amendment rights. It would be especially critical to bar any reference to either the Nuremberg rules supporting the right to dissent to unjust wars or the Geneva Convention's prohibitions against undeclared wars. The defendants hoped that they could tackle broader issues and "boost . . . the antiwar movement, [proving] that Johnson . . . had made a big mistake."[13]

The government chose its prosecutor, John Wall, brilliantly. He was the ideal person to help the judge narrow the scope of the trial. Wall was young, dogged, relentless, and humorless. He combined every quality Decca detested most. She found him so "unpleasant . . . uptight and horrid" that she could hardly look at his "pallid, mouse-blond face."[14] As bad as Wall was, the judge, Francis Ford, was worse. Born in 1882 and eighty-five years old by the time the trial commenced, Ford was both Southie tough (he made a point of both his impoverished South Boston background and his Harvard education) and old school autocratic. He displayed an unmistakable bias toward the prosecution, was nasty to the defense, and created a general atmosphere of "gloom and doom" throughout the four-week trial, Decca said.[15]

The trial's venue was as carefully chosen as its prosecutor. Few of the defendants had a connection to Boston. Raskin was in D.C., Spock was in New York, and Coffin was in New Haven. Moreover, few of the public protests cited in the case as evidence of conspiring to interfere with the draft took place in Boston. Boston was chosen in the hope of a jury that would be less sympathetic to the defendants than in New York or D.C. The prosecution ultimately engineered a jury that was not only all white, but also all male, an important point of contention in later appeals.

Decca moved to Boston for the duration of the trial, staying in the smallest, least expensive room that the Parker House hotel—only two blocks from the courthouse—had to offer. The jury was sequestered on a floor in the Parker House as well, and other people connected to the trial were also staying there. The Parker House had an old-fashioned, world-class, cream-sauce style restaurant and dark, clubby bar. Had Decca been staying there as part of a magazine assignment, on someone else's dime, she'd have eagerly enjoyed both. But this was no junket, so she ate in cheap restaurants nearby and kept a large bottle of booze in her room.

Approaching the first big book commission of her life, Decca was disciplined and earnest, studious and timely. She was great fun outside the courthouse, making jokes, creating perfect nicknames for the prosecution, buoying everyone's spirits. She played the central role among observers in creating a shared culture of derision that she looked back on nostalgically, as a "snug world" of comrades, "not unlike life aboard a cruise ship."[16] In court, on the other hand, she was a professional on a "mission." She "took the trial very seriously," Ferber recalled.[17] Decca, in fact, was so absorbed with her responsibilities that she never took breaks. She did not learn, throughout that month's time, where the courtroom bathrooms were located. "I literally haven't got time to go," she wrote a friend.[18]

In her contract for *The Trial of Dr. Spock*, Decca accepted the tightest deadline of her writing life. The book was due to Gottlieb and Knopf six months after the trial's conclusion. Probably persuaded that readers would lose interest unless the book followed the case quickly, Decca needed to work three or four times faster than her usual pace, and without a coauthor or collaborator. She also faced the pressure of knowing that numerous competing magazine and newspaper pieces were appearing on the trial, many of them excellent.

Decca's typical approach to a book or long magazine article was to design, in effect, a personal curriculum for a graduate degree in her subject. As she worked on the Spock book, her day began in her cramped hotel room at 7:00 a.m., writing up notes from the day before. She left early to walk the few blocks through Boston's narrow downtown streets, making sure she arrived before the trial's 9:00 start (lines for observers were long, started early in the long marble hallways, and made no exceptions for journalists). She never left before the trial's 4:00 p.m. finish. She then spent hours typing up notes, almost always in the form of a letter to Bob, a technique she'd perfected at Maine Chance. She typically grabbed a quick bite around 8:00, then went straight back to her room to clip newspaper articles about the trial from 9:00 or so until she fell asleep, sometimes still clutching her scissors. She felt under "enormous" pressure. If she was not sorting through her "sea of papers" then she felt she ought to be interviewing clerks, going through *The Boston Globe*'s enormous archives, or visiting key resistance sites, such as Boston's Arlington Church, where some of the defendants had given particularly memorable speeches and helped collect draft cards. She sometimes had other journalists up to her room for a nightcap, everyone sitting on her thin monastic bed. On weekends she dashed out of Boston, usually to New York, but kept working on her notes on the train and conducted interviews once she arrived. Sometimes, her family visited. Even Benjy showed up, unannounced, without luggage or a place to sleep. Michael Ferber thought Benjy was "sort of strange," but also "sweet," and he let Benjy crash on his couch.[19]

Decca grumbled about her workload. But she had to admit to "rather adoring it" as well.[20] Finally immersed again in a meaningful project, working with like-minded people and making new friends, doing something that mattered, energized her more than it exhausted her. Even though most days of the trial were filled with "anticlimactic motions about technicalities," the hallway outside the courtroom was packed each morning with thirty or more reporters from magazines, national newspapers, and the foreign press. Local papers such as *The Boston Globe*, which proved especially sympathetic to the defendants (even sending a "lifestyle" reporter to report on the defendants' clothes), never missed a day. All the major Left periodicals, such as *Ramparts*, also sent reporters, as did *The New Yorker*, *Esquire*, and even *The Yale Review* (a nod to Coffin's status at Yale).[21] Decca was both a journalist among journalists and *the* author of *the* book on the case. She often asked other journalists for help and insights; most were happy to lend her a hand. She was sharper and more square-shouldered than she'd been in months and it felt great.

The trial ran from May 19, 1968, to June 14, 1968, one of the most explosive periods in modern American history: just weeks after both Martin Luther King, Jr., and Black Panther Bobby Hutton were killed, the Civil Rights Act was signed into law, Columbia University students shut down their school, students went on strike across the nation in anti-war mobilizations, Black Panther Party Minister of Information Eldridge Cleaver announced his candidacy for president, and the Berrigans and their associates destroyed draft records in Maryland. Yet excepting the one day when defendants were allowed to speak to their motives, all testimony on the war itself was barred as irrelevant.[22] Instead of being the "landmark case to set the limits of dissent," the trial was "strangely devoid of drama," as one reporter put it.[23] Decca sadly declared it a "fizzle."[24]

If the trial fizzled, however, her book about it could not. Decca did her best. She opened with the drama of the defendants finding out from news coverage that they'd been indicted and then covered their first, largely bewildered meeting in Leonard Boudin's West Village living room, being introduced to one another while holding porcelain cups of tea laced with bourbon. Decca then followed with mini biographies of the defendants, using as much of their human-interest material as she could before proceeding to the necessary, but drier, sections on the history of conspiracy law. Conspiracy defendants, she carefully explained, need not be found guilty of any illegal actions. They only have to plan together, even *think* together in some instances, to commit such actions. As she detailed, a misdemeanor offense immediately becomes a felony if planned by two or more people, whether it is carried out or not, giving the government "extraordinary," if admittedly rarely applied, power. In this case, since the defendants had done nothing coercive, secret, or criminal, they stood "accused of *conspiring* to do something that, as a matter of explicit policy, the government does *not* consider an indictable crime." The range of activity that constituted conspiracy was particularly broad. "I asked," Decca wrote, if it were true that "even applauding what others said, if done enthusiastically rather than politely, was considered evidence of criminal intent. . . . 'That is substantially correct,' answered Mr. Wall."[25] Even more ludicrous, as Decca's book carefully explicated, were Judge Ford's directions to the jury at the end of the trial, which included ten special provisions to be applied in the event of a guilty verdict (suggesting that such a verdict was inevitable) and a lengthy lecture on the legal irrelevance of motive and intent. The defense objected that Ford's instructions virtually guaranteed a verdict. No one was surprised when the jury shortly found four of the five defendants guilty. The only surprise was that Marcus Raskin, somewhat unaccountably, was found not guilty.[26]

Working harder than she'd ever worked before, Decca met her deadlines. She submitted her manuscript in time for publication in the early fall of 1969, barely a year from the end of the trial. Decca tried to balance her reputation and her responsibility. While much was ridiculous about the trial, little was funny. For readers expecting another uproarious exposé, like *The American Way of Death*, she hoped that her thorough accounting would satisfy them instead.

Bob was usually unstinting in his praise of Decca. She counted on him as her cheerleader. But he was also straightforward. He pronounced the final book "workmanlike." Even Benjy, usually such an enthusiast, could come up with nothing better than "solid."[27]

Fortunately for Decca, reviewers were kinder.[28] *The Trial of Dr. Spock* received dozens of favorable reviews from mainstream newspapers in major cities such as New York, Los Angeles, and Washington, D.C., as well as a surprising amount of coverage in smaller cities such as Fairbanks, Alaska; Appleton, Wisconsin; Dover, Ohio; and Gaffney, South Carolina. Most reviewers heaped praise on the very thing Decca was most anxious about—whether the narrative would fizzle or sizzle—calling it "engaging" and "entertaining," a "fascinating account," "lively," and, some remarked, so compelling that they "can't put it down." Even critics as famously cantankerous as Alan Dershowitz (already an attention-grabbing contrarian) praised her book as "vivid" and perceptive.[29]

By the time the book appeared, the balance of public opinion on the war had tipped and an appeals court ruling had overturned the convictions of Spock and Ferber (in large part because of Judge Ford's bias in the case and his bizarre instructions to the jury) and sent Coffin and Goodman for a retrial, on technicalities, which no one expected would ever take place. A majority of Americans, by fall of 1969, felt that the war had been a mistake.[30] Militant opposition to the war at induction centers, on college campuses, and in Washington, D.C., had become so routinely visible on television screens across the nation that the actions of the Boston Five seemed restrained, even genteel, by comparison. In this context, Decca's insistence on what some called "advocacy journalism" drew comments—"she never conceals her bias," for example—but little condemnation.[31]

Decca never claimed to be objective. "Objectivity: I've always had an objective," she liked to quip. Reporting, she insisted, required evaluating sources, assessing evidence, discerning the biases of others. It could not be done by "pathetic cabbages without opinions—everybody comes with their ideas."[32] The idea of "giving equal weight to all information that comes one's way," seemed to her both stupid and dishonest, evidence of a "totally blank mind" and bad writing as well.

Decca often obsessed over reviews, reception, and sales of her work. She typically clipped all publicity, wrote responses to fan mail and reviews, and enlisted her friends to do likewise. This time she did not.

In the spring of 1969, just as she was in the final edits of her book, she had learned that her sister Nancy had been diagnosed with an abdominal lump which had been sent out for testing, a very slow process at that time. Nancy had suffered agonizing back and leg pain for years and believed she had sciatica. But the lump turned out to be a large liver tumor. Nancy tried, as always, to make a joke of it, naming the tumor "lumpling" and "Lord Redesdale" and insisting it had a personality with its own contrary quirks. The situation, however, was very serious. After considerable back-and-forth with her sisters, Decca raced to Versailles, leaving in such a hurry that she failed to notice her passport was days from expiring.

Nancy's house was small and boxy, furnished with delicate, uncomfortable French furniture. In the back was a large walled garden where Nancy had planted a profusion of colorful flowers, "as if 1,000 Edwardian hats had fallen into it."[33]

When the doctors confirmed cancer, they also advised that Nancy—struggling to finish a biography of Frederick the Great—not be told of the diagnosis, on the grounds that it might make her despondent. Decca's jobs in Versailles were shopping, which had to be done multiple times a day to ensure the freshest breads and produce; weeding; cutting and arranging flowers from Nancy's garden;

and arguing with her sisters about their refusal to tell Nancy how ill she was.

"I long to avoid all friction," Decca wrote Debo, before leaving Oakland for France. Decca kept her word. She tried to persuade her sisters by example, as gently as she could. "I should far prefer to know" if she were in Nancy's position, she told them, "for masses of reasons."[34] Although she came to feel that it was "verging on wicked not to tell Nancy . . . a sort of awful betrayal," she honored their rules.[35] So determined was she to avoid all conflict that she got along even with Diana. "We don't, of course, talk about anything but the parsley-weeding and Nancy's illness," she explained to friends back in Oakland.[36] Decca could not help noticing that after thirty-four years of not seeing her, Diana still seemed remarkably beautiful. At fifty-nine, she had retained her "marvellous [sic] figure" and striking aqua eyes. She was, Decca noted, "like a beautiful, aging bit of sculpture."[37] Diana was also surprised at how "easy and natural" it was to be together after decades without contact. In her diary, Diana wrote: "Decca has kept her childlike face but her voice has changed, not the accent but the tone of voice. I felt an unexpected sympathy, even affection for her, & was surprised."[38]

Nancy kept up the bravest of fronts, despite terrible pain. She especially enjoyed having all her sisters around her. At least once a day they all dissolved into the same "shrieks" of laughter, over the same silly things, that had connected them so closely in childhood. They still roared about things that struck them—though often no one else—as "too too" hilarious. Nancy shrieked as loudly as any of them; sometimes, Decca noticed, she shrieked the loudest of them all.

Unlike all the other sisters, Nancy was now very much alone. It was a tribute to the sisters' bond that they realized how that must feel for her, especially now that she was ill, and that they rallied around her as they did. Gaston Palewski, for whom Nancy had waited, in vain, for three decades and who had of late become more of a friend than a lover, announced his intention to wed a very wealthy French duchess, Hélène de Talleyrand-Périgord, and he cruelly let Nancy learn of it from the newspapers. Nancy covered for him, as she'd always done, telling her sisters that he'd come to Versailles to inform her in person (he hadn't) and that she didn't mind in the least (she did).[39] Secrecy and a stiff upper lip were still the norm for Decca's sisters, but Decca now found it all very strange. "She never says anything about the pain," she wrote Aranka from Versailles. "You know how they are; one can only tell if her face goes grey."[40]

Decca longed for letters when she traveled. "One craves letters," she said.[41] She was constantly haranguing her friends to write more often and share better details. Now she felt especially "cut off," she told them, from "news of Berkeley." She was just leaving for Versailles when protests over the university's demolition of housing to build athletic fields erupted. Students and Berkeley activists, defending what they called People's Park, were attacked by police, who killed one protester and blinded a bystander. Governor Reagan called in 7,500 heavily armed National Guard troops to defend a less than three-acre plot of disputed land. It was not only Bob's new legal work with People's Park and the Oakland Seven trial she wanted to hear about. Decca was desperate for letters from home to help steady an internal equilibrium that only her sisters could upset. She had managed her time with her sisters well. And she cherished the chance to see them all. But in all the ways that mattered, she was no longer one of them. The world that she'd so painstakingly created simply didn't exist for her sisters. It had been "bliss" to see them, but it had thrown her off-kilter. "There's no point to discussing it [the movement] with Nancy as she's completely against the students," Decca wrote to her friends.[42] As soon as Nancy seemed stable, Decca gratefully returned to Berkeley via Paris and New York, spending time with Dinky, who was pregnant again, Aranka, and many of her East Coast friends.

Decca traveled so often now that missing political events that mattered greatly to her became a pattern. In July 1969, when the U.S. Appeals Court verdict on the Spock trial came in, Decca was back home in Oakland. In October when the National Moratorium Against the War organized some of the largest demonstrations ever seen in North America, she was in London on book business. Fortunately, she no longer needed to be present to feel she was contributing. Being called in to write the book on the "political trial of the decade" had given her a new sense of herself. She had more confidence, more faith in her own judgments. She worried less about what others thought.

At this time, the catch phrase "Do Admit" began to pepper her correspondence. "Do admit they were a rather rum bunch," Decca said of her family. "Do admit it's really rather heaven." "Do admit that the undertakers are a lark." "Do admit" dominated her letters in spite of the fact, which she knew all too well, that few people found things as funny as she did or looked at things in quite the Decca way.[43] "Do Admit" was redolent of Decca's privileged British background and commandeering style. And in that sense, perhaps, it avoided argument, rather than joining it. It could be seen as part of what one old friend called that "curiously cadenced sing-song" of Mitford-speak, with its many repeats of "such," "too," and "so": a linguistic world in which things are too "divine" or too "dread," where people who generally can't stand one another are always "longing" to meet for tea, and where everything is perfect, so lovely, so awful.[44] "Do admit" also smacks of the very American "Say Uncle"—give up, give in, surrender. And in that sense, it is a kind of rhetorical wish fulfillment: Just give in; don't make me fight with you about this. Do give up.

However bossy Decca was in her personal life, in her writing she nevertheless *worked* for agreement. Her style married traditional strategies to highly inventive ones to win her reader over. Comedy was her most effective weapon, but she now used it more sparingly.

An increased stylistic confidence was particularly evident in the article Decca turned to next, even as she was preparing a foreword to the paperback edition of *The Trial of Dr. Spock*. This essay, on the Famous Writers School, gave her "more pleasure from start to finish than any other" she had written, she later said.[45]

Like so many of her favorite pieces of writing, "Let Us Now Appraise Famous Writers" came to Decca by chance. She was traveling like mad, racing back and forth between California, New York, London, and Paris. In demand again as a speaker, she gave talks on draft resistance, Vietnam, the government's use of conspiracy, and the suppression of protest. She was constantly packing and repacking, writing on the go, accepting invitations, editing on planes, trying to keep up with U.S. news from England and France.

"Let Us Now Appraise Famous Writers" started with a story Bob told her in the car on the way home from the airport after another long flight from London in the winter of 1969. He had taken the case of a seventy-two-year-old widow on social security. She had been talked into surrendering her life's savings for a Famous Writers School correspondence course that promised a new and exciting career as a writer. The salesman (one of the eight hundred "rapacious" traveling salesmen the Famous Writers School deployed across the nation to earn commissions from "gullible" housewives) had come to her house, been alternately charming and then high pressure, and ultimately harangued her to the point of exhaustion, spinning visions of the wonderfully inspired and creative life ahead of her. It seemed that the only way to get him to stop was to agree. He extracted a signed contract and a two-hundred-dollar deposit for an eight-hundred-dollar course. The widow, who spoke more German than English, instantly regretted signing and tried to get her money back. When the Famous Writers School refused to refund her deposit, she turned to Bob Treuhaft. By the time Bob and Decca pulled their sedan into the driveway on Regent Street, Decca was hooked. I am "into yet another conspiracy," she told her friend Barb Kahn.[46]

This was not just "another" conspiracy, however. The "chicanery" of the Famous Writers School struck a nerve. Decca became relentless in her pursuit of the "Famous Brutes." She was determined to "topple their whole house of cards."[47]

As she did whenever she was passionate about a subject, Decca researched every angle of the Famous Writers School. She learned that they "accepted" everyone who applied, had an enrollment of approximately sixty-five thousand students, a teaching faculty of fifty-five people who gave "feedback" by form letter, and that the company had generated roughly $50 million in tuition revenue. They spent almost $11 million on advertising. Their roster of "Guiding Faculty," pictured in all their advertising, included Faith Baldwin, Paul Engle, Clifton Fadiman, and most prominently, Bennett Cerf, president of Random House, writer, and beloved celebrity on television's *"What's My Line?"* The Guiding Faculty, Decca discovered, never laid eyes on students' work, never met with the Teaching Faculty and never appeared at the school. They received very handsome salaries, purely for supplying credible names used to sucker in students.[48]

Decca's best technique was always to let her adversaries dig their own graves, with their own expressions. Most damning in her new article were the words of the Famous Writers themselves. Decca researched each of them in *Who's Who* and found that most of their addresses were listed. With her typed list of names and addresses in front of her, she sat down at her desk, pulled her large desk phone forward, dialed Directory Assistance, and proceeded to call them, one after the other. All wanted to talk. They seemed to so relish the sound of their own voices that they became careless. They all gave their "cooperation in constructing a noose to hang themselves with," Decca happily announced to her friend and sometimes editor, Vivian Cadden.[49] Once again, she was gleefully shooting fish in a barrel.

Decca was not merely out to expose the school's shady methods. She wanted to break them. In the case of Bennett Cerf especially, she planned to "destroy the brute."[50]

By the time she was through with the Famous Writers School, no reputable magazine would carry their advertisements, the Federal Trade Commission had launched an investigation, cartoonists and talk-show hosts mocked the Guiding Faculty mercilessly, the corporation that owned the school went bankrupt, and stock in the school was wiped out. It closed. While by no means her most "important" battle, this was "one of the few clear-cut successes . . . of my muckraking career," Decca declared.[51]

Many people, and Cerf's biographer in particular, have wondered why Decca was so bent on destroying the Famous Writers School and so particularly incensed about Cerf.[52] While the Guiding Faculty were "super-respectable right-wing asses," Decca had locked horns with many right-wing asses. Few had produced the same rage.[53] Her attitude toward the Famous Writers School makes perfect sense in context, however. Decca could not help comparing a celebrity like Cerf, who used his fame for personal gain at others' expense, to someone like Spock, who put his reputation on the line for the greater good. Decca refused to call herself a "feminist": aspects of the movement such as consciousness-raising were too close to the "grubbing about" into feelings she abhorred. Nevertheless, she bristled if anyone suggested she wasn't all in for women's liberation. When a friend said that Decca hadn't "a feminist bone in her body," she responded testily: "Perhaps true, but I do have splashes of cartilage."[54] Her feminist "cartilage" reserved a special place in hell for men who took advantage of women. She had not forgotten what being a widow was like, or the precarious feeling of being suddenly on her own, without enough money. She had been moved to write *The American Way of Death* not only in defense of consumers, but especially in defense of poor widows, coerced by salesmen lacking compassion or scruples. Cerf and his cronies looked suspiciously like those devious undertakers to Decca.

Her knowledge of the moral vacuity of traveling salesmen dated back to Esmond's training to sell silk stockings door to door for the Silkform company, an occupation for which he had shown frighteningly good instincts. Decca had not only worked alongside Esmond, carefully watching how he wore his targets down with a mixture of charm and alarm, but she'd also studied his sales training manuals, with their sexist instructions in how to "mesmerize" the "victim" with "a deft combination of mental torture and physical manipulation designed to reduce the subject to a state of helpless passivity, bereft of independent will, and ready to sign anything as a condition of freedom from torment."[55] At the time, Decca felt a little bad for the victims they coerced into purchases they did not need and could not afford. But she and Esmond were young, poor, and unscrupulous. Esmond drew Decca into many clever hijinks, as she then thought of them—stealing toothpaste from the Myers, not paying the electric bill for months in London's East End, milking employers whenever possible. It all seemed part of the fun.

Thirty years later, Decca saw things differently. Her long study of consumers' rights and sales practices made it impossible for her to view traveling salesmen—almost always male and almost always preying on women of little means—as comic.[56] What was funny then was not funny now. There may have been a touch of shame, showing up as rage, in her feelings about the Famous Writers School.

Her relentless pursuit of the school was also a direct result of its own efforts to stop her article. Cerf interfered first at *The Atlantic*, then at *Mc-Call's*, then at *Life*, threatening not only to withhold all advertising dollars but also to keep well-known writers Cerf worked with from publishing in those venues. The July issue of *The Atlantic*, which initially wavered on publishing Decca's essay but finally refused to cave to Cerf and canceled all advertising from the Famous Writers School, "had the largest newsstand sale of any in the magazine's history," Decca merrily noted.[57]

Decca thoroughly enjoyed taking down the Famous Writers School. But it was not her main prey.

From the moment she took on the book on the Spock trial, her interest in the criminal justice system grew. Social analyses coming out of the prisons, Decca felt, were providing some of the most trenchant thinking about what was wrong with the country and how it had to change. "Black militancy and New Left ideas are seeping into the prisons . . . a new type of offender: civil-disobedients, Panthers, collegiate narc. users etc. are coming into the prisons. Hence, new and more sophisticated demands by prisoners," she wrote.[58]

Decca may have been the first person, or one of the first, to use the phrase "prison abolition." From the beginning, she opposed the idea of prison reform. "It's really the common-sense defying irrationality of the prison system that gets me more than anything," she wrote in 1970. "I do not believe, she added, that the presumption of innocence and other aspects of the process are working for the poor and black, & I don't think they get justice in the courts."[59] The system, she could see, was too broken to be fixed by reforms; too structured by racism and injustice to be rebuilt. The cycle of "liberal reform," she argued, begins when there are prison uprisings and riots, becomes briefly heated, results in much discussion and tiny changes, and is invariably, she wrote, "followed by a restatement of the penological nostrums of preceding decades."[60]

In the early summer of 1973, Nancy's condition took a turn for the worse. Decca rushed to Versailles and found her sister "quite changed, her face all grey, can't get up—in fact, can't be moved without truly awful agony. No jokes, no gossip, nothing but—well, here's how it is," Decca wrote Bob. "Mostly she's fearfully sleepy . . . The awful thing is the well-known stoicism has faded & she cries a lot."[61] So in the spring and early summer of 1973, Decca was once again out of the country, regretfully missing the chance to watch the televised Watergate hearings with Bob and her friends. For many liberals, the question of whether government officials would be punished for crimes was paramount. And the bravery of her friend Kay Graham, who refused to bend to power or pressure, moved Decca deeply.

Nancy held on longer than any of her doctors expected. They had finally diagnosed her condition as a rare form of Hodgkin's disease for which few effective treatments then existed. Her cancer had spread to her spine, compressing it, and causing excruciating pain. Watching Nancy's agony was "miserable." Unlike her earlier stay in Versailles, when she deferred to her sisters' dictates, Decca now made her own decisions. She did not argue with her sisters, but she did not to listen to them either. Something, Decca determined, *had* to be done "to alleviate the pain."

Decca called Nancy's doctors. They told Nancy's nurse that Nancy's morphine could be doubled, twice a day. Without consulting anyone, Decca took matters into her own hands. She told the nurse, who didn't "speak French," "to give 4 double injections a day," twice what the doctors had prescribed. "So she did," Decca added, "& I hope . . . that all this morphine will send her into a coma soon. I do hope the Dr. won't be livid when he finds out."[62] Nancy died a few days later. There is no indication that Decca's sisters knew about the morphine dose, at least not for many years. She told another friend what she'd done, describing it as "the only useful thing I did" in Nancy's care.[63] To the same friend, Decca boasted that she'd probably avoid the kind of dreadful death that Nancy endured because she was too "self-indulgent" and "lazy" to hang on to life as Nancy had done. Besides, she said boastfully, she was smoking and drinking "like mad." That would ensure that her "lights & livers" would "give out in no time." "Don't you agree?" she asked, at the close of her letter. "Do forgive," she added later, about a contentious thing she'd said. "Do come," she wrote.

17

"A Bit of a Black Cloud"

I would never want to live in England again.[1]
—JESSICA MITFORD

Decca hated working but she hated not working more. "Talk about me needing a Project to keep me alive," she joked.[2] She began the work that led to her next book, on prisons, almost as soon as she finished *The Trial of Dr. Spock.*

It was clear to Decca as early as 1970, when she attended an eight-day conference on the criminal justice system in Washington, D.C., that prisons would be next.[3] She participated in a workshop experience that included a simulated arrest and time in solitary confinement. In solitary, she was placed directly opposite a cell where a minor, held for "adjustment," was screaming in "rage and misery, shrieks and obscenities interspersed with deep, racking sobs." That led to an essay called "Women in Cages," published in *McCall's*.[4] "I don't really want to do a book on prisons but the awful thing is I think I'll have to. It's like quicksand, and I'm getting sucked under," she told Virginia Durr. "Women in Cages" was one of the only times that female prisoners were her focus.

In some ways, a book on prisons was a natural outgrowth of her concern with judicial overreach, and her decades of involvement in legal cases (some of them Bob's) that stripped Black men like Jerry Newson and Willie McGee of their rights. Her prison work also grew from her support for the prisoners' rights movement, especially active in northern California and led first by Black Muslims and then by Black Panthers and activists like Dinky's partner, James Forman. Decca was afraid for Forman. With so many Black militants targeted by law enforcement, it was easy to imagine that Forman might be arrested, or worse. She felt that the prisoners' rights movement emerged "out of the whole rebellion against government and authority that distinguished the student movement etc. of the 60s." As soon as her Spock conspiracy trial work was done, she began meeting with prisoners.

Everything Decca wrote in the 1970s was designed to make radical arguments compelling to nonradicals, to bridge political and moral divides. "What I try to do mostly, is write things that I hope will be useful in the struggle," she said.[5] Her most clear-cut successes came in fighting profiteering: in the funeral industry, the Famous Writers School, and other exploitative businesses.[6] Nevertheless, she was "not one to go into consumer advocacy for the sake of it," she said.[7] Aware that "the mere exposure of bureaucratic absurdities is insufficient in and of itself to force change," she wanted to get to the root of social problems, not just their excesses.[8] Some of her stuff, she felt, was "very often extremely trivial."[9] "I wish we could drive the prisons bankrupt," she said, while wryly acknowledging that "that's not likely" to occur.[10]

The ACLU asked her to write an exposé on the unauthorized use of inmates in medical experiments. Decca claimed that she "never had so much difficulty with a piece" as she did with that one, but the article, published as "Kind and Usual Punishment in California" by *The Atlantic* in 1971, proved widely influential.[11]

Decca had now become very close to Maya Angelou, who she'd known for years, but now considered her "sister." Angelou was tough as nails, unapologetically ambitious, a gorgeous writer, a total rule breaker, and funny as hell. She and Decca sang bawdy songs, dished about agents and editors, read each other's drafts and often discussed ways to fight racism as writers. Decca rarely took others' advice. But she never dismissed Angelou's views. Angelou adored Decca. They fed on one another's cultural differences. Decca had often said that "being bored" was "the thing I'm most afraid of."[12] Angelou could be prickly and imperious. Some people found her impossible. But she was always brilliant, bold, and never boring.

Exposés by white muckrakers such as herself, Decca thought, were limited. "Do-gooding suggestions of people like me about prisons won't do much good," she wrote, "unless they express the views of the prisoners."[13] Accordingly, Decca began spending much of her time inside prisons, mostly men's prisons, listening to the incarcerated. She read their writing, sent articles, and tried to amplify their voices. She began corresponding with prisoners, almost all male, about the "total failure of prison 'reform'" and learning what their lives were like.[14] She sent books such as George Jackson's *Soledad Brother* and Angelou's *I Know Why the Caged Bird Sings*, along with supportive notes to men who wrote her that "I haven't got any 'real' hopes" left. She learned about prisoners who'd "died from the lack of medical care," and about beatings, torture, psychological abuse, and solitary confinement. Much of her correspondence was devoted to prisoners' efforts to file appeals and assert their legal rights: the right to be interviewed, the right not to be transferred arbitrarily, the right to communicate with outsiders, the right to consent to drug testing or refuse such consent, the right to control the funds deposited for their use, and more.[15]

Like most American leftists, Decca had absorbed books such as *Soledad Brother*. In 1971, after months of wrangling with prison officials, she was able to visit Jackson in prison. Her interview, "A Talk with George Jackson," appeared in *The New York Times Book Review* in June 1971, just two months before Jackson was killed by prison guards in San Quentin. Unusual among the many political essays about Jackson, Mitford's interview was a writer-to-writer conversation, largely about things like revision, typewriting, word choice, working with editors, and literary influences. Jackson's love of words was something that Decca had not expected. It drew her closer to him. Toward the end of the interview, Decca noted, Jackson predicted that he'd be murdered by the authorities, on the "first chance" they could get.[16]

Decca's essays attracted attention, especially from incarcerated people, and convinced her to take on a book on the prison system. "I can see that now," she wrote to Virginia Durr, "I shall have to muddle around in the federal prison system."[17] She was, of course, not "muddling." However unlikely she might have appeared to some people—a white, middle-aged, mostly law-abiding, humorous, middle-class writer— Decca was suited to write about prisons in the early 1970s. For *The American Way of Death*, she had created the persona of a smart, slightly dowdy, vaguely eccentric housewife, carrying a small notebook in her large black handbag, the better to catch scoundrels who were fleecing good-hearted consumers. She had largely abandoned that character when writing *The Trial of Dr. Spock*. Now, faced with the challenge of trying to get her readers to identify with incarcerated men, she dropped it altogether. The more she could link her writing to her activism, the less inclined she felt to rely on the fictionalized version of herself as narrator she'd crafted for so long (and to which her fans were devoted).

Decca's ambitions caused some friction with old friends. Few women in the 1970s were equally famous as social activists and mainstream writers. Decca and Maya Angelou were exceptions. As Decca's professional opportunities expanded, some of her oldest friends, including Dobby Walker and Marge Frantz, carped about her attitude. Decca's "profound sense of confidence" had now returned, and with it, a renewed reluctance to solicit advice. That confidence was the core of her "irresistible charisma" for many, but for those who'd known her longest, and remembered Decca's periods of insecurities and self-doubt, it could also seem jarring, especially where money was concerned.[18] For her part, however, Decca never let herself be goaded into apologizing for wanting to make a good living as a writer. If celebrity male writers, including some of the "brutes" at the Famous Writers School, garnered high advances and stayed in good hotels, then she too should be paid what she was worth. While no book of hers would ever again achieve the phenomenal success of *The American Way of Death*, every subsequent book did earn a higher advance (often doubling each time). As she entered middle age, she was more comfortable financially and professionally than she'd imagined possible. And that suited her just fine, thank you very much. She was not going backward.

Angelou always pushed Decca to feel comfortable about demanding her due. She never apologized for success and always fought to win.[19] "Nobody could turn me 'round," Angelou said. "I knew I was going to do something."[20] Angelou encouraged Decca to go after fellowships and visiting professorships, the sort of perks that typically went to white men with degrees, and Decca could always turn to Angelou for full-throated support when she needed backing. They traveled together often, and Decca, usually the brave one, found herself in the novel role of being goaded into being more daring, following Angelou's fearlessness. Once, to Decca's lifelong regret, Angelou persuaded her to ride an elephant. Absolutely dreadful, Decca maintained.

Whenever the young Mitford girls found a phrase that tickled their funny bones, they tended to use it unremittingly. Decca never lost that habit. Especially useful terms such as "tease," "frenemy," "good hater," "concrete upper lip," "loom," "extraorder," and "Abyssinia" (I'll be seeing ya') were so ubiquitous in Decca's speech that her friends adopted them without noticing they'd done so. Around her fifty-sixth birthday, on September 11, 1973, Decca added "kaleidoscopic" and "contrast-y" to her personal lexicon.[21]

One contrast, of course, was shuffling between her comfortable study and the cells of survivors of torturous, involuntary medical experiments. Another contrast was feeling settled in the life she'd built and yet also feeling restless about her work, as well as identifying as an American but often feeling very English, being treated as a celebrity and feared as a subversive. There were contrasts between her old friends in the Party and a new bicoastal world of writers, and between her irrepressible humor and a growing sense of gloom. She often now described herself as feeling under a "black cloud." She was torn between the socializing she adored—"Decca and Bob knew anyone who was anyone nationally in radical politics; the couple threw the best leftist parties around," as one local left-wing lawyer recalled—and her desire to work.[22] She felt the contrast between her preternatural energy and a middle-aged body that, undeniably, had never received very much care and was now feeling its years. Decca believed that her prison work was vitally important. But it depressed her deeply. "PRISONS. I know," she wrote Virginia Durr, "it is a drear enough subject—funerals were so much jollier."[23] Nancy's "terrible" suffering—"still awfully vivid"—was followed by other family illnesses. There were stresses in Dinky's relationship. Decca was concerned about both Benjy's mental health and his financial instability. There were increasing feuds with her sisters.[24] Decca had long been a heavy drinker. Now she was drinking more often alone and starting earlier every day.

Bob's attempt to make Decca's fifty-sixth birthday a big celebration contrasted with both their responses to the news. On September 11, 1973, the democratically elected government of Chile was toppled in a bloody military coup eerily reminiscent of Spain in the 1930s. Salvador Allende, Chile's much-admired Socialist president, was assassinated and replaced by a brutal dictator, backed by the United States, as had also occurred in Spain.[25] Decca's left-wing circle was painfully reminded that peace was fragile, hard-won gains easily reversed, and few people could be trusted. Some of her friends sunk into despair. It was impossible for Decca not to wonder if all the talk of revolution really prophesied any fundamental change.

Once she committed to a book on prisons, Decca jumped into her research "feetfirst," as one of her former editors put it.[26] She met with other prison activists including white women like Ysabel Rennie, a suburban housewife from Ohio whom Decca deeply admired for her relentless efforts to change her state's penitentiary, and Fay Stender, Decca's second real "frenemy" (her first was Betty Friedan) whose fearless advocacy of Black Panthers Decca respected but whose tendency to sentimentalize her clients Decca found ridiculous.[27] Other friends and associates included Alan Dershowitz, then still a liberal, Johnny Cash, and Hillary Clinton, whose friendship Decca renewed (Clinton had interned at Bob's law firm in the summer of 1971) in hopes of enlisting her in prison reform work. She pored over books and articles, clippings and interview transcripts, court records, legal articles, legislative reports and bills, testimonials, budgets, accounting documents, memoranda, meeting minutes, hearing records, news clippings—any material that might prove relevant.[28] She had files of contacts, corrections officials, historians, ex-convicts, and lawyers.[29] If she wasn't reading about prisons, she was on her desk phone, conducting interviews.

Trade journals and internal documents of corrections officials began to pile up. Thanks to both disgruntled guards and incarcerated friends, Decca received masses of documents never intended for her eyes, including the private minutes of prison meetings; internal memos and proposals; reams of appeals, briefs, and parole materials; psychological case files and studies; prison budgets for food and recreational equipment; and more. She infiltrated corrections conferences, collecting "Charm and Personal Improvement" course materials, riot shield brochures, tear gas grenade samples, surveillance system and gas mask discounts, samples of "flavor fresh" fruit syrup concentrates, and riot control handouts. On her big adding machine, she tallied the yearly expenses spent on prisoners and calculated that Harvard cost less per annum. She uncovered a $10,000 donation Johnny Cash had made to prisoners at Folsom after his famous 1960 performance. Cash had channeled the money, as he was directed, through Folsom's Inmate Welfare Fund. Decca discovered that the inmates had never seen a dime of it, and she was able to force Folsom to spend it—to Cash's great relief—on the incarcerated men.[30]

"Technical literature in most fields is written," Decca noted "so that the average reader, won't understand."[31] Undertakers had given Decca easy targets with their euphemisms. The corrections industry now did the same, calling solitary confinement "adjustment," prisons "correctional facilities," wardens "institutional superintendents," convicts "clients," and confinement "therapy."

"To identify those reforms worth supporting one must listen to the voice of the prisoner," Decca asserted.[32] Accordingly, she established close friendships with more than one hundred prisoners, all male, with whom she kept up an extensive and intense correspondence.[33] "These letters sustained me through the often nightmarish task of preparing this book," she said.[34] She read her new correspondents' articles, poetry, legal documents, books, and essays. She sent them her article drafts asking for their feedback as well as her draft manuscript of *Kind and Usual Punishment*.[35] They opened her eyes to the psychological grind of imprisonment's arbitrary rules. Prisoners and ex-prisoners, Decca later said, were "practically my only social circle for a long long time" in the 1970s.[36] These new friendships broadened Decca's perspective, but they took a toll on her spirits. She never left a prisoner's letter unanswered. Virtually every prison letter occasioned follow-ups: sending books or materials; mailing manuscripts to editors or agents; filing petitions, briefs, or lawsuits; writing letters to parole boards or organizations that might help; arranging free legal counsel. Sometimes, after release, she helped get former prisoners jobs. "I seem to have got involved with so much correspondence, lawsuits, and campaigns that it has become like a full time job," she lamented.[37] Sometimes she felt like a balloon with no air.

Decca was profoundly disturbed by the then widespread practice of coercing incarcerated people into participating in abusive medical experiments. She learned of inmates who developed severe scurvy from inadequate prison food and then were studied, but not treated, when they inevitably suffered "joint pains, swelling of the legs, dental cavities, recurrent loss of new dental fillings, excessive loss of hair, hemorrhages in the skin and whites of the eyes, excess fluid in the joint spaces, shortness of breath, scaly skin, mental depression, and abnormalities in emotional responses."[38] She traced the enormous profits pharmaceutical companies gleaned from such studies and the prestige that academic researchers received at the expense of prisoners' health. She published her findings and traveled to D.C. to testify to Congress and explain how meaningless so-called voluntary consent was when the incarcerated lacked both relevant information and also any other means to make money. "Decca doesn't futz around," her editor remembered of her address to the legislators.[39]

Decca wasn't interested in the usual "hard luck stories" other prison critics told. She, instead, wanted readers to see incarceration itself as "essentially a reflection of the values, and a codification of the self-interest, and a method of control, of the dominant class in any society."[40] Corporate crime, federal crime, white-collar crime were ubiquitous, but almost never punished. Why was Russell G. Oswald, the official who ordered troops into Attica prison resulting in forty-three deaths, not charged with murder? Why were the incarcerated demonized, and wasn't it a crime, she asked, to keep separating "us" and "them"?[41]

The core of Decca's exposé was a little-known feature of American prisons, standard in all California prisons, called the indeterminate sentence. It allowed judges to sentence those found guilty for a vaguely defined "term prescribed by the law," which prison administrators could shorten or lengthen at will.[42] Decca objected that it kept the "prisoner in perpetual suspense" and constantly subject to an exercise of authority that could never be called to account since it existed without limits. Moreover, authorities used it, virtually without exception, to lengthen sentences, never to shorten them. Indeterminate sentencing was total social control and guaranteed that "the whole criminal justice system . . . [operated] as an instrument of class and race oppression."[43] For *Kind and Usual Punishment*, Decca prepared her own index. The first entry read "abolition of prisons."[44] She wanted her readers to see American prisons as "a form of legal concentration camp to isolate and contain the rebellious and the political militant."[45]

Decca was amazed that Knopf had scheduled a first U.S. printing of twenty-five thousand. Optimistic, she thought. Two years prior, the Attica uprising had shone a harsh lens on U.S. prison conditions and generated enormous attention. Now, Decca feared that national interest had "died down" and perhaps she'd "sort of missed the boat."[46] She knew that she was asking more of her readers than she'd done before. A book on prisons could never be as funny as a book on funerals. Most of her readers probably felt, as she put it, "a frisson of self-congratulation that all these violent wretches" were behind bars and they were not.[47]

372

As *The New York Times* remarked: "Everyone was against death, and wholeheartedly so; but by no means is everyone opposed to prisons."[48]

In fact, her book was widely reviewed.[49] For the most part, it was warmly received, described as "wonderfully readable," "tough-minded," and "trenchant."[50] To her surprise, she was sometimes faulted for not taking a strong *enough* position on abolition.[51] She "hides behind quotations from others and never tackles the issue frontally . . . In the end . . . Mitford steps back from the abolition position," *The New York Times* wrote.[52] Those who did not find the book particularly compelling compared it unfavorably to *The American Way of Death*.[53] Not as funny, they complained. Harder to get through. Demonstrating their lack of understanding of how muckraking works, a few reviewers faulted the book for describing a problem but not solving it.[54]

Neither *The Trial of Dr. Spock* nor *Kind and Usual Punishment* sold as well as either her memoir or *The American Way of Death*. She was making so much money now from essays and lecturing, however, that she could afford to write what she wanted, and *Kind and Usual Punishment* had been supported by a Guggenheim Fellowship of $12,000, almost half of her advance.[55] She was increasingly busy as a reviewer, and she was in constant demand as a speaker, garnering speaker's fees that ranged from a few hundred to a few thousand dollars. She was fielding requests for movie rights, including a negotiation for movie rights to *Boadilla*, Esmond's book about the Spanish Civil War, a deal that seemed poised to bring in as much as £10,000 (the equivalent of £110,000 today).[56] She found that she was now famous enough to sell six dozen boxes of her papers, "the junk heap of research material" she kept in her attic. The University of Texas paid her $10,000.[57]

As she was putting final touches on *Kind and Usual Punishment*, Decca received a surprise invitation to be a visiting Distinguished Professor at San Jose State University. The offer came in the "boring lingo" of what she called "Sociologese," but was a thrill nevertheless, especially given the large sum—$10,000—that San Jose offered her for a large lecture course on *The American Way of Death* and a small honors seminar on muckraking.[58] San Jose quickly raised the offer to $11,000, considerably more than she had received as an advance for *The Trial of Dr. Spock*, and a third of her advance for *Kind and Usual Punishment*. "Was somebody pulling my leg," Decca asked Bob. "Which of my fun-loving friends would have access to San Jose State University writing paper?" Since Decca had "never attended a university, a high school, or even an elementary school," she found it all "a trifle terrifying," as she told Bob Gottlieb. "I've never actually even taken a course, except in typewriting when I was 23 and did v. badly in, let alone given one."[59] But for someone who dearly loved an audience and a microphone, it was a "wild, improbable, yet wonderful fantasy," she admitted.[60] "You'd better go for it," Bob said.[61] She hired a young assistant ("a reformed airline stewardess from South Carolina") to help her plan her classes and gather materials.[62] She spent the latter half of the summer planning, then went on an extensive book tour for *Kind and Usual Punishment*, and arrived in San Jose in late September 1975, absolutely exhausted.

She had designed her lecture class, "The American Way," as "something resembling a variety show," with many guest speakers and students doing final projects in whatever ways they thought would showcase their talents. The seminar, "Techniques of Muckraking," would be a workshop, she decided, with students encouraged to investigate local institutions. The first red flag was raised before her classes started. The university president, who objected to the word "muckraking," changed her seminar title to "Sociology 169H." "Boring as hell," Decca said, and promptly changed it back.[63] Her classes proved wildly popular, with standing room only in her lecture course. She taught "caskets, courts, convicts, con men." She invited her students to translate paragraphs of Sociology "into English." In place of examinations, she urged students to produce whatever "artifact" they liked—"Poem, song, one-act play, a cartoon strip." One made a miniature velvet-lined coffin, complete with tiny brass handles and hardware. Decca was a gifted lecturer. She made every person in the audience feel as if she were talking just to them. Her enthusiasm was unchecked. Her manner was dramatic and comedic. "At last I've found my true vocation!" she exclaimed, after her first lecture at San Jose.[64]

The university didn't see it that way. It was hardly prepared for someone who scrutinized its procedures and disrespected its policies, and who did so in such rolling, patrician tones. Soon after arriving, Decca was asked both to sign a loyalty oath and to produce fingerprints for the university. "There's not a word about either in my contract," she pointed out, and refused. When the dean insisted she comply, Decca dug in her heels. The wrangling became increasingly intense, with university lawyers appearing at her lunch table, in her classrooms, at the door of her faculty apartment. On the advice of her lawyer, Decca eventually signed the loyalty oath. She steadfastly declined the fingerprint requirement, a refusal that so enraged the university administration that they pronounced her "de-hired." That's not a thing, Decca said, and insisted on teaching regardless. The administration then told her students that they would not receive any credit for her courses. Then it refused to pay Decca any money.

"We Want Jessica!" Students demonstrated by the hundreds with toeprint stickers proclaiming "Mitford Thumbs Her Toes at the Trustees." The "Finger Flap," Decca believed, had tapped into "long-smoldering, deeply felt resentments" over "petty, arbitrary, bureaucratic treatment they received in daily doses from those in authority." Administrators were unyielding. Decca finished out the semester in a state of high dudgeon and also great fun. She was only able to squeeze her salary out of the university by taking the administrators to court. An angry judge asked them: "Has she performed the duties for which she was hired?" "Yes," they glumly replied. Then "pay the Lady her money!" the judge yelled.[65]

Coverage of Decca's "Finger Flap" was so extensive that she shortly received an honorary doctorate (Litt.D., which sounded a lot like her nickname, "Little D," to her) from Smith College and a teaching offer from Yale. Yale's offer of $2,000 paled in comparison to San Jose's, but Yale proved to be much more flexible, allowing Decca to put off the appointment until the spring of 1976. By pressing hard for expenses, she successfully negotiated a free, spacious furnished apartment in Yale's Calhoun College, library privileges, round-trip airfare to and from California, and most of her meals. She calculated that by taking a "doggie bag" from lunch every day she could eat practically free all semester. The extra time, she figured, would also let her round up lecture opportunities at East Coast colleges, revisiting invitations she'd previously turned down as too far to travel from California.[66]

She and Bob had already put off a long-planned sabbatical year for Bob. Now, however, with Yale safely pocketed for later, they went ahead with their plans for a year in England. Early in 1974 they moved into a London house rented from their friend Sally Toynbee, and Decca intended to settle down, at last, to finishing the second memoir she'd been promising her editor for years.

Throughout the year, they visited with friends and family, providing just the distractions Decca needed to avoid her writing. Pressed by Debo, Decca declined to see Diana again. "It's not exactly politics now," she explained. "It's more that having really adored her all through childhood, it makes it 10 times more difficult to have just casual meetings . . . rather agony," Decca added.[67] They obsessed about Watergate—watching the House impeachment hearings live whenever they could find them on British television. Bob gardened, planting a "child's garden . . . all planted higgledy-piggledy," with a riot of brightly colored blooms. Decca worked on an article for *The*

Atlantic on the "Finger Flap" at San Jose.[68] By August she had finally run out of distractions and switched back to her memoir again. She told Marge Frantz that "somehow that wretched book, which I note from my notes has started/stopped many a time beginning literally in 1960, is starting to work."[69] She felt that the memoir was taking an increasingly gloomy turn, however. She simply couldn't bear to write about Nicholas's death, she confessed, not even mentioning the earlier deaths of her daughter Julia or Esmond, and she did not want to dwell on death or loss.

Then, in the fall of 1974, James Forman suffered some form of a psychotic break. Dinky took him to New York, hoping that his friends there would help him accept treatment. When he remained adamantly opposed, Dinky felt forced to leave him. Decca was in a "fog of the most awful despair . . . a mood of gloom the likes of which I can hardly remember," until she could convince Dinky to bring her sons and seek refuge with her and Bob in England.[70] Decca tried to joke—she could "hardly hear myself drink" with her grandsons about, she said.[71] But tending to her daughter and grandsons meant not doing "a stroke of work" on her book. Nevertheless, it "was worth <u>everything</u>," she said.[72]

Clifford Durr died in the spring of 1975, and Decca, who'd only been back in Oakland a few months, traveled to Washington, D.C., to offer a eulogy at his June memorial, attended by over seven hundred people. Only two weeks after Durr's memorial, Aranka passed away, quite suddenly. Bob rushed to New York, while Decca struggled with the sudden loss of another family member. She and Aranka had had a rocky start in the early years of Decca's marriage but had come to be very good friends later on. Decca had grown to admire Aranka's tenacity and her loyalty. Decca's world seemed to be contracting. "Do admit," she wrote to Debo, it leaves "one with a blank & drab feeling."[73]

In October, Decca was surprised to receive a two-month residency fellowship from the Rockefeller Foundation at its renowned Bellagio

Study and Conference Center in northern Italy. She reveled in "the total comfort" of gorgeous scenery, lush accommodations, fabulous meals, plentiful alcohol, a "cocoon of luxury," she told Marge Frantz.[74] Most of the other scholars had puffed up their résumés and project proposals to snag the fellowship: "a pretty fraudulent lot," she pronounced. Among the group was Gerda Lerner, whom Decca dismissed as a "grim feminist who talks sociologese." "Boring," like Susan Brownmiller, Decca pronounced.[75] Maya Angelou managed to get a Bellagio fellowship at the same time as Decca, so for the most part, they formed a society of two (four with their husbands).[76]

Within a few days of arriving at Bellagio, however, "a row of huge proportions" erupted between Maya's husband Paul du Feu—"a bit of a barroom brawler," as Decca described him—and a member of the British Parliament, whom du Feu claimed had made a racist remark. "I didn't realize Paul was married to that black girl," the MP said in his own spectacularly failed self-defense. Angelou and du Feu demanded that their meals be served to them in their rooms for the duration of their stay and that the MP be shown the door. The MP—"easily the Most Important Person in the Room," Decca said—tried to apologize. According to Angelou, he also tried to slap her behind. Angelou punched him full in the face. Within a day, to Decca's surprise, the Bellagio directors had asked the MP to leave. "I did rather adore the whole drama," Decca admitted. "It livened things up no end."[77] Once again, though, Decca got very little done on her memoir. She was tired, she said, of being "browbeaten into deadlines." For the first time in her professional life, she began needing regular extensions.[78]

There was no time for the book when she got home from Bellagio. Within a day, Decca was packing for her trip to New Haven. Yale was just then mired in controversy over Decca's old friend, Communist historian Herbert Aptheker. Yale had asked him to teach a college seminar on W. E. B. Du Bois, then disinvited him when the Trustees balked. Decca sent a furious statement to the *Yale Daily News* and considered canceling her course. She decided, instead, to make a scene about Aptheker as soon as she arrived, something like the "Finger Flap," she figured.

At Yale, Decca created her usual "non-stop social life," with dinner invitations most nights and busy lunches on campus with students and colleagues.[79] Oblivious to Yale's rigid social hierarchies, she befriended whoever amused her. Students often filled her apartment, chatting away comfortably on the heavy oak sitting-room chairs, cocktails in hand.

For her course, Decca was asked to accept eighteen students from over two hundred who applied. "Pure torture," she said. The mix she finally settled on included some who planned to become journalists (including William Buckley's son, an applicant she came to regret admitting because they fell out instantly), to those whose applications most amused her. Her favorite was from a student who said he wanted to be a journalist because he was "tall enough to look over walls & thin enough to hide behind trees." From day one, she said she was "loving the students."[80] But "some of my students were much too nice . . . to be muckrakers. They hadn't the instincts of gutter fighters. They didn't want to go for the jugular. They wanted to write in a peaceable way."[81] Some showed muckraking instincts, including one who worked on the Aptheker scandal. Decca shared his material with Bob, hoping he'd take a legal interest in Aptheker's case. "I can hardly imagine anything more pleasurable than having my husband suing Yale while I'm still here," she said.[82]

Decca was fifty-nine, approaching sixty. She made no effort to hide her age, leaning into the image of a middle-aged matron "having tea in a village," as one student put it. She wore double-knit suits, no hair dye or jewelry (except her simple gold wedding band and an occasional piece of Mexican silver), and she carried a large handbag and wore enormous dark-rimmed glasses. Her wavy brown-gray hair was slightly layered, curling naturally just below her ears. The less hip she fashioned herself, however, the more her students adored her. She seemed "more radical and genuinely young" than anyone else on campus, one former student remembered.[83] She was also more up on current affairs than anyone at Yale, they said, and she gave her students credit for radical thoughts. She also expected them to be as amusing and entertaining as any of the well-known wits, artists, and subversives in her circle. "You just died to make her laugh," one of her favorite students remembered. "We all died to make her laugh." Her message to her students was to "be amused" by life and at the same time to "assume everyone is lying." You must "see through humbug," she told them.[84] A few of her students, who were particularly sensitive, thought that Decca seemed lonely. They noticed that she drank excessively throughout the day. One student wondered if she might have been drinking before leading class.[85] "I can see I shan't be doing too much on my book," Decca said, soon after getting to Yale.[86]

On an unseasonably springlike day, February 25, she received the manuscript of a new biography of Unity and began reading it immediately. The book "stirred up a family row of huge proportions," ushering in a gloom that settled over Decca for years and from which she never completely recovered.[87] It created a "bit of a black cloud" that Decca could not budge.[88] Decca's trips to see Nancy, followed by subsequent friendly visits during her recent year in England, had led her to think that she was now on better footing with her sisters Pamela and Deborah. The manuscript in her hands was destined to dash any recent goodwill and to reveal, unfortunately, that her sisters did not trust her and probably never would accept her as one of their own.

The book Decca had received was written by a British author named David Pryce-Jones, whose father, Alan, Decca had known for decades. The younger Pryce-Jones had been in their Oakland home, seen various Mitford family artifacts, and became fascinated by Unity. Decca had warned him that no one in the family, except her, would cooperate with him. But he persisted and Decca thought he'd "do really well" and avoid "the sort of sensational horror-tale that others might" go after, she told Debo.[89] He seemed "to have a strange sort of sympathy, or affinity, with the actual Boud [Unity]."[90] Pryce-Jones proved himself an exceptional investigator. He completed what Decca called "a tour de force of research," tracking Unity in various languages and countries, interviewing hundreds of people, even gaining access to the German doctors who treated Unity immediately after her suicide attempt.

Aside from Decca, none of the immediate family would speak to him. Decca's sisters worked assiduously to suppress the book, and they discouraged anyone they could from speaking to Pryce-Jones. Andrew Cavendish used his vast connections to get an advance copy of the book and pressured its publisher to remove the passages he found most offensive. Debo, Andrew, Diana, Pamela, and Mosley fought the book so hard that they drew more attention to it than it might otherwise have received.[91]

Nevertheless, Pryce-Jones published *Unity Mitford: A Quest*, in 1976, shortly after Decca's time at Yale.[92] He was not a particularly compelling writer, and the book was difficult to read. But it created a stir. Diana, Pamela, and Debo called it "very nasty," referred to Pryce-Jones as "the worm," and made it known that the biography was, in their view, a "pornographic" account that got almost everything about Unity wrong.[93] They blamed Decca for its existence, insisting that her encouragement had been instrumental.

Immediately after the book appeared, Debo, Pamela, and Diana sent a joint letter to *The Times*, laying out their objections to Pryce-Jones's slant. Their upset over the book—"Nazis all the way," Debo complained—seemed to grow rather than dissipate with every passing day.

A few weeks later, Pamela accused Decca of having stolen a massive family scrapbook—"the size of a table"—to provide Pryce-Jones with precious photographs and news clippings.[94] "I suppose you gave it to him," Pamela wrote Decca. "Did you borrow it, perhaps, as I believe you are writing your own life? . . . We would all like to have it back."[95] Decca was furious over being accused of stealing from her sisters. She was deeply hurt to see how little they thought of her integrity. "I was absolutely enraged," she wrote back in early October, "by your foul letter, implying that I've stolen one of Debo's scrapbooks."[96] Decca then sent a carbon of this letter to Debo but received no reply. She followed with another letter to Debo, later that month, asking if "perhaps this all means it's curtains for us." She was *terrifically sad*," she told Debo, "in floods of tears." She closed her letter, sadly, "with love."[97] To a family friend, Decca wrote that she was "v. much laid low, in a decline, over the sisterly row." "The depression over all this has been intense."[98]

Debo did not respond immediately to this second letter either. Instead, she wrote to Diana, enclosing a copy of Decca's letter and saying that the idea of breaking with Decca made her very "SAD." She would nevertheless need to "think v. carefully before answering," she confided. Diana wrote back with complaints about Decca's "horrid little husband," her "ghastly" views, and *Hons and Rebels*: "ninety per cent lies & rubbish," Diana grumbled. Finally, in November, Debo responded to Decca. "For goodness sake don't let's quarrel. It would be *too sad*," she wrote, suggesting that they "face the fact that we are deeply divided" about many things, but that "underneath the ties are v. strong."[99]

By December, Decca was back in England, this time to film a BBC documentary about her life, produced by her friends Michael Barnes and Clare Douglas. She had dinner with Pamela and then with Debo and was glad, and relieved, to have seen them both. In May, she went back to England briefly. She was invited to Chatsworth for what she assumed would be another reconciliation dinner. Instead, Decca felt grilled about the scrapbook again, accused still of stealing it, and treated like a criminal. She ran from the dinner in tears. In 1974, Decca had described her reaction to Forman's breakdown as "a mood of gloom the likes of which I can hardly remember." This was far worse.[100] For months she was in a sad haze, feeling as if she had "an interminable & incurable illness, or a sort of non-stop condition of mourning."[101] She was so "fully, chronically sad," in fact, that she wrote a multipage single-spaced typed letter to her niece Emma Tennant, Debo's daughter, laying out her side of the story.[102] Decca wrote at least four drafts of this letter, all of which Bob advised her not to send. She sent it anyway. Normally, Decca avoided talking about her feelings. Now she could not stop. The hurt, she told her niece, was "debilitating . . . a sort of physical feeling when you wake up each morning of actual pain."[103] Decca told all her friends about the row, as well as her cousin Clementine. "As I'm sure you'll have gathered from the family grapevine, a terribly deep & I fear perhaps irremediable quarrel has developed between me & the sisters." "I'm fearfully sad," she added, "it's sort of an ongoing nightmare."[104] Then, a few days after Thanksgiving, she received a telegram from Debo that read, "EUREKA PHOTOGRAPH BOOKS HAS TURNED UP. HENDERSON." Inexplicably, in November 1977, the contested scrapbook reappeared, exactly where it had always been sitting, on a large table in Debo's private drawing room at Chatsworth. "There it was, just as if it had never been away, the most extraorder thing, complete, and its old self," Debo wrote happily. "It is a GREAT LIFTING OF WEIGHT I promise you," Debo wrote. "All's well that starts Peace Talks," she added gaily.[105]

Decca had now spent nearly a year grieving the loss of her sisters.

383

"I was deeply miserable and v. shaken," she wrote Debo.[106] It had been "one of the worst things that's happened . . . (in a long life of awful things)." Yet she now responded to her sister warmly, asked for "details of the Find" and told Debo that she was still hoping for "Peace Talks." She was "amazed" and "*incredibly pleased*," she said. Instead of pressing for the apology she was clearly owed, she humbly asked if "true friendship is still possible" or if the scrapbook turning up didn't change the fact that, as far as Decca could tell, Debo "loathed my book & the BBC film" both? While expressing her disinclination for "a row of any sort," Debo did not take responsibility for what had happened, nor did she apologize for the dreadful spring dinner, which she said left her shaken and sleepless as well. About the scrapbook having been there all along, she would only say that things had a way of appearing and disappearing at Chatsworth and that it "was very odd indeed" and that "I am very sorry indeed if you still think I wrongfully accused you."[107]

The book that Decca thought Debo might have loathed was her second memoir, *A Fine Old Conflict*, which Decca had finally been able to finish and publish. The title derived from the way Decca initially misheard the famous lines of the Communist "Internationale," mistaking "'Tis the final conflict" for "'Tis a Fine Old Conflict." She told Kay Graham that the book had taken her seventeen years of thinking and three years to write and that it left her "drained" and disappointed. "It's not nearly as good as I hoped it would be."[108] It rehashed some of the family stories, but her family was not its intended audience. The book was written for other radicals, part of Decca's long dialogue with American activists about how best to be good allies in the struggle to change the world.

Where *Hons and Rebels* began with Decca's childhood and ended as Esmond departed Washington, D.C., *A Fine Old Conflict* covered considerably more ground, beginning with Decca's family in "the

Swinbrook fortress," running away, and the "rather uphill work" of "escaping from the private Mitford cosmic joke . . . into the real world of activism, family, and writing." It covered Decca's life up to the phenomenal success of *The American Way of Death* in 1963 and reprinted her 1956 booklet *Lifeitselfmanship: Or How to Become a Precisely-Because Man* as an appendix. Part of Decca's motivation for writing the book, she explained in its introduction, was to defend activism and advocacy. She wanted to convey the "fascination, difficulties, and frequent joys" of being an activist. She especially wanted "to lay to rest some of the myths created by the 'I-Was-Duped' school of American ex-Party members." While the American Communist Party "made some abysmal mistakes," she wrote, it left a "heritage" of struggle for all "future radical movements." Without it their calls for revolutionary change could never have occurred.[109] She wished that readers would see the joy in a life dedicated to anti-authoritarian political struggle.

A Fine Old Conflict was expansive and thoughtful and funny in parts, heartfelt in others. Several reviewers pronounced it a "marvelously high-spirited account" that "jollifies expertly" and from which "one gets the impression that life in the party was a lark." Mitford, *The Washington Post* reviewer wrote, makes "a convincing case that for her at least life in the party was chockfull of joy."[110]

A few reviewers thought the book was *too* upbeat. "Perhaps a shade too delightful," John Leonard noted.[111] This was certainly the view of old Party comrades such as William and Louise Patterson, to whom Decca had sent a draft of the book. "I don't think *A Fine Old Conflict* a positive contribution to the struggle to which I believe we are both dedicated," Patterson wrote. "I am not happy with it."[112] Decca could only tell Patterson how "saddened" she was by his letter," since she'd written the book, she said, for her radical friends.[113]

Decca's sisters hated the book. They wondered why she still published under "the name of Mitford" since she seemed so critical of the family. Debo noted that Decca left out any mention of the "most *searing* things in her life"—the death of her daughter Julia, and the death of her son Nicky, a charge that others had made about her handling of Esmond's death in her first memoir but that Debo, of all people, should have well understood.[114]

A Fine Old Conflict came out first in England in the spring and then in the United States in September. Four days after her sixtieth birthday, Decca went on an "incredibly grueling" monthlong book tour that included television appearances on the *Today* show and *Dick Cavett*. She found that she had less energy and enthusiasm for such touring than she'd had in the past.[115] But the book did well, selling a very respectable twenty-two thousand copies in the U.S. and another six to eight thousand in England in its first month on the market. The memoir reignited the sisters' feud. Decca hungered to get along with her sisters but didn't want to be bullied by them. She felt she had a right to tell her own story as she saw fit. Amused by the now thriving Mitford Industry, Decca saw no reason she could not play a part in it. "Why should you be the final arbiter of everything about the family," she asked Debo.[116]

When Decca published her memoir, Diana also published her autobiography, called *A Life of Contrasts*. It is a peculiar book, well written but maddeningly smug, its most recurrent trope a series of "I told you so" statements about Oswald Mosley being "very wise" and everyone else being stupid.[117] Diana's voice comes through clearly— she shared Decca's ability to strike a conversational tone—making the reading experience especially chilling. Diana insisted that Hitler was a charming man and that what the Nazis did was no different from what many others had done. "Hitler was not unique." The violence "of the thirties," she claimed, was not directed at the Jews. It "was Jews attacking Kit's [Oswald Mosley's] people in dark lanes etc.," Diana declared.[118] She was unrepentant about the role she and

Mosley played in supporting fascism. The Jews, Diana wrote, were to blame for their misfortunes: "It was a tragedy that world Jewry did not make a great effort in the thirties to accommodate its co-racialists from center Europe elsewhere in the world."[119] Unity was a "a heroine . . . a tragic heroine" whose choices showed "extraordinary courage."[120] And yet, Debo and Pam concurred with Diana that it was Decca, not Diana, who had a "strange view of the past" and whose version of history could not be trusted.[121]

Decca's "love of conflict" and her "appetite for tracking and destroying the enemy" was the heart of her muckraking.[122] "Gottlieb claims I see all life as a conflict," she noted rather proudly, "with me in adversary position against all comers."[123] But that love of conflict did not apply to Decca's relations with her loved ones. With those, while she would not back down if she felt she was right, she would also do almost anything to avoid a row. When asked by Debo to do so, she gave many of her materials to Debo's archive, even knowing that Debo would restrict others' access. Evidently, she was determined not to rock the boat. "I know you think I thrive on rows, but I don't. I long to be friends."[124] As she was approaching her sixty-third year, chasing the enemy, let alone her family and friends, seemed to be losing its luster. Her attitude about England changed now. She began to describe it as cheap and uncivil. "English inefficiency" rankled her. She detected a persistent "dank smell of poverty in the air." She told her friend Sally Belfrage that "I would never want to live in England again."[125]

Decca was diagnosed with phlebitis, a potentially dangerous and painful blood clot in her leg. She and Bob were visiting friends in the Hamptons when it happened, and Decca went to see the doctor there. "In the course of examination," she told Philip Toynbee, "the Dr. said in a tentative sort of way, 'Do you like an occasional glass of wine?' 'Do I!' said I, 'absolutely, whenever available'—thinking he was going to say well you'll have to cut that out. Instead, he said that's v. good as alcohol acts as a blood-thinner, so the more the better."[126] Decca wanted all the "Thinner," as she now called it, she could get. By the spring of 1979, as she told Maya Angelou, "gloom has set in" again and would not lift. "Too many really vile things have happened lately for my liking."[127] The vile list included not only her sisters' behavior, but also the murders of San Francisco Mayor George Moscone and Supervisor Harvey Milk, followed by a very light sentence for their killer, Dan White. A few days later, Decca's "Frenemy" Fay Stender was shot six times in her home by an assailant who claimed she'd betrayed George Jackson. And after years of erratic behavior, which Decca had long called Benjy's "Troubles," she had to face that something serious was wrong with him. His symptoms came and went, and he was sometimes very much himself and other times "antagonistic to everyone." One of the difficulties, Decca noted affectionately, was that he had always had "a screw loose," which made it "difficult to distinguish between his built-in eccentricity & this new development."[128] She had long thought of his condition as "the strangeness," a kind of mystery.[129] Worry about him, she confided in Dinky, now "has occupied my waking thoughts & stopped me from sleeping much."[130] Benjy was now diagnosed as manic-depressive and prescribed Lithium, which he refused to take.[131] He left his wife, stopped playing or tuning pianos, and disappeared somewhere in the Midwest, leaving Decca in despair.

She kept working. She cranked out a series of articles, including two on an overpriced New York restaurant, which did give her a "joy of the chase" lift, as well as more money than she'd ever been paid, and the satisfaction of closing the restaurant. Small beans, but fun for her at the time. She also wrote a most unlikely piece on an archaeological dig in Egypt.[132] She had been approached by GEO magazine, which told her they'd send her anywhere if she'd write a piece for them about it. Having recently met an archaeologist who'd invited her to come see his dig, she responded, only half seriously, "How about Egypt"? "Done," the GEO editor replied. Egypt was both an adventure and a departure from her muckraking work, and Decca looked forward to a relaxing trip and writing experience. Instead, she found herself immersed in the chaos of a badly organized expedition run by individuals she compared to "the inmates of a lunatic asylum." She did her best to produce a piece on the "mounds of ancient rubble" that might interest GEO's readers, without exposing her to libel about the archaeologists.

While neither essay churned up any social change of significance, Decca included both pieces in a book of essays she published in 1979, *Poison Penmanship: The Gentle Art of Muckraking*, a collection of her essays, with commentary, intended to be used as a textbook on investigative reporting (and published in England as *The Making of a Muckraker*). The idea had come to her early in her time at Yale, when she was making notes on the stories behind her essays and thinking about "how one chooses a subject, all the technique bit from interviewing to picking other people's brains."[133] She derided the project occasionally as "mammon, mammon all the way" but in fact she greatly enjoyed writing it and was proud to reflect on the work she had done.[134] With the publication of *Poison Penmanship*, alongside the wild success of *The American Way of Death*, as well as her subsequent books and teaching credentials, she was the reigning queen of American muckraking. Because she designed it as a textbook, *Poison Penmanship* cemented her standing both in universities and with the general public as the authority on the genre for many years to come.

Poison Penmanship, published in 1979, however, was the last time Decca was able to publish a successful, truly influential work of muckraking.

18

"Writing About the Dead" [1]

One lives on and plunges into causes & other interesting things. [2]
—JESSICA MITFORD TO VIRGINIA DURR, 1983

Being in the classroom was blissful for Decca. She was too new to teaching for course preparation to be the tedium it is to most seasoned professors. A great performer, Decca was always willing to clown to get her point across. She was informal and passionate. Students were wild for her. She loved how they doubled over laughing at stories that her friends, who'd heard them many times, now only smiled at. The students were marvelous, she felt, "exceptionally bright and inventive." [3]

That no further long-term teaching offers materialized after Yale, even with an article in *The Atlantic*, "My Short and Happy Life as a Distinguished Professor," operating almost as an advertisement for her

Jessica with a muckrake.
Photograph by Jock McDonald.

Jessica, Constancia, and Robert in 1944.
Unknown photographer, photo courtesy of Constancia Romilly, Benjamin Treuhaft, and Ben Weber.

Constancia, Robert, Nicholas, Benjamin, and Jessica, at a family Christmas.
Unknown photographer, photo courtesy of Constancia Romilly, Benjamin Treuhaft, and Ben Weber.

Jessica with Nicholas, Benjamin, and Constancia, October 1947.
Unknown photographer, photo courtesy of Constancia Romilly, Benjamin Treuhaft, and Ben Weber.

Jessica, Robert, and family dog at Christmas.
Unknown photographer, photo courtesy of Constancia Romilly, Benjamin Treuhaft, and Ben Weber.

White mob outside Gary house, Richmond, California.
Unknown photographer, photo courtesy Ohio State University Library and Mitford family.

Jessica and Realtor Neitha Williams with broken window at Williams's office.
Unknown photographer, photo courtesy Ohio State University Library and Mitford family.

essica with Buddy Green and an unidentified woman (possibly Green's wife), 1978.
Unknown photographer, photo courtesy of Constancia Romilly, Benjamin Treuhaft, and Ben Weber.

The Garys at home.
Unknown photographer, photo courtesy Ohio State University Library and Mitford family.

Jessica with Willie McGee
(poster by Pele de Lappe).
*Unknown photographer, photo
courtesy of Constancia
Romilly, Benjamin Treuhaft, and Ben Weber
and Ohio State University Library.*

Jessica (lower right) and the white
women's delegation to Mississippi to
fight for Willie McGee, 1951.
*Unknown photographer, photo courtesy of
Constancia Romilly, Benjamin Treuhaft,
and Ben Weber.*

Jessica with Jerry Newson defense committee.
Unknown photographer, photo courtesy of Constancia Romilly, Benjamin Treuhaft, and Ben Weber.

Jessica and her mother, Sydney,
on Inch Kenneth, 1959.
*Unknown photographer, photo courtesy of
Constancia Romilly, Benjamin Treuhaft,
and Ben Weber.*

Mitford family house on
Inch Kenneth.
Photo courtesy of the author.

Jessica on Inch Kenneth.
*Unknown photographer, photo courtesy of
Constancia Romilly, Benjamin Treuhaft,
and Ben Weber.*

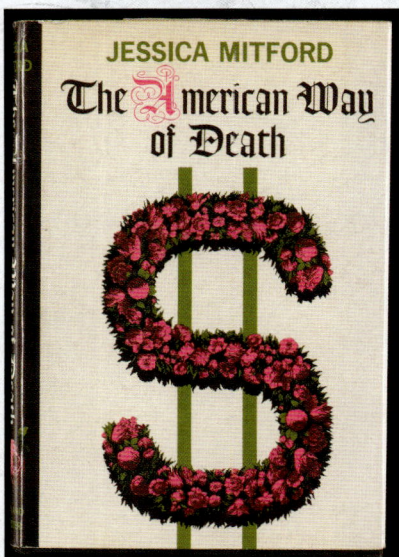

JESSICA MITFORD

The American Way of Death

Original cover for
The American Way of Death
(design by Janet Halverson).
Photo courtesy of Harry Ransom Research Center,
University of Texas, Austin.

Original cover for *A Fine Old Conflict* (painting by Edward Sorel).
Photo courtesy of Harry Ransom Research Center,
University of Texas, Austin.

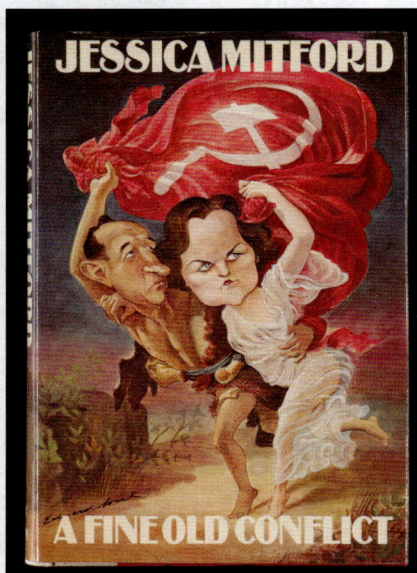

JESSICA MITFORD

A FINE OLD CONFLICT

Jessica signing copies of
A Fine Old Conflict.
Unknown photographer, photo courtesy of Mary
Evans Picture Library.

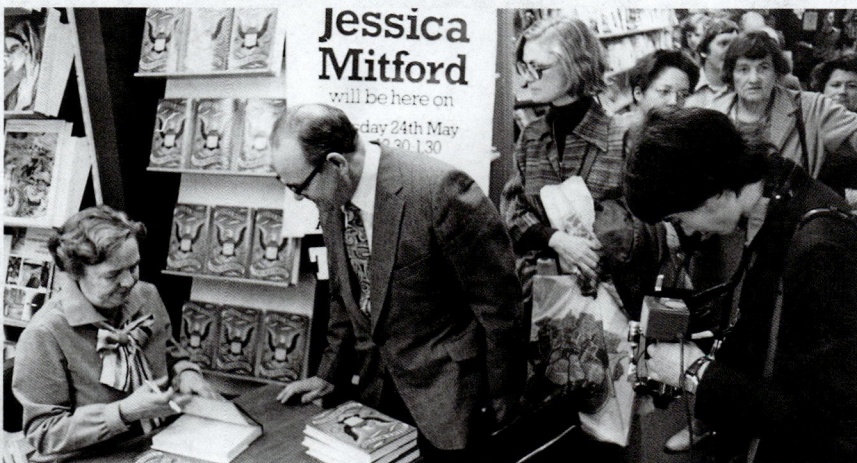

Jessica
Mitford
will be here on
day 24th May
2.30-1.30

Jessica at
Chatsworth, 1965.
*Unknown photographer,
photo courtesy of Constancia
Romilly, Benjamin Treuhaft,
and Ben Weber.*

David, Unity, and Sydney at
Old Mill Cottage during the
war, 1945.
*Unknown photographer, photo courtesy
of Constancia Romilly, Benjamin
Treuhaft, and Ben Weber.*

Jessica and Deborah
in 1955.
*Unknown photographer,
photo courtesy of Constancia Romilly,
Benjamin Treuhaft, and Ben Weber.*

Don Bachardy drawing of Jessica, 1964.
Courtesy of Don Bachardy.

Courtroom 3 Floor 12, McCormack Building.
Photograph by Carol M. Highsmith, photo courtesy of Library of Congress, Prints and Photographs Division.

Jane Spock, Michael Ferber, Benjamin Spock, Marcus Raskin, and William Sloane Coffin at a press conference at Arlington Street Church, January 29, 1968.
Unknown photographer, photo courtesy of Brearley Collection, Boston Public Library.

Dr. Benjamin Spock addressing an anti-draft rally in Boston Common, July 10, 1968.
Unknown photographer, photo courtesy of Brearley Collection, Boston Public Library.

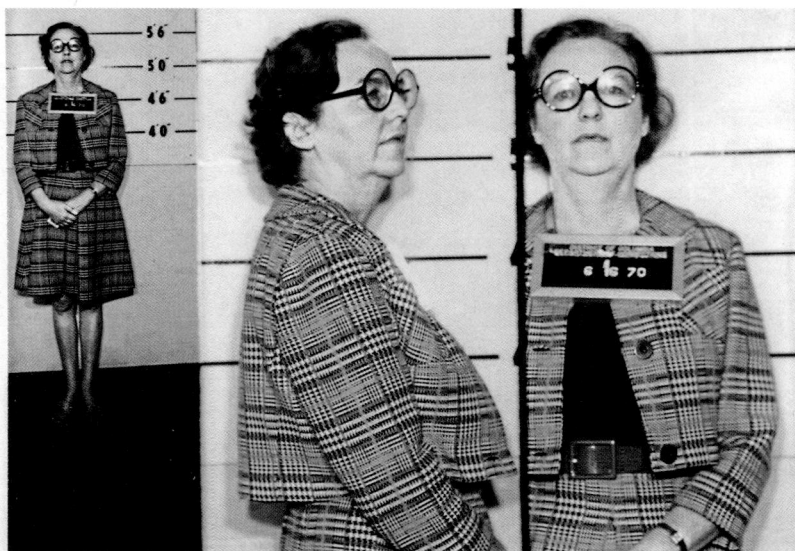

Jessica, prison mugshot, early 1970s, possibly taken during workshop on incarceration.
Unknown photographer, photo courtesy of Constancia Romilly, Benjamin Treuhaft, and Ben Weber.

Jessica with Woody Allen, filming a cameo as herself in *Play It Again, Sam.*
Unknown photographer, photo courtesy of Constancia Romilly, Benjamin Treuhaft, and Ben Weber.

Jessica at a microphone, one of her favorite places.
Unknown photographer, photo courtesy of Mary Evans Picture Library.

Maya Angelou and Jessica Mitford, North Carolina, 1986.
Photograph by Mary Ellen Mark.

Robert Treuhaft, Maya Angelou,
and Jessica playing Boggle.
*Unknown photographer, photo courtesy of
Constancia Romilly, Benjamin Treuhaft,
and Ben Weber.*

Marge Frantz, still frame from
video, Kelly Anderson videographer.
*Photo courtesy of Smith College Libraries, Special
Collections, Voices of Feminism Oral History Project,
Sophia Smith Collection.*

Jessica and Virginia Durr in
DC, 1991 or 1992.
*Unknown photographer, photo courtesy
of Constancia Romilly,
Benjamin Treuhaft, and Ben Weber.*

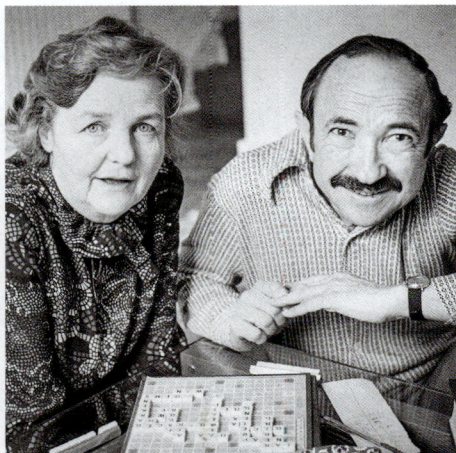

Jessica and Robert, playing Scrabble.
Photograph by Jane Bown,
photo courtesy Guardian *archive.*

Jessica playing Julia Child, 1982.
Unknown photographer, photo courtesy of Constancia Romilly,
Benjamin Treuhaft, and Ben Weber.

Jessica and Robert, 1993.
Photograph by Victoria Sheridan for the Oakland Tribune, *photo courtesy Oakland Museum of California.*

Constancia, Terry
Weber, Chaka, James,
and Ben Weber, 1980.
*Unknown photographer, photo
courtesy of Constancia Romilly,
Benjamin Treuhaft,
and Ben Weber.*

Benjamin Treuhaft.
*Unknown photographer, photo courtesy of
Constancia Romilly, Benjamin Treuhaft,
and Ben Weber.*

Jessica, Virginia Durr, and Constancia
at Constancia's wedding, June 1980.
*Unknown photographer, photo courtesy of Constancia
Romilly, Benjamin Treuhaft, and Ben Weber.*

James Forman with Chaka Forman
and James Forman Jr. at
James Forman Jr.'s Yale Law
School graduation, May 1992.
*Unknown photographer, photo courtesy of
Constancia Romilly, Benjamin Treuhaft,
and Ben Weber.*

Jessica, at a Decca and the Dectones performance, 1995.
Unknown photographer, photo courtesy of Constancia Romilly, Benjamin Treuhaft, and Ben Weber.

Jessica with a feather mask and fancy glasses.
Photograph by Janet Fries/Getty Images.

Jessica winking.
Photograph by Neil Hanshaw.

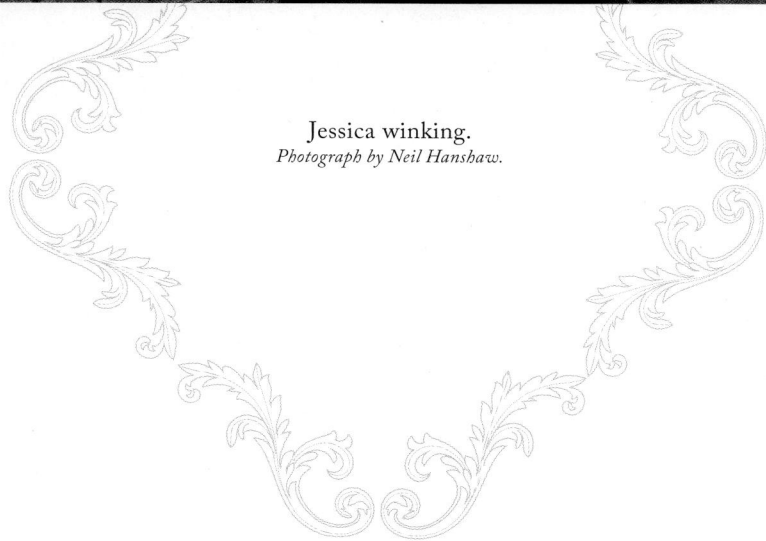

services, was terribly disappointing.[4] But Decca did not complain. As much fun as San Jose and Yale had been, she "maintained her political fervor," as Peter Sussman puts it, and moved on to new projects and political work.[5] Various possibilities presented themselves, from a book about writers and their experiences with editors (her editor Bob Gottlieb thought it sounded dull), to a book on evangelists (about whom Decca knew next to nothing), to a book on the Brixton race riots, which happened during one of her increasingly frequent visits to London. She also considered other subjects connected to her work on prisons or the law.[6] Still very much absorbed by the legal cases she'd been involved in, from HUAC to Spock to George Jackson and Angela Davis, she floated the idea of a book on lawyers and their clients, even writing up a proposal for *Their Day in Court*, although she ultimately decided not to pursue it.

Meanwhile, she continued writing frequent book reviews and commissioned short pieces, responding to the ever-expanding Mitford Industry and, although she hated flying, taking airplane trips almost monthly, often for the lectures she now considered the mainstay of "how I make my drab living." She turned sixty-four at the end of 1981, and claimed to be "getting TOO OLD to travel & adore getting home," yet at least twice a year she traveled to England, which entailed an eleven-to-twelve-hour flight from San Francisco, if a nonstop could be found.[7] In addition, she took yearly family trips to Mexico, visited Maya Angelou, who had accepted a professorship in North Carolina, and took as many trips to see Dinky and family in Atlanta as she could arrange.[8] Benjy remained unpredictable and worrisome, sometimes appearing in Oakland and sometimes showing up where Decca and Bob were traveling. One never knew with him.

Early in 1981, Decca was asked by the Cobden House Trust to be its distinguished Human Rights Day lecturer. Her talk, a major fundraiser for the National Council for Civil Liberties (the British equivalent to the ACLU), was scheduled to take place on December

10. It was an enormous honor, typically offered to heads of state, and Decca agonized over it for months. Poring over previous Cobden House lectures, which she found exceedingly boring, she decided to eschew the usual platitudes. Her talk, "Law & Disorder: A Transatlantic View," was intended to expose British racism. She particularly hoped to illuminate so-called race blindness as a smug form of wishful thinking, unresponsive to realities on the ground. She was still struggling with the talk when she arrived in England on Wednesday, December 2, at the start of the coldest English December on record. Deborah Rogers, her British agent, loaned Decca an office conveniently located a few blocks from the British Museum and Goodge Street Tube Station. She also lent Decca a typewriter and the assistance of her clerical staff. Decca worked on the lecture every day and into the weekend. The Cobden Trust requested a synopsis for publicity, which Decca had to admit she did not have ready. In the evenings, she enlisted help from prominent friends such as Baroness Helena Kennedy, an eminent human rights lawyer and member of Parliament, and television anchor Jon Snow. Over long dinners, with lots of drinks, they tried out different angles and read relevant documents.

When finally completed, the speech ran to nearly thirty-five pages. It used defendants well known to Decca, such as Angela Davis, to ask whether justice was possible when institutional racism was baked into the system. Finding a few occasions for jokes, mostly at the Queen's, her family's, and Ronald Reagan's expense, Decca made a case for the importance of looking for bias in legal proceedings. Don't lean on good intentions, she cautioned. The British, Decca ventured, were dishonest with themselves about racism. They'd allowed it to become another "horrid subject the English don't like confronting."[9]

Decca's point was that if she, a product of the insular, right-wing British rural aristocracy, could unlearn racism, then anyone could. She also suggested that every white person was a "black man's burden" and needed to undertake a personal transformation. She did not, she told her very white, very liberal audience, want to sound "governessy." But of course, she did. She was relieved to see that her audience appeared to take her chastisements in stride. They offered what she heard as resounding applause. "All I did was to blast," she remarked soon after. "But anyway they loved it, perhaps people like being blasted?"[10]

In fact, they did not like it. She expected Cobden House to publish the talk in pamphlet form in Britain, as they did with most of their annual lectures. However, the Cobden board found Decca's lecture, they said, too anecdotal, and not sufficiently new. They rejected it. Decca then sent "Law & Disorder: A Transatlantic View" to numerous venues, including *The Nation* and *Mother Jones*, as well as to her former Yale student Corby Kummer at *The Atlantic*—her customary habit of doubling up on her efforts so that nothing went to waste. In the end, despite her efforts, it remained unpublished in both countries, something to which she would now have to grow more accustomed.[11]

At that moment, however, her plate remained very full. In 1963, James Dean Walker—a fit young white man with Hollywood-level good looks and an admitted wild streak—had been convicted of killing a policeman in an altercation following a bar fight (a fight in which, Walker acknowledged, he'd pistol-whipped another man with a gun). The case was rife with irregularities, including the suppression of both exculpatory evidence and witness testimony, and the judge's clear bias. Evidence that Walker's gun had never been fired was disallowed. Nevertheless, Walker was found guilty and sentenced to life imprisonment. After years as a model prisoner, and a convert to Christian Evangelism, Walker wrote up his story as "testimony . . . of the two widely and different roads . . . the broad and the narrow." It was published and distributed by a national church and Walker was allowed out of Cummins State Prison Farm (the most notorious and "hellish" prison in the state) on furloughs.[12] Walker preached to audiences at hundreds of churches for over a year until, one day in 1975, he simply vanished. Four years later, in 1979, he was arrested on a petty drug charge, which appeared to be entrapment. Walker faced interstate extradition back to Arkansas. He had many supporters who all believed that he'd be murdered by retaliatory wardens. Walker was, after all, a convicted "cop killer" and an escapee. The horrific conditions in Arkansas prisons had become public, and the prison from which Walker had escaped had been pronounced unconstitutional. His chance of surviving a return to Cummins for very long seemed slim.[13]

Decca was first alerted to Walker's case by Tom Murton, former warden and state prison superintendent on whom Robert Redford's popular 1980 film *Brubaker* was based. Murton had been one of Decca's consultants for *Kind and Usual Punishment*.[14] Along with numerous other Californians, including actors Shirley MacLaine and Mike Farrell, Decca was quickly caught up in Walker's story. "I've finally found something to do with my trivial life," she declared.[15] She threw herself into Walker's case, amassing material, traveling to Nevada, California, and Arkansas on Walker's behalf, corresponding with his girlfriend, organizing fundraisers, writing to governors, judges, lawyers, and friends—whoever she thought might have some pull. The case has "got me by the throat," she told Shirley MacLaine.[16] Decca and Bob were supposed to embark on a Mediterranean cruise, paid for by *The Sunday Telegraph* in return for an article. When it became clear that she couldn't both go on the cruise and work on the case, she gave up the cruise.

She began corresponding directly with Walker. He told her that he had "hopes of getting a book written . . . [about] my experience with the 'Southern Justice' system." Would you, he asked, "be interested in collaborating on the work?"[17] "Too much else on deck at the moment, also collaboration is not my forte," Decca replied. She offered to find him an editor, however, suggested he begin with an article, offered to read it, and promised to put that in front of editor friends at *The Atlantic, The Nation,* and elsewhere.[18]

Hillary Clinton had stayed in friendly, if infrequent, communication, mostly trading holiday cards. Bill Clinton had recently been elected for his first term as governor of Arkansas and was already viewed as a possible future president. Decca asked Hillary to intervene for Walker. Hillary hedged. The Arkansas prisons, she insisted, were now vastly improved and perfectly safe for Walker.[19] Decca pressed. Hillary replied that she'd looked into the Walker case, and it seemed to her "without merit."[20]

In November 1980, Decca published an essay about the case in the regional *New West* magazine. Shortly after it appeared, Bob Gottlieb encouraged her to write a book about Arkansas prisons. Walker had, by then, "acquired the status of Joe Hill, Sacco and Vanzetti and the Scottsboro Boys," so a book by Decca, he suggested, would be a sure thing.[21] Gottlieb may also have been looking to align Decca's work with the "New Journalism" practiced by Truman Capote with his blockbuster *In Cold Blood*, or, more recently, Norman Mailer, with *The Executioner's Song* in 1979.

Decca said that she couldn't "puzzle out a way to make a book out of it" and did not want to write "another loser" of a book that no one "but me is remotely interested in."[22] She asked Gottlieb to create an outline for the book and send it to her. The principal problem was that "the theme still eludes me," and she could not write it simply as a narrative of events. "I know from bitter experience," she explained to Gottlieb, "how hopeless it is to write anything, from a 1,000-word article to a book, without a clear vision." At the same time, it seemed a shame to waste "all those trips, notebooks, letters hither & yon."[23]

She followed her *New West* article with a short piece for the *Los Angeles Times*, just as the Iranian hostage crisis was unfolding. "We've been noting Carter on telly & in newspapers, speaking of the 'bar-

baric cruelty' of the Iranians to the hostages: random beatings, one chap had a tooth knocked out, solitary confinement, mental torture such as withholding mail from home etc. All this happens DAILY in the Ark. Prisons. In fact in most prisons."[24]

She avoided the religious angle and played down Walker's religion as a likely turnoff for her readers. To her, the spiritual seeking of California's counterculture was self-indulgent nonsense. As she put it, "I don't think I could ever take myself seriously enough to go grubbing about looking for my soul" and she didn't see why anyone else should do so either.[25]

Decca was as baffled by the commitment to armed struggle on the part of a small cadre of self-styled revolutionaries as she was by Spiritualism and consciousness-raising. On October 20, 1981, Kathy Boudin, once Dinky's close friend and the daughter of Bob and Decca's friend Leonard Boudin, was arrested for felony murder. The failed robbery of a Brink's truck that Boudin participated in dominated the news. The robbery was conceived by the Black Liberation Army as "political action by enemy combatants in a war the United States was waging against black militancy," but it was almost universally described as the crazed actions of former activists turned terrorists, as historian Susan Reverby explains.[26] Decca was appalled by Kathy's involvement. "WICKED and STUPID, is all I can say," she wrote Maya Angelou. "Kathy has managed in one deft moment to rehabilitate the discredited FBI, possibly ensure passage of the 'terrorist' bill which would re-establish HUAC in a new & more palatable form, plus senselessly murdering the three people. . . . I can't say how gloomy I am about it all . . . Madness reigns . . . I've been in a state of semi-shock over it all."[27]

"Gloom" and "semi-shock" overshadowed many periods of Decca's life in the 1980s, especially as so many of her loved ones were dying. Most upsetting to her was Philip Toynbee's death in June 1981. She'd known he was ailing, both from years of alcoholism and, more recently, from cancer. Once Decca resumed visiting England, Toynbee had become an increasingly important friend to her, and not only as a tie to her past. She counted on Toynbee and his wife for support and, following the scrapbook row with her sisters, had come to consider them her real family in England. A 1980 reissue of Toynbee's memoir of Esmond, *Friends Apart*, had just recently brought them even closer. Toynbee was only one year older than Decca. His death, which happened quite suddenly on June 15, rocked her. She and Bob dashed to England for the funeral.

Grieving with his friends and family, Decca marveled at how varied Toynbee's life had been: from a privileged youth, to an accomplished young scholar and activist—the first, and possibly last, open Communist to be elected president of the Oxford Union—to an avant-garde novelist and poet, to England's best-known literary reviewer.[28] Late in life, Toynbee converted to Christianity and established a subsistence commune that foreswore both meat and capitalist excess (although he was happy, whenever Decca was in town, to let her tease him about G-D and escape with her to the nearest pub for a burger and a beer).

Ironically, in June 1980, Toynbee had written Decca with a terrific tease. "Believe it or not," he wrote, "I've just been asked to write your *Times* obituary. In some ways I see that this is tremendously one up on you—unless, of course, you've also been asked to write mine. On the other hand, it does give me a good deal of freedom, doesn't it: I mean either you'll never read it or you'll read it From Beyond where all is forgiven." In the process, he asked Decca for a chronological list of her books, into which she slipped one that did not exist, just to see if he'd catch it: *Fair Game: Genuine Sportsmen's Clubs or Cover for Vigilante Operation*. "Exactly the sort of plunking book I might have written, if I had," she noted.[29]

The Observer planned to run a special commemoration for Toynbee, with remembrances by many of his friends, including Patrick Leigh Fermor, Stephen Spender, Decca, and others. She was given one night to write her three-hundred-word piece. She stayed up all night drinking coffee and vodka but was unhappy with it when it was done. "Life itself had to chug along despite inner gloom & misery," she wrote her friend and first cousin Anne Farrer Horne, so perhaps it was for the best that she couldn't stop to grieve since "one HAS to do it willy nilly so it takes one's mind off" one's grief.[30]

As she always did when hurting, Decca stayed in constant motion, moving between Oakland and England, between projects and between political causes. Both of her children married. Constancia married Terry Weber in June 1980. Benjy remarried, to musician Sue Draheim in March 1981. My life, she told Bob Gottlieb in 1981, was "more weddings than funerals."[31] But that wasn't strictly true. She juggled more bad news than good news across those years. Nancy's excruciating illness and death was followed by Dobby's husband, Mason's, death, then Fay Stender's suicide, then Vivian Cadden's husband's death in 1981, and in 1981 as well, a sudden stroke of Diana's that revealed a brain tumor (Diana surprised everyone by recovering, though slowly).[32] Decca and Debo began sharing notes on what they did—and did not—want at their own funeral. "My funeral: . . . me plan is to have a flying wedge of my former students whose one job at the funeral will be to keep their ears cocked for the word BUT [as in, but she was a poor dresser], & forcibly remove But-sayers."[33]

Increasingly, Decca was referring to herself as old. She often joked about dying: "'tis the season to be creaking," she quipped.[34] Her life remained as "hectic" as ever—up at dawn to drive to Sacramento on Walker business, back to Oakland in the afternoon for a 6:00 p.m. flight to London. But now she admitted that it was a "wee bit demanding."[35] She became more emotional, "overwhelmed with sadness" at unexpected times. She found herself "absolutely clobbered" by things that she would have met stoically in the past.[36] Once or twice she even found herself crying in public.

Early in 1980, British producer Julian Jebb approached the sisters. He wanted to make a documentary about Nancy, largely as told by all her survivors. Decca learned that Debo and Diana would have final say over content. Still smarting over Debo's self-anointment as "arbiter" of all things Mitford, and very much concerned that the Mitford Industry tended to either glamorize or make light of her family's fascist leanings, Decca put on the brakes. When Jebb asked to interview her in Oakland, she welcomed him and answered every question he posed. Then she insisted on reading a letter of Nancy's on tape, a letter that painted Tom as a socialist sympathizer and that Decca felt set the record straight about her brother's politics. "I don't think it is fair for Decca to use this," Diana wrote Debo. Jebb allowed Diana a chance to rebut it, also filming her insistence that she and Mosley had never been anti-Semitic. It wasn't all Jews Mosley hated, Diana patiently explained, with her pretty blue eyes wide, just the awful ones who wouldn't support Hitler.[37]

The Mitford Girls opened on July 15, 1981. Decca flew to England for Jebb's production and she and Bob led "a safari of various cousins & London chums to see it" (traveling a hundred miles south from London to Sussex). The audience all had buttons reading "I'm a Mitford Girl." The sisters had ones reading "I really am a Mitford Girl." Bob's button read "I'm married to a real Mitford Girl." Decca thought it was all silly, but she wore her button nevertheless.[38] She reviewed *The Mitford Girls* for *The Sunday Times*, for which she was paid £750 (much more than she received in royalties for the musical). She criticized the production's silliness about Hitler and fascism as altogether too focused on "crazy larks."[39] Even Debo had to admit that the musical was shallow. "La Triviata," she called it.

Deborah published her first of many books on Chatsworth in October 1982. Decca drafted a review of Debo's book slamming "those

Dukes of Devonshire" for their colonial "plunder" and attitudes.[40] Then she thought better of it and submitted a final, warm, bland copy. That same month, *Masterpiece Theatre* released an eight-part miniseries based on Nancy's first two novels, *The Pursuit of Love* and *Love in a Cold Climate*, and Decca reviewed that for *TV Guide*, recycling some material from her first memoir on what it was like "to be a real-life Mitford . . . in those far-off years between the two world wars."[41]

Writing about the family was lucrative (*TV Guide* paid her $1,000), but a sidelight. Most of Decca's energy went to articles on Southern racism. "Return to the South" was a very substantial essay written for *Harper's* but rejected by them (her second such rejection in this period). She successfully published an article in *McCall's* in 1981 on the Atlanta murders of young Black boys, a string of more than two dozen murders.[42] Known as the Atlanta Child Murders, the killings terrorized parents of children of color. Decca's article, "How Will We Ever Teach Them to Trust Adults Again?" began with profiles of her own Atlanta grandchildren, ages thirteen and eleven, and described the "eerie experience" of Atlanta's "deserted playgrounds . . . streets in which there is not a single youngster in sight."[43]

She tried moving on to other subjects but found that she could not let the Walker case go. Hundreds of unmarked graves had been found behind the Arkansas prison farm. A guard in Walker's prison had broken an inmate's neck and called it "horseplay." Death certificates were being falsified to hide other inmate murders. Decca traveled to Little Rock and set up a base in the Camelot Inn, just off the highway. She hired a local researcher and began conducting interviews. Her interview process was laborious—for each interview she typed up her questions in advance, then took extensive notes by hand, then spent her evenings typing in the responses and typing up summaries. She then sent copies of the interview transcripts back to her subjects, to be checked for accuracy. "I set out to write a simple article, & have become obsessed. Pity, but there you are," she said.[44]

Bill Clinton had promised Decca he'd ensure Walker's safety, but in a stunning upset in 1980, he lost his reelection bid to a Republican rival, Frank White. Walker was extradited back to Arkansas and placed in solitary confinement. He was still in solitary confinement when Decca wrote Clinton, after his December 1982 victory returning him to the governor's mansion, to implore him to finally do something for Walker.[45] "My God, Governor Clinton, do something, please," Decca pleaded.[46] Decca published two more articles on Walker. She wrote members of the California Congress. She took the case to the Center for Investigative Reporting in Oakland, hoping to interest young reporters. To her great excitement there was a flurry of interest from Hollywood, with two different deals on the table simultaneously, but both were ultimately "a total washout."[47] By early 1982, she was obliged to admit that "the Walker case per se is fairly deadish." She added, "All is gloom."[48]

Decca stuck with the case, although she had believed that she'd be done with it in 1980 when her first article on it was published.[49] "How wrong I was," she wrote years later. "The case dragged on—now simmering on a back burner, now furiously aboil—for five more years, dragging me with it all the way."[50] *60 Minutes* showed interest, then lost it. Hollywood waxed cold, then hot, then cold again. For years, various newspapers announced an upcoming film, starring Mike Farrell as Walker, but it never came to fruition.[51] In spite of everything, in 1983 some of Walker's supporters accused Decca of trying to profit from Walker's story. Spitting mad, Decca had her film agent at the time, Renee Wayne Golden, sign an affidavit attesting that Decca's only interest had ever been "to aid Mr. Walker in his fight to stay alive."[52]

Decca was prone to passionate disputes over minor things at this time. She spent years pursuing a plagiarism suit over a few paragraphs lifted from her first memoir and also picked other fights that struck her friends as pointless. In 1981 she admitted to her friend, attorney

Barney Dreyfus, that "compromise is not much in my nature."[53] Her sense of perspective was not helped by ongoing difficulties getting publishers to accept her work. She didn't know what to do with all her years of work on Walker and continued toying with the idea of a book on his case.[54]

Worst of all, Decca was losing faith in muckraking. Her belief in the power of writing and the force of facts had sustained her activism. In 1982 she was no longer so certain. Was the arc bending toward justice? Had prisons really changed? "From the point of view of the man or woman in the prison cell, life has, if anything changed drastically for the worse," she noted sadly.[55]

Decca always claimed that she could only work on one thing at a time, especially as her method required total immersion. But from 1981 to 1983 she worked on two large projects at once, and she had her feet in two completely different worlds.

She didn't set out to write a book about Philip Toynbee, she said, but found herself backing into it, because she thought it should be done and "nobody else was keen to do it." Philip combined, she said, "all my favourite characteristics: he was a gifted and very funny raconteur, and a perfect target for teasing . . . but there was also his serious dedication to the causes" of socialism and anti-fascism.[56] He was outrageous, preternaturally energetic, and brilliant. She wanted him properly remembered so that readers could see "the complexity of him via interviews, letters, etc. from his friends & family," she said.[57] Toynbee was Decca's "one remaining link with the vanished pre–World War II life."[58] She loved his fierce political commitments and his refusal to give up, his right, as he put it, to "drink and kiss and lie in the sun."[59] Writing a memoir of Toynbee also made her the "arbiter" of the past, his past at least. Toynbee's own memoir of Esmond had gotten him exactly right, Decca felt. She may have now been repaying that debt. Both of her earlier memoirs were geared toward explaining: How did I get here? Toynbee's memoir, on the other hand, was elegiac, nostalgic, and less focused on any theme. It did not take advantage of Decca's love of skewering the enemy or her gift of mockery.

Gottlieb was not sure it would work. Not only was this not the sort of thing at which Decca excelled, Toynbee was completely unknown in the United States. Gottlieb urged Decca to make it a larger book and to add more characters. Decca refused. She wanted to focus on Toynbee. Gottlieb was not the sort of editor to tell a writer, especially a writer of Decca's caliber, what they should do. Even if he wanted to dissuade her, Gottlieb knew that "it wouldn't work. . . . You can't suggest ideas to someone like Decca. . . . That's what she wanted to do."[60] He wrote Decca carefully in the spring of 1982, saying he wasn't sure if Toynbee was best suited to a book—perhaps an article or something else? If she wanted to do it, he would publish it, he assured her, but needed her to understand that he couldn't pay as he had for some of her other books. "If we're not gouged for Large Monies, we can afford to publish wonderful books with limited sales possibilities."[61]

Before his death, Toynbee had become one of the most important members of Decca's transatlantic Writing Committee. He provided terrific feedback but also used to tease her that there wasn't enough about him in her writing: "Nothing about ME?" he would write in the margins. "Here goes, Philip," Decca said to the paper she rolled into her typewriter.[62]

Toynbee was a large man, resembling, Patrick Leigh Fermor wrote, "a huge, raw-boned aristocratic lumber-jack or stevedore," with a strong face, full lips, and thick black hair. Decca described him as like a "wolfhound puppy" in his uncontrollable energy and wild enthusiasms (which earned him the nickname of Plunger).[63] Unlike either Esmond or Decca, he wore his heart on his sleeve. Why, Decca could now wonder, had he been so sure his personality would have been crushed by Decca and Esmond when they were young? Was the balance then as uneven as he claimed?

Toynbee had married twice, first to old British money and later to an American named Sally, whom Decca came to love. He had children from both marriages. His daughter Polly became one of Decca's closest friends. Philip Toynbee wrote novels and poetry, and worked on a multi-volume verse novel called *Pantaloon*, which was highly praised in some modernist circles. He also fought terrible depression and eventually succumbed to alcoholism.

Decca's memoir stressed Toynbee's lifelong struggle, as he put it, to be a "good man." That was her main thread. Toynbee insisted on taking action on his ideas, whether hoarding suicide pills in case of nuclear war or turning his country home into a commune for those Decca dismissed as "the flotsam and jetsom of British society."[64] Like her, he'd always been an "Action Man."

Strikingly, the portrait that emerges of Toynbee could often just as easily stand as a portrait of Decca. She praised his "endless jokes, games, songs," his "sense of the ridiculous," his "constant exploitation of potentially comic situations." She wrote about his "mischief"—"It seemed as though the child who lurks within every adult was particularly alive and frisky in Philip." She noted his "extraordinary capacity for work, an intellectual vigour that never deserted him . . . time-consuming friendships, family life into which he poured endless energy." He was, she wrote, "remarkably efficient and professional." She liked that "he was never averse to an appreciative audience" and also that he "never adopted the facile, pop-psychological view that Communism and Fascism were two sides of the same coin."[65] It was, she wrote, the "web of contradictions that made Philip such a pleasure—and sometimes such a pain."[66] Was she describing Toynbee, or herself?

Decca worked on *Faces of Philip* all through 1983, while also advocating for James Dean Walker. In the summer of 1983, on August 11, a panel ruled that Walker was unsafe in Arkansas and had to be transferred out. At the end of October, he was transferred out of Arkansas into federal prison. Decca worked hard to try to get him released.

Shortly after turning in her final copy of *Faces of Philip*, Decca was invited to be part of a six-woman delegation to El Salvador and Nicaragua, a fact-finding tour sponsored by the Project of National Interest and the USOCA (U.S. Out of Central America) Committee. She traveled to El Salvador during the height of its civil war and of Americans' opposition to U.S. funding of the country's right-wing dictatorship. There were widespread efforts to stop the Salvadoran government's practice of "disappearing" dissidents. Activists organized solidarity protests throughout the 1980s under the slogan "El Salvador is Spanish for Vietnam." For many, El Salvador was *the* political issue of the decade. Decca left for Central America in late January of 1984, after "boning up like mad" on the area's history, about which she felt "ABYSMALLY ignorant."[67] She departed California feeling fine. But while in El Salvador she suffered a stroke that paralyzed one side of her body. She was rushed back home.

Decca made light of her condition. "The only really awful news this end is that I've got to give up smoking . . . stroke-inducing they say. . . . However I am cutting down; it's now 10:30 a.m. and I've only had six."[68] She joked about Debo being forced to pay for a long-distance call to check on her. Her galleys arrived for *Faces of Philip*, and Decca told friends that she was more than up for the task of corrections. But to a couple of close confidants, she admitted that she could not hold a pen. Her recovery was, in fact, slow and difficult, lasting many months. Nevertheless, she produced two short pieces on her time in Central America, both published in March 1984, "El Salvador on the Precipice" and "The Salvadoran Way of Death."[69] Some months later, when she spoke to the Abraham Lincoln Brigade about how many volunteers had gone to Nicaragua to assist the Revolution and how "similar" she found it to Spain, Decca's voice was clear and strong. Her left leg, however, was still supported by a large metal brace, beginning under her knee, with rods running down her leg and under her brown Oxford shoe. She neither hid her brace—in fact, she wore a dress—nor accepted any help getting upstairs to the stage.[70]

Soon after her stroke, Benjy suffered a serious relapse of his bipolar condition. He still refused to take medicine, was divorcing his wife, and had antagonized all his clients, pushing everyone away as he always did when ill. "The beastliness of it all is indescribable. He simply turns into a totally different and horrible person," Decca told Gottlieb.[71] Decca was angrier than she was sympathetic. Benjy's illness seemed to her like something he could conquer if he would only try. She told him to stay away until he stopped being Hyde; she could not bear his dark side. How could someone as talented, charming, and lovable as Benjy allow himself to succumb to an illness that changed his personality? Why would someone like Michael Straight—Decca's old friend from Washington—not only act as a spy for the Russians but admit it all now, in 1983, when it could have been just left in the past?[72] Around this time, Pele de Lappe, one of Decca's closest friends, remarked that Decca had a "tendency to laugh off one's problems . . . not being sympathetic . . . it's almost as if she would rather not get involved . . . it ruffles things up."[73]

More Mitford Industry products appeared. A new biography of Nancy, which Decca considered "vague" and "plodding," received praise from her sisters.[74] Diana's branch of the family also completed a doorstop family biography of the Mitfords, *The House of Mitford*, which, as Peter Sussman writes, "reflected the extreme right-wing views of Diana and rationalized the Mosleys' anti-Semitic history."[75] Decca refused to cooperate with it.[76] But when galleys found their way to her in 1984 she saw that it relied heavily on her *Hons and Rebels*. "Decca detested the book and toyed with the idea of filing another lawsuit," according to Sussman.[77] Virginia Durr was also working on her own autobiography, published in 1985. And Decca was cooperating with a young, untried scholar, Kevin Ingram, who'd come forward to write Esmond's biography. She hosted him in her home and gave him unrestricted access to her files and papers.[78] She took Ingram under her wing, introduced him to all her friends, and provided the kind of limitless encouragement that had so endeared her to her writing students at San Jose and Yale.

Predictably, perhaps, reviews of *Faces of Philip* were scant. Not all were positive. *Library Journal* praised the book's "glimpses of upper-class British life," but panned the book overall as "sketchy and unsatisfying. . . . Mitford's narrative barely grazes the surface of Toynbee's personality. She admits that this slim study is 'a lot less ambitious' than a biography and indeed it is." *The Times Literary Supplement* thought the book altogether too light: "The story of Peter Pan, as written by Tinker Bell," as if Decca wanted "to keep Toynbee in the world of the madcap Mitfords." A reviewer in India liked the book but suggested, with great insight, that the experience of reading it was one of being reminded of the "tribal cosiness" of the British upper class, to which outsiders can never belong and from which insiders, whatever their political rebellions, will never really escape. Those reviewers who liked Toynbee, and/ or Mitford, found things to praise. The *Financial Times* pronounced it "funny, unsentimental" and "moving." The *New York Times* reviewer, Clancy Sigal, found the book "deeply affecting." The *San Francisco Chronicle* review, anonymous but almost certainly written by someone Mitford knew, diplomatically noted that "Mitford is always delightful to read." The reviewer for the *Los Angeles Times* was even more diplomatic, opting only to summarize but not to evaluate Decca's effort.[79]

Decca now embarked on an even more nostalgic project. She decided to write a book about Grace Darling, an English heroine from the mid-1800s. A lighthouse keeper's daughter who performed a seemingly impossible rescue and saved nine shipwrecked passengers in a September 1838 gale off the rocky Farne islands on the east coast of northern England, Darling was known throughout Britain, but completely "unknown in America," as Decca was the first to admit.[80] Was she trying to introduce her American readers to her English past? Was she turning her back on her readers, or merely indulging a whim and filling up her time? Why another small, wistful book?

Decca knew that her choice of subject would strike her left-wing friends as "WEIRD" and perhaps "a ridiculous waste of time & energy." She maintained that the "whole thrust of my book will be an exploration of this early Victorian press phenomenon, the 'Yellow Press.'"[81] She was probably writing the book for the sheer pleasure of it. She also claimed the book was Bob's idea. Decca loved to belt out the "Grace Darling" song with Maya Angelou. They sang it often, in simulated patriotic fervor, warming to the song's rousing nationalist conclusion: "Go tell the wide world over, / What English pluck can do: / And sing of brave Grace Darling, / Who nobly saved the crew." "How about Grace Darling?" Bob had suggested after one of their duets.

Decca's book was originally intended for a series that could pay her only £6,500 (about £18,000 today). If she went with a slightly longer book, outside the series, Viking was prepared to nearly double that advance. Decca wanted the money for travel to England and to hire a British researcher. She talked it over with her editor friend Billy Abrahams, who helped her negotiate terms for it to be in a new imprint he was heading. It was the first project in decades that Decca had not taken to Bob Gottlieb, but Gottlieb, at the time, was leaving Knopf for *The New Yorker*.

Under normal circumstances, losing her longtime editor would have been a blow. Gottlieb's defection was the least of Decca's problems just then, however.

She and Bob had remained good friends with Bob's former law partner Victor Rabinowitz and his much younger wife, African American filmmaker and activist Joanne Grant. During Forman's breakdown, when Dinky had come over to England, Grant had been the first friend to rush to Dinky's side. She was almost family to Decca. In the early spring of 1985, Decca learned, evidently from Bob, that he'd been having a long-running affair with Grant. For years, they had met secretly, traveled to the same vacation spots, slipped away together when the two couples were together, hid their attraction to one another when the two couples were sharing houses, meals, attending the same fundraisers, being at the same conferences. They had allowed their spouses to misassume, misunderstand, misperceive, and misremember, always gaslighting, covering their tracks, acting as if nothing was going on.

The affair came to light when Bob decided to end it. He told Decca about the affair and said that he did not want to separate from her.

Decca had always been perplexed and saddened by the breakups of others' marriages. She took their divorces quite hard. When Carl Bernstein and Nora Ephron separated, in 1980, she wrote: "I suppose I'm simply bone stupid about things like this, absolutely cannot fathom why & how they could separate . . . I'm just terribly sad over it . . . they seemed so wonderfully well suited to each other."[82]

No couple had seemed to her, however, as happy and well suited as she and Bob. They were the couple that others looked up to, people wanted to be around, that seemed to have mastered the trick of being both lovers and friends. They were famously supportive of one another's careers, able to work together on many kinds of projects, quick to finish one another's sentences and thoughts, fierce in each other's defense. They loved to play games, and to travel, and to gossip together about everyone they knew. When one of them walked into the room where the other was seated, both of them lit up.

Decca was a loyal person, and not very sexual. This kind of betrayal gutted her and also made little sense to her. She was completely unseated. And she was also ashamed. Over all the years of tensions with her sisters, who never let Decca forget that they were thinner, richer, and more elegant than she was, Decca had always been able to take comfort in having the best marriage of them all. While her sisters' husbands and lovers all lied and cheated—womanizers all—Decca had been able to take pride in Bob's fealty and fidelity. Her marriage, like her writing success, was proof that she had chosen wisely and built a better life.

Decca left very little record of either the affair or her devastation. She spoke of it only to three people: Sally Belfrage, Maya Angelou, and Constancia. It was typical of Decca to say least about whatever hurt her most. In this case, she may have been careful to keep gossip in check so that she could stay with Bob, should she choose to, and most of their friends would never find out what had gone on between them. Decca could not bear to be seen as weak, or a victim. A wrong that could not be righted was not a story she'd have wanted to share. Pity was intolerable to her.

She did not want to leave her marriage. But forging ahead in the face of Bob's betrayal also seemed impossible, especially at first. "The SQUALOR of it all & all the lies etc. tend to come back on me in waves at unexpected moments, causing me to lash out at B. [Bob] perhaps unfairly," she confided to Sally Belfrage.[83] Bob, moreover, set conditions on their staying together. He would give up Joanne. But Decca would have to agree not to torture him about what he'd done. She could not bring it up out of context and she could not punish him for it if they were going to continue together. "He gets v. annoyed when I bring up the subject so I've rather stopped doing it," she told Sally.[84]

There is no question that Decca and Bob continued to act as a team, even during the worst of this time, when it was not yet clear that their marriage would survive. Bob accompanied Decca to England that summer, and he helped with her research into Grace Darling. While in England, Bob took it upon himself to champion Decca over the long-simmering feud with her sisters. At the end of a visit with Debo, who threw herself enthusiastically into Decca's

Grace Darling work, Bob took Debo aside to say that she owed Decca an apology. Decca described what happened next to her niece Emma, who'd been her confidante throughout the scrapbook fracas. "Debo said NOT ONE WORD. She got in her car. Bob said, 'Were you going to say something?' Answer: 'Goodbye, Bob,' & she drove off."[85] However it was that Decca and Bob framed Bob's betrayal— whether in 1960s countercultural terms or in the old-fashioned "boys will be boys" double standard or in some private negotiation of their own fashioning—Decca was unwilling to lose his continued support. Bob's best qualities had always been his delight in her success, a twinkling sense of humor, brilliance, and loyalty. He was loyal to her now, even if he'd been disloyal to her with Grant. Decca genuinely appreciated his intervention with Debo. "Thanks to Bob's bold spur-of-the moment intervention scrapbook-wise (& her response all of which I told you)," Decca wrote her niece, "everything was v. sunny—back to the old Honnish friendship of yore (or almost)— anyway ordinary vs. prickly & guarded, semi-suspicious."[86] She held fast to the idea of Bob as a loyal spouse and to Debo as a loving and trusted Hon.

Decca planned an enormous birthday party for Bob in Oakland. The surprise of the evening was James Dean Walker, just released from prison pending his third (and ultimately final) trial in 1986. As hard as Decca tried to put the Walker case behind her, she found herself returning to it. She wrote yet another article on his case, which was rejected by *The New York Times*, *Vanity Fair*, the *San Francisco Chronicle*, and finally, *Mother Jones*, which wanted Decca to make herself more of a character in the piece and which she just couldn't manage, especially not right then.

Her Grace Darling project, on the other hand, proved a good distraction. She loved the research, and here she did insert herself into the book, once again creating a caricature of the researcher as hunt-

411

ress. Some of her research touched on her mother's maritime childhood, as well as her family's ancestral lands in Northumberland. Instead of thinking about those cold northern waters as Esmond's grave, she could now focus on those who'd been plucked from that ocean and about what it might have been like for her mother, as a child, to sail those waters and risk shipwreck. The Farne island, where Grace Darling's lighthouse station stood, was, like the Hebrides, a rocky and isolated spot, difficult to access. It helped her think about her mother's years on Inch Kenneth and what those must have been like.

Her proposal for the book had suggested a focus "on the amazing press hoop-la" accorded Grace Darling in her day, compared to "(for example) the Beatles in our era." But as she worked, Decca followed her nose. She became fascinated by numerous aspects of the story: media and celebrity, profit and tragedy, newspaper history, gender and class ideologies of heroism, and more. Her book, *Grace Had an English Heart*, was not a biography, which she considered an "ambitious" and confining genre that required one to "probe deeply into the subject's antecedents and childhood, the literary influences that shaped his writings and re-cord details of his comings and goings from cradle to grave," and which must always, she felt, "let the reader draw [their] own conclusion."[87] It was not a history. Nor was it a travel book. Although she did not know it, Decca was helping to usher in the genre of meditations on lost female celebrities, a critical aspect of the feminist movement.

She was much more aware of contributing to the field of media history. Written at a time when the Mitford Industry was wreaking havoc, her book was informed by questions about how the press creates, then hounds, celebrity women. As a journalist, she was especially interested in the history of journalistic work, in their "scramble for scoops" and their pay: a penny a line. A self-described news junkie, who lived for the sound of a newspaper clattering onto the porch ("once, ages ago when I was about 30 & thought I might be dead soon . . . I'm sorry to say my last thoughts were not so much for Bob & children as I'll never see to-morrow's paper"), Decca was fascinated to learn that a professional jour-nalist in Grace Darling's day was one who "spent his days rushing from place to place, often walking six or seven miles a day in search of news."[88] He would then spend his nights, with sheets of onionskin and an early form of carbon paper, bearing down on six copies of highly elaborated and adjectival prose—he was paid by the line after all and needed "to stretch out his story to the maximum possible length in order to garner extra pennies for his day's work"—in hopes that one of the half dozen main London papers would use his stuff.[89] As a devotee of carbon paper and xeroxing, Decca was particularly intrigued by the six thin sheets to match the six London dailies.

The Grace Darling story engaged some of Decca's muckraking in-stincts. The wreck had occurred when a new steamship, the *Forfarshire*, crashed. Decca uncovered information about its boilers and those who were tasked with maintaining them. On January 28, 1986, she recounted, "just as I was ploughing through interminable evidence at the coroner's jury about failures of rivets in boilers, the space shuttle [*Challenger*] blew up so I was nipping off to the telly to watch all that. There are some striking parallels: brand new technology of steamships, thought to be more or less invulnerable—until the rivets gave way. Ditto, technology of space shuttles, declared to be totally safe, until some wee little fault in the manufacture of the O-rings was detected after the event."[90]

There was a Grace Darling Museum in the town of Bamburgh, and Decca spent time browsing its two small rooms. She found grandiose language to puncture and "mass-produced souvenirs and knick-knacks" to mock: "entrepreneurial ingenuity of nineteenth-century manufacturers, alert even in those far-off days to the commercial value of a famous name: Grace Darling Cadbury chocolates, Grace Darling mugs, Grace Darling pen-wipers." She imagined an historic public subjected to "pens, shoes, fireplace implements, hearth tidies, doorstops, napkin rings, soap, chocolates, and all kinds of decorative tableware . . . jugs, mugs, tankards, plates, trays of all shapes and sizes, in a range of materials from lusterware to porcelain to lowly earthenware, prices to suit all purses," all bearing an idealized image of Grace Darling battling the waves.[91]

Freed from all genre constraints, sometimes Decca just included whatever she found intriguing, adding pages of passages from newspapers of the day as they covered weather, French policy, advertisements, notices, conditions in Ireland, and crime. Having stumbled onto a story of a thief trying to get out of a sheep-stealing charge by claiming it really wasn't a sheep at all, but venison, she felt "I think I must put some of that sort of thing in the book . . . Flavour of the times."[92]

Decca did not realize that she had become "Topic A" among her sisters. Somehow, they learned of Bob's affair, presumably from something Decca let drop to Debo, who had offered to help with the Grace Darling research. Diana's pitying response—"It sounds very bad, poor Decca"—dripping with Schadenfreude, cannot have been something Decca sought or wanted.[93] With Bob having come to England to help with the book, Decca thought that things might be getting back to normal between them.

Decca and Bob continued their shared political commitments, just as they'd always done. In early 1987 they flew to Atlanta for the huge civil rights march in Forsyth County, a former sundown county. Following an earlier march on January 17 that was attacked by white supremacists, the march they attended featured many national civil rights leaders, including John Lewis, Rev. Joseph Lowery, president of the Southern Christian Leadership Council, Gary Hart, Andrew Young, Ben Hooks, Ralph Abernathy, Dick Gregory, Jesse Jackson, and Coretta Scott King. Buses were arranged to take people to and from Atlanta, but so many demonstrators showed up that there was not nearly enough transportation. Quickly assessing the situation, Dinky spirited Decca and Bob onto one of the VIP buses, designated for Reverend Lowery and others. "This is Jessica Mitford," Dinky said, moving through the crowd, "This is Jessica Mitford." Demonstrators parted to make way for her. In *Grace Had an English Heart*, Decca surmised that Grace had an "intense dislike of the public spotlight" and "did nothing to advance her fame and acclaim, she positively shrank from it."[94] Decca never shared that sentiment.

The book appeared, as its publishers planned, precisely in time for the 150th anniversary of Grace Darling's rescue. Published by Viking in England in 1988 (with color illustrations and more than fifty black-and-white illustrations) and by Dutton in the United States in 1989 (with color illustrations only), *Grace Had an English Heart: The Story of Grace Darling, Heroine and Victorian Superstar*, was a hit in Britain, especially when Decca was onstage during book tours. The British press was enthusiastic. Rebecca Fraser, in *The Times*, noted that *Grace Had an English Heart* was "a marvellously eccentric . . . romp" written in the "Mitfordese" of Decca's "whimsical" childhood. She called it a muckraking book "without a terrific lot of muck to rake" and lauded Decca for setting "out on a quest for the truth behind the legend." The *Financial Times* praised the book as "humourous," and a "virtual feast," adding that Mitford shared her every discovery with the reader. *The Sunday Times* pronounced the book "dazzlingly funny" (just what Decca would most want to hear) and the *Daily Mail*'s reviewer found "a laugh on every page." Some of the British reviewers evidently couldn't resist puns of their own, saying that fans would go "overboard" and that Mitford "sail[s] smartly" through the sea of other books.[95]

Given the book's obscure subject, there were a surprising number of reviews of *Grace Had an English Heart* in the United States, and in a testament to Mitford's fame and regard, it was taken up by papers in Washington, D.C., Los Angeles, Chicago, Orlando, New York, and elsewhere. Most were kind. *Library Journal* noted that the book had Mitford's "customary, wry view of human foibles," and that it might encourage its readers to compare Grace Darling's fame to that of "contemporary media celebrities." *The Washington Post* called it an "engagingly breezy little book" and this light praise was echoed in other reviews, such as the *Los Angeles Times*, which called the book "tart and witty," and the *Chicago Tribune*, which described it as "drolly offbeat." *The New York Times*, however, found less to praise in a book that seemed, finally, to its reviewer a kind of "hodgepodge" reminiscent of the small museum in Bamburgh.[96]

Decca's book came out just as the feminist movement was advocating the recuperation of lost heroines and just as feminists around the world were reimagining and telling their stories. It was occasionally advertised alongside Brenda Maddox's biography of Nora Joyce, a classic of feminist recuperation, published the same year. But Decca was either unaware of that recuperative turn in feminist thought or, perhaps, uninterested by it.

Neither the recuperative turn, nor the anti-pornography movement, spoke to Decca. When California feminists, including Ann Simonton, tried to enlist Decca in the anti-pornography movement, Decca found them "almost over the brink."[97] And yet, Decca was speaking to issues at the heart of contemporary feminism, even if feminists were not addressed by her.

After her book appeared, she returned to the Grace Darling Museum and to Bamburgh to celebrate its publication and the sesquicentennial anniversary of Grace Darling's rescue. In September 1988, just before her seventy-first birthday, Decca stood again on Longstone rock, in the wind and the rain. Bob was with her, as were other family and friends. Her sister Debo "adored" Decca's book and was once again affectionate, even doting.[98] Decca knew that September storms were the fiercest in that area. "So, don't you think that if our boat is wrecked & all are drowned it would be smashing publicity for my book? Be praying for bad weather, Barb," she wrote one of her closest friends.[99]

19

"Toddling Towards the End"[1]

I do *have an attitude toward death—I am against it.*[2]
—JESSICA MITFORD

More than a year after *Grace Darling*'s publication, Dutton (which Decca considered incompetent) had only about five thousand orders, a fraction of what she was accustomed to. Decca didn't complain. She returned to traveling and writing other things.

Visiting Virginia Durr early in 1988, she gave an interview to a small Southern newspaper, lacerating the local country Club for excluding Jews. Decca also exposed the president of Montgomery's chapter of the English-Speaking Union as a racist who routinely used racial slurs to denigrate Black citizens. The article, she proudly told a friend, "caused a) flurry in the dove-cote, b) put the cat amongst the pigeons, or c) shit in the electric fan, depending on whether you prefer 19th Cent. English, early 20th Cent. English, or modern American."[3] Being able to stir up trouble, even at seventy-one, was essential for Decca. Growing old gracefully was about the worst thing she could imagine. As much as she liked to tease that she was "toddling towards the end" and that she'd finish off her life by lazying about on the couch, no one who knew Decca paid that any attention. "I love being a feisty old dame," she truthfully said.[4]

Decca still loved public speaking. "Get your own audience," she once told a young friend standing a little too close to her microphone.[5] Her joy in lecturing was infectious, even when her topics were designed to provoke outrage. She now received a steady stream of invitations to address writers, arts organizations, political campaigns, unions, universities, journalists, memorial societies, health-care organizations, politicians, gerontological groups, community groups, literary societies, ladies' clubs, museums, libraries, festivals, church groups (Unitarians, mostly), and consumer cooperatives. She took no trip purely for pleasure, always tacking on an interview or speaking gig, sometimes juggling multiple side trips at once. The older she got, the more she craved both activity and the presence of young people—"that's what cheers me up," she said.[6] Her favorite tag line, lifted from a flyer for one of her talks, was now "She's not one of the Old Boys."[7] She treasured the fan letters she received after talks and saved notes that thanked her for "humor and clarity," for being such "a fine speaker," a "great inspiration," giving a "brilliant performance," or "absolutely the hit of the event."[8]

Decca could not accept every invitation that clattered through the mail slot of Regent Street's front door. Occasionally she let one of her lecture bureaus make arrangements for her, but she preferred to handle speaking invitations herself, scribbling a note across each and leaving it out for Bob to peruse. If Bob thought it looked good, she'd negotiate terms and have her assistant, Katie Edwards, handle the rest. For political events, fundraisers, causes she cared about (such as Central American or Nicaraguan solidarity work, health-care reform, civil rights, or free speech), Decca might speak for free (as long as all her expenses were covered). In other cases, she tried to get the highest possible honorarium out of her hosts. From the late 1980s onward, she set her "standard" minimum at $3,000, a sum she almost never received (and which is roughly equivalent to £5,500 today). She often padded honoraria, requesting travel reimbursement and arranging to receive that from more than one organization per trip. Occasionally she requested first-class travel airfare from England, then had a printer friend "forge a bill" if she was in fact traveling from Oakland.[9] A 1989 essay called "The Mitford Way of Travel" shared some of her tricks for dodging fees, securing upgrades, getting others to pack and carry her bags, making long-distance calls for free, and getting extra expenses paid.

Decca sat down with every speaking or writing contract and went over every line to make sure her expenses were covered, deadlines were reasonable, she could not be censored or edited without her consent, and that publishers included a kill fee if for any reason a commissioned piece was rejected.

Previously, that kill fee clause had been a formality, hardly ever invoked. Around 1985, however, when *Life* magazine commissioned then quashed an essay on Nicaragua and *Vanity Fair* ultimately rejected her long essay on James Dean Walker, Decca found that she could no longer count on her work being accepted. "DAMN DAMN DAMN," she wrote her friend, the writer Kay Boyle, after one such rejection.[10]

One of her most frequent speaking subjects, perhaps inspired by some of her own experiences, was now censorship. Maya Angelou's book *I Know Why the Caged Bird Sings* had been banned by a California high school, and Decca's vigorous defense of Angelou led to more research and lectures on freedom of speech.[11] She became a staunch supporter of free expression, including sexual expression, and an equally fierce opponent of anti-pornography feminists whom, she believed, mistook speech

419

for action. Among her most frequently consulted folders was a thick file she kept on "Censorship." One of the stock speeches she kept in her files now was called "Sex and the First Amendment: Porn Bashers from Jesse Helms to Andrea Dworkin," a talk she tried to publish in *The Nation*, and elsewhere.

In July 1988, in England preparing for the publication of *Grace Darling*, Decca spoke to Doug Foster, editor of *Mother Jones*, and negotiated an essay on four Black, newly elected members of Parliament, "a stunning achievement" after sixty years of an all-white Parliament. Despondent over the reelection of Margaret Thatcher—"Oh Maggie!" Decca would shout at her television—she considered the diversification of Parliament the one "bright spot amid the encircling gloom."[12] Foster was a good friend, and Decca was relieved to have the essay bound for his hands, in spite of the fact that *Mother Jones* had rejected two recent essays by her. After reviewing her outline with Foster and receiving his enthusiastic sign-off, Decca conducted interviews, extensive background research, and drafted the piece. Foster sent back two full pages of notes and a request for a total rewrite. "Not riveting," he stated reluctantly.[13] Surely a *complete* redo wasn't needed, Decca thought. She sent the essay to another friend, Peter Jenkins, editor of *The Independent* (and husband of Decca's dear friend Polly Toynbee). Although Jenkins was as "keen on her" as Foster, he also thought the essay was weak. Unwilling to waste her own work, she undertook a full round of revisions for Foster. "Take it or leave it," she said. Foster thought it needed a third round of revisions. He left it, apologizing profusely.

Decca said she was too "swamped" to dwell on it.[14] She had accepted an assignment from *Traveler* magazine to describe a cruise for American tourists on the Volga River—Vodka, she called it—under Soviet rule. Perhaps, she thought, she could work in reflections on cultural difference and even on Communism. Unfortunately, the trip was a "total bust" and Decca was worried "that if I tell it like it was, the mag. might turn it down."[15] She wrote up the cruise as she'd experienced it: a mind-numbing week of tight quarters, bad food, boring lectures, jaded tourists, and throughout, "interminable waits while the tour leaders got their act together." Luckily, *Traveler* accepted Decca's essay.[16] She was also busy finalizing arrangements and publicity for the reissue of *Poison Penmanship* (originally published in 1979). Hill & Wang brought it back out in 1988, but it failed to garner the national attention Decca and her publisher would have liked.

Decca's pace would have punished people half her age. Her energy was still extraordinary. Yet, attempts to glorify aging struck her as ridiculous. "Actually it's very debilitating," she said, though it didn't seem so for her.[17] When her frenemy Betty Friedan published *The Fountain of Age*, describing aging as "empowering," Decca was merciless. Mocking Friedan's focus on how it *felt* to be an older woman—sexually, socially, and professionally—Decca's book review countered that the real issue was not getting in touch with some mystical womanly strength but rather joining the fight for "a single-payer system in which the government would replace the multibillion-dollar insurance industry" and older women could get decent health care.[18] Her message was unmistakable: Puleeze, Betty, get over yourself.

Decca did not agonize over her weight or thickened middle, never pretended to be other than who she was. Instead, she actively sought out young people to mentor and she tried to keep her focus off herself. When she lost a couple of teeth, her dentist encouraged her to get implants. "You don't want to look like a toothless old woman," he cautioned. "Why not," she replied, "as I am in fact a toothless old woman?"[19] She would have been embarrassed to be more concerned with her drooping eyelids than with someone else's health-care costs. Decca's attitude toward aging had roots, of course, in her upbringing, in the British aristocratic aversion to anything faux, the belief that it was always better to have an Aubusson with moth holes than a new machine-loomed rug made of nylon. In refusing to make a fuss about growing older, Decca was actually in sync with her background. She did not know how often her sisters lamented aging to one another, how much they obsessed about it, the measures they took to try to deflect it.

All the Mitford women tended to become more, not less, themselves as they aged, leaning into whatever qualities they had hitherto found most useful. Sydney had become even more practical as she aged, caring for the sheep on Inch Kenneth and keeping her ancient Aga stove going. Nancy had remained elegant, cold, brilliant, and snobbishly well-read until she died. Diana remained beautiful, thin to the vanishing point, superior, chatty, disdainful of others, and unapologetically fascist all her life. She suffered terrible headaches and lost her hearing, but her bearing and beliefs never changed. Pamela, the family rock, similarly clung to old habits, including staying out of the limelight. Debo's lifelong determination to be a duchess, locked in from childhood, led to her brilliant restoration of Chatsworth and the many economic innovations that allowed her to retain it. All hewed closely to the paths carved in their youth.

As a 1993 graduation speaker for the UC Berkeley Communications Department, Decca urged "plodding determination" as the key to success.[20] Her audience, used to humor that Decca admitted was sometimes "sourcastic," no doubt thought she was joking. She didn't strike many people as a plodder. But Decca never saw herself quite as others did. She knew she was intimidating, without fully understanding why. She saw herself as someone who worked hard and enjoyed life, but who lacked the "stellar quality" she saw, and deferred to, in a dazzling, dramatic friend like Maya Angelou.[21]

A term such as "steadfast" would have been more accurate than "plodding." Decca's consistency of character kept her grounded and made her instantly recognizable. It could also make her inflexible, even arrogant. Her sense of herself included her passionate advocacy on behalf of social justice, of course. She was even prouder of her ability to laugh at herself and the world, to not take herself too seriously, to avoid complaining or self-involvement. Her mother had a "slightly drooping mouth," which always made her look sad.[22] Decca's face was open and round, her mouth always turned upward. But the weight of being upbeat now began to show. Her eyes were heavily hooded and no longer electric blue. If no one was looking, they were often sad. She was still full of mischief, but there seemed less to laugh about.

As she moved into her seventies, Decca had a stock of essays or lectures ready to go: on Central America, muckraking, censorship and free speech, activism, and aging and creativity. Most were not getting published. She was placing travel essays, book reviews, forewords for others' books—all the sorts of pieces that were nearly impossible to re-use and therefore her least favorite forms.[23] Decca was extremely well connected. She knew everyone from Alice Walker to Salman Rushdie and from Dorothy Bryant to Carl Bernstein. Her frequent book reviews were often an occasion to defend her friends, sometimes against other friends, and just as often, a chance to skewer her enemies.[24] She rose to each battle, but they were short news-cycle affairs, not the kind of long-term campaign she preferred. Increasingly, her essays relied on stories she'd already told. Asked to write a foreword for her old friend Cedric Belfrage's book on HUAC and the Red Scare, Decca reminisced about meeting Belfrage when she and Bob were traveling on illegal passports, a story she'd often told in the past.[25]

Struggling to choose the next good subject is the bane of writers. It is typical for even the most accomplished writers to agonize over what's next. The impulse to accept the advice of agents or editors can be potent. Decca drew a sharp line between projects done for money, those done to further social change, and those, such as her last two books, done purely for love. She put up a steel wall on subject suggestions from anyone other than Bob and her closest friends. Agents and editors, in her view, were "supposed to be at one's beck and call and to follow through on one's instructions."[26] They were never to suggest content. "They are NOT to tell a person what to write. . . . The editor is essentially a helpmeet, who can be immensely useful if he/she sticks to the job of being an encourager, a goad when needed, and above all an intelligent & sympathetic dispassionate reader who can spot various deficiencies. . . . But never, ever, should the editor dictate the subject matter."[27]

By December 1988, four months after launching *Grace Darling*, Decca had her next book subject. Her agent, Renee Wayne Golden, a Hollywood lawyer, gave it to her.

The new topic was American childbirth. The book was to be in the mode of *The American Way of Death*.

On the surface, it seemed a very unlikely choice. Decca had, in fact, become interested in midwives through two friends, Peewee and Ted Kalman, whose daughter Janice had trained as a midwife but could not get a California license. Janice had an enviable track record as a practitioner. But she was being threatened with criminal prosecution, jail time, and fines. The Kalmans were terrified. Decca wrote a couple of local articles attempting to explain the "implacable hostility" of doctors and medical boards toward midwives. "Why?" she queried, are they so aggressive? "Follow the money."[28] Golden urged her to write up a proposal broadening the subject. Like embalming and expensive funerals, a book on childbirth could point out peculiarly American ideas, Golden thought, since most other countries encouraged midwifery. Birth was an expensive business that obstetricians did not want to give up. In 1989, the average cost of an insured hospital birth was $7,800, and a cesarean birth, $16,000.[29] Midwife-assisted births cost a fraction of that and reduced cesarean rates from roughly 20 percent to less than 2 percent.[30] No wonder that "the medical monopoly is trying to push midwives out," as one exposé at the time put it.[31] Decca should be able, Golden thought, to expose profiteering and exploit the narrative potential of conflicts with greedy physicians.

Golden arranged meetings with "the cream of the publishing industry" on February 17, 1989. Wanting Decca to be at her most charming,
Golden had the good sense to locate the meetings in Vivian Cadden's
large, airy, Manhattan apartment, where Decca could be comfortable and
relaxed. It had now been twenty-five years since Decca's last smash success and she knew she would not be dealing with Robert Gottlieb (now
at *The New Yorker*) and probably not dealing with Billy Abrahams either,
since her books for him had not come close to earning back her advances.
Decca woke before dawn, very nervous and "madly trying to scribble
down" bullet points that would sell unknown editors on the merits of the
new project.

Golden arrived at 7:30 a.m., direct from a red-eye flight, to find an
anxious author who'd been up, fretting, for hours. She set Decca straight.
You are not auditioning for the publishers, Golden told her. On the contrary, she had Decca repeat, "it's for ME to audition THEM." Just prior
to the meetings, Golden had set a bidding floor of $100,000, a bigger
initial advance than Decca had ever received. All day, editors traipsed
in and out of Cadden's Eighty-Fifth Street apartment: Delacourt/Ban-
tam, Simon & Schuster, Crown, Random House, Addison Wesley, and
Harper & Row all made cases for why they would do the best job with
Decca's new book.[32] As Decca had "general chitchat" with editors—"she
talked the bejeezus out of them," Golden later said—Golden fielded
phone offers in the background. Throughout the day, bids rose from
$100,000 to a $200,000 offer from Crown. The Random House team
came last. They offered $500,000 for the hardback rights to the book, "a
shower of gold the likes of which I've never seen," Decca marveled, an
amount that might nearly double when paperback rights were added in
(and that was somewhat ironic given Decca's earlier takedown of Random House founder Bennet Cerf).[33] Golden later claimed that when
Random House arrived, she held up five fingers as a silent signal of the
offer she wanted. The actual substance of the book, Golden claimed,

"never came up." The editors were vying for *Decca*, hoping for another sleeper hit like *The American Way of Death*.[34] She's a "miracle worker," Decca said of Golden.

Oddly, neither Decca nor her "miracle worker" agent had thought to look at her Dutton contract for *Grace Had an English Heart*. As was common, when it signed up *Grace Darling*, Dutton had retained the right of first refusal for whatever book Decca wrote next. Decca liked Billy Abrahams but was otherwise unhappy with Dutton. No one from Dutton had been invited to Golden's daylong auction. Golden now went to Dutton with Random House's offer and extracted an advance of $525,000 from them for the hardback rights to *The American Way of Birth*, enough money to leave Decca "secure in old age, & lots to leave my children & Oys [grandchildren]."[35] "I was very lucky," Golden later said.[36] Liking Dutton a bit better now, Decca signed a contract in the spring of 1989 with a deadline of June 1, 1991. It was a quick turnaround for a book requiring much research into areas about which Decca was "abysmally ignorant."[37] But the money was incredible.

Written when thirty-seven to forty million Americans still lacked health-care coverage and an additional fifty-three million Americans were underinsured, Decca planned to highlight "money and greed."[38] She intended "the whole thrust of my book . . . [to] be for the embattled midwives vs. medical establishment."[39] She hired Ted Kalman as a researcher, paying him ten dollars an hour and mileage (only Bob, her children, and a few of her closest friends knew about her "outsize" advance), scheduled interviews, and began investigations. Avoiding "hard luck" stories, just as she'd done with *Kind and Usual Punishment*, Decca focused her attention on policy questions, public opinion, and profits. Janice Kalman felt that Decca was "a wonderful advocate," who "used her privilege to good ends," could draw national attention to good causes, was consistent in her commitment to social justice, and just "so sassy" and fun to be with.[40]

Where *The American Way of Death* had opened new ground,

propelled by the explosive energy of exposé, Decca's new book did not uncover secrets. The long history of attacks on midwives as witches, beginning in medieval times, was already well known in the late 1980s and early 1990s. So was the American medicalization of childbirth, and the medical profession's disgraceful treatment of nurses, patients, and poor people. Indefensible increases in cesarean birth, approaching 25 percent nationally, and the overuse of fetal monitors were already well documented, as were skyrocketing medical costs and social inequities in health care. Decca's research was solid, but lacked the get-a-load-of-this quality of *The American Way of Death*.

The real energy in childbirth debates had come from years of feminist work into the ways men profited—in every sense of the term—from seizing control of reproduction and birth. Barbara Ehrenreich and others had published muckraking exposés. Laurel Thatcher Ulrich, along with other historians, had delved into the gendered history of American medicine. And for twenty years, the fight for women's health care as a fundamental right had galvanized feminist struggles. As the widely distributed and much-beloved book *Our Bodies, Ourselves* put it, more than a decade earlier, "We have needs that are not being met . . . [by] a medical system that can quickly dehumanize us during this most deeply human of experiences."[41]

It is hard to know how much of that work was familiar to Decca or Golden. Decca had been at odds with prominent feminists such as Andrea Dworkin and Catharine MacKinnon for years, frequently attacking their views of pornography as lending dangerous support to right-wing ideologues such as Jesse Helms. While the anti-pornography feminists and the women's health feminists were vastly different, Decca tended to lump them all together. She included well-known radical natural childbirth advocates such as Ina May Gaskin in her derisive dismissal of what she called feminism's "mushy" politics.[42] She couldn't stand talk about "sisterhood." Any celebration of pregnancy or childbirth she saw as part of the "new hifalutin sisterly gush." It brought out the instant snark in her.[43] It is possible that in spite of having many good friends who were feminists—including Marge Frantz, Maya Angelou, Angela Davis, Bettina Aptheker, Dorothy Bryant, Susan Griffin, and Grace Paley—Decca may have been unaware of the extent to which she was now stepping onto well-trod terrain.

Decca was a fighter. She was not a particularly flexible thinker. She was better at holding positions than at nuancing them. Having accepted the Communist dictum decades ago that gender politics were bourgeois, she stuck to that view, despite modeling a very feminist life. For someone as averse to personal sharing as Decca was, the bedrock feminist principle that "the personal is political" would always be off-putting. She was not unaware of how confounding her intransigence was. "Several devoted friends say I haven't got . . . feminist [bones]," she sometimes lamented.[44]

By the time Decca finished her book, she considered it "on the whole pro their pt of view," but predicted that "feminists may rather loathe it."[45] It might have been better if feminists *had* loathed her book. Most feminists simply ignored it. Ultimately, *The American Way of Birth* understood its targets better than its audience. Going from grave to cradle, or tomb to womb, as Decca liked to quip, could have made her, as one British newspaper put it, "the absolute expert on the American way of birth and of death."[46] But when *The American Way of Birth* finally appeared in 1992, it lacked either a clear connection to feminism or the key feature of *The American Way of Death*. Writing about live women made it hard to be funny, Decca learned. "There aren't many jokes in it," she acknowledged about her new book.[47] The book's strongest thread was Decca's animosity toward doctors: "a pretty boring & often wicked lot . . . supremely venal, money-grubbing, self-aggrandizing bores/monsters."[48]

Reviews were tepid.[49] One in *The New Republic* said *The American Way of Birth* was underresearched (a charge Decca never before had to face). It described Decca as a "curmudgeon who has lost her edge."[50] Many praised the book's emphasis on health care, its relevance to the upcoming Bush-Clinton election, and how well Mitford's narrative explained the safety of midwife-assisted births over forceps, fetal monitors, C-sections, and other high-tech interventions.[51] *The New York Times*, however, described the book as "much less amusing" than Mitford's other writing: highly dogmatic and ideological" and "a bit loopy."[52] A review in the *Chicago Tribune* was especially harsh. Reviewer Jean Griffin wrote: "If you need a primer on childbirth from the Middle Ages to the present day, with heavy emphasis on the goodness of midwives and the badness of (male) obstetricians, this is the book for you. But if you have read even a smattering of the literature on this subject published over the past 20 years or so, you won't find much new here. For the most part, the book is disappointingly general and pedantic, relying on already published reports."[53] *Newsweek* described the book as "personable"—faint praise indeed—and added that "none of this is new."[54] "Mitford misses the mark," another reviewer wrote: "a lot of bark but very little bite."[55] "Capably written," observed *The Atlantic*.[56]

Decca had a chance to respond to these critiques. With the paperback of *The American Way of Birth* scheduled to appear just after a national election that put health care front and center of national discussions, extensive edits were needed. Instead, Decca used the revisions not to answer her detractors but to explain the differences between the "managed competition" model being put forward by Clinton and the kind of system that existed in Canada. "Managed competition," she warned, would lead to "large-scale, corporate health-care entities run by a few large insurance companies," which is precisely the situation we find ourselves in now, where almost all large health insurance providers are owned by huge insurers.[57] Decca profoundly distrusted Bill Clinton, partly because of his refusal to intervene on behalf of James Dean Walker years earlier and partly because she found him "absurd" and overblown, and not good enough for Hillary, who Decca considered "smashing."[58] Somewhat reluctantly, Decca supported Governor Jerry Brown's presidential bid over Clinton's.[59] So, Decca made Clinton the villain in her paperback, just as he was being hailed by many as the hero of health-care reform.

In 1992, the BBC decided to film a documentary based on *The American Way of Birth*. They sent two young filmmakers, Liesel Evans and Steve Ruggi, to California. Evans, like Decca, was an "Honorable" who eschewed her rank and a socialist who detested titles. Both shared her politics, and she quickly came to adore them. They ended their documentary with an instrumental version of the Communist Party anthem "The Internationale." The film began with the Beach Boys' "Surfer Girl" and dramatic crashing-wave beach shots, very much a product of its times. The film gave equal attention to every oddball idea of birth, from ocean births with dolphins, to high-tech births with robots, all presented against a backdrop of psychedelic color and noise. The film contained some truly peculiar moments. One scene featured shots of Decca fondling the fake breasts of a man wearing an "empathy belly" (meant to teach men what the experience of pregnancy is really like from breasts to bladder). It also included inexplicable images of fighter jets, as well as a gratuitously grisly scene of a baby being extracted by C-section, and long shots of Decca, primly seated in a grimy-looking booth at San Francisco's "Real Good Karma Natural Food Restaurant," under enormous graphic murals of naked women enjoying natural childbirth.[60] Decca loved the film. Since it would not air in the United States (and never has), she rented an enormous theater—she could now afford to do so—and invited all her friends to a special screening.

At this time, Charlotte Mosley, Diana's daughter-in-law, stepped up to edit Nancy's letters. Decca was concerned that there might be another family attempt to whitewash the political past. "The whole point of letters is to reveal the writer & her various opinions & let the chips fall where they may. Censoring them for fear of offending the subjects is in my view absolutely wrong," Decca said.[61] Ultimately, she felt that

Mosley had done a "superb" job. But when she then asked Decca to contribute to a volume of letters among all the sisters and sent her samples, Decca declined to "be in the same book" with Diana.[62] It was painful, Decca said, to finally see some of the "v. catty items about me & Bob" that those letters contained.[63] She was struck to realize how much Nancy's insistence on working and having her own income had been "a huge influence on me, then and forever."[64]

Decca went through major spats with some of her closest friends at this time. She even fell out with Dobby Walker, "one of my very best friends, ever, anywhere." The slight that enraged Decca seemed quite small to other people. Dobby had asked Decca for a professional recommendation, based on Decca's "name recognition." Dobby did not ask Bob. Decca exploded. How dare Dobby suggest that Bob—"loved & admired throughout the Bay Area and by all generations"—had any less name recognition than her, or, for that matter, any less recognition than famous lawyers such as Leonard Boudin and Charles Garry? He was, Decca insisted, on par with any of them. She not only refused to provide the recommendation but then refused to act as a reference for a position Dobby badly wanted.[65]

Decca knew she was famous. And she nurtured her renown. Why then her rage at Dobby's request? To Decca, it must have been critically important that Bob also be thought of as famous. She may have needed that, unconsciously, to justify staying with him, remaining in her marriage. Perhaps she was reminding herself of what a good team they were. A famous team. An equally famous team. She may have needed that enough to push a good friend away.

When she fell out with Dobby, Decca had already lost a good friend, writer and activist Kay Boyle, to another disheartening dispute she called a "Deep freeze."[66] Boyle had been encouraging a biographer named Joan Mellen for years, asking all her friends to speak with her. After Mellen had done years of research work, conducted interviews, and undertaken extensive and expensive travel, Boyle suddenly pulled the plug. "Don't speak to Joan," Boyle now said. Decca was incensed. This "sudden dumping of you is too extraordinary," Decca told Mellen. "I don't specially like being ordered to talk/not talk to whom I may choose."[67] However much Decca cherished her friendships, if she believed her friends were wrong, she said so. "All cards on table etc. can be a splash of salt, just makes life more interesting, & friendship more enduring."[68] "All cards on table" did not work with Boyle or Dobby.

This strategy also nearly cost Decca her most important late-life friendship with her "sister," Maya Angelou. On August 25, 1991, Angelou published an Op-Ed in *The New York Times* strongly supporting the Supreme Court appointment of Clarence Thomas to replace the celebrated Black justice Thurgood Marshall.[69] She acknowledged Thomas's opposition to affirmative action, busing, and reparations as "lamentable." Yet, Angelou maintained that a Black conservative was still better than a white one. Despite Thomas's pattern of "indifference to African-American issues," Angelou believed that having a "culture in common with us" would eventually align him with Black causes. Moreover, she argued, the ancestors would connect Thomas to "the black youngsters of today."[70]

Anita Hill had not yet gone public—that would occur in October—but opposition to Thomas's appointment was stormy. On July 11, the Congressional Black Caucus had voted overwhelmingly against his appointment.[71] Almost all Black scholars, lawyers, legislators, and activists, and virtually every left-wing progressive in the country, opposed his appointment.[72] Decca considered Angelou's Op-Ed a "disgraceful effort." She was "appalled." When Angelou asked Decca her view, she gave it. Your Op-Ed is "disturbing" and "uncharacteristic of you," Decca wrote, attempting to tamp down her tone. While Decca frankly told friends, "Maya seems to have lost her way hopelessly," she tried to be measured, just as she'd been when Angelou exploded in Bellagio.[73] As desperate as she was to hold on to Angelou, however, Decca was equally determined to stand up to her this time: "true friendship does include being able to discuss differences of opinion on substantive matters."[74] When Angelou did not respond to her entreaties to "PLEASE GET IN TOUCH," Decca experienced a "terror that you would forever be on non-speakers . . . approaching the misery of death."[75] She reached out to Angelou continuously, calling, writing, and faxing. But she did not alter her view of Thomas.[76]

For Decca, friendship and talking were coterminous. She considered computers awful—"don't expect ME to master one of those dread machines"—and clung to phone calls and the intimacy of letters as long as she could.[77] "FAX machines!!! Never says I," she declared in 1988. Her attitude changed in late 1992, however, when the young BBC producers, Evans and Ruggi, had to install a fax machine in Decca's dining room so that they could quickly exchange script edits with the BBC team in London. Within days, Decca was "besotted" by the "amazing" machine—a "miracle" to be able to correspond almost instantly (she would have adored both email and the end of the long-distance phone charges).[78] She had always used letters to flesh out her ideas. She'd always answered them, as she'd been trained to do, by return of post. Now she answered faxes within the hour, expecting others to do the same and driving some friends and family, such as Debo, to insist on a moratorium on faxing. Decca was so taken with the possibilities of instant, free communication that she struck up a lively exchange by fax with Miss Manners, on proper fax etiquette. When Angelou, with whom Decca did finally get back on speakers, accepted George Bush's White House invitation and then Bill Clinton's request for an inaugural poem, Decca controlled her impulse to fire off instant fax comments. She told Angelou the invitations to the White House were wonderful, the poem was wonderful, and when a small scandal ensued over plagiarism charges, Decca was completely supportive.[79] As she wrote to Sally Belfrage, "the thing about Maya is that she's absolutely impervious to criticism of any kind," as Decca now well knew. Decca did not give in often, but even she could be no match for Angelou, one of the only people with whom Decca occasionally dropped her dukes.

Some of Decca's friends—Marge Frantz in particular—accused Decca of selling out in the wake of *The American Way of Birth*.[80] They said she'd become too bourgeois, dazzled by money and comfort. In 1991, Debo, who was attended by approximately seven hundred staff at Chatsworth, complained on British television that Decca—still in the same modest Oakland house—was living like an aristocrat. "She can't do a thing for herself," Debo groused.[81] Decca had not changed. She'd always been delighted with the privileges of wealth—good food, expensive alcohol, soft beds, first-class travel—provided she did not have to change her principles or pay for such excesses herself. More than any of her other friends, Angelou had always understood this and encouraged Decca to get her hands on everything she could.

In truth, Decca was extremely generous with her new wealth, lavishing money on her children and grandchildren, giving money away to her friends. She and Bob had purchased a building in New York and for years they subsidized a couple living in it. When Dinky and Terry moved from Atlanta to New York in the fall of 1990, Decca and Bob undertook all expenses (and stresses) to remodel part of the building for them. Yet, Decca also remained as frugal as ever when it came to herself. She rented the cheapest quarters she could find in England and flew coach when she was paying her own airfare. She was happy to give Dinky thousands of dollars but, at the same time, hounded her to fill out a fake invoice declaring the money as payment for research expenses, so that she could write it off her taxes.

When she was honored as a New York Public Library Literary Lion on November 8, 1990, along with Rita Mae Brown, Stanley Kunitz, August Wilson, Gwendolyn Brooks, Alfred Kazin, Gloria Naylor, Art

Buchwald, and others, Decca wore a borrowed outfit. The floor-length dark dress, with sparkles and appliqued swirls, probably looked elegant on Maya Angelou, whose dress it was. On Decca, with dark beads and a cane, it looked more like something a hippie would wear when required, as Decca put it, to don her "unaccustomed best." Decca was not in high heels. Her hair was not styled. She was seated with Brooke Astor, in pink satin and gold, and surrounded by Barbara Bush (in a shimmering red-and-purple gown), Fran Lebowitz (in a tuxedo) and Henry Kissinger; yet she was not in the least intimidated. If anything, she was bored. For her, the event was stiff and artificial, with people too dressed up to actually enjoy themselves, in rooms too noisy for the kind of chatting she loved. She may have thought of herself as a somewhat plodding writer, who had to work hard for everything she had, and who traded in facts and information rather than brilliant bursts of imagination and art. But she was always sure of herself, and sure about her preferences. Some writers would kill to be Literary Lions. To Decca, it was "in all a weird & forgettable moment."[82]

Decca did love parties, being honored, being in large groups of friends and comrades. She relished informal events where people could laugh, carry on conversations, and argue: the kinds of parties she and Bob always threw and that, on occasion, could get out of hand (Decca, who was drinking to excess, did not rein them in). In throwing Decca and Bob a fiftieth wedding anniversary party, on June 20, 1993, in the First Unitarian Church of Kensington (invariably called "the FUCK"), Benjy and Dinky honored Decca and Bob's taste. Decca had specified that there be "no seated dinner with interminable courses of horrible catered food." She wanted funny speeches (short ones), poems, songs, parodies, and roasts.[83] The celebration included a photocopied songbook, distributed to each guest, filled with comic and sometimes original tunes. "Oh Lord, I Wish I Was a Single Girl Again" came first, followed by "The Red Flag," "Piano Tuner's Lament," "Right, Said Fred" [Decca's favorite song], "The Grace Darling Song," and others, all accompanied by Black pianist and composer Charles Darden.

In 1994, Benjy found a way to turn his manic energy into a project and defy the Cuban embargo. His campaign combined serious politics and hijinks. Under the banner "Senda Piana to Havana," Benjy was attempting to replace termite-ridden old Steinways and Russian pianos (Cuba's humidity made any wooden object vulnerable to infestation) with used pianos in better condition. Decca kept her fax machine whirring with appeals for funds and news of his pranks. For years, Cubans had been repairing decaying pianos with airline cable and tape. World-class musicians were being trained on trash.[84] As a British documentary captured on film, Benjy dressed up as a piano to attempt entry into the American embassy in Havana. Denied permission, he paraded in full piano costume up and down the city's Malecón.

Decca turned to music around this time as well, first to let off steam and have some fun, then, perhaps, more seriously. For years, she'd been belting out songs with Maya Angelou whenever they were invited to sing—and sometimes when they were not invited at all. Their favorite song, "Right, Said Fred" was a silly ballad about two hapless movers who keep pausing their labors to have a "cup of tea." Their other favorite was the Beatles' "Maxwell's Silver Hammer." Decca performed both with such verve at a book fair in the Bay Area that she caught the attention of a local musician, Kathie Goldmark, who was inspired to form a band around Decca—"Decca and the Dectones." The band was just quirky enough (its lead instrument was a kazoo) and Decca was still just famous enough for Decca and the Dectones to be popular. They performed at local nightclubs in the Bay Area and at New York's Town Hall on May Day 1995. They recorded an album under Goldmark's "Don't Quit Your Day Job" label. Decca told everyone that she was now a "rock star." She dressed up, wore fancy Elton John–style glasses, and warbled away on stage in complete delight. Christopher Cerf, Bennet Cerf's son, threw a fundraising party for Decca and her band. Bob Gottlieb was one of the guests. "Can't you stop her?" he pleaded to Bob Treuhaft. "My dear," Gottlieb told Decca, "in all the years that I've attended every sort of musical event, never, ever have I heard anything quite so a-tonal, so lacking in the rudiments of rhythm, so out of tune as your performance."[85]

In addition to the band, Decca found the energy for many new projects and ideas in the middle years of the 1990s. She tried a weekly column, "Jessica Mitford's Diary" for *The Times* (she could write about anything she wanted and completed four of them, then stopped). She collected material for a possible new book on white racism. She taught courses at San Francisco State and the University of Michigan (which she combined with as many Midwestern lectures as she could). She participated in a lengthy interview project intended first for *Vanity Fair* and then *The New Yorker*, but that never appeared. She wrote a substantial article on the British aristocracy (beginning with a defense of David Cannadine's work) that was also intended for *Vanity Fair* and that also never appeared. Her biggest project was a revised and updated version of *The American Way of Death*, intended to survey all the changes in dying, death, and burial/cremation over the last thirty years.

It was a remarkably ambitious agenda given both her age and the fact that she had never taken particularly good care of her health. Decca avoided doctors, who she feared would poke and prod, tell her to exercise or, even worse, to give up drinking. When she was finally persuaded to see a doctor at seventy-three years old, Decca had her first mammogram, was put on thyroid medicine, and was told her cholesterol was way too high, which she attributed to a childhood in the Cotswolds with constant cream, butter, and cheese. She refused to take it very seriously. She continued drinking but began a moderate program of exercise on a stationary bicycle, trying to log a mile or so a day.

Compared to some of her circle, it seemed to Decca that she and

Bob were doing quite well. Bob's affair had been put firmly in the past, and was not spoken of, and both were in better health than many of their friends or family. In June 1992, a friend of Decca's, food writer and author M. F. K. Fisher (who had lived in a cottage on David Pleydell-Bouverie's ranch for more than twenty years), passed away after years of failing health and pain. Decca hoped that "Dink wld never let that happen to me—she knows all the ways to put one out of one's misery."[86] In November 1993, Decca's cousin "Rudben" died. Later that same month her good friend Jill Tweedie, who was only fifty-seven, passed away. "Horridness of Grim Reaper," Decca said.[87] In April 1994, Decca's sister Pamela died, unexpectedly, at the age of eighty-six, after a lifetime of robust health. Pamela had not only been the healthiest sister, she'd also been the calmest, most steadying, most reliable of them all. In London, Pamela fell down a set of stairs and broke her leg. It was a bad break and required pins. The surgery went well, and she seemed to be recovering. Then, without warning, she died of an embolism. "So—that's that," Decca wrote her children, "a quick & merciful death."[88] Although she had never quite gotten over the scrapbook fracas, or over Pamela's closeness to Diana, Decca loved Pamela.[89] It is "gloom all around," she wrote Debo.[90] Nevertheless, she did not fly to England for the Swinbrook funeral.[91]

Decca dealt with her anxieties about dying by mocking them. Increasingly, she began to plan both her own obituary and her own memorial service. She lined up different friends to write her obituary when the time came and drafted detailed instructions if the wrong people got the assignment. Decca had long joked about having an elaborate ceremony with plumed horses drawing a glass hearse, a band playing, and all the local streets closed off in her honor. She could "splurge," she teased, on "the Southern Wisteria" casket "with its delicately embroidered needlework interior" or on "the Sheridan" casket, with its "two-needle shirred pillow."[92] In fact, she had already made arrangements for the simplest and least expensive cremation possible, a cost she was proud to bring in at $562—for when the time came.

Decca's thinking about death prior to 1995 had mostly been professional. In 1995, her interest began to look prescient.

She had fallen twice in 1994, breaking first her ankle, then her wrist. She was unsteady because she was drinking. Her family urged her to go to "one of those drying-out places," but Decca knew herself too well to attempt "all that appalling Frank Talk."[93] She decided to quit drinking on her own, in spite of being so dependent now that she was often drinking before 7:00 a.m. On November 22, 1994, she announced that she was done with alcohol. To everyone's shock, and Bob's especially, from that moment on she did not have a drink. "To my surprise," she wrote Debo, she "didn't even miss it."[94]

Her ankle refused to heal. Then, in May 1996, Bob became dangerously ill following oral surgery. When he stopped eating, lost the ability to speak, and couldn't understand what was going on around him, an ambulance was finally called. On May 29, a large abscess was removed from his jaw, sepsis was diagnosed, and after a brief decline, he began improving. By mid-June he was back to his office daily.

Decca had started a walking regimen to strengthen her ankle. She began with just a block or two, and with the assistance of a walker. Within months she was able to log miles in Berkeley and Oakland, with the help of paid walking companions and a cane. But her ankle continued to bother her, and her hip ached. She attributed that to her bad gait from the sore ankle. The pain did not subside. In late June, she began coughing up blood, even when she was just clearing her throat, which seemed to be always bothering her. She assumed it was nothing and didn't mention it to Bob or Dinky, but reported it to her doctor and to Lisa Pollard, a local musician, who'd been helping Bob and was walking with Decca. Over the next days, Decca's health deteriorated. Dinky flew in from New York, arriving July 3. She persuaded Decca that hospital tests were needed (Decca was reluctant) and accompanied her mother to have them done.

The tests revealed lung cancer and extensive metastasis, including cancer in her brain. The doctor showed them scans of Decca's bones. They seemed covered in white spots. "That's cancer," the doctor said. "That too." "So are those." It was especially bad in her hip.

Dinky and Decca sat in the doctor's office together as Decca took in the news. She did not cry. She did not shake. She did not rail. Told that she might live another eight months or so, and given her treatment options, Decca had only two questions: "Can I work, and for how long?" and "Can I go to Wellfleet in August with my family?" She agreed to radiation only, no chemotherapy or other measures, so that she could function as long as possible and finish her book. Lisa Pollard thought Decca gave in to sobbing only once, closed in a car with Bob, as she shared her diagnosis with him. "She wasn't one to share sadness," Dinky said.

Shortly before her diagnosis Decca had said that what she could not stand was a "self-pitying whiner." Now she asked for chocolate mousse and visits from her friends. She quietly endured radiation to slow the cancer's spread.[95] In spite of everything she felt "v. well," she said, and was only in pain from her hip and ankle.[96] She was given pain pills and antidepressants. She did not drink. She still counted on finishing *The American Way of Death* and also going to Cape Cod, where she looked forward to seeing both of her grandsons, as well as old friends. She made plans. She worked. She initiated lawsuits. "We all operated under the rule of Dec," Lisa Pollard said. Decca sent out mailers and flyers to anyone—Debo especially—who she thought might contribute to Benjy's Senda Piana to Havana project and was pleased to see his fundraising rise in direct proportion to her declining health, "on ground that you can't refuse a dying person's request," she quipped to Debo.[97] Debo wanted to fly out immediately, but Decca dissuaded her, saying she hoped to come to England in the fall or for Christmas. "But DO come to me funeral," she wrote, "about 9 months or a year off accdg to the Dr. I thought I'd make SCI [Service Corporation International, her old funeral industry adversary] give me a free one with all the best? I'll let you know as plans progress."[98]

On July 10, unable to sleep, Decca wrote Bob, asleep upstairs, a letter. "Bob—it's so ODD to be dying, so I must just jot a few thoughts— starting with fact that I've SO enjoyed life with you in all ways. . . . Mainly, of course, you've been incredibly GOOD to me all through life and have TAUGHT me more than I can say, not to mention being incredibly kind & forgiving of faults such as Impatience. I must say I'm glad it's me first as I v. much doubt I'd bother to go on much if it was you. Also there really is a small bonus—I wonder if you agree? In knowing ahead of time so one can think things out a bit (not just finish book—you know what I mean)." Toward the end of a letter that reminisced lovingly about their meeting and their past, with no recrim- inations, no snark, no resentment, she added: "You'll need someone—I mean you've got all those household skills, cooking etc., pity to waste don't you agree? Be thinking of someone agreeable. You won't have to as they'll come flocking I bet. I do have some ideas but fear to mention for fear of annoying or being intrusive, none of my business you'll say."[99]

Over the next few weeks, her condition worsened. The doctors short- ened their prognosis—her "deadline" Decca called it—from eight months, to six, then to three. So many friends came to "chat" and sing that it was like a "sort of nonstop party," Decca said. "Needless to say I'm taking full advantage, everyone's bringing meels on wheels, delicious things for me & all marvelous helpers who are absolutely smoothing every path here."[100] As the cancer progressed, Decca was persuaded to reenter the hospital for more radiation. But swelling had already produced pressure on Decca's brain. She had a stroke-like episode that left her nearly paralyzed on one side of her body and impeded her speech. She was done with treatment and wanted to go home. A hospital bed was set up in her front room. The family was called. Maya Angelou was called. "Get out here," they were told. Encircling her bed, friends and family sang Decca's favorite songs. Decca had trouble moving or speaking. But whenever someone got the words wrong, she'd rouse herself to correct them.

In the evening of July 22, Decca had Debo reached by telephone. Decca's words were undecipherable, but she seemed to hear her sister well. After the phone call, friends and family surrounded her bed again and sang.

On July 23, 1996, Decca died, in her living room, at home. Her grandson Chaka was holding her hand. Dinky, Benjy, Katie Edwards, Marge Frantz, and others, were at her bedside. Bob, too anxious and upset to stay still, had walked in and out of Decca's room dozens of times throughout her last day.

IMMEDIATELY AFTER HER DEATH, DECCA'S fax machine began churning. The Associated Press asked someone "who knew her" to confirm that Decca had died. Reporters from both local and national papers faxed in requests for quotes they could use from the family. There were faxes from fact-checkers, faxes of condolences, poems (Susan Griffin sent a poem she'd written for the occasion and Debo faxed Poe's "Annabel Lee," which Decca had loved to recite), reminiscences, and dozens of obituary drafts sent to the family with requests for edits, comments, or additions before printing. All day the next day, "the phone has been ringing off the hook," assistant Karen Leonard noted, "because every funeral director in the county seems to be calling me," offering to "do" Decca's funeral.[101]

Decca managed a few post-death pranks. Her friends snuck a perfect Decca Tease into her *New York Times* obituary (not an easy feat since celebrity obituaries are always prewritten and only slightly updated as needed at the last minute). It claimed that she'd asked for the most elaborate funeral possible, complete with a carriage, horses, and embalming, with "streets blocked off, dignitaries to declaim sobbingly over the flower-smothered bier, proclamations to be issued."[102] Like the obituary in *The Times*, most of Decca's obituaries, of which there were dozens, were both warm and riddled with errors. The constancy of Decca's myriad contradictions, her lifelong insistence on being a both/and person, seemed to confound many of the obituary writers, who wanted to sum her up simply.

Decca's second post-death tease was also preplanned. Karen Leonard, at Decca's direction, followed her death with a letter, from Decca, to the president of the SCI Corporation, the nation's largest funeral conglomerate, suggesting that he should reimburse the family the $425 they paid for Decca's funeral, considering all the publicity she'd brought them over the years.[103]

The first memorial for Decca was in San Francisco, attended by over six hundred people, "standing room only."[104] Speakers included Shana Alexander, Doug Foster, Pat Holt, Buddy Green, Benjy, Molly Ivins, and Maya Angelou, who came in a limo and left in a huff, evidently upset over who had the microphone.[105] It was, overall, the kind of party Decca liked best. Two friends, Dugald Stermer and attorney Anne Weills, arranged another post-death Decca Tease. They hired a glass hearse—filled with Decca's writings—six plumed horses, and a top-hatted driver to lead a cortege through closed San Francisco streets. Lisa Pollard's Green Street Mortuary Band followed the hearse, playing dirges, hymns, "When the Saints Come Marching In," and Decca's favorite songs.

The London memorial was organized by a committee of English friends. Originally slated for November, it had to be postponed, partly to accommodate Maya Angelou's travel schedule. The committee rented a large theater, with a deposit secured by Debo. Bob put up $3,000 toward the fundraising. The organizers planned a series of speeches, video clips, readings from Decca's works, and an exhibition in the theater lobby, designed to educate mourners about "the availability of cheap funerals," complete with information about cardboard coffins and green burials.[106]

Someone at *The Times* caught wind of the planning and wrote a "corker" of a story, representing the planned memorial as a total "circus." The "star turn," the paper claimed, "will be given to four undertakers parading their wares" and "anybody who is interested will be able to order a coffin . . . and coffins for pets will be on offer" as well.[107]

Debo had a fit. She would not, she told Dinky, have any part in such a "publicity stunt designed to surprise and shock." Moreover, she added, she'd never been to a non-Christian memorial and wasn't keen to see one.[108] Dinky understood how much Decca and Debo "loved each other, in spite of deep differences and hostilities," and she did everything that she could think of to placate Debo.[109] The exhibition plans were scrapped. A ticketed event, by invitation only, the London memorial also drew six hundred people. But Debo did not attend.

Bob helped make sure that Decca had the last word. He retired from his practice and devoted a year to finishing the revised edition of *The American Way of Death*, with help from Decca's assistants. The new edition appeared in 1998 and has never been out of print. "Even in death, the Associated Press noted, "Mitford continues to serve as the Scourge of those who would profit obscenely from dying." Decca's muckraking, *Business Week* had to admit, remains "a jolt to the funny bone" and a serious jolt at that.

Equally famous for birth and death by the time she died, Decca had been able to turn both to her advantage. Although she was born quietly at home on her family's British estate, she made her childhood and family into an American legend and a cautionary tale. And although her expertise in dying and medical care could not conquer her cancer, Decca died on her own terms, exactly as she wanted to go, leaving pranks behind her as she departed. It was her nearly eighty years of life, Decca knew, that really mattered, nearly eighty years lived exactly as she chose to live them, in defiance—and in brilliant use—of both the accident of birth and the inevitability of death.

ACKNOWLEDGMENTS

I t is a great privilege to thank all of those who helped me tell Jessica Mitford's story. I am honored that so many who admired and adored her have trusted me to put her important choices into context.

This book was completed during a pandemic which has also been a period of many personal losses: both of my parents (Bernard and Rosalyn Kaplan, fierce anti-fascists who believed in the power of stories to inspire) and four of my closest friends (Amy Kaplan, Deborah "Shocky" Greenberg, Adam Levinson, and Robert Finch—all great storytellers). It went into production just as our country's cruel administration began trying to push us into tyranny. I appreciate everyone who helped me "forge ahead," as Mitford would say, in the face of those challenges.

Institutional support was provided by Northeastern University, and I am especially grateful to Acting Dean Ronald Sandler, English Department Chair Neal Lerner, and Dean Kellee Tsai for her support of the Humanities, WGSS, and *Signs*. Northeastern University's skilled audio-visual and IT staff, Terry Beadle especially, turned family snapshots into high-resolution images and MacJerry Lubin helped me archive thousands of digitized archival documents. The research support provided by my endowed chair helped underwrite research and digitization. I am grateful to Northeastern University President Joseph E. Aoun and Zeina Aoun, for many years of encouragement across two different coasts.

At Northeastern, I have been fortunate to have a strong feminist scholarly community in Women's, Gender, and Sexuality Studies, thanks to the outstanding work of Suzanna Walters, with whom I also edit the journal *Signs*. Suzanna knows more about creating strong feminist formations than anyone I know, and it has been a joy to work with her in WGSS, the journal, and the Feminist Public Intellectuals Project; she is both fierce and fun. I also want to thank the entire *Signs* team, and particularly Miranda Outman and Andrew Mazzaschi. At WGSS we all benefit from the incredible skill and patience of Kiki Samko, who has my sincere thanks. The English Department staff has also provided myriad forms of assistance, and I am especially grateful to Linda Collins and Jennifer Lobisser, brilliant contract sentries.

Mitford's primary archives, at the Ransom Center at the University of Texas at Austin, and at Ohio State University in Columbus, total nearly four hundred boxes of material, plus hundreds of audio and video recordings. They also include additional odd items Mitford saved, such as massive scrapbooks and small containers of human remains. This biography would have been inconceivable without those archives, and I am immensely grateful to Susan Floyd in Texas and the incomparable Emily Corey in Columbus Ohio for their stellar work digitizing documents. Emily Corey worked in the beginning of the project and then gamely came back on board at the end to help with fact-checking and proofreading; she is a consummate professional and a great friend.

Over the years, many Northeastern University graduate students became invaluable members of "Team Decca." In the early years of the project, Brent Griffin, Lana Cook, Laura Hartmann, Lauren Kuryloski,

Sarah Payne, Abbie Levesque, Rachel Molko, Aleks Galus, William Quinn, Tabitha Clark, Hailley Delaine Danielson-Owczynsky and Rhiannon Callahan were indispensable in digitizing, archiving, transcribing, transferring digital materials between different formats, assembling bibliographies, inventorying material, and doing background research. In the later years of the project, background research, bibliographies, fact-checking, and proofreading were aided immeasurably by the able hands of Adam Tomasi and Elisa Fuhrken. Adam and Elisa particularly made Decca their own; I appreciate their curiosity and passion for Decca and the importance of anti-fascist allies. The chronological bibliography of Mitford's writing, the only such record of her work I am aware of, is largely the work of Adam and, especially, Elisa, who also assembled this book's bibliography. Nikita Allgire helped with the project in Berkeley California.

Foundations, libraries, and Humanities centers provided critical resources, release time from teaching, and the camaraderie of other writers with whom I was able to discuss this work. I was awarded a National Endowment for the Humanities "Public Scholar" grant in the initial cohort of NEH "Public Scholar" Fellows, and I am especially grateful to Mark Silver who facilitated our year. Like all NEH fellows, I look forward to a vigorous return of that program. At the Suzy Newhouse Center for the Humanities at Wellesley I spent a wonderful year as the Mary L. Cornille Distinguished Scholar in Residence in the company of Anne Harrington, Beth Desombre, Duncan White, Eugene Marshall, Kate Grandjean, Kristin Williams, Marje Abe, and Yasmine Ramadan. My time at the Newhouse was made especially productive by Program Coordinator Jane Jackson and my two Wellesley research assistants, Molly F. Tyler and Hana L. Glasser. I am grateful to Director Carol Dougherty for her kind invitation to come to the Newhouse. I also received support for this project as the Fannie Hurst Visiting Professor at Washington University, and as a recipient of a New England Regional Fellowship Consortium grant which assisted my research at the Schlesinger, Smith, Houghton and Massachusetts Historical Society libraries. An early research fellowship at the Ransom Center at Austin was also instrumental. At Northeastern I received a fellowship at the Humanities Center, for a year the Center devoted to "Authority and Subversion" and I am grateful to Center Director Lori Lefkovitz and the other fellows— Candice Delmas, Ekaterina Botchkovar, Risa Kitagawa, Williams S. Miles, Summer Marion, Matthew Bowser, and Patricia Mabrouk—as well as Gabrielle Fiorenza, Center manager. Although I was unable to accept it, I was honored to be offered a yearlong fellowship at the extraordinary Leon Levy Center for the Study of Biography.

The libraries listed under Principal Archives were all exceptionally helpful. I would like to thank Ellen Shea and Marilyn Dunn at the Schlesinger; Nanci Young, Leslie Fields, and Kate Long at Smith; Pat Fox, Richard P. Watson, and Bridget Gayle Ground at the Ransom Center; and Eric Johnson, Jolie Braun, and Rebecca Jewett at OSU.

This book benefited from discussions with students in a number of seminars, including "American Women Writers" and "Public Humanities." I also benefited from discussions with students in a recent dissertation workshop and students in my graduate and undergraduate courses on muckraking. I benefited especially from an Independent Study on Literary Journalism that Jonathan Fitzgerald talked me into; I probably learned more from him than he did from me.

I had the occasion to give talks on Mitford and receive audience responses and questions from the Faculty Research Group of Civil Rights and Restorative Justice; Dorothy Helly and Graduate Center lectures, the American Literatures and Cultures Workshop, and King's College in London. I also benefited from an early ASA panel I organized with two of the nation's leading scholars of muckraking, Cecilia Tichi and Brooke Kroeger. This book began when the Women Writing Women's Lives seminar brought in Constancia Romilly to discuss Peter Sussman's book of Decca's letters. I am grateful to everyone at WWWL, and to Sydney Stern and Carla Peterson in particular.

Biographers International is a terrific resource for biographers. It is a great pleasure to have found "my people" on its splendid board of directors.

I am indebted to the many friends and family who became interested in Decca and remained interested in me: Margaret Burnham, Joseph Allen Boone, Rae Chesny, Erin Cramer and Neil Heathcote, Lucinda Crofton, Eric Daigneault, Irene Echenique, Alice Echols, Jeff Elmer, Gretchen Gerzina, Nicole and Ryan Hart (and BunBun), Coppelia Kahn, my sister Clair Kaplan, Kitty Kelley, Deborah Kruger, Kate Clifford Larson, Lindy Lohmann, Megan Marshall, Roxanne Davis May, Monica Miller, Durba Mitra, Marilyn Neimark, Sue Quinn, Necee Regis, Susanne Salem-Schatz, Lari Schwartz (my other sister), Kathy Shorr, Alisa Solomon, Claudia Springer and Geoff Adams, my nephew David Kaplan Taylor and my niece Brett Snyder, Sara Young and David Watson (thanks for plucking us from the river and trying to make something of us), and Rafia Zafar. Particular forms of help for which I am grateful were provided by Emma Walters, Jessica Salky, Jon Deer, my cousin Elisabeth Kaplan and Bob Horton (excellent archivists), Peter Tighe, Lorna Kaplan, Liz Grant, Elisabeth Dupuis, Duane Wesemann, Diane Weisenberg, Gail Reid, and Lissa Warren.

Everyone I interviewed for this book was generous and thoughtful. Almost without exception each, at some point, said "Decca was Decca." Aware that I had never met her, many tried to explain how unique Decca was, how funny, and tough and brave. They wanted me to understand that she both glittered and glowered. I especially want to single out Mitford's sister, the late Duchess of Devonshire, who gave me a full day in 2008, Decca's grandsons Chaka and James, her assistant Catherine (Katie) Edwards, and, most especially, her daughter Constancia "Dinky" Romilly, who let me turn to her over and over again with questions which must have been tedious.

Many people helped me navigate visits to the places important to Decca. I thank Rosie Pearson at Asthall, Susan Lyall at Swinbrook, the Duchess of Devonshire at Chatsworth, Ben Weber at Regent Street in Oakland, Inch Kenneth owner Claire Barlow and caretakers Carol Perry and Wayne Hamilton, Almudena Cros and Kevin Ingram in and around Madrid, Roxanne May in Oakland, and owners Kim and Curry Hammack, as well as James Lyon and Patricia Sullivan at Pea Level, the Durr family home in Wetumpka Alabama, where I was also able to meet and talk to Lucy Hackney, Lulah Colan, and Tilla Durr.

I am a member of a wonderful biographers' discussion group, which includes Sara Catterall, Eve Kahn, Amy Reading, Christine Cipriani, and Allison Gilbert, all of whom provide enthusiasm and support. While writing this book I was also a member of two writing groups which I could depend on for great feedback, criticism, and suggestions. I thank Nancy Cott, Susan Reverby, and Ann Braude as well as Carol Oja and Susan Ware (who read every chapter and helped with the title). The Susans have my special gratitude.

In addition to my writing groups, a number of friends read the book manuscript either in whole or in part and I am deeply grateful for their feedback: Susan Ware, Amy Reading, Amanda Vaill, Katie Edwards, Liese Mayer, Peter Sussman, and Steve Larsen.

I would like to thank my amazing team of women at Harper-Collins: Michele Cameron in design, Robin Bilardello and Frances Ross in art, copy editor Jane Cavolina, Frieda Duggan in production editorial, Alison Elliott-Yarden in audiobooks, Kelsey Young in foreign rights, Yelena Nesbit and Katie O'Callaghan in publicity and marketing, Associate Editor Edie Astley, and of course, my editor, Sara Nelson, who generously made sure this book did not get orphaned and who championed its many photographs.

Troublemaker was initially acquired by the extraordinary Gail Winston, with whom I had the privilege of working on *Miss Anne in Harlem*. Gail does not throw praise around lightly, but she provides just the right encouragement where and when it is needed. Her interest in Mitford's story and her early enthusiasm for the project meant the world to me. I had the good fortune to land at Hurst in the UK and Commonwealth and be able to work with a dream team of women who are committed to Decca's legacy and fighting spirit. My editors Lara Weisweiller-Wu and Mei Jayne Yew immediately grasped what I was trying to do and why this story of allyship and activism matters. Raminta Uselytė is a genius of a publicist—fun, fierce, and creative. I would also like to thank Daisy Leitch in Production, and Kathleen May and Rubi Kumari in Sales & Marketing.

Robin Hultgren took my author photo, as she has done for every trade book I've published. Neil Giordano came through once again, doing incredible work on the photo permissions for this book.

In Brettne Bloom I have the best agent in the business, and I've now had the pleasure of working with her on three books. She is smart, kind, and fierce and she loves a good story. I never want to do a book without her. She is a true friend.

Peter Sussman, the editor of Mitford's letters, was far more generous than he had to be and far more generous than is usual. He not only made time for me whenever I had questions, but he turned over his excess research materials to me so that I could use them in this book. Then he read portions of the manuscript and offered his usual hard-nosed editing, which I appreciate. Most importantly, Peter and Pat took me into their circle of friends, and I treasure that. I would never have attempted this book without Peter's support.

Mitford's children, Constancia "Dinky" Romilly and Benjamin Treuhaft have been nothing but gracious, forbearing, cooperative, available, and generous. They have never asked me to leave anything out of this story, never failed to promptly answer any of my dozens of emails, and never refused assistance they were able to provide. From the day that I first met them in New York, they have been steadfast about my doing this, even as the timeline stretched. Getting to know them both, and Dinky especially, has been a great joy. This book would have been impossible had they not been so open and helpful.

My husband, Steve Larsen, is a writer's dream partner. He built me and Decca a Tiny House to retreat to so that my labrador Otis and I always had a quiet place to work. He accompanied me on trips to England, Scotland, Inch Kenneth, and Austin, as well as on numerous swim treks and daily ocean, river, and pond swims where email could not reach me. He generously took over household tasks so that I could write, did all the cooking and kept up our homes. He also read the manuscript, offering his smart, insightful, understated feedback, and learning more about Decca and the British aristocracy than he ever thought possible. As a union organizer Steve was trained as a professional troublemaker. But his anti-authoritarianism is innate. It manifested, I'm told, even in his early childhood. This book is dedicated to Steve and his troublemaking ways, with love and gratitude.

NOTES

A note about family names: Mitford's sisters will generally be referenced in the following notes with the last name of Mitford, rather than their married names or titles, but exceptions to that rule are made when other names, used by the addressee or a publisher, may be more convenient to locate referenced sources. The same principle is applied to other family members with multiple names, such as Cavendish and Devonshire.

Principal Archives and Abbreviations

CH   Chatsworth House Archives
FBI   Jessica Mitford's FBI Records
HER   Herefordshire Archive and Records Centre, Herefordshire, England
HO   Houghton Library, Harvard University
HRC   Jessica Mitford Papers, Harry Ransom Research Center, University of Texas, Austin
JM-CK   Jessica Mitford Papers in personal collection of the author, donated by Peter Sussman, Leah Garchik, Jerry Garchik, Tilla Durr, Edmund Romilly, Constancia "Dinky" Romilly, and others
MF   Marge Frantz Papers, Smith College Library
NYU   Robert Treuhaft Papers, Tamiment Library & Robert F. Wagner Labor Archives, New York University
OSU   Jessica Mitford Papers, Ohio State University. (In July 2024 OSU renumbered their massive Mitford collection of more than 238 boxes. Box and folder numbers listed here correspond to the published Finding Aid preceding that renumbering.)
PdL   Pele de Lappe Papers, San Francisco State University Labor Archives and Research Center
SR   Selden Rodman Papers, Beinecke Library, Yale University
VD   Virginia Durr Papers, Schlesinger Library, Radcliffe Center for Advanced Study

Interviews conducted by the author

Thomas Alpert
Bettina Aptheker
Judith Bernal (Glassner/Viorst)
Anne de Courcy
Mary Clemmey
Almudena Cros
Deborah Devonshire
Tilla Durr
Katie Edwards
Marge Frantz
Chaka Forman
James Forman, Jr.
Michael Ferber
Leah Garchik
Jerry Garchik
Renee Golden
Lennie Goodings
Robert Gottlieb
Jonathan Guinness
Marina Guinness
Selina Hastings
Kevin Ingram
Coppelia Kahn
Kathy Kahn
Janice Kalman
Helena Kennedy
Corby Kummer
Jonathan Mandell
Victor Navasky
Dan Okrent
Rosie Pearson
Lisa Pollard
Jamie Raskin
Lauren Robertson
Constancia Dinky Romilly
Edmund Romilly
Robert Scheer
Seattle Burial Cooperative
John Simon
Jon Snow
Peter Sussman
Polly Toynbee
Marina Warner
Ben Weber
Maud Winchester

A Note to the Reader

1. An excellent selection of these letters has been published as *Decca: The Letters of Jessica Mitford*, edited by Peter Sussman, Decca's neighbor, friend, and coworker on prison reform and other topics. Recently re-released in paperback, this collection of letters was first issued by Knopf in 2006, published by Mitford's friend and longtime editor, Robert Gottlieb, and assembled with the assistance of her husband, Robert Treuhaft.

Introduction: "God Careth for Us"

1. Jessica Mitford, *Hons and Rebels*, 20.
2. "Queen of the Muckrakers," *Time*, July 20, 1970. This article also called Mitford a "scourge," another term she cheerily adopted. https://time.com/archive/6814812/the-press-queen-of-muckrakers/.
3. Jessica Mitford to Maya Angelou, April 30, 1992, JM-CK.
4. Jessica Mitford, *Poison Penmanship*, 4.
5. Mitford, *Hons and Rebels*, 3–4.
6. Quoted by Sussman, *Decca*, ix.
7. Quoted by Sussman, *Decca*, x.
8. Writing to Alex Haley about *her* roots, Decca described the "Dull Fellows" who escorted debutantes to balls. See Jessica Mitford to Alex Haley, no date [late March], 1988, JM-CK.
9. In addition to the primary rooms of Chatsworth, there are dozens of workrooms, hallways, storage rooms, servants' rooms, utility rooms, and other ancillary rooms increasing the room count at Chatsworth well into the hundreds, not including the many additional structures dotting the estate. Some of the house's many rooms are pictured in Deborah Cavendish, Duchess of Devonshire, *Chatsworth: The House* (London: Frances Lincoln, 2002).
10. Biographies of Diana include Jan Dalley, *Diana Mosley: A Life* and Anne De Courcy, *Diana Mosley: Mitford Beauty, British Fascist, Hitler's Angel*. Diana Mosley published *A Life of Contrasts* in 1977. Biographies of Nancy include Harold Acton, *Nancy Mitford: A Memoir*; Selina Hastings, *Nancy Mitford: A Biography*; Laura Thompson, *Life in a Cold Climate: Nancy Mitford, A Portrait of a Contradictory Woman*; Lisa Hilton, *The Horror of Love: Nancy Mitford and Gaston Palewski in Paris and London*; Charlotte Mosley edited two large volumes of Nancy's letters in 1993 and 1996: *Love from Nancy: The Letters of Nancy Mitford* and *The Letters of Nancy Mitford and Evelyn Waugh*. Diana Alexander published *The Other Mitford: Pamela's Story* in 2012. Biographies of Unity include David Pryce-Jones, *Unity Mitford: A Quest* and David R. L. Litchfield, *Hitler's Valkyrie: The Uncensored Biography of Unity Mitford*. Deborah Mitford [Cavendish] published a series of books about Chatsworth, as well as memoirs, and books of essays, including *All in One Basket* in 2001 and *Wait for Me!* in 2010. In 2008 a collection of Deborah's letters was published as *In Tearing Haste: Letters Between Deborah Devonshire and Patrick Leigh Fermor*. Group biographies of the Mitfords include Jonathan Guinness, *The House of Mitford*; Sophia Murphy, *The Mitford Family Album*; Mary S. Lovell, *The Sisters: The Saga of the Mitford Family*; Laura Thompson, *The Six: The Lives of the Mitford Sisters*. Charlotte Mosley edited a large volume of letters between the sisters in 2007: *The Mitfords: Letters Between Six Sisters*. A BritBox series based on Lovell's book aired in 2025. See Maureen Ryan, "A Mitford Sisters First Look: 'Outrageous' Takes on the 1930's Brilliant, Scandalous Siblings," *Vanity Fair* (August 14, 2024).
11. Cannadine, *The Decline and Fall of the British Aristocracy*, 13; David Cannadine, *Aspects of Aristocracy*, 156, 243.
12. Nancy Mitford to Tom Mitford, n.d., as cited by Hastings, *Nancy Mitford*, 23.

13. Mitford, *Hons and Rebels*, 19.

14. Mitford, *Hons and Rebels*, 19.

15. Mitford, *Hons and Rebels*, 73, 59–60. Much later, Decca returned often to what she called Britain's "peculiar obsession" with class, insisting that it remained "alive and well." See her unpublished manuscript, *The Unbearable Lightness and Discreet Charm of the British Aristocracy*, OSU, Box 99, folder 865.

16. Mitford, *Hons and Rebels*, 73.

17. Sharon Jayson, interview with Michele Borba, "Is Selfie Culture Making Our Kids Selfish," *New York Times*, June 23, 2016.

18. Justin Kaplan, *Lincoln Steffens: A Biography*, 164, cited by Mitford, *Poison Penmanship*, 26.

19. The principal exception to this is Peter Sussman's book of letters, cited above, a splendid collection without which this biography would not have been possible. Additional works on Jessica Mitford include Leslie Brody, *Irrepressible: The Life and Times of Jessica Mitford*, Meredith Whitford, *Jessica Mitford: Churchill's Rebel*, and two U.S. dissertations: Anthea Fursland, "Jessica Mitford: A Levinsonian Study," Wright Institute, 1990, and Laura McCreery, "Queen of the Muckrakers: Jessica Mitford's Contributions to American Journalism," San Jose State University, 1995.

Prelude: "The Gooey Parts"

1. Jessica Mitford, interview, "VHS," undated, in author's possession, JM-CK.

2. Jessica Mitford, *The American Way of Death Revisited*, 43. A trocar is an extractive tool used in embalming.

3. Jessica Mitford to Duchess of Devonshire [her sister, often called Debo], February 15, 1962. "On speakers" is Mitford-speak for being on speaking terms with someone. "Hen" is one of the many nicknames that Decca used for her sisters; Hen or "Henderson" was a reference to the chickens that they loved.

4. Jessica Mitford to Candida Donadio [her agent], March 2, 1962, OSU, Box 147, folder 1222.

5. Jessica Mitford to Candida Donadio, March 2, 1962, OSU, Box 147, folder 1222.

6. Jessica Mitford to Sally Belfrage, August 22, 1985, OSU, Box 195, folder 1545.

Chapter One: "The Feudal Remnant and the Fem"

1. Jessica Mitford, letter to Marge Frantz, May 15, 1986, OSU, Box 204, folder 1619.

2. Jessica Mitford, foreword to Nancy Mitford, *The Pursuit of Love* and *Love in a Cold Climate*.

3. Baize is a coarse thick cloth, like felt, meant to muffle noise and protect the privacy of masters' conversations from servants on the other side of the swinging door. In British literature, the green baize door is a trope for the dividing line between the wealthy and everyone else. Jane Austen used the trope often and wrote that aristocratic privacy was always an illusion, even if a necessary one, since aristocratic houses were so heavily staffed by non–family members.

4. Nancy Mitford, *The Pursuit of Love*, 1, 15, 65, 11.

5. Nancy Mitford, *The Pursuit of Love*, 33; Nancy Mitford, *The Water Beetle: Essays*.

6. My thanks to Amanda Vaill for pointing out that these nicknames are abbreviations of Cockney nicknames, and a good example of how layered aristocratic speech can be.

7. Jessica Mitford, *Hons and Rebels*, 3, 17, 28, 36, 40, 26, 39. Decca later wrote that she sold the appendix, in a glass jar, to her sister Deborah for a pound. Deborah says she would not have had a pound and could afford only one of the stitches, for which she paid a shilling. Deborah Mitford, Duchess of Devonshire, *Wait for Me!: Memoirs*, 65.

8. Mitford, *Hons and Rebels*, 38.

9. Mitford, *Hons and Rebels*, 38, 3.

10. The house was 25 Lowndes Square, adjoining the Lowndes Square gardens. The building still stands, though it is now broken up into many apartments.

11. Bowles published the first issue of *Vanity Fair* on November 14, 1868, with a promise to "display the vanities of the week," every week. With its emphasis on "Truth" and its invention of political cartoons of a particularly high quality, *Vanity Fair* clearly influenced Mitford's later muckraking, as his later publication, *The Candid Review*, dedicated to bringing about "a better conduct of Public Affairs," probably did as well. Unlike *Vanity Fair* and *The Candid Review*, *The Lady* was entirely market driven, a commercial magazine of "quality" feminine reading matter, featuring—and still known for—advertisements for domestic help. Naylor, *The Irrepressible Victoria*. Bowles sold *Vanity Fair* in 1889, still during what Peter Clarke calls the "golden age of newspapers" in Britain. Clarke, *Hope and Glory*, 144. Until this past April, *The Lady* was still operating and owned by the family.

12. In World War II, Batsford House served as a barracks, housing as many as three hundred soldiers. The BBC's production of *The Pursuit of Love* and *Love in a Cold Climate* starring Rosamund Pike is filmed at Batsford and provides the best means to see the house, as it was then. Currently in private hands, Batsford House is not open to the public.

13. Mitford's two-volume *Memories* ("monstrously boring," Decca lamented), and his *Tales of Japan* were immensely popular. *Tales of Japan* remains in print today. Mitford's final volume of *Memories* was published posthumously, soon after his death. Mitford, *Hons and Rebels*, 28.

14. Sixteen years Bertie's junior, Clementine Ogilvy Mitford (1854–1932) was the second daughter of the Earl of Airlie and Blanche Stanley. (The Stanleys were a "sharp-tongued family" renowned for literary and cultural figures including Bertrand Russell, and for their advocacy of education for girls). Lady Stanley, as quoted by Jonathan Guinness, *The House of Mitford* (London: Phoenix, 2004), 64. While Guinness's politics appear to cleave closely to those of his mother, Diana, and his stepfather, Oswald Mosley, and his interpretations of family history to be coloured accordingly, *House of Mitford* is comprehensively researched and relies on many documents denied other researchers; basic biographical and factual information contained in this important source appears largely reliable.

15. Nancy Mitford, ed., *Noblesse Oblige*, 52.

16. In her fiftieth year, after achieving renown as a writer, Mitford wrote an exposé on Weight Watchers that set out to mock—"I came to scoff," she wrote—but could not help confirming the view that overweight "is a very real and widespread problem." Jessica Mitford, "The Importance of Being Skinny," *Los Angeles Times*, November 26, 1967, B34.

17. "Because so much of the courtship [of young couples] happened in homes of the couple's parents, privacy was at a premium." Frost, *Promises Broken*, 100. Mary Lovell argues that the "only" reason Sydney married David was "love." "There can be no other reason," Lovell maintains. Lovell, *The Sisters*, 100. But for a woman approaching twenty-five, as Sydney was by the time they married, there were, in fact, endless pressures to marry and few candidates to choose from. Rather than marrying for "only" one reason, women of Sydney's class married for myriad reasons, with love, as we now understand it, fairly far down the list.

18. "In fact," a courtship historian writes, "dating as we know it was nonexistent and all interactions between the sexes were expected to take place in public or under adult supervision. Social encounters were heavily monitored by chaperones until late in the century. Phegley, *Courtship and Marriage in Victorian England*, 37.

19. Ostentation was looked upon by the established gentry as the first sign of respectability. Pigram

and Edwards, *Cotswold Memories*, 15. Excess differentiated the gentry from the undernourished villagers. Clarke, *Hope and Glory*, 91.

20. The Heimlich maneuver was not invented for almost one hundred more years, in 1974.

21. Guinness, *The House of Mitford*, 174–75. All references to Sydney's diary, to which I was not granted access by Chatsworth House, where the diary is housed, are from her grandson Jonathan Guinness.

22. Maternal death rates in England were especially high in the 1870s (more than seventy per one thousand women), the highest rates in England's recorded history. See Geoffrey Chamberlain, "British Maternal Mortality in the 19th and early 20th Century," *Journal of the Royal Society of Medicine*, 99 (11) (November 2006), 559–63, https://www.ncbi.nlm.nih.gov/pmc/articles /PMC1633559/.

23. Julia Budworth, *Never Forget: George S. Bowles, A Biography*, 30–31. Budworth, editor of *The Lady*, (who passed away in 2024), was Sydney's niece, the son of her brother George. Editing is very much in the family; George was the editor of *Granta*. This birth was three years after David's birth in 1878. Jessica lived until Sydney was eight. She died in 1887, as the result of an abortion meant to avert another difficult childbirth. Two years earlier, in 1885, she successfully gave birth to Sydney's youngest sister, Dorothy, always known as Weenie. Jessica Bowles was thirty-five when she died. Tap had the following inscribed on her tombstone: "She was as near perfect wife and mother as may be. She governed her household faithfully and prudently, she ruled her children wisely and lovingly; of her husband she was the brighter, sweeter and nobler part and to him was ever as a constant motive, to be a better man and to do a better thing, for her sake. For eleven happy years were their lives knit together as one." Bowles, *The Irrepressible Victorian*, 122.

24. "The Milner-Gibsons (1806–1986)," https://milnergibson.wordpress.com/2013/08/03/the-milner -gibsons/.

25. Cortazzi, *Mitford's Japan*, xxiv.

26. Cohen, *Family Secrets*, 124.

27. Gibson's wife, Arethusa, was something of a progressive. She opened her home to artists and writers—Charles Dickens, among others, lived with her at various times—and was considered politically radical. Her interests and arts patronage influenced all her children, and Tap, especially, showed a great interest in the theater. Budworth, *Never Forget*, 38–39. Susan Bowles had two other children, a daughter and a son, who she did not give up. According to Budworth, Gibson supported Susan all her life, with a small house and income, and Tap, Sydney's father, visited her occasionally as an adult. He was always aware, Budworth writes, of the circumstances of his birth.

28. Bowles, *Flotsam & Jetsam: A Yachtsman's Experiences at Sea and Ashore*, 116, 22–23. *Flotsam & Jetsam* is a remarkable text, filled with both tirades and travelogues—like a right-wing version of Walt Whitman.

29. Jessica Mitford, interview, 1986–87, in author's possession, JM-CK. Bertie's and Tap's anti-Semitic attitudes percolated down to almost all members of the Mitford family, and many of their biographers have been at great pains to try to excuse, and dismiss, these attitudes. Sir David Warren, British ambassador to Japan from 2008–2012, maintains that Mitford "was not an anti-Semite." Warren also notes that Mitford "had a Japanese mistress and fathered an illegitimate child" in Japan. Sir David Warren, rev. of Robert Morton, *A.B. Mitford and the Birth of Japan as a Modern State: Letters Home* (Riverside, CA: Renaissance Books, 2017), in *Japan Society* 70, vol. 12, no. 4 (August 2017), 2–3.

30. Bertie believed, Jan Dalley writes, "that racial origins determined almost everything." According to Dalley, "Chamberlain's book gave high-octane fuel to the growth of the Nazi creed," and Diana and Unity's descent from Bertie, one of Chamberlain's great supporters, "was of huge importance" to Hitler. "He used to mention it constantly." Dalley, *Diana Mosley: A Life*, 7, 8, 9.

31. Bowles, *The Log of the 'Nereid,'* 149–50. *The Log* is a work of philosophical and political ruminations, combined with a memoir of sailing around the world. Jonathan Guinness writes that "too much can be—and has been—made of this diatribe. It does not imply that Thomas had a prejudice against Jews as such. . . . All that happened was that he saw a group of people who seemed to him to be unattractive, and said so." Guinness, *House of Mitford*, 161.

32. Guinness, *House of Mitford*, 147.

33. This was a highly unusual view. In the nineteenth century, "white bread, considered socially superior, had widely supplanted the former rye or mixed-grain bread." Mingay, *A Social History of the English Countryside*, 116. Sydney's siblings were equally persuaded. Her brother, Geoffrey, founded the Liberty Restoration League, whose slogan was "Freedom, not Doctordom," and proselytized against "murdered food," pasteurization, "de-vitalised, de-natured, de-hydrated, de-everythinged" and "chemicals and heat and processes and tins." Geoffrey believed that commercial food production was destroying British masculinity. Sounding like a cross between Arnold Schwarzenegger and Rachel Carson, he argued that "deadened soil" had created "she-men" and that only bacteria and compost could restore England's manhood: "It is now the worm's turn to re-form the manhood of England," he wrote. Bowles, *Rebel*, 60–63.

34. Guinness, *House of Mitford*, 141.

35. Mitford, *Hons and Rebels*, 27.

36. Because it has often been noted that the *Nereid* was a 150-ton ship, a misleading picture of the *Nereid* as much larger than it was has become commonplace. Probably the ship's displacement number—a measurement of the amount of water the ship displaced or moved through—and not the actual weight of the ship, the *Nereid*'s size was not in excess of other personal sailing yachts owned by wealthy people at the time. Sydney always looked back on it as rather "small." Sydney Redesdale, unpublished memoir, *The Dolphin*, CH.

37. Sydney Redesdale, unpublished memoir, *The Dolphin*, 3, CH.

38. Sydney Redesdale, unpublished memoir, *The Dolphin*, 5–7, CH.

39. Sydney Redesdale to Jessica Mitford, 7 December 1955, OSU, Box 212, folder 1699. Sydney continued to spend summers yachting with her father—she had very little choice. Lovell claims that Sydney "loved" the sea and sought out every opportunity to sail. I find no evidence of this. When Sydney had to travel by sea, she did so, as there wasn't any other choice. Neither she nor David owned boats larger than small launches much later in life, when they were necessary in Scotland. And Decca and her sisters were rarely on boats, though when Decca was eight or nine, she vowed, "I'm going to buy a yacht twice as big as Dweedle's," her grandfather's. Jessica Mitford to Sydney Redesdale, September 1926, OSU, Box 211, folder 1697. Decca and Sydney narrowly avoided the *Titanic* disaster, having booked passage on the *Titanic*, but changed their travel plans shortly before the ship sailed.

40. Bowles, *Flotsam and Jetsam*, 3.

41. Bowles, *Flotsam and Jetsam*, 3, 24.

42. Tello gave birth to a son, then three other children of Tap's. After the voyage, he got Tello a job on *The Lady*, of which she became the editor in three years, and supported her, though he did not marry her, all their adult lives. Jonathan Guinness believes that Tap failed to marry Tello because he was not, in fact, the father of her first child, conceived on the ship. Guinness' hypothesis is

about a naval lieutenant who serenaded Tello once as her probable suitor and the child's likely father, in spite of the fact that neither Tap, nor Tello, were ever at pains to hide the nature of their relationship and that all her children, along with Tello, were later supported by Tap. Observing, quite rightly, that "lovemaking on board the Nereid" would have been very difficult to hide, Guinness considers it more credible that Tello would have sneaked off the ship to have sex with a total stranger. See Guinness, *House of Mitford*, 171.

43. Bowles, *Log of the 'Nereid,* 102.
44. Edmund Gosse, entry on Bertram Mitford for the *Dictionary of National Biography*, as quoted by Cortazzi, *Mitford's Japan*, ix.
45. Mitford, *Memories*, vol. 2, 588, 590.
46. Devonshire, *Wait for Me!: Memoirs*, 20
47. In Ceylon, Decca later noted, her father "sort of had the 'white man's burden' experience." Mitford, interview, 1986–87. Rudyard Kipling had summed up imperial sentiments about the workers in his 1899 "The White Man's Burden": "Take up the White Man's burden / Send forth the best you breed / Your new-caught sullen children / Half devil and half child." Rudyard Kipling, "The White Man's Burden," *McClure's Magazine*, February 1899.
48. Peebles, *The Plantation Tamils of Ceylon*, 54–55; G. C. Mendis, *Ceylon Under the British*, 148.
49. David to his sister Iris, August 3, 1900, as quoted by Guinness, *House of Mitford*, 214.
50. Sydney Redesdale, diary, as quoted by Guinness, *House of Mitford*, 220, 219, 215.
51. Pugh, *Britain Since 1789*, 147–48; Clarke, *Hope and Glory*, 79.
52. Mingay, *Social History of the English Countryside*, 187. For more recent challenges to this narrative of aristocratic "continuous decline" and arguments for the remarkable resilience of the British aristocracy, see David Cannadine and others.
53. In spite of such obvious indications of wealth, Mary Lovell describes the family's finances as "merely adequate in a world where there were no electrical appliances, detergents or easy-care fabrics." Lovell, *The Sisters*, 21. It is not uncommon for the wealthy to decry as poverty what to others would be enormous luxury.
54. "Lawns and Lawn History," The Lawn Institute. For the irony of American imitations of this British tradition, see especially Jenkins, *The Lawn: A History of an American Obsession*. While Batsford house is no longer open to the public, its gardens have now become an arboretum that the public can visit.
55. David Mitford to Clementine Mitford, as quoted by Jonathan Guinness, *House of Mitford*, 223.
56. Ironically, Swastika was where Unity was conceived.
57. Devonshire, *Wait for Me!*, 16.
58. Devonshire, *Wait for Me!*, 25.
59. Devonshire, *Wait for Me!*, 9.
60. Nancy Mitford, *Highland Fling*, 97.
61. Mitford, interview, 1986–87, JM-CK.
62. The Northumberland lands that Bertie Mitford inherited were approximately eighteen thousand acres, http://www.tynedalelife.co.uk/2011/12/did-you-know/.

Chapter Two: "That Dread Place"

1. Jessica Mitford to Nancy Mitford, October 13, 1971, OSU, Box 212, folder 3; Jessica Mitford, *A Fine Old Conflict* (Knopf, 1977; repr., New York: Vintage, 1978), fn. 13.
2. Mitford, *Hons and Rebels*, 57.
3. Many enormous country houses such as Batsford were sold when David sold. Designed to be

staffed by servants who were paid very little, the labor for such large houses vanished after World War I with the onset of substantial labor shortages. According to one British historian, by March 1919, the year David sold Batsford, so many large country estates were being sold that the country was undergoing a "revolution in landowning." Over one million acres of land were sold in 1919 by aristocrats who could not profit from them. Between 1918 and 1921, "6–8 million acres changed hands." Yet the social structure of the British countryside was based on large landowners and underpaid tenants, a structure that held fast even as land ownership changed. See Mingay, *A Social History of the English Countryside*.

4. Documents still held at Asthall, including the real estate surveys of the late teens and middle 1920s, prepared by London auctioneers John D. Wood & Co., indicate the extent of the estate that David inherited. It included almost all the houses and buildings in the village, excepting Asthall manor. The town housed around four hundred people, many of them paying rent or working for the Redesdales. Some of the houses were provided rent-free, such as to the vicar and the estate manager, but other tenants paid rent on the houses and the lands they farmed. I am deeply grateful to Rosie Pearson, current owner of Asthall Manor, for allowing me to spend so much time in the house, tour it at will, photograph it, and peruse the estate documents in her possession.

5. Devonshire, *Wait for Me!*, 7.

6. Mitford, *Hons and Rebels*, 2.

7. Nancy Mitford, *The Pursuit of Love* (1945; repr., New York: Vintage, 2001), foreword by Jessica Mitford, 18.

8. Mitford, *Hons and Rebels*, 6.

9. Philip Toynbee, *Friends Apart: A Memoir of Esmond Romilly & Jasper Ridley in the Thirties*. Evelyn Waugh, one of the chief chroniclers of the "Bright Young Things" (and one of Nancy's closest friends), described them as "cosmopolitan, sympathetic to the arts, well-mannered, above all ornamental even in rather bizarre ways." Evelyn Waugh, review of Cecil Beaton, *The Wandering Years*, in *The Spectator*, July 21, 1961, reprinted in Gallagher, ed., *The Essays, Articles, and Reviews of Evelyn Waugh*. They were, historian D. J. Taylor writes, "glamorous, well-connected" and "exclusive" young aristocrats. Their world of "cocktails, jazz, licence [*sic*], abandon and fragrantly improper behavior" was made possible by many forms of social change in the interwar period. Taylor, *Bright Young People*, 4. Decca was particularly awed by Nancy's ability to maneuver Farve into allowing the Bright Young Things—outsiders all—to visit. "On weekends they would swoop down from Oxford or London in merry hordes, to be greeted with solid disapproval by my mother, and furious glares from my father." Jessica Mitford, *Hons and Rebels*, 31.

10. Jessica Mitford, interview, "The Honorable Rebel"; James Lees-Milne, interview, undated, Selina Hastings, *Nancy Mitford: A Biography*, 5.

11. Nancy Mitford, *The Water Beetle*; Jessica Mitford, *Hons and Rebels*.

12. Mitford, *Hons and Rebels*, 65, 66, 72.

13. Jessica Mitford, interview, cited in obituary, Jessica Mitford, *The Telegraph*, July 25, 1996.

14. Jessica Mitford to Sydney Redesdale, May 15, n.y.; Jessica Mitford to David Redesdale, February 9, 1932; Jessica Mitford to David Redesdale, late 1933, OSU, Box 211, folder 1697.

15. Mitford, *Hons and Rebels*, 72.

16. Mitford, *Hons and Rebels*, 69.

17. Mitford, *Hons and Rebels*, 72.

18. Mitford, *Hons and Rebels*, 12.

19. Jessica Mitford to Nancy Mitford, October 13, 1971, Mosley, ed. *The Mitfords*, 556.

20. Martin Pugh, *We Danced All Night: A Social History of Britain Between the Wars*, 207.

21. Jessica Mitford to Nancy Mitford, October 13, 1971, Mosley, ed., *The Mitfords*, 555. Diana, on seeing this letter to Nancy, declared such resentment, which Nancy shared, to be "rubbish:" "If Decca had really wanted to be a scientist she could have 'gone on' at Muv & I bet you finally she wd have got her way." Diana Mosley to Deborah Mosley, October 21, 1971, Mosley, ed. *The Mitfords*, 558.

22. Selina Hastings and Charlotte Mosley date this as 1927. Mary Lovell, and Decca herself, both date this as 1928. However, Decca's two memoirs cannot always be precisely relied upon in regard to dates, since the memoirs were often written without immediate access to some of the family letters stored at Chatsworth, under what were laughingly called "Maximum Archival Conditions."

23. A bed-sitter is a single room with a shared bathroom. Young aristocratic women, like Decca, often romanticized the image of the London bed-sitter as a modern emblem of freedom from constraints and chaperones. Mitford, *Hons and Rebels*, 33.

24. Mitford, *Hons and Rebels*, 33; Nancy Mitford to Diana Mitford, n.d., Mosley, ed. *The Mitfords*, 14. This letter is also published in Mosley, ed., *Love from Nancy*. (Hastings either misattributes Nancy's addressee in this letter as Tom, or Nancy wrote Tom and Diana identical letters. See Hastings, *Nancy Mitford*.) This story, while very likely true, was also a tease. Nancy had left art school, as she confided to Diana, because her teachers were so discouraging. "The professor has been so beastly. . . . They are so awful to you, they come up & say what a very depressing drawing, I wonder how you manage to draw so foully, have you never had a pencil in your hand before." But telling her younger sisters the truth would have been admitting to failure, which Nancy always tried to avoid.

25. Mitford, *Hons and Rebels*, 33.

26. Mitford, *Hons and Rebels*, 26.

27. Mitford, *Hons and Rebels*, 33–34. She saved the Drummonds letter all her life.

28. Mitford, *Hons and Rebels*, 54–55, 57.

29. Mitford, *Hons and Rebels*, 59.

30. Mitford, interview, 1986–87; Jessica Mitford, interview, "VHS," undated, JM-CK.

31. Andrew Cavendish [Devonshire], "The Aristocracy–Born to Rule," Episode 1, 1875–1914, BBC Documentary, Sam Organ Producer.

32. Mitford, *Hons and Rebels*, 55–59.

33. Mitford, *Hons and Rebels*, 4, 3.

34. Deborah to Nancy, August 30, 1962. Thompson, *The Six*, 50. Thompson wrote an earlier biography of Nancy. Her largely anecdotal group biography of the sisters takes most of them, including Diana, on faith. Yet, she distrusts Decca's claims, more or less as her sisters did: "Jessica, again, was making merry with the facts," she asserts. Thompson, *The Six*, 57.

35. Devonshire, *Wait for Me!*, 4–5.

36. Bingham, *The Cotswolds*.

37. Deborah Mitford, "Debutantes: 1939," BBC, minute 15.40.

38. Devonshire, *Wait for Me!*, 4–5.

39. Charles Spencer, "Enemies of the Estate," *Vanity Fair*, January 2010.

40. Diana Mosley, *A Life of Contrasts*, 12.

41. Lovell, *The Sisters*, 104, 406 and passim; Thompson, *The Six*, 59 and passim.

42. Diana Mitford to Deborah Mitford, December 15, 1976, Mosley, *The Mitfords*, 637.

Chapter Three: "It Will All Be Terrific Fun"

1. Jessica Mitford, *Hons and Rebels* (1960), 140.
2. Mitford, *Hons and Rebels*, 75.
3. Mitford, *Hons and Rebels*, 76; Ingram, *Rebel*, 78–79; Interview with Kevin Ingram, Madrid, May 2018.
4. Mitford, *Hons and Rebels*, 100, 77.
5. Ingram, *Rebel*, 72, 104.
6. Esmond Romilly, as quoted by Whitford, *Churchill's Rebels*, 51, Kindle.
7. Toynbee, *Friends Apart*, 114, 86, 95, 107.
8. Toynbee, *Friends Apart*, 18.
9. "A Hurry–Esmond Romilly (Aged 15) Views the World," *Sunday Referee*, April 28, 1934, as quoted by Ingram, *Rebel*, 82.
10. Jason Gurney, *Crusade in Spain*, as quoted by Baxell, *Unlikely Warriors*, 26. The historical record of British support for fascism is complicated by competing fascist organizations and fascists, who, like Oswald Mosley, also were opportunists in shifting between anti-immigrant and anti-Semitic positions, based on perceptions of whatever might offer the greatest "emotional appeal of something to hate." Griffiths, *Fellow Travellers of the Right*, 106.
11. Mitford, *Wigs on the Green*, 128.
12. Baxell, *Unlikely Warriors*, 34.
13. Baxell, *Unlikely Warriors*, 37, 40.
14. Romilly, *Boadilla*, 18.
15. I am enormously grateful to Almudena Cros, of AcrossMadrid Tours, for arranging a special tour for me of all the sites where Romilly fought in Madrid. I am also grateful to Cros, who is president of the Association of Friends of the International Brigades (AABI), for sharing her vast knowledge of Romilly, the Spanish Civil War, and the International Brigades with me. I will never forget hiking miles in nearly hundred-degree heat with Cros, then nearly nine months pregnant, who continually had to wait for me to catch up with her.
16. Romilly, *Boadilla*, 113.
17. Mitford, *Hons and Rebels*, 93, 118.
18. Jessica Mitford, as the Paget Twins, to Sydney Redesdale, February 3, 1937.
19. Devonshire, *Wait for Me!*, 79.
20. In her biography of the Paget twins, Ariane Bankes writes that "Celia always claimed that Decca had a touch of the delinquent about her—she was ruthless and would stop at nothing to get her way." *The Dazzling Paget Sisters*, 31. Kindle edition.
21. Jessica Mitford to Sydney Redesdale, no date, [February 1937], from Bayonne. Sussman, *Decca*, 22–23.
22. Bankes, *The Dazzling Paget Sisters*, pp. 30–32, Kindle.
23. Jessica Mitford to Sydney Redesdale, no date, late February 1937, Sussman, *Decca*, 23–24.
24. Devonshire, *Wait for Me!*, 80.
25. Ingram, *Rebel*, 171.
26. Sussman, *Decca*, xiii.
27. Mitford, *Hons and Rebels*, 140.
28. Toynbee, *Friends Apart*, 114, 86, 95, 107.
29. Mitford, *Hons and Rebels*, 140–41.
30. Mitford, *Hons and Rebels*, 140–41.

31. Mitford, *Hons and Rebels*, 142.
32. Mitford, *Hons and Rebels*, 140.
33. Jessica Mitford to Lady Redesdale, n.d., [Late February], [from Paris]. Sussman, *Decca,* 24.
34. Variations of "Hen" include both "Henderson" and "Hon," the latter used by Decca in the U.S. title of her memoir *Hons and Rebels*, which may have contributed to the misimpression that "Hon" was short for "Honorable," an official title for a Lord's daughter that Decca always rejected and refused to adopt, except ironically, as in her book's title.
35. This account of Decca and Esmond's passage to Spain draws largely from Mitford's *Hons and Rebels*, as well as from Esmond Romilly's *Boadilla: An Account from the Spanish Civil War*, and my time in Spain and the Basque country. I am particularly grateful to Kevin Ingram, who lives in Madrid, for helping me piece together Esmond and Decca's time in Spain and France.
36. Mitford, *Hons and Rebels*, 146.
37. Philip Toynbee believed that their first few days were spent as the personal guests of the Basque president, at his "own house," but there is little evidence that such a stay occurred. They may have been invited and intending to stay, as they would have reported to Toynbee in one of their frequent letters to him. See Toynbee's *Friends Apart*, 99.
38. Mitford, *Hons and Rebels*, 148.
39. Lovell, *The Sisters*, 228.
40. Mitford, *Hons and Rebels*, 149, 147.
41. Jessica Mitford to Lady Redesdale, [late February 1937], [from Paris], Sussman, *Decca*, 23.
42. Jessica Mitford to Deborah Mitford, April 6, 1937, Mosley, *The Mitfords*, 88. Deborah sold some other clothes, for £2.10, and told Debo she didn't want the purple Worth dress to go for "so little." Worth is credited with inventing the notion of couturier and the idea that a dress should show its designer. The House of Worth—in the hands of his sons by the time of Decca's coming out—was the most expensive, and coveted, clothing designer in the world.
43. Deborah Mitford to Jessica Mitford, July 14; July 21, 1937, OSU, Box 197, folder 1559; Deborah Mitford to Jessica Mitford, July 14, July 21, 1937, OSU, Box 197, folder 1559; Deborah Mitford to Jessica Mitford, April 2, 1937, Mosley, *The Mitfords*, 86–87.
44. Jessica Mitford to Deborah Mitford, April 6, 1937, Mosley, *The Mitfords*, 87–88.
45. Unity Mitford to Jessica Mitford, March 3, 1937, Mosley, *The Mitfords*, 80–81. Unity and Jessica called each other "Boud." "Boud" was derived from Boudledige (pronounced bowdledidge).
46. Nancy Mitford to Jessica Mitford, March 14, 1937, Mosley, *The Mitfords*, 81–83. Nancy and Jessica called each other "Susan."
47. Romilly, *Boadilla*, 196.
48. Ingram, *Rebel*.
49. Toynbee, *Friends Apart*, 86.
50. Toynbee, *Friends Apart*, 115.
51. Sussman, *Decca*, 3. (Nancy and General Palewski, Diana and Oswald Mosley, Unity and Hitler, Deborah and the Duke.)
52. Jessica Mitford, interview, as quoted by Ingram, *Rebel*, 152.
53. Lannon, *The Spanish Civil War*, 7, 91.
54. Baxell, *British Volunteers*, 46.
55. Graham, *The War and Its Shadow*, 12, 1.
56. Graham, *The War and Its Shadow*, 20, 34, 21.

57. Graham, *The War and Its Shadow*, 47.
58. Diana Mitford to Deborah Mitford, June 2, 1938, 123; Diana Mitford to Deborah Mitford, June 2, 1938, Mosley, *The Mitfords*, 123; Diana Mitford to Unity Mitford, August 18, 1938, Mosley, *The Mitfords*, 135.
59. Unity Mitford to Jessica Mitford, March 3, 1937, Mosley, *The Mitfords*, 80–81; see "Hitler a Fickle Lover," *Philadelphia Inquirer*, November 21, 1945, 1; Pryce-Jones, *Unity Mitford*, 5–6, 155, 190–91.
60. Lady Redesdale, *Daily Telegraph*, as quoted, Lovell, *The Sisters*, 203.
61. Graham, *The War*, 35–36, 57.
62. Graham, *The War*, 64.
63. Lannon, *The Spanish Civil War*, 80.
64. Baxell, *British Volunteers*, 49. An "Appreciation," published just after Browne's death, along with some of her drawings from Spain, lamented the "tragedy" of her death as, in part, the loss of "the very best type of the new woman"—the woman who was brave, honest, "humane," and committed to the ideals of "livingness," which meant finding through "workers and peasants" the "real and rooted life" that the "clamorous and false significances which modern European civilization tries to foist upon" obscures. "Appreciation," Anonymous, Drawings by Felicia Brown, published 1936, after her death. Reproduced online by William Brown, a descendant, at https://archive.org/details/DrawingsFeliciaBrowne. According to a note in the "Appreciation," "a party of ten volunteers, including Felicia, set out at night to blow up a rebel munition train. Attacked, four to one, by a Fascist patrol, they retreated. A wounded man had to be left behind. Felicia returned to help him, but the rebels riddled them both with bullets," Artists' International Association Bulletin, No. 19.
65. Watling, *Tomorrow Perhaps the Future*, 3, 11.
66. The *News Chronicle*, a daily, had sent three journalists to Spain and was strongly anti-fascist. In 1960 it was absorbed into *The Daily Mail*.
67. Mitford, *Hons and Rebels*, 149.
68. Mitford, *Hons and Rebels*, 156.
69. Mates, *The Spanish Civil War and the British Left*, 30.
70. Mitford, *Hons and Rebels*, 163, 164.
71. Mitford, *Hons and Rebels*, 155.
72. Baxell, *British Volunteers*, 109, 117–18.
73. OSU; Chatsworth House Archives; Mitford, *Hons and Rebels*, 159–61; Ingram, *Rebel*.
74. Mitford, *Hons and Rebels*, 153.
75. Mitford, *Hons and Rebels*, 161.
76. Lannon, *The Spanish Civil War*, 45.
77. Stevenson had sent Nancy and Peter ahead to France to persuade Decca and Esmond to continue on to England. "Impossible," Decca told them. Jessica Mitford to Deborah Mitford, April 6, 1937, Mosley, *The Mitfords*, 87.
78. Mitford, *Hons and Rebels*, 161.
79. Lady Redesdale to Jessica Mitford, March 3, 1937, OSU, Box 211, folder 1697.
80. Romilly, *Boadilla*, 66, 78, 87.
81. Unity Mitford to Jessica Mitford, April 11, 1937, Mosley, *The Mitfords*, 90–91.
82. Jessica Mitford to Deborah Mitford, May 23, 1937, Mosley, *The Mitfords*, 99.
83. Unity Mitford to Jessica Mitford, May 16, 1937, Mosley, *The Mitfords*, 94–95.

84. Jessica Mitford to Deborah Mitford, May 23, 1937, Mosley, *The Mitfords*, 98.
85. Nancy Mitford to Jessica Mitford, May 26, 1937, Mosley, *The Mitfords*, 97.
86. Unity Mitford to Jessica Mitford, August 10, 1937, Mosley, *The Mitfords*, 113.
87. Deborah Mitford to Jessica Mitford, June 13, 1937, Mosley, *The Mitfords*, 100–101; Deborah Mitford to Jessica Mitford, June 20, 1937, Mosley, *The Mitfords*, 103; "chinless," Deborah Mitford to Jessica Mitford, June 30, 1937, Mosley, *The Mitfords*, 104; Deborah Mitford to Jessica Mitford, June 30, 1937, Mosley, *The Mitfords*, 104.
88. Jessica Mitford to Nancy Mitford [August 1937], Mosley, *The Mitfords*, 30.
89. Jessica Mitford to Nancy Mitford, [August 1937] [from Dieppe], Sussman, *Decca*, 30–31.
90. Esmond Romilly to Jessica Mitford, n.d. [August 1937], OSU, Box 119, folder 127.
91. Esmond Romilly to Jessica Mitford, Saturday Morning [1937], OSU, Box 119, folder 1027.
92. Toynbee, *Friends Apart*, 106.
93. Toynbee, *Friends Apart*, 113.
94. Jessica Mitford to Deborah Mitford, December 28, 1937, Mosley, *The Mitfords*, 121. Deborah had contracted measles just before the baby's birth and therefore could not go to visit.
95. When one did become available, aristocrats formed the core of England's passionate anti-vaccination movement. Sydney was especially opposed to "pumping dead germs" into "the Good Body." See Durback, *Bodily Matters*.
96. See Brincker, "A Historical, Epidemiological and Aetiological Study of Measles," *Proceedings of the Royal Society of Medicine* 21, no. 807 (1938): 33–54.
97. Mary Lovell writes that "Decca took her baby to the local clinic for inoculation;" such inoculation did not become available in England until 1968, however. See Lovell, *The Sisters*, 259.
98. Mitford, *Hons and Rebels*, 182.
99. Mitford, *Hons and Rebels*, 182.
100. Toynbee, *Friends Apart*, 115–16.
101. Jessica Mitford to Deborah Mitford, May 31, 1938, Mosley, *The Mitfords*, 123.
102. Mitford, *Hons and Rebels*, 182–83.
103. Decca would have made a deliberate decision not to use the family cemetery at St. Mary's Church in Swinbrook. Nancy, Unity, and Diana are buried at St. Mary's, as are David, Sydney, and many other family members.
104. Mitford, *Wigs on the Green*, 52.
105. Mitford, *Hons and Rebels*, 254.

Chapter Four: "Let's Go to America"

1. Esmond Romilly, "Blue Blood Adventurers Discover America," *Washington Post*, January 28, 1940, B2.
2. Jessica Mitford, *Hons and Rebels*, 266.
3. Mitford, *Hons and Rebels*, 266.
4. Toynbee, *Friends Apart*, 155. He also said that Decca and Esmond were the only people with whom he belonged.
5. Mitford, *Hons and Rebels*, 266.
6. Mitford, *Hons and Rebels*, 278.
7. Esmond Romilly, "Escape from England," *The Commentator*, October 1939, 126.
8. Esmond Romilly, "Escape from England," 128.
9. Jessica and Esmond Romilly, interview, *Time*, April 3, 1939, Vol. 33 Issue 14, 56.
10. Mitford, *Hons and Rebels*, 188.

11. Mitford, *Hons and Rebels*, 199.
12. Sydney Redesdale to Jessica Mitford, June 12, 1937, OSU, Box 211, folder 1697.
13. Sydney Redesdale to Neville Chamberlain, November 11, 1938, OSU, Box 211, folder 1697.
14. Lovell, *The Sisters*, 242.
15. Mitford, *A Fine Old Conflict*, 15.
16. Bernard Gutteridge, letter to Ingram, Kevin Ingram, *Rebel*, 168.
17. Mitford, *Hons and Rebels*, 190, 192; Ingram, *Rebel*, 178.
18. Mitford, *Hons and Rebels*, 189.
19. "Blue Blood Adventurers Discover America." The article misreports the year of their arrival as 1938 and the money they had as 200 pounds.
20. They never paid these bills, though friends whose names had been added to the accounts appealed to Esmond and Decca, for months after their arrival in America, to send money for the outstanding accounts.
21. The party took place behind Rutland Gate, the Mitford family's large London home, in the annex, a small building, containing a house and garage, in the back. Toynbee, *Friends Apart*, 136.
22. Esmond's biographer, Kevin Ingram, believes that Nevile was "in love" with Esmond and, hence incapable of denying Esmond anything. Interview with Kevin Ingram, Madrid, in author's possession.
23. Roughton, who owned the Rotherhithe house at No. 41 in which Esmond and Decca rented the top floor, was a poet and Communist who inherited wealth and started a journal in 1936 called *Contemporary Poetry & Prose*. He was Esmond's partner in a short-lived venture to start an alternative news agency. Roughton, who was purportedly gay, committed suicide in Dublin in June 1941.
24. "Two Young Adventurers Explore New York," *Washington Post*, February 4, 1940, B4.
25. The Southampton docks were then the largest in the world and as many as 5.5 million passengers came through them a year at this time. Thousands of passengers might be boarding different large ships on any given day from the dock's many wharves. "Port of Achievement," Imperial War Museum, Southern Railway, 1946, Huntley Archives, No. 8489.
26. Some historians have claimed that they booked second-class passage. Both Decca and Esmond, however, confirm that they booked steerage, third-class. See, for example, Esmond Romilly, "Escape from England."
27. Reforms passed in 1907 mandated washroom facilities, some ventilation, and proper nutrition.
28. Mitford, *Hons and Rebels*, 200.
29. "Blue Blood Adventurers Discover America," B2.
30. "Weather"; "100 Jews Each Day Must Leave Reich: Order Is Effective in Berlin Tomorrow— Violates the Recent Refugee Compact, Hopeful View Was General 100," *New York Times*, February 26, 1939, 1, 23.
31. Mitford, *Hons and Rebels*, 199.
32. When it was built, the Shelton, with over a thousand rooms, was the tallest hotel in the world; its stepped architectural form, which maximized grandeur while minimizing mass, helped define the future of modern skyscrapers.
33. Jessica Mitford to Sydney Redesdale, 9 March 1939, JM-CK.
34. Some have claimed that they were at the Shelton a month. Letters and their own statements indicate otherwise.
35. Jessica Mitford to Sydney Redesdale, March 23, 1939, JM-CK.
36. "Hitler Drives On: Hitler's Push to the East and Five Momentous Questions," *New York Times*,

March 19, 1939, 63; "Old World Is Nervous as Italy Takes Albania," *New York Times*, April 9, 1939, E3.

37. Jessica Mitford to Sydney Redesdale, August 1939, JM-CK.

38. Jessica Mitford to Sydney Redesdale, March 9, 1939, JM-CK. Decca loved this particular dress. It features in almost all 1939 photographs of her, including a lovely group of pictures by famous *Life* photographer David Scherman, who quickly became one of Decca and Esmond's friends.

39. Jessica Mitford to Sydney Redesdale, April 9, 1941, from Toronto, Sussman, *Decca*, 78.

40. Mitford, *Hons and Rebels*, 204.

41. Peter Leeman to Esmond Romilly, October 3, 1939, OSU Box 119, folder 1035.

42. See Tinniswood, *The Long Weekend* and Jenkins, *The Lawn*. F. Scott Fitzgerald famously poked fun at the practice of ostentatious and derivative American architecture on Long Island in *The Great Gatsby*.

43. Esmond Romilly to Philip Toynbee, OSU, Box 119, folder 1035. Being British was such an advantage in America, Esmond pointed out to Philip Toynbee, in a rare backward glance (he was not generally one to hold grudges), that the "lecture tour idea of ours would have been a colossal success."

44. For a recent article on British "sartorial shabbiness," as a "code of honour . . . their collars are frayed, the tweed jackets darned, their shoes scuffed," see Sarah Sands, "Threadbare Is the Classiest Look of All," *The Independent*, October 3, 2010. In her 1956 send-up of aristocratic attitudes, Nancy Mitford explains that little could be more undignified for the aristocracy than seeming to care about money. See Nancy Mitford, "The English Aristocracy," *Noblesse Oblige*. Sands explains that this aesthetic, in part, is "rooted in a sense that anything worthwhile is inherited."

45. Peter Nevile to Esmond Romilly, September 10, 1939, OSU, Box 119, folder 1035.

46. Mitford, *Hons and Rebels*, 260–61.

47. Toynbee, *Friends Apart*, 135.

48. Philip Toynbee to Esmond Romilly, [March?] 29, 1939, OSU, Box 119, folder 1035.

49. "Two Young Adventurers Explore New York," *Washington Post*, February 4, 1940, B4.

50. This section references the extensive and international coverage of their elopement. The scrapbook files that Decca kept of this extensive newspaper coverage have gone missing from OSU. I have been able to reconstruct most of the newspaper coverage in Britain and the U.S., partly archivally and also because Sydney also kept scrapbooks of the British side of this coverage, which were made available to me at Chatsworth.

51. "Blue Blood Adventurers Discover America," B2.

52. "Lord Redesdale Daughter Works in New York Shop," *Boston Globe*, April 11, 1939, 22.

53. "Blue Blood Adventurers Discover America," B2; "Two Britons in 'Hobohemia,'" *Washington Post*, January 28, 1940.

54. "Blue Blood Adventurers Discover America," B2.

55. Selden Rodman to Esmond Romilly, November 7, 1939, OSU, Box 119, folder 1035.

56. Mitford, *Hons and Rebels*, 237.

57. Mitford, *Hons and Rebels*, 257.

58. Mitford, *Hons and Rebels*, 205–7.

59. "Blue Blood Adventurers Discover America," B2; "Two Young Adventurers Explore New York, *Washington Post*, B4; English Adventurers Stalk Job in Wilds of New York," *Washington Post*, February 11, 1940, B7; "English Adventurers Explore Capital," *Washington Post*, February 25, 1940, B6.

60. Esmond Romilly to Peter Nevile and Philip Toynbee, May 10, 1939. OSU, Box 119, folder 1035.

61. Esmond Romilly to Philip Toynbee, May 10, 1939, OSU, Box 119, folder 1035. Their combined yearly salary of $1,353 was hardly wealth, translating into about $25,000 a year in today's dollars. But Esmond had never made much money, didn't really understand money, and could easily declare, as he did to Philip Toynbee, that "money means nothing to me." Esmond Romilly to Philip Toynbee, 1939.

62. Gelernter, *1939: The Lost World of the Fair*, 12.

63. "English Adventurers Stalk Job in Wilds of New York," B7.

64. Jessica Mitford to Sydney Redesdale, August 2/3, 1939, Sussman, *Decca*, 32.

65. Jessica Mitford to Sydney Redesdale, September 27, 1939, Sussman, *Decca*, 33–34.

66. Mitford, *Hons and Rebels*, 230–31.

67. Nancy Mitford to Jessica Mitford, September 21, 1939, OSU, Box 212, folder 1707.

68. Mitford, *Hons and Rebels*, 239.

69. Mitford, *Hons and Rebels*, 237–38.

70. Selden Rodman's diary, Beinecke Library, Yale University, SR.

71. Ingram, *Rebel*, 190.

72. Esmond Romilly, "England's Next Prime Minister," *Common Sense*, vol. 8 (October 1939), 6–9. Frances Pandyck, from *The American Mercury*, wrote Esmond soon after this article appeared, soliciting a "sadistic" portrait of Winston Churchill. Whether or not the editor meant to write "satiric," Esmond declined. Pandyck to Esmond Romilly, November 16, 1939.

73. Jessica Mitford to Sydney Redesdale, Sept 6, 1939, Sussman, *Decca*, 33.

74. Jessica Mitford to Sydney Redesdale, Sept 6, 1939, Sussman, *Decca*, 33.

75. Kennedy, *Freedom from Fear*, 427.

76. Peter Nevile to Esmond Romilly, October 11, 1939, OSU, Box 119, folder 1035. "How I envy you both being out of the country," Philip Toynbee wrote, November 25, 1939.

77. Zinn, *A People's History of the United States*, 407. See also, Feingold, *The Politics of Rescue*.

78. September 1 and 3; see Kennedy, *Freedom from Fear*, 426–27.

79. See Offner, *American Appeasement*.

80. Selden Rodman's Diary, SR.

81. See, for example, Charles A. Lindbergh, "Appeal to Isolationism," *Vital Speeches*, 751–52. Partial revisions of the Neutrality Act in November did succeed in rolling back some of those restrictions. See Welles, *The Time for Decision*, 148.

Chapter Five: "America Is Such Heaven"

1. Sullivan, ed., *Freedom Writer*, 423.

2. Articles such as "Peer's Daughter Stays in Germany," only added to her anxiety. *Washington Post*, October 3, 1939.

3. Jessica Mitford to Sydney Redesdale, September 6, 1939.

4. Mitford, *Hons and Rebels*, 228.

5. Esmond Romilly to Selden Rodman, November 6, 1939, OSU, Box 211, folder 1045.

6. Mitford, *Hons and Rebels*, 253.

7. He regretted his recruitment almost immediately, trying thereafter to avoid all contact with his Soviet handlers, much to the frustration of those who had recruited him, and produced almost nothing of value for the Russians. He presented as a well-connected, transparent Washington liberal. Straight took over the editorship of *The New Republic* from his parents in 1940. He

revealed his largely inconsequential work as a spy in 1963. From 1969–1977 he served as Deputy Chairman of the National Endowment for the Arts. He died in 2004.

8. Arthur Sears Henning, "F.D.R. Backers Swell Ranks of 'Sixth Column,'" *Chicago Daily Tribune*, March 26, 1942, 1; "Reports Biddle Urges Politics as Usual in War," March 8, 1942, 6. Straight also served as vice chair of the Fight for Freedom committee, which pushed for the United States to declare war against Germany.
9. Goodwin, *No Ordinary Time*, 43.
10. Kennedy, *Freedom from Fear*, 377; "well-being . . ." comes from Cohen, *Making a New Deal*, 2–3.
11. Sullivan, *Freedom Writer*, 3, 418.
12. Esmond Romilly to Selden Rodman, November 6, 1939, SR, copy in OSU, Box 211, folder 1045.
13. Mitford, *Hons and Rebels*, 253.
14. Mitford, *Hons and Rebels*, 253.
15. Dorothy married Leonard Knight Elmhirst in 1925. She and Elmhirst founded Dartington in 1926. Esmond and Giles Romilly, *Out of Bounds*, 17.
16. They wed on September 12, 1939.
17. Mitford, *Hons and Rebels*, 253.
18. Binny, later known as Belinda, went on to become a psychiatrist and a civil rights activist. She traveled to Selma in 1965 to provide first aid and medical assistance to the marchers and was one of the people who treated John Lewis when his skull was fractured by police officers on the Edmund Pettus Bridge. Belinda, and other medical volunteers, treated the wounded in the home of a local minister. Straight wrote of the incident for *The Washington Post*: "The injured began to pour into the kitchen," she wrote. "The little house rocked with cries of anguish. Stumbling, limping, bleeding, retching—more and more staggered in. Some were blinded, others could scarcely breathe, some in terror did not know who or where they were. Over the choking fumes rose the sobs and cries of horror of the relatives." See her obituaries in *The Washington Post* and *Vineyard Gazette*: https://www.washingtonpost.com /local/obituaries/belinda-straight-psychiatrist-and-civil-rights-activist-dies-at-95/2015/12/22 /db7e0f9c-a801-11e5-8058-480b572b4aae_story.html; https://vineyardgazette.com/obituaries /2015/12/15/dr-belinda-straight-civil-rights-activist.
19. See "Folk School to Give Ballad Here Friday," *Washington Post*, December 1, 1940, 16; "Madame Chairman," *Washington Post*, July 27, 1940, 8; "Miss Lenroot to Speak," *Washington Post*, May 22, 1941, 17; "Mrs. Fletcher to Entertain," *Washington Post*, March 10, 1940, 55; "Steven Kennedy to Sing," *Washington Post*, January 28, 1940, F6.
20. Straight, *After Long Silence*, 141.
21. Mitford, *Hons and Rebels*, 257.
22. Interview with Michael Straight, cited by Ingram, *Rebel*, 196.
23. Interview with Michael Straight, cited by Ingram, *Rebel*, 196.
24. Straight, *After Long Silence*, 141.
25. Mitford, *Hons and Rebels*, 250.
26. Mitford, *Hons and Rebels*, 248.
27. Virginia Durr, interview with Sullivan, *Freedom Writer*, 7.
28. Durr, *Outside the Magic Circle*, 5, 6, 19.
29. Durr, *Outside the Magic Circle*, 31–32.
30. Virginia Durr, interview with Sullivan, *Freedom Writer*, 6.
31. Durr, *Outside the Magic Circle*, 79.

32. Virginia Durr, interview with Sullivan, *Freedom Writer*, 418.
33. "Charges of 'petticoat government' really annoyed her [Eleanor's] husband . . . Therefore she never took credit, never referred to her influence on him, and never mentioned her occasionally successful efforts at persuasion. Nor did FDR credit his wife for many positions he gratefully accepted from her." Cook, *Eleanor Roosevelt*, 382.
34. Jessica Mitford to Virginia Durr, June 18, 1963, Schlesinger, VD.
35. Mitford, *A Fine Old Conflict*, as quoted by Sullivan, *Freedom Writer*, 16.
36. Mitford, *Hons and Rebels*, 253, 254.
37. Virginia Durr, interview.
38. As cited by Sussman, *Decca*, 45.
39. "Hitler's Admirer Stricken," *Washington Post*, October 21, 1939; "Unity Mitford Ill in Reich," *New York Times*, October 21, 1939; "Hitler Girlfriend Reported Ill of Sleeping Potion," *Washington Post*, October 30, 1939; "Miss Mitford Tried to Take Life," *New York Times*, October 30, 1939; "Peer's Daughter Quarrels with Hitler," *Chicago Tribune*, October 30, 1939; "Reich Denies Unity Is Ill," *New York Times*, October 31, 1939; "Hitler's Girlfriend Believed Suicide," *Washington Post*, November 5, 1939.
40. Jessica Mitford to Sydney Redesdale, November 23, 1939, Miami, Florida, Sussman, *Decca*, 34.
41. Mitford, *Hons and Rebels*, 261.
42. Mitford, *Hons and Rebels*, 274.
43. Unity had constantly reassured Hitler that England would not declare war. Some historians believe that Hitler relied on this assurance, even imagining that Unity was channeling official British policy or able to act as a courier. But Unity had no ties, either official or unofficial, to British government or military advisors. Her only ties, through Diana, were to the British Fascist Union and Mosley, who never paid her any heed.
44. Guinness, *House of Mitford*, 428.
45. Some believe this could only have been achieved by the Foreign Office giving Unity's case top priority. See Litchfield, *Hitler's Valkyrie*, 231. "[S]afe-conduct through enemy lines" was an "extraordinary measure," Decca later wrote.
46. Mitford, *Hons and Rebels*, 262–63, 270.
47. Jessica Mitford to Sydney Redesdale, November 23, 1939, Sussman, *Decca*, 34–35.
48. Jessica Mitford to Tom Mitford, December 24, 1939, Sussman, *Decca*, 35.
49. Jessica Mitford to Tom Mitford, December 24, 1939, Sussman, *Decca*, 35.
50. Jessica Mitford to Unity Mitford, January–February, 1940. Sussman, *Decca*, 39.
51. Deborah Mitford, Duchess of Devonshire, "My Sister and Hitler: Unity Mitford's War," *The Guardian*, December 7, 2002.
52. "Unity Mitford, Ill, on Way to England," *New York Times*, January 3, 1940; "Loss of Unity Mitford's Memory," *New York Herald Tribune*, January 5, 1940, 2.
53. *Washington Post*, January 4, 1940, 7; "Unity, Hitler's Friend, *Boston Globe*, January 4, 1940.
54. "Miss Mitford Back, Army Guards Pier," *New York Times*, January 4, 1940, 9.
55. "Loss of Memory," *New York Herald Tribune*, January 5, 1940, 2.
56. "Miss Mitford Back, Army Guards Pier," *New York Times*, January 4, 1940, 9.
57. January 26, 1940, *The Daily Mail*, as cited in Pryce-Jones, *Unity Mitford*, 247. See also Litchfield, *Hitler's Valkyrie*, 232.
58. Lovell, *The Sisters*, 309.
59. Her article went on: "The English have no notion of the Jewish danger. Our worst Jews work only behind the scenes. We think with joy of the day when we will be able to say England for

the English! Out with the Jews! Heil Hitler! P.S. please publish my name in full, I want everyone to know I am a Jew hater." *Der Sturmer*. David Pryce-Jones details Unity's tours of the Munich apartments; see *Unity Mitford: A Quest*.

60. Jessica Mitford to Lady Redesdale, February 1, 1940, from Miami, Sussman, *Decca*, 39.

61. See especially "Heil, Heil, the Gang's All Here," *Washington Post*, May 8, 1977.

62. Mitford, *Hons and Rebels*, 273.

63. Jessica Mitford to Esmond Romilly, November 9, 1941, from Seminary Hill, OSU, Box 119, folder 1027.

64. Jessica Mitford to Unity Mitford, January 1940, from Miami, Mosley, *The Mitfords*, 154.

65. Unity Mitford to Jessica Mitford, February 20, 1940, from Old Mill Cottage, High Wycombe, Mosley, *The Mitfords*, 154.

66. Mitford, *Hons and Rebels*, 263.

67. Mitford, *Hons and Rebels*, 267, 269.

68. Mitford, *Hons and Rebels*, 270.

69. In her memoir, Decca incorrectly dates the start of this news storm as the Christmas holidays, but the news did not break until January.

70. "Roosevelt Evokes British Approval," *New York Times*, January 4, 1940. Unity's news coverage became transatlantic news in itself, with the *Chicago Tribune* charging, "Hitler's Friend Causes Rumpus in London Press," and *The New York Times* reporting that the Lord Provost of Glasgow, Patrick Joseph Dollan, had spoken out about Unity's spotlight. "It is simply disgusting," he remarked, "that this attention should be paid to a little flapper who really ought to have her pants spanked instead of getting publicity." "Hitler's Friend Causes Rumpus in London Press," *Chicago Tribune*, January 6, 1940, 2; Incidents in European Conflict," *New York Times*, January 6, 1940, 2.

71. James B. Reston, "A Fair Nazi Is Back in England" *New York Times*, January 7, 1940, 77.

72. "Friend Says Hitler's English Girl Admirer Shot Self in Head," *Los Angeles Times*, January 3, 1940, 1.

73. Jessica Mitford to Sydney Redesdale, February 1, 1940, from Miami, Sussman, *Decca*, 39.

74. "A Fair Nazi Back in England," "Miss Freeman Mitford," and "She Went Home," *New York Times*, January 7, 1940, 77, 73, 77.

75. "Unity's Sister a Miami Waitress," *Chicago Tribune*, January 7, 1940.

76. "Highball Sir? Asks Unity's Sister," *Washington Post*, January 7, 1940, 8.

77. Mitford, *Hons and Rebels*, 272.

78. "Blueblood Adventurers Discover America" and "Two Britons in Hobohemia" *Washington Post*, January 28, 1940, 1, 8; "Unity Reported Wounded Twice," *Washington Post*, January 28, 1940, 11.

79. Litchfield, *Hitler's Valkyrie*, 5. Cannadine writes: "The varied, extreme, and ultimately self-destructive behavior of the Mitford family illustrates . . . embroiled patrician marginality in a particularly concentrated and poignant way. . . . In their flamboyant way they reflected many of the obscure psychological and political motives which were to afflict certain sections of the British aristocracy . . . [they were] textbook declining gentry." See Cannadine, *The Decline and Fall of the British Aristocracy*, 550–51.

80. Jessica Mitford to Lady Redesdale, July 22, 1940, Seminary Hill, Sussman, *Decca*, 41.

81. Mitford, *Hons and Rebels*, 261.

82. Jessica Mitford to Lady Redesdale, February 26, 1940, Miami, Sussman, *Decca*, 40.

83. Oswald Mosley was arrested on May 23, 1940. Diana was arrested on June 29, 1940. They left behind four sons, including their youngest, Max, who was eleven weeks old at the time of

Diana's arrest. Churchill intervened personally to allow the Mosleys to be held in prison together, in December 1941.

84. Mitford, *Fine Old Conflict*, 23; Seminary Hill, boundaried by highways 395 and 495, is about ten miles from central Washington, and just south of both Arlington Cemetery and Reagan National Airport.

85. The RCAF was a joint British/Canadian force which did not become independent from Britain until 1943 and which, in 1940, was very actively recruiting pilots. Esmond, who badly wanted to fly a bomber, was at an advantage in Canada that he might not have had in Great Britain. See Leslie Roberts, *There Shall Be Wings* and Francis, *The Flyer: British Culture and the Royal Air Force, 1939–1945*.

86. Durr, *Outside the Magic Circle*, 138–39.

87. Mitford, *Hons and Rebels*, 277. Decca noted, presciently, that to join the military and submit to its disciplines, Esmond had "to overcome the habits of a lifetime," 278.

88. Esmond Romilly to Jessica Mitford, July 23, 1940, OSU, Box 119, folder 1027.

89. Esmond Romilly to Jessica Mitford, July 19 [1940] from Ottawa, OSU, Box 119, folder 1027.

90. Esmond Romilly to Jessica Mitford, July 19 [1940] from Ottawa, OSU, Box 119, folder 1027.

91. The interstate system was built in the 1950s. Prior to the interstates, and before the national wartime imposition of a 35 mph limit to save gas and rubber, people traveled across country on a hodgepodge of different local roads and highways, with no set or coordinated speed limits, in cars that required much more frequent service and attention than cars today, and without a system of roadside services designed for "easy-on" and "easy-off" service to drivers.

92. Durr, *Outside the Magic Circle*, 139. Information also comes from interviews with Constancia ("Dinky") Romilly.

93. Diane M. Blair, "No Ordinary Time: Eleanor Roosevelt's Address to the 1940 Democratic National Convention," *Rhetoric and Public Affairs* 4, no. 2 (2001), 203–22.

94. Jessica Mitford to Esmond Romilly, July 25, 2940, Seminary Hill, OSU, Box 119, folder 1027.

95. Jessica Mitford to Esmond Romilly, July 31, 1940, Seminary Hill, OSU, Box 119, folder 1027.

96. Virginia Durr, "Interview," for "The Making of a Muckraker."

97. Mitford, *Fine Old Conflict*, 24; Durr, *Outside the Magic Circle*, 150.

98. Jessica Mitford to Esmond Romilly, July 25, 1940, Seminary Hill, OSU, Box 119, folder 1027.

99. Jessica Mitford to Esmond Romilly, July 31, 1940, Seminary Hill, OSU, Box 119, folder 1027.

100. Jessica Mitford to Esmond Romilly, undated, early September 1940, Seminary Hill, OSU, Box 119, folder 1027. There is no record of such a store and it is possible Mitford later misremembered the name. Garfinckel's is the store which most closely fits Decca's recollections and descriptions of a high-end establishment catering to the wives of politicians.

101. Jessica Mitford to Esmond Romilly, undated, early August 1940, Seminary Hill.

102. Jessica Mitford to Esmond Romilly, September 8, 1940, Seminary Hill, OSU, Box 119, folder 1027.

103. "English Adventurers Explore Capital," *Washington Post*, February 25, 1940; "English Adventurers Learn the Hard Way," *Washington Post*, February 18, 1940; "Young Esmond Tries His Hand at Being a Waiter—Is Fired After Two Days," *Washington Post*, March 10, 1940. Toynbee was especially critical of the series, calling it "coy and shameless, a cosy picture of a gallant little English couple fighting against heavy odds to keep their heads above the deep and alien waters of America." Toynbee, *Friends Apart*, 259.

104. Esmond Romilly to Jessica Mitford, July 15, [1940], on Hotel Buffalo stationery.

Chapter Six: "A Prolonged Dull . . . Ache"

1. Jessica Mitford, *Hons and Rebels*, 282.
2. By war's end, Great Britain lost nearly half a million soldiers and about as many were wounded, https://www.britannica.com/event/World-War-II/Costs-of-the-war.
3. Mitford, *Hons and Rebels*, 283.
4. Jessica Mitford to Esmond Romilly, Sunday, October 19 [1941], (from the Durrs), OSU, Box 119, folder 1027.
5. Mitford, *Hons and Rebels*, 277.
6. American Institute of Public Opinion polls, https://news.gallup.com/opinion/polling-matters /232949/american-public-opinion-holocaust.aspx. In November of 1938, according to a Gallup poll, 72 percent of Americans said "no" when Gallup asked: "Should we allow a large number of Jewish exiles from Germany to come to the United States to live."
7. Gallup poll, https://news.gallup.com/opinion/polling-matters/232949/american-public-opinion -holocaust.aspx.
8. Durr, *Outside the Magic Circle*, 142, 141.
9. Mitford, *Hons and Rebels*, 277.
10. Mitford, *Hons and Rebels*, 276.
11. Mitford, *Hons and Rebels*, 277.
12. Jessica Mitford to Esmond Romilly, n.d. [July 1940], OSU, Box 119, folder 1027.
13. Esmond Romilly to Jessica Mitford, September 22, 1941, OSU, Box 119, folder 1027.
14. Mitford, *Hons and Rebels*, 282.
15. Jessica Mitford to Esmond Romilly, Friday [January or early February 1941], OSU, Box 119, folder 1027.
16. Jessica Mitford to Esmond Romilly, September 8, 1940.
17. Mitford, *Hons and Rebels*, 278.
18. Jessica Mitford to Esmond Romilly, November 9, [1941], OSU, Box 119, folder 1027.
19. Esmond Romilly to Jessica Mitford, September 22, 1941, OSU, Box 119, folder 1027. Esmond Romilly to Jessica Mitford, February 2, 1941, OSU, Box 119, folder 1027.
20. Decca treasured these and saved them all her life, keeping them long after she'd turned over all her other papers to archives.
21. Canada entered the war in September 1939, a few days after Great Britain declared war.
22. See "The British Commonwealth Air Training Plan," Bomber Command Museum, http:// www.bombercommandmuseum.ca/bcatp.html; "Commonwealth Air Training Plan", Elgin Military Museum, http://www.theelginmilitarymuseum.ca/commonwealth-air-training-plan.html; "RCAF Students Learning Gunnery at Special School", (31 May 1941) 200 UN 13-971 - Universal News, https://www.youtube.com/watch?v=t8v8qI2dIuU; "British Commonwealth Air Training Program" City of Mossbank, http://mossbank.ca/british-commonwealth-air-training -program/; "The British Commonwealth Air Training Plan", Veteran's Affairs Canada, http:// www.veterans.gc.ca/eng/remembrance/history/second-world-war/british-commonwealth-air -training-plan. Esmond Romilly to Jessica Mitford, July 29 [1940], OSU, Box 119, folder 1027.
23. Esmond Romilly to Jessica Mitford, July 29 and August 4, 1940, OSU, Box 119, folder 1027.
24. Mitford, *Hons and Rebels*, 278.
25. Durr, interview.
26. Jessica Mitford to Esmond Romilly, September 8, 1940, OSU, Box 119, folder 1027.
27. Bill Morris, January 2006 Oral History, "Born, Bombed and Buried in Bermondsey," in the

WW2 People's War, Oral History archive, BBC, https://www.bbc.co.uk/history/ww2peopleswar/stories/88/a8943988.shtml, November 12, 2018.

28. Drew Middleton, "Eyewitness Account: Fiery Glow Turns London into Fantastic Dreamworld," *Washington Post*, October 8, 1940, 1, 4.

29. Raymond Daniell, "Capital is Shaken: Factories, Docks, Public Utilities and Workers' Quarters Bombed," *New York Times*, September 8, 1940.

30. Esmond Romilly to Jessica Mitford, September 15, 1940, from Regina, OSU, Box 119, folder 1027.

31. Ingram, *Rebel*, 210. Almost a year later, Esmond wrote Decca praising the way that British "people stood the raids, got ready for the invasion, endured the boredom, fear, regimentation of their lives with patience and courage that could hardly have been bettered."

32. Esmond Romilly to Jessica Mitford, September 1940, from Training School in Regina Saskatchewan, OSU, Box 119, folder 1027.

33. Jessica Mitford to Esmond Romilly, September 8, 1940, OSU, Box 119, folder 1027.

34. Esmond Romilly to Jessica Mitford, October 25, 1940, OSU, Box 119, folder 1027.

35. Esmond Romilly to Jessica Mitford, Saskatchewan, possibly late September 1940, marked by archive: 9/27/40. Ingram says it was operated on when he was five and that the military doctor thought it might have left him deaf in one ear. Ingram, *Rebel*, 208. Esmond Romilly refers to age of operation in letter of July 21 [1940], OSU, Box 119, folder 1027.

36. Esmond Romilly to Jessica Mitford undated ten-page letter, marked only Monday Morning. [Ingram has it as 7 October.] Ingram, *Rebel*; OSU, Box 119, folder 1027.

37. Esmond Romilly to Jessica Mitford, October 25, 1940. As he put it: "I even think I'll ask Mrs. Romilly to use her influence if necessary with her bro-in-law." OSU, Box 119, folder 1027.

38. Esmond Romilly to Jessica Mitford, Saskatchewan, possibly late September 1940, marked by archive: 9/27/40, OSU, Box 119, folder 1027.

39. Quoted by Ingram, *Rebel*, 212. Ingram cites this as a letter from September 22, 1940.

40. Jessica Mitford to Esmond Romilly, September 8, 1940, OSU, Box 119, folder 1027.

41. Esmond Romilly to Jessica Mitford, September 22, 1941, as quoted by Ingram, *Rebel*.

42. Durr, interview, quoted by Ingram, *Rebel*, 215.

43. Jessica Mitford to Esmond Romilly, Tuesday [1941], OSU, Box 119, folder 1027.

44. Esmond Romilly to Jessica Mitford, March 2, 1941, OSU, Box 119, folder 1027.

45. Sussman, *Decca*, 47.

46. Esmond Romilly to Jessica Mitford, June 27, 1941, as quoted by Ingram, *Rebel*.

47. Esmond Romilly to Jessica Mitford, 12+ page shipboard letter, undated, OSU, Box 119, folder 1027.

48. Jessica Mitford to Esmond Romilly, no date, [February 1941], OSU, Box 119, folder 1027.

49. Aristocrats eat asparagus with their left hands, not with utensils.

50. Jessica Mitford to Esmond Romilly, n.d. [winter 1941], OSU, Box 119, folder 1027.

51. Jessica Mitford to Esmond Romilly, June 26 [1941], OSU, Box 119, folder 1027.

52. Jessica Mitford to Esmond Romilly, August 1, 1941, OSU, Box 119, folder 1027.

53. Rodman Diary, SR.

54. Rodman Diary, SR.

55. Jessica Mitford to Esmond Romilly, July 14 [1941], OSU, Box 119, folder 1027.

56. Jessica Mitford to Esmond Romilly, July 14 [1941], OSU, Box 119, folder 1027.

57. Esmond Romilly to Jessica Mitford, August 23, 1941, OSU, Box 119, folder 1027.

58. Toynbee, *Friends Apart*.
59. This would mean that the baby had been conceived in July or August of 1941, about 5 months after Dinky's birth.
60. Jessica Mitford to Esmond Romilly, August 16 [1941], OSU, Box 119, folder 1027.
61. Jessica Mitford to Esmond Romilly, August 1, 1941, OSU, Box 119, folder 1027.
62. Durr, *Outside the Magic Circle*, interview.
63. Jessica Mitford to Esmond Romilly, August 1, 1941, OSU, Box 119, folder 1027.
64. Jessica Mitford to Esmond Romilly, August 1, 1941, OSU, Box 119, folder 1027.
65. Esmond Romilly to Jessica Mitford, September 26, 1941.
66. Esmond Romilly to Jessica Mitford, October 28, 1941[?], OSU, Box 119, folder 1027.
67. Esmond Romilly to Jessica Mitford, October 16, 1941, September 22, 1941.
68. Roughton said the reason for his suicide was the German-Soviet nonaggression pact.
69. Jessica Mitford to Esmond Romilly, October 29 [1941], OSU, Box 119, folder 1027.
70. Jessica Mitford to Esmond Romilly, November 9, [1941], OSU, Box 119, folder 1027.
71. Jessica Mitford to Esmond Romilly, October 29 [1941], OSU, Box 119, folder 1027.
72. Jessica Mitford to Esmond Romilly, November 9, [1941], OSU, Box 119, folder 1027.
73. Esmond Romilly to Jessica Mitford, October 16, 1941, OSU, Box 119, folder 1027.
74. Esmond Romilly to Jessica Mitford, November 11, 1941, OSU, Box 119, folder 1027.
75. Esmond Romilly to Jessica Mitford, November 23, 1941, Ingram, *Rebel*, 232.
76. Esmond Romilly to Jessica Mitford November 23, 1941, Ingram, *Rebel*, 232.
77. Jessica Mitford to Esmond Romilly, November 8, 1941, telegram, OSU, Box 119, folder 1027.
78. Jessica Mitford to Esmond Romilly, November 15, 1941, OSU, Box 119, folder 1027.
79. Jessica Mitford to Esmond Romilly, December 1, 1941, OSU, Box 119, folder 1027.
80. Earlier that fall, Esmond had twice flown over the North Sea to assist British Air Sea Rescue by searching for survivors, or wreckage, of planes shot down by the Germans. He had never been able to spot anything in the ragged, gray water.
81. Durr, *Outside the Magic Circle*.
82. Jessica Mitford, *Hons and Rebels*, 281. Mitford's second memoir, *A Fine Old Conflict*, devotes hardly more space than this. "He was killed in action in November 1941," it reads, 22.

Chapter Seven: "A Concrete Upper Lip"

1. Mitford, *A Fine Old Conflict*, 22.
2. Esmond is now memorialized, along with 20,274 other military casualties, in Parcel 60 of the Runneymede Memorial Cemetery, as Pilot Officer Esmond Mark David Romilly, Service Number J/5677, 58th Squadron, Royal Canadian Air Force. Dedicated 1953. Parcel 60 is in the southwest corner of the cemetery, near the entrance.
3. Nellie Romilly to Sydney Redesdale, March 31, 1942, OSU, Box 119, folder 1032.
4. In addition to multiple communications from Wing Commander Ronald Clark, Decca received letters of official notification from Wing Commander T. C. Macfarlane (December 3, 1941), from two different divisions of the Department of National Defence Air Service of Canada, the Canadian Red Cross, the Royal Air Force, the Royal Air Force Delegation, the Air Council, the Royal Canadian Air Force Casualties Division, Air Ministry, and others. See OSU Box 121, folder 1054 especially.
5. Sutherland and Cantwell, *The RAF Air Sea Rescue Service 1918–1986*.
6. Esmond Romilly to Jessica Mitford, November 11, 1941, OSU, Box 119, folder 1027.
7. Selden Rodman, Diary, SR.

8. Selden Rodman to Jessica Mitford, December 7, 1941, OSU, Box 120, folder 1045.
9. Peter Nevile to Jessica Mitford, December 8, 1941, OSU, Box 121, folder 1046.
10. Durr, *Outside the Magic Circle*, 141.
11. Jessica Mitford to Sydney Redesdale, January 17, 1942, OSU, Box 211, folder 1698.
12. Denial is widely considered to be the first stage of grieving. Elisabeth Kübler-Ross popularized the five stages of grief as a more or less chronological progression through denial, anger, bargaining, depression, and acceptance. As far as I can tell, Decca skipped bargaining altogether, indulged in almost no depression, and never let go of her anger. See Kübler-Ross, *On Death and Dying*.
13. Romilly, *Boadilla*, 113, 114.
14. Toynbee, *Friends Apart*, 158.
15. Toynbee, *Friends Apart*, 14.
16. See, for example, Mrs. Isabelle Denison to Jessica Romilly, October 22, 1940, OSU, Box 121, folder 1046. Mrs. Denison, of the American Branch of the International Migration Service, wrote in response to many inquiries by Jessica and Esmond about Giles's disappearance. "My Dear Mrs. Romilly," she wrote, "we are glad to tell you that through our Norwegian correspondent has come the information that a man named 'Romilly Giles, born September 19, 1916, in London, is a prisoner of war in Germany."
17. Decca's copy of the Memorandum was dated July 1940. She kept it until her death. OSU, Box 121, folder 1046.
18. Virginia Durr to Sydney Redesdale, n.d. [early 1942], OSU, Box 211, folder 1698.
19. Since these letters ended up in Mitford's own papers, she evidently found out about them at some point. I have seen no evidence that she was angry with Durr about them. Virginia Durr to Sydney Redesdale, no date, OSU, Box 211, folder 1698, and Virginia Durr to Sydney Redesdale, May 6, 1942, OSU, Box 211, folder 1698.
20. Sydney Redesdale to Virginia Durr, March 25, 1942, OSU, Box 211, folder 1698.
21. Sydney Redesdale to Jessica Mitford, January 18, 1942, OSU, Box 211, folder 1698.
22. England's Defence Finance Regulations, issued under the Emergency Powers Defence Act of 1939, controlled the export of British pounds. Considered a nonresident because of living in the United States, Decca would have had virtually no access to British assets, her own or her mother's. Exchange controls were not relaxed until after 1943. "Britain to Retain Exchange Control," *New York Times*, November 27, 1946, 5. See also, Bank of England, "The UK Exchange Control: A Short History," *Quarterly Bulletin*, September 1, 1967, 251–52.
23. Decca kept a clipping of one such article all her life, a short piece from *The Derby Evening Telegraph*, titled "They Once Called Him Unworthy," which rehearsed some of the negative views of Esmond's rebelliousness and unconventionality and concluded: "Now, when Giles is a prisoner and Esmond is missing, perhaps they feel differently." Rosemary Meynell, undated clipping [late 1941], Box 121, folder 1046.
24. "By the time Esmond and I met," Decca told Esmond's biographer, Esmond "had an implacable loathing of her." Jessica Mitford to Kevin Ingram, October 13, 1981, OSU, Box 120, folder 1043.
25. Nellie Romilly, unsigned poem, "Written after a dream," December 4, 1941, OSU, Box 211, folder 1698.
26. Giles Romilly, "My Brother: Poem from a Prison Camp," *Evening Standard*, August 8, 1942, Box 121, folder 1046. Selden Rodman's homage, published years later, paid tribute to that instinct as well, and to Esmond's sacrifice, which "gave the chance to others by your soldier's death." Rodman's elegy also paid tribute to Esmond's playfulness, his competitive streak, his rebelliousness,

and irreverence. Rodman, "In Memoriam," *The Amazing Year*, 26–27. Rodman's diary covered spring 1945–1946, so the August 4 poem for Esmond would have been written in 1945.

27. Jessica Mitford to Aranka Treuhaft, fall 1957, n.d. "Virginia Durr is always saying," Decca wrote her mother-in-law, "that whereas most English people have a 'stiff upper lip' mine has turned to concrete, she's always accusing me of having a concrete upper lip." OSU, Box 217, folder 1749.

28. Ira Katznelson, *Fear Itself*, 316; Kennedy, *Freedom from Fear*, 519–22.

29. Katznelson, *Fear Itself*, 316.

30. Walter Lippman, "Today and Tomorrow: Wake Up, America," *Washington Post*, December 9, 1941, 19.

31. Virginia Durr, *Outside the Magic Circle*, 142–43 and passim.

32. Mitford, *A Fine Old Conflict*, 38.

33. Winston Churchill, *The Grand Alliance*, 1950, 538. Churchill's diary recorded feeling "saved and thankful." Goodwin, *No Ordinary Time*, 290; Churchill, *The Second World War*, 539–40.

34. Virginia Durr to Sydney Redesdale, n.d., [February 1942]. Mary Lovell cites this letter as coming from folder 1032, but the letter does not appear there and is now missing from the archives. See Lovell, *The Sisters*, 351 and n27, 561.

35. Fox, *Watching the English*, 297, 301. From its ruling class, Jeremy Paxman suggests, a whole nation absorbed the notion that "the emotions are there to be controlled" except in those cases—principally involving pets and furry animals—in which extremes of sentimentality are the rule. Paxman, *The English*, 5; 242.

36. According to A. A. Gill, "heroic self-control" is "England's most admirable achievement." *The Angry Island*, 8.

37. Deborah Cavendish to Jessica Mitford, December 12, 1941, Mosley, ed., *The Mitfords*, 186. The day before she wrote her letter to Decca, Deborah also wrote Diana about not knowing what to say. "It is so dreadful about Esmond isn't it, I don't know what to say to poor Squalor, I don't even know how to begin the letter because I can't start Dearest Cheerless like I usually do. Thank goodness she has her pig [Mitford-speak for a baby, derived from watching guinea pigs] anyhow. It is so much worse for her because of her being so queer one feels she would mind even more than most people." Deborah to Diana, November 11, 1941 [passed by prison censor on December 12], Mosley, ed., *The Mitfords*, 185–86.

38. Fox, *Watching the English*, 178; Gill, *The Angry Island*, 214.

39. Jessica Mitford to Sydney Redesdale, June 11, 1948, OSU, Box 211, folder 1698.

40. Reputed by many to be Esmond's father.

41. Goodwin, *No Ordinary Time*, 302.

42. Bob Treuhaft, interview with Mary Lovell, *The Sisters*, 347.

43. Straight later misremembered this day, in his memoir, as occurring on New Year's Day, not on Christmas, but Decca's White House visit was Christmas Day and Churchill's address followed on December 26.

44. Michael Straight, *After Long Silence*, 166. The main purpose of Straight's memoir was to reveal his long-hidden secret that he'd been a Russian spy and to explain why he had done so.

45. Straight, *After Long Silence*, 166.

46. Decca was always contradictory about this question. She told numerous people, including Selden Rodman and Virginia Durr, that she was convinced Esmond was Churchill's son and took that as a given. She also told some people, including Kevin Ingram, Esmond's chosen biographer, that there was no reason to make too much of it. See Virginia Durr to Selden Rodman, 1950s letters with no date. Virginia Durr believed that Esmond was "without doubt Churchill's son."

According to Constancia, Decca believed that story. Constancia also expressed her incredulity that anyone would think it matters one way or another whether he was or not. She expressed no confirmation of such rumors. Interview with Constancia Romilly.

47. According to Mary Lovell, the Mosleys two house servants were sex offenders, chosen, Diana said, "because they are clean and honest." *Sisters*, 364.

48. Various sources list an array of other uses to which Decca is purported to have given this money, and some say it all went for a pony for one of Virginia's daughters (it would be a very rare pony that would cost $500 in 1942). Mary Lovell writes that Decca gave the money to the Communist Party, which would have been even more unlikely, given her lack of Party connections at the time.

49. Goodwin, *No Ordinary Time*, 307–308.

50. Durr, *Outside the Magic Circle*, 141.

51. Jessica Mitford to Sydney Redesdale, February 22, 1942, Sussman, *Decca*, 93.

52. Jessica Mitford to Selden Rodman, [March] 1943.

53. Durr, *Outside the Magic Circle*, 143.

54. Durr, *Outside the Magic Circle*, 146.

55. Goodwin, *No Ordinary Time*, 296.

56. See Zinn, *A People's History of the United States*, 416.

57. Strayer was founded in 1892 in Baltimore. Its D.C. branch was opened in 1904. In D.C., especially during World War I, Strayer helped train the high number of government employees that were needed almost overnight. It is now headquartered in D.C. and has been beset by controversy over high student loan debt, low graduation rates, and scandal in 2013 over fraudulent transcripts for foreign students.

58. The British RAF, founded in 1918, played a decisive role in training pilots in World War II, as well as procuring equipment, supervising air crews, and influencing U.S. policy. It also oversaw the Air Sea Rescue division which had searched for Esmond. See Killebrew, *The Royal Air Force in the American Skies;* Patrick Bishop, "How the RAF Won the War," BBC History Magazine, https://www.historyextra.com/period/second-world-war/raf-centenary-anniversary-won -second-world-war-weapon/; "90 Americans in RAF Become U.S. Aviators," *New York Times* (April 13, 1943), 10.

59. Mitford, *A Fine Old Conflict*, 27, 28.

60. Durr, *Outside the Magic Circle*, 151.

61. Durr, interview (with Ida Landauer), Tape #1, OSU, Box 139, folder 1156.

62. Durr, *Outside the Magic Circle*, 146.

63. Jessica Mitford to Sydney Redesdale, July 30, 1942. Anne Hopkins, later Anne Hopkins Aiken, became one of the founders of American Zen Buddhism and the Buddhist Peace Fellowship. During the time she lived with Decca, she would have been writing her master's thesis in Sociology for Northwestern University, OSU, Box 211, folder 1698.

64. Jessica Mitford to Sydney Redesdale, October 31, 1942, OSU, Box 211, folder 1698.

65. Emily Post, "Rooms for Rent?" *The Atlanta Constitution*, June 13, 1943, 19. See also "Summer Boarders," *Boston Globe*, August 28, 1940, 15; "Life with Mother Taylor," *New York Times*, April 4, 1943, 1; "Boarder Shot in Argument Over Radio," *Washington Post*, June 1, 1941; and "Landlady Turns Other Cheek After Star-Boarder Slaps It," *Pittsburgh Courier*, March 2, 1940.

66. Jessica Mitford to Sydney Redesdale, October 31, 1942. OSU, Box 211, folder 1698.

67. Bridget Clarke, "Requisitioned Houses in Wartime," St. John's Wood Memories, www .stjohnswoodmemories.org.uk/content/memories/world_war_1_world_war_2/requisitioned

_houses_in_wartime; "Land and Property Requisitioned for War in the 20th Century," National Archives, 25 October 2018, www.nationalarchives.gov.uk/help-with-your-research/research -guides/land-requisitioned-war/; "Rutland Gate: Early Development of Rutland Gate, 1836- c.1847," in *Survey of London: Volume 45, Knightsbridge*, ed. John Greenacombe (London, 2000), 144–51; British History Online, http://www.british-history.ac.uk/survey-london/vol45/pp144 -151. In May 1942, their country house at Wycombe was requisitioned and "turned into a hostel for 25 women." Sydney Redesdale to Jessica Mitford, May 20, 1942, OSU Box 211, folder 1698.

68. Nancy Mitford to Violet Hammersley, October 1, 1940, and December 2, 1940, Mosley, ed., *Love from Nancy*.

69. Nancy Mitford to Violet Hammersley, December 26, 1940, *Love from Nancy*, 108.

70. Mitford, *A Fine Old Conflict*, 30.

71. Mitford, *A Fine Old Conflict*, 30.

72. Mitford, *A Fine Old Conflict*, 31.

73. Jessica Mitford to Betty Friedan, January 6, 1964, OSU, Box 147, folder 1222.

74. Robert Treuhaft Report, Harvard Twenty-fifth Reunion. Mitford reprinted Bob's report in *A Fine Old Conflict*, 35.

75. Treuhaft, Oral History. See also Bob Treuhaft to Aranka Treuhaft.

76. Graham was another woman who refashioned herself completely, going from dutiful wife to fearless publisher who would not back down on releasing the Watergate documents and covering the scandal.

77. Jessica Mitford to Kay Graham, December 1942, OSU.

78. Jessica Mitford to Doris ("Dobby") Walker, April 6, 1973, OSU, Box 1, folder 1.

79. Treuhaft, Oral History, 14, 8.

80. Treuhaft, Oral History, 14, 8.

81. Treuhaft, Oral History.

82. At the time of his death, Bob's father, Albin, had already, and just recently, left the family, having made a bad investment in a restaurant and been caught in an affair with a waitress. He had taken out a substantial life insurance policy, planning to commit suicide, just prior to finding out he had terminal cancer, and he was unaware that had he committed suicide, the policy would not have paid out.

83. Scrabble was not commercially marketed until 1948, but numerous anagrammatic word games preceded it. Decca was a lifelong Scrabble aficionado and a brilliant player. There was almost always a Scrabble board set up in mid-play in her home.

84. Sussman, *Decca*, 51.

85. Mitford, *A Fine Old Conflict*, 43.

Chapter Eight: The "New Life"

1. Jessica Mitford to Constancia Romilly, February 26, 1959, Sussman, *Decca*, 187.

2. Jessica Mitford to Constancia Romilly, October 31, 1958; January 7, 1959 [mismarked 1958], courtesy of Constancia Romilly and Peter Sussman, in author's collection.

3. Jessica Mitford To Constancia Romilly, January 7, 1959. Decca usually avoided introspection. But she could be thoughtful about emotions with her daughter Constancia, especially if she felt that she was struggling. Her love for her daughter brought out what Decca derided as "poor old Mama's efforts to philosophize." "The Pursuit of Happiness," she added in this same letter, "is rather a chimera." Sussman, *Decca*, 184.

4. Jessica Mitford to Constancia Romilly, February 26, 1959, Sussman, *Decca*, 187.

5. Mitford, *Fine Old Conflict*, 55.

6. Jessica Mitford to Constancia Romilly, October 31, 1958.

7. Mitford, *Fine Old Conflict*, 51.

8. Harris, et al., *The Home Front*, 115. By 1944, 2.75 million women with children under 14 had entered the U.S. workforce. See Hartmann, *The Home Front & Beyond*, 84.

9. Mitford, *Fine Old Conflict*, 44.

10. The building has now been torn down to make way for a school.

11. The San Francisco housing shortage was so severe that in February 1943, a month before she arrived, San Francisco's mayor had asked city hotels to provide cots for soldiers in dining rooms and ballrooms. See also Sinclair, *San Francisco*, 36.

12. Lingeman, "Don't You Know There's a War On?," 69.

13. Marjorie Cartwright and Frances Veeder, oral histories, in Harris, *The Homefront*, 191, 178.

14. Lingeman, "Don't You Know," 81.

15. This placed Decca's salary a few hundred dollars above the national average, but San Francisco salaries were especially high, as were all salaries in California. Bob later reported that he believed she was only earning about $1,200 at the time. Treuhaft, Oral History.

16. In her memoir, Decca called her Mrs. Tibbs.

17. Hartmann, *The Home Front & Beyond*, 84. On the problems that women workers with children faced in San Francisco, see also Takaki, *Double Victory*, 46, 98, and passim.

18. Mrs. Betts charged only an additional forty dollars a month for day care. The going rate was closer to one hundred dollars a month.

19. Mitford, *Fine Old Conflict*, 44.

20. Starr, *Embattled Dreams*, 78.

21. Samuel Redman, "During World War II, Thousands of Women Chased Their Own California Dream." *Smithsonian*, November 29, 2017. See also C. Taeuber, "Wartime Population Changes in the United States," *Milbank Memorial Fund Quarterly* 24, no. 3 (1946): 236; E. Lee and A. Lee, "Internal Migration Statistics for the United States," *Journal of the American Statistical Association* 55, no. 292 (1960); United States Census Bureau, "Before and After 1940: Change in Population Density," August 16, 2012, https://www.census.gov/dataviz/visualizations/010./.

22. Twelve million new enlistees signed up after Pearl Harbor, and many of them left families behind to serve. See Polenberg, *War and Society*, 138.

23. Polenberg reports that divorce rates increased each year from 1940 to 1945. See Polenberg, *War and Society*, 138. Polenberg neglects to mention that marriage soared in the same period. See Cott, *Public Vows: A History of Marriage and the Nation*, 187. On rising divorce rates, see 195 and passim.

24. See Cott, *Public Vows: A History of Marriage and the Nation*, 185.

25. Johnson, *The Second Gold Rush*, Kindle, 37 of 3968.

26. It is now known as the Twitter Building because it houses the offices of Twitter, or X as it is now called.

27. Mitford, *Fine Old Conflict*, 39.

28. See Mitford, *Fine Old Conflict*, 39.

29. The correspondence between Decca and Bob has largely disappeared, though both refer to it and quote from it in later writings. The quotes in this paragraph come from Mitford, *A Fine Old Conflict*, 45–46.

30. In a foreword to a guidebook about San Francisco, Decca acknowledged San Francisco's "glamor," only to concentrate almost entirely on the superiorities of the grittier and less glamorous Oakland. See Mitford, Foreword, Adams, *San Francisco*.

31. Jessica Mitford to Sydney Redesdale, April 11, 1943, OSU, Box 211, folder 1698.

32. FBI reports, April [n.d.] 1943 and April 9, 1943. These reports were filled with errors. A March 1943 report, done in the FBI's Miami office, for example, described Churchill as Decca's "uncle." FBI Papers.

33. California Communist Party leader Dorothy Healey later recollected that "so unquestioning was our support for the war that a few months later [after Executive Order 9066] we raised no objections when Japanese American citizens, including some of our own comrades, like Karl Yoneda, along with his non-Japanese wife, Elaine Black, were sent to relocation camps in the western desert. *The People's World* fired its sole Japanese American employee in the early months of the war. Healey, *California Red*, 87. On the Party, internment, and racism towards Asians, see also David Jenkins, "The Union Movement, the California Labor School and San Francisco Politics," an oral history conducted in 1987 and 1988 by Lisa Rubens, Regional Oral History Office, International Longshoremen's and Warehousemen's Union Oral History Series, Bancroft Library, University of California Berkeley, 1993. Order 9066, for example, was authorized by Durr's brother-in-law, Hugo Black.

34. Angelou, *I Know Why the Caged Bird Sings*, 178.

35. Clark, *Rosie the Riveter Revisited*, 42.

36. The list of consumer goods that were not manufactured during the war, in fact, was long. Doris Kearns Goodwin writes that "government regulations extended into almost every aspect of American life. Shortages of iron and steel prohibited the manufacture of a wide range of consumer items, including electric refrigerators, vacuum cleaners, sewing machines, electric ranges, washing machines and ironers, radios and phonographs, lawn mowers, waffle irons, and toasters. The use of stainless steel was prohibited in tableware. Shoe manufacturers were ordered to avoid double soles and overlapping tips; lingerie makers were limited to styles without ruffles, pleating, or full sleeves." Goodwin, *No Ordinary Time*, 394; Nancy Walker, *Shaping Our Mothers' World: American Women's Magazines*; Nancy Walker, *Women's Magazines, 1940–1960: Gender Roles and the Popular Press*.

37. David Kennedy credits the substantial Republican gains of the 1942 election, for example, largely to "frustration" and "smoldering resentment" towards the "nettlesome" Office of Price Administration. See his *Freedom from Fear*, 782; Charles E. Egan, "OPA Gives its Critics a Chance," *New York Times*, August 22, 1943, E7; Goodwin, *No Ordinary Time*, 231.

38. *The Washington Post* was such a harsh critic of the pleasure-driving ban that, in the summer of 1943, its editorial page issued something of an apology to both the OPA and the Petroleum Administration for War for having gone too far in its objections to government controls over resources needed for war. See "Gasoline Rationing," *Washington Post*, August 28, 1943, 4.

39. Mark Sullivan, "Defense Rulings: Have Been Offensive," *Washington Post*, January 15, 1943, 8.

40. "The Basic Problem," *New York Times*, March 26, 1943, 18.

41. "Exposing the Tyrant," *Chicago Daily Tribune*, September 10, 1943, 16.

42. Bob agreed with her. In 1942 he lamented that "nobody seems to want to do anything drastic about winning the war. People have the crazy notion that we'll muddle through somehow, without any radical change in our way of being." Robert Treuhaft to Aranka Treuhaft, postmarked November 6, 1942, OSU, Box 216, folder 1742.

43. Mitford, *Fine Old Conflict*, 49.

44. Mark Sullivan, "Business Experience: Reorganizing OPA," *Washington Post*, July 19, 1943, 10.
45. Goodwin, *No Ordinary Time*, 384.
46. Andrew H. Bartels, "The Office of Price Administration and the Legacy of the New Deal, 1939–1946," *The Public Historian*, vol. 5, no. 3, 1983, 5–29; Harvey C. Mansfield, *A Short History of OPA*, 1947.
47. Lingeman, "Don't You Know," 269; Kennedy, *Freedom from Fear*, 620.
48. Kennedy, *Freedom from Fear*, 641. The president's efforts to hold back inflation cast new light on the problems and limits of the OPA. Subsidies were intended to help hold the line on prices, but maintaining civilian supplies was a hurdle that hampered all efforts at price control, *The New York Times* reported. Turner Catledge, "OPA Runs into Trouble on 'Hold the Line' Order," *New York Times*, June 6, 1943.
49. Kennedy, *Freedom from Fear*, 640.
50. Mitford, *Fine Old Conflict*, 47–49.
51. Decca had great respect for McTernan and sided with him in the many battles between progressives and conservatives that were splitting the OPA. When McTernan was fired in late July 1943, not long after this incident, Decca rightly realized that her own position was in jeopardy. "Firing him is just another dirty manoeuvre of those in OPA who are really against strong enforcement," Decca angrily noted. Jessica Mitford to Aranka Treuhaft, July 30, 1943. McTernan went into private practice after being fired from the OPA and became famous as a left-wing lawyer, working for over fifty years in partnership with Ben Margolis, who defended the Hollywood Ten. His clients included Angela Davis (for whom he won reinstatement at UCLA), and the United Farm Workers, and others. McTernan, who was a Communist Party member for some years, had six cases before the U.S. Supreme Court and served on the national board of the ACLU. His brother, Francis McTernan, defended Decca when she was called up before HUAC. Mitford's friend, Cedric Belfrage, lauded McTernan in his book *The American Inquisition* for his bravery.
52. Mitford, *Fine Old Conflict*, 44.
53. Jessica Mitford to Sydney Redesdale, March 3, 1943. The Belfrages had not yet set up an outpost in Cuernavaca, which later became a home to many progressives, including those blacklisted from Hollywood in the 1950s, but numerous left-wing activists, including some refugees from Spain, had already established themselves. Sussman, *Decca*, 97.
54. Mitford, *Fine Old Conflict*, 45.
55. "14,045,000 Hear Churchill Address," *Boston Globe*, May 19, 1943, 1; "Congress Pleased by Churchill Talk: Address Found Encouraging," *New York Times*, May 20, 1943, 3; "Cities to be 'Ashes': Churchill Says Britain Will Join in Scourging [Japan]," *New York Times*, May 20, 1943, 1.
56. Jessica Mitford to Sydney Redesdale, April 11, 1943, Sussman, *Decca*, 97–98.
57. The UFWA had grown to over 130 chapters by 1943, representing close to 20,000 federal workers. Arnesen, *Encyclopedia of U.S. Labor and Working-Class History*.
58. Mitford, *Fine Old Conflict*, 51.
59. FBI Report on Jessica Mitford, OSU and Peter Sussman archive, San Francisco File, SAC, SF. FBI.
60. In her memoir, Mitford noted the union's reputation, wrote that she hoped it was true [that it was Communist] and that the union would be "a step towards finding the Communist Party." Of course, she'd already found it by then and was already involved. Here, as in many other cases, Mitford compresses and alters chronology to suit the demands of narrative. Mitford, *Fine Old Conflict*, 49.
61. Mitford, *Fine Old Conflict*, 53.

62. Dobby was later a partner in Bob's law firm.
63. Jessica Mitford to Sydney Redesdale, May 30, 1943, OSU, Box 211, folder 1698.
64. Jessica Mitford to Sydney Redesdale, July 11, 1943. The Dies committee (House Committee on Un-American Activities) chaired by Martin Dies (Democrat from Texas) was formed in May 1938 to investigate so-called disloyalty on the part of American citizens. It played an important role in arguing for the relocation of Japanese-Americans and it led to the creation of the House Unamerican Activities Committee (HUAC) chaired by Joseph McCarthy. Citizens investigated by Dies, regardless of the committee's findings, often found themselves ostracized from their communities, fired from their jobs, even thrown out of their churches and civic groups. OSU, Box 211, folder 1698.
65. Sullivan, ed., *Freedom Writer*, 13.
66. Virginia Durr, Oral History, 1974, Oral History Research Office, Columbia University, transcription, OSU, Box 140, folder 1158.
67. Durr, *Outside the Magic Circle*, 103.
68. Virginia Durr, Oral History, March 13, 14, and 15, 1975, interview G-0023–23-2, Oral History Program, Southern Oral History Program Collection, interview with Sue Thrasher. University of North Carolina, Chapel Hill. (#4007), series, "Documenting the American South."
69. Durr, *Outside the Magic Circle*, 168, 165.
70. Mitford, *Fine Old Conflict*, 51.
71. Mitford, *Fine Old Conflict*, 52.
72. Sussman, *Decca*, 102.
73. Robert Treuhaft to Aranka Treuhaft, June [28] 1943, OSU, Box 216, folder 1742.
74. Jessica Mitford to Sydney Redesdale, June 28, 1943, OSU, Box 211, folder 1698.
75. This was exceedingly rare. One study suggests that as few as 1 percent of men in 1940 were doing any significant amount of domestic labor and that, of those, the great majority were between forty-five and fifty-four years of age and, hence, probably less involved in any of the tasks that childrearing made necessary. See Donna Scanlon, https://blogs.loc.gov/inside_adams/2010107 /men_housework_1940-1950 and United States Census, 1940.
76. Mitford, *Fine Old Conflict*, 55.
77. Mitford, *Fine Old Conflict*, 57.
78. The National War Labor Board was still new, having been established in 1942 to supersede the NLRB in wartime and to help avoid strikes and lockouts during the war. While some unions resented the board's authority, as they resented the OPA, the board's support for equal pay for the same work was seen as progressive by many, and the board was understood as a champion of women workers and Black workers. W. H. Lawrence, "War Labor Board Created; Davis Heads 12-Man Body," *New York Times*, January 13, 1942, 1; Alfred Friendly," War Labor Board of 12 Set Up by Roosevelt," *Washington Post*, January 13, 1942, 1; National War Labor Board Press Release, No. B 693, June 4, 1943, in "Chapter 24: Equal Pay for Women," The Termination Report of the National War Labor Board: Industrial Disputes and Wage Stabilization in Wartime, January 12, 1942–December 31, 1945, vol. 1, 290–91.
79. Virginia Durr, undated interview [with Ida Landauer], OSU, Box 139, folder 1156.
80. Mitford, *Fine Old Conflict*, 62, 63, and passim.

Chapter Nine: "A Serious Person"
1. Mitford, *A Fine Old Conflict*, 50. "A serious person of single-aim sincerity" was a quote (a misquote in fact) that Decca took from Esmond's book on Spain, *Boadilla*.

2. Jessica Mitford to Carl Bernstein, September 17, 1988, OSU, Box 177, folder 1357.

3. Jessica Mitford to Sydney Redesdale, June 28, 1943, OSU, Box 211, folder 1698.

4. Mitford, *Fine Old Conflict*, 25.

5. According to David Jenkins, Communist Party member and first director of the California Labor School, membership in the Party in San Francisco, in the early 1940s, was between three to four thousand people out of approximately ten thousand Party members in the state. Party membership numbers vary widely across different estimates and are notoriously inaccurate, following the need for Party members to keep their affiliation secret. See Jenkins, "The Union Movement," Oral History, 140. Jenkins reports that the two key longshoremen's unions, the ILWU, and the Longshoremen's Union, had over seventeen thousand members combined.

6. California Labor School Spring 1944 Catalogue. California Labor School, Labor Archives and Research Center, J. Paul Leonard Library, San Francisco State University, http://digital -collections.library.sfsu.edu/digital/collection/p16737coll1/id/524/rec/4. See also California Labor School, Social Networks and Archival Context Project, https://snaccooperative.org /view/17402626.

7. Jenkins "The Union Movement," Oral History, 147, 133.

8. At the same time that the California Labor School was founded, similar schools were attempting this new model in Boston, Philadelphia, Chicago, and New York. The California Labor School struck a particularly reciprocal relationship with the Jefferson School in New York, often exchanging speakers. See Gettleman, "The Lost World of United States Labor Education: Curricula at East and West Coast Communist Schools, 1944–1957," *American Labor and the Cold War*, 205–15.

9. "Literally every union in the Bay Area endorsed us and gave us a monthly stipend," Jenkins noted. Jenkins "The Union Movement," Oral History, 151. Philip Foner, George Hitchcock, Tillie Olsen, Erik Erikson, Pele de Lappe, Dorothy Erskine, Pablo O'Higgins, Celeste Strack, Ralph Stackpole, Anton Refregier, and others, all taught at the California Labor School.

10. The Summer 1944 catalogue shows more than ten classes available each weekday evening, from News Writing to Russian to Recreational Dance to Public Speaking, to Race Relations and Public Health. California Labor School 1944 Summer Term Catalog, California Labor School, Labor Archives and Research Center, J. Paul Leonard Library, San Francisco State University, http://digital-collections.library.sfsu.edu/digital/collection/p16737coll1/id/524/rec/4.

11. Pele de Lappe, *Pele: A Passionate Journey Through Art & The Red Press*, 38.

12. Healey, *California Red*, 60.

13. Marge Frantz, "Seeing Red: Stories of American Communists," 1983, Documentary, American Film Institute, Directed by Jim Klein and Julia Reichert, produced by Aaron Ezekeil and Julia Reichert, New Day Films, 1983.

14. The USSR's shocking nonaggression pact with Hitler was not broken until Hitler's 1941 invasion of Russia.

15. Denning, *The Cultural Front*, 11.

16. Denning, *The Cultural Front*, 4.

17. Esmond as quoted by Mitford, *A Fine Old Conflict*, 49–50.

18. Decca's good friend Pele de Lappe describes some of the collective meals and housing arrangements in *Pele: A Passionate Journey Through Art & The Red Press*.

19. Robert Treuhaft to Aranka Treuhaft, June 19, 1943. "Club" was then a term for communist groups, sometimes called cells. OSU, Box 216, folder 1742.

20. Mitford, *Fine Old Conflict*.

21. Dobby Walker to Carl Bernstein, in Carl Bernstein, *Loyalties*, 75. Carl Bernstein is best known for his Pulitzer Prize-winning reporting on Watergate.
22. Jessica Mitford to Dobby Walker, May 6, 1973, OSU, Box 1, folder 2.
23. Mitford, *Fine Old Conflict*, 50.
24. Most sources put Walker's joining the Party at seventeen, but a few put it later, after passing the bar, which would be much closer to meeting Decca.
25. See Doris Brin Walker, "How I Happened to Become the Guild's First Woman President," *Guild Practitioner* 64 (2007), n. p.
26. According to Bettina Aptheker, Walker was "intensely conscientious." Aptheker, *The Morning Breaks*, 69.
27. "Heroic" was one of Decca's terms for Walker. See Jessica Mitford to Doris Brin Walker, May 7, 1951.
28. Jessica Mitford to Aranka Treuhaft, July 30, 1943, OSU, Box 216, folder 1742.
29. Robert E. Treuhaft Papers, TAM 664, Tamiment Library and Robert F. Wagner Labor Archive, Elmer Holmes Bobst Library, New York University, Box 1, folder 18, letters from B. T. Oliver and Bob's responses.
30. Her new boss was John T. McTernan. McTernan later became legendary for fighting the House Un-American Activities Committee, winning Angela Davis's reinstatement at the University of California, and trying numerous landmark Supreme Court cases over civil and social rights.
31. Mitford, *Fine Old Conflict*, 50, 54. "I roared about the Union of S. African Republics," Decca wrote her mother. "I meant <u>trade</u> union meetings." Jessica Mitford to Sydney Redesdale, August 21, 1944, OSU, Box 211, folder 1698.
32. Robert Treuhaft, Oral History.
33. Mitford, *Fine Old Conflict*, 139.
34. Robert Treuhaft, Oral History. This was a time when women's hats were essential accessories in high fashion. See, for example, "Green Favored for Hats; Aranka Showing Also Features New Shade Called Eggnog," *New York Times*, March 13, 1947, 13.
35. Jessica Mitford to William L. Patterson, August 9, 1977, OSU, Box 211, folder 1689.
36. Jessica Mitford to Aranka Treuhaft, July 30, 1943, OSU, Box 216, folder 1742.
37. Robert Treuhaft, Oral History.
38. A transcontinental flight in 1943 would have required three stops and cost upwards of $4,000 in today's currency. It is highly unlikely that Bob or Decca could have paid for this flight and much more probable that the flight was another gift from Aranka.
39. Jessica Mitford to Aranka Treuhaft, October 8, 1943, OSU, Box 216, folder 1742.
40. Mitford, *Fine Old Conflict*, 62.
41. Mitford, *Fine Old Conflict*, 63.
42. Robert Treuhaft, Oral History.
43. Rose Podmaka, "Seeing Red: Stories of American Communists," 1983, Documentary.
44. Communist Party membership card, in Bob's personal papers, Robert E. Treuhaft Papers, TAM 664, Tamiment Library and Robert F. Wagner Labor Archive, Elmer Holmes Bobst Library, New York University.
45. Landon R. Y. Storrs, "Red Scare Politics and the Suppression of Popular Front Feminism: The Loyalty Investigation of Mary Dublin Keyserling," *Journal of American History* (September 2003), 510. "Social connections" were at the heart of American Communism, and the "centrality of relationships" both created and reinforced political bonds," write Kathleen A. Brown

and Elizabeth Fave, "Social Bonds, Sexual Politics, and Political Community on the U.S. Left, 1920s–1940s," *Left History* 7, no. 1 (Spring 2000), 9–45.

46. Lillian Carlson, "A California Girlhood," *Red Diapers*, 25–26.

47. Unidentified speaker; California Party leader Dorothy Healey, "Seeing Red: Stories of American Communists," 1983, Documentary.

48. Robert Treuhaft, Oral History.

49. Mitford, *Fine Old Conflict*, 66 and passim.

50. Mitford, *Fine Old Conflict*, 64.

51. See Buhle, *Marxism in the United States*, 194.

52. Mitford, *Fine Old Conflict*, 65.

53. "Communist Party Membership by Districts, 1922–1950," *Mapping American Social Movements Through the 20th Century*, Civil Rights and Labor History Consortium, University of Washington.

54. Mitford, *Fine Old Conflict*, 67.

55. The *Daily People's World*, still publishing weekly as *People's World*, was founded in 1938 as a Communist daily. It changed its name over the years from *Daily People's World* to *People's World*, lost subscribers from a high of more than twenty thousand in its early days to a low of a few thousand, and merged with the *Daily World*, once the *Daily Worker*, which was founded in 1924.

56. Richmond, *A Long View from the Left*, 272–73.

57. Richmond calculated that launching an urban daily would require roughly $15 million in 1938. The paper had $37,500. See Richmond, *Long View*, 271. Nevertheless, *The People's World* quickly became, as Marxist historian Michael Denning puts it, "the voice of the California left." *Cultural Front*, 414.

58. Mitford, *Fine Old Conflict*, 75.

59. Pele de Lappe, "Remembering Decca: A Fine Old Life," in Pele de Lappe Papers, Box 1, folder 12, San Francisco State University Labor Archives and Research Center.

60. See Benjamin Aaron, "Catalyst: The National War Labor Board of World War II," *Case Western Reserve Law Review* 39, no. 2 (1988): 519–43; W. H. Lawrence, "War Labor Board Created; Davis Heads 12-Man Body," *New York Times*, January 13, 1942, 1; National War Labor Board Press Release, No. B 693, in chap. 24, "Equal Pay for Women," The Termination Report of the National War Labor Board: Industrial Disputes and Wage Stabilization in Wartime," January 12, 1942–December 31, 1945, vol. 1, 290–91; Orleck, *Rethinking American Women's Activism*, 40; Pedrick and Scham, *Inside Affirmative Action*.

61. The Women's Commission of the Party local disapproved, asking for "more seriousness and concern" in dealing with women's issues.

62. See Pele de Lappe, *Pele: A Passionate Journey Through Art & The Red Press*.

63. Pele and Bert had been in Washington, in 1937, while Bert worked a brief period for the National Labor Relations Board. While they knew Al and Sylvia Bernstein there, they seem not to have met Bob and Decca until both were also in San Francisco.

64. Undated interview (VHS), transcribed, Pele de Lappe with Edith and unidentified male interviewer, circa 1986–87.

65. Weigard, *Red Feminism*, 31.

66. Jenkins, "The Union Movement," Oral History.

67. Mitford, *Fine Old Conflict*, 80, 81, 71.

68. "Operation Harvest Festival," as the Nazis called it (Polish prisoners dubbed it "Bloody

Wednesday"), by most estimates, killed over forty thousand prisoners, surpassing even the killings at Babi Yar.

69. Mosley had had phlebitis on and off for years and would bind his leg when the problem recurred. Some, including his oldest son, believe that he deliberately exacerbated the condition, in prison, in hopes of being released. See Mosley, *Rules of the Game*, 501.

70. "British Workers Assail Decision to Free Mosley," *New York Herald Tribune*, November 19, 1943, 7A. See also "Mosley Release Protests Mount," *Washington Post*, November 19, 1943, 3; "Mosley Is Freed Secretly, Goes into Seclusion," *New York Herald Tribune*, November 21, 1943, 1; Padraic King, "They Say Sir Oswald Mosley Had Champagne in Jail," *Daily Boston Globe*, November 28, 1943, C5; George Padmore, "British Colonials Irked by Release of Fascist Mosley," *Chicago Defender*, December 4, 1943, 21; "Mosleys Miss Welcome Mat," *Atlanta Constitution*, December 10, 1943, 26.

71. "Opposition to Sir Oswald Mosley's Release from Prison Increases," *Boston Globe*, November 19, 1943, 2; "Britain Takes Action to Explain Proposal to Release Mosley," *Washington Post*, November 20, 1943, 2; "Britain Releases Mosley Quietly: Protests Grow in Intensity," *New York Times*, November 21, 1943, 33; "British Reds See Fascist Threats," *New York Times*, November 22, 1943, 10. Clementine Churchill wrote her husband Winston (who was in Egypt) about the "large but good-tempered" protests. Mary Soames, ed., *Speaking for Themselves: The Personal Letters of Winston and Clementine Churchill* (New York: Doubleday, 1998), 488.

72. Nancy Mitford to Diana Mosley, December 21, 1943, Mosley, ed. *The Mitfords*, 193.

73. As a joke, Nancy pasted one of them on a postcard to Diana. See Mosley, ed., *Love From Nancy*, 119.

74. Jessica Mitford to Sydney Redesdale, November 23, 1943, OSU, Box 211, folder 1698.

75. Jessica Mitford to Sydney Redesdale, November 23, 1943, OSU, Box 211, folder 1698.

76. Mosley, *A Life of Contrasts*, 198.

77. De Courcy, *Diana Mosley*, 275.

78. Lovell, *The Sisters*, 378. Lovell, often generous to the right-wing side of the family, was given extensive access to Mitford family archives and granted access to Sydney's papers that other researchers have not received. Sonia Purnell, Clementine's latest biographer, maintains that "despite her blood ties to the Mitfords, Clementine felt little sympathy. Her perspective was simple: the Mosleys and Mitfords were fascists and should not be indulged." See Purnell, *Clementine*, 249.

79. Sydney Redesdale to Jessica Mitford, January 1, 1944, OSU, Box 211, folder 1698.

80. Jessica Mitford, *Fine Old Conflict*, 57.

81. Jessica Mitford to Winston Churchill, November 24, 1943. "The *Chronicle* story caused quite a stir in the union," Decca was pleased to note. OSU, Box, 163, folder 1290.

82. Mitford, *Fine Old Conflict*, 61. In *A Fine Old Conflict*, Decca expressed some regret about her behavior, writing: "Rereading the letter today, I find it painfully stuffy and self-righteous—and also, as Nancy later pointed out in her understated fashion, 'not very sisterly. . . . No doubt, these views—as comes through strongly in my letter—were admixed with deep bitterness over Esmond's death and a goodly dash of familial spitefulness." Interestingly, she also writes there that she hoped her letter might bring her closer to an invitation to join the Communist Party. But of course, by November 1943, she'd accepted that invitation and was very active as a new member. This is another instance of Decca allowing narrative to trump chronology in her memoir, as her next chapter is about joining the Communist Party. Pele de Lappe, interview, transcribed, OSU.

83. In 1946, the JAFRC was accused of being a Communist front organization and brought before HUAC. When the board refused to turn over any of its records for investigation, all board members were jailed.

84. "Off speakers" is Mitford-speak for no longer talking to someone.

85. Mitford, *Fine Old Conflict*, 139–40. Brackets within quote are Decca's.

86. Jessica Mitford to Sydney Redesdale, March 27, 1944 [arrived April 21, 1944, as letters between England and America often took a month, or longer, to arrive], OSU, Box 211, folder 1698.

87. Nancy Mitford to Jessica Mitford, March 11, 1944.

88. Inexplicably, Nancy and Decca often called one another "Susan," which others found confusing. Jessica Mitford to Nancy Mitford, April 24, 1944, Chatsworth House Archives.

89. Jessica Mitford to Aranka Treuhaft, May 1944, n.d., OSU, Box 216, folder 1743.

90. Jessica Mitford to Nancy Mitford, n.d., circa May 1945; Jessica Mitford to Sydney Redesdale, June 15, 1944. Benjy was named "Tito" after Josip Broz Tito, the Yugoslavian Communist revolutionary who led the Yugoslav Partisans against the German Nazis and served, after the war, as prime minister and then president, from 1944 to his death in 1980. While many historians now see him as dictatorial, he was considered quite heroic in the immediate after-war era.

91. This letter was forwarded to Decca by Sydney. David's nostalgia for a prewar world was common in both England and America. The Cavendish family, into which Deborah had married, stood for the old England of tradition, aristocracy, land, stability, and empire. But even Cavendish power, privilege, and wealth could be undone by war. On May 6, Andrew's brother, Billy Hartington, heir to the dukedom of Devonshire, married Kathleen "Kick" Kennedy, daughter of Joseph and Rose, sister to Bobby, John, Ted, Eunice, Joe Jr., Rosemary, Patricia, and Jean. The media loved the young, plucky, photogenic pair. By September 9, however, Billy was dead, killed in Belgium four months after the wedding, and just days after Britain's troops liberated Brussels from Germany. Four years later, still in her early twenties, Kick was killed in a plane crash. See especially Devonshire, *Wait for Me!: Memoirs* and Leaming, *Kick Kennedy*.

92. Gettleman, "The Lost World of United States Labor Education," 207.

93. Classes offered in San Francisco that were not offered in Oakland included: American History, American Political Parties, Current Events ("especially designed for swing shift workers and housewives"), Philosophy, Latin America and the U.S., Race Relations and Politics, Our Underground Allies, Social Criticism in Modern Literature (featuring works by Richard Wright, John Dos Passos, Romain Rolland, Theodore Dreiser, Anna Sehers, Mikhail Sholokov, and others), Russian, Spanish, Creative Writing, Radio Script Writing, Basic Design, Furniture Making, Composition, Color, Mimeograph, Musical History. Spring 1944 catalogue.

94. California Labor School, Oakland, 1945 Fall Catalogue. San Francisco State University Labor Archives Research Center.

95. Jenkins, "The Union Movement," Oral History.

96. Jessica Mitford to Sydney Redesdale, June 15, 1944, OSU, Box 211, folder 1698.

97. Jessica Mitford to Aranka Treuhaft, June 15, 1944, OSU, Box 216, folder 1743.

98. Jessica Mitford to Sydney Redesdale, August 21, 1944, OSU, Box 211, folder 1698.

99. Mitford, *Fine Old Conflict*, 99.

100. Jessica Mitford to Sydney Redesdale, August 21, 1944, OSU, Box 211, folder 1698.

101. de Lappe, *Pele: A Passionate Journey*, 36.

102. Years later, when Decca and Bob's youngest son, Benjamin, was diagnosed as bipolar their familiarity with Bert stood them in good stead.

103. U.S. Census (194), Haight Street Enumeration District No. 38-352, April 22, 1940: Clayton

Street Enumeration District No. 38-352, April 23, 1940; Brian Godfrey, "Inner-City Revitalization and Cultural Succession: The Evolution of San Francisco's Haight-Ashbury District,"
Yearbook of the Association of Pacific Coast Geographers 46 (1984): 79–91; San Francisco History
Center, "Haight Street between Ashbury and Clayton, looking west, 1944," Found SF, n.d.,
http://www.foundsf.org/index.php?title=Haight_Street_1940s.
104. The house last sold, in 2015, for $2,450,000.
105. Jessica Mitford to Sydney Redesdale, August 21, 1944, OSU, Box 211, folder 1698.
106. Interviews with Helena Kennedy and Jon Snow, summer 2016 and 2017, Wellfleet.
107. Jessica Mitford to Aranka Treuhaft, April, n.d., 1945, OSU, Box 216, folder 1743.
108. Mitford, *Fine Old Conflict*, 103, 104.
109. Jessica Mitford to Aranka Treuhaft, September n.d., 1945, OSU, Box 216, folder 1743.
110. Mitford, *Fine Old Conflict*, 79.
111. Pamela Jackson to Jessica Mitford, April 18, 1945, OSU, Box 208, folder 1651.
112. Jessica Mitford to Sydney Redesdale, May 15, 1945, OSU, Box 211, folder 1698.
113. Jessica Mitford to Sydney Redesdale, May 21, 1945, OSU, Box 211, folder 1698.
114. Sydney Redesdale to Jessica Mitford, March 24, 1945, OSU, Box 211, folder 1698.
115. The water temperature off Inch Kenneth, warmed by summer currents, reaches about 59 degrees
Fahrenheit in August.
116. Jessica Mitford to Sydney Redesdale, May 21, 1946, OSU, Box 211, folder 1698.
117. Jessica Mitford to Sydney Redesdale, May 15, 1945. Accounts of Romilly's rescue from
Colditz differ widely. Some sources claim that Romilly was rescued by the Russians when
they liberated the prison in May. Others give credit to the Americans. Romilly's own account,
however, makes clear that he effected a dramatic escape, rappelling down Colditz's stone walls,
just days before Russian liberators arrived. See Giles Romilly and Michael Alexander, *Hostages
of Colditz*, first published in 1954 as *The Privileged Nightmare*; Reinhold Eggers, *Escape from
Colditz* (City: Publisher, date); P. R. Reid, *Colditz: The Full Story* (London: Pan Books, 1984).

Chapter Ten: "A Terrific Hater"
1. Mitford, *Hons and Rebels*, 273, 280.
2. Mitford, *Hons and Rebels*, 273–74, 280.
3. Claud Cockburn, "Island Fling: A Souvenir of the Mitford Country," *Punch*, March 30, 1960,
tear sheets at OSU, Box 126, folder 1078. Cockburn, in fact, tried to engineer a sale back to
David of Decca's share. She was, of course, enraged. I am grateful to Jolie Braun for rushing me
a digital copy of this essay.
4. Mitford, *A Fine Old Conflict*, 116, 112.
5. Mitford, *Fine Old Conflict*, 76.
6. Mitford, *Hon and Rebels*, 280–81.
7. Mitford, *Hon and Rebels*, 280–81.
8. Nancy Mitford to Jessica Mitford, April 13, 1945.
9. Julian Jebb, "Nancy Mitford: A Portrait by Her Sisters," BBC, 1980.
10. Nancy's letters during this period have only added to a perception of her subordination to
Palewski. "I can't live without that military gentleman," she wrote Diana on August 28, 1947.
There is no question that Palewski dominated Nancy, and that she encouraged him to do so.
But some of her biographers, I believe, have missed the tease of some of her letters, failing to
notice that her frequent reference to being "under his thumb," for example, is almost certainly
also a sexual double entendre, designed to express her delight in the first relationship of her life

that brought her sexual satisfaction. "'Are you under my thumb?' he always says, & of course I am." Nancy to Diana, August 28, 1947. See Hilton, *The Horror of Love*; Hastings, *Nancy Mitford*.

11. Nancy was nearly phobic about fat. She and Diana both maintained their girlish figures throughout their lives. They were often snide about anyone, especially the Queen, who failed to do likewise.

12. Nancy had written *The Pursuit of Love* in only three months, largely as a guest in others' country houses. The tragedy of Tom's death, which came in the middle of writing the novel, occurred during one of those visits. Nancy took the news quietly and insisted on appearing at dinner that night, making no reference to the death and keeping up her end of lively conversation, as good houseguests were expected to do. Her behavior contributed to the myth that writing the novel had been painless and easy. With its proceeds, Nancy moved to Paris to be as close to Palewski as possible. There, she never made a fuss about how little time he had for her, how often he stood her up, or the attention that he paid to other women. While she continued writing furiously in France in an effort to support herself, she cultivated the image of a wealthy woman of leisure, buying Dior dresses that used dozens of yards of material [the most elaborate ballroom-style wedding gowns today typically use less than ten yards of fabric, if that], and fashioning an image of a fuss-free romance and lifestyle.

13. Orville Prescott, review, *New York Times*, August 28, 1963, 18.

14. Jessica Mitford to Sydney Redesdale, January 3, 1946.

15. The firm, which changed often, began in San Francisco as Gladstein, Andersen, Resner, Sawyer & Edises and included George R. Anderson, Herbert Resner, Bob, Norman Leonard, Ewing Sibbett and Myer C. Symonds and maintained a San Francisco office at 240 Montgomery Street. Its Oakland offices were downtown, on Broadway, in a building with a Deco facade and stained-glass foyer. In 1948, Bob and Bert Edises spun off their own firm but remained closely associated.

16. Jessica Mitford to Sydney Redesdale, August 26, 1947, OSU.

17. See Marilynn S. Johnson, "Mobilizing the Homefront: Labor and Politics in Oakland, 1941–1951," Cornford, ed. *Working People of California*; Philip J. Wolman, "The Oakland General Strike of 1946," *Southern California Quarterly* 57, no. 2 (July 1975).

18. Treuhaft, Oral History, interview with Robert G. Larsen, Berkeley Oral History Project, Berkeley Historical Society, 1988–89, 46, 38.

19. House Un-American Activities Committee (HUAC), "Report on the CRC as a Communist Front Organization" (Washington: D.C.: Government Printing Office, 1947).

20. East Bay Civil Rights Congress, "Report on Police Brutality," June 18, 1949. I am grateful to Adam Tomasi, for locating a copy of this report.

21. Jessica Mitford to Aranka Treuhaft, May 3, 1948.

22. Robert Treuhaft, Oral History, 43. Because of its leadership and tactics, the CRC is considered a forerunner of organizations like SNCC and CORE.

23. Aubrey Grossman Obituary, *San Francisco Chronicle*, December 10, 1999, https://www.sfgate .com/news/article/Aubrey-Grossman-2891336.php.

24. From comprising 3 percent of Oakland's population before the war, the Black population of Oakland rose to 12.4 percent by 1950. "Mobilizing the Homefront," and Daniel Cornford, ed. *Working People of California* (Berkeley: University of California Press, 1995), 349; M. I. Gershenson, "Wartime and Postwar Employment Trends in California," *Monthly Labor Review* 64 (April 1947): 577, 584; U.S. Department of Labor, War Manpower Commission, "Summary of Monthly Narrative Reports, June 14, 1945."

25. Mitford, *Fine Old Conflict*, 100.
26. Mitford, *Fine Old Conflict*, 100.
27. Jessica Mitford, "Why I Live Where I Live," undated and unpublished essay written for *Esquire*, OSU, Box 99, folder 871.
28. Mitford, *Fine Old Conflict*, 107, 99.
29. Mitford, *Fine Old Conflict*, 103.
30. Personal communication with Constancia Romilly, December 1, 2020. Decca gave his birthday, in telegram to Sydney, as October 20. Jessica Mitford to Sydney Redesdale, October 21, 1947, Chatsworth House Archive.
31. She wrote Aranka that "caudal anaesthetic . . . Greatest boon to childbearers ever invented," n.d., 1946, OSU.
32. Jessica Mitford to Aranka Treuhaft, October 21, 1947. Although her induced labor was uncomfortable—and almost certainly comprised of procedures, such as the enemas, which were also unnecessary—when Decca later wrote about American childbirth practices in *The American Way of Birth*, induction was hardly mentioned.
33. Jessica Mitford to Sydney Redesdale, January 27, 1948, Chatsworth House Archive; Mitford, *Fine Old Conflict*, 102.
34. "The other night he said 'Hi, Bob' quite distinctly," Decca insisted. Jessica Mitford to Aranka Treuhaft, March 3, 1948, OSU.
35. Mitford, *Fine Old Conflict*, 149.
36. Jessica Mitford to Sydney Redesdale, July 1950.
37. Jessica Mitford to Nancy Mitford, 1947. Decca may have sensed Nancy's duplicity and renewed relationship with Diana. In spite of having been the one most responsible for Diana's jail term—something Diana never learned during Nancy's life—Nancy had now made Diana her chief confidante and closest friend. She wrote Diana constantly, visited often, and gave herself license to gossip, often quite nastily, with Diana about everyone else, including Decca. Nancy may have resented Decca's silence. She must have known what a breach it was to talk about Decca to Diana, of all people. "I think she [Decca] hates me at heart. We've become sort of bogy-men to her. What a bore—in a way, though really less boring than cheerful American goodwill to all." Nancy Mitford to Diana Mitford, 1947.
38. Constancia Romilly to Sydney Redesdale, 27 January 1948, Chatsworth House Archive.
39. Sussman, *Decca*, 107.
40. Mitford, *Fine Old Conflict*, 150.
41. In *Fine Old Conflict*, Mitford wrote that she'd flown "direct from London" (in those days a fifty-hour journey), but there were no such direct flights at the time. The first commercial flights from London to San Francisco took place in 1957.
42. Mitford, *Fine Old Conflict*, 151.
43. Jessica Mitford to Aranka Treuhaft, May 3, 1948. Sydney had to fly from London to New York and then New York to San Francisco. In spite of the many amenities then available to airline passengers, this was a grueling trip.
44. Mitford, *Fine Old Conflict*, 153.
45. Nancy Mitford to Diana Mitford, July 17, 1948, Chatsworth House Archives.
46. Diana Mitford to Nancy Mitford, July 21, 1948; Diana Mitford to Nancy Mitford, May 2, 1948, Mosley, *The Mitfords*, 245, 251.
47. Jessica Mitford to Sydney Redesdale, June 11, 1948.
48. Beverly Gage, *G-Man: J. Edgar Hoover and the Making of the American Century*, 356.

49. "Indicted Reds Get Wallace Support," *New York Times*, July 22, 1948.
50. Belknap, "Foley Square Trials," Belknap, *American Political Trials*.
51. Jessica Mitford to Sydney Redesdale, August 13, 1948, Chatsworth House Archives.
52. Patterson et al., eds., *We Charge Genocide*, 12, 125, 19.
53. Patterson, *The Man Who Cried Genocide: An Autobiography*, 178.
54. Dailey, *White Fright: The Sexual Panic at the Heart of America's Racist History*, 42; Patterson et al., *We Charge Genocide*, 149.
55. Patterson et al., *We Charge Genocide*, 165.
56. See Alexander, *The New Jim Crow*.
57. Horne, *Communist Front? The Civil Rights Congress*, 320. One of the CRC's main lawyers, Charles Garry, was later a central lawyer for the Black Panther Party.
58. Horne, *Communist Front?*, 74.
59. Heard, *The Eyes of Willie McGee*, 3.
60. Leandra Zarnow, "Braving Jim Crow to Save Willie McGee: Bella Abzug, the Legal Left, and Civil Rights Innovation, 1948–1951," *Law & Social Inquiry* 33, no. 4 (Fall 2008): 1003–41.
61. Zarnow, "Braving Jim Crow."
62. The NAACP affirmed the civil liberties of Communists in 1950, but by 1956, declaring itself "An American Organization" and adorning its statements with enormous American flags, the organization not only attacked Communists but insisted it had been doing so going back to the 1940s. See, for example, "NAACP: An American Organization," Conference Proceedings (New York: NAACP, June 1956). In *A Fine Old Conflict*, Decca collapsed the 1956 and 1950 resolutions, one of the many instances in which dates in her memoir are best treated as approximations. See *A Fine Old Conflict*, 113.
63. Harry Haywood, "World War II and the Merchant Marines," Gwendolyn Midlo Hall, ed., *A Black Communist in the Freedom Struggle*, 259.
64. Patterson letter, in Horne, *Communist Front?*, xxx.
65. Horne, *Communist Front?*, 338, 340.
66. Among Gelders's many connections as an activist was muckraking's founding father Lincoln Steffens, one of the writers behind the organization supporting political prisoners that gave Gelders part of his political beginnings.
67. Personal communication, Coppelia Kahn. Kahn co-owned a commune, or coop "ranch," in California with Frantz, and others, for decades. The commune, called Chamokome, still survives. Kahn remembers Frantz as "a powerhouse, but quiet about it . . . humming with knowledge on many fronts, omnicompetence . . . so lucid. In a meeting she was the ideal participant: moved things along, cleared the air, found the focus."
68. Marge Frantz, interview, Smith College Oral History, 70.
69. Robert Treuhaft, interview, date and interview team not provided, transcribed by Lauren Kuryloski, tape from Peter Sussman, possibly circa 1985.
70. See Kendi, *How to Be an Antiracist*, especially 202–16; Peggy Mcintosh, "White Privilege: Unpacking the Invisible Knapsack," *Peace and Freedom Magazine*, July/August 1989, 10–12; Eddo-Lodge, *Why I'm No Longer Talking to White People About Race*.
71. CRC, "I Shall Not Live at Peace with Jim Crow Campaign Pledge," cited by Horne, *Communist Front?*, 58. Also see Kendi, *How to Be an Antiracist*.
72. Marge Frantz, quoted by Sussman, *Decca*, 104, Oral History, Smith.
73. Mitford, *Fine Old Conflict*, 127.
74. Mitford, *Fine Old Conflict*, 115.

75. Horne, *Communist Front?*, 27.

76. Jessica Mitford to Sydney Redesdale, April 29, 1950, Chatsworth House Archives.

77. Jessica Mitford to Sydney Redesdale, April 29, 1950, Chatsworth House Archives.

78. Mitford, *Fine Old Conflict*, 122.

79. Press Release, May 22, 1950. Public News Service, draft in OSU, Box 27, folder 144.

80. Treuhaft, Oral History, 1988–89, 49.

81. Jessica Mitford to Sydney Redesdale, May 11, 1950.

82. Green and Murdock, *The Jerry Newson Story*, 44. Priced at twenty-five cents.

83. Jessica Mitford lecture, 1981; Sussman, *Decca*, 103.

84. Mitford, *Fine Old Conflict*, 119–20.

85. In a letter to her mother, of September 14, 1950, Decca noted that she'd helped to write the booklet.

86. Mitford, *Fine Old Conflict*, 116.

87. Jessica Mitford to Sydney Redesdale, September 13, 1951.

88. Jessica Mitford to Sydney Redesdale, March 6, 1950.

89. Jessica Mitford to Sydney Redesdale, May 11, 1950; June 4, 1950; June 15, 1950.

90. The ranch had been purchased from Frieda Lawrence, widow of D. H. Lawrence, by two young Communists, Jenny and Craig Vincent. Elizabeth Cleary, "The Unique Past of San Cristóbal Valley Ranch," *Taos News*, September 28, 2014, https://www.taosnews.com/la-vida/the-unique-past-of-san-crist-bal-valley-ranch/article_ca2a418a-2d2d-511b-9b97-fc48074d8a60.html.

91. Jessica Mitford to Sydney Redesdale, September 14, 1950.

92. Jessica Mitford to Sydney Redesdale, August 20, 1950.

93. Jessica Mitford to Sydney Redesdale, August 10, 1950.

94. Nancy Mitford to Diana Mosley, July 17, 1948.

95. Robert Treuhaft, interview, October 1999, NYU Tamiment Library, TAM 664, B2, f.8.

96. Mitford, *Fine Old Conflict*, 142. The CRC folded by the mid-1950s, at which point Benjamin would still have been too young for any such activities. These references can only have been to Constancia and Nicholas, but after Nicholas's death, in 1955, Mitford did not speak of him. This was written long after the fact of these events and after Nicholas's death. Probably Mitford has substituted Benjy for the Nicholas she won't mention.

97. Mitford, *Fine Old Conflict*, 144.

98. Jessica Mitford to Sydney Redesdale, January 1, 1951.

99. Mitford, *Fine Old Conflict*, 161, 173; Horne, 91, 89. The other three women in Decca's original group of four were Eve Friedan, Billie Wachter, and Louise Hopson.

100. Jessica Mitford to Sydney Redesdale, April 2, 1951, Chatsworth House Archives, clipping included. "Minister Said Nothing Can Help McGee—Then Came Good News."

101. "Report by Delegation of White Women to Mississippi," OSU, Box 27, folder 148.

102. Buddy Green to Jessica Mitford, March 19, 1951, OSU, Box 27, folder 148.

103. *Memphis Commercial Appeal*, March 27, 1951, Horne, *Communist Front?*, 86.

104. Patterson et al., *We Charge Genocide*, "Petitioners," ix–x. *We Charge Genocide* was presented in Paris in December 1951.

105. "Lynch Trial Makes Southern History," June 2, 1947; "The End of Willie McGee," May 21, 1951.

106. Horne, *Communist Front?*, 74, 79.

107. "Willie McGee and the Traveling Electric Chair," Radio Diaries, https://soundcloud.com /radio-diaries/radio-diaries-mcgee.

108. Laurel has recently become famous as the star of a nostalgic home improvement show, called *Home Town*, in which a lovable young white couple tries to reinvigorate Laurel by rescuing its historic houses and restoring them, one by one. Once one of the most prosperous lumber towns in the southern Piney Woods, Laurel's historic wealth was seen in its parks—Frederick Law Olmsted was brought in to design them—in its art museums, and especially in its many architecturally significant homes, built when Laurel was producing as much as a million board feet of lumber a day. *Home Town* celebrates that past and celebrates Laurel as a great place "to come home to." "Something about our small town life could make people all across the country nostalgic for a place they've never even been," says the show's human star, Erin Napier. "It's a show about finding your place in a small town at its heart," https://www.countryliving.com/life /entertainment/a37399/hgtv-home-town/. *Home Town* seems not to refer to Laurel's lynchings, to Howard Wash killed in 1942, to the long legal lynching of Willie McGee, or to Laurel's troubled racial past. "Mississippi Mob Lynches a Slayer," *New York Times*, October 17, 1942, 49. "It was bad," as one Black city councilman, born in 1947, says. "It was rough." "Laurel Councilman Remembers Bad Times," February 18, 2010, https://www.wdam.com/story/12005929/black -history-month-laurel-councilman-remembers-bad-times/.

109. "Willie McGee and the Traveling Electric Chair," Radio Diaries; Heard, *The Eyes of Willie McGee*, 334–35.

110. Jessica Mitford to Sydney Redesdale, September 23, 1951, Chatsworth House Archives. Decca's letter included a photo of how she looked that day from a newspaper clipping.

111. Sussman provides an excellent account of this. See *Decca*, 105.

112. Mitford, *Fine Old Conflict*, 200, 204.

Chapter Eleven: "A Most Un-Duchessy Life"

1. Chatsworth House Archives.

2. Halberstam, *The Fifties*, x.

3. Richmond, *A Long View from the Left*, 301.

4. David Caute, *The Great Fear*, 77, 102.

5. Rabinowitz, *Unrepentant Leftist*, 100–101.

6. Rabinowitz, *Unrepentant Leftist*, 158.

7. Fast, *Being Red*, 179, 347. Fast was one of the most prominent writers in the Communist Party and played a leading role in the Peekskill resistance. In 1957, after he renounced the Party, Decca was furious with him, and he became a model for her of the "I was duped" school of former Communists, a group with whom she had no patience at all.

8. Mitford, *A Fine Old Conflict*, 116.

9. Virginia Durr to Ann Durr, March 7, 1954, Sullivan, ed., *Freedom Writer*, 65.

10. Caute, *The Great Fear*, 215, 447.

11. Jessica Mitford to Sydney Redesdale, June 6, 1952.

12. Healey, *California Red*, 132.

13. Caute, *The Great Fear*, 211.

14. Navasky, *Naming Names*, ix, 347.

15. Eva Maas [Lapin], *Looking Back on a Life in the Left*, 83.

16. Chernin, *In My Mother's House*, ebook edition, location 3940.

17. Healey, *California Red*, 140.
18. Richmond, *Long View*, 310.
19. Belfrage, *The American Inquisition*, 103.
20. Oshinsky, *Polio: An American Story*, 4, 81, 161–62, 218, 256, and passim. By 1952, polio numbers had been doubling every few years and now approached almost sixty thousand cases.
21. Patrick Cockburn, "Polio: The Deadly Summer of 1956," *The Independent*, October 23, 2011. "Polio was peculiar in that it produced visceral fear only equaled by AIDS today," Cockburn (the son of Decca's friend Claud) wrote.
22. Oshinsky, *Polio*, 161.
23. Jessica Mitford to Aranka Treuhaft, no date, fall 1951.
24. Edward Cavendish had suffered a sudden heart attack, at the age of fifty-five, while chopping wood. Devonshire, *Wait for Me!*, 138.
25. He died in September 1944 at the age of twenty-six, shortly after marrying Kathleen (Kick) Kennedy.
26. Devonshire, *Wait for Me!*, 139. Andrew and Deborah had to sell large properties and many valuable artworks to pay down this debt. Nevertheless, they managed to retain many significant artworks that are still on display today.
27. The Estate includes an additional twenty-three thousand acres in the surrounding county.
28. Statistics are drawn from Devonshire, *Chatsworth: The House*, 42–43. See also Mosley, ed., *The Mitfords*, 266–67. In addition to Chatsworth, the young couple now owned Hardwick Hall, the legendary home of Bess of Hardwick, once the wealthiest woman in Great Britain, a massive sixteenth-century house famous for its use of glass and its artworks, as well as Lismore Castle in Ireland, an enormous gray structure looking like every child's drawing of a castle, on the banks of the River Blackwater. Lismore had been used into the late 1940s by Andrew's Uncle Charlie. After his early death (also from alcoholism) it was used by his widow, Adele Astaire, Fred Astaire's sister and dancing partner before her marriage.
29. Murphy, *A Mitford Family Album*, n. p. Murphy is Deborah's youngest daughter.
30. Jessica Mitford to Deborah Devonshire, October 19, 1951.
31. Mitford, *A Fine Old Conflict*, 159.
32. In her memoir, *A Fine Old Conflict*, Mitford misdates this visit as occurring in 1950.
33. Deborah Devonshire to Diana Mosley, February 8, 1952, Mosley, ed., *The Mitfords*, 276–77.
34. Devonshire, *Wait for Me!*, 153–54.
35. Marge Frantz, personal interview.
36. Devonshire, *Wait for Me!*, 153.
37. Jessica Mitford to Sydney Redesdale, June 6, 1952. Henderson refers back to their beloved chickens, or hens, the source of their calling themselves "hons" and the source for the name "Hons Cupboard."
38. Mitford, *A Fine Old Conflict*, 158–59. I spent the better part of an unusually hot June day in 2008 with the duchess, a few years before her death. She was a gracious hostess and very generous with her time, giving up a full day on her calendar to chat with her sister's biographer. She was also one of the most interviewed women in history—she had given dozens of interviews, especially about the family, and she tended to fall into what was clearly a script when asked about her sisters. Later, looking at various video interviews, I was able to verify that, indeed, some of her answers were nearly word for word in various interviews, mine included. After hours talking together in her crowded chintz drawing room, I despaired of getting anything fresh from her about the family. Just before lunch (beef aspic, bloody roast beef and potatoes), however, I happened to ask her a question about Marge Frantz, Decca's CRC coworker and

one her closest lifelong friends. The veil dropped. The Duchess insisted that she had never heard of Marge Frantz and that she couldn't have been important to Decca. When I read her a few sections of letters to Marge from Peter Sussman's book (which she admitted to not having read), she was shocked. She expressed consternation that Decca would have kept back any of her authentic life. I mentioned the clothing and careless hair. "I'm not like that"; "I look at the inner person; Decca knew that," the Duchess snapped, her eyes welling. "Why would she do that?" she repeated. The Communists were all "boring," she added suddenly. Interview with Deborah Mitford, June 25, 2008, Edensor House, Chatsworth Estate.

39. Jessica Mitford, quoted by Jovanka Beckles, "The Gary Family: Fighting for Equality and Standing for Their Rights," Parts One and Two, Radio Free Richmond, no date, http://www.radiofreerichmond.com/jovanka_beckles_the_gary_family_of_richmond_fighting_for_equality_and_standing_for_their_rights_part_1; http://www.radiofreerichmond.com/jovanka_beckles_the_gary_family_of_richmond_fighting_for_equality_and_standing_for_their_rights_part_2.

40. On Oakland as an "industrial garden," see especially Self, *American Babylon: Race and the Struggle for Postwar Oakland*.

41. On "beloved community," see especially, Eig, *King*. On the violence that civil rights activists faced in the fight for racial justice, see especially Raymond Arsenault, *John Lewis*, and Greenberg, *John Lewis*.

42. Mitford, *Fine Old Conflict*, 129–30.

43. The figure of eight hundred comes from Eileen Mary Roarback, "The Defense of the Self: Autobiographical Response of American Intellectuals to the McCarthy Era," PhD diss., American Studies, University of Iowa, May 1999; Mitford, *Fine Old Conflict*, 130.

44. Mitford, *Fine Old Conflict*, 133.

45. Self, *American Babylon*, 78.

46. Jessica Mitford to Sydney Redesdale, June 6, 1952.

47. Healey, *California Red*, 139.

48. Richmond, *Long View*, 305–306.

49. Sabin, *In Calmer Times*, xxx.

50. "Dinky wrote to Winston Churchill," Decca told her mother, "about the Rosenbergs before they were killed, she signed it 'your loving niece, Constancia Romilly' but he never answered." Jessica Mitford to Sydney Redesdale, September 16, 1953.

51. See for example, Steve Crabtree, "The Gallup Brain: Americans and the Korean War," Gallup, February 4, 2003, https://news.gallup.com/poll/7741/gallup-brain-americans-korean-war.aspx; Lydia Saad, "Gallup Vault: Americans Not Keen on A-Bomb During Korean War," Gallup, August 17, 2017, https://news.gallup.com/vault/216317/gallup-vault-americans-not-keen-bomb-during-korean-war.aspx; Edward A. Suchman, Rose K. Goldsen, and Robin M. Williams, Jr., "Attitudes Toward the Korean War," *Public Opinion Quarterly* 17, no. 2 (Summer 1953): 171.

52. Jessica Mitford to Sydney Redesdale, February 1954.

53. Sydney Redesdale to Jessica Mitford, February 28, 1954, Chatsworth House Archive.

54. Wells was an orphan. He had been sent to reform school at age eight and to San Quentin at nineteen for receiving a stolen suit. Wells was finally paroled, after forty-six years in prison, in 1974. See "In Jail 46 Years, Man Wins Parole," *New York Times*, July 8, 1974, 30.

55. CRC circular, August 31, 1950, as cited by Hamm, "Wesley Robert Wells and the Civil Rights Congress," in *Racializing Justice, Disenfranchising Lives*, Marable, et al., eds., 24. At another

point, Hamm attributes this phrase to Buddy Green's foreword to Wells's life story, but I do not find this phrase in that foreword.

56. Jessica Mitford, foreword to Charles Garry, *Street Fighter in the Courtroom*, manuscript draft, OSU, Box 98, folder 852.

57. William Kunstler, "Charles Garry: Streetfighter in the Courtroom," Documentary, Produced by Roxanne Bezjian, 1992, https://www.youtube.com/watch?v=cmnY2Wdjaas. Decca also appears briefly in the beginning of the documentary, channeling some of Garry's famous sartorial playfulness by dressing in red, white, and blue.

58. Wesley Robert Wells, Fact Sheet, "The Facts of My Case."

59. Jessica Mitford to Sydney Redesdale, September 16, 1953.

60. Wells, *My Name Is Wesley Robert Wells*, with a foreword by Buddy Green, 4, xxx. The CRC succeeded in staying Wells's execution and helping him achieve clemency. But it could not free him from prison. Wells spent two more decades in prison before he was finally released from Vacaville on July 1, 1974. By then, his case had become central to the anti-prison organizing work of the Black Panther Party. Some, including Theodore Hamm, call Wells the "first Black Panther." He was in his early sixties and had spent forty-six years of his life in prison, many of those years in solitary confinement. After his release, Wells lived only eighteen months before dying of a heart attack.

61. Healey is quoted by Hamm, "Wesley Robert Wells," 29. Hamm provides the figures on the number of doctors who signed the 1954 letter.

62. Jessica Mitford to Vivian Hallinan, August 30, 1967. She added, to Hallinan, that she was "nearly expelled" from the CRC at the time (doubtful given how indispensable she then was) "for devoting all my time to the Doctor's effort [to free Wells], instead of organizing CRC street demonstrations and the like." The coalition supporting Wells developed at a critical moment for the Communist Party, which was experiencing steep drops in its membership. Party leader and Spanish Civil War veteran Steve Nelson supplies the following membership figures: 75,000–80-80,000 in 1945; 20,000 in 1956, before Khrushchev's revelations; 5,000 in 1958. Nelson, *American Radical*, 393.

63. Jessica Mitford to Sydney Redesdale, July 20, 1953

64. Jessica Mitford to Aranka Treuhaft, December 5, 1953.

65. Jessica Mitford, "A 'Roach' Remembers," C5.

66. Durr, *Outside the Magic Circle*, 256.

67. Virginia Durr to Esther [Esther Josephine Frank, wife of Joe Gelders and mother of Marge Frantz], April 6, 1954; Sullivan, *Freedom Writer*, 70; Virginia Durr, *Outside the Magic Circle*, 270.

68. Comments by Clifford Durr, Virginia Durr, Oral History, Columbia University Oral History Collection, 1976, Part 3, 164, 166–70. See also Durr, *Outside the Magic Circle*, 263–65.

69. Virginia Durr to Jessica Mitford, May 1, 1954

70. Jessica Mitford to Sydney Redesdale, December 10, 1953.

71. Belfrage, *The American Inquisition*, 229.

72. Nancy Mitford, "How to Catch a King: May 1954," *Atlantic Monthly*, May 1954, Part One, 25–34. Nancy appeared opposite Ernest Hemingway's "The Paris Years," but only she was mentioned on the cover.

73. Jessica Mitford to Aranka Treuhaft, no date. [1957?]

74. This friend was Bettina Aptheker. Decca told Aptheker the story many years later, and in the context of discussions about sexual violence. Leslie Brody, typed interview with Bettina Aptheker, August 2008, OSU, Box 2, 28 of 83. In my conversations with Bettina Aptheker,

she confirmed what Decca had told her only days after the event—that she'd been raped. Interview with Bettina Aptheker, January 26, 2024.

75. Jessica Mitford to Sydney Redesdale, October 25, 1954.

76. Clonfert was never rebuilt. It lies in ruins to this day, with trees now growing up through the middle of the house, but the outer walls standing firm.

77. Jessica Mitford to Sydney Redesdale, February 16, 1955.

78. Leslie Brody interview with Pele de Lappe, no date, typed interview.

79. Redwood Memorial Gardens is no longer an active cemetery. It has been taken over by a local historical society. According to its website, Nicholas remains buried there, in a site that is registered but not marked.

80. Leslie Brody interview with Doris Brin Walker, no date, typed interview, OSU.

81. Leslie Brody interview with Doris Brin Walker, no date, typed interview, OSU.

82. Jessica Mitford to Aranka Treuhaft, March 7, 1955.

Chapter Twelve: "Going Home Again"

1. Mitford used the phrase "Going Home Again" for one of the chapters of her memoir, *A Fine Old Conflict*. Although it is the chapter that has the least to do with the ostensible subject of her book—joining and then leaving the Communist Party—it is the longest chapter by far.

2. Jessica Mitford to Sydney Redesdale, February 21, 1956.

3. Jessica Mitford to Sydney Redesdale, July 19, 1955, Chatsworth.

4. Jessica Mitford to Sydney Redesdale, July 19, 1955, courtesy of Constancia Romilly.

5. Jessica Mitford to Sydney Redesdale, July 19, 1955.

6. Jessica Mitford to Sydney Redesdale, August 6, 1955, Chatsworth House Archive.

7. Jessica Mitford to Aranka Treuhaft, n.d. [1954], OSU, Box 217, folder 1748.

8. Decca told Aranka how much she hated flying in a letter of November 14, 1956. While she eventually flew quite often, she never liked it and always avoided it whenever she could. Jessica Mitford to Aranka Treuhaft, November 14, 1956. Decca took the Pacemaker train from Chicago to New York, an all-coach train with prime lounge and dining service. Jessica Mitford to Constancia Romilly, August 11, 1955. The Pacemaker service advertised "low-cost luxury," Decca's ideal.

9. Jessica Mitford to Aub [Grossman], Ed Grogan, Bert Edises, & spouses, August 25, 1955.

10. Potter, *Lifemanship*, 14–15.

11. Mitford, *Fine Old Conflict*, 234.

12. Jessica Mitford to Dobby and Mason, September 11, 1955. Decca often used her birthday as a chance to write to friends and catch them up on her life. Her birthday was frequently her most reflective mood of the year.

13. Jessica Mitford to Dobby and Mason, September 11, 1955.

14. Sydney felt that not-roaring was a condition too restrictive to broach; consequently, Decca did not see her father and he never met her family.

15. While most often associated with anti-Asian racism, the phrase "Yellow Peril" was used throughout Europe, and in Germany especially, to denigrate Jews and advance notions of white and Aryan supremacy. See Florian Hessel, "'Yellow Peril' and the Globalization of German Anti-Semitism," *Intellectual Anti-Semitism*.

16. Deborah Mitford Cavendish to Nancy Mitford, August 30, 1955, Mosley, ed., *The Mitfords*, 286.

17. Jessica Mitford to Aranka Treuhaft and Edith Treuhaft, October 23, 1955.

18. Nancy Mitford to Deborah Mitford, September 6, 1955, Mosley, ed., *The Mitfords*, 286.

19. Nancy Mitford to Diana Mosley, September 8, 1955, Mosley, ed., *The Mitfords*, 287.

20. According to Selina Hastings, *Noblesse Oblige* sold fifteen thousand copies on its first British publication and ten thousand copies in the United States within its first week. Hastings, *Nancy Mitford*, 225. "Even Nancy was surprised at the book's success," one of her biographers writes. "It was a worldwide smash hit" and it made "Nancy a cult figure." Lovell, *The Sisters*, 452.

21. Bob Treuhaft to Aranka Treuhaft, September 1, 1955, OSU, Box 217, folder 1784.

22. Jessica Mitford to Dobby and Mason, September 11, 1955. In fact, Sydney had twelve staff people on the island, including her cook, housemaid, boatman, and livestock tenders.

23. Bob Treuhaft to Aranka Treuhaft, September 11, 1955, OSU, Box 217, folder 1784.

24. David J. Garrow, "The Origins of the Montgomery Bus Boycott," *Southern Changes* 7 (October–December 1985): 21–27; Branch, *Parting the Waters*. See also Margot Adler, "Before Rosa Parks, There Was Claudette Colvin," March 15, 2009, NPR, Weekend Edition Sunday, https://www.npr.org/2009/03/15/101719889/before-rosa-parks-there-was-claudette-colvin. See also Giddings, *Ida: A Sword Among Lions* and Giddings, "It's Time for a 21st-Century Anti-Lynching Movement," *The Nation*, August 27, 2014; Phillip M. Hoose, *Claudette Colvin*; Gray, *Bus Ride to Justice: The Life and Works of Fred Gray, Revised Edition*.

25. Jessica Mitford to Pele, Dobby, and husbands, September 20, 1955. According to Charlotte Mosley, the death duties for Chatsworth amounted to "eighty per cent" of the estate. "In order to raise money to pay off the debt, Andrew sold thousands of acres in Scotland and Derbyshire, as well as important works of art, including paintings by Rembrandt, Holbein, Memling, Claude and Rubens. Hardwick Hall, which had been in the family for fifteen generations, went to the National Trust in lieu of duty." Mosley, ed., *The Mitfords*, 266–67.

26. Constancia Romilly, personal interview, April 2, 2021.

27. Mitford, *Fine Old Conflict*, 235.

28. Deborah Mitford to Nancy Mitford, September 12, 1955.

29. Nancy Mitford to Raymond Mortimer, September 8, 1955, Mosley, ed., *Love from Nancy*, 344.

30. Mitford, *Fine Old Conflict*, 235.

31. Jessica Mitford to Sydney Redesdale, September 20, 1955.

32. Mitford, *Fine Old Conflict*, 235.

33. Jessica Mitford to Aranka Treuhaft, September 18, 1955.

34. Mitford, *Fine Old Conflict*, 238.

35. Jessica Mitford to Adam Lapin and Steve Murdock, September 28, 1955.

36. Mitford, *Fine Old Conflict*, 238, 241.

37. Mitford, *Fine Old Conflict*, 242.

38. Personal interview, Constancia Romilly, April 4, 2021.

39. Decca Treuhaft, "We Visited Socialism," *The People's World* magazine, February 17, 1956, 4.

40. Mitford, *Fine Old Conflict*, 272.

41. Jessica Mitford to Pele, Steve, Bob & Dorothy Neville, October 29, 1955.

42. Mitford, *Fine Old Conflict*, 246.

43. Mitford, *Fine Old Conflict*, 246.

44. Nancy Mitford to Diana Mosley, October 22, 1955, Mosley, ed., *The Mitfords*, 289.

45. Nancy Mitford to Diana Mosley, October 22, 1955.

46. Nancy Mitford to Diana Mosley, October 22, 1955.

47. Mitford, *Fine Old Conflict*, 248.

48. Nancy Mitford to Evelyn Waugh, November 1955, Mosley, ed., *Love from Nancy*, 346.

49. Mitford, *Fine Old Conflict*, 248.

50. Mitford, *Fine Old Conflict*, 249.
51. Jessica Mitford to Bob Treuhaft, November 8, 1955.
52. Mitford, *Fine Old Conflict*, 229.
53. Jessica Mitford to Bob Treuhaft, November 12, 1955.
54. Jessica Mitford to Bob Treuhaft, November 3, 1955; Jessica Mitford to Bob Treuhaft, November 11, 1955.
55. Jessica Mitford to Sydney Redesdale, from ship, November 28, 1955.
56. Personal emails, March 23–25, 2021.
57. New York's divorce laws were some of the most restrictive in the nation and did not loosen until the 1960s, and this gave Kliot considerable leverage, although he had brought very little into the marriage. See Isabel Marcus, "Locked In and Locked Out: Reflections on the History of Divorce Law Reform in New York State," *Buffalo Law Review* 37, 1988; Laura Oren, "No-Fault Divorce Reform in the 1950s: The Lost History of the 'Greatest Project' of the National Association of Women Lawyers," *Law and History Review* 36, no. 4, September 24, 2018.
58. Mitford, *Fine Old Conflict*, 255. Decca was still traveling in December of 1955 when Rosa Parks, a friend of Virginia and Clifford Durr, was arrested in Montgomery for refusing to give up her seat. The Durrs were the ones to bail Parks out of jail. Based in part on the earlier Baton Rouge bus boycotts, the Montgomery boycotts were not purely spontaneous, as they have too often been portrayed by the media, but resulted from years of careful planning and discussions about how best to fight Southern prejudices and Jim Crow practices.
59. Mitford, *Fine Old Conflict*, 259.
60. Virginia Durr to Jessica Mitford, February [n.d.], 1956, Sullivan, ed., *Freedom Writer*, 95.
61. Virginia Durr to Jessica Mitford, February 13, 1956, Sullivan, ed., *Freedom Writer*, 106–107.
62. Jessica Mitford to Aranka Treuhaft, March 29, 1956, OSU, Box 217, folder 1749.
63. Interview with Judith Viorst, May 3, 2021.
64. Mitford, *Fine Old Conflict*, 261. Jessica Mitford to Sydney Redesdale, May 13, 1956.
65. According to Dorothy Healey, the Party lost about thirty thousand members across the first half of the 1950s, going from fifty thousand to about twenty thousand by the end of 1955, when Decca returned from England. See Healey, *California Red*, 150.
66. As quoted by Sussman, *Decca*, 109.
67. Mitford, *Fine Old Conflict*, 269.
68. Jessica Mitford to Sydney Redesdale, October 8, 1956.
69. Jessica Mitford did not date *Lifeitselfmanship*, except by year. Her FBI file gives the date of July 20 for its first publication. If that is accurate, she would have begun the pamphlet earlier, probably in April or May; Sussman, *Decca*, xii.
70. Jessica Mitford to Sydney Redesdale, October 8, 1956, Chatsworth House Archives.
71. Mitford, *Fine Old Conflict*, 272, 277.
72. Mitford, *Fine Old Conflict*, 271.
73. Vivian Gornick, "They Were True Believers," *New York Times*, 9.
74. Jerry Harris, "First Reaction: U.S. Communist Leaders Confront the Khrushchev Revelations": 502–12.
75. Nelson, *American Radical*, 387. Other members said very similar things. "I was convulsed with tears," Party leader Dorothy Healey wrote of learning of Stalin's "deliberate policy of torture and murder . . . It was unbearable," she said. Healey, *California Red*, 153–55.
76. See Healey, *California Red* and Nelson, *American Radical*.
77. Mitford, *Fine Old Conflict*, 273.

78. Pele Murdock (née de Lappe), interview with Leslie Brody, October 2006, OSU, uncatalogued materials.
79. Mitford, *Fine Old Conflict*, 246, 257, 259.
80. Richmond, *A Long View*, 376.
81. Jessica Mitford to Sydney Redesdale, October 8, 1956, Chatsworth House Archives.
82. Jessica Mitford to Aranka Treuhaft, November 14, 1956, OSU; Jessica Mitford to Sydney Redesdale, January 4, 1957, Chatsworth House Archives.
83. Conversion per Bureau of Labor Statistics.
84. Jessica Mitford to Sydney Redesdale, October 21, 1956, Chatsworth House Archives.
85. See Jessica Mitford to "Dear Neighbor" [Murdocks] June 27, 1957; Jessica Mitford to Aranka Treuhaft, March 16, 1958, OSU.
86. Mitford, *Fine Old Conflict*, 373.
87. After five dozen venues turned down requests from the Party to rent convention space, shabby quarters had been secured in an old Russian Orthodox church used by a catering service. On the Chateau Gardens as a setting for this convention, see Rosenberg, "The Communist Party Convention."
88. Mitford, *Fine Old Conflict*, 275.
89. Healey, *California Red*, 163.
90. Dorothy Day, "On Pilgrimage," *The Catholic Worker*, March 1, 1957, 5, 7.
91. Mitford, *Fine Old Conflict*, 275, 277.
92. Deborah Mitford Cavendish to Diana Mosley, May 20, 1957.
93. Virginia Durr to Hugo and Josephine Black, June 5, 1957; Hugo Black to Virginia Durr, n.d., [June 1957], both in Sullivan, ed., *Freedom Writer*, 145–46.
94. Jessica Mitford to Marge Frantz, June 19, 1957.
95. Jessica Mitford to Aranka Treuhaft, March 16, 1958.
96. According to their FBI files, they resigned on April 14, 1958.
97. Mitford, *Fine Old Conflict*, 279–80.
98. Treuhaft, Oral History, 70–73.
99. Maas [Lapin], *Looking Back on a Life in the Left*, 87, 95–96.

Chapter Thirteen: "Action Man"
1. Jessica Mitford to Constancia Romilly, January 16, 1962, courtesy of Constancia Romilly and Peter Sussman, in author's collection.
2. Jessica Mitford to Constancia Romilly, February 15, 1960, courtesy of Constancia Romilly and Peter Sussman, in author's collection.
3. Jessica Mitford to Constancia Romilly, October 31, 1958; January 7, 1959 [mismarked 1958], courtesy of Constancia Romilly and Peter Sussman, in author's collection.
4. Jessica Mitford to Constancia Romilly, January 29, 1960, courtesy of Constancia Romilly and Peter Sussman, in author's collection.
5. Jessica Mitford to Constancia Romilly, January 29, 1960, courtesy of Constancia Romilly and Peter Sussman, in author's collection.
6. Jessica Mitford to Constancia Romilly, October 31, 1958; January 7, 1959 [mismarked 1958], courtesy of Constancia Romilly and Peter Sussman, in author's collection.
7. Jessica Mitford to Constancia Romilly, July 16, 1957.
8. Jessica Mitford to Aranka Treuhaft, September 18, 1958, OSU.
9. Jessica Mitford to Robert Treuhaft, April 30, 1959, OSU, Box 221, folder 1775.

10. Jessica Mitford to Aranka Treuhaft, May 20, 1958.

11. Jessica Mitford to Constancia Romilly, July 23, 1957.

12. Mitford, *A Fine Old Conflict*, 283; Jessica Mitford to Robert Treuhaft, April 30, 1959. Bacon was a fierce advocate of progressive children's literature; she persuaded the Communist Party to publish children's books. See also Jessica Mitford to Robert Treuhaft, April 26, 1959.

13. Mitford, *A Fine Old Conflict*, 283.

14. Mitford, *Hons and Rebels*, 5.

15. Jessica Mitford to Virginia Durr, June 18, 1963, VD.

16. Mitford, *A Fine Old Conflict*, 286.

17. Mitford, *Poison Penmanship*, 42, 40. Mitford reprinted not the published version of the essay but her more disjointed draft version, wanting her readers to see what good editing could accomplish (though she did not include the more streamlined, published version for comparison).

18. Freeman, *At Berkeley in the 60s*, 17.

19. Thomas Powell, "Biological Warfare in the Korean War: Allegations and Cover-up," *Socialism and Democracy* 31, no. 1, March 2017; *United States v. Powell*, 156 F. Su526 (N.D. Cal. 1957), November 1, 1957; Fuyuan Shen, "John William Powell and 'The China Weekly Review': An Analysis of His Reporting and His McCarthy Era Ordeal," August 1994, 148; *United States v. Powell*, 171 F. Su202 (N.D. Cal. 1959), February 3, 1959. Eventually, Charles Garry was also brought into the case, giving Decca another occasion to collaborate with him.

20. Jessica Mitford to Constancia Romilly, October 1, 1958.

21. Jessica Mitford to Pele de Lappe and Steve Murdock, June 21, 1958, OSU. Almost one hundred years old, the Belmar is still operating as a hotel but has seen better days. Famous for its bar and as a supposedly very haunted site, it still has a large, young, mostly local following.

22. Jessica Mitford to Sydney Redesdale, June 30, 1958, Chatsworth House Archives.

23. *Times (London)*, March 31, 1960, 15.

24. "Leftist Daughter Left Nothing by Her Father," *Chicago Tribune*, July 10, 1958, W10.

25. "The Mitfords: Red Sheep Left Out of Will," *Globe and Mail*, July 9, 1958, 21. Associated Press (London), "One of 'Mitford Girls' Disinherited by Father," *New York Times*, July 10, 1958, 6. The AP article misstated Nicky's name, misstated Benjy's name, and misrepresented the relationship between Farve and Hitler (wrongly claiming they'd been great friends). Other papers repeated and elaborated the errors. *The Philadelphia Enquirer*, for example, also gave Decca seven other sisters and erroneously claimed that she had named one of her children Lenin, *Philadelphia Enquirer*, July 11, 1958, 9.

26. Carolyn Anspacher, "Lord Redesdale Will Cuts Bay Wife—'Split by Hitler,'" *San Francisco Chronicle*, March 10, 1958, clipping in Jessica Mitford's files, OSU.

27. Bob did tell the *Detroit Free Press* that Decca would not have accepted money from her family had it been offered her. "Penniless Heiress," *Detroit Free Press*, July 11, 1958, 9; Peg Johnson, "Redesdale Will Cuts Off Madcap Jessica," *Washington Post*, July 10, 1958, D1.

28. Jessica Mitford to Pele de Lappe and Steve Murdock, July 9, 1958.

29. Mitford, *A Fine Old Conflict*, 286.

30. On African American legacies of mutual aid, self-help, and cooperation, see especially, Ransby, *Ella Baker and the Black Freedom Movement: A Radical Democratic Vision*.

31. Treuhaft, Oral History.

32. Mitford, *Fine Old Conflict*, 287.

33. Treuhaft, Oral History, 287.

34. Mitford, *Poison Penmanship*, 51.

35. Jessica Mitford to Aranka Treuhaft, October 20, 1958.

36. Mitford, *Poison Penmanship*, 51.

37. Jessica Mitford to Candida Donadio, July 7, 1961. Donadio was Decca's literary agent at the time.

38. Jessica Mitford to Candida Donadio, July 7, 1961.

39. Roul Tunley, "Can You Afford to Die?," *Saturday Evening Post*, June 17, 1961.

40. Jessica Mitford to Constancia Romilly, September 17, 1958; November 18, 1958; October 13, 1958; Jessica Mitford to Constancia Romilly, January 12, 1959.

41. Jessica Mitford to Constancia Romilly, October 31, 1958.

42. Decca's FBI file indicates that she did not receive her own passport, in fact, but rather permission to travel under Bob's passport. Any travel to Communist countries was expressly forbidden for both Bob and Decca.

43. Mitford, *Fine Old Conflict*, 289.

44. Jessica Mitford to Robert Treuhaft, April 30, 1959.

45. Jessica Mitford to Robert Treuhaft, April 15, 1959.

46. Jessica Mitford to Robert Treuhaft, April 29, 1959, OSU, Box 221, folder 1775.

47. Jessica Mitford to Robert Treuhaft, April 30, 1959, OSU, Box 221, folder 1775.

48. Jessica Mitford to Robert Treuhaft, April 20, 1959; Jessica Mitford to Robert Treuhaft, April 26, 1959. MacGibbon had represented numerous friends of Decca's, including Philip Toynbee. Gollancz publishing, founded in 1927 by Victor Gollancz, a German-Polish Jew, was a well-respected left-wing British publisher of nonfiction and literature. Early authors included George Orwell, Ford Madox Ford, Daphne du Maurier, Frank Kafka, and many others. Houghton Mifflin bought the company in 1989 and sold it three years later. Now a division of Orion Publishing, owned by Hachette, Gollancz continues to publish mostly science fiction. Diana made various anti-Semitic remarks to Sydney about Decca publishing with a Jewish publisher, remarks that Decca saw on her mother's desk on Inch Kenneth.

49. Jessica Mitford to Marge Frantz, May 2, 1959.

50. Mitford, *Fine Old Conflict*, 291; Jessica Mitford to Robert Treuhaft and Constancia Romilly, May 4, 1959.

51. Mitford, *Hons and Rebels*, 141.

52. Mitford, *Hons and Rebels*, 284.

53. Jessica Mitford to Marge Frantz, June 10, 1959.

54. Jessica Mitford to Constancia Romilly and Robert Treuhaft, July 10, 1959.

55. Sussman, *Decca*, 190.

56. Jessica Mitford to Constancia Romilly, April 21, 1960.

57. *The Times*, Thursday, March 31, 1960, 15; Fanny Butcher, "The Literary Spotlight," *Chicago Daily Tribune*, June 5, 1960, C6; Virginia Bright, "Jessica Mitford Talks of New Book: Her Autobiography Didn't Please Kin," *Boston Globe*, July 10, 1960, 27; Charles Poore, untitled review, *New York Times*, June 9, 1960. See also Leonard Lyons, *Daily Defender*, May 31, 1960, 5; Elizabeth Janeway, "The Mitfords: Home Was Something to Run Away From," *New York Times*, June 26, 1960, 5, 20; Ann Wyman, "She Had a Course in Shoplifting," *Boston Globe*, June 26, 1960, A27.

58. Mitford, *Fine Old Conflict*, 295.

59. Jessica Mitford to Nancy Mitford, March 28, 1960; Mitford, *Fine Old Conflict*, 293.

60. Diana Mosley, letter to the editor, *Times Literary Supplement*, April 8, 1960.

61. Nancy Mitford to Jessica Mitford, March 11, 1960; Mitford, *Fine Old Conflict*.

62. Jessica Mitford to Nancy Mitford, November 16, 1971. In looking back on her sisters' reactions to the book, Decca also noted that she did eventually receive an angry letter from Pamela, disputing her accounts.

63. Deborah Mitford to Nancy Mitford, March 16, 1960, Chatsworth House Archives.

64. Deborah Mitford to Nancy Mitford, March 28, 1960, Chatsworth House Archives.

65. Nancy Mitford to Jessica Mitford, March 30, 1960, Chatsworth House Archives.

66. Nancy Mitford to Pamela Mitford, March 31, 1960, Chatsworth House Archives.

67. Jessica Mitford, "Rebels with a Hundred Causes: The Indignant Generation," manuscript version, OSU, Box 97, folder 832, 27.

68. "Proceed with Caution" was commissioned by *Life* for the hefty sum of $500 (nearly $5,000 in today's currency) and published on August 4, 1961, with "Jessica Mitford" as her byline. It is a light essay, with a slant that is supposed to be that of a puzzled British person encountering the oddities of American life—sort of an American Way of Travel. Decca loved the fact that *Life* included her paragraph about the family practice of defrauding the phone company with coded messages in fake collect calls: "Esther Annie Mehl," "Alice Okey," and so on. "I never really expected *Life* to run that paragraph," Decca later exclaimed. (*Poison Penmanship*, 59). Mitford was not always accurate with dates. In her essay collection *Poison Penmanship*, she erroneously gave the publication date of this article as June 1961.

69. Catherine Fosl, interview with Anne Braden, June 17, 1999, Anne Braden Oral History Project, Louie B. Nunn Center for Oral History, University of Kentucky Libraries, n.p., 00:13.00.

70. Braden's deliberate retention of what her biographer called "the persona of a rank-and-file activist . . . churning out leaflets and making phone calls until late into the night" was one of the models of an alternative form of activism—different from obedience to Party authority—that Decca absorbed from the student and civil rights movements of the 1960s. See Grant, *Ella Baker: Freedom Bound*; Catherine Fosl, *Subversive Southerner: Anne Braden and the Struggle for Racial Justice in the Cold War South*; and Julie A. Clements, "Participatory Democracy: The Bridge from Civil Rights to Women's Liberation," *Public Purpose* 1 (2003).

71. Belfrage, *Freedom Summer*, xiii. Belfrage, the daughter of Decca's friends Cedric and Molly Castle Belfrage, was not part of the original Freedom Ride, but participated a few years later in Freedom Summer, 1964.

72. Arsenault, *Freedom Riders: 1961 and the Struggle for Racial Justice*, 5.

73. Calvin Trillin, "Back on the Bus: Remembering the Freedom Riders," *New Yorker*, July 25, 2011. Trillin was in Montgomery and locked in the First Baptist Church overnight with Mitford, who refers to him, in later writings; Carson, *In Struggle: SNCC and the Black Awakening of the 1960s*, 37; Branch, *Parting the Waters: America in the King Years*, 446.

74. Branch, *Parting the Waters*, 446. Two white women students were dragged from a car belonging to Kennedy's administrative assistant and beaten senseless. After ten long minutes, the local police arrived and began arresting the Freedom Riders (those who were still conscious) for inciting a riot. A white couple who tried to protect the Riders—Frederick and Anna Gach—were arrested for interfering with the police. McWhorter, *Carry Me Home*, 210. The Gach case was taken by Clifford Durr and Decca spent the next few months raising money for their defense.

75. McWhorter, *Carry Me Home*, 210.

76. Durr, *Freedom Writer*, 250.

77. Jessica Mitford, "Whut They're Thanking Down There," *Esquire*, May 1, 1962. Decca's original title was "You-All and Non-You-All: A Southern Potpourri," and she hated the title that *Esquire*

gave her piece. When she reprinted the article in *Poison Penmanship*, she reverted to the original title although *Esquire* did not use it.

78. Len Holt, as quoted by Diane McWhorter, *Carry Me Home*, 210.
79. Carson, *In Struggle*, 36.
80. "You-all and Non-You-All," *Poison Penmanship*, 74.
81. "You-all and Non-You-All," *Poison Penmanship*, 73.
82. The house remains in the family, and I am grateful to have been able to spend time there. When Decca and Bob found out that the seller was trying to keep the house white-owned, they canceled the deal. It was only revived after they laid down a series of conditions and gave the seller numerous lectures on racial justice.
83. Jessica Mitford to Virginia Durr, December 1, 1960.
84. Eventually that attic came to hold hundreds of boxes later sold to archives in Texas and Ohio; that material is the principal primary source for this book.
85. "Whut They're Thanking Down There," *Esquire*, May 1962.

Chapter Fourteen: "The Making of a Muckraker"

1. Jessica Mitford, draft of speech for the Student Nonviolent Coordinating Committee (SNCC), Harry Ransom Research Center (HRC), Box 11, folder 11; Jessica Mitford to Candida Donadio, September 16, 1963, HRC, Box 11, folder 6.2.
2. Jessica Mitford, "So What's Wrong with Being a New Yorker," *San Francisco Chronicle*, May 14, 1961, 7–8; Jessica Mitford, "Something for the Boys," review of Rosalind Erskine, *The Passion Flower Hotel*, *New York Times Book Review*, September 30, 1962, BR3; Jessica Mitford, "Below Stairs," review of E. S. Turner, *What the Butler Saw: Two Hundred and Fifty Years of the Servant Problem*, *New York Times Book Review*, April 21, 1963, BR22. She criticized Turner for misunderstanding as "amusing" the subject of caste and class and for betraying the "patronizing and pretentious attitudes of her parents' class, oblivious to the "unending drudgery" of domestic work and the "near-slavery of below stairs life." Mitford's publisher, Simon & Schuster, was also the publisher of Erskine's novel. It is likely that they arranged for Mitford's review, which ran opposite a very large ad announcing: "The Funniest Book Ever Written About Sex? Jessica Mitford Says *The Passion Flower Hotel* is in a class all by itself for sheer immoderate comedy." The success of *Hons and Rebels* had evidently landed Mitford squarely on her publisher's promotion team.
3. Mitford, *Fine Old Conflict*, 297.
4. Mitford, *Fine Old Conflict*, 297.
5. Evelyn Waugh, "Embellishing the Loved Ones," review of *The American Way of Death*, *Sunday Times* (London), September 29, 1963. OSU, Box 4, folder 22.
6. Roul Tunley, "Can You Afford to Die?," *Saturday Evening Post*, June 17, 1961.
7. They also anticipated the work of consumer activists such as Esther Peterson and built on the work of organizations such as the National Consumers League as well as the history of African American cooperatives pioneered by Ella Baker and others.
8. Bernal, *Geography of a Life*, 250. I am grateful to Judy Bernal, now Judith Dunn, for confirming her own memories of Decca with me. Interview with Judith Dunn [Viorst] [Judy Bernal], February 20, 2022.
9. Mitford, *Fine Old Conflict*, 297.
10. Mitford, *Fine Old Conflict*, 298.
11. Sussman, *Decca*, 265.

12. Mitford's archives at the Ransom Center in Austin Texas contain many of these subscription labels bearing the names of her family and friends.

13. Jessica Mitford to Sydney Redesdale, October 19, 1961.

14. One of the nation's largest cemeteries outside of Los Angeles had its own gift shop. Decca purchased as many Forest Lawn wall plaques as she could fit in her luggage, planning to give them as Christmas presents to her Writing Committee and other friends. The Forest Lawn coloring book depicted two children, holding hands as they passed through the Forest Lawn gates, where "twenty-nine scenes of Forest Lawn treasures" awaited them. Forest Lawn offered Decca many examples of astoundingly poor taste.

15. Jessica Mitford to Kathleen Kahn, November 24, 1961.

16. Jessica Mitford to Candida Donadio, July 7, 1961.

17. This list of preferred terminology comes from Service Corporation International, the nation's then largest funeral conglomerate. Decca and Bob found many similar lists in the trade journals of the industry. Mitford, *The American Way of Death Revisited*, 194.

18. Mitford, *Poison Penmanship*, 4. Jessica Mitford to Constancia Romilly, January 16, 1962; Jessica Mitford to Kathleen Kahn, February 3, 1962.

19. Mitford, *The American Way of Death Revisited*, 43, 44–49, 54–57, 27, 58.

20. Lovell Thompson to Jessica Mitford, Sussman, *Decca*, n. 16, 275.

21. Jessica Mitford to Candida Donadio, March 2, 1962.

22. Jessica Mitford to Constancia Romilly, March 3, 1962.

23. Mitford, *Fine Old Conflict*, 300.

24. Houghton Mifflin had offered $2,500, which Gottlieb doubled to $5,000, equivalent to roughly $50,000 in today's currency, a still moderate advance for a book that would turn out to be the bestselling book in the nation.

25. Mitford, *Fine Old Conflict*, 301.

26. Gottlieb, *Avid Reader: A Life*, 58.

27. L. Rust Hills, "The Structure of the American Literary Establishment," *Esquire* (July 1963), 41. Hills provided a "power chart" of New York publishing. He put Donadio dead center in the "red" zone of "hot" literary figures. Gottlieb was not quite there yet, but he would be very soon, largely thanks to the explosive success of Decca and Bob's book.

28. Jessica Mitford to Candida Donadio, March 2, 1962.

29. Robert Gottlieb, interview, "Portrait of a Muckraker," produced by Stephen Evans, Ida Landauer, and James Morgan, KQED San Francisco, 1990, transcript, OSU, Box 239, folder 69.

30. Bob's lifelong willingness to give Decca center stage is corroborated by numerous family, friends, and neighbors. I am especially grateful to James and Chaka Forman for their view of their grandparents' marriage and collaboration. Decca gave in to the publication credits, but the book's original acknowledgments, left out of subsequent editions, made Bob's role clear. "Large portions of this book could well be labeled, 'By Robert Treuhaft, as told to Jessica Mitford.' My husband, the family expert on funerals because of his participation in the Bay Area Funeral Society, worked with me for many months gathering material. . . . He pioneered the subject of cemeteries, about which almost nothing has been written except in industry journals. He gave invaluable direction. . . . I should never have attempted this book without his help." The original dedication, which Bob later removed when he published a posthumous "revisited" edition of the book, read: "Dedicated to my husband: ROBERT TREUHAFT, with much gratitude for his untiring collaboration in all phases of the preparation of this book." Mitford, *The American Way of Death*.

31. Jessica Mitford to Barbara Kahn, June 30, 1962.

32. Jessica Mitford to Virginia Durr, July 4, 1962.
33. Jessica Mitford to Barbara Kahn, July 15, 1962.
34. Jessica Mitford to Barbara Kahn, July 13, 1962.
35. Jessica Mitford to Barbara Kahn, July 13, 1962.
36. Jessica Mitford to Miriam Miller, August 24, 1962.
37. Jessica Mitford to Peter Nevile, September 25, 1962.
38. "Good old Hen wanted to come," Deborah noted approvingly, "but the journey from San Francisco would have taken at least two days and as the doctor thought Muv might die at any moment, it was likely she would arrive too late." Devonshire, *Wait for Me!*, 231.
39. Nancy Mitford to Jessica Mitford, May 19, 1963; Deborah Mitford to Jessica Mitford, May 13, 1963.
40. Jessica Mitford to Deborah Mitford, June 2, 1963.
41. Nancy Mitford to Jessica Mitford, June 12, 1963.
42. Nancy Mitford to Mark Ogilvie-Grant, May 14, 1963, Mosley, ed. *Love from Nancy*.
43. Mitford, *The American Way of Death Revisited*, 79–80.
44. Jessica Mitford to Deborah Mitford Cavendish, June 2, 1963.
45. Jessica Mitford to Nancy Mitford, June 12, 1963.
46. Dan Green, interview, circa 1994–1995, conducted for "Portrait of a Muckraker," 1996, produced by Stephen Evans, Ida Landauer, and James Morgan. Interviewers unidentified, but almost certainly Landauer and either Morgan or Evans. Dan Green went on to become a publicity director and, ultimately, one of the most influential figures in book publishing.
47. Gottlieb, interview, "Portrait of a Muckraker," transcript, OSU, Box 239, folder 69.
48. Sussman, *Decca*, 266.
49. See also Clarence Seidenspinner, "Light upon Shadows," *Chicago Tribune*, August 25, 1963, K2; Richard Gilman, "The Loved One's in the Slumber Room, Laid Out in Style," *New York Times*, August 25, 1963, 4; Orville Prescott, review, *New York Times*, August 28, 1963, 25; Victor O. Jones, "Undertakers Hoist Selves by Own Pomp," *Boston Globe*, September 25, 1963, 20; George S. Schuyler, "News and Reviews," *Pittsburgh Courier*, November 30, 1963, 12.
50. Gottlieb, *Avid Reader*, 58.
51. Mitford, *Fine Old Conflict*, 307.
52. Jessica Mitford to Robert Treuhaft, October 31, 1963.
53. Jessica Mitford to Aranka Treuhaft, September 17, 1963.
54. Jessica Mitford to Deborah Mitford, October 7, 1963.
55. Bernal, who later became well known as a psychologist and academic, eventually teaching at both Penn State University and King's College, was also British. At the time Decca hired her, Judy Bernal was married to China scholar Martin Bernal. Bernal latter argued for the Afro-Asiatic roots of classical civilization and, along with Judy, became good friends with both Decca and Bob at the time. Decca was a bit dubious about Bernal initially, "sort of a deb type actually," she said, but she was too busy to dictate answers to her many fan letters and allowed her new assistant, she told her sister, "to make up the answers herself." Jessica Mitford to Deborah Mitford, October 7, 1963.
56. Mitford, *Fine Old Conflict*, 306.
57. Jessica Mitford to Robert Treuhaft, October 21, 1963. "Happiness is a warm train," her letter to Bob began.
58. Gottlieb, *Avid Reader*, 58.
59. Jessica Mitford to Robert Treuhaft, October 21, 1963.

60. Jessica Mitford to Robert Treuhaft, October 18, 1963.
61. Sussman, *Decca*, 267. *Tocsin* was a right-wing local newsletter, edited by Keith George.
62. Mitford, *The American Way of Death Revisited*, xvii.
63. Jessica Mitford to unidentified recipient, n. d., HRC.
64. Jessica Mitford to Barbara Kahn, October 17, 1963. The Brown Palace had printed hotel stationery with her name embossed on it for her use. Decca was thrilled with the "mad writing paper" and her evident reputation for letter-writing. See also Jessica Mitford to Robert Treuhaft, October 18, 1963. Decca reported to Bob, in her letter, that an old friend had come by with the bottle of whiskey, to help her get along. Decca returned to her complaint about university women in an October 21, 1963, letter to Bob and used the phrase "flavored hats" to describe the pastel-shaded hats then favored by middle-class white women. Decca had to leave a few book events early because of drinking too much and had to apologize, after others, for being drunk. See Jessica Mitford to David [probably Lowe], August 26, 1963. "I am calming nerves by writing to you," Decca admitted to her friend Barbara Kahn. October 22, 1963.
65. James B. Utt, Address to Congress, October 17, 1963.
66. Mitford, *Fine Old Conflict*, 312–13.
67. "How Not to Read a Book," *New York Times*, October 20, 1963, 10E.
68. Dan Green, interview for *Portrait of a Muckraker*, HRC, 80–90–93, #68.
69. Jessica Mitford, notes for speech, untitled, undated, HRC, Box 11, folder 11.
70. Mitford, *Fine Old Conflict*, 310. Jessica Mitford to Barbara Kahn, November 13, 1963.
71. Sussman, *Decca*, 268.
72. Decca was so taken with the range of people who wrote her fan letters that she attempted to incorporate them into some of her public lectures. See Jessica Mitford, notes for *Tribune* speech, HRC, Box 11, folder 11. She kept all her fan letters and often filed them under categories of "boring" or "interesting."
73. Mitford, *Fine Old Conflict*, 317.
74. Jessica Mitford to Deborah Mitford, November 24, 1963, Chatsworth House Archives.
75. Jessica Mitford to Deborah Mitford, November 24, 1963, Chatsworth House Archives.
76. Jessica Mitford to Robert Treuhaft, June 23, 1964.
77. Ann Marie Hourihane, review of Deborah Devonshire, *Wait for Me!*, *Irish Times*, September 2010; Nancy Mitford to Jessica Mitford, December 18, 1961, Mosley, ed., *The Mitfords*, 383. On the tensest day of the Cuban missile crisis, October 27, 1962, known as "Black Saturday," Deborah was in Washington for an exposition of drawings from Chatsworth. In spite of all the urgency of the ongoing crisis, Kennedy attended the dinner for the exposition opening at the National Gallery. When Kennedy visited his sister Kathleen's grave at Chatsworth in June 1963, Nancy remarked to Decca that "it makes an excellent excuse" for him to spend time with Debo. The sisters were well aware that Deborah's access to Kennedy was facilitated by numerous family connections, including many provided by her husband, Andrew (who was, himself, notorious as a womanizer). Andrew's uncle, Harold Macmillan, was British prime minister while Kennedy was in the White House. See Deborah Mitford to Diana Mosley, undated letter, November 1 or 2, 1962, Chatsworth House Archives, and also Nancy Mitford to Jessica Mitford, June 27, 1963.
78. Jessica Mitford to Robert Treuhaft, June 23, 1964; Schlesinger, *Robert Kennedy and His Times*.

Chapter Fifteen: "Do Something"
1. Jessica Mitford to Barbara Kahn, July 24, 1964.
2. Mitford, *Poison Penmanship*; Jessica Mitford to unnamed doctor, Sussman, *Decca*, 344.

3. In short order, Mitford published a number of related pieces, including "Americans Don't Want Fancy Funerals" in *The Saturday Evening Post*, an essay for *Nova* called "My Way of Life Since *The American Way of Death*," an essay on Evelyn Waugh's *The Loved One* called "Something to Offend Everyone," *Show*, December 1964, and others.

4. Nelson, *American Radical*, 399.

5. Maas, *Looking Back on a Life in the Left*, 135.

6. Adrienne Rich, "When We Dead Awaken: Writing as Revision," *College English* 34, no. 1 (October 1972): 18–30.

7. Jessica Mitford to Barbara Kahn, July 24, 1964. A few days after Decca wrote this letter, the bodies of Chaney, Goodman, and Schwerner were found.

8. Mitford, "My Way of Life Since *The American Way of Death*; Mitford, *Poison Penmanship*.

9. Jessica Mitford to Barbara Kahn, July 24, 1964.

10. Jessica Mitford, "Why I Decided to Write About Funerals," *The Bookseller*, September 1963; Jessica Mitford, "My Way of Life Since *The American Way of Death*"; Mitford, "Something to Offend Everyone"; Jessica Mitford, "Waugh Is Hell, or Anyhow, He Was Once," *Life*, November 13, 1964.

11. SNCC activist Tracy Sugarman, in "The Risk," *American Experience*, PBS, season 26, episode 6, aired June 24, 2014.

12. SNCC Digital Gateway, "Chuck McDew," https://snccdigital.org/people/chuck-mcdew/.

13. Constancia was romantically involved at this time with Charles McDew, a Black activist and SNCC leader. Carson, *In Struggle*, 70.

14. Carson, *In Struggle*, 52–53, 72–73, 98–103, 194–200, April 18, 1964, SNCC Memo, "From the Finance Office to Members of the Executive Committee of SNCC," Civil Rights Movement Archive; Constancia Romilly to Tom Tolg, November 7, 1963; Constancia Romilly to Tom Tolg, February 27, 1964.

15. Personal interview, Constancia Romilly, July 24, 2022.

16. Treuhaft, Oral History, 10, 46.

17. Sussman, *Decca*, 104.

18. Brad Cleaveland, "A Letter to Undergraduates," *Slate Supplement* 1, no. 4, 1964.

19. Freeman, *At Berkeley in the 1960s*, 84.

20. Self, *American Babylon*; Gitlin, *The Sixties*, 164; Cohen and Zelnik, eds., *The Free Speech Movement*, 27.

21. By the spring of 1964 an enhanced Klan presence existed across Mississippi, likely in response to the white volunteers coming south to register voters.

22. Moses's quote appears in Nelson and Readdean, "Freedom Summer," and has also been quoted often in histories of the movement. See Freeman, *At Berkeley in the 60s: The Education of an Activist*. During Freedom Summer there were a thousand arrests, at least eighty beatings, and over sixty bombings of Black churches and homes, Freeman writes. The SNCC volunteers may have felt unprotected by their whiteness, yet some scholars, such as Todd Gitlin, believe that "the white shield was a partial success," at least in drawing more attention to racial violence. Gitlin, *The Sixties*, 151.

23. Jessica Mitford, "Rebels with a Hundred Causes: The Indignant Generation," unpublished typescript, 1961, OSU, Box 97, folder 832.

24. Dorothy Zellner, interview, Nelson and Readdean, "Freedom Summer." One of the FSM student volunteers later reflected that their lessons in listening gave them a critical perspective on white supremacy and an understanding that unlearning racism would not come easily. White

students, he wrote, "listened to African Americans, learned from them, followed African American leadership, and in the process were forever transformed." Waldo Martin, "Holding One Another: Mario Savio and the Freedom Struggle in Mississippi and Berkeley," in Cohen and Zelnik, eds., *The Free Speech Movement*.

25. Mitford, *Hons and Rebels*, 19.

26. Jessica Mitford to Virginia Durr, October 9, 1965.

27. Treuhaft, Oral History.

28. Jessica Mitford to Edith Treuhaft, December 9, 1964.

29. "The Berkeley Student Protests, 1964–1965: A Chronology," Online Archive of California (OAC), "The 'Free Speech' Crisis at Berkeley, 1964–1965: Some Issues for Social and Legal Research," https://oac.cdlib.org/view?docId=kt9r29p975;NAAN=13030&doc.view=frames&chunk.id=div00002&toc.depth=1&toc.id=&brand=oac4. Numbers for those arrested that night vary from a low of 768 (counting Bob) to a high of 860. Because the arrests came in waves and continued over many hours, an exact count may be difficult to obtain. Decca put the number at 860.

30. Treuhaft, Oral History.

31. Bob's FSM role was such a source of pride, in fact, for Decca that she had a later falling out with her dear friend Dobby Walker over what she felt was Walker's failure to acknowledge Bob's importance to the movement. Thirty years after the mass arrests, Decca was still "steaming with anger" over Dobby suggesting "that Bob hasn't got NAME RECOGNITION! How ridic. . . . representing the FSM students & being the first arrested . . . Those are just some name rec. examples of a very high order." Jessica Mitford to Dobby Walker, October 20, 1995.

32. Malcolm Bernstein, "The FSM: A Movement Lawyer's Perspective," Cohen and Zelnik, eds., *The Free Speech Movement*, 433.

33. Jessica Mitford to Aranka Treuhaft Kliot, December 9, 1964.

34. Douglas B. Ward, "The Geography of the *Ladies' Home Journal*: An Analysis of a Magazine's Audience, 1911–1955," *Journalism History* 34, no. 1 (2008). Ward's data ends in 1955 but readership for the magazine continued to climb for the next ten years, making the estimate of 10 to 11 million readers a conservative one. Jean E. Hunter puts the figure at 15 million readers a month. See J. E. Hunter, "A Daring New Concept: *The Ladies' Home Journal* and Modernism Feminism, *NWSA Journal*, 2, no. 4 (Autumn 1990), 583–602.

35. *Ladies' Home Journal*, June 1964, Special Issue: "Woman: The Fourth Dimension." Contributors included Marya Mannes, Arlene Eisenberg, Johanna Davies, and Suzanne Massie, all white women.

36. *The American Way of Death* sold hundreds of thousands of copies and has never gone out of print. It appeared above Carson's *Silent Spring* or Friedan's *The Feminine Mystique* on major bestseller lists. Its first print runs sold out as fast as the publisher could produce them. On August 23, 1964, for example, the *Chicago Tribune* reported that *The American Way of Death* was no. 2 on the paperback bestseller list and *The Feminine Mystique* was no. 6. Friedan's book preceded Mitford's by approximately six months. It spent six weeks on *The New York Times* bestseller list, compared to sixteen weeks for *The American Way of Death*, which also ranked consistently higher on the list than *The Feminine Mystique*. *The American Way of Death* was the no. 1 bestseller for many weeks. *The Feminine Mystique* never reached higher than no. 7 on the *Times* bestseller list. Over time, both Carson's and Friedan's books sold millions of paperback copies. Edwin McDowell, "'*Silent Spring*,' 20 Years a Milestone," *New York Times*, September 27, 1982, C16; Grace Lichtenstein, "Women's Lib Wooed by Publishers," *New York Times*,

August 17, 1970, 32; Ben Wattenberg, "Betty Freidan and 'The Feminine Mystique'," PBS, 2000; Ray Walters, "Paperback Talk," *New York Times*, June 28, 1981, 71; Jacob Munoz, "The Powerful, Complicated Legacy of Betty Friedan's 'The Feminine Mystique'," *Smithsonian*, February 4, 2021; "Best Seller List," *New York Times*, January 26, 1964, BR8; "Paperback Best Sellers," *Chicago Tribune*, August 23, 1964, K10.

37. "Royalties Aren't the Only Reward," *New York Times*, December 1, 1963.

38. The "Seven Sister" magazines (*Better Homes and Gardens*, *Family Circle*, *Good Housekeeping*, *McCall's*, *Redbook*, *Women's Day*, and *The Ladies' Home Journal*) could not count 6411 Regent Street as subscribers—that distinction went to journals such as *Casket & Sunnyside* and *Mortuary Management*—but Decca had written for many of the women's magazines before, felt she knew what was called for, and also strongly believed that it was her duty to address general readers and try to reach them.

39. Jessica Mitford, "The American Way of Success," *Ladies Home Journal*, Special Issue: Woman: The Fourth Dimension," ed., Betty Friedan, June 1964, 22, 25. As was often true when Decca did not take an assignment too seriously, her essay shamelessly recycled bits of her life story already published elsewhere, which made it that much easier to write.

40. Alvin Toffler, "What the Husbands Think." Such extreme caution and pervasive sexism were the norm not only in the mainstream but also on the Left. Even SNCC—a radical organization of youth—was mobilizing in 1964 under the banner of "One Man, One Vote," careful not to rock the gender boat too strongly. Official SNCC stationery not only carried the "One Man, One Vote" motto in 1964 but buttons and other publicity materials such as bumper stickers with that slogan were being widely disseminated by SNCC in preparation for the Freedom Summer campaign. Constancia was one of the SNCC workers using that stationery and disseminating those materials. Friedan's defensiveness may well, as Daniel Horowitz (and others) argue, have been a carefully constructed persona, designed to make it easier "for white suburban women readers to identify" with Friedan. Daniel Horowitz, *Betty Friedan*, 2. Decca also constructed such a persona at times, especially in *The American Way of Death*. While she and Friedan and also Rachel Carson worked to revolutionize American policy and practice, all three had to be careful not to seem too radical to their readers.

41. Jessica Mitford, American Way of Success," *Ladies' Home Journal*, June 1964, 22, 25. "The Women Your Husband Works With . . . ," an advertisement for "Great Books," appears on 13.

42. See, for example, Mitford, "Waugh Is Hell." While Mitford remained indebted to Waugh's work on cultures of death and dying and had traveled to Hollywood, all expenses paid, to consult with Christopher Isherwood, Terry Southern, Tony Richardson, Vanessa Redgrave, and others, on the film adaptation of Waugh's 1948 satire *The Loved One*, she did not shy from attacking him for coming to "lament the passing of the very fixtures which he once sought so heroically to destroy."

43. Mitford, "Comment on Three Funeral Pieces," *Poison Penmanship*, 103.

44. Jessica Mitford to Robert Treuhaft, July 1964; Jessica Mitford, "It's a Pairfect Day for the Games," *Venture*.

45. Jessica Mitford to Julie Andrews, December 2, 1965.

46. Here, she forecast the platform such shows could provide to right-wing extremists, and she decried the power that self-professed authorities might wield, anticipating by many decades the influence of such "Talkicians" as Rush Limbaugh and Tucker Carlson. Jessica Mitford, "Hello There! You're on the Air!" *Harper's Magazine*, May 1, 1966.

47. Jessica Mitford to Barbara Kahn, March 30, 1965.

48. Jessica Mitford, "Maine Chance Diary," *McCall's*, 130.

49. Mitford, "Maine Chance," 138.
50. Fannie Hurst was well known for subsisting on a diet of only six hundred calories a day to stay slim, although her bestselling short stories usually took a feminist slant on women and society. Her memoir, *No Food with My Meals*, capitalized on her dieting fame. Fannie Hurst, Daily Diet Notes 1940s, Fannie Hurst Papers, Brandeis University.
51. Jessica Mitford to Robert Treuhaft, November 16 and November 15, 1965. Jessica Mitford to Barbara Kahn, November 16, 1965. Amongst the guests at Maine Chance when Decca was there were a smattering of career women, including Peggy Goldwater, wife of Barry Goldwater.
52. Jessica Mitford to Robert Treuhaft, November 15 and 16, 1965.
53. Jessica Mitford to Barb Kahn; Jessica Mitford to Bob Treuhaft.
54. Mitford, "Maine Chance," 138.
55. Mitford, "Maine Chance," 129.
56. Mitford, "Maine Chance," and *Poison Penmanship*, 132.
57. One journalist who followed in Mitford's footsteps ten years later, also going undercover as an overweight client, wrote that "Maine Chance is also known—but definitely not advertised—as a dehydration farm, since no alcohol is served on the premises." Sondra Gottlieb, "Slimming in Arizona with the Very Rich," *Maclean's*, October 1, 1974.
58. Jessica Mitford, "Maine Chance."
59. Her essay on Maine Chance was republished in *Nova* in October 1966 under the title "How to Lose Five Pounds for a Thousand Dollars." An essay titled "The Importance of Being Skinny" was published in the *Los Angeles Times* on November 26, 1967, and then republished as "The Skinny Crusade: Is There a Weight Watcher Watching You" in the *New York Post* on December 2, 1967, and again as "Weight Watchers' Demands: Last Pound of Flesh" in *The Boston Globe* on December 10, 1967, and as "Group Therapy for Fat People" in the *San Francisco Sunday Examiner & Chronicle* on December 17, 1967.
60. Jessica Mitford, "Pretty, Lascivious, Undignified," *Vogue*, March 15, 1966.
61. Forman, *The Making of Black Revolutionaries*, 265.
62. Julian Bond, foreword, James Forman, *Making Black Revolutionaries*, xi–xii.
63. Interview, Constancia Romilly, July 24, 2022; Jessica Mitford to Barbara Kahn, December 21, 1965, and December 29, 1965.
64. Jessica Mitford to Barbara Kahn, December 21, 1965. The memoir became Forman's *The Making of Black Revolutionaries*. Decca found parts of it predictable, but she kept that criticism from Forman and Dinky.
65. Jessica Mitford to Barbara Kahn, December 19, 1965.
66. Jessica Mitford to Pele de Lappe, December 30, 1965.
67. See Jessica Mitford to Sydney Redesdale, May 11, 1950; Treuhaft, Oral History, 51–52. (Even many years later, Bob still viewed Newson's as "the big case of the decade.").
68. Jessica Mitford to "friends" (form letter for Bob's campaign), OSU.
69. J. Frank Coakley, *For the People: Sixty Years of Fighting for Law and Order* (City: Western Star Press, 1992), 38; Treuhaft, Oral History, 89.
70. Bob Treuhaft, Oral History, 109.
71. Bob Treuhaft, Oral History, 110.
72. R. Jeffrey Lusting, "The War at Home: California's Struggle to Stop the Vietnam War," in Marcia Eymann and Charles Wollenberg, eds., *What's Going On?: California and the Vietnam War* (Berkeley: University of California Press, 2004), 66.
73. Interview with Robert Scheer, March 3, 2022.

74. Jessica Mitford to Leonard Boudin, June 24, 1966. See also Braudy, *Family Circle: The Boudins and the Aristocracy of the Left.*

75. Jessica Mitford to Bob Gottlieb, December 14, 1966; Jessica Mitford to Barbara Kahn, February 6, 1967.

76. Ironically, some of her enthusiasm was shared most openly in her letters to her sisters. See Jessica Mitford to Nancy Mitford, April 6, 1967. See also Jessica Mitford to Barbara Kahn, February 6, 1967.

77. David L. Brunsma, "Interracial Families and the Racial Identification of Mixed-Race Children: Evidence from the Early Childhood Longitudinal Study," *Social Forces* 84, no. 2 (December 2005), 1131. According to a Gallup poll in 1958, almost 95 percent of all Americans opposed interracial marriage in the 1950s. Cultural attitudes began to shift over the next twenty years, but slowly and by small margins. See also Lester, *Loving Before Loving.*

78. Jessica Mitford to Nancy Mitford, May 4, 1967.

79. Jessica Mitford to Nancy Mitford, April 6, 1967.

80. Jessica Mitford to Miriam Miller, June 26, 1967.

81. Deborah Mitford to Nancy Mitford, March 13, 1967.

82. Deborah Mitford to Nancy Mitford, March 13, 1967.

83. Diana Mosley to Deborah Mitford, March 15, 1967. Diana and Debo went on, in their correspondence, to speculate that Nancy, the most liberal of the sisters after Decca, also "minded very much." Evidence suggests that they were right. At about this time, Nancy was invited by some of her literary friends to meet North Vietnamese writers at a literary event in Paris. "No, I will not," she firmly declared to Debo. "You may disapprove of people being set fire to without wanting to meet them." Nancy Mitford to Deborah Mitford, March 28, 1968. Diana never apologized for her racism, fascism, or anti-Semitism. She insisted all her life that the Holocaust was an exaggeration, and that Hitler had the right idea. Diana Mosley, interview with Sue Lawley, November 1989, BBC, Desert Island Discs.

84. Nancy Mitford to Jessica Mitford, April 10, 1967.

85. *Ramparts* ad, "Good Neighbor Plan," *Ramparts.* Mitford's *Ramparts* ads ran for a few months in 1966 and 1967. Clippings of some of the ads are in OSU, Boxes 126 and 127. Eventually a conventional real estate company took over the sale of the island.

86. Self, *American Babylon*, 205.

87. Paul Cobb, public lecture, 1968, as quoted in *Oakland Tribune*, July 2, 1968 and Donald K. Tamaki, "Oakland Politics and Powerless Pressure Groups," Institute of Governmental Studies, University of California, Berkeley, September, 1970, 8, both as quoted by Self, *American Babylon*, 211.

88. Forman, *The Making of Black Revolutionaries*, 527.

89. On the overlap of these youth movements, see especially Murch, *Living for the City: Migration, Education, and the Rise of the Black Panther Party.*

90. Palewski had been, for some years, seeing a wealthy woman fourteen years his junior, with whom he'd had a son in 1961. Violette de Talleyrand-Périgord was beautiful, much younger than Nancy, and fabulously rich. Although Palewski had always told Nancy that he could not marry a divorced woman—and, hence, could never marry her—because it would damage his career, when Talleyrand-Périgord finally got a divorce, Palewski married her in 1969.

91. One of Nancy's biographers believes that "despite the apparent control with which she wielded her icicle pen, coldness was not innate in her: it was her way of dealing with blazing emotion." Thompson, *Life in a Cold Climate*, 360. I find scant evidence that Nancy's coolness was other than what it seemed.

92. Jessica Mitford to Virginia Durr, August 9, 1967.
93. Jessica Mitford to Virginia Durr, August 9, 1967.
94. Jessica Mitford to Peter Nevile, September 25, 1962.
95. Jessica Mitford to Virginia Durr, August 18, 1967.
96. See Jessica Mitford to Lord Haig, September 26, 1967. Haig was the children's trustee. Decca had witnessed Giles spending enormous amounts of money and was very concerned for his children's welfare.
97. Personal interview with Edmund Romilly, November 9, 2016. Yet, Edmund was also drawn to the family, staying with Dinky and Forman in 1969 and with Decca and Bob at various times as a young man.
98. One of her dearest friends, Evie Frieden, who had been part of Decca's original white women's delegation in support of Willie McGee, had also recently died of leukemia.
99. In early 1967, 60 percent of Americans still supported the war effort. By fall of 1967, the tables were beginning to turn, with half of Americans beginning to question the war. Boyle, *The Shattering*, 264.
100. See especially Jessica Mitford to Vivian Hallinan, August 30, 1967.
101. "A Call to Resist Illegitimate Authority," October 7, 1967. The statement was signed by over twenty-five thousand individuals, including Linus Pauling.
102. See especially, Benjamin Spock, "Oral History: The Conspiracy to Oppose the Vietnam War," in *It Did Happen Here: Recollections of Political Repression in America*, ed. Bud and Ruth Schultz (Berkeley: University of California Press, 1989).
103. Jessica Mitford, "Harsh Punishment Questioned," *Los Angeles Times*, July 30, 1966, B4.
104. Jessica Mitford to Cedric and Mary Belfrage, March 18, 1968.
105. Jessica Mitford to Cedric and Mary Belfrage, March 18, 1968.

Chapter Sixteen: "Do Admit"

1. The courtroom still looks now almost exactly as it looked in 1968. According to Michael Ferber, the only visible difference is the space between the judge's bench and the lawyer's tables, which is far greater now than it was in 1968.
2. Jessica Mitford to Cedric and Mary Belfrage, March 18, 1968.
3. As quoted by Sokol, *The Heavens Might Crack: The Death and Legacy of Martin Luther King, Jr.* and Boyle, *The Shattering: America in the 1960s*, 281.
4. Fred Graham, "Department of Justice Wants Draft & Foes' Trial Focused on Conspiracy Charge," *New York Times*, March 26, 1968, 5.
5. Elinor Langer, "The Oakland 7," *The Atlantic*, October 1969.
6. Leonard Boudin, interview for *The Making of a Muckraker*, circa 1985, OSU, Box 139, folder 1154.
7. Jessica Mitford, interview for *The Making of a Muckraker*, circa 1985, OSU, Box 139, folder 1154. The conspiracy charges which Attorney General Ramsey Clark, generally considered a liberal, brought against the Boston Five were designed not only to intimidate resisters, as were the Oakland charges, but also to scare the roughly half of all Americans who now refused to support the war in Vietnam. Ramsey Clark later said that his appointment by President Johnson was a "shock" not only because he was only thirty-seven years old, but also because he'd already been opposed to the death penalty, opposed to wiretapping, and opposed to any "absolute obedience to authority," which was just what Johnson and others wished to reinstate. Ramsey Clark, interview with Michael Ratner, Michael Smith, and Heidi Boghasian,

April 28, 2008, reprinted in Smith, *Lawyers for the Left*, 146. Some people suspected that Clark, pressured by Johnson to suppress protest, had chosen his defendants on the assumption that no jury would convict them.

8. The Oakland Seven jury—a mix of housewives, civil servants, blue- and white-collar workers, and a retired Marine colonel—acquitted all defendants in late March 1968.

9. Langer, "The Oakland 7."

10. In late 1967 when the defendants in both conspiracy cases were indicted, roughly half the country still supported the war. By the time both trials took place, those numbers dropped dramatically, as they would continue to do every month, until by the end of the decade only a third of all Americans expressed support for the war. Gallup Polls, 1967–1969.

11. Boudin, interview, "Making of a Muckraker."

12. Michael Ferber, *Conspiracy*, unpublished manuscript. I am grateful to Michael Ferber for sharing his memories and unpublished narrative of the trial with me.

13. Ferber, *Conspiracy*.

14. Jessica Mitford to Virginia Durr, June 19, 1968, VD.

15. Jessica Mitford, interview, "Making of a Muckraker."

16. Mitford, *The Trial of Dr. Spock*, 118, 116.

17. Michael Ferber, personal interview, October 8, 2023.

18. Jessica Mitford to Barbara Kahn, May 23, 1968.

19. Michael Ferber, personal interview, October 8, 2023.

20. Jessica Mitford to Barbara Kahn, May 23, 1968; Jessica Mitford to Pele de Lappe, April 14, 1968.

21. Decca's "main press pals" came from *The Boston Globe*, *Ramparts*, *The Washington Post*, *Esquire*, *The Michigan Daily*, *The Yale Review*, and *The New Yorker*, an eclectic mix reflecting her ability to fit in with very different constituencies.

22. Fred Graham, "Judge Bars Legality of Vietnam War as Issue in Spock Trial," *New York Times*, April 18, 1968.

23. "Spock Trial May Be Thriller," *Washington Post*; Homer Bigart, "The Spock Trial," *New York Times*, May 26, 1968, E15.

24. Jessica Mitford to Virginia Durr, June 19, 1968.

25. Jessica Mitford, *The Trial of Dr. Spock*, 64, 69, 73.

26. Mitford, *The Trial of Dr. Spock*, 199–202.

27. Jessica Mitford to Virginia Durr, April 17, 1969.

28. A few reviews, as was typical for her, were written by friends and comrades, including Helen Sobell (wife of jailed dissident Morton Sobell, whom Decca had long defended) and Alan Pryce-Jones (a friend whose son David's later biography of Unity would cause a major rift between Decca and her sisters). Helen Sobell, *Science & Society* 34, no. 4 (1970): 497–99; Alan Pryce-Jones, "Mitford Eyes Spock Case," *Oakland Tribune*, October 12, 1964. Sobell was released from prison in April 1969.

29. Harry E. Fuller, "Dr. Spock, 'Boston Five' Court Trial Dissected," *Salt Lake Tribune*, October 19, 1969, 2E; Christopher Lehmann-Haupt, "Guilty as Charged by the Judge," *New York Times*, September 8, 1969; Herbert Kenney, "Background to the Spock Case," *The Boston Globe*, September 24, 1969; Francis D. Wormuth, "The Trial of Dr. Spock," *Western Political Quarterly* 23, no. 2 (June 1970); *The Daily Reporter*, Dover, Ohio, February 7, 1970; Alan Dershowitz, "The Trial of Dr. Spock," *New York Times*, September 14, 1969.

30. October 1969 Gallup Poll: 68 percent.

31. Herbert Packer, "The Conspiracy Weapon," *New York Review of Books*, November 6, 1969. *Time* magazine's anonymous reviewer was a notable exception. Amid sexist descriptions of Mitford's prose as "kittenish," the reviewer slammed the book as "hollow and partisan." Anonymous, "Books: One Disappointing Trial," *Time*, October 3, 1969.

32. Mitford, *Poison Penmanship*, 24. Jessica Mitford, interview for "The Making of a Muckraker," circa 1984–1985, OSU, Box 139, folder 1154.

33. Nancy Mitford to Deborah Mitford, June 8, 1968.

34. Jessica Mitford to Deborah Mitford, May 13, 1969.

35. Jessica Mitford to Deborah Mitford, July 17, 1969.

36. Jessica Mitford to Pele de Lappe and Steve Murdock, May 26, 1969.

37. Jessica Mitford to Pele de Lappe and Steve Murdock, May 26, 1969.

38. Diana Mosley's diary, as quoted by Mosley, *The Mitfords*.

39. "One simply does not know how much she minds," Deborah wrote to Pamela, "as she is such a private person . . . it must be miserable for her." Deborah Mitford to Pamela Mitford, April 1, 1969. See also Hastings, *Nancy Mitford*.

40. Jessica Mitford to Aranka Treuhaft, May 22, 1969.

41. Jessica Mitford to Doris ("Dobby") Walker, received February 19, 1974, undated, OSU. All of her life she corresponded and collected correspondence (which is how she came to leave more than twelve thousand of her own letters behind after her death).

42. Jessica Mitford to Pele de Lappe and Steve Murdock, May 26, 1969.

43. See, for example, Jessica Mitford to Virginia Durr, March 10, 1970; Jessica Mitford to Nancy Mitford, October 31, 1971; Jessica Mitford to Nancy Mitford, March 7, 1972; Jessica Mitford to Doris [Dobby] Walker, April 6, 1973.

44. Toynbee, *Friends Apart*.

45. Mitford, *Poison Penmanship*, 170.

46. Bennett Cerf, one of the principal beneficiaries of the Famous Writers School, referred to the customers their salesmen targeted as both "gullible" and also as "semi-literates and other incompetents." When he asked Mitford to leave those comments out of her article, she refused. Mitford, *Poison Penmanship*, 166. Jessica Mitford to Barbara Kahn, December 3, 1969.

47. Jessica Mitford to Deborah Rogers, April 1, 1970.

48. Jessica Mitford, "Let Us Now Appraise Famous Writers," *The Atlantic*, July 1970.

49. Jessica Mitford to Vivian Cadden, January 1, 1970.

50. Jessica Mitford to Barbara Kahn, February 17, 1970.

51. Mitford, *Poison Penmanship*, 177, 170.

52. Personal communication with Gayle Feldman, October 11, 2016.

53. Jessica Mitford to Deborah Rogers, April 1, 1970.

54. Jessica Mitford to Marge Frantz, May 25, 1986.

55. Mitford, *Daughters and Rebels*, 248.

56. "A form of courtship," Alfred Fuller of the Fuller Brush Company called such selling. See Howard R. Stanger, "The Larkin Clubs of Ten: Consumer Buying Clubs and Mail-Order Commerce, 1890–1910," *Enterprise & Society* 8, no. 1 (2008). I am grateful to Elisa Fuhrken for research into traveling sales.

57. Jessica Mitford, *Poison Penmanship*, 177.

58. Jessica Mitford to Barbara ____ [last name unknown], October 15, 1970.

59. Jessica Mitford to Bill Outsi (an official with the National Parole Board in Ottawa), November 30, 1970.

60. Jessica Mitford, "Prisons: The Menace of Liberal Reform," *New York Review of Books*, March 9, 1972.
61. Jessica Mitford to Bob Treuhaft, June 13, 1973.
62. Jessica Mitford to Marge Frantz, June 21, 1973.
63. Jessica Mitford to Eleanor Fried Furman, July 10, 1973.

Chapter Seventeen: "A Bit of a Black Cloud"

1. Jessica Mitford to Sally Belfrage, March 18, 1976.
2. Jessica Mitford to Miriam Miller, July 21, 1977.
3. Jessica Mitford, "Women in Cages: District of Columbia Women's Detention Center," *McCall's*, September 1972.
4. Mitford, "Women in Cages."
5. Jessica Mitford to Alex ("Comrade E"), May 18, 1978.
6. Mitford's 1959 advance for *Hons and Rebels* from Houghton was $1,500. The advance on the London edition that same year was 250 pounds. The original Simon & Schuster advance for *The American Way of Death* was $5,000, split equally between her and Bob and more than three times her first advance. Decca also signed a lecture contract, coincident with the publication of *The American Way of Death* with Colston Leigh. That contract called for $750 for individual lectures and a $1,500 a week minimum, ensuring that she made much more money lecturing than from the book. Decca's advance for *The Trial of Dr. Spock* was $7,500, signed April 11, 1968, and requiring that the full manuscript be turned in no later than April 12, 1969. In addition to the $7,500 advance, her contract provided for $1,500 in expenses. Her London contract, signed in June 1969, was for 1,250 pounds. On June 9, 1971, for an unnamed book on prisons, Knopf paid an advance of $30,000 for approximately 100,000 words, due a little over a year later, July 1, 1972 (the equivalent today of just over $250,000). This would have been one of the first deadlines she did not meet, and given the amount of research she needed to do for the book, it was a wildly optimistic deadline. In November 1973 Mitford signed an additional contract for a Vintage paperback of *Kind and Usual Punishment* for $6,000. Her December 1973 British contract for *Kind and Usual Punishment* was for an advance of 450 pounds. For *A Fine Old Conflict*, her contract called for 100,000 to 125,00 words, and a delivery date of April 1, 1976, a deadline she also did not make. Her advance was $40,000. In 1977 she sold the paperback rights for $7,750. Most of Mitford's contracts excluded film and dramatic rights, as well as translation rights, which she reserved and for which she was paid significant additional monies. For example, in 1979 Warner Brothers paid $5,000 for initial one-year rights to both *Hons and Rebels* and Esmond's *Out of Bounds*. The Warner Bros. contract specified that if they did engage a scriptwriter, Mitford would be brought on as a consultant for an additional fee of $10,000. Their contract also specified that if they exercised their option, the payment would be $50,000 with $25,000 additional if they produced a sequel, and, in the case of television, $1,250 per episode for a one-hour episode. All contracts are in OSU, Box 148, folders 1232.1–1232.6.
7. Interview for "Portrait of a Muckraker," transcript, OSU, Box 139, folder 1155. This interview is marked as "Interview #1."
8. Mitford, *Poison Penmanship*, 216.
9. Mitford, interview for "Portrait of a Muckraker," transcript, 20 & 18, OSU, Box 139, folder 1154.
10. Mitford, interview for "Portrait of a Muckraker," transcript, 20 & 18, OSU, Box 139, folder 1154.

11. "Kind and Usual Punishment in California," *Atlantic Monthly*, March 1, 1971.

12. Mark Lapin, as quoted by Brody, *Irrepressible*, 279.

13. Jessica Mitford to Raymond Benedict (California State prison), July 12, 1971.

14. Jessica Mitford to Raymond Benedict (California State prison), July 12, 1971.

15. Jim Keyes to Jessica Mitford, January 26, 1972, San Quentin, HRC, Box 59, folder 7; Richard R. Nichols to Fay Stender, August 10, 1972, Folsom Prison, HRC, Box 48, folder 2. For some prisoners, such as her friend Roney Nunes, she ultimately collected large boxes of legal paperwork, appeals, and reports. See Roney Nunes papers in Boxes 30, 32, 39, and 51, HRC.

16. Jessica Mitford, "A Talk with George Jackson," *New York Times Book Review*, June 13, 1971; Mitford, *Poison Penmanship*, 191.

17. Jessica Mitford to Virginia Durr, March 7, 1971.

18. Interview with Christopher "Cricket" Lyman, February 8, 2024.

19. Maya Angelou, "In Self-Defense," *Letter to My Daughter*, 102–103.

20. Maya Angelou, interview with George Plimpton, quoted in Linda Wagner Martin, *Maya Angelou: Adventurous Spirit*, ebook, page 20.

21. Jessica Mitford to "Old Thing" [Marge Frantz], June 1, 1974. Some of Decca's closest friends understood this aspect of her. Shortly after her husband, Clifford's, death, in 1975, Virginia Durr wrote to Decca that "few people could have survived the contradictions and ups and downs of your life and still stayed sane and continued to function and be creative." She said that looking back on how Decca handled Esmond's death was helping her to deal with Cliff's. Virginia Durr to Jessica Mitford, June 21, 1975. See, for example, Jessica Mitford to Dobby Walker, May 24, 1977, OSU; and Jessica Mitford to Anne Farrer Horne [Idden], June 19, 1978.

22. Pearlman, *Call Me Phaedra: The Life and Times of Movement Lawyer Fay Stender*, 88.

23. Jessica Mitford to Virginia Durr, March 7, 1971.

24. Jessica Mitford to Deborah Mitford, September 23, 1973.

25. President Nixon cautioned, "The greatest danger is that the Allende government might consolidate and be successful. We must avoid, at all costs, the possibility of other countries in Latin America following the Allende government example." Quoted by Vincenc Navarro, "What Happened in Chile: Parallels to Spain," "Dominio Público" *PÚBLICO*, September 19, 2013, translated by Collen Boland and published online at https://www.vnavarro.org/?p=9827&lang=en.

26. Barbara Blakemore [*McCall's* editor], Ida Landauer, interview for "Portrait of a Muckraker," interview transcript, OSU, Box 139, folder 1155.

27. Jessica Mitford to Deborah Mitford, October 8, 1973, Chatsworth House Archives. On Rennie, see "The Ohio Pen's Avenging Angel," *Columbus Monthly*, August 1, 2009. Decca admired Stender's Prison Law Project and defense of Jackson and the Soledad Brothers but took Stender to task in *Kind and Usual Punishment* for describing prisoners as "the salt of the earth." She especially objected to language that Stender used in a preface to a book of prison letters (edited by another friend of Decca's), where she wrote: "'I certainly feel that person for person, prisoners are better human beings than you would find in any random group of people. They are more loving. They have more concern for each other. They have more creative potential.'" Mitford, *Kind and Usual Punishment*, 7; Fay Stender, preface, *Maximum Security: Letters*, ed. Eve Pell (New York: Dutton, 1972). In 1979, an ex-felon broke into Stender's home, forced her to sign a statement saying she'd betrayed George Jackson, and shot her six times. Stender survived, paralyzed to her waist and wheelchair bound. She lived long enough to testify against her attacker. She killed herself after his trial and sentencing. The attack filled Decca with "gloom," and in an act of solidarity

and contrition, she offered to shelter Stender's children. Jessica Mitford to Maya Angelou and Paul du Feu, May 30, 1979.

28. Her printed research materials (excluding books), for this project alone, fill well over three dozen densely packed banker's boxes.
29. Mitford's prison guard correspondence is in HRC, Box 47, folder 7.
30. Mitford, *Kind and Usual Punishment*, 296–97.
31. Mitford, *Kind and Usual Punishment*, 6. As she noted, the state commission report concluded that no real change had occurred at Attica: "The cycle of misunderstanding, protest, and reaction continues, and confrontation remains the only language in which the inmates feel they can call attention to the system. The possibility that the Attica townspeople will again hear the dread sound of the powerhouse whistle is very real." *Attica: The Official Report*, 470.
32. Jessica Mitford to Robert Gottlieb, February 12, 1973, HRC, Box 66, folder 6.
33. Her prison correspondence from this period fills more than three banker's boxes. One of her longest standing correspondences was with Roney Nunes, a prison activist in San Luis Obispo [convicted of robbing a drive-in at gunpoint, he was originally incarcerated in 1957] with whom she began corresponding in 1971.
34. Mitford, *Kind and Usual Punishment*, viii.
35. These included "An Eye for an Eye," *New York Times Book Review*, October 3, 1971; "Kind and Usual Punishment in California," *Atlantic Monthly*, March 1, 1971; "A Talk with George Jackson," *New York Times*, June 13, 1971; "Prisons: The Menace of Liberal Reform," *New York Times Book Review*, March 9, 1972; "Women in Cages," *McCall's*, September 1972; "Experiments Behind Bars: Doctors, Drug Companies, and Prisoners," *The Atlantic*, January 1, 1973; "Prisons and Funerals," *New York Times*, September 5, 1973; and "The Torture Cure," *Harper's*, August 1, 1973.
36. Jessica Mitford, interview for "Portrait of a Muckraker," transcript, tape 3, 21, OSU, Box 139, folder 1154.
37. Jessica Mitford to Muriel Woodring, September 17, 1971, HRC, Box 59, folder 3.
38. Mitford, "Experiments Behind Bars: Doctors, Drug Companies, and Prisoners" in *The Atlantic*, January 1, 1973.
39. Barbara Blakemore [*McCall's* editor], Ida Landauer, interview for "Portrait of a Muckraker," transcript, OSU, Box 139, folder 1155.
40. Mitford, *Kind and Usual Punishment*, 71.
41. Mitford, *Kind and Usual Punishment*, 97.
42. Mitford, *Kind and Usual Punishment*, 80, 87.
43. Jessica Mitford, "Kind and Usual Punishment in California," *The Atlantic*, 52.
44. Mitford, *Kind and Usual Punishment*, 341.
45. Mitford, *Kind and Usual Punishment*, 188.
46. Jessica Mitford to Dobby Walker, April 6, 1973.
47. Jessica Mitford to Bill Outsi, November 30, 1970.
48. Christopher Lehmann-Haupt, "On the Shame of Our Prisons," *New York Times*, September 19, 1973, 45.
49. Remarkably, while almost every reviewer mentioned *The American Way of Death*, there was not one reviewer who mentioned *The Trial of Dr. Spock*. *The American Way of Death* was invariably referred to as her "last" or her "previous" book, as if *The Trial of Dr. Spock*, a book that in its own way did as much to cement Decca's sense of herself as did *The American Way of Death*, had simply never existed.

50. David J. Rothman, review of *Kind and Usual Punishment, New York Times*, September 9, 1973; Joan Hanauer, review, UPI, *Chicago Tribune*, September 23, 1973, E7. Hanauer's review was syndicated in papers in many cities, including Lubbock, Texas; Fort Walton Beach, Florida; Ogden, Utah; Eureka, California; Pomona, California, and elsewhere. Reuters syndicated reviews in Cameron, Texas, and the *South China Post*. There were also reviews syndicated through the Newhouse News Service, which opened in 1961 and operated for decades, less successfully than Reuters or UPI; see also Heidi Steffens, review, *Off Our Backs* 3, no. 11 (October 1973): 13. One of the early feminist journals, *Off Our Backs*, had recently devoted a special issue to women in prisons. While some have wondered about Mitford's appeal to feminists, Steffens gushed "I'm in love with Mitford." Wally Trabing, Jessica Mitford interview, "Mostly About People," *Santa Cruz Sentinel*, October 11, 1973, 13. Mitford kept her copy of the *Off Our Backs* issue, "Women in Prisons," vol. 2, no. 8 (April 1972) with her papers. HRC, Box 24, folder 1.

51. "She fails to advocate the abolition of the prison," one law professor wrote. Daniel Nobel, review of *Kind and Usual Punishment, Buffalo Law Review* 23, no. 1 (Fall 1973): 307–312.

52. David J. Rothman, review of *Kind and Usual Punishment, New York Times*, September 9, 1973; review of the paperback, *New York Times*, November 10, 1974; Edwin W. Tucker, *Justice System Journal* 1, no. 1 (Winter 1974), 85–88.

53. In another *New York Times* review (ultimately there were four), Christopher Lehmann-Haupt wrote that *Kind and Usual Punishment* was not "half as effective as her earlier book," "On the Shame of Our Prisons."

54. See, for example, *Harvard Law Review* 87, no. 2 (December 1973), 509; Marc Plattner, "Neo-Abolitionism," *Commentary*, January 1974, 80.

55. Decca was one of only about 21 women, out of 175 total recipients, to receive a Guggenheim for 1973 and one of the very few women to receive one for nonfiction.

56. See June 1972 letter from agent Deborah Rogers. She was also involved in numerous lawsuits for prisoners' rights, half a dozen of which went to federal courts. "I won those lawsuits in federal court . . . down the line," Decca later said. Interview for "Portrait of a Muckraker," transcript, OSU Box 139, folder 1154. She added that the Nixon Supreme Court ultimately ruled against all of them, confirming that prison administrators could determine prison access.

57. Jessica Mitford to Edith Treuhaft, November 15, 1973. Subsequently, Decca was persuaded to sell the remainder of her materials to Ohio State, where the bulk of her papers now reside. Evidently, Ohio State offered a considerably better price ($10,000 was equivalent to nearly $70,000 today).

58. Jessica Mitford to Constancia Romilly, November 9, 1975; Jessica Mitford to James Forman, Jr., October 1, 1990.

59. Jessica Mitford to Robert Gottlieb, May 25, 1973.

60. Jessica Mitford, "My Short and Happy Life as a Distinguished Professor," *The Atlantic*, October 1974, reprinted in *Poison Penmanship*, 192.

61. Mitford, "My Short and Happy Life as a Distinguished Professor," 193.

62. Mitford, "My Short and Happy Life as a Distinguished Professor," 195.

63. Jessica Mitford to Aranka Treuhaft, September 22, 1973.

64. Mitford, *Poison Penmanship*, 197.

65. Mitford, *Poison Penmanship*, 192–216.

66. Hobart & William Smith, for example, paid her $1,000 plus her travel expenses for a couple of days of visiting. (This is equivalent to more than $5,000 today.)

67. Jessica Mitford to Deborah Mitford, September 19, 1974.

68. Jessica Mitford to Aranka Treuhaft, October 2, 1974.

69. Jessica Mitford to Marge Frantz, August 29, 1974.

70. Jessica Mitford to Dobby Walker, September 25, 1974; Jessica Mitford to Marge Frantz, December 28, 1974.

71. Jessica Mitford to Marge Frantz, December 28, 1974.

72. Jessica Mitford to Marge Frantz, October 1, 1974.

73. Jessica Mitford to Deborah Mitford, June 21, 1975.

74. Jessica Mitford to Doris Brin Walker and Other Friends, October 18, 1975; Jessica Mitford to Marge Frantz, November 4, 1975.

75. Jessica Mitford to Marge Frantz, November 4, 1975.

76. She didn't want the other fellows "sucking up" to Maya. Jessica Mitford to Marge Frantz, November 4, 1975.

77. Jessica Mitford to Constancia Romilly, November 9, 1975.

78. Jessica Mitford to Marge Frantz, November 12, 1975.

79. Jessica Mitford to Dobby Walker "& All," January 19, 1976.

80. Jessica Mitford to Deborah Mitford, February 14, 1976.

81. Interview for "Portrait of a Muckraker," transcript, OSU, Box 139, folder 1155. This interview is marked as "Interview #1." A number of the students in the class did, in fact, go on to careers in journalism, including Corby Kummer, Jonathan Mandell, Chris Buckley, and others.

82. Jessica Mitford to Bob Treuhaft and Dobby Walker, March 29, 1976, OSU, Box 131, folder 1110.

83. Interview with Corby Kummer, January 12, 2024; interview with Christopher "Cricket" Lyman, February 8, 2024.

84. Interview with Corby Kummer, January 12, 2024.

85. I am grateful for the memories and insights of Yale students in Decca's class, including Jonathan Mandell, Christopher "Cricket" Lyman, Corby Kummer, David Scobey, and Tom Alpert. Interviews with Decca's Yale students were conducted in the fall and winter of 2023–2024.

86. Jessica Mitford to Dobby Walker "& All," January 19, 1976.

87. Jessica Mitford to Sally Belfrage, October 25, 1976.

88. "I'm in a bit of a black cloud myself as it looks like total warfare with the remaining sisters." Jessica Mitford to Philip Toynbee, June 17, 1977.

89. Jessica Mitford to Barbara and Ephraim Kahn and Miriam Miller, June 22, 1973.

90. Jessica Mitford to Deborah Mitford, January 25, 1974.

91. While most of the family's efforts at suppression were unsuccessful, Andrew Cavendish did prevail on the publishers to omit at least one paragraph about Unity's sexual life in Germany, which included claims of rampant promiscuity with German officers and sexual acts, such as fellatio, performed at Hitler's request.

92. Jessica Mitford to David Pryce-Jones, February 26, 1976. According to Mary Lovell, Pryce-Jones "did a huge amount of new research, tracking down childhood friends, people who had known Unity in Germany in the late thirties, and even medical staff who had nursed her after her attempted suicide." Lovell, *The Sisters*, 495. Decca repeated the phrase "tour de force of research" in a letter to Debo, discussing Pryce-Jones's many interviews and finding "hitherto secret documents & papers," something Decca always admired. Jessica Mitford to Deborah Mitford, August 17, 1976.

93. Diana Mosley to Deborah Mitford, June 16, 1976; Pamela Mitford to Jessica Mitford, September 22, 1976.

94. Jessica Mitford to Deborah Mitford; Pamela Jackson to Jessica Mitford, September 22, 1976.
95. Pamela Jackson to Jessica Mitford, September 22, 1976, OSU, Box 208, folder 1651.
96. Jessica Mitford to Pamela Jackson, October 4, 1976.
97. Jessica Mitford to Deborah Mitford, October 26, 1976.
98. Jessica Mitford to Sonia Orwell, November 17, 1976.
99. Deborah Mitford to Jessica Mitford, November 10, 1976.
100. Jessica Mitford to Marge Frantz, December 28, 1974.
101. Jessica Mitford to Deborah Mitford, 23 November 1977.
102. Jessica Mitford to unnamed addressee [probably Polly Toynbee], July 4, 1977.
103. Jessica Mitford to Emma (the Good) Tennant, July 20, 1977.
104. Jessica Mitford to Clementine Churchill, August 21, 1977.
105. Deborah Mitford to Jessica Mitford, November 29, 1977.
106. Jessica Mitford to Deborah Mitford, November 19, 1976.
107. Deborah Mitford to Jessica Mitford, February 13, 1978.
108. Jessica Mitford to Kay Graham, November 26, 1976.
109. Mitford, *A Fine Old Conflict*, 10, 3, 320.
110. *Virginia Quarterly* 54, no. 2 (Spring 1978): 47; John Leonard, "Books of the Times," *New York Times*, September 8, 1977; Ronald Radosh, *The Nation*, January 28, 1978, 85; Katherine Evans, *Washington Post*, October 2, 1977.
111. John Leonard, "Books of the Times," *New York Times*, September 8, 1977.
112. William L. Patterson to Jessica Mitford, September 9, 1977.
113. Jessica Mitford to William L. Patterson, August 9, 1977 & September 13, 1977.
114. Deborah Mitford to Diana Mosley, May 6, 1977. Decca was well aware that she'd "simply air-brushed Nicky" out of her book. "I simply couldn't bear to go into all that in a book," she told Kay Graham many years later. "I know it must seem v. odd," she wrote Dinky and Benjy a few years before her death, "that in writing *A Fine Old Conflict* I sort of air-brushed Nicky out of it entirely, not one mention of him—although he was such a star & hugely important factor in our life . . . to relive his death (which one has to, if writing about a person) was a bit more than I cld. bear." Jessica Mitford to Katharine Graham, April 9, 1990; Jessica Mitford to Constancia and Benjamin, March 1993.
115. Jessica Mitford to Michael and Clare Barnes, October 14, 1977.
116. Jessica Mitford to Deborah Mitford, October 26, 1976.
117. Diana Mosley to Deborah Mitford, March 31, 1975.
118. Diana Mosley to Deborah Mitford, March 31, 1975.
119. Mosley, *A Life of Contrasts*, 123–24; 128, 135. Mary S. Lovell writes that Diana "did not condone the horrors perpetrated by his [Hitler's] regime." One could say, however, that by blaming the Jews for their own deaths, creating endless moral equivalencies between Nazis and other ideologies, and minimizing/discounting the Holocaust (Nazi concentration camps are treated as if they are prisoner-of-war camps in the book), Diana Mosley very much condoned the horrors of Nazism. See Lovell, *The Sisters*, 501. Those who are critical of Diana, Lovell describes as "the uncharitable," 502. Lovell was given seemingly unrestricted access to the archives at Chatsworth. Some of her research materials for her book were then donated to Chatsworth, after her book was written, where they remained largely closed to other researchers.
120. Diana Mosley to Deborah Mitford, March 2, 1976.
121. Deborah Mitford to Jessica Mitford, February 13, 1978.

122. Mitford, *Poison Penmanship*, 4.

123. Jessica Mitford to Marge Frantz, August 29, 1974.

124. Jessica Mitford to Robert Gottlieb, January 9, 1980.

125. Jessica Mitford to Robert Treuhaft, December 4, 1976. Jessica Mitford to Sally Belfrage, March 18, 1976.

126. Jessica Mitford to Philip Toynbee, September 30, 1978.

127. Jessica Mitford to Maya Angelou and Paul du Feu, May 30, 1979.

128. Jessica Mitford to Aranka and Edith Treuhaft, January 28, 1975.

129. Jessica Mitford to Aranka and Edith Treuhaft, February 27, 1975.

130. Jessica Mitford to Constancia Romilly, July 24, 1979.

131. Lithium had been used to treat depression as early as the 1950s as an alternative to electroshock treatments, which were still very much in use with some manic-depressive patients. The side effects of lithium were severe and included a range of dangers from rashes to heart attacks to stomach problems and nerve damage. Sehar Raza, M.D. and Stacy Doumas, M.D., "Lithium: Past, Present, and Future," *Psychiatric Times*, May 24, 2023. Diagnoses of bipolar disorder were not commonly given until after 1980.

132. Jessica Mitford to Alex or "Comrade E," May 18, 1978. For the first essay on the Sign of the Dove, Decca was paid $200 a page, "Most I've ever got," she boasted. Jessica Mitford to Clare and Michael Barnes, April 12, 1977. This would be the equivalent of about $1,000 a page today.

133. Jessica Mitford to Robert Treuhaft, January 20, 1976.

134. Jessica Mitford to Philip Toynbee, September 30, 1978.

Chapter Eighteen: "Writing About the Dead"

1. Jessica Mitford to Robert Gottlieb, April 2, 1982. Mitford is here quoting Philip Toynbee, about whom she'd decided to write a book. The full quote read: "There is at least one simple distinction between writing about the dead & writing about the living. Not only have the dead that completeness which makes them more amenable subjects for a book, but also they are incapable of reacting to what is written about them." Mitford decided that "this will be the epigraph to my book," although she did not use the quote as her epigraph when her book about Toynbee, *Faces of Philip*, was published in 1984.

2. Jessica Mitford to Virginia Durr, November 30, 1983, VD.

3. Jessica Mitford, "My Short and Happy Life as a Distinguished Professor," *The Atlantic*, October 1974, reprinted in Mitford, *Poison Penmanship*.

4. Decca did, in fact, receive an offer to be a distinguished visiting professor at the University of Michigan many years later. In the fall of 1993 she spent three weeks teaching an intensive seminar in "Investigative Journalism" to approximately eight students who worked on a variety of projects including Scientology, students raped by football players, affirmative action, AIDS discrimination, and private security firms. She was paid $15,000. OSU, Box 132, folders 1113–19.

5. Sussman, *Decca*, 544.

6. Brixton was (and is) a largely Black, working-class area in South London where police had been harassing residents with "stop-and-search" tactics very like those Bob had fought against in Oakland. Decca and Bob happened to be in London when the riots took place in April 1981 (although Decca spent most of her time there in bed with the flu and a very high fever).

7. Jessica Mitford to Kay Boyle, January 4, 1982.

8. Jessica Mitford to Virginia Durr, April 3, 1986. (Angelou accepted the position of Reynolds Professor of American Studies at Wake Forest University in 1981.)

9. Jessica Mitford, final draft, "Law & Disorder: A Transatlantic View," Cobden House Lecture, OSU, Box 135, folder 1134.

10. Sussman, *Decca*, n.15, 552.

11. In 1980 Decca had written about having a review (of a book by Lillian Hellman) rejected because it used—quoting the author—the word "fucking." "I suppose," Decca wrote, "that every freelance writer has experienced the soaring hopes occasioned by the commissioning of an article, followed by the thudding letdown of a rejection after the finished piece is submitted." Since these words were written at the start of a published essay about not publishing a review, Mitford was more tongue in cheek than serious here (even if she did not end up publishing where she'd first intended). Those soaring hopes and thudding letdowns were just not, at the time, a part of her typical professional life. Jessica Mitford, "The Review No One Would Publish," *Berkeley Monthly*, December 1980, 51.

12. James Dean Walker, *Through Death's Doorway* (West Frankfurt, Illinois: Trumpet Press, 1971).

13. The *Holt v. Sarver* judgments of 1969 and 1970 (which became the basis for the popular 1980 film *Brubaker*, starring Robert Redford as reform-minded administrator Tim Murton) found the "entire Arkansas prison system to be so inhumane as to be in violation of the Eighth and Fourteenth amendments' prohibition against cruel and unusual punishment." "Holt v. Sarver," Encyclopedia of Arkansas, https://encyclopediaofarkansas.net/entries/holt-v-sarver-4165/. See also Kyle Williams, "Questions Remain in Nearly 60 Year Old Murder," KAUF radio, NPR Affiliate radio, April 19, 2021; "The Unusual Saga of James Dean Walker, KAUF radio, NPR Affiliate radio, May 17, 2021; Dave Haberman, "Finding Justice: Judge Myron Bright and James Walker," *North Dakota Law* 2, no. 1, August 2008. A third trial in 1985 eventually freed Walker on a plea deal. He died on January 24, 2023.

14. Jessica Mitford to Miriam Miller, July 16, 1980.

15. Jessica Mitford to Miriam Miller, July 16, 1980.

16. Jessica Mitford to Shirley MacLaine, July 12, 1980.

17. James Dean Walker to Jessica Mitford, June 11, 1980.

18. Jessica Mitford to James Dean Walker, June 20, 1980.

19. Jessica Mitford to Hillary Rodham Clinton, May 10 and June 20, 1980. Hillary Rodham Clinton to Jessica Mitford and Robert Treuhaft, April 30, 1980; Hillary Rodham Clinton to Jessica Mitford, July 12, 1980.

20. Hillary Rodham Clinton to Jessica Mitford, July 12, 1980.

21. Doug Smith, "James Dean Walker: The California Connection," *Arkansas Gazette*, Sunday, March 22, 1981, Section 11E.

22. This letter is quoted by Peter Sussman, who does not supply the name of its addressee. I have not been able to locate the original. See Sussman, *Decca*, n. 192, 537.

23. Jessica Mitford to Robert Gottlieb.

24. Jessica Mitford to Marge Frantz, January 23, 1981.

25. Jessica Mitford to Sally Belfrage, July 14, 1980.

26. Reverby, *Co-Conspirator for Justice*, 113–14. Boudin had been underground for eleven years when the Brink's robbery and arrest occurred, having vanished after a bomb explosion in a New York townhouse killed three members of the Weathermen in March 1970.

27. Jessica Mitford to Maya Angelou, October 23, 1981.

28. Mitford, *Faces of Philip*, 5; also published in England by William Heinemann. Toynbee's literary reviews ran for thirty years in *The Observer*, and he was famous for being able to absorb a book and write an insightful and engaging review—an "outstanding" one, Decca often said—in a day.

29. Mitford told this story in numerous letters and publications, including the beginning of *Faces of Philip*.
30. Jessica Mitford to Anne Farrer Horne [known as Idden], June 17, 1981.
31. Jessica Mitford to Bob Gottlieb, May 26, 1981.
32. Diana had surgery, recuperated at Chatsworth, and ultimately made a full recovery, something that no one, Diana included, had expected. Decca stayed as up to date as she could on all aspects of Diana's health, in spite of her refusal to speak with her or see her again after Nancy's death. For her part, Diana did the same. While always claiming not to care what Decca said or thought, she pressed Debo to send her all of Decca's letters to Debo or to Pamela, read them all, and commented on each one.
33. Jessica Mitford to Deborah Mitford, March 11, 1986.
34. Jessica Mitford to Rudbin [her cousin, Joan Ferrer], January 7, 1981.
35. Jessica Mitford to Kay Graham, April 5, 1981.
36. Jessica Mitford to Victor Navasky, October 26, 1983.
37. Diana Mitford to Deborah Mitford, February 4, 1980; Jessica Mitford to Deborah Mitford, March 11, 1980. As it turned out, Diana not only had the last word in the film but was given that last word by Decca. Decca read out a letter Diana had written her after Nancy's funeral, commenting on camera about how "very nice" it was of Diana to send it. In spite of that generosity, Diana and Deborah could not be appeased. Diana wrote to Deborah: "I am well aware that her life is in many ways rather awful . . . I put her out of my mind." Then Diana went on to admonish Deborah to cut Decca off. "If someone behaved to you or Woman as she has to me all these years, I should not wish to have friendship with that person," Diana wrote.
38. Much of the play was based on *Hons and Rebels* (Decca had her agent add up exactly how many words came from each of the sisters' writing: Decca, 8,000; Nancy, 2,837; Diana, 1,093; Deborah, 226; Pamela, 276), and Decca had her British agent, Deborah Rogers, fight for a significant share of the royalties, more, Decca insisted, than her sisters were getting. Deborah Rogers to Jessica Mitford, January 29, 1981.
39. Jessica Mitford, "Swingtime for Hitler in Chichester," *Sunday Times*, July 26, 1981.
40. Jessica Mitford, "Chatting About Chatsworth," *San Francisco Chronicle*, December 5, 1982; Jessica Mitford, draft review, "My Sister's House Has Many Mansions," typescript, OSU, Box 92, folder 746.
41. Jessica Mitford, "All in the Family: One Fascist, One Socialist, One Novelist, and One Duchess," *TV Guide*, March 27–April 2, 1982, 10–12; Jessica Mitford, "The Way We Really Were," draft for *TV Guide*, no date, typescript, OSU, Box 91, folder 716. The British version of the series aired in England in 1980 and in France in 1981.
42. When *Harper's* initially rejected "Return to the South," Decca shopped it to *The New Yorker*, which passed without much explanation, and then to *The Atlantic* (which said it was too long). *Harper's* then changed their minds and said they were interested, but before it could be published the acquiring editor left the magazine and the essay was orphaned and ultimately abandoned.
43. Jessica Mitford, "How Will We Ever Teach Them to Trust Adults Again?," *McCall's*, June 1981.
44. Jessica Mitford to Paul Halvonik, November 8, 1980.
45. Jessica Mitford to Bill and Hillary Clinton, December 20, 1982.
46. Jessica Mitford to William Clinton, n.d. [early 1983].
47. Jessica Mitford to Leeta Harris [Walker's girlfriend], et al, February 21, 1982.
48. Jessica Mitford to Staff, Center for Investigative Reporting," January 23, 1982.
49. Jessica Mitford, "Appointment in Arkansas," *New West*, November 3, 1980.

50. Jessica Mitford, unnamed, unpublished manuscript, n.d. [1985–86], 33, OSU, Box 11, 1019.

51. "Screenwriter Working on Walker Movie," *Tahoe Tribune*, July 15, 1985, n.p. (from Jessica Mitford's clipping files), OSU, Box 118, folder 1015.

52. Renee Wayne Golden to Jessica Mitford, James Dean Walker, Leeta Harris, Deborah Halvonik, and Oscar Fendler, *Esquire*, March 22, 1983.

53. Jessica Mitford to Barney Dreyfus, June 3, 1981.

54. Decca's obsession with this case was not hers alone. Others also described being unable to set it aside. Mike Farrell came to feel that it was something of a Rorschach test for those who became involved, and he surmised that it seemed to give almost everyone something they needed. He wrote, "Those who love you and think you're sexy, and those who think you got a raw deal, and those who don't know but think that justice was served, and those who think you're a no-good smart-ass who ought to fry, and those who think you are a brother in Christ, and those who think you are good cause to get involved in, and those who think you are a potential meal ticket and those who get their rocks off knowing a con, and those who see in you some aspect of themselves . . . remember that there is one guy who, once in a while, has the slightest hint of an awareness (he thinks) of the vast loneliness you swim in, and thinks, no matter what the facts all are, that you are very impressive man." Mike Farrell to James Dean Walker, n.d., OSU, Box 115, folder 1002.

55. Jessica Mitford, "An Update on the 'Prison Business:' A 'Change for the Worse,'" *The Nation*, October 30, 1982, 424–46. This article, like so many of her published pieces, began as a lecture, in this case for the California Bar Association Convention.

56. Mitford, *Faces*, 21.

57. Sussman, *Decca*, 545.

58. Mitford, *Faces*, 10.

59. Toynbee, as quoted by Mitford, *Faces*, 29.

60. Robert Gottlieb, personal interview, 2017.

61. Robert Gottlieb to Jessica Mitford, April 5, 1982.

62. Mitford, *Faces*, 11.

63. Fermor as quoted by Mitford, *Faces*, 22.

64. At about the same time Toynbee established a commune in England, Decca's best friend Marge Frantz established one, along with numerous other Berkeley radicals, north of Berkeley; Mitford, *Faces*, 5. Decca also called them "parasitic scroungers" 144.

65. Barnes interviewed Toynbee for his documentary. And in that interview, Barnes proceeded from the same misassumption, which Toynbee was very quick to correct: "I think this business of mixing up fascists and communists is one of the great illusions of all time . . . I think this [false idea] has grown up partly because of the Mitford sisters themselves . . . tender hearted people do not become fascists . . . sensible people do not become fascists." Interview transcript, OSU, 35, 213.

66. Mitford, *Faces*, 100, 49, 57, 63, 140, 87, 110, 112, 97, 101, 62.

67. Jessica Mitford to Robert Gottlieb, January 8, 1984.

68. Jessica Mitford to Robert Gottlieb, April 10, 1984.

69. Jessica Mitford, "The Salvadoran Way of Death," *San Francisco Chronicle*, March 11, 1984, 7–8; 17; "El Salvador on the Precipice," *The Observer*, March 25, 1984. The second article was a slightly shorter version of the first, similar to it in many ways.

70. Tape 3, "Mitford Field Tape: Lincoln Brigade," OSU, 89-14.

71. Jessica Mitford to Robert Gottlieb, August 1984.

72. Straight, *After Long Silence*.

73. Pele de Lappe, video interview, unnamed interviewer, OSU 89-11.

74. Jessica Mitford to Deborah Mitford, January 7, 1982.

75. Guinness *House of Mitford*; Sussman, *Decca*, 546.

76. Jessica Mitford to Ann Farrer Horne, August 25, 1984.

77. Sussman, *Decca*, 546.

78. Durr, *Outside the Magic Circle*. Ingram published *Rebel: The Short Life of Esmond Romilly* with Weidenfeld in England in 1985 and, that same year, with E. P. Dutton (Selina Hastings's publisher) in the United States. Ingram stayed close to Decca for the rest of her life and was shocked to find himself, without intending to be, at her deathbed in 1996. Personal interview with Kevin Ingram, Madrid, May 4, 2018.

79. Linda Simon, review of *Faces of Philip*, *Library Journal*, July 1984, 1320; D. A. N. Jones, "The Revolutionary Habit," *Times Literary Supplement*, July 27, 1984, 850–51; NJN, "Private Lives on a Platter," *Times of India*, July 29, 1984, 8; Peter Vansittart, "Books: English Eccentric: *Faces of Philip: A Memoir of Philip Toynbee* by Jessica Mitford," *Financial Times*, July 7, 1984, 14; anonymous reviewer, *San Francisco Review of Books*, 9.2 (November–December, 1984); Mary Dryden, "A Mitford on the Tribulations of a Toynbee," *Los Angeles Times*, November 18, 1984, U14; Clancy Sigal, "Trapped Between Greatness and Niceness," *New York Times*, January 13, 1985.

80. Mitford, *Grace Had an English Heart*. The book was published under the imprint of "William Abrahams." Abrahams, always known to Decca as Billy, was at the time a dear friend who lived nearby and whom Decca and Bob saw often, with his partner, Peter.

81. Jessica Mitford to Sally Belfrage, August 8, 1985.

82. Jessica Mitford to Robert Gottlieb, January 9, 1980.

83. Jessica Mitford to Sally Belfrage, August 8, 1985.

84. Jessica Mitford to Sally Belfrage, August 8, 1985.

85. Jessica Mitford to Emma Tennant, July 15, 1985.

86. Jessica Mitford to Emma Tennant, October 8, 1985.

87. Mitford, *Faces of Philip*, viii; Jessica Mitford to Kevin Ingram, October 13, 1981.

88. Jessica Mitford to Anne Farrer Horne, quoted in Sussman, *Decca*, xiv; Mitford, *Grace Had an English Heart*.

89. Mitford, *Grace Had an English Heart*, 48, 47, 49.

90. Jessica Mitford to Emma Tennant, March 6, 1986.

91. Mitford, *Grace Had an English Heart*, 55, 58, 118–19.

92. Jessica Mitford to Emma Tennant, October 8, 1985.

93. Diana Mosley to Deborah Devonshire, July 18, 1985.

94. Mitford, *Grace Had an Engish Heart*, 11.

95. Rebecca Fraser, "Heroine of the High Seas," *Sunday Times* (London), September 4, 1988; Lucinda De La Rue, "The Model of a Maiden," *Financial Times*, December 3, 1988, 18. Reviews in *Sunday Times*, *Daily Mail*, and *Sunday Telegraph* all taken from U.S. jacket copy.

96. Susan Thatch Dean, review of *Grace Had an English Heart*, *Library Journal*, March 1, 1989, 78; Marcus Cunliffe, "The Angel of the Lighthouse," *Washington Post*, March 12, 1989 [Cunliffe taught at George Washington University but, as he explained in his review, was born and raised in Northumberland, where he knew the Grace Darling legend well]; Elaine Kendall, "Amazing Grace," *Los Angeles Times*, April 2, 1989, 3; Michele Slung, "Rowing Her Boat ("Help!") into History," *New York Times*, Book Review, April 16, 1989, 22.

97. Jessica Mitford to Ann Simonton, May 21, 1986.

98. Jessica Mitford to Annie Fursland, August 23, 1989.

99. Jessica Mitford to Barbara Kahn, August 20, 1988.

Chapter Nineteen: "Toddling Towards the End"

1. Jessica Mitford to Bob Treuhaft, March 1986, Sussman, *Decca*, 544.
2. Jessica Mitford, "My Funeral," undated, unpublished typescript manuscript draft, HRC, Box 9, folder 3. Decca added here that being against death was "to no avail."
3. Jessica Mitford to Peter Stansky, January 31, 1988.
4. Quote from *Britain Daily Express*, repeated by Decca, quoted by Sussman, *Decca*, 626.
5. Interview with Lisa Pollard, July 13, 2024.
6. Ken Kelley, "Lion in Winter," interview with Jessica Mitford, *Diablo*, February 1994.
7. Jessica Mitford, untitled manuscript, unpublished, February 4, 1996, OSU, Box 170, folder 1323.
8. Sandy Silver, Women's International League for Peace and Freedom, September 3, OSU, Box 169, folder 1320; Frank Vogel, Biennial Conference of the Continental Association of Funeral and Memorial Societies, to Jessica Mitford, July 18, 1992; Neil Morgan, editor, *San Diego Tribune*, April 13, 1990, OSU, Box 169, folder 1317; Harold Lawrence to Jessica Mitford, March 16, 1992.
9. Jessica Mitford, memo to Bob Treuhaft, January 21, 1987, OSU, Box 168, folder 1315.
10. Jessica Mitford to Kay Boyle, February 5, 1985.
11. Associated Press, "Vista School Board Bans Angelou's . . . 'Caged Bird,'" *Oakland Tribune*, January 13, 1989.
12. Interview with Lauren Robertson; Jessica Mitford, "To Be Young, Black, Gifted—And a British M.P.," typescript manuscript, unpublished, 1988, OSU, Box 99, folder 861.
13. Doug Foster to Jessica Mitford, September 6, 1988, OSU, Box 99, folder 861.
14. Jessica Mitford to Miriam Miller, July 29, 1988.
15. Jessica Mitford to Barbara Kahn, August 5, 1988.
16. Jessica Mitford, "Relax-nost: A Volga Cruise in the Era of Glasnost," final manuscript draft, typescript; and Jessica Mitford to Maria Matthiessen, August 15, 1988, OSU, Box 98, folder 833.
17. Kelley, "Lion," *Diablo*.
18. Jessica Mitford, "At Peace with Old Age: Betty Friedan Confronts the Aging Process," *San Francisco Chronicle*, September 13, 1993, 1, 7. Mitford also faults Friedan for succumbing "to the inevitable temptation to chuck in" all her "massive" research, which was a failing that reviewers often mentioned in Decca's just published *The American Way of Birth*. Friedan published *The Fountain of Age* in 1993, just as Decca also published the paperback of *The American Way of Birth*, placing them together again on advertisements, announcements, and book review pages.
19. Jessica Mitford to Marge Frantz, January 19, 1991.
20. Jessica Mitford, graduation speech final draft, May 25, 1993, OSU, Box 169, folder 1320. Decca repeated that advice, as an essential quality, in her introduction to *Poison Penmanship*. "Plodding determination and an appetite for tracking and destroying the enemy" were the qualities needed, she wrote. Mitford, *Poison Penmanship*, 4.
21. Jessica Mitford to Tilla Durr, October 19, 1993.
22. James Les-Milne, Obituary for Sydney Redesdale, *The Times*, 1963, as quoted by Jessica Mitford, unpublished autobiographical essay, OSU, Box 91, folder 716, manuscript, 3. This is an early draft, I believe, of the beginning of Mitford's *Hons and Rebels*, intended for repurposing into a reference book.
23. See, for example, "Teach Midwifery, Go to Jail," *This World*, October 21, 1990, 7–9, 12; "Advice for the Next Creation," *New York Times*, November 8, 1992.
24. See, for example, Jessica Mitford, "Prime Time for Communists?," *New York Times*, April 16,

1989, regarding Decca's old friend Elinor Langer's review of Decca's old friend Carl Bernstein's *Loyalties*.

25. Jessica Mitford, "Foreword," Cedric Belfrage, *The American Inquisition*.

26. Jessica Mitford to the Maases, June 21, 1991, OSU, Box 208, folder 1656.

27. Jessica Mitford to Shana Alexander, December 12, 1993. When she taught journalism, Decca often referred back to her Houghton Mifflin editors' demand that she pull the embalming sections from *The American Way of Death*. Her teaching notes included the injunction to "trust yrself not editor if there's a substantial disagreement." University of Michigan lecture notes, circa 1993, OSU Box 132, folder 1114.

28. Mitford, "Teach Midwifery, Go to Jail."

29. Laurel Druley, "The Childbirth Monopoly: Why the Medical Industry is Dragging Its Feet when it Comes to Midwives," *Mother Jones*, June 2, 1998.

30. In 1995, 97 percent of Americans polled said that their babies were born in the hospital; 2 percent reported Birth Centers. Only 1 percent of those polled checked "somewhere else," indicating a home birth. Roper Center for Public Opinion Research, Commonwealth Fund Poll, July 1995.

31. In 1998, when Golden pressed Decca to write the book, there were approximately two hundred American midwives who were arrested or otherwise prevented from practicing, according to one exposé. See Druley, "The Childbirth Monopoly"; Janice Kalman, et al, "A Feminist Perspective on the Study of Home: Application of a Midwifery Care Framework," *Journal of Nurse-Midwifery* 39, no. 3 (May/June 1994).

32. Jessica Mitford to Constancia Romilly, September 18, 1994.

33. Jessica Mitford to Sally Belfrage, February 22, 1989.

34. Interview with Renee Wayne Golden, Los Angeles, March 8, 2018. Personal communication by email with Katie Edwards, April 16, 2018.

35. Jessica Mitford to Mary Clemmey [British agent and friend], March 20, 1990.

36. Interview with Renee Wayne Golden, Los Angeles, March 8, 2018.

37. Jessica Mitford to Billy Abrahams, May 7, 1989. Abrahams was not among the many editors fired in what one senior female editor described as a "bloodbath" at Dutton when the publishing house, shortly after Decca signed her contract, was absorbed by Penguin. Edwin McDowell, "Dutton's Adult Unit to Be Absorbed," *New York Times*, November 1, 1989, D19. See also Michael Arndt, "E. P. Dutton Merges with Parent," *Chicago Tribune*, November 1, 1989.

38. Edward Shorter, "Deliverance," *New York Times Book Review*, 3; Jessica Mitford, quoted in Veronique Mistiaen, "Rebel with a Cause: That Muckraker Jessica Mitford Skewers America's Way of Birthing," *Chicago Tribune*, December 20, 1992, F3; Mitford, *The American Way of Birth*, 75, 254.

39. Jessica Mitford to Billy Abrahams, May 7, 1989; Mitford, *The American Way of Birth*.

40. Interview, Janice Kalman, July 7, 2024.

41. Ehrenreich and English, *Witches, Midwives and Nurses*; Ehrenreich and English, *For Her Own Good*; Ulrich, *A Midwife's Tale*; The Boston Women's Health Collective, *Our Bodies, Ourselves*, 2nd ed. (New York: Simon & Schuster, 1976), 249, 248, 250. Now considered a "feminist classic," *Our Bodies, Ourselves*, a product of the Bread and Roses collective, was first published in 1970, has now sold over four million copies, and has been translated into thirty-three languages.

42. Jeffrey Davis, and Jeffrey Hogan, "A Mitford Way of Reporting," *Mother Jones*, November/ December 1992. (Gaskin's widely influential book, *Spiritual Midwifery*, had been published

nearly twenty years prior to *The American Way of Birth*.) Decca visited Gaskin's farm and birthing center with Ted Kalman and was delighted to find it "mercifully devoid of the sort of mushy malarky" she had feared. Her relief did not, however, translate into unqualified endorsement of Gaskin and it did not keep Decca from mocking her.

43. Jessica Mitford to John Kenneth and Catherine Galbraith, August 5, 1989.
44. Jessica Mitford, as quoted by Davis and Hogan, "A Mitford Way of Reporting," *Mother Jones*, 13.
45. Jessica Mitford to Emma (the Good) Tennant, April 21, 1992.
46. "Editor's Note," Jessica Mitford, "Burial Writes," *The Mail*, Sunday, November 13, 1995.
47. Jessica Mitford, as quoted by Davis and Hogan, "A Mitford Way of Reporting," 13.
48. Jessica Mitford to Kay Boyle, March 3, 1990. This letter was written during the brief period when Decca and Boyle attempted a reconciliation. It did not last. When Boyle died a few years later, Decca did not attend any of the memorials or celebrations, saying it would be hypocritical to do so, given their falling out.
49. A few reviews did praise the book's depth of research, measured tone, and its wit. See especially *Kirkus Reviews*, August 15, 1992. Many were more negative. Describing *The American Way of Birth* as "a bit dated," for example, a Canadian review says that "in some chapters she seems to be just letting us read over her shoulder as she shifts through her research." Marni Jackson, "Muckraker in the Delivery Room," *Toronto Star*, December 19, 1992, E14.
50. Judith Walzer Leavitt, "Alienated Birth," *New Republic*.
51. Morton Mintz, "Births of a Nation," *Washington Post*, November 1, 1992, 6.
52. Shorter, "Deliverance," 3.
53. Jean Latz Griffin, "Mitford Stops Short in Her Book on Childbirth," *Chicago Tribune*, November 13, 1992, C3.
54. Laura Shapiro, "From Here to Maternity," *Newsweek*, November 15, 1992, 79.
55. Don Walker, "Mitford Misses the Mark," *Milwaukee Journal*, November 22, 1992, E11.
56. "Brief Reviews," *The Atlantic*, December 1992, 151
57. Mitford, *American Way of Birth*, afterword, Plume edition (November 1993), 278.
58. Jessica Mitford to Virginia Durr, July 4, 1991.
59. Jessica Mitford to Sally Belfrage, April 23, 1992.
60. "The American Way of Birth," *Birthright*, BBC 2, Steve Ruggi, director, 1993, aired February 27, 1993, in England.
61. Jessica Mitford to Deborah Mitford, September 18, 1994.
62. Jessica Mitford to Charlotte Mosley, January 21, 1993 and February 8, 1994. Mosley did eventually bring out an important collection of the letters of all six sisters to one another, which she published, with Decca's family's cooperation and participation, in 2007.
63. Jessica Mitford to Deborah Mitford, May 14, 1993.
64. Jessica Mitford to Deborah Mitford, May 14, 1993.
65. Jessica Mitford to Virginia Tilla Durr, December 6, 1995.
66. Quoted by Sussman, *Decca*, 631n6.
67. Jessica Mitford to Joan Mellen, January 24, 1989.
68. Jessica Mitford to Maya Angelou, December 12, 1991.
69. Jessica Mitford to Sally Belfrage, April 29, 1991.
70. Maya Angelou, "I Dare to Hope," *New York Times*, August 25, 1991, 15.
71. Richard L. Berke, "Black Caucus Votes to Oppose Thomas for High Court," *New York Times*, July 12, 1991, A1. See also Herb Boyd, "Clarence Thomas and his Right-Wing Bedfellows," *New York Amsterdam News*, August 31, 1991, 4.

72. See, for example, the special issue of *The Black Scholar* 22, nos, 1 and 2 (Spring 1992), in which thirty-five Black writers and scholars explained why Thomas was unacceptable. Nearly alone, Angelou continued to speak in defense of Thomas.
73. Jessica Mitford to Dolly McPherson, September 4, 1991.
74. Jessica Mitford to Maya Angelou, July 8, 1992.
75. Jessica Mitford to Maya Angelou, September 9, 1991; Jessica Mitford to Maya Angelou, December 12, 1991.
76. After Hill's testimony, the opposition to Thomas was so fierce that it seemed to Decca that he couldn't possibly be confirmed, given how large his opposition was, how extreme his and his wife's views were, and how widespread the feminist outcry to his treatment of women became. The feminist arguments against Thomas were less important to Decca than his dismal civil rights record. She, in fact, made light of the issue of sexual harassment and assault (in spite of having herself been terrifyingly assaulted). She saw the issues of censoring sexist and censoring racist remarks as "totally different," and to her, the former was never very serious. "The whole thing about Judge Thomas is that he was a hopeless choice (totally political, as all have pointed out) and shld have been rejected as an incompetent & a liar by those disgraceful senators." Jessica Mitford to James Forman, Jr., July 20, 1992.
77. Jessica Mitford to Ted Kalman, December 21, 1988.
78. Jessica Mitford to Shana Alexander, December 4, 1992.
79. The charges were made by Norton Tenille and received remarkably little press coverage. See John Meroney, "Maya Angelou's Inaugural Poem: Plagiarized or Inspired?," *Chronicles*, December 1993; Norton F. Tennille, "A Rock, A River, A Tree / A Poetic Controversy," *Harper's*, March 1994; Jessica Mitford to Sally Belfrage, November 25, 1993; Martin Walker, "Angelou's Poetic Source Queried," *The Guardian*, November 25, 1993, 26; reprinted in *Sydney Morning Herald*, November 26, 1993, 18. Meroney's article was far and away the most critical of Angelou. Tennille spent quite some time trying to get Angelou's publishers to give him some credit for inspiring the poem, then retreated.
80. Interview with Marge Frantz; interview with Constancia Romilly.
81. Jessica Mitford to Polly Toynbee, January 11, 1991. Mitford reported Debo's statements.
82. Jessica Mitford to Shana Alexander, November 15, 1990. In this letter, written a week after the event, Decca unaccountably describes her outfit as a "top loaned by Maya," rather than a dress.
83. Jessica Mitford to Constancia Romilly, May 16, 1993. Program for Decca and Bob's 50th Wedding Anniversary Party, courtesy of Jerry and Leah Garchik.
84. NVL Arts and Ovation, *Tuning with the Enemy*, produced and directed by Tricia O'Leary and Helen Gallacher, 1998. Benjy had been charged, officially, with "tuning with the enemy" by the United States State Department.
85. Jessica Mitford to Christopher Cerf, May 3, 1995.
86. Jessica Mitford to Dolly McPherson and Maya Angelou, June 29, 1992.
87. Jessica Mitford to Sally Belfrage, November 25, 1993.
88. Jessica Mitford to Constancia Romilly and Ben Treuhaft, April 12, 1994.
89. The only available biography of Pamela, written by a former member of her staff, is also unsympathetic to Decca. While containing useful factual information about the particulars of Pamela's life, Diana Alexander's book, *The Other Mitford: Pamela's Story*, which contains a foreword by Jonathan Guinness, will not countenance the possibility of Pamela's lesbianism—dismissing it as a another of Decca's "notoriously inaccurate" speculations, although the other sisters all confirmed Decca's description of her relationship to Giuditta Tommasi as a "marriage." Alexander

writes that those who dismiss the idea of Pamela's lesbianism are "kinder" to Pamela's memory. She offers, as proof of Pamela's abiding heterosexuality, that "men certainly continued to find her attractive," 117. Alexander concludes that "the frustration of the others towards Jessica . . . is not hard to understand," 126. In Alexander's opinion, Decca was too quick to take offense and lacked the "incredible niceness and charm," of Diana, 133. She found Decca rude, and the other sisters more mannered, despite noting Diana's "failure to condemn some of the nastier elements of the Nazi regime, particularly anti-Semitism," 124. *The Other Mitford: Pamela's Story*, 117, 126, 124.

90. Jessica Mitford to Deborah Mitford, April 16, 1994.

91. Pamela's ex-husband Derek, who had abandoned her many years ago, left Pamela a small fortune on his death in 1982. It allowed Pamela to live the quiet country life she preferred, at Woodfield House in Caudle Green in the Cotswolds, with staff and many comforts.

92. Jessica Mitford, "My Funeral," manuscript draft, typescript, unpublished.

93. Jessica Mitford to Deborah Mitford, December 23, 1994.

94. Jessica Mitford to Deborah Mitford, December 23, 1994; Jessica Mitford to Deborah Mitford, January 12, 1995. Andrew had been a serious alcoholic but had quit drinking years ago.

95. Constancia remembered that Decca had one treatment, found it excruciating, and did not go back. Interview with Constancia Romilly, May 16, 2024.

96. Jessica Mitford to Deborah Mitford, July 6, 1996; Pollard interview, 2024.

97. Jessica Mitford to Deborah Mitford, July 13, 1996.

98. Jessica Mitford to Deborah Mitford, July 6, 1996. SCI was Service Corporation International, the enormous corporation that had been buying up family funeral homes for years.

99. Jessica Mitford to Bob Treuhaft, July 10, 1996. Bob lived almost another fifteen years, dying on November 11, 2001, at the age of eighty-nine. While women did come calling, as Decca predicted, Bob lived alone from Decca's death until his own.

100. Jessica Mitford to Deborah Mitford, July 11, 1996.

101. Karen Leonard, quoted in "Funeral Directors Want Piece of Mitford," *The Record* (Stockton, CA), July 25, 1996, A2.

102. Obituary, *New York Times*, July 24, 1996; Molly Ivins, "Queen of the Muckrakers," *New York Times*, August 25, 1996.

103. Karen Leonard to Robert Waltrip, July 24, 1996.

104. Some reports put the number of attendees as high as eight hundred.

105. Various newspapers later reported that Angelou's abrupt and angry departure was in response to the open mic portion of the program, where a representative of the funeral industry was allowed to speak. But Katie Edwards, Decca's assistant, remembers that Angelou was responding angrily to what she saw as second-tier friends, Virginia Durr's daughter Tilla especially, getting too much time to speak. Interview with Katie Edwards.

106. Jon [Snow], Mary [Clemmey], Mike [Barnes], Liesel [Evans], & Ursula to Bob, by fax, February 11, 1997.

107. "Diary," *The Times*, February 8, 1977, clipping; Jon [Snow], Mary [Clemmey], Mike [Barnes], Liesel [Evans], & Ursula to Bob, by fax, February 11, 1997.

108. Deborah to Dinky Romilly, February 11, 1997, by fax; Bob to Alexander Cockburn, March 4, 1997. "I could not face it," Deborah Mitford later wrote, "So I stayed at home with my own thoughts about my remarkable dear old Hen." Devonshire, *Wait for Me!*, 302.

109. Constancia Romilly to Bob and Benjy Treuhaft, February 11, 1997.

SELECTED BIBLIOGRAPHY

"90 Americans in RAF Become U.S. Aviators." *New York Times* (April 1943): 10.

"100 Jews Each Day Must Leave Reich: Order Is Effective in Berlin Tomorrow—Violates the Recent Refugee Compact, Hopeful View Was General 100." *New York Times* (February 1939): 1, 23.

"14,045,000 Hear Churchill Address." *Boston Globe*, 1943: 1.

"A Hurry—Esmond Romilly (Aged 15) Views the World." *Sunday Referee* (April 1934).

Aaron, Benjamin. "Catalyst: The National War Labor Board of World War II." *Case Western Reserve Law Review* 39, no. 2 (1988): 519–43.

Acton, Harold. *Nancy Mitford: A Memoir*. 1st U.S. ed. New York: Harper & Row, 1975.

Adler, Margot, "Before Rosa Parks, There Was Claudette Colvin." *NPR* (2009).

Alexander, Diana. *The Other Mitford: Pamela's Story*. Stroud, Gloucestershire: The History Press, 2012.

Alexander, Michelle. *The New Jim Crow: Mass Incarceration in the Age of Colorblindness*. New York: New Press, 2012.

"An Eye for an Eye." *New York Times Book Review* (October 1971).

Angelou, Maya. "I Dare to Hope." *New York Times* (1991): 15.

———. *I Know Why the Caged Bird Sings*. New York: Random House, 1971.

———. "In Self-Defense." *Letter to My Daughter*. New York: Random House, 2008.

———. Interview with George Plimpton. Quoted in Linda Wagner Martin, *Maya Angelou: Adventurous Spirit*, New York: Bloomsbury, revised edition, 2015: 20.

Anonymous. "Books: One Disappointing Trial." *Time* (October 1969).

———. "Drawings by Felicia Browne." *Internet Archive*, 1936. https://archive.org/details /DrawingsFeliciaBrowne.

———. *San Francisco Review of Books* 9, no. 2 (November–December 1984).

Anspacher, Carolyn. "Lord Redesdale Will Cuts Bay Wife – 'Split by Hitler.'" *San Francisco Chronicle* (1958).

Aptheker, Bettina. *The Morning Breaks: The Trial of Angela Davis*. Ithaca: Cornell University Press, 1997.

Arndt, Michael. "E.P. Dutton Merges with Parent." *Chicago Tribune* (1989).

Arnesen, Eric. *Encyclopedia of U.S. Labor and Working-Class History*. New York: Routledge, 2007.

Arsenault, Raymond. *Freedom Riders: 1961 and the Struggle for Racial Justice*. Oxford University Press, 2006.

———. *John Lewis: In Search of the Beloved Community*. New Haven: Yale University Press, 2024.

Atlantic Monthly, Cover, 193, no. 5 (May 1954), part one.

Attica: The Official Report. New York State Special Commission on Attica. New York: Bantam, 1972.

Bank of England. "The UK Exchange Control: A Short History." *Quarterly Bulletin* (September 1967): 251–52.

Bankes, Ariane. *The Dazzling Paget Sisters: Identical Twins at the Heart of the Twentieth Century*. McNally, 2025. Kindle.

Bartels, Andrew H. "The Office of Price Administration and the Legacy of the New Deal, 1939–1946." *Public Historian* 5, no. 3 (1983): 5–29.

"The Basic Problem." *New York Times* (March 1943): 18.

Baxell, Richard. *British Volunteers in the Spanish Civil War: The British Battalion in the International Brigades, 1936–1939*. Routledge, 2004.

———. *Unlikely Warriors: The British in the Spanish Civil War and the Struggle Against Fascism*. London: Aurum, 2012.

Beckles, Jovanka. "The Gary Family: Fighting for Equality and Standing for Their Rights." Parts 1 & 2. *Radio Free Richmond*, n.d.

"Before and After 1940: Change in Population Density." *United States Census Bureau*, 2012.

Belfrage, Cedric. *The American Inquisition, 1945–1960*. New York: Bobbs-Merrill, 1973.

Belfrage, Sally. *Freedom Summer*. New York: Viking Press, 1965.

Belknap, Michael R. "Foley Square Trials." *American Political Trials*, Belknap, ed. Westport: Greenwood Press, 1994.

Berke, Richard L. "Black Caucus Votes to Oppose Thomas for High Court." *New York Times* (1991).

Bernal, Martin. *Geography of a Life*. Exlibris, 2012.

Bernstein, Carl. *Loyalties: A Son's Memoir*. New York: Simon and Schuster, 1989.

Bernstein, Malcolm. "The FSM: A Movement Lawyer's Perspective." *The Free Speech Movement*, ed. Robert Cohen and Reginald E. Zelnik. Oakland: University of California Press, 2002.

"Best Seller List." *New York Times* (January 1964): BR8.

Bezjian, Roxanne. "Charles Garry: Streetfighter in the Courtroom," 1992.

Bingham, Jane. *The Cotswolds: A Cultural History*. New York: Oxford, 2009.

Bishop, Patrick. "How the RAF Won the War." *BBC History Magazine*, 2018: 10.

Black Scholar 22, no. 1 & 2 (Spring 1992).

Blair, Diane M. "No Ordinary Time: Eleanor Roosevelt's Address to the 1940 Democratic National Convention." *Rhetoric and Public Affairs* 4, no. 2 (2001).

"Blueblood Adventurers Discover America." *Washington Post* (January 1940).

"Boarder Shot in Argument Over Radio." *Washington Post* (June 1941).

Bond, Julian. "Foreword." *The Making of Black Revolutionaries; a Personal Account*. By James Forman. Seattle: University of Washington Press, 1997: xi–xii.

The Boston Women's Health Collective. *Our Bodies, Ourselves*, Second Edition. New York: Simon and Schuster, 1976.

Bowles, Thomas Gibson. *Flotsam & Jetsam: A Yachtsman's Experiences at Sea and Ashore*. New York: Funk & Wagnalls, 1883.

———. *The Log of the 'Nereid.'* London: Simpkin, Marshall, 1889.

Boyd, Herb. "Clarence Thomas and his Right-Wing Bedfellows." *New York Amsterdam News* (1991): 4.

Boyle, Kevin. *The Shattering: America in the 1960s*. New York: W. W. Norton, 2021.

Branch, Taylor. *Parting the Waters: America in the King Years, 1954–1963*. New York: Simon & Schuster, 1988.

Braudy, Susan. *Family Circle: The Boudins and the Aristocracy of the Left*. New York: Anchor, 2003.

"Brief Reviews." *The Atlantic* (December 1992): 151.

Bright, Virginia. "Jessica Mitford Talks of New Book: Her Autobiography Didn't Please Kin." *Boston Globe* (1960): 27.

Brincker, J.A.H., "A Historical, Epidemiological and Aetiological Study of Measles," *Proceedings of the Royal Society of Medicine* XXI, n. 807, (1938): 33–54.

"Britain Releases Mosley Quietly: Protests Grow in Intensity." *New York Times* (November 1943): 33.

"Britain Takes Action to Explain Proposal to Release Mosley." *Washington Post* (November 1943): 2.

"Britain to Retain Exchange Control." *New York Times* (November 1946): 5.

"The British Commonwealth Air Training Plan." The Bomber Command Museum, n.d.

"British Reds See Fascist Threats." *New York Times* (November 1943): 10.

"British Workers Assail Decision to Free Mosley." *New York Herald Tribune* (November 1943): 7A.

Brody, Leslie. *Irrepressible: The Life and Times of Jessica Mitford*. Berkeley: Counterpoint, 2010.

Brown, Kathleen A. and Elizabeth Fave. "Social Bonds, Sexual Politics, and Political Community on the U.S. Left, 1920s–1940s." *Left History* 7, no. 1 (2000): 9–45.

Brunsma, David L. "Interracial Families and the Racial Identification of Mixed-Race Children: Evidence from the Early Childhood Longitudinal Study." *Social Forces* 84, no. 2 (December 2005): 1131.

Budworth, Julia. *Never Forget: George S. Bowles, A Biography*. privately published: Julia M. Budworth, 2001.

Buhle, Paul. *Marxism in the United States*. London: Verso, 1987.

Butcher, Fanny. "The Literary Spotlight." *Chicago Daily Tribune*, 1960: C6.

Canada, Veterans Affairs. 2020. "Second World War—Veterans Affairs Canada." www.veterans.gc.ca. January 23, 2020.

Cannadine, David. *The Decline and Fall of the British Aristocracy*. New Haven: Yale University Press, 1990.

———. *Aspects of Aristocracy*. New Haven: Yale University Press, 1984.

Carlson, Lillian. "A California Girlhood." *Red Diapers: Growing up in the Communist Left*, ed. Judy Kaplan and Linn Shapiro. Urbana: University of Illinois Press, 1998.

Carson, Clayborne. *In Struggle: SNCC and the Black Awakening of the 1960s*. Cambridge: Harvard University Press, 1981.

Catledge, Turner. "OPA Runs into Trouble on 'Hold the Line' Order." *New York Times* (1943).

Caute, David. *The Great Fear: The Anti-Communist Purge Under Truman and Eisenhower*. New York: Simon & Schuster, 1978.

Chamberlain, Geoffrey. "British Maternal Mortality in the 19th and early 20th Century." *Journal of the Royal Society of Medicine* 99 no. 11 (November 2006).

Chernin, Kim. *In My Mother's House: A Memoir*. New Haven: Ticknor & Fields, 1983.

"Chuck McDew," "SNCC Digital Gateway," https://snccdigital.org/people/chuck-mcdew/.

Churchill, Winston. *The Grand Alliance*. Houghton Mifflin, 1950.

———. *The Second World War*, Volume III, Houghton Miller, 1932.

"Cities to be 'Ashes': Churchill Says Britain Will Join in Scourging [Japan]." *New York Times* (May 1943): 1.

City of Mossbank. n.d. "British Commonwealth Air Training Program." Mossbank.

Clark, Sherna Berger. *Rosie the Riveter Revisited: Women, the War, and Social Change*. New York: Twayne Publishers, 1987.

Clarke, Bridget. "Requisitioned Houses in Wartime." *St John's Wood Memories*, 2013.

Clarke, Peter. *Hope and Glory: Britain 1900-2000*, 2nd ed., New York: Penguin, 2004.

Cleaveland, Brad "A Letter to Undergraduates." *SLATE Supplement* 1, no. IV (1964).

Clements, Julie A. "Participatory Democracy: The Bridge from Civil Rights to Women's Liberation." *Public Purpose* 1 (2003).

Coakley, J. Frank. *For the People: Sixty Years of Fighting for Law and Order*. Western Star Press, 1992.

Cockburn, Claud. "Island Fling: A Souvenir of the Mitford Country." *Punch* (1960).

Cockburn, Patrick. "Polio: The Deadly Summer of 1956." *The Independent* (2011).

Cohen, Deborah. *Family Secrets: Shame & Privacy in Modern Britain*. New York: Oxford, 2013.

Cohen, Lizabeth. *Making a New Deal: Industrial Workers in Chicago, 1919-1939*. Cambridge University Press, 1990.

Cohen, Robert, and Reginald E. Zelnik. *The Free Speech Movement Reflections on Berkeley in the 1960s*. University of California Press, 2002.

"Commonwealth Air Training Plan." *Elgin Military Museum*, http://www .theelginmilitarymuseum.ca/commonwealth-air-training-plan.html.

"Congress Pleased by Churchill Talk: Address Found Encouraging." *New York Times* (May 1943): 3.

Cook, Blanche Wiesen. *Eleanor Roosevelt: The War Years and After*, Volume 3. New York: Penguin, 2016.

Cornford, Daniel, ed. *Working People of California*. Berkeley: University of California Press, 1995.

Cortazzi, Hugh. *Mitford's Japan: Memories and Recollections, 1866–1906*, revised ed. London: Japan Library, 2002.

Cott, Nancy. *Public Vows: A History of Marriage and the Nation*. Cambridge: Harvard University Press, 2000.

Crabtree, Steve. "The Gallup Brain: Americans and the Korean War." *Gallup* (2003).

Cunliffe, Marcus. "The Angel of the Lighthouse." *Washington Post* (1989).

Dailey, Jane. *White Fright: The Sexual Panic at the Heart of America's Racist History*. New York: Basic Books, 2020.

Dalley, Jan. *Diana Mosley: A Life*. London: Faber and Faber, 1999.

Daniell, Raymond. "Capital is Shaken: Factories, Docks, Public Utilities and Workers' Quarters Bombed." *New York Times* (1940).

David, Darrah. "Hitler's Friend Causes Rumpus in London Press: Sensationalism Attacked and Defended." *Chicago Daily Tribune (1923–1963)* (January 1940): 2.

Day, Dorothy. "On Pilgrimage—March 1957." *The Catholic Worker* 3, no. 6 (March 1978).

Dean, Susan Thatch. "Review of *Grace Had an English Heart.*" *Library Journal*, (March 1989): 78.

De Courcy, Anne. *Diana Mosley: Mitford Beauty, British Fascist, Hitler's Angel.* New York: William Morrow, 2003.

de Lappe, Pele. *Pele: A Passionate Journey Through Art & The Red Press.* Self-Published: Pele de Lappe, 1999.

De La Rue, Lucinda. "The Model of a Maiden." *Financial Times* [London] (December 1988): 18.

Denning, Michael. *The Cultural Front: The Laboring of American Culture in the Twentieth Century.* New York: Verso, 1996.

Dershowitz, Alan. "The Trial of Dr. Spock." *New York Times* (1969).

Devonshire, Andrew. "The Aristocracy – Born to Rule: 1875–1914," Episode 1, BBC 2, Episode 1, 2002.

Devonshire, Deborah. *Chatsworth: The House.* London: Frances Lincoln, 2012.

———. *In Tearing Haste: Letters Between Deborah Devonshire and Patrick Leigh Fermor.* London: John Murray, 2008.

———. *Wait for Me!: Memoirs.* New York: Farrar, Straus and Giroux, 2010.

"Diary." *The Times* (London), (February 1997).

"Did You Know." *Tynedale Life*, 2011.

"Discussion of New Books." *Virginia Quarterly*, 54, no. 2 (Spring 1978): 47.

Druley, Laurel. "The Childbirth Monopoly: Why the Medical Industry is Dragging Its Feet When It Comes to Midwives." *Mother Jones* (June 1998).

Dryden, Mary. "A Mitford on the Tribulations of a Toynbee." *Los Angeles Times* (November 1984): U14.

Durback, Nadja. *Bodily Matters: The Anti-Vaccination Movement in England, 1853–1907.* Durham: Duke, 2005.

Durr, Virginia Foster. *Freedom Writer: Virginia Foster Durr, Letters from the Civil Rights Years.* Edited by Patricia O'Sullivan. Athens: University of Georgia Press, 2006.

———. *Outside the Magic Circle: The Autobiography of Virginia Foster Durr.* edited by Hollinger F. Barnard. Tuscaloosa: University of Alabama Press, 1985.

Eddo-Lodge, Reni. *Why I'm No Longer Talking to White People About Race.* New York: Bloomsbury, 2017.

Egan, Charles E. "OPA Gives its Critics a Chance." *New York Times* (August 1943): E7.

Ehrenreich, Barbara and Deirdre English. *For Her Own Good: Two Centuries of the Experts' Advice to Women.* New York: Anchor Press, 1978.

———. *Witches, Midwives and Nurses: A History of Women Healers.* New York: Feminist Press, 1972.

Eig, Jonathan. *King.* New York: Farrar, Straus and Giroux, 2023.

"English Adventurers Explore Capital." *Washington Post* (February 1940).

"English Adventurers Learn the Hard Way." *Washington Post* (February 1940).

"English Adventurers Stalk Job in Wilds of New York." *Washington Post* (February 1940): B7.

Estes, Billie Sol. "Good Neighbor Plan." *Ramparts* (n.d).

Evans, Katherine. "Why Couldn't You Marry a Duke Like Your Sister?" *Washington Post* (October 1977): E5.

Evans, Stephen, Ida Landauer, and James Morgan. *Portrait of a Muckraker: The Stories of Jessica Mitford.* Filmmakers Library, 1990.

"Exposing the Tyrant." *Chicago Daily Tribune* (1923–1963), 1943: 16.

Eymann, Marcia, and Charles Wollenberg, eds. *What's Going On?: California and the Vietnam Era.* Berkeley: University of California Press, 2004.

Fast, Howard. *Being Red: A Memoir.* Boston: Houghton Mifflin, 1950.

Feingold, Henry. *The Politics of Rescue: The Roosevelt Administration and the Holocaust.* New Brunswick: Rutgers, 1970.

"Folk School to Give Ballad Here Friday." *Washington Post* (December 1940): 16.

Forman, James. *The Making of Black Revolutionaries; a Personal Account.* Seattle: University of Washington Press, 1997.

Fosl, Catherine. *Subversive Southerner: Anne Braden and the Struggle for Racial Justice in the Cold War South.* Louisville: University of Kentucky Press, 2006.

Fox, Kate. *Watching the English: The Hidden Rules of English Behaviour.* London: Nicholas Brealey, 2008.

Francis, Martin. *The Flyer: British Culture and the Royal Air Force, 1939–1945.* Oxford: Oxford University Press, 2008.

Fraser, Rebecca. "Heroine of the High Seas," *Sunday Times* [London] (September 1988).

Freeman, Jo. *At Berkeley in the 60s: The Education of an Activist, 1961–1965.* Bloomington: Indiana University Press, 2004.

"Friend Says Hitler's English Girl Admirer Shot Self in Head." *Los Angeles Times* (January 1940).

Friendly, Alfred. "War Labor Board of 12 Set Up by Roosevelt." *Washington Post* (January 1942): 1.

Frost, Ginger Suzanne. *Promises Broken: Courtship, Class, and Gender in Victorian England.* Charlottesville: University Press of Virginia, 1995.

Fuller, Harry E. "Dr. Spock, 'Boston Five' Court Trial Dissected." *Salt Lake Tribune* (October 1969): 2E.

Fursland, Anthea Rosemary. *Jessica Mitford: A Levinsonian Study of Midlife.* 1990. ProQuest Dissertations & Theses.

Gage, Beverly. *G-Man: J. Edgar Hoover and the Making of the American Century.* New York: Viking, 2022.

Gallup, Inc. 2018. "American Public Opinion and the Holocaust." Gallup.com. April 23, 2018. https://news.gallup.com/opinion/polling-matters/232949/american-public-opinion -holocaust.aspx.

Garrow, David J. "The Origins of the Montgomery Bus Boycott." *Southern Changes* 7 (October–December 1985): 21–27.

Gaskin, Ina May. *Spiritual Midwifery,* 4th ed. Summertown: Book Publishing Company, 2002.

"Gasoline Rationing." *Washington Post* (August 1943): 4.

Gelernter, David. *1939: The Lost World of the Fair.* New York: Free Press, 1995.

Gershenson, M. I. "Wartime and Postwar Employment Trends in California." *Monthly Labor Review* 64, no. 4, (April 1947): 576–88.

Gettleman, Marvin. "The Lost World of United States Labor Education: Curricula at East and West Coast Communist Schools, 1944–1957." *American Labor and the Cold War.* Edited by in Robert W. Cherny, William Issel, and Kiera Walsh Taylor. New Brunswick: Rutgers University Press, 2004.

Giddings, Paula J. *Ida: A Sword Among Lions: Ida B. Wells and the Campaign Against Lynching.* New York: Amistad, 2008.

———. "It's Time for a 21st-Century Anti-Lynching Movement." *The Nation* (August 2014).

Gili, Jonathan. "Debutantes: 1939." BBC, minute 15.40, 2001.

Gill, A.A. *The Angry Island.* Simon & Schuster, 2005.

Gilman, Richard. "The Loved One's in the Slumber Room, Laid Out in Style." *New York Times* (August 1963): 4.

Gitlin, Todd. *The Sixties: Years of Hope, Days of Rage*. New York: Bantam Press, 1993.

Godfrey, Brian. "Inner-City Revitalization and Cultural Succession: The Evolution of San Francisco's Haight-Ashbury District." *Yearbook of the Association of Pacific Coast Geographers* 46, 1984.

Goodwin, Doris Kearns. *No Ordinary Time: Franklin and Eleanor Roosevelt: The Home Front in World War II*. New York: Simon & Schuster, 1994.

Gornick, Vivian. "They Were True Believers." *New York Times* (April 2017): 9.

Gosse, Edmund. Quoted by Hugh Cortazzi. *Mitford's Japan: Memories and Recollections 1866–1906*, revised edition. London: Japan Library, 2002.

Gottlieb, Robert. *Avid Reader: A Life*. New York: Farrar, Straus and Giroux, 2016.

Gottlieb, Sondra. "Slimming in Arizona with the Very Rich." *Maclean's* (October 1974).

Graham, Fred P. "Department of Justice Wants Draft & Foes' Trial Focused on Conspiracy Charge." *New York Times*, (March 1968): 5.

———. "Judge Bars Legality of Vietnam War as Issue in Spock Trial." *New York Times*, (April 1968): n.p.

Graham, Helen. *The War and Its Shadow: Spain's Civil War in Europe's Long Twentieth Century*. Brighton: Sussex Press, 2012.

Grant, Joanne. *Ella Baker: Freedom Bound*. New York: Wiley, 1998.

Gray, Fred. *Bus Ride to Justice: The Life and Works of Fred Gray*. Revised Edition. Montgomery: New South Books, 2013.

Green, Buddy and Steve Murdock. *The Jerry Newson Story*. Self-published.

"Green Favored for Hats; Aranka Showing Also Features New Shade Called Eggnog." *New York Times* (March 1947): 13.

Greenberg, David. *John Lewis: A Life*. New York: Simon & Schuster, 2024.

Griffin, Jean Latz. "Mitford Stops Short in Her Book on Childbirth." *Chicago Tribune* (November 1992): C3.

Griffiths, Richard. *Fellow Travelers of the Right: British Enthusiasts for Nazi Germany, 1933–1939*. London: Constable & Co., 1980.

Guinness, Jonathan. *The House of Mitford*. London: Hutchinson, 1984.

Gurney, Jason. *Crusade in Spain*. Readers Union, 1976. Quoted by Richard Baxell, *Unlikely Warriors: The British in the Spanish Civil War and the Struggle Against Fascism*. London: Aurum, 2012: 26.

Haberman, Dave. "Finding Justice: Judge Myron Bright and James Walker." *North Dakota Law* 2, no. 1 (August 2008).

Halberstam, David. *The Fifties*. New York: Ballantine, 1993.

Hamm, Theodore. "Wesley Robert Wells and the Civil Rights Congress." *Racializing Justice, Disenfranchising Lives*. Manning Marable, et al., eds. London: Palgrave Macmillan, 2007.

Hanauer, Joan. review, UPI, *Chicago Tribune* (September 1973): E7.

Harris, Jerry. "First Reaction: U.S. Communist Leaders Confront the Khrushchev Revelations." *Science & Society* 61 (Winter 1997/1998): 502–512.

Harris, Mark Jonathan, Franklin D. Mitchell, and Steven J. Schechter. *The Homefront: America During World War II*. New York: Putnam's, 1984.

Hartmann, Susan M. *The Home Front & Beyond: American Women in the 1940s*. Boston: Twayne, 1982.

Hastings, Selina. *Nancy Mitford: A Biography*. London: Hamish Hamilton, 1985.

Haywood, Harry. "World War II and the Merchant Marines," Gwendolyn Midlo Hall, ed., *A Black Communist in the Freedom Struggle*. Minneapolis: University of Minnesota Press, 2012.

Healey, Dorothy. *California Red: A Life in the American Communist Party*. Urbana: University of Illinois Press, 1993.

Heard, Alex. *The Eyes of Willie McGee: A Tragedy of Race, Sex, and Secrets in the Jim Crow South*. New York: HarperCollins, 2010.

"Heil, Heil, the Gang's All Here." *Washington Post* (May 1977).

Hennings, Arthur Sears. "F.D.R. Backers Swell Ranks of 'Sixth Column.'" *Chicago Daily Tribune* (March 1942): 1.

"Highball Sir? Asks Unity's Sister." *The Washington Post* (January 1940).

Hills, L. Rust. "The Structure of the American Literary Establishment." *Esquire* (July 1963).

Hilton, Lisa. *The Horror of Love: Nancy Mitford and Gaston Palewski in Paris and London*. Berkeley: Pegasus, 2012.

"Hitler Drives On: Hitler's Push to the East and Five Momentous Questions." *New York Times* (March 1939): 63.

"Hitler's Admirer Stricken." *Washington Post* (October 1939).

"Hitler's Fickle Lover." *Philadelphia Inquirer* (November 1945).

"Hitler Girlfriend Reported Ill of Sleeping Potion." *Washington Post* (October 1939).

"Hitler's Girlfriend Believed Suicide." *Washington Post* (November 1939).

"Holt v. Sarver," *Encyclopedia of Arkansas*, https://encyclopediaofarkansas.net/entries/holt-v -sarver-4165/, accessed February 24, 2024.

Hoose, Phillip M. *Claudette Colvin: Twice Toward Justice*. New York: Farrar, Straus and Giroux, 2009.

Horne, Gerald. *Communist Front? The Civil Rights Congress, 1946–1956*. New York: International Publishers, 1988.

Horowitz, Daniel. *Betty Friedan and the Making of the Feminine Mystique*. Amherst: University of Massachusetts Press, 1998.

Hourihane, Ann Marie. "Review of Deborah Devonshire, *Wait for Me!*." *Irish Times* (September 2010).

"How Not to Read a Book." *New York Times* (October 1963): 10E.

Hunter, Jean E. "A Daring New Concept: *The Ladies' Home Journal* and Modern Feminism." *NWSA Journal* 2, no. 4 (1990): 583–602.

"In Jail 46 Years, Man Wins Parole." *New York Times* (July 1974): 30.

"Incidents in European Conflict." *New York Times* (January 1940).

Ingram, Kevin. *Rebel: The Short Life of Esmond Romilly*. New York: Dutton, 1985.

Jackson, Marni. "Muckraker in the Delivery Room." *Toronto Star* (December 1992): E14.

Janeway, Elizabeth. "The Mitfords: Home was Something to Run Away From." *New York Times* (June 1960): 5–20.

Jayson, Sharon. "Is Selfie Culture Making Our Kids Selfish?." *New York Times* (2016).

Jebb, Julian. "Nancy Mitford: A Portrait by Her Sisters," BBC, 1980.

Jenkins, David. "The Union Movement, the California Labor School, and San Francisco Politics, 1926–1988." Commerce, Industry, and Labor Oral Histories Individual Interviews. The Regents of the University of California, Bancroft Library, Berkeley.

Jenkins, Virginia Scott. *The Lawn: A History of an American Obsession*. Washington, D.C.: The Smithsonian Institution, 1994.

Johnson, Marilynn S. *The Second Gold Rush: Oakland and the Bay Area in World War II*. Berkeley: University of California Press, 1993.

Johnson, Peg. "Redesdale Will Cuts Off Madcap Jessica." *Washington Post* (July 1958): D1.

Jones, D.A.N. "The Revolutionary Habit." *Times Literary Supplement* (July 1984): 850–51.

Jones, Victor O. "Undertakers Hoist Selves by Own Pomp." *Boston Globe* (September 1963): 20.

Kalman, Janice, Sylvia Bortin, Marina Alzugaray, and Judy Dowd. "A Feminist Perspective on the Study of Home: Application of a Midwifery Care Framework," *Journal of Nurse-Midwifery* 39, no. 3 (May/June 1994): 142–49.

Kaplan, Justin. *Lincoln Steffens: A Biography*. New York: Simon & Schuster, 1974.

Katznelson, Ira. *Fear Itself: The New Deal and the Origin of Our Time*. New York: Liveright, 2013.

Kellams, Kyle. "The Unusual Saga of James Dean Walker." *KAUF radio*, NPR Affiliate radio, 2021.

Kendall, Elaine. "Amazing Grace." *The Los Angeles Times* (April 1989): 3.

Kendi, Ibram X. *How to Be an Antiracist*. New York: Random House, 2019.

Kennedy, David M. *Freedom from Fear: The American People in Depression and War, 1929–1945*. New York: Oxford, 1999.

Kenney, Herbert. "Background to the Spock Case." *Boston Globe* (September 1969).

Killebrew, Tom. *The Royal Air Force in the American Skies: The Seven British Flight Schools in the United States During World War II*. Denton: University of North Texas, 2015.

King, Padraic. "They Say Sir Oswald Mosley Had Champagne in Jail." *Daily Boston Globe* (November 1943): C5.

Kipling, Rudyard. "The White Man's Burden." *McClure's Magazine* (February 1899).

Klein, Jim and Julia Reichert. "Seeing Red: Stories of American Communists." *New Day Films*, 1983.

Kübler-Ross, Elisabeth. *On Death and Dying*. New York: Routledge, 1969.

"Landlady Turns Other Cheek After Star-Boarder Slaps It." *Pittsburgh Courier* (March 1940).

Langer, Elinor. "The Oakland 7." *The Atlantic* (October 1969).

Lannon, Frances. *The Spanish Civil War, 1936–1939*. Oxford: Osprey, 2002.

"Lawns and Lawn History." The Lawn Institute. n.d.

Lawrence, W.H. "War Labor Board Created; Davis Heads 12-Man Body." *New York Times* (January 1942): 1.

Leaming, Barbara. *Kick Kennedy: The Charmed Life and Tragic Death of the Favorite Kennedy Daughter*. New York: St. Martin's Press, 2016.

Leavitt, Judith Walzer. "Alienated Labor - The American Way of Birth by Jessica Mitford." *New Republic* 207. Washington: New Republic, 1992.

Lee, Everett S., and Anne S. Lee. "Internal Migration Statistics for the United States." *Journal of the American Statistical Association* 55, no. 292 (1960): 664–97.

"Leftist Daughter Left Nothing by Her Father." *Chicago Daily Tribune (1923–1963)* (1958): 1.

Lehmann-Haupt, Christopher. "Guilty as Charged by the Judge." *New York Times* (September 1969).

———. "On the Shame of Our Prisons," *New York Times* (September 1973): 45.

Leonard, John. "Books of the Times." *New York Times* (September 1977).

Leonard, Karen. Quoted in "Funeral Directors Want Piece of Mitford," *The Record* (Stockton, CA) (July 1996): A2.

Lester, Joan Steinau. *Loving Before Loving: A Marriage in Black and White*. Madison: University of Wisconsin Press, 2021.

Lichtenstein, Grace. "Women's Lib Wooed by Publishers." *New York Times* (August 1970): 32.

"Life with Mother Taylor." *New York Times* (April 1943): 1.

Lindbergh, Charles A. "Appeal to Isolationism." *Vital Speeches of the Day* (1939): 751–52.

Lingeman, Richard. *Don't You Know There's a War On?: The American Homefront, 1941–1945.* New York: Nation Books, 1970.

Lippman, Walter. "Today and Tomorrow: Wake Up, America." *Washington Post* (December 1941): 19.

Litchfield, David R.L. *Hitler's Valkyrie: The Uncensored Biography of Unity Mitford.* Stroud, Gloucestershire: History Press, 2013.

"Lord Redesdale Daughter Works in New York Shop." *Daily Boston Globe (1928-1960)* (1939): 22.

"Loss of Memory," *New York Herald Tribune* (January 5, 1940): 2.

Lovell, Mary S. *The Sisters: The Saga of the Mitford Family.* New York: W.W. Norton, 2001.

Lusting, R. Jeffrey. "The War at Home: California's Struggle to Stop the Vietnam War." *What's Going On?: California and the Vietnam War.* Edited by Marcia Eymann and Charles Wollenberg. Berkeley: University of California Press, 2004.

Lyons, Leonard. "LYONS DEN." *Daily Defender (Daily Edition) (1956-1960).* Chicago, Ill: Real Times, Inc, 1960: 5.

Maas, Eva [Lapin]. *Looking Back on a Life in the Left.* Self-published: Eva Maas, 1998.

"Madame Chairman." *The Washington Post* (July 1940): 8.

Mansfield, H. C. "A Short History of OPA." *Superintendent of Documents,* 1948.

Marable, Manning, Ian Steinberg, and Keesha Middlemass, eds. *Racializing Justice, Disenfranchising Lives: The Racism, Criminal Justice, and Law Reader.* New York, New York; Palgrave Macmillan, 2007.

Marcus, Isabel. "Locked In and Locked Out: Reflections on the History of Divorce Law Reform in New York State." *Buffalo Law Review* 37, 1988.

Martin, Jonathan, and Robert Powell. *Escape from Colditz.* British Broadcasting Corporation BBC, 2003.

Martin, Waldo. "Holding One Another: Mario Savio and the Freedom Struggle in Mississippi and Berkeley." *The Free Speech Movement: Reflections on Berkeley in the 1960s.* Edited by Robert Cohen and Reginald E. Zelnik. University of California Press, 2002.

Mates, Lewis H. *The Spanish Civil War and the British Left: Political Activism and the Popular Front.* London: Tauris Academic Studies, 2007.

McCreery, Laura. *Queen of the Muckrackers: Jessica Mitford's Contributions to American Journalism.* 1995. ProQuest Dissertations & Theses.

McDowell, Edwin. "Dutton's Adult Unit to be Absorbed." *New York Times,* (November 1989):D19.

———. "'Silent Spring,' 20 Years a Milestone," *New York Times,* (September 1982): C16.

McIntosh, Peggy. "White Privilege: Unpacking the Invisible Knapsack," *Peace and Freedom Magazine* (July/August 1989): 10–12.

McWhorter, Diane. *Carry Me Home: Birmingham, Alabama: The Climactic Battle of the Civil Rights Movement,* revised edition. New York: Simon & Schuster, 2012.

Mendis, G.C. *Ceylon Under the British.* New Delhi: Asian Educational Services, 2005.

Meroney, John. "Maya Angelou's Inaugural Poem: Plagiarized or Inspired?" *Chronicles* (December 1993).

Middleton, Drew. "Eyewitness Account: Fiery Glow Turns London into Fantastic Dreamworld." *Washington Post* (October 1940): 1–4.

"The Milner-Gibsons." *Wordpress*, 2013. https://milnergibson.wordpress.com/2013/08/03/the
    -milner-gibsons/.
Mingay, G.E. *A Social History of the English Countryside*. London: Routledge, 1990.
Mintz, Morton. "Births of a Nation." *Washington Post* (November 1992): 6.
"Miss Lenroot to Speak." *Washington Post* (May 1941): 17.
"Miss Mitford Back, Army Guards Pier." *New York Times* (January 1940): 9.
"Miss Mitford Tried to Take Life." *New York Times* (October 1939).
Mitford, Deborah. *All in One Basket*. Farrar, Straus and Giroux, 2001.
———. "My Sister and Hitler: Unity Mitford's War," *The Guardian* (December 2002).
———. *Wait for Me! Memoir*. Farrar, Straus and Giroux, 2010.
Mitford, Jessica. *A Fine Old Conflict*. New York: Knopf, 1977.
———. *American Way of Birth*, Plume Edition (November 1993).
———. *The American Way of Death*. New York: Simon & Schuster, 1963.
———. *The American Way of Death Revisited,* first published 1963. New York: Vintage, 2000.
———. "The American Way of Success," *Ladies' Home Journal*, Special Issue: Woman: The
    Fourth Dimension." Edited by Betty Friedan, (June 1964): 22–25.
———. "An Update on the 'Prison Business:' A 'Change for the Worse.'" *The Nation* (October
    1982): 424–46.
———. "Appointment in Arkansas." *New West* (November 1980).
———. "A Talk with George Jackson." *New York Times Book Review* (June 1971).
———. "At Peace with Old Age: Betty Friedan Confronts the Aging Process." *San Francisco
    Chronicle* (September 1993): 1–7.
———. "'Below Stairs,' Review of E.S. Turner What the Butler Saw: Two Hundred and Fifty
    Years of the Servant Problem." *New York Times Book Review* (April 1963): BR22.
———. "Burial Writes." *The Mail* (November 1995).
———. "Chatting About Chatsworth." *San Francisco Chronicle* (December 1982).
———. *Daughters and Rebels: an Autobiography*. Houghton Mifflin, 1960.
———. *Faces of Philip: A Memoir of Philip Toynbee*. New York: Knopf, 1984.
———. "Foreword," Cedric Belfrage, *The American Inquisition, 1945–1960: A Profile of the
    'McCarthy Era'*. New York: Thunder's Mouth Press, 1989.
———. "Foreword." *The Pursuit of Love* and *Love in a Cold Climate*. By Nancy Mitford. New
    York: Vintage, 2001.
———. "El Salvador on the Precipice." *The Observer* (March 1984).
———. "Experiments behind Bars: Doctors, Drug Companies, and Prisoners." *Atlantic
    Monthly (1971)* 76, no. 1 (1973): 64.
———. *Grace Had an English Heart: The Story of Grace Darling, Heroine and Victorian Superstar*.
    New York: Dutton, 1989.
———. "Group Therapy for Fat People." *San Francisco Sunday Examiner* (December 1967).
———. "Harsh Punishment Questioned." *Los Angeles Times* (July 1966): B4.
———. "Hello There! You're On the Air!" *Harper's Magazine* (May 1966).
———. *Hons and Rebels*. New York: New York Review of Books, 2004; first published 1960.
———. "How To Lose Five Pounds for a Thousand Dollars." *Nova* (October 1966).
———. "How Will We Ever Teach Them to Trust Adults Again?" *McCall's* (June 1981).
———. "The Importance of Being Skinny." *Los Angeles Times* (November 1967): B34.
———. "Kind and Usual Punishment in California." *The Atlantic* 227, no. 3, Atlantic Monthly
    Co. (1971): 45.

———. "Maine Chance Diary." *McCall's* (1966): 130.

———. "My Short and Happy Life as a Distinguished Professor." *Atlantic Monthly* (October 1974).

———. "My Way of Life Since *The American Way of Death*." Written for *Nova* (possibly unpublished) (1964).

———. *Poison Penmanship: The Gentle Art of Muckraking*. New York: Farrar, Straus and Giroux, 1979.

———. "Pretty, Lascivious, Undignified." *Vogue* (March 1966).

———. "Prime Time for Communists?" *New York Times* (April 1989).

———. "Prisons: The Menace of Liberal Reform." *New York Review of Books* (March 1972).

———. "The Review No One Would Publish." *Berkeley Monthly* (December 1980): 51.

———. "The Salvadoran Way of Death." *San Francisco Chronicle* (March 1984): 7–8; 17.

———. "The Skinny Crusade: Is There a Weight Watcher Watching You?" *New York Post* (December 1967).

———. "So What's Wrong with Being a New Yorker?" *San Francisco Chronicle* (May 1961): 7–8.

———. "Something for the Boys," Review of Rosalind Erskine *The Passion Flower Hotel*. *New York Times Book Review* (September 1962).

———. "Something to Offend Everyone." *Show* (December 1964).

———. "St. Peter Don't You Call Me: American Burial Standards—Classy But Expensive." *Frontier* (November 1958).

———. "Swingtime for Hitler in Chichester." *Sunday Times* [London] (July 1981).

———. *The Trial of Dr. Spock, The Reverend William Sloane Coffin, Jr., Michael Ferber, Mitchell Goodman, and Marcus Raskin*. New York: Alfred A. Knopf, 1969.

———. "The Torture Cure," *Harper's* (August 1973).

———. "Weight Watchers' Demands: Last Pound of Flesh." *Boston Globe* (December 1967).

———. "Whut They're Thanking Down There." *Esquire* (May 1962).

———. "Why I Decided to Write About Funerals." *The Bookseller* (September 1963).

———. "Women in Cages: District of Columbia Women's Detention Center," *McCall's* (September 1972).

———. "The Women Your Husband Works With . . ." *Ladies' Home Journal* (June 1964): 13.

Mitford, Nancy. *The Blessing*. New York: Vintage, 2010, first published 1951.

———. *Christmas Pudding and Pigeon Pie*. New York: Vintage, 2013, first published 1932; 1940.

———. *Don't Tell Alfred*. New York: Vintage, 2010, first published 1960.

———. *Highland Fling*. London: Capuchin, 2010, first published in 1931.

———. Charlotte Mosley. *Love from Nancy: The Letters of Nancy Mitford*. Houghton Mifflin, 1993.

———. et al. *Love in a Cold Climate*. Directed by Tom Hooper, *BBC Worldwide*, 2001.

———. "The English Aristocracy," *Noblesse Oblige: Sophisticated Fun About the Speech and Manners of the English Upper Class*. New York: Harper & Bros., 1956.

———. *Noblesse Oblige: Sophisticated Fun About the Speech and Manners of the English Upper Class*. New York: Harper & Bros., 1956.

———. et al. *The Letters of Nancy Mitford and Evelyn Waugh*. Houghton Mifflin Co., 1996. Ed. Charlotte Mosley.

———. *The Pursuit of Love & Love in a Cold Climate*. New York: Vintage, 2001, first published 1945 and 1949.

———. *The Water Beetle: Essays*. New York: Atheneum, 1986, originally published 1962.

———. *Wigs on the Green*. New York: Vintage: 2010, originally published 1935.

"The Mitfords: Red Sheep Left Out of Will." *Globe and Mail* (July 1958): 21.

Morris, Bill. "Born, Bombed and Buried in Bermondsey." WW2 People's War Oral History archive, BBC, 2006.

Mosley, Charlotte, ed. *The Mitfords: Letters Between Six Sisters*. New York: HarperCollins, 2007.

Mosley, Diana. Interview with Sue Lawley, BBC, Desert Island Discs, November 1989.

———. "Letter to the Editor." *Times Literary Supplement* (April 1960).

———. *A Life of Contrasts: An Autobiography*. London: Hamish Hamilton, 1977.

Mosley, Nicholas. *Rules of the Game/Beyond the Pale: Memoirs of Sir Oswald Mosley and Family*. Elmwood Park, Illinois: Dalkey Archive Press, 1991.

"Mosley Release Protests Mount." *Washington Post* (November 1943).

"Mosleys Miss Welcome Mat." *Atlanta Constitution* (1943): 26.

"Mostly About People." *Santa Cruz Sentinel* (October 1973): 13.

"Mrs. Fletcher To Entertain." *Washington Post* (March 1940): 55.

Munoz, Jacob. "The Powerful, Complicated Legacy of Betty Friedan's 'The Feminine Mystique.'" *Smithsonian Magazine* (February 2021).

Murch, Donna Jean. *Living for the City: Migration, Education, and the Rise of the Black Panther Party in Oakland*. Chapel Hill: University of North Carolina Press, 2010.

Murphy, Sophia. *The Mitford Family Album*. London: Sidgwick & Jackson, 1985.

National War Labor Board Press Release, No. B 693, in Chapter 24. "Equal Pay for Women." *The Termination Report of the National War Labor Board: Industrial Disputes and Wage Stabilization in Wartime*, Volume I. (January 1942–December 1945): 290–91.

Navarro, Vincenc. "What Happened in Chile: Parallels to Spain." Translated by Collen Boland. *PÚBLICO* (September 2013).

Navasky, Victor S. *Naming Names*. New York: Hill and Wang, 2003.

Naylor, Leonard E. *The Irrepressible Victorian: The Story of Thomas Gibson Bowles: Journalist Parliamentarian, and Founder Editor of the Original Vanity Fair*. London: Macdonald, 1965.

Nelson, Steve. *American Radical*. Pittsburgh: University of Pittsburgh Press, 1981.

NJN, "Private Lives on a Platter." *Times of India* (July 1984): 8.

Nobel, Daniel. "Review of *Kind and Usual Punishment*." *Buffalo Law Review* 23, no. 1 (Fall 1973): 307–312.

Offner, Arnold. *American Appeasement: U.S. Foreign Policy and Germany*. New York: W.W. Norton, 1976.

"The Ohio Pen's Avenging Angel." *Columbus Monthly*, (2009).

"One of 'Mitford Girls' Disinherited by Father." *New York Times* (July 1958): 6.

Oren, Laura. "No-Fault Divorce Reform in the 1950s: The Lost History of the "Greatest Project" of the National Association of Women Lawyers." *Law and History Review* 36, no. 4 (September 2018).

Orleck, Annelise. *Rethinking American Women's Activism*. New York: Routledge, 2015.

Oshinsky, David M. *Polio: An American Story*. New York: Oxford, 2005.

Packer, Herbert. "The Conspiracy Weapon." *New York Review of Books* (November 1969).

Padmore, George. "British Colonials Irked By Release of Fascist Mosley." *Chicago Defender* (December 1943).

"Paperback Best Sellers." *Chicago Tribune*, 1964: K10.

Patterson, William L. *The Man Who Cried Genocide: An Autobiography.* New York: International Publishers, 1971.

———. et al., eds., *We Charge Genocide: The Historic Petition to the United Nations for Relief From a Crime of the United States Government Against the Negro People.* Civil Rights Congress, 1951.

Paxman, Jeremy. *The English: A Portrait of a People.* Woodstock: Overlook Press, 2000.

Pearlman, Lise. *Call Me Phaedra: The Life and Times of Movement Lawyer Fay Stender.* Berkeley: Regent Press, 2018.

Pedrick, Karin Williamson and Sandra Arnold Scham. *Inside Affirmative Action: The Executive Order that Transformed America's Workplace.* New York: Routledge, 2018.

Peebles, Patrick. *The Plantation Tamils of Ceylon.* London: Leicester University Press, 2001.

"Peer's Daughter Quarrels with Hitler." *Chicago Tribune* (1939).

"Peer's Daughter Stays in Germany." *Washington Post* (October 1939).

"Penniless Heiress." *Detroit Free Press* (1958): 9.

Phegley, Sarah. *Courtship and Marriage in Victorian England.* Santa Barbara: Praeger, 2012.

Pigram, Ron and Dennis F. Edwards. *Cotswold Memories: Recollections of Rural Life in the Steam Age.* Kent: Unicorn Books, 1990.

Plattner, Marc F. "Kind and Usual Punishment, by Jessica Mitford (Book Review)." *Commentary (New York).* New York, N. Y: American Jewish Committee, 1974.

Polenberg, Richard. *War and Society: The United States, 1941–1945.* Westport: Greenwood Press, 1972.

Poore, Charles. "Untitled Review. *New York Times* (June1960).

Post, Emily. "Rooms for Rent?" *Atlanta Constitution* (June 1943):19.

Potter, Stephen. *Lifemanship: Some Notes on Lifemanship with a Summary of Recent Research in Gamesmanship.* New York: Holt, 1955.

Powell, Thomas. "Biological Warfare in the Korean War: Allegations and Cover-up." *Socialism and Democracy* (Routledge) 31:1, (March 2017).

Prescott, Orville. "Book of the Times; The High Cost of Dying." *New York Times* (August 1963): 25.

"Prisons and Funerals." *New York Times* (September 1973).

Pryce-Jones, Alan. "Mitford Eyes Spock Case." *Oakland Tribune* (October 1964).

Pryce-Jones, David. *Unity Mitford: A Quest.* London: Weidenfield and Nicolson, 1976.

Pugh, Martin. *Britain Since 1789: A Concise History.* New York: St. Martin's, 1999.

———. *We Danced All Night: A Social History of Britain Between the Wars.* London: Vintage Books, 2009.

Purnell, Sonia. *Clementine: The Life of Mrs. Winston Churchill.* New York: Viking, 2013.

"Queen of the Muckrakers." *The Times* (July 1970).

Rabinowitz, Victor. *Unrepentant Leftist: A Lawyer's Memoir.* Urbana: University of Illinois Press, 1996.

Radosh, Ronald. "Life of the Party." *The Nation* (January 1978): 85.

Ransby, Barbara. *Ella Baker and the Black Freedom Movement: A Radical Democratic Vision.* Chapel Hill: University of North Carolina Press, 2003.

Raza, Sehar, Stacy Doumas, and Saba Afzal. "Lithium: Past, Present, and Future." *Psychiatric Times* 40, no. 5 (2023): 45.

"RCAF Students Learning Gunnery at Special School." *Universal News* (May 1941).

Redesdale, Algernon Bertram Freeman-Mitford. *Memories: V. 2.* Hutchinson, 1915.

Redman, Samuel. "During World War II, Thousands of Women Chased Their Own California Dream." *Smithsonian Magazine* (November 2017).

"Reich Denies Unity is Ill." *New York Times* (October 1939).

Reid, P.R., *Colditz: The Full Story*. New York: St. Martin's Press, 1984.

"Reports Biddle Urges Politics as Usual in War: Senator Reveals New Dealers' Meeting." *Chicago Daily Tribune (1923-1963)*, 1942: 6.

Reston, James B. "A Fair Nazi Back in England." *New York Times* (January 1940).

———. "Miss Freeman Mitford." *New York Times* (January 1940).

———. "She Went Home." *New York Times* (January 1940).

Reverby, Susan. *Co-Conspirator for Justice: The Revolutionary Life of Dr. Alan Berkman*. Chapel Hill: University of North Carolina Press, 2020.

Richmond, Al. *A Long View from the Left: Memoirs of An American Revolutionary*. New York: Houghton Mifflin, 1972.

Roarback, Eileen Mary. "The Defense of the Self: Autobiographical Response of American Intellectuals to the McCarthy Era." PhD Dissertation, American Studies, University of Iowa, May 1999.

Roberts, Leslie. *There Shall Be Wings: A History of the Royal Canadian Air Force*. Toronto: Clarke, Irwin & Company, 1959.

Rodman, Selden. "In Memoriam: Esmond Romilly: 1918-1941." *The Amazing Year: A Diary in Verse*. New York: Scribner's, 1947.

Romilly, Esmond. *Boadilla: A Personal Account of a Battle in Spain*. London: Hamish Hamilton, 1937.

———. "Blue Blood Adventurers Discover America." *Washington Post* (January 1940): B4.

———. "England's Next Prime Minister," *Common Sense* 8 (October 1939): 6–9.

———. "Escape from England." *The Commentator* (October 1939): 126–28.

———. and Giles Romilly. *Out of Bounds: The Education of Giles Romilly and Esmond Romilly*. London: Umbria Press, 2015.

———. "Interview." *The Times (of London)* (March 1960): 15.

Romilly, Giles and Michael Alexander. *Hostages of Colditz*. New York: Praeger, 1973.

———. "My Brother: Poem from a Prison Camp." *Evening Standard* (August 1942).

"Roosevelt Evokes British Approval." *New York Times* (January 1940).

Rosenberg, Bernard. "The Communist Party Convention." *Dissent* (Spring 1957).

Rothman, David J. "Kind And Usual Punishment: The American Way of Jail. The Prison Business. By Jessica Mitford. 340 Pp. New York: Alfred A. Knopf. $7.95." Review, *New York Times*. 1973.

"Royalties Aren't the Only Reward." *New York Times* (December 1963).

Ruggi, Steve. "The American Way of Birth," BBC 2, 1993.

"Rutland Gate: Early Development of Rutland Gate, 1836–c.1847," in *Survey of London: Volume 45, Knightsbridge*, ed. John Greenacombe. London, (2000): 144–151.

Ryan, Maureen. "A Mitford Sisters First Look: 'Outrageous' Takes on the 1930's Brilliant, Scandalous Siblings." *Vanity Fair* (August 2024).

Saad, Lydia. "Gallup Vault: Americans Not Keen on A-Bomb During Korean War," *Gallup* (August 2017).

Sabin, Arthur J. *In Calmer Times: The Supreme Court and Red Monday*. University of Pennsylvania Press, 1999.

Sands, Sarah. "Threadbare is the Classiest Look of All." *The Independent* (October 2010).

Scanlon, Donna. "Men's Housework, 1940–1950." Library of Congress, n.d.

Schlesinger, Arthur. *Robert Kennedy and His Times*. New York: Houghton Mifflin, 1978.

Schuyler, George S. "News and Reviews." *Pittsburgh Courier* (November 1963): 12.

Seidenspinner, Clarence. "Light Upon Shadows." *Chicago Tribune* (August 1963): K2.

Self, Robert O. *American Babylon: Race and the Struggle for Postwar Oakland*. Princeton: Princeton University Press, 2003.

Shapiro, Laura. "From Here to Maternity: Two Feminists Take on Birth and Menopause," *Newsweek* 120, November 19, 1992.

Shen, Fuyuan. "John William Powell and 'The China Weekly Review': An Analysis of His Reporting and His McCarthy Era Ordeal." *ERIC Institute of Education Sciences* (August 1994): 148.

Shorter, Edward. "Deliverance." *New York Times Book Review* (1992).

Sigal, Clancy. "Trapped Between Greatness and Niceness." *New York Times* (January 1985).

Simon, Linda. "Review of "Faces of Philip'." *Library Journal* (July 1984): 1320.

Sinclair, Mick. *San Francisco: A Cultural and Literary History*. Northampton: Interlink, 2004.

Slung, Michele. "Rowing her Boat ("Help!") Into History." *New York Times* (April 1989): 22.

Smith, Doug. "James Dean Walker: The California Connection." *Arkansas Gazette* (March 1981): 11E.

Smith, Michael Steven. *Lawyers for the Left: In the Courts, In the Streets, and On the Air*. New York: OR Books, 2019.

Soames, Mary, ed. *Speaking for Themselves: The Personal Letters of Winston and Clementine Churchill*. New York: Doubleday, 1998.

Sobell, Helen. "Mitford, 'The Trial of Dr. Spock, The Reverend William Sloane Coffin, Jr., Michael Ferber, Mitchell Goodman, and Marcus Raskin' (Book Review)." *Science & Society (New York. 1936)*. New York: Science and Society, Inc, 1970: 497–99.

Sokol, Jason. *The Heavens Might Crack: The Death and Legacy of Martin Luther King, Jr*. New York: Basic Books, 2018.

Special Cable to, the G. "Opposition to Sir Oswald Mosley's Release from Prison Increases." *Daily Boston Globe (1928-1960)* (November 1943): 2.

Spencer, Charles. "Enemies of the Estate." *Vanity Fair* (January 2010).

Spock, Benjamin. "Oral History: The Conspiracy to Oppose the Vietnam War." *It Did Happen Here: Recollections of Political Repression in America*, ed. Bud and Ruth Schultz. Berkeley: University of California Press, 1989.

"The Spock Trial." *New York Times* (May 1968): E15.

"Spock Trial May Be Thriller." *Washington Post* (1968).

Stanger, Howard R. "The Larkin Clubs of Ten: Consumer Buying Clubs and Mail-Order Commerce, 1890-1910." *Enterprise & Society* 8, no. 1 (2008).

Starr, Kevin. *Embattled Dreams: California in War and Peace, 1940–1950*. New York: Oxford University Press, 2002.

Stender, Fay. "Preface." *Maximum Security: Letters*, ed. Eve Pell. New York: Dutton, 1972.

"Steven Kennedy to Sing." *Washington Post* (January 1940): F6.

Storrs, Landon R. Y. "Red Scare Politics and the Suppression of Popular Front Feminism: The Loyalty Investigation of Mary Dublin Keyserling." *Journal of American History* (September 2003): 510.

Straight, Michael. *After Long Silence*. New York: Norton, 1983.

Suchman, Edward A., Rose K. Goldsen, and Robin M. Williams, Jr. "Attitudes Toward the Korean War." *Public Opinion Quarterly* 17, no. 2 (Summer 1953): 171.

Sullivan, Mark. "Business Experience: Reorganizing OPA." *Washington Post* (July 1943):10.

———. "Defense Rulings: Have Been Offensive." *Washington Post* (January 1943): 8.

Sullivan, Patricia. *Days of Hope: Race and Democracy in the New Deal Era*. Chapel Hill: University of North Carolina Press, 1996.

"Summer Boarders." *Daily Boston Globe* (1940): 15.

Survey of London: Volume 45, Knightsbridge. Ed. John Greenacombe (London, 2000), *British History Online*. Web.

Sussman, Peter. *Decca: The Letters of Jessica Mitford*. New York: Knopf, 2006.

Sutherland, Jon and Diane Cantwell. *The RAF Air Sea Rescue Service 1918–1986*. Great Britain: Pen and Sword, 2010.

Taeuber, C. "Wartime Population Changes in the United States." *Milbank Memorial Fund Quarterly* 24, no. 3 (n.d.): 236.

Takaki, Ronald. *Double Victory: A Multicultural History of America in World War II*. Boston: Little Brown, 2000.

Tamaki, Donald K. "Oakland Politics and Powerless Pressure Groups." Institute of Governmental Studies, University of California, Berkeley (September 1978).

Taylor, D. J. *Bright Young People: The Lost Generation of London's Jazz Age*. New York: Farrar, Straus and Giroux, 2007.

Tennille, Norton F. "A Rock, A River, A Tree/A Poetic Controversy." *Harpers* (March 1994).

"They Once Called Him Unworthy." *Derby Evening Telegraph* (n.d).

Thompson, Laura. *Life in a Cold Climate: Nancy Mitford, A Portrait of a Contradictory Woman*. London: Headline, 2003.

———. *The Six: The Lives of the Mitford Sisters*. New York: St. Martin's, 2015.

Tinniswood, Adrian. *The Long Weekend: Life in the English Country House*. New York: Basic, 2016.

Toffler, Alvin. "What the Husbands Think." *Ladies' Home Journal* 81. New York: Meredith Corporation, 1964.

Toynbee, Philip. *Friends Apart: A Memoir of Esmond Romilly & Jasper Ridley in the Thirties*. London: Sidgwick & Jackson, 1980.

Treuhaft, Decca. "We Visited Socialism." *The People's World* (February 1956): 4.

Treuhaft, Robert E. *Left-Wing Political Activist and Progressive Leader in the Berkeley Co-op*. Oral history conducted by Robert G. Larsen, Berkeley Oral History Project, Berkeley Historical Society, 1990, Consumers Cooperative of Berkeley Oral History Collection.

Trillin, Calvin. "Back on the Bus: Remembering the Freedom Riders." *The New Yorker* (July 2011).

Tucker, Edwin W. "Kind and Usual Punishment: The Prison Business." *Justice System Journal*. Institute for Court Management of the National Center for State Courts, 1974.

"Tuning with the Enemy." Produced and directed by Tricia O'Leary and Helen Gallacher, 1998.

Tunley, Roul. "Can You Afford to Die?." *Saturday Evening Post* (June 1961).

"Two Britons in 'Hobohemia.'" *Washington Post* (January 1940).

"Two Young Adventurers Explore New York." *Washington Post* (February 1940): B4.

Ulrich, Laurel Thatcher. *A Midwife's Tale: The Life of Martha Ballard Based on Her Diary, 1785–1812*. New York: Alfred A. Knopf, 1990.

United States v. Powell, 156 F. Supp. 526 (N.D. Cal. 1957), November 1, 1957, https://law.justia.com/cases/federal/district-courts/FSupp/156/526/2137284/.

United States v. Powell, 171 F. Supp. 202 (N.D. Cal. 1959), February 3, 1959, https://law.justia
.com/cases/federal/district-courts/FSupp/171/202/1555749/.

"Unity, Hitler's Friend, *Boston Globe*, January 4, 1940.

"Unity Mitford Ill in Reich." *New York Times* (October 1939).

"Unity Mitford, Ill, on Way to England." *New York Times* (January 1940).

"Unity Reported Wounded Twice." *Washington Post* (January 1940).

"Unity's Sister a Miami Waitress: Mum on Mystery Illness." *Chicago Daily Tribune (1923–1963)*
(1940): 3.

Vanity Fair, vol. 1, ed. Thomas Gibson Bowles, November 14, 1868.

Vansittart, Peter. "Books: English Eccentric: *Faces of Philip: A Memoir of Philip Toynbee* by
Jessica Mitford." *Financial Times* (July 1984): 14.

Walker, Don. "Mitford Misses the Mark." *Milwaukee Journal* (November 1992): E11.

Walker, Doris Brin. "How I Happened to Become the Guild's First Woman President." *Guild
Practitioner* 64 (2007), n.p.

Walker, James Dean. *Through Death's Doorway*. West Frankfurt, Illinois: The Trumpet Press, 1971.

Walker, Martin. "Angelou's Poetic Source Queried." *The Guardian* (November 1993): 26.

Walker, Nancy. *Shaping Our Mothers' World: American Women's Magazines*. University Press of
Mississippi. 2000.

———. *Women's Magazines, 1940–1960: Gender Roles and the Popular Press*. Bedford/St.
Martins: Boston. 1998.

Walters, Ray. "Paperback Talk." *New York Times* (June 1981): 71.

Ward, Douglas B. "The Geography of the *Ladies' Home Journal*: An Analysis of a Magazine's
Audience, 1911–1955." *Journalism History* 34, no. 1 (2008).

Warren, Sir David. "Review of Robert Morton, *A.B. Mitford and the Birth of Japan as a Modern
State: Letters Home*." *Japan Society* 12, no. 4 (August 2017).

Watling, Sarah. *Tomorrow Perhaps the Future: Writers, Rebels, and the Spanish Civil War*. New
York: Vintage, 2024.

Wattenberg, Ben. "Betty Freidan and 'The Feminine Mystique.'" PBS, 2000.

Waugh, Evelyn. "Embellishing the Loved Ones." Review of *The American Way of Death*. *Sunday
Times* (of London) (September 1963).

———. "Review of Cecil Beaton, *The Wandering Years*." *The Essays, Articles, and Reviews of
Evelyn Waugh*. Edited Donat Gallagher, London: Harmondsworth, 1986.

Weigard, Kate. *Red Feminism: American Communism and the Making of Women's Liberation*.
Baltimore: Hopkins, 2001.

Welles, Sumner. *The Time for Decision*. New York: Harper, 1944.

Wells, Wesley Robert. "The Facts of My Case: Written from the Death House." Self-published,
1953.

———. *My Name is Wesley Robert Wells*. San Francisco: San Francisco Civil Rights Congress,
1951.

Whitford, Meredith. *Jessica Mitford: Churchill's Rebel* (Sydney: Endeavour Press, 2013).

Williams, Kyle. "Questions Remain in Nearly 60-Year-Old Murder." KAUF radio, NPR
Affiliate radio, April 19, 2021.

Wolman, Philip J. "The Oakland General Strike of 1946," *Southern California Quarterly* 57, no. 2
(July 1975): 147–78.

"WOMAN: THE FOURTH DIMENSION." *Ladies' Home Journal* 81. New York: Meredith Corporation, 1964.

Wormuth, Francis D. "The Trial of Dr. Spock." *Western Political Quarterly* 23, no. 2 (June 1970).

Wyman, Ann. "She Had a Course in Shoplifting." *Boston Globe* (June 1960): A27.

"Young Esmond Tries His Hand at Being a Waiter – Is Fired After Two Days." *Washington Post* (March 1940).

Zarnow, Leandra. "Braving Jim Crow to Save Willie McGee: Bella Abzug, the Legal Left, and Civil Rights Innovation, 1948–1951," *Law & Social Inquiry* 33, no. 4 (Fall 2008): 1003–41.

Zinn, Howard. *A People's History of the United States*. New York: Harper, 2016.

JESSICA MITFORD'S WRITING: A CHRONOLOGICAL BIBLIOGRAPHY

PUBLISHED

1940. and Esmond Romilly (coauthored but single byline). "Blueblood Adventurers Discover America," *Washington Post*, January 28.

1940. and Esmond Romilly. "English Adventurers Learn the Hard Way," *Washington Post*, February 18.

1940. and Esmond Romilly. "Two Young Adventurers Explore New York," *Washington Post*, February 1.

1940. and Esmond Romilly. "English Adventurers Stalk Job in Wilds of New York," *Washington Post*, February 11.

1940. and Esmond Romilly. "English Adventurers Explore Capital," *Washington Post*, February 25.

1940. "Young English Adventurers Make a Door-to-Door Tour of Washington," *Washington Post*, March 10.

1940. and Esmond Romilly. "Young Esmond Romilly Tries His Hand At Being a Waiter – Is Fired After Two Days," *Washington Post*, March 10.

1956. "Lifeitselfmanship, or How to Become a Precisely-Because Man," self-published, (later included as an Appendix to *A Fine Old Conflict* (1977).

1956. "The British Peace Movement: An Enthusiastic First-hand Report," *Daily's People World*, January 27.

1956. "We Visited Socialism," *People's World*, February 17: 4.

1957. "Trial by Headline," *The Nation*, 185.13, October 26: 279–82.

1958. "St. Peter, Don't You Call Me," *Frontier*, November: 8–10.

1960. *Daughters and Rebels; the Autobiography of Jessica Mitford*. Boston: Houghton Mifflin.

1960. *Hons and Rebels*. United Kingdom: Gollancz.

1960. "Sheilah and Jessica Crossed the Tracks in Opposite Directions," *This World/San Francisco Sunday Chronicle*, June 5.

1960. "A Small Girl's Memories of Her Tory Parents," "Just Browsing," Chicago Daily Tribune, July 10.

1960. "The Last of the Great Victorian Wits: Sir Max . . . ," review of Portrait of Max: An Intimate Memoir of Sir Max Beerbohm, by S. N. Behrman, People's World, December 3.

1961. "Foreword," San Francisco, An Informal Guide, by Ben Adams. New York: Hill & Wang.

1961. "The Higher 'The Wall Between' Got, the Colder Were the Feet," This World/San Francisco Sunday Chronicle, April 23.

1961. "So What's Wrong With Being a New Yorker?" This World/San Francisco Sunday Chronicle, May 14.

1961. "Proceed with Caution: Amid the Big U.S. Push to Lure Foreign Tourists, a Sharp–Eyed Englishwoman Warns Them About Motor Trips," Overseas Life, 51.5, August 4. [Mitford dates this as June in Poison Penmanship and titles it "Proceed with Caution" there.]

1961. "The Indignant Generation," The Nation, 192.21, May 27.

1962. "Whut They're Thanking Down There," Esquire, 57.5, May: 94–99. [Mitford titles this "You-All and Non-You-All: A Southern Potpourri" in Poison Penmanship.]

1962. "Something for the Boys," review of the Passion Flower Hotel, by Rosalind Erskine. New York Times Book Review, September 30.

1963. "Americans Don't Want Fancy Funerals," Saturday Evening Post, November 23.

1963. "Below Stairs," New York Times, April 21.

1963. "The Undertaker's Racket," The Atlantic, 211.6, June 1.

1963. "Why I decided to write about Funerals," The Bookseller, September 21: 1470–71.

1963. "Americans Don't Want Fancy Funerals," Speaking Out: The Voice of Dissent, November 23.

1964. "The American Way of Death: The Facts about the Funeral Furor," Good Housekeeping, 158.2, February: 69–82.

1964. "The American Way of Success," Ladies' Home Journal, 81.5, June: 22, 25.

1964. "Waugh is Hell, or Anyhow, He Was One," review of A Little Learning, by Evelyn Waugh, Life Book Review, 57.20, November 13: 12–14.

1964. "Something to Offend Everyone," Show, 4.11, December: 41 & ff.

1965. "Have the Undertakers Reformed?" The Atlantic, 215.6, June 1.

1965. "The Disease that Dr. Kildare Couldn't Cure," McCall's, 92.12, September. [Mitford titles this "Don't Call it Syphilis" in Poison Penmanship.]

1965. "The Rest of Ronald Reagan," Ramparts, 4.7, November.

1965. "Raising Kids without Fear or Freud," review of Your Child is a Person, by Stella Chess, Alexander Thomas, and Herbert G. Birch. Life, 59.21, November 19.

1965. "The Good Grief," review of Death, Grief and Mourning, by Geoffrey Gorer, The Nation, 201.22, December 27: 533–35.

[1965]. "The Formaldehyde Frolics," Holiday, review of film "The Loved One," based on Evelyn Waugh's novel.

1966. "The American Way of Aging," McCall's, 93.4 March. [Mitford retitles this "Main Chance Diary" in Poison Penmanship.]

1966. "Pretty, lascivious, undignified," Vogue, 147.5, March 15: 92–93. [OSU's Finding Aid lists this under the title "The Individuality of Women."]

1966. "A Question of Custody," McCall's, 93.8, May.

1966. "Harsh Punishment Questioned," Los Angeles Times, July 30.

1966. "Hello There! You're on the Air!" Harper's Magazine, 232, May 1.

1966. "How to Lose Five Pounds for a Thousand Dollars," Nova, October: 70 & ff.

1966. "Funds for Justice." In "Letters" with Oscar G. Chase and Imgard Lenel. *The Nation*, 203.4, August 8: 106.

1967. "Jessica Mitford." *Authors Take Sides on Vietnam: Two Questions on the War in Vietnam Answered by Authors of Several Nations*. Edited by Cecil Woolf and John Bagguley. New York: Simon and Schuster.

1967. "It's a Pairfect Day for the Games!" *Venture Magazine*, 4.1, February/March: 33–36.

1967. "The Skinny Crusade: Is There a Weight Watcher Watching You?" *New York Post*, December 2.

1967. "Weight-Watchers' Demands: Last Pound of Flesh," *Boston Globe*, December 10.

1967. "Group Therapy for Fat People," *San Francisco Sunday Examiner & Chronicle*, December 17.

1968. "The Case for Cremation," *Good Housekeeping*, 166.2, February.

1969. *The Trial of Dr. Spock : The Reverend William Sloane Coffin, Jr., Michael Ferber, Mitchell Goodman, and Marcus Raskin*. New York: Knopf.

1969. "Guilty As Charged by the Judge," *The Atlantic*, 224.2, August 1.

1970. "Let Us Now Appraise Famous Writers," *The Atlantic*, 226.1, July 1.

1971. "Kind and Usual Punishment in California," *The Atlantic*, 227.3, March 1.

1971. "A Talk with George Jackson," *New York Times Book Review*, June 13.

1971. "The Keeper and the Kept—A Report from the Kept," review of *An Eye for an Eye*, by Jack Griswold, Mike Misenheimer, Art Powers, and Ed Tromanhauser, *New York Times*, October 3.

1971. "Join the Ranks." in "Letters" with Robert Boyd and Robert Hunter, *The Nation*, 213.5, August 30: 130.

1971. "The Fingerers Fingered," *The Atlantic*, 228.6, December 1.

1972. "Foreword." *Making the World Safe for Hypocrisy*. By Edward Sorel. Chicago: Swallow Press.

1972. "Prisons: The Menace of Liberal Reform," review of *Struggle for Justice: A Report on Crime and Punishment in America*, by Hill & Wang, and review of *Maximum Security: Letters from the California Prison*, edited by Edith Pell, *New York Review of Books*, March 9.

1972. "One for Two," letter to the editor, *San Francisco Chronicle*, June 29.

1972. "Women in Cages: District of Columbia Women's Detention Center," *McCall's*, 99.12, September.

1972. "Misplaced Confidence," letter to the editor, *San Francisco Chronicle*, June 29.

1973. *Kind and Usual Punishment; the Prison Business*. New York: Knopf.

1973. "The Funeral Industry and the Prison Industry," *Fellowship (New York)*, 39.11, November: 10–11.

1973. "Experiments Behind Bars: Doctors, Drug Companies, and Prisoners," *The Atlantic*, 76.1, January 1.

1973. "The Torture Cure," *Harper's*, 247.1479, August 1.

1973. "Prisons and Funerals," *New York Times*, September 5.

1974. "My Short and Happy Life As a Distinguished Professor," *The Atlantic*, 234.4, October 1.

1975. "Professor Mitford and the Fingerprint Flap," *The Observer*, January 5.

1975. "A Different View of the Shah of Iran," *San Francisco Examiner*, February 16.

1976. "The Importance of Being Skinny," *Los Angeles Times*, November 26.

1977. *The American Prison Business*. Harmondsworth, Middlesex, England: Penguin Books. [UK edition of *Kind and Usual Punishment*.]

1977. *A Fine Old Conflict*. New York: Knopf.

1977. "Foreword." *Streetfighter in the Courtroom*, by Charles Garry. New York: E.P. Dutton.

1977. "Memoirs of a Not-So-Dutiful Daughter," *New York Times*, April 17.

1977. "Checks and Balances at the Sign of the Dove," *New York Journal*, May 30.

1977. "If You Think Your Family Is Crazy . . . or Taking Tea With Hitler," *Ms. Magazine*, 6.3, September.

1977. "The Best of Frenemies," *New York Times*, September 13. [In *Poison Penmanship*, Mitford cites this as the *Daily Mail*.]

1977. "The Dove Strikes Back: A Morality Play in Five Acts," *New York*, 10.38, September 19.

1977. "Dauntless Decca in D.C.: Raising Hell on the Home Front," *Washington Post*, October 2.

1977. "The Funeral Salesmen," *McCall's*, 105.2, November.

1977. "Hospital Trip," review of *Patients*, by Polly Toynbee, *New York Times*, December 18.

1978. *The American Way of Death*. New York: Simon and Schuster.

1978. "How Big-Name Lawyers Got Stung," *New West*, January 30: 47–50. [Mitford titles this "Waiting for O'Hara" in *Poison Penmanship*].

1978. "Loss and Gain: Voices from the American Old Left," review of *The Romance of American Communism*, by Vivian Gornick, *Newsday*, February 19.

1978. "The Life of the Party: Interviews with U.S. ex-Communists," review of *The Romance of American Communism*, by Vivian Gornick, *Los Angeles Times*, March 5.

1978. "A Brutish Little Gift from Britain," review of *The English Gentleman*, by Douglas Sutherland, *San Francisco Examiner & Chronicle*, December 3.

1979. *Poison Penmanship : The Gentle Art of Muckraking*. [1st ed]. New York: Knopf.

1979. *The Making of a Muckraker*. London: Michael Joseph.

*1979. "Knee-deep in Muck in Egypt," *GEO*, April 22. [Mitford titled this "Egyptomania: Tut, Muck, and the Rest of the Gang" in *Poison Penmanship*].

1979. "A Ship Without a Sail," review of *Nancy Cunard*, by Anne Chisholm, *New York*,12.12, May 14: 65.

1979. "Memoirs of a Social Engineer, Part II," review *of The Shaping of a Behaviorist*, by B.F. Skinner, *Los Angeles Times*, May 20.

1979. "Can't Get No Satisfaction," *New York Magazine*, 12.32, August 13.

1979. "Review of *The Mirage*, by Zay N. Smith and Pamela Zekman," *Chicago Sun-Times*.

1979. "Cudgeling up to a Collection of Snore-core Curmudgeony," review of *The Trouble With Nowadays: A Curmudgeon Strikes Back*, by Cleveland Amory," *Los Angeles Tribune*, August 19.

1980. "Bake and Shake," *New York*, 13.3, January 21: 50.

1980. "Appointment in Arkansas," *New West*, November 3.

+1980. "The Review No One Would Publish," review of *Maybe*, by Lillian Hellman, *Berkeley Monthly*, December. [This review was originally intended for the *Oakland Tribune* which would not publish it because Mitford used the F-word in it.]

1981. "A California Cliffhanger: Will Justice Be Done?" *Los Angeles Times*, February 15.

1981. "Jail-House Chic," *Panorama*, March.

1981. "How Will We Ever Teach Them to Trust Adults Again?" *McCall's*, 108.9, June.

1981. "A Self-mocking Search for Truth," review of *Philip Toynbee*, by Philip Toynbee, *Observer* (London), June 21.

1981. "Innocence Lost: One Librarian's Experience with 'Mitford Remembers,'" *Library Journal*, 106.18, October 15: 1997–99.

1982. "Expiring?" Letter to the editor, *People's World*, January 30.

1982. "Susan Sontag's God that Failed," *Soho News*, March 2.

1982. "All In The Family: One Fascist, One Socialist, One Novelist and One Duchess," *TV Guide*, 30.13, March 27.

1982. "Rebecca West at the Century's Start," review of *The Young Rebecca: Writings of Rebecca West 1911–17*, by Rebecca West, and *1900*, by Rebecca West, *Los Angeles Herald Examiner*, May 2.

1982. "Nuclear Power Brokers," review of *The Nuclear Barons*, by Peter Pringle and James Spigelman, *The Nation*, 234.18, May 8: 566–67.

1982. "Another Lady Di, Another Time, Another Party," review of Philip Ziegler's *Diana Cooper: The Biography of Lady Diana Cooper*, *Newsday*, May 9.

1982. "A Woman of the Century," review of *The Young Rebecca: Writings of Rebecca West 1911–17*, by Rebecca West, *New York*, 15.19, May 10: 59–60.

1982. "The Young Rebecca West," review of *The Young Rebecca West: Writings of Rebecca West 1911–17*, *Tribune*, May 23.

1982. "'Racist Onslaught' Against A TV Film," letter to the editor, *New York Times*, June 11.

1982. "Buyer Beware: It's Your Funeral," *San Jose Mercury News*, August 8.

1982. "An Update on the 'Prison Business,'" *The Nation*, 235.14, October 30: 424–26.

1982. "Chatting About Chatsworth," review of *The House: Living at Chatsworth*, by Duchess of Devonshire (Deborah Mitford Cavendish), *San Francisco Chronicle Review*, December 5.

1982. Letter to the editor re: review of *When the Wind Blows*, *People's World*, December 6.

1983. "From Washington with Love," *San Francisco Sunday Examiner & Chronicle*, February 13.

1983. "Dame Rebecca Had Style," *Los Angeles Times*, March 23.

1983. "Return to Mitford Country," *Diversion*, May: 213–19.

1983. "Mitford on Thatcher's Britain," *This World/San Francisco Sunday Chronicle*, July 24.

1983. "An Immodest Proposal," *Village Voice*, September 6.

1984. *Faces of Philip: A Memoir of Philip Toynbee*. New York: Knopf.

1984. "The Salvadoran Way of Death," *This World/San Francisco Sunday Chronicle*, March 11.

1984. "El Salvador on the Precipice," *Observer* (London), March 25.

1984. "The Toynbee Roller Coaster," *Observer* (London), June 24.

1984. "An Open Letter to the Democratic National Convention Delegates," *San Francisco Chronicle Review*, July 15.

1984. "From Here to London, Campaign Takes Off: American-style Democracy is Envy of British Pundits," *San Jose Mercury News*, July 15.

1984. "For the Love of Eleanor," review of *A World of Love: Eleanor Roosevelt and Her Friends 1943–1962*, by Joseph P. Lash, *Vanity Fair*, 47.10, October.

1984. "Travail & Leisure," *San Francisco Sunday Examiner & Chronicle*, October 7.

1984. "The Love Lives of H.G. Wells," review of *H.G. Wells in Love*, by H.G. Wells, *Vanity Fair*, 47.11, November.

1984. "Everything in Common But a Language," *New Statesman*, November 30.

1984. "Contribution to 'Books Worth Giving,'" review of *Shrinklits: Seventy of the World's Towering Classics Cut Down to Size*, by Maurice Sagoff. *Berkeley Monthly*, December.

1984. "Personal Treasure," review of *Modern Pig-Sticking*, by Major A. E. Wardrop, *Vanity Fair*, 47.12, December.

1984. "Faces of Philip," *Chicago Tribune*, December 2.

1985. "Investigating Investigative Reporters," *Mother Jones*, January 6.

*1985. "Black Eloquence," *Sunday Times*, March 13.

1985. "The Saga of Swinbrook," "Great Escapes"/*San Francisco Sunday Examiner & Chronicle*, March 25.

1985."Til Death Do Ye Part," *Consumers Digest*, March/April.

1985. "A Mitford Goes to Merseyside," *Observer* (London), May 10.

1985. "A Love Affair with Language," review of *Paths from a White Horse*, by Peter Vansittart, *Observer* (London), August 18.

1986. "Commentary in Defense of Nancy Mitford," review of *Nancy Mitford: A Biography*, by Selina Hastings, *San Francisco Chronicle*, September 21.

1986. "Wit Amid the Encircling Gloom," review of *22 Stories*, by Penelope Gilliatt, *San Francisco Chronicle*, November 2.

1987. "'Just Do As We Say': Jessica Mitford on Rushdie in Nicaragua," *The Guardian*, February 20.

1987. "A Moment in the Life of a Country," review of *The Jaguar Smile*, by Salman Rushdie, *San Francisco Chronicle*, February 22.

1987. "Lawyers of the Left: Their Embattled Guild Has Survived to Fight Again," *Washington Post*, May 24.

1987. "Lawyers of the Left," *This World/San Francisco Sunday Chronicle*, June 28.

1987. "Grace Darling—The Lighthouse Heroine," *Architectural Digest*, September.

1987. "Christmas: Pro and Con," *Image (San Francisco Examiner)*, December 20.

1987. "And There We Were, Marching Through Georgia." *Oakland Tribune*, February 8, 1987.

1988. "Bizarre but Brilliant: The Vision of Steadman," review of *Scar Strangled Banger*, by Ralph Steadman, *Weekend Australian*, May.

1988. "Getting a Focus on a Rolling Stone," review of *I.F. Stone: A Portrait*, by Andrew Parker, *San Francisco Chronicle*, February 28.

+1988. "Twentieth Century Literature," *Personal Views*, Fall: 290–91.

*1988. "In Peril on the Sea," *Country Living*, October.

1988. "A 'Roach' Remembers: We Radicals Got into Hot Water but Look Who Went to the Cooler," *Washington Post*, October 30.

1988. "The Passionate Truth," letter to the editor, *San Francisco Chronicle*, December 9.

*1988. "RELAX-nost: A Volga Cruise in the Era of Glasnost," *Traveler*.

1989. *Grace Had an English Heart: The Story of Grace Darling, Heroine and Victorian Superstar.* New York, N.Y: Dutton.

1989. "The Mitford Way of Travel," *Male and Femail*, (London Daily Mail) January 7.

1989. "Always Have the Final Say: New York," *The Guardian*, February 11.

1989. "Foreword." *The American Inquisition, 1945–1960: A Profile of the "McCarthy Era,"* by Cedric Belfrage. New York: Thunder's Mouth Press, 1989.

1989. "Old School Spies," review of *A Divided Life*, by Robert Cecil, and *The Master Spy*, by Phillip Knightley, *Washington Post*, March 26.

1989. "Prime Time for Communists?" letter to the editor, *New York Times*, April 16.

1989. "Grace Had An English Heart: The Story of Grace Darling, Heroine and Victorian Superstar," *Belles Lettres*, 4.3, April 30: 8.g

1990. "Letter to the Editor re: Herb Caen," *San Francisco Chronicle*, March 1.

1990. "Teach Midwifery, Go to Jail," *This World/San Francisco Sunday Chronicle*, October 21.

1992. *The American Way of Birth*. New York, N.Y: Dutton.

1992. "The American Way of Birth," *Newsweek*, December 28.

1992. "The American Way of Birth," *Good Housekeeping*, 215.4, October.

1992. "She's Come for an Abortion. What Do You Say?" *Harper's*, 285, January 1.

1992. "Letter to the Editor 13 -- no Title," *New York Times*, May 3.

1992. "You Communist Bitch!" *San Francisco Focus*, July.

1992. "Sea Worthies," *Travel-Holiday*, September: 67–71, 125.

1992. "Advice for the Next Creation," *New York Times Book Review*, November 8.

1993. "Afterword For the Paperback Edition of the American Way of Birth," *Birth Gazette*, 9.3, June 30: 15–18.

1993. "Jessica Mitford's Diary," *The Times* (London), September 18.

1993. "Jessica Mitford's Diary," *The Times* (London), September 25.

1993. "Jessica Mitford Diary," *The Times* (London), October 2: 5.

1993. "Jessica Mitford's Diary," *The Times* (London), October 9: 4.

1993. "Letter to the Editor re: 'On the Electronic Plantation,'" *This World/San Francisco Chronicle*, March 22.

1993. "I Was Sacked!" *Elle*, March.

1993. "The Fingerflap," *California Lawyer*, September 1: 96.

1993. "At Peace with Old Age," Review of *The Foundation of Age*, by Betty Friedan, *San Francisco Chronicle*, September 12.

1993. "At Her Wit's End: Nancy Mitford's Letters," review of *The Letters of Nancy Mitford*, by Evelyn Waugh and Nancy Mitford, *The Times* (London), September 12.

1993. "Zsa, Zsa, Marlene and . . . Jessica," *Daily Telegraph*, September 28.

1993. "U.S. Cuba Policy Is Ill-Conceived," *San Francisco Chronicle*, November 2.

1993. "The Never-Ending Quest for Youth," *Daily Telegraph*, November 6.

1994. "Obituary: Sally Belfrage," *The Independent (London)*, March 16.

1994. "When It's Its," letter to the editor, *The Spectator*, April 30.

1994. "Delighted Read," letter to the editor, *The Spectator*, May 21.

1994. "Introduction." *Censored: The News That Didn't Make the News And Why: 1994 Project Censored Yearbook*, by Carl Jensen and Project Censored. New York: Thunder's Mountain Press.

1995. "Customs in Exile," review of *The Oxford Book of Exile*, by John Simpson, *The Mail*, April 9.

1995. "Burial Writes," review of *Dancing on the Grave: Encounters with Death* by Nigel Barley & *Who Lies Where: Guide to Famous Graves* by Michael Kerrigan, *The Mail*, November 13.

1995. "Frontline Defenders." *A Free Library in This City: The Illustrated History of the San Francisco Library*, by Peter Booth Wiley. San Francisco: Weldon Owen.

1996. "Of Danger Ne'er Afraid," *The Guardian* (London), July 25.

1997. "Money Men In At The Death," *The Guardian* (London), February 8.

1997. "Death, Incorporated," *Vanity Fair*, 429, March.

1998. *The American Way of Death Revisited*. Rev. ed. New York: Alfred A. Knopf.

2001. "Foreword." *The Pursuit of Love and Love in Cold Climate*, by Nancy Mitford. New York: Vintage.

2004. *Hons and Rebels*. New York: The New York Review of Books.

UNPUBLISHED

1961. "The Longest Meeting." Manuscript version, OSU, Box 96, folder 804.

1961. "Rebels with a Hundred Causes: The Indignant Generation." OSU, Box 94, folder 832, 27.

+1963. "What the Undertaker's are Saying about *The American Way of Death*," *San Francisco Chronicle*, OSU, Box 99, folder 870.

+1964. "My Way of Life Since The American Way of Death" (for *Nova*). Manuscript version, OSU, Box 97, folder 818.

+1968. "Untitled" (Editorial for *Liberation*). OSU, Box 96, folder 800.

[1972]. "D.C. Prison." OSU, Box 14, folder 77.

1973. "Cheaper than Chimpanzees." *The Atlantic*, 231.1. OSU, Box 14, folder 80—manuscript.

[1978.] "Nasty, Short, and Brutish." Review of *The English Gentleman*, by Douglas Sutherland. Manuscript version, OSU, Box 92, folder 741.

[1979.] "King of Burn and Scatter" (for *The Sunday Telegraph*). Manuscript version, OSU, Box 96, folder 796.

1979. "Return to the South" (for *Harper's*). Manuscript version, OSU, Box 98, folder 835.

1981. *Their Day in Court* (book proposal). Manuscript version, OSU, Box 99, folder 858.

1981. "Foreword" to *Conspiracy to Advocate* by William Schneiderman. Manuscript version, OSU, Box 93, folder 752.

[1983]. "Dog Pee Article" (for *Sunday Times*). Manuscript version, OSU, Box 93, folder 759.

1988. "To Be Young, Black, Gifted—and a British M.P." (for *Mother Jones*). Manuscript version, OSU, Box 99, folder 861.

1988. "*Orphan Island* Film Proposal" (based on the book *Orphan Island* by Rose Maccaulay, 1925). Manuscript version, OSU, Box 97, folder 823.

1993. "Tricks of Memory," (for *Longevity*). Manuscript version, OSU, Box 99, folder 864.

UNPUBLISHED, UNDATED

"Review of *A Little Learning* by Evelyn Waugh." Manuscript version, OSU, Box 96, folder 803.

"The Book Business, Limited," n.d. Manuscript version (for *San Francisco Chronicle*), OSU, Box 92, folder 737.

"Boring From Without, or The Rest of Ronald Reagan." n.d. Manuscript version, OSU, Box 92, folder 738.

"Dig That Crazy Grave." n.d. OSU, Box 92, folder 741.

"Doggess: The Dictionary Game." n.d. Manuscript version, OSU, Box 93, folder 760.

+"Foreword (or Afterword) for Book About Howard Gossage." n.d. Manuscript version, OSU, Box 95, folder 779.

+Foreword to "San Francisco: An Informal Guide." n.d. Manuscript version, OSU, Box 98, folder 841.

"My Funeral." n.d. Manuscript version, Harry Ransom Humanities Research Center (HRC), Box 9, folder 3.

"A Global Village of the Dead." Manuscript version, OSU, Box 93, folder 757.

"Ordeal by Jury." n.d. OSU, Box 97, folder 822.

"Post-Mortem." n.d. OSU, Box 97, folder 825.

Review of *The Autobiography of Bertrand Russell*, by Bertrand Russell (for *The Atlantic*). Manuscript version, OSU, Box 91, folder 727.

"Seems I've Read This Before." Manuscript sent to Scott Meredith Literary Agency. n.d. OSU, Box 98, folder 843.

"The *Daily Peoples World* and the Current Discussions." n.d. Manuscript version, OSU, Box 27, folder 153.

"The Lure of the Falklands." n.d. Manuscript version, OSU, Box 98, folder 857.

"The Unbearable Lightness and Discreet Charm of the British Aristocracy" (for *Vanity Fair*), n.d. Manuscript version, OSU, Box 99, folder 865.

"Why I Live Where I Live" (series for *Esquire*). Manuscript version, OSU, Box 99, folder 871.

Dates in brackets are based on internal evidence and provided by the author. All box and folder numbers correspond to Inventory listings prior to July 2024.

+Entries marked + are manuscript copies from Mitford's archives for which publication could not be verified and which may have been intended for publication but remained unpublished.

*Entries marked * are published clippings located in Mitford's archives for which external copies could not be located to supply additional bibliographical information.

Mitford wrote dozens, possibly hundreds, of letters to the editor, some unpublished, many of which are contained in her archives; with a few exceptions, letters to the editor are not listed here.

Because Mitford wrote so many book reviews, often for regional or small publications, book review listings here may not be comprehensive.

INDEX

Abernathy, Ralph, 297, 414
abortion, 458n23
Abraham Lincoln Brigade, 171–172, 405
Abrahams, Billy, 408, 425, 426, 530n37
Abzug, Bella, 208–209, 217
ACLU, 209, 364–365, 483n51
"Action Man" nickname, 275, 294, 404
activism
    Black, 7, 321, 323, 337–338
    privilege and, 9
    Southern, 294–295, 320–322
    student movement, 282, 294–295, 324–325, 355
    by women, 367
    women and, 294–295
    See also allyship; civil rights; communism;
        prison abolition
Acton, Harold, 190
Adamson, Joy, 292
Addison, Goldstein and Walsh, 313
Addison Wesley, 425
advocacy, 13, 426, 457n14
advocacy journalism, 352
African Americans
    Communists, 201
    cooperatives, 506n7
    Jim Crow and, 208, 238, 263
    in Oakland, 201, 491n24
    police brutality and, 200, 204, 210
    racial discrimination, 176, 337
    racial injustice, 213
    redlining, 323
    segregation, 211, 294, 323
    voter participation, 335
    wartime labor force, 153–154, 201
    See also civil rights; racism
aging, 421–422
Aikin, Anne Hopkins, 139, 479n63
Airlie castle, 22
air travel, 71, 248–249, 486n38, 492n41,

492n43, 499n8
Albania, Italian invasion of, 83
Alexander, Babe, 85
Alexander, Diana, 532n89
Alexander, Hursel, 209, 213
Alexander, Shana, 443
Allen, Louis, 321
Allende, Salvador, 369, 519n25
Allhusen, Dorothy, 48–49, 106
allyship, 4, 6, 7, 9–10, 234–236, 239–240, 282,
    294–296, 321, 323. *See also* civil rights
Ambassador Hotel, 314
"America First," 85
Americans
    1950s world of, 223
    appeal of Communism to, 3, 167, 486n45
    appeal of socialism to, 167
    culture of consumption, 308
    enthusiasm of, 73, 87
    hypocrisy of, 155–156, 482n42
    See also United States
"The American Way" lecture class, 374–376,
    379–380
The American Way of Birth (film), 430
American way of death, 176, 286–287
American Zen Buddhism, 479n63
Andrews, Julie, 329
Angelou, Maya
    Bellagio fellowship, 378, 432
    at California Labor School, 166
    feminism, 428
    Jessica and, 3–4, 146, 153, 365, 367, 388, 396,
        408, 410, 422, 432–434, 435, 436, 442
    Jessica's memorial, 443, 533n105
    I Know Why the Caged Bird Sings, 365, 419
    Thomas op-ed, 432–433
anti-authoritarianism, 41, 282, 295, 324, 344,
    385, 452
anti-colonialism, 5

Goldmark, Kathie, 436
Gollancz, Victor, 290, 504n48
Gollancz publishing, 289, 504n48
"the Good Body," Sydney Redesdale and, 5, 15, 17, 24, 144
Goodman, Andrew, 324
Goodman, Mitchell, 341, 352
Goodwin, Doris Kearns, 88, 482n36
"Gooey Parts," Jessica Mitford and the, 11–13
Gornick, Vivian, 267
Gottlieb, Robert (Bob), 307–308, 311, 314, 316, 322, 333, 342, 348, 374, 387, 391, 395, 398, 403, 408, 425, 437, 455n1, 507n27
Grace Darling Museum, 413–414, 416
Graham, Helen, 57
Graham, Katharine (Kay), 116, 143, 162, 335, 384, 480n76
Grand "Tor," Jessica Mitford and Esmond Romilly on, 82
Grant, Duncan, 309
Grant, Joanne, 409, 410
Granta (periodical), 458n23
Gray, Fred, 263
The Great Gatsby (Fitzgerald), 468n42
Green, Buddy, 213, 214, 218, 234–235, 239, 443
Green, Dan, 311, 312, 314, 316
Green Street Mortuary Band, 443
Greenwich Village, 72–73
Gregory, Dick, 321–322, 414
grief, stages of, 477n12
Griffin, Susan, 428, 442
Grossman, Aubrey, 199–200, 208, 215
Guggenheim Fellowship, 373, 521n55
Guinness, Bryan, 6, 39
Guinness, Jonathan, 457n14, 459n31, 459n42, 532n89
Guthrie, Woody, 175

Hachette, 504n48
Hackney, Sheldon, 273
the Haight, San Francisco, 149, 187
Halberstam, David, 223
Haley, Alex, 455n8
Hamm, Theodore, 498n60
Hammersley, Violet, 140
Hardwick Hall, 496n28, 500n25
Harper & Row, 425
Harper's (periodical), 400, 526n42
Hart, Gary, 414
Hartington, William (Billy), Marquess of, 228, 489n91, 496n25
Hastings, Selena, 462n22, 500n20, 528n79
Hawkins, Willette, 209, 220, 244
Haywood, Harry, 209
Healey, Dorothy, 178, 225, 227, 229, 236–237, 271, 482n33, 501n65, 501n75
health care, American, 426–430
Heimlich maneuver, 458n20

Hellman, Lillian, 182, 525n11
Helms, Jesse, 427
"Hen"/"Henderson" nicknames, 12, 36, 84, 132–133, 233, 456n3, 464n34, 496n37
hereditary privilege, 28
Highlander School, 89, 120, 242
Hill, Anita, 432, 532n76
Hill & Wang, 421
Hiss, Alger, 215
Hitler, Adolf, 6, 24, 38, 68, 132, 399, 459n30
annexation of Czechoslovakia, 75
Diana and, 39, 69, 386, 523n119
European attacks, 101
forced evacuation of Jews, 72
invasion of Poland, 83, 84–85
invasion of Russia, 119, 485n14
march into Prague, 73
Unity and, 40, 55, 57, 62, 63, 69, 94–95, 98, 99, 471n43
Holloway Prison, 102, 135, 179, 180
Hollywood Ten, 483n51
Holocaust, 137
Holt, Pat, 443
Holt v. Sarver, 525n13
Home Town (TV show), 495n108
"Hon" nickname, 229, 464n34
Honnish, in Mitford-speak, 36, 56, 141
Hons' Cupboard, 36, 229, 257, 289, 496n37
Hons Society, 36
Hooks, Ben, 414
Hoover, J. Edgar, 206
Hopkins, Anne, 139, 479n63
Hopson, Louise, 494n99
Horne, Ann Farrer, 208, 218, 398
Horowitz, Daniel, 512n40
Horton, Myles, 242
Hotel Claremont, 231
Hotel des Basques, 61
Hotel Torrontegui, 54
Houghton Mifflin, 12, 289, 307, 504n48, 507n24, 518n6
The House of Mitford (Guinness), 457n14
House of Worth, 464n42
House Un-American Activities Committee (HUAC), 77, 200, 223–226, 241–243, 324, 391, 423, 483n51, 484n64, 486n30, 489n83
The Hoyden (yacht), 28
HUAC. *See* House Committee on Un-American Activities
Hughes, Langston, 182
Hungary, 257–259, 270, 280
and revolution, 283
hunger marches, 5
Hunter, Jean E., 511n34
Hurst, Fannie, 330, 513n50
Hutton, Bobby, 350
Huxley, Julian, 309
Hyndman, Tony, 68

ABOUT THE AUTHOR

Carla Kaplan is an award-winning writer; the Davis Distinguished Professor of American Literature at Northeastern University; and a Guggenheim and 'Public Scholar' Fellow. She is the author of the *New York Times* Notable Books *Miss Anne in Harlem* and *Zora Neale Hurston: A Life in Letters*, among others.